ESSAY

Reading with the Writer's Eye

HANS P. GUTH
San Jose State University

RENÉE V. HAUSMANN
University of the District of Columbia

Wadsworth Publishing Company
A Division of Wadsworth, Inc.
Belmont, California

We gratefully acknowledge the suggestions and helpful advice of the following reviewers:

Samuel I. Bellman, California State Polytechnic University, Pomona
Eileen B. Evans, Western Michigan University
Robert F. Geary, James Madison University
Michael L. Johnson, University of Kansas, Lawrence
Virginia Thigpen, Volunteer State Community College

English Editor: Kevin J. Howat
Production Editors: Leland Moss and Sally Schuman
Designer: MaryEllen Podgorski
Copy Editor: William Waller

Printed in the United States of America
2 3 4 5 6 7 8 9 10—88 87 86 85 84

ISBN 0-534-03086-6

Library of Congress Cataloging in Publication Data
Guth, Hans Paul, 1926–
    Essay, reading with the writer's eye.

    Bibliography: p.
    Includes index.
    1. College readers.   2. English language—
    Rhetoric.   I. Hausmann, Renée.   II. Title.
PE1417.G87   1984   808'.0427   83–17005
ISBN 0-534-03086-6

CONTENTS

PART TWO
Patterns for Writing

PART THREE
Audiences for Writing

Reading with
the Writer's Eye

PREFACE

To the Instructor

Essay is designed to help students learn to read with the writer's eye. Each selection is included because it can help teach the student reader something about what good writing is and what it means to be a writer. The selections range from the best current nonfiction prose to familiar classics of the expository essay. The questions that accompany the selections are designed to help the reader see how a successful piece of writing works; they focus attention on why and how writers do what they do.

The overall organization of the book mirrors three major stages or dimensions of the process of writing:

- SOURCES FOR WRITING—What gives writing substance? The emphasis here is on *content*—on where writers turn for material, how they draw on observation and experience, how they become involved in a topic.

- PATTERNS FOR WRITING—What gives writing shape? The emphasis here is on *structure*—on how writers sort out material or organize evidence, on how they use and adapt familiar patterns of exposition for their own purposes.

- AUDIENCES FOR WRITING—What does a writer do for the reader? The emphasis here is on *strategy and style*—on how writers respond to the needs and expectations of their readers, on how their sense of audience influences their choice of rhetorical and stylistic means.

The following features of *Essay* are designed to make the book different from more routine collections of readings—more helpful to teachers trying to make their students better readers and better writers:

1. FIRST-RATE PROSE FOR THE STUDENT READER

The authors represented in this book have something to say and say it well. (No pap.) *Essay* steers clear of the snippets and the ponderous sociological thinkpieces that are the rock and the whirlpool awaiting editors of freshman readers. This book aims at converting students to the cause of good reading by offering them lively, invigorating, and thought-provoking prose—prose worth reading. Whatever their widely publicized academic deficiencies, today's students are often eager to study and to learn. This book takes them seriously as students and as readers. It asks them to pay serious attention to essays whose authors write for the common reader but respect their readers' intelligence, broaden their horizons, test their commitments, and stimulate their imagination.

2. READING WITH THE WRITER'S EYE

The apparatus in this book focuses the student reader's attention on the why and how of writing. How do the forms and techniques of writing serve the writer's purpose? What was the writer trying to do, and how did the writer do it? A successful essay takes shape in the fruitful interaction of the why and the how. As a result, the questions asked about the readings in this book do not divorce form from content, technique from meaning, or the medium from the message. With each essay, a brief "Guide to Reading" helps students read with an eye for what the writer set out to do and how the writer dealt with the topic. Following the essay, questions labeled "The Writer's Agenda" take students through the essay to make them see how a competent piece of writing takes shape. The aim is to make students see a successful piece of writing as a purposeful whole that takes shape as the writer does justice to the subject and works out the strategy that serves the writer's purpose.

3. COMBINED RHETORICAL AND THEMATIC PLAN

Each of the thirteen units in *Essay* illustrates a major rhetorical category with essays linked by a common theme. The common thematic focus encourages students to think of expository patterns or rhetorical forms not as ends in themselves but as means fit for characteristic uses—as means to be chosen and adapted to serve the writer's purpose. We confuse the ends and the means when we make it appear to students as if writers wrote *in order* to describe, to narrate, to classify, to compare and contrast. Writers describe or classify or compare in order to do justice to a topic. Our students need to see what situations, for instance, might bring process analysis or cause-and-effect thinking into play, or what the typical uses and pitfalls are of schemes of classification. The combined rhetorical and thematic table of contents will help the instructor keep the subject matter of an essay from seeming merely optional or interchangeable, used to flesh out ready-made expository patterns or rhetorical forms.

4. A MINI-RHETORIC FOR THE STUDENT WRITER

Essay is designed to do more than conventional collections of readings to provide the missing link between reading and writing. Each of the thirteen units starts with a "Writer's Guide" designed to bridge the gap between general rhetorical principles and the students' own writing. The "Writer's Guides" provide pointed practical advice, many sample outlines, and graphic demonstration of writing strategies. "Prewriting Activities" at the end of each guide range from sentence practice and paragraph work to discovery frames for exploring a topic and working up the material for a theme. Questions "For Discussion or Writing" following each selection provide a wide range of assignments for student papers growing out of class discussion, reacting to or branching out from the reading, and implementing the rhetorical strategies being studied. Each unit concludes with a short "Pro and Con" selection meant as a springboard for further discussion and writing and well suited as stimulus for in-class writing.

5. SPECIAL HELPS FOR BETTER READING

Essay provides special help for poorly prepared students trying to become more proficient readers. Author biographies providing "Background" for each selection go beyond conventional biographical data to set the scene for the reading selection and fill in essential context for the student reader. Editorial footnotes often provide help with historical or literary references beyond the ken of the less-than-well-read student. Suggestions for "Using the Dictionary" go beyond a routine listing of vocabulary items to teach the student reader to make full use of dictionary resources. For each major selection, the Instructor's Manual provides a "Vocabulary Review"—a multiple-choice (usually 20-item) reading check that presents key words in the context of a sentence. These vocabulary reviews help teach students to read for context clues and provide the instructor with a quick check on reading and comprehension.

In preparing *Essay* as a textbook for a composition course, we have at various points felt the need to go beyond the tried and only half-true. We do not believe that in the teaching of writing old wood always burns brightest. In traditional underfunded and undervalued composition programs, much dedicated work was done with often disappointing results. The current renaissance of rhetoric and the general upgrading of composition as an academic subject have given many teachers of writing a renewed sense of purpose. As rhetoricians today, we are paying more serious attention than we did in more genteel and self-satisfied days to why and how writers write. We ask what, in our students' writing, makes the difference between dreary, unreadable imitation prose and writing that is worth reading—and worth correcting and revising. This book is dedicated to the countless teachers of composition around the country who take the student seriously as a reader and as a writer. May they frequently find in this book evidence of the power of the truly written word to inform, to illuminate, to challenge, and to inspire.

SOURCES FOR WRITING

WHERE DOES good writing come from? Good writing has its sources in the author's observation, experience, and reading. A basic prerequisite for every writer is the ability to pay attention, to take things in. We expect an effective writer to take a stand, to say something that is worthwhile. In much of the writing you do in a composition course, you will be asked to support a thesis, or central idea. Often the first question for the student writer is: "How do I *arrive* at a thesis? How do I form an opinion that is more than a superficial impression? How do I reach the point where I can state and support a worthwhile idea with confidence?"

Part One of this book focuses on the resources that you should mobilize for your writing. Learn where to turn for material. Know how to set an essay in motion. The readings in Part One are grouped under three headings:

1 ✦ OBSERVATION

Good writing is rooted in first-hand observation. Good writers have learned to look for themselves and to reach their own conclusions. They have learned to trust their own eyes and ears. When writing about places, people, and events, effective writers know how to move in for a *closer look*. They know how to describe a scene in such a way that we see it before our eyes. Many readers are tired of writing that sounds trite, second-hand, and insincere. It is high praise when such a reader says, as did a reader of a book about wildlife in the Rockies, that the author "watched carefully and reported truthfully" on what she saw.

2 ✦ EXPERIENCE

Good writing draws on personal experience. Good writers know how to bring ideas and issues to life by drawing on what they have experienced in their own lives. Some of the strongest writing we read deals with an achievement, conflict, grievance, or loss that had a personal meaning for the author. The use of material from personal experience is not limited to writing whose main purpose is autobiographical: Some writing about serious public issues is done by impartial outsiders, but often the most effective or persistent voices are those of people who are in some way personally involved. Learn how to draw on personal experience as a major resource for your writing. Effective writers know how to make abstract ideas real by the use of examples from personal experience and observation. They know how to clinch an argument by vividly presenting a case in point as a witness who can say: "I saw it happen. I experienced it myself."

3 ✦ POINTS OF VIEW

A good writer is an alert listener and reader. Much effective writing is part of an ongoing dialogue: We write in *response* to someone else's opinion or initiative. Someone makes a case, and we want to show why we agree. Someone makes a proposal, and we want to show what is wrong with it. Much genuine writing is part of a pattern of action and reaction. We feel the need to come to terms with a disturbing new idea, or to head off an ill-considered scheme, or to correct a stereotype. Study the writing of authors with a strong personal point of view. How does a writer become involved in the discussion of an issue? How does an effective writer take a stand? How does an effective writer support a thesis or strong central idea in such a way that it will hold its own in the rough-and-tumble of public debate?

U N I T 1

OBSERVATION:
Special Places

The Common Theme: The writers in this unit are alert, open-eyed observers who describe for us something they care about: a place that was a good place to be or a place that they would long remember. Each of these writers has an eye for striking, authentic detail; they know how to make a setting real for the reader. Gretel Ehrlich, in "Wide Open Spaces," writes about finding a new life as a sheepherder in Wyoming. Donald M. Murray, in "Culture Trading on the Old Silk Road," writes as a traveler open to new impressions, puzzled and intrigued by what he sees abroad. N. Scott Momaday, in "The Way to Rainy Mountain," searches his childhood memories for clues to a half-forgotten past.

WRITER'S GUIDE 1:
Writing from Observation

A good writer is first of all a good observer. If you want to write effectively, you have to learn to notice things, to take things in. Weak writing is thin writing, full of generalities and clichés. Effective writing is done by people who have learned to look for themselves, who have learned to pay attention to the world around them. If you have no profound new ideas about censorship or democracy or marriage, you can still become an interesting and effective writer by remembering a first basic rule: Use your own eyes and ears.

An essential part of an effective writer's training is writing based on honest first-hand observation. Student writers sometimes feel that they have nothing to write about or nothing to say. They begin to solve this problem when they ask themselves: "What is out there? What do I see? What do I hear?" Writing becomes real when the writer begins to do justice to the sights and sounds around us, to the shape and texture of things, to the way things around us look and move.

Writing that records honest first-hand observation is called **description**. Description is seldom an end in itself. Not only in description, but also in argument or persuasion, the effective writer knows how to make places, things, and people graphic and vivid for the mind's eye. As you study and practice writing based on observation, remember the following guidelines:

(1) *Bring in authentic first-hand detail.* Instead of just calling something beautiful or interesting or colorful, show it to the reader. Provide the details that enable your readers to imagine themselves in your place as a first-hand observer at the scene. When we read a passage like the following about small towns off the tourist track in California, we know that the details do not come from a travel folder or a Chamber of Commerce brochure. We read about these places with the feeling: "She was there."

> Every so often along 99 between Bakersfield and Sacramento there is a town: Delano, Tulare, Fresno, Madera, Merced, Modesto, Stockton. Some of these towns are pretty big now, but they are all the same at heart, one- and two- and three-story buildings artlessly arranged, so that what appears to be the good dress shop stands beside a W. T. Grant store, so that the big Bank of America faces a Mexican movie house. *Dos Peliculas, Bingo Bingo Bingo.* Beyond the downtown (pronounced *down*town, with the Okie accent that now pervades Valley speech patterns) lie blocks of old frame houses—paint peeling, sidewalks cracking, their occasional leaded amber win-

dows overlooking a Foster's Freeze or a five-minute car wash or a State Farm Insurance office; beyond those spread the shopping centers and miles of tract houses, pastel with redwood siding, the unmistakable signs of cheap building already blossoming on those houses which have survived the first rain.

—Joan Didion, *Slouching Towards Bethlehem*

As we read this passage, we know that we can trust this writer to remember and bring in authentic detail: a hotel that still has tile floor in the dining room and dusty potted palms and big ceiling fans; a golden anniversary where the guests of honor sat on straight-backed chairs in front of a sheaf of gladioluses in 110-degree heat; the arched sign over the main street of a small town, saying "Water—Wealth, Contentment—Health."

(2) *Move in for a close look.* Every writer has to learn to **focus** on one thing at at time—to concentrate, to pay attention. Many things that are not superficially interesting *become* interesting when we bother to look. Here is an expert at close observation writing about a twenty-five-cent goldfish. Note the many details that a less attentive observer would have overlooked:

Ellery is a deep red-orange, darker than most goldfish. He steers short distances mainly with his slender red lateral fins; they seem to provide impetus for going backward, up, or down. It took me a few days to discover his ventral fins; they are completely transparent and all but invisible—dream fins. He also has a short anal fin, and a tail that is deeply notched and perfectly transparent at the two tapered tips. He can extend his mouth, so that it looks like a length of pipe; he can shift the angle of his eyes in his head so he can look before and behind himself, instead of simply out to his side. His belly, what there is of it, is white ventrally, and a patch of this white extends up his sides—the variegated Ellery. When he opens his gill slits he shows a thin crescent of silver where the flap overlapped—as though all his brightness were sunburn.

—Annie Dillard, *Pilgrim at Tinker Creek*

(3) *Make your details add up to an overall impression.* We tire of details that remain scattered or miscellaneous. We want things to fall into place; we want to see details become part of a larger picture. In effective description, well-chosen details help create a mood or set a scene that we will remember. Together, the details build a strong **dominant impression**; they are relevant to some overall result the writer is trying to achieve. The following sentences are from successive para-

graphs of a chapter called "Flood"; the author is trying to impress on us the force and speed of the rain-swollen waters. Note the many words like *smash, hurtle, lurch, zip, stream,* or *pour* that reinforce the dominant impression:

> I look at the creek at my feet. It smashes under the bridge like a fist, but there is no end to its force; it hurtles down as far as I can see till it lurches round the bend, filling the valley. . . .
>
> The water arches where the bridge's supports at the banks prevent its enormous volume from going wide, forcing it to go high. . . .
>
> Everything imaginable is zipping by, almost too fast to see. . . . There are dolls, split wood and kindling, dead fledgling songbirds, bottles, whole bushes and trees, rakes and garden gloves. . . .
>
> The whole world is in flood, the land as well as the water. Water streams down the trunks of trees, drips from hat-brims, courses across roads. The whole earth seems to slide like sand down a chute; water pouring over the least slope leaves the grass flattened, silver side up, pointing downstream. . . .
> —Annie Dillard, *Pilgrim at Tinker Creek*

In this example, the untamed energy of the floodwaters becomes the keynote that unifies the author's description. Try summing up the keynote or unifying central impression at the beginning of a paper. When the main point or central idea of a paper is summed up in one or two pointed sentences, we call it the **thesis** of a paper. Each of the following might serve as the thesis of a well-focused descriptive paper:

> THESIS: The beauty of nature is not just in sunsets and sweeping panoramas. *A camping trip gives us a chance to watch and enjoy the little things*—insects around a lantern, the frogs in a pond.
>
> THESIS: We often think of the vast gray ocean as bleak and lifeless. *A tide pool gives us a chance to look at a concentrated sample of busy, colorful ocean life.*

(4) *Set up a clear pattern for your readers to follow.* When you describe a scene, help your readers find their bearings. Suppose you want to take them to a neighborhood park for an old-fashioned barbecue. Choose a vantage point from which you survey what you describe. For instance, place yourself at one of the tables where tickets or des-

serts or souvenir buttons are sold. Then let your eyes move from there over the picnic tables, the family groups, the band, the adjoining stands, the people who come by for food and drink.

Effective description often follows a clear, consistent pattern in **space**. Suppose you are describing a city that is struggling to reverse the familiar pattern of urban blight. An overall scheme like the following will seem to have grown naturally out of the subject you describe:

A Tale of Three Cities

I. *Starting at the center,* we see the new financial and commercial downtown, with its banks and glossy shops and pedestrian malls.

II. *Moving away from the center,* we see the older neighborhoods around the core of the city, with their aging two-story frame houses and vacant lots and old-style alleys.

III. *Following the expressways farther out,* we see the suburban ring of tract houses with their two-car garages and trimmed lawns.

Often effective description brings movement into a static scene by combining spatial order with **chronological** order—a clear sequence in time. A pattern like the following combines spatial and chronological order:

Once More to the Lake

I. Approaching the lake on the hillside trail

II. Exploring the lakeside

III. Canoeing to the island in the center of the lake

IV. Returning to shore for the campfire as night falls

(5) *Find the right word.* Effective description uses fresh, specific language that makes the things being described take shape before our eyes. A passage like the following uses words that are simple and unpretentious but that carry accurate information and bring the right picture to the reader's mind:

> I handed the man a quarter, and he handed me a *knotted plastic bag bouncing with water* in which a green plant floated and the goldfish swam. This fish, two bits' worth, has *a coiled gut, a spine radiating fine bones,* and a brain.
> —Annie Dillard, *Pilgrim at Tinker Creek*

Look at the way the author uses the words *bouncing, coiled,* and *radiating:* Each is the right word for what the author wants us to see; these are highly "visual" words. Words that are exceptionally effective in calling up sights, sounds, smells, and other sense impressions are **concrete** words. *Lurch, veer,* and *stir* are more concrete than the colorless general word *move. Hover, soar,* and *swoop* are more concrete than *fly. Caw, twitter,* and *trill* are concrete words for the sounds of birds; *hum, whir, clunk,* and *wheeze* are concrete words for noises made by machines. The more general and colorless words give us only a fuzzy general picture. Concrete words help writers make us see what they saw and hear what they heard.

(6) *Bring the reader's imagination into play.* A writer with an active imagination can help revive our dulled, blunted senses and make us notice the color, pattern, and life in the world around us. Imaginative comparisons help us go beyond the literal resources of language; they help us verbalize impressions and feelings that are hard to put into words. Look at the comparisons that help bring the following description of a laundromat to life:

A middle-aged man whose clothes are in a small washing machine is standing in front of it reading a sports column in the *News,* but most of the other patrons who are between putting-in and taking-out chores seem to be mesmerized by the *kaleido-scopic activity inside the machines.* In one washing machine, a few striped sheets and pillowcases are spinning, creating a dizzying optical effect. In another, *a lively clothes dance is taking place—three or four white shirts jitterbugging with six or eight pairs of gray socks.* In a third, the clothes, temporarily obscured by a flurry of soapsuds, still cast a spell over their owner, who doesn't take her eyes off the round glass window in the front of the machine. The clothes in the dryers—here a few towels, there some men's work pants—seem to *be free-falling, like sky divers drifting down to earth.*
—Susan Sheehan, "Laundromat," *The New Yorker*

To sum up: Writing becomes real to us and holds our attention when it was done by a writer with open eyes and quick ears, someone who has learned to draw on authentic first-hand observation. In books about writing, description is sometimes treated as a somewhat optional aid to other kinds of writing. It is treated as a supporting device that makes explanation or argument more vivid or more understandable. But in the training of an effective writer, writing from observation plays a more fundamental role: It takes us to one of the basic sources of writing. A good writer is more receptive and more observant than other people. A good writer takes in things that others overlook.

PREWRITING ACTIVITIES 1

1. Take a close look at a scene, taking notes on the place and the people. Be the *camera eye*—do a series of vignettes or snapshots of a scene like the following: a busy downtown intersection, a hub of campus life, a hometown scene, skid row, a thoroughfare in the big city. What did you see? What did you hear? Include telling details; record your candid impressions. (Some of your entries may be sentence-length, some paragraph-length.)

2. Practice packing a sentence with a detail from close first-hand observation. For *sentence practice,* write two or more sentences in each of the following three categories. Study the student-written examples before writing your own sentences.

A sentence providing a *capsule portrait* of a person:

a. A girl with thick glasses and jet-black, long straight hair was reading a worn, thick literature book in her math class.

b. A bald, elderly man with tuning forks, brushes, and a wrench in the back pocket of his baggy old pants hit a sour "C" octave on our antique piano as I walked into the living room.

A sentence summing up the *atmosphere of a place:*

c. The self-service station has a sullen cashier sitting behind dark glass in a burglarproof, bulletproof cubicle with "Pay before pumping gas" posted all over it.

d. The gym was filled with the sounds of bouncing basketballs, squeaking tennis shoes, grunting players, and a constantly criticizing coach.

A sentence giving *details first* and then going on to a general label:

e. The slow rumble of the ball rolling down the alley; the loud crash as the pins are scattered in every direction; the "Yippee" from the thrower of the ball as he realizes he has got a strike: this is a bowling alley.

f. The white acoustical tile, the floor-to-ceiling mirror, the high-backed piano, and the thick door with double-plate glass window: this is a musicians' practice room.

3. For *sentence practice,* write four or five sentences that each make us visualize a person, an object, a scene, or an event by presenting a vivid *imaginative comparison.* Study the following examples before writing your own sentences:

a. On the site of the new building, a crane extends upward into the sky, *like a giraffe reaching for green leaves at the top of the tree.*

b. The great fantastic arch of the Delaware River bridge loomed ahead of me *like a preposterous giant's toy.*

c. The candidate *surfed* to the speaker's table *on a nice wave of applause.*

BACKGROUND: Gretel Ehrlich was born in Santa Barbara, California, in 1946. She was a student at Bennington College and at UCLA. She became a producer and director of award-winning documentary films and was for a time an adviser to the Navajo Film Commission. In the following essay, she takes up a topic that was for a long time a major theme in American history and literature: the wide open spaces of the West, which gave people a chance to get close to the land, to work with their hands, and to meet other people as individuals. She wrote the essay four years after she had gone to Wyoming in search of "new and unpopulated territory." Instead of leaving after a while, as she had planned, she went to work helping a sheep rancher shear, brand, and delouse his thousands of sheep. She threw away her old clothes and bought new. The following, in a slightly shortened form, is her account of what it was like for her to live and work in open country.

Gretel Ehrlich

Wide Open Spaces

GUIDE TO READING: As you read the essay, take note of the many authentic details from the author's first-hand observation. At the same time, however, pay special attention to how she *uses* these details to support the general impressions she has formed of the place and its people. What is special about the setting—what are the features that make this part of the country different from others? What is the relation between the place and the people that the author describes—how does the harsh setting in which these people live help shape their outlook and behavior?

IT'S MAY, and I've just awakened from a nap, curled against sage-brush the way my dog taught me to sleep—sheltered from wind. A weather front is pulling the huge sky over me, and from the dark a hailstone has hit me on the head.

I'm trailing a band of 2000 sheep across a stretch of Wyoming bad-land, a 50-mile trip that takes five days because sheep shade up in the hot sun and won't budge until it cools. Bunched together now, and excited into a run by the storm, they drift across dry land, tumbling into draws like water and surging out again onto the rugged, choppy plateaus that are the building blocks of this state.

3   The name "Wyoming" comes from an Indian word meaning "at the great plains," but the plains are really valleys, great arid valleys, 1600 square miles' worth of them, with the horizon bending up on all sides into mountain ranges. This gives the vastness a sheltering look.

4   Winter lasts six months here. Prevailing winds spill snowdrifts to the east, and new storms from the northwest replenish them. This white bulk is sometimes dizzying, even nauseating, to look at. At 20, 30, 40 degrees below zero, it is not only your car that doesn't work but also your mind and body.

5   The landscape hardens into a dungeon of space. During the winter, while I was riding to find a new calf, my legs half froze to the saddle, and in the silence that such cold creates, I felt like the first person on earth, or the last.

6   Today the sun is out—only a few clouds billowing. In the east, where the sheep have started off without me, the benchland tilts up in a series of red-earthed, eroded mesas, planed flat on top by a million years of water. Behind them, a bold line of muscular scraps rears up 10,000 feet to become the Big Horn Mountains. A tidal pattern is engraved into the ground, as if left by the sea that once covered this state. Canyons curve down like galaxies to meet the oncoming rush of flat land.

7   To live and work in this kind of open country, with its 100-mile views, is to lose the distinction between background and foreground. When I asked an older ranch hand to describe Wyoming's openness, he said, "It's all a bunch of nothing—wind and rattlesnakes—and so much of it you can't tell where you're going or where you've been and it don't make much difference."

8   John, a sheepman I know, is tall and handsome and has an explosive temperament. He has a perfect intuition about people and sheep. They call him "Highpockets" because he's so long-legged; his graceful stride matches the distances he has to cover.

9   "Open space hasn't affected me at all. It's all the people moving in on it," he said. The huge ranch he was born on takes up much of one county and spreads into another state. For him to put 100,000 miles on his pickup in three years and never leave home is not unusual.

10   Most of Wyoming has a "lean-to" look. Instead of big, roomy barns and Victorian houses, there are dugouts, low sheds, log cabins, sheep camps and fence lines that look like driftwood blown haphazardly into place. People in Wyoming still feel pride because they live in such a harsh place, part of the glamorous cowboy past, and they are determined not to be the victims of a mining-dominated future.

11   Most characteristic of the state's landscape is what a developer eu-

phemistically describes as "indigenous growth right up to your front door"—a reference to waterless stands of salt sage, snakes, jackrabbits, deerflies, red dust, a brief respite of wildflowers, dry washes and no trees.

Sagebrush covers 58,000 square miles of Wyoming. The biggest city 12 has a population of 50,000, and there are only five settlements that could be called cities in the whole state. The rest are towns, scattered across the expanse with as much as 60 miles between them, their populations 2000, 50 or 10. They are fugitive-looking, perched on a barren, windblown bench, or tagged onto a river or a railroad, or laid out straight in a farming valley with implement stores and a block-long Mormon church.

In the eastern part of the state, which slides down into the Great 13 Plains, the new mining settlements are boomtowns, trailer cities, metal knots on flat land.

Despite the desolate look, there's a coziness to living in this state. 14

There are so few people (only 470,000) that ranchers who buy and sell cattle know each other statewide. The kids who choose to go to college usually go to the state's one university, in Laramie. Hired hands work their way around Wyoming in a lifetime of hirings and firings. And, despite the physical separation, people stay in touch, often driving two or three hours to another ranch for dinner.

Seventy-five years ago, when travel was by buckboard or horseback, 15 cowboys who were temporarily out of work rode the grub line—drifting from ranch to ranch, mending fences or milking cows, and receiving in exchange a bed and meals. Gossip and messages traveled this slow circuit with them, creating an intimacy among ranchers who were three and four weeks' ride apart.

One old-time couple I know, whose turn-of-the-century homestead 16 was used by an outlaw gang as a relay station for stolen horses, recall that if you were traveling, desperado or not, any lighted ranch house was a welcome sign.

Even now, for someone who lives in a remote spot, arriving at a 17 ranch or coming to town for supplies is cause for celebration. To emerge from isolation can be disorienting. Everything looks bright, new, vivid. After I had been herding sheep for only three days, the sound of the camp-tender's pickup flustered me. Longing for human company, I felt a foolish grin take over my face, yet I had to resist an urgent temptation to run and hide.

Things happen suddenly in Wyoming: the change of seasons and 18 weather; for people, the violent swings into and out of isolation. But goodnaturedness goes hand in hand with severity. Friendliness is a tradition. Strangers passing on the road wave hello.

A common sight is two pickups stopped side by side far out on a 19 range, on a dirt track winding through the sage. The drivers will share a cigarette, uncap their Thermos bottles, and pass a battered cup, steaming with coffee, between windows. These meetings summon up the details of several generations, because in Wyoming private histories are largely public knowledge.

20   In most parts of Wyoming, the human population is visibly outnumbered by the animal. Not far from my town of 50, I rode into a narrow valley and startled a herd of 200 elk. Eagles look like small people as they eat car-killed deer by the road. Antelope, moving in small, graceful bands, travel at 60 m.p.h., their mouths open as if drinking in the space.

21   The solitude in which Westerners live makes them quiet. They telegraph thoughts and feelings by the way they tilt their heads and listen; pulling their Stetsons into a steep dive over their eyes or pigeon-toeing one boot over the other, they lean against a fence and take the whole scene in. These detached looks of quiet amusement are sometimes cynical, but they can also come from a dry-eyed humility as lucid as the air is clear.

22   Conversation goes on in what sounds like a private code. A few phrases imply a complex of meanings. Asking directions you get a curious list of details. While trailing sheep, I was told to "ride up to that kinda upturned rock, follow the pin wash, turn left at the dump, and then you'll see the waterhole."

23   I've spent hours riding to sheep camp at dawn in a pickup when nothing was said and eaten meals in the cookhouse when the only words spoken were a mumbled "Thank you, ma'am" at the end of dinner. The silence is profound. Instead of talking, we seem to share one eye. The landscape is engorged with detail, every movement on it chillingly sharp. The air between people is charged.

24   Spring weather is capricious and mean. It snows, then blisters with heat. There have been tornadoes. They lay their elephant trunks out in the sage until they find houses, then slurp everything up and leave. I've noticed that melting snowbanks hiss and rot, viperous, then drip into calm pools where ducklings hatch and livestock, being trailed to summer range, drink.

25   With the ice cover gone, rivers churn a milkshake brown, taking culverts and small bridges with them. Water in such an arid place (the average annual rainfall where I live is less than eight inches) is like blood. It festoons drab land with green veins: a line of cottonwoods following a stream; a strip of alfalfa, and on ditchbanks, wild asparagus growing.

26   I try to imagine a world of uncharted land, in which one could look over an uncompleted map and ride a horse past where all the lines have stopped. There is no real wilderness left; wilderness, yes, but true

wilderness has been gone on this continent since the time of Lewis and Clark's overland journey.

Two hundred years ago, the Crow, Shoshone, Arapaho, Cheyenne, and Sioux roamed the intermountain West, orchestrating their movements according to hunger, season, and warfare. Once they acquired horses, they traversed the spines of all the big Wyoming ranges—the Absarokas, the Wind Rivers, the Tetons, the Big Horns—and wintered on the unprotected plains that fan out from them. Space was life. The word was their home. 27

What was life-giving to native Americans was often nightmarish to sod-busters who arrived encumbered with families and ethnic pasts to be transplanted in nearly uninhabitable land. The great distances, the shortage of water and trees, and the loneliness created unexpected hardships for them. 28

In her book *O Pioneers!* Willa Cather gives a settler's version of the black landscape:[1] "The little town behind them had vanished as if it had never been, had fallen behind the swell of the prairie, and the stern frozen country received them into its bosom. The homesteads were few and far apart; here and there a windmill gaunt against the sky, a sod house crouching in a hollow." 29

The emptiness of the West was for others a geography of possibility. Men and women who amassed great chunks of land and struggled to preserve unfenced empires were, despite their self-serving motives, unwitting geographers. They understood the lay of the land. 30

But by the 1850s, the Oregon and Mormon trails sported bumper-to-bumper traffic. Wealthy landowners, many of them aristocratic absentee landlords, known as remittance men because they were paid to come West and get out of their families' hair, overstocked the range with more than a million head of cattle. By 1885, the feed and water were desperately short, and the winter of 1886 laid out the gaunt bodies of dead animals so closely together that when the thaw came, one rancher from Kaycee claimed to have walked on cowhide all the way to Crazy Woman Creek, 20 miles away. 31

Territorial Wyoming was a boy's world. The land was generous with everything but water. At first there was room enough and food enough for everyone. And, as with all beginnings, an expansive mood set in. The young cowboys, drifters, shopkeepers, and schoolteachers were heroic, lawless, generous, rowdy, and tenacious. The individualism and optimism generated during those times have endured. 32

Cattle barons tried to control all the public grazing land by restrict- 33

---

[1][Willa Cather (1873–1947) grew up in the grasslands of Nebraska. In books like *O Pioneers!* (1913) and *My Antonia* (1918) she told the story of European immigrants who farmed the uncharted plains of the Midwest.]

ing membership in the Wyoming Stock Growers Association, as if it were a country club. They ostracized from roundups and brandings cowboys and ranchers who were not members, then denounced them as rustlers.

34   One cold-blooded murder of a small-time stockman kicked off the Johnson County cattle war, which was no simple good guy–bad guy shootout but a complicated class struggle between landed gentry and less affluent settlers—a shocking reminder that the West was not an egalitarian sanctuary after all.

35   Fencing ultimately enforced boundaries, but barbed wire abolished space. It was stretched across the beautiful valleys, into mountains, over desert badlands, through buffalo grass.

36   The "anything is possible" fever—the lure of any place—was constricted. The integrity of the land as a geographical body, and the freedom to ride anywhere on it, was lost.

37   I punched cows with a young man named Martin, who is the great-grandson of John Tisdale. His inheritance is not the open land that Tisdale knew and prematurely lost but a rage against restraint.

38   In all this open space, values crystallize quickly. People are strong on scruples but tenderhearted about quirky behavior. A friend and I found one ranch hand, who's "not right in the head," sitting in front of the badly decayed carcass of a cow, shaking his finger and saying, "Now, I don't want you to do this ever again!"

39   When I asked what was wrong with him, I was told, "He's goofier than hell, just like the rest of us."

40   Perhaps because the West is historically new, conventional morality is still felt to be less important than rock-bottom truths. Though there's always a lot of teasing and sparring around, people are blunt with each other, sometimes even cruel, believing honesty is stronger medicine than sympathy, which may console but often conceals.

41   The formality that goes hand in hand with the rowdiness is known as "the Western Code." It's a list of practical do's and don'ts, faithfully observed. A friend, Cliff, who runs a trapline in the winter, cut off half his foot while axing a hole in the ice. Alone, he dragged himself to his pickup and headed for town, stopping to open the ranch gate as he left, and getting out to close it again, thus losing, in his observance of rules, precious time and blood.

42   Later, he commented, "How would it look, them having to come to the hospital to tell me their cows had gotten out?"

43   The roominess of the state has affected political attitudes. Ranchers keep up with world politics and the convulsions of the economy but are basically isolationists. Used to running their own small empires of land and livestock, they're suspicious of big government.

44   It's a "don't fence me in" holdover from a century ago. They still

want the elbow room their grandfathers had, so they're strongly conservative, but with a populist twist.

Summer is the season when we get our "cowboy tans"—on the   45
lower parts of our faces and on three fourths of our arms. Excessive
heat, in the 90s and higher, sends us outside with the mosquitoes.

After the brief lushness of summer, the sun moves south. The range   46
grass is brown. Livestock has been trailed back down from the mountains. Waterholes begin to frost over at night. Last fall Martin asked me
to accompany him on a pack trip. With five horses, we followed a river
into the mountains behind the tiny Wyoming town of Meeteetse.
Groves of aspen, red and orange, gave off a light that made us look
toasted.

One of our evening entertainments was to watch the night sky. My   47
dog, who also came on the trip, a dingo bred to herd sheep, is so used
to the silence and empty skies that when an airplane flies over he
always looks up and eyes the distant intruder quizzically.

The sky, lately, seems to be much more crowded than it used to be.   48
Satellites make their silent passes in the dark with great regularity. We
counted 18 in one hour's viewing. How odd to think that while they
circumnavigated the planet, Martin and I had moved only six miles into
our local wilderness, and had seen no other human for the two weeks
we stayed there.

At night, by moonlight, the land is whittled to slivers—a ridge, a   49
river, a strip of grassland stretching to the mountains, then the huge
sky. One morning a full moon was setting in the west just as the sun
was rising. I felt precariously balanced between the two as I loped
across a meadow. For a moment, I could believe that the stars, which
were still visible, work like cooper's bands, holding everything above
Wyoming together.

Space has a spiritual equivalent, and can heal what is divided and   50
burdensome in us. My grandchildren will probably use space shuttles
for a honeymoon trip or to recover from heart attacks, but closer to
home we might also learn how to carry space inside ourselves in the
effortless way we carry our skins. Space represents sanity, not a life
purified, dull, or "spaced out" but one that might accommodate intelligently any idea or situation.

 USING THE DICTIONARY: Check the information in your dictionary on three kinds of words with which the average reader of this essay might need help: (a) Look up the following examples of **regional** vocabulary—words likely to be familiar to people in the part of the country the author writes about:

1. *plateau* (2) 2. *mesa* (6) 3. *canyon* (6) 4. *range* (3) 5. *dry wash* (11) 6. *log cabin* (10) 7. *buckboard* (15) 8. *relay station* (16) 9. *sodbuster* (28) 10. *sod house* (29) (b) Look up the following examples of **historical** terms. Check especially for helpful information about their origins or associations: 11. *indigenous* (11) 12. *desperado* (16) 13. *ostracize* (33) 14. *drifter* (32) 15. *landed gentry* (34) 16. *egalitarian* (34) 17. *absentee landlord* (31) 18. *sanctuary* (34) 19. *isolationist* (43) 20. *populist* (44) (c) Look up examples of words more likely to appear in **formal** writing than in informal speech: 21. *replenish* (4) 22. *euphemistic* (11) 23. *respite* (11) 24. *expanse* (12) 25. *desolate* (14) 26. *traverse* (27) 27. *encumbered* (28) 28. *circumnavigate* (48) 29. *precarious* (49) 30. *lope* (49)

THE WRITER'S AGENDA:

This essay is a good example of how an effective writer uses authentic details *for a purpose*. Answer the following questions about how the author uses details from first-hand observation to support her general conclusions about the land and its people:

1. In the first nine paragraphs, the author presents to us the **dominant impression** that gives unity to her essay as a whole. In this introduction, she presents and develops the keynote of *spaciousness* already struck in the title of the essay. Point out terms and expressions that echo this key idea of "wide open" country, where everything is on a large scale. Point out specific details that support and reinforce this key idea in these introductory paragraphs.

2. A second section of the essay begins with "Most of Wyoming has a 'lean-to' look." In the next four paragraphs, the author focuses on features of the *physical setting* that make it a harsh place to live. Point out details about architecture, vegetation, wildlife, and geography that all support this point.

3. In the section starting "Despite the desolate look . . ." the author goes on to talk about a first major trait of the *people*. What is that trait, and how does she explain it? In the next five or six paragraphs, trace the network of **related terms** that all echo or reinforce this first major point. At the end of this section, the author goes on to a second psychological trait that she explains as the result of solitude. What is it, and why may it seem contradictory when compared with the first?

4. Several paragraphs in the central section of the essay sketch major *historical developments* that have had a lasting effect on the politics

and the people of the state. Identify several major historical stages. Explain some of the attitudes or competing forces that played a major role in each.

5. In her *conclusion,* the author returns to the dominant overall impression that has unified her many observations of the place and the people. How does she make sure that the concluding four or five paragraphs are not merely weak repetition of what she has already said? At the very end, she spells out a central idea that was implied in much of what she said earlier. State it in your own words.

6. Like other writers of effective description, Gretel Ehrlich makes a special effort to make what she has observed real and vivid for her readers. She frequently uses **figurative** language—imaginative comparisons that help us share not only in the sights and sounds but also in the feelings and reactions of the observer. Study examples of figurative language in the following sample passages. What does each example make us see and hear and feel? What does it draw on for comparison?

a. Today the sun is out—only a few clouds billowing. In the east, where the sheep have started off without me, the benchland tilts up in a series of red-earthed, eroded mesas, planed flat on top by a million years of water. Behind them, a bold line of muscular scraps rears up 10,000 feet to become the Big Horn Mountains. A tidal pattern is engraved into the ground, as if left by the sea that once covered this state. Canyons curve down like galaxies to meet the oncoming rush of flat land.

b. Spring weather is capricious and mean. It snows, then blisters with heat. There have been tornadoes. They lay their elephant trunks out in the sage until they find houses, then slurp everything up and leave. I've noticed that melting snowbanks hiss and rot, viperous, then drip into calm pools where ducklings hatch and livestock, being trailed to summer range, drink.

FOR DISCUSSION OR WRITING:

1. People are often wary of the outsider who forms superficial impressions. If you were an oldtimer in the area that the author describes, how do you think you would react to her account? If you had to defend her against charges of being a superficial observer, on which passages or which details would you draw?

2. Gretel Ehrlich touches on several traditional traits of the American national character that observers have traced to the frontier experience: neighborliness; tolerance for eccentricity; quietness, or dislike of

too much talk. Concentrate on one of these. To judge from your own observation, is it still strong, or has it changed or disappeared? Discuss detailed examples from first-hand observation.

3. We are often told that Americans today are very mobile; they move on from place to place. To judge from your own observation and experience, do Americans care much or little about the area or the region where they live? Are the places where they live or grew up very special to them? Discuss some detailed evidence from your own observation.

4. Describe a part of the country that for you has a definite regional flavor—that is different in appearance or mood from other parts of the country. Concentrate on the physical setting—the landscape, the weather, and the like. Select details that allow you to build up a strong overall impression.

5. Do you know fairly well some occupation that brings people close to sights and sounds not familiar to outsiders? For instance, have you ever worked in a service station, hospital, family grocery? Describe the setting, concentrating on what the people working there see and hear and feel. Aim at a unifying overall impression.

BACKGROUND: Donald M. Murray (born 1917) was a student at Syracuse University and the University of Kentucky and became a teacher of American literature at Northern Illinois University in DeKalb. He says, "I have traveled a good deal, combining travel with teaching or study." He taught for two years at the University of Hong Kong as a Fulbright scholar and spent a summer studying in Taiwan. In 1980, he went to the Chinese mainland to teach American literature at Xian in the People's Republic of China. Although China had been an ally of the United States during World War II, the two countries were for many years shut off from each other after the victory of the Communist party under Mao Zedong in the Chinese civil war. During the "Cultural Revolution," the zealous young Red Guards led the fight against foreign influences, especially those from the capitalistic West. The Chinese students that Murray was asked to teach knew a few nineteenth-century British writers like Charles Dickens, the author of *Oliver Twist,* or W. M. Thackeray, the author of *Vanity Fair.* They knew a few American writers like Jack London, author of *The Call of the Wild.* Their visiting American professor set out to introduce them to the wider range of American literature, from Henry David Thoreau to Stephen Crane to Robert Frost. The article that Murray wrote about his experiences as an American professor in China was published in *Today's Education* and reprinted in the *Chicago Tribune.*

Donald M. Murray
Culture Trading on the Old Silk Road

GUIDE TO READING: Through the centuries, travelers have returned from distant places to share their impressions with their readers. We expect such a writer to be a good *observer*—quick to notice striking details and able to recreate vividly the highlights of a trip. In reading this essay, pay special attention to the details and incidents that give the writing substance. Look for examples of authentic, open-minded observation. At the same time, however, pay attention to the pattern that takes shape as the writer becomes our *guide* in strange new territory. What conclusions has the author drawn? How has he sorted out his impressions?

1   CHINA SEEMS to be full of people who are studying English—both language and literature.

2   I came here to teach, so naturally I expected to see some students—people sitting in rows and listening to me for 50 minutes. But students are everywhere. They pop up in temples, from behind Buddhas. They accost me in parks, like panhandlers: "Good morning, sir, I am a student. I welcome this opportunity to practice my English. How old are you?"

3   On loan from a U.S. university, I'm teaching in a provincial university in Xian, China—once a stop on the Silk Road that carried traders between China and the West. I have a heavy load of classwork and a lot of very bright students. I like them.

4   When I'm through with class, however, I'm not through with students. They stalk me in the corridor, often cornering me near the foul-smelling latrine. Book in hand, they come up to me on the campus. They seep into my apartment after dinner.

5   The other day I was taking my customary lap around the track at 7 a.m. The runner behind me pounded up a little closer and without salutation puffed out, "When the Queen says, 'Hamlet, thou hast thy father much offended,' does she mean. . . .?" And I don't even teach Shakespeare.

6   Such incidents have been so common, both on and off campus, that I find it necessary to classify the questioners. Maybe then I can decide whether I am being exploited or am engaged in some sort of trading enterprise.

7   In one large category are all the kind, innocent folk who catch me on the street and, just to be friendly, lay a few words of English on me.

8   "Hel-lo," says a giggly six-year-old, pushed to the front by a group of his buddies. I answer, and he explodes with laughter. Then they all shout, "Hel-lo, bye-bye!"—expending their English vocabulary in two shots.

9   A young man in a crowded bus gives me his seat. (He does so because the Chinese are polite and because I'm foreign.) He beams and asks my age, a question which is not impolite here. It is also all the English he knows.

10   Some have more words.

11   A frail old man approaches me on a city street. I am holding a map, and he asks, "May I help you?" Then he talks, rapidly. (Is he afraid of being observed fraternizing with a foreigner? He has lived through the Cultural Revolution that began in 1968, when this was absolutely forbidden.) He talks about his happy experience with American army officers stationed here before the Liberation of 1949. Would I know any of them? Let's see, one was Colonel Campbell, from New York. . . .

12   An elderly academic on a southern campus buttonholes me. Is the Ku Klux Klan really strong in America? Why do they roll eggs on the

White House lawn at Easter—and where do they roll them to? (These last I couldn't answer.)

Such questioners are delightful innocents. They're different from the pushy fellow in the park who announced his intention of practicing on me.   13

Other questioners are honest culture-traders. They take, but they also give—services or society.   14

A bus driver on his day off guides me around his city. He is a plump, simple man, who tells me with swelling pride that he is the monitor of his evening class in English. We become great friends.   15

Then another fellow steps up, utters authoritative words in Chinese. Very abruptly, my friend says good-bye. I am puzzled and sad, but don't interfere. Is the new man an official of preventing too-close friendship?   16

Whatever he is, he isn't around when, on a warm spring night, a friend and I are wandering through back streets. A young woman emerges from the shadows and says, "What do you want?"   17

My friend, who (as he tells me later) has jumped to conclusions too often, answers, "I don't know, what do *you* want?"   18

She wants a chance to practice her English. (It turns out that she intended to say something like "Where do you want to go?") We help her, and she invites us to her home, to a party in celebration of her brother's getting a scholarship to a Canadian university. It is a lovely evening.   19

That is a trade. And it is a trade when, in another town, a bright young man at a bus station says frankly, "I can help you, and I want to practice my English." He gets me a reduced-price ticket (almost everything can be got at reduced price, but it takes a knowledgeable Chinese to get it), and he waits hours at the bus station to help me when I get back from my trip. Then, in exchange, we get together later, and I "translate" a Peter-Paul-and-Mary song for him: Although he speaks good English, the American cultural background balked him. We sit in the lobby of a tiny guesthouse in southern China with the sunshine pouring in, playing "It's raining, it's pouring/The old man is snoring" over and over.   20

As for the people I work for at the university, they're traders, too. They ask for a year of my life, all of my privacy, some of my freedoms, about 10 years' worth of my energy, and a grand tolerance about latrines and bookless libraries. In return, they give me bright, charming young people to work with and numerous perks like free transportation to tombs and temples and towns all over China. It's a complex deal.   21

Is it profitable or not? For my own sake and for the sake, perhaps, of other American teachers who will take this trade route, I've tried to decide.   22

I'd have to take into account first of all my strong feeling of com-   23 passion for my students and my continuing, ineradicable sense of frustration at not being able to do much for them.

24 The facilities are incredibly poor. Libraries consist of the works of Mao Zedong (now gathering dust) and, in my field, a few ragged nineteenth-century volumes that look as if they came from some missionary's attic: Dickens; Thackeray (English translation of *Vanity Fair* published in Moscow). Even these are not properly catalogued or really available to students.

25 Classrooms look like something out of *Oliver Twist,* with their rickety desks jammed together, bad light, and grime. Students have piled their rice bowls on the table; apparently they virtually live here. Glowing portraits of Mao and Hua[1] are the only decorations, and even Mao is coming down in some rooms.

26 At first I wanted to change it all. I begged books of my friends back home. Then I discovered how undependable the mail is. Now I just try to live with the situation. But the frustration persists, like a chronic headache.

27 What is worse than such facilities (I don't even mention student housing and food) is the political instruction (one afternoon a week when I came here, now stepped up to two). Among other things, it leaves students with the impression that Marxism is the only known pattern of human thought ("Who's Freud?"[2] "What's existentialism?"). The censorship makes a lot of films and books unavailable and elevates Jack London and Anna Louise Strong to the status of Great American Writers.

28 All this seemed, when I arrived, to be changing. After all, I and others were invited to come here and teach. And we have been, so far, under only those restraints due from guest to host.

29 But our problems are numerous. "If the poem doesn't teach anything, why study it?" "Did the publication of *Sister Carrie*[3] bring about many changes in the System?"

30 Then there is the traditional Chinese conception of education. This keeps students tight-lipped in class when they should be asking questions and deludes them into thinking that a teacher is to pour out facts, a student to receive them passively.

31 Cramped by their physical facilities and by certain new or old modes of thought, the students are nevertheless hungry for the knowledge and methods that the West has to offer. And their heritage of traditional attitudes sometimes aids them in acquiring these things.

[1] [a successor to the Chinese leader]

[2] [Sigmund Freud (1856–1939), Austrian psychologist famous for his study of dreams; the founder of modern psychoanalysis]

[3] [Published in 1900, *Sister Carrie,* by the American novelist Theodore Dreiser, caused a stir by its frank treatment of previously taboo subjects.]

Good Chinese students—and they are all, in this sense, good— 32
apply themselves with tremendous zeal to the tasks set. They learn facts
fast. They are polite, prompt, and—unless hospitalized—present.

Imagine an American student rising when I walk over to him in the 33
classroom to speak; imagine several American students leaping up to
get me a cup of tea; imagine them doing little personal errands like
taking my spare pants to the tailor to get the zipper fixed. Imagine a
class that is always on time, always (well, almost always) prepared. The
respectful attention these students pay is—to an American teacher—
irresistible.

I suspect, however, that to some extent they just want to hear a 34
native speaker's speech. Most of them learned English from books and
from Chinese teachers, so they badly need contemporary vocabulary,
inflection, idiom. One of my students wrote that his sister had married
"a coxcomb and a fop." Another says "I don't know" with Chinese
tones: *I* is like an exclamation; *don't* is neutral; and *know* starts low,
dips, and comes up. This is beautiful to hear, but it isn't English. All
these things the students want to correct, so they turn me on like a tape
recorder. Probably they'd be just as happy to hear the same lecture,
over and over again, the whole term.

Well, no. They're hungry for ideas as well as sounds. I've seen faces 35
shine like lamps when they got an understanding of Stephen Crane's
bright images or Frost's homely ambiguities or Thoreau's tricky puns.
And it happens more often than in a comparable American class.

These students' eagerness, their industry, their politeness—all 36
make teaching them rewarding. Further, teaching them improves pedagogical skills.

For one thing, almost the entire foundation of culture that I 37
share—or at least assume that I share—with American students just
isn't here. I can't refer to Darwin,[4] or the Beatles, or Peoria.

To be alone in the classroom without my family, so to speak, 38
was scary at first. I remembered Jonathan Edwards' declaration to the
sinner:[5]

". . . you have nothing to stand upon, nor anything to take hold of; 39
there is nothing between you and hell but the air."

I recall the joy I felt when it occurred to me, while teaching *Life on* 40
the Mississippi, that the marble boat built in the lake of the Summer
Palace in Beijing was a side-wheeler. What happiness to be able to
relate Mark Twain thus materially to the Ch'ing dynasty! But alas, many
of my students haven't seen the marble boat. Except for those who are

---

[4] [Charles Darwin (1809–82), British biologist and author of *The Origin of Species,*
an early defense of the theory of evolution]

[5] [Jonathan Edwards (1703–58), Puritan preacher famous for his sermon *Sinners in
the Hands of an Angry God*]

old enough to have ridden the trains as Red Guards during the Cultural Revolution, they haven't traveled in their own country. Nor do they know Chinese history before 1949 or ancient literature. The Tang poets? Their fathers were jailed for loving such things.

41   I learned to briefly present essential background and to ignore much of the ephemeral and local in literature. I got closer to the nub. I honed my tools of analysis by practice in a cultural void.

42   I learned, besides, to identify and attack the specific problems of Asian people, their methods of learning and their old-fashioned attitudes toward learning.

43   The verb *nian shu* (literally *read book*) means both to study and to read aloud so as to commit to memory. On the athletic field, as soon as it becomes light, I see not only the joggers and the practitioners of *tai chi* physical conditioning, but a lot of students pacing slowly up and down, book in hand, reading aloud. They are memorizing language patterns or facts.

44   A typical—and symbolic—stance is that taken by the students who stand facing a wall (so as not to be disturbed by joggers?) and read aloud. It is weird to hear "Richard Cory,"[6] in a Chinese accent, echoing from the wall of the campus pigpen at 6 A.M.

45   Once in class I paused before discussing a poem that had been assigned. "Read it over first, to refresh your minds on it," I said, meaning "read it silently." The class suddenly burst into speech, full-throated but strangely mechanical because of the coordination of the voices. I almost jumped out of my seat. Panicky, I wondered: How do you turn them off?

46   They have to get over *nian shu* if they want to learn from the West. They have to learn to analyze instead of memorize.

47   In helping them do this, I myself gained a few things besides skills—for instance, a distinct appreciation of our American advantages. These need no elaboration. I will only say that when I go home, I will write criticism of the government all over my office door (in big characters), just to reassure myself that it's legal to do so. And I will go over to the library and plant a great big kiss on the card catalogue.

48   I will also, however, go home with a keen sense of some American limitations. How provincial we are about China. How little we know about the turmoils under the surface here, the nature of the widespread poverty, the variety among the people called Chinese. Finally, how little we know about the kind of historical continuity found here. In Chicago, the old part of town is the part that dates from maybe the 1890's. To go to Old Town in Xian, I go through a gate in an eighth-century wall and visit the site of a village 6,000 years old. In China one

---

[6][An often anthologized poem by the American poet E. A. Robinson (1869–1935)]

gets what Henry James called "a sense of the past."[7]

Culture trading on the Old Silk Road has its hardships, then, espe- 49
cially on the campus. But an American teacher receives great rewards,
in the shape of strokes for the ego, improvement of the teacher's craft,
deeper knowledge of the Middle Kingdom, and humility and pride
concerning our own country.

Access to the route may not last. Some people here fear that the 50
radicalism of the Cultural Revolution may return and that the foreign
teachers and their bourgeois culture may not long be welcome. I'm all
for carrying our wares through the Wall while we can. The trading is
profitable.

 USING THE DICTIONARY: During its history, English has taken
over many thousands of words from other languages, including especially Latin and Greek. Often our language uses several *related words* from the same Latin or Greek word root.
Look up both words in each of the following pairs. How are
the two words related? Explain how the second and more
familiar word could help a student understand or remember
the less common word used in this essay. 1. *salutation—
salute* (5) 2. *expend—expense* (8) 3. *fraternize—fraternity*
(11) 4. *authoritative—authority* (16) 5. *ineradicable—
erase* (23) 6. *persist—persistent* (26) 7. *delude—delusion*
(30) 8. *pedagogical—pediatrician* (36) 9. *stance—station-
ary* (44) 10. *provincial—province* (48)

THE WRITER'S AGENDA:

The writer of this article wants to share with his readers what he has
learned during his trip. He shares with us many striking impressions.
But he has also sorted things out in his mind to arrive at some general
conclusions. Study the pattern that takes shape as the author shares
with us his impressions of China.

1. Look at details showing us that the author is an alert observer:
(a) A good observer has a quick eye for how people act and a quick ear
for what they say. Describe several of the amusing or puzzling *encounters* that the visitor had with Chinese people. (b) Describe several
strange details about the *setting* or physical environment—things that
are likely to catch a foreign visitor's eye.

---

[7] [Henry James (1843–1916), American novelist, one of whose major themes was the
meeting between American and Old World culture]

2. The first four paragraphs of this article already sum up a strong *general impression*. The writer from the beginning sets up a general perspective that prepares us for much of what follows later. State the overall impression in your own words. Show how it is echoed or developed in the first four paragraphs.

3. To make sense of what we observe, we often *classify* things—we sort them out into categories. The author early in the essay sets up two large categories for the "questioners" who approach him. What are the two categories? What characteristics set them apart? What examples does he give for each?

4. Visitors to a foreign country often experience mixed emotions. They return with a mixture of favorable and *unfavorable impressions*. In the central part of the essay, the author talks about things that made his work difficult. He discusses his frustration at not being able to do more for his students. What were the major problems or obstacles? What were the physical or material difficulties? What were the psychological difficulties?

5. In the central part of the essay, the author at the same time talks about *advantages* or rewards that compensated for his difficulties. He talks appreciatively about the personal qualities of his students. What did he like about their attitudes toward education and toward teachers? What are some of the labels he applied to them? What to you is the key quality that impressed him again and again about these students?

6. The author of this article tries to be an *open-minded* observer— neither judge or accuser, nor advocate or eager supporter. To some extent, we have to reach our own answers to questions we are likely to ask about a country like China. After reading this article, how would you answer the following questions: (a) What is the standard of living? (b) What is the nature or extent of censorship or indoctrination? (c) How liberal or how repressive is the political system?

7. The author's **tone** suits an article whose aim is to inform but also to entertain the reader. The writer uses a moderately formal kind of English—serious, but with an occasional lighter touch. What makes sentences such as the following informal or humorous? For each, what would be a more formal or more serious way of saying the same thing? (a) "Kind, innocent folk catch me on the street and lay a few words of English on me." (b) "A giggly six-year-old is pushed to the front by a group of his buddies." (c) "I will plant a great big kiss on the card catalog." (d) "The teacher receives rewards in the shape of strokes for the ego."

FOR DISCUSSION OR WRITING:

1. Visitors to foreign countries often experience culture shock. They see things that are strange and bewildering. If you had been in the author's shoes, which of his experiences would have been most strange or bewildering to you?

2. The author comments on the limited background of his students—their limited familiarity with Western culture. How well would you do on a test designed to check your own cultural background? Answer *one* of the following in a well-developed paragraph: (a) What is Marxism? (b) Who was Freud? (c) What is existentialism? (d) Who was Jack London? (e) Who was Darwin?

3. The author says about his Chinese students, "They have to learn to analyze instead of memorize." He implies that American students are taught to think rather than merely to commit things to memory. To judge from your own experience as a student, is he right?

4. How good a guide to American ways and ideas would you make for a visiting student from China? Explain and discuss one of the following: (a) American ideas about a citizen's right to criticize the government; (b) familiar American ideas about the role the ego plays in people's behavior.

5. Americans traveling in foreign countries often think of themselves as people with good intentions, "ambassadors of good will." Have you encountered evidence of this positive self-image in American movies and television shows or in your reading? How or to what extent does Murray fit this familiar stereotype?

6. Describe a lifestyle or way of life that might be new or different to at least some of your fellow students. Draw on your own first-hand observation of a setting and of people's behavior and attitudes.

7. Americans are often accused of knowing too little about foreign countries. Do you think the charge is justified? Draw on your experience and reading for material you can use in answering this question.

BACKGROUND: N. Scott Momaday (born 1934) is a member of the Kiowa tribe and first became widely known when he published a collection of Kiowa tales, *The Journey of Tai-me* (1968), later republished as *The Way to Rainy Mountain*. Momaday was born in Lawton, Oklahoma, and studied at the University of New Mexico and Stanford University. He became a Professor of English at the University of California, first at Santa Barbara and then at Berkeley. His novel *The House Made of Dawn* won the Pulitzer Prize in 1969. Many of his poems recreate with haunting beauty the songs and legends of his people; they have appeared in collections such as *The Gourd Dancer* (1976). The following essay, after which the book *The Way to Rainy Mountain* was named, was first published in *The Reporter*.

N. Scott Momaday
The Way to Rainy Mountain

GUIDE TO READING: Momaday is a writer who vividly recalls scenes and people from the past. In reading the essay, pay special attention to vividly remembered characteristic details that make places and people real for the reader. At the same time, ask yourself: "Why does the writer remember these details? What is their meaning for him?"

1   A SINGLE KNOLL rises out of the plain in Oklahoma, north and west of the Wichita range. For my people, the Kiowas, it is an old landmark, and they gave it the name Rainy Mountain. The hardest weather in the world is there. Winter brings blizzards, hot tornadic winds arise in the spring, and in the summer the prairie is an anvil's edge. The grass turns brittle and brown, and it cracks beneath your feet. There are green belts along the rivers and creeks, linear groves of hickory and pecan, willow and witch hazel. At a distance in July or August the steaming foliage seems almost to writhe in fire. Great green and yellow grasshoppers are everywhere in the tall grass, popping up like

corn to sting the flesh, and tortoises crawl about on the red earth, going nowhere in the plenty of time. Loneliness is an aspect of the land. All things in the plain are isolate; there is no confusion of objects in the eye, but *one* hill or *one* tree or *one* man. To look upon that landscape in the early morning, with the sun at your back, is to lose the sense of proportion. Your imagination comes to life, and this, you think, is where Creation was begun.

I returned to Rainy Mountain in July. My grandmother had died in in the spring, and I wanted to be at her grave. She had lived to be very old and at last infirm. Her only living daughter was with her when she died, and I was told that in death her face was that of a child. 2

I like to think of her as a child. When she was born, the Kiowas were living the last great moment of their history. For more than a hundred years they had controlled the open range from the Smoky Hill River to the Red, from the headwaters of the Canadian to the fork of the Arkansas and Cimarron. In alliance with the Comanches, they had ruled the whole of the Southern Plains. War was their sacred business, and they were the finest horsemen the world has ever known. But warfare for the Kiowas was pre-eminently a matter of disposition rather than of survival, and they never understood the grim, unrelenting advance of the U.S. Cavalry. When at last, divided and ill provisioned, they were driven onto the Staked Plains in the cold of autumn, they fell into panic.[1] In Palo Duro Canyon they abandoned their crucial stores to pillage and had nothing then but their lives. In order to save themselves, they surrendered to the soldiers at Fort Sill and were imprisoned in the old stone corral that now stands as a military museum. My grandmother was spared the humiliation of those high gray walls by eight or ten years, but she must have known from birth the affliction of defeat, the dark brooding of old warriors. 3

Her name was Aho, and she belonged to the last culture to evolve in North America. Her forebears came down from the high country in western Montana nearly three centuries ago. They were a mountain people, a mysterious tribe of hunters whose language has never been classified in any major group. In the late seventeenth century they began a long migration to the south and east. It was a journey toward the dawn, and it led to a golden age. Along the way the Kiowas were befriended by the Crows, who gave them the culture and religion of the Plains. They acquired horses, and their ancient nomadic spirit was suddenly free of the ground. They acquired Tai-me, the sacred sun-dance doll, from that moment the object and symbol of their worship, and so 4

[1] [The Staked Plains, English for the Spanish *Llano Estacado,* is the name of the great arid plateau of southeast New Mexico, northwest Oklahoma, and west Texas.]

shared in the divinity of the sun. Not least, they acquired the sense of destiny, therefore courage and pride. When they entered upon the Southern Plains they had been transformed. No longer were they slaves to the simple necessity of survival; they were a lordly and dangerous society of fighters and thieves, hunters and priests of the sun. According to their origin myth, they entered the world through a hollow log. From one point of view, their migration was the fruit of an old prophecy, for indeed they emerged from a sunless world.

5   Though my grandmother lived out her long life in the shadow of Rainy Mountain, the immense landscape of the continental interior lay like memory in her blood. She could tell of the Crows, whom she had never seen, and of the Black Hills, where she had never been. I wanted to see in reality what she had seen more perfectly in the mind's eye, and drove fifteen hundred miles to begin my pilgrimage.

6   Yellowstone, it seemed to me, was the top of the world, a region of deep lakes and dark timber, canyons and waterfalls. But, beautiful as it is, one might have the sense of confinement there. The skyline in all directions is close at hand, the high wall of the woods and deep cleavages of shade. There is a perfect freedom in the mountains, but it belongs to the eagle and the elk, the badger and the bear. The Kiowas reckoned their stature by distances they see, and they were bent and blind in the wilderness.

7   Descending eastward, the highland meadows are a stairway to the plain. In July the inland slope of the Rockies is luxuriant with flax and buckwheat, stonecrop and larkspur. The earth unfolds and the limit of the land recedes. Clusters of trees, and animals grazing far in the distance, cause the vision to reach away and wonder to build upon the mind. The sun follows a longer course in the day, and the sky is immense beyond all comparison. The great billowing clouds that sail upon it are shadows that move upon the grain like water, dividing light. Farther down, in the land of the Crows and Blackfeet, the plain is yellow. Sweet clover takes hold of the hills and bends upon itself to cover and seal the soil. There the Kiowas paused on their way; they had come to the place where they must change their lives. The sun is at home on the plains. Precisely there does it have the certain character of a god. When the Kiowas came to the land of the Crows, they could see the dark lees of the hills at dawn across the Bighorn River, the profusion of light on the grain shelves, the oldest deity ranging after the solstices. Not yet would they veer southward to the caldron of the land that lay below; they must wean their blood from the northern winter and hold the mountains a while longer in their view. They bore Tai-me in procession to the east.

8   A dark mist lay over the Black Hills, and the land was like iron. At the top of a ridge I caught sight of Devil's Tower upthrust against the

gray sky as if in the birth of time the core of the earth had broken through its crust and the motion of the world was begun. There are things in nature that engender an awful quiet in the heart of man; Devil's Tower is one of them. Two centuries ago, because they could not do otherwise, the Kiowas made a legend at the base of the rock. My grandmother said:

"Eight children were there at play, seven sisters and their brother. 9 Suddenly the boy was struck dumb; he trembled and began to run upon his hands and feet. His fingers became claws, and his body was covered with fur. There was a bear where the boy had been. The sisters were terrified; they ran, and the bear after them. They came to the stump of a great tree, and the tree spoke to them. It bade them climb upon it, and as they did so, it began to rise into the air. The bear came to kill them, but they were just beyond its reach. It reared against the tree and scored the bark all around with its claws. The seven sisters were borne into the sky, and they became the stars of the Big Dipper." From that moment, and so long as the legend lives, the Kiowas have kinsmen in the night sky. Whatever they were in the mountains, they could be no more. However tenuous their well-being, however much they had suffered and would suffer again, they had found a way out of the wilderness.

My grandmother had a reverence for the sun, a holy regard that now 10 is all but gone out of mankind. There was a wariness in her, and an ancient awe. She was a Christian in her later years, but she had come a long way about, and she never forgot her birthright. As a child she had been to the sun dances; she had taken part in that annual rite, and by it she had learned the restoration of her people in the presence of Tai-me. She was about seven when the last Kiowa sun dance was held in 1887 on the Washita River above Rainy Mountain Creek. The buffalo were gone. In order to consummate the ancient sacrifice—to impale the head of a buffalo bull upon the Tai-me tree—a delegation of old men journeyed into Texas, there to beg and and barter for an animal from the Goodnight herd. She was ten when the Kiowas came together for the last time as a living sun-dance culture. They could find no buffalo; they had to hang an old hide from the sacred tree. Before the dance could begin, a company of soldiers rode out from Fort Sill under orders to disperse the tribe. Forbidden without cause the essential act of their faith, having seen the wild herds slaughtered and left to rot upon the ground, the Kiowas backed away forever from the tree. That was July 20, 1890, at the great bend of the Washita. My grandmother was there. Without bitterness, and for as long as she lived, she bore a vision of deicide.

Now that I can have her only in memory, I see my grandmother in 11 the several postures that were peculiar to her: standing at the wood stove on a winter morning and turning meat in a great iron skillet; sitting at the south window, bent above her beadwork, and afterwards, when her vision failed, looking down for a long time into the fold of her hands; going out upon a cane, very slowly as she did when the weight of age came upon her; praying. I remember her most often at prayer. She made long, rambling prayers out of suffering and hope, having seen many things. I was never sure that I had the right to hear, so exclusive were they of all mere custom and company. The last time I saw her she prayed standing by the side of her bed at night, naked to the waist, the light of a kerosene lamp moving upon her dark skin. Her long black hair, always drawn and braided in the day, lay upon her shoulders and against her breasts like a shawl. I do not speak Kiowa, and I never understood her prayers, but there was something inherently sad in the sound, some merest hesitation upon the syllables of sorrow. She began in a high and descending pitch, exhausting her breath to silence; then again and again—and always the same intensity of effort, of something that is, and is not, like urgency in the human voice. Transported so in the dancing light among the shadows of her room, she seemed beyond the reach of time. But that was illusion; I think I knew then that I should not see her again.

12   Houses are like sentinels in the plain, old keepers of the weather watch. There, in a very little while, wood takes on the appearance of great age. All colors wear soon away in the wind and rain, and then the wood is burned gray and the grain appears and the nails turn red with rust. The window panes are black and opaque; you imagine there is nothing within, and indeed there are many ghosts, bones given up to the land. They stand here and there against the sky, and you approach them for a longer time than you expect. They belong in the distance; it is their domain.

13   Once there was a lot of sound in my grandmother's house, a lot of coming and going, feasting and talk. The summers there were full of excitement and reunion. The Kiowas are a summer people; they abide the cold and keep to themselves, but when the season turns and the land becomes warm and vital they cannot hold still; an old love of going returns upon them. The aged visitors who came to my grandmother's house when I was a child were made of lean and leather, and they bore themselves upright. They wore great black hats and bright ample shirts that shook in the wind. They rubbed fat upon their hair and wound their braids with strips of colored cloth. Some of them painted their faces and carried the scars of old and cherished enmities. They were an old council of warlords, come to remind and be reminded of who they were. Their wives and daughters served them well. The women might indulge themselves; gossip was at once the mark and compensation of their servitude. They made loud and elaborate

talk among themselves, full of jest and gesture, fright and false alarm. They went abroad in fringed and flowered shawls, bright beadwork and German silver.They were at home in the kitchen, and they prepared meals that were banquets.

There were frequent prayer meetings, and nocturnal feasts. When I 14 was a child I played with my cousins outside, where the lamplight fell upon the ground and the singing of the old people rose up around us and carried away into the darkness. There were a lot of good things to eat, a lot of laughter and surprise. And afterwards, when the quiet returned, I lay down with my grandmother and could hear the frogs away by the river and feel the motion of the air.

Now there is a funeral silence in the rooms, the endless wake of 15 some final word. The walls have closed in upon my grandmother's house. When I returned to it in mourning, I saw for the first time in my life how small it was. It was late at night, and there was a white moon, nearly full. I sat for a long time on the stone steps by the kitchen door. From there I could see out across the land; I could see the long row of trees by the creek, the low light upon the rolling plains, and the stars of the Big Dipper. Once I looked at the moon and caught sight of a strange thing. A cricket had perched upon the handrail, only a few inches away. My line of vision was such that the creature filled the moon like a fossil. It had gone there, I thought, to live and die, for there, of all places, was its small definition made whole and eternal. A warm wind rose up and purled like the longing within me.

The next morning, I awoke at dawn and went out on the dirt road to 16 Rainy Mountain. It was already hot, and the grasshoppers began to fill the air. Still, it was early in the morning, and birds sang out of the shadows. The long yellow grass on the mountain shone in the bright light, and a scissortail hied above the land. There, where it ought to be, at the end of a long and legendary way, was my grandmother's grave. She had at last succeeded to that holy ground. Here and there on the dark stones were ancestral names. Looking back once, I saw the mountain and came away.

 USING THE DICTIONARY: N. Scott Momaday writes about the past in a solemn, reverential style. For each of the following, what would be a simpler word or expression that would serve for a more casual or ordinary occasion? 1. *isolate*—adj. (1) 2. *pillage* (3) 3. *forebears* (4) 4. *kinsmen* (9) 5. *tenuous* (9) 6. *consummate* (10) 7. *impale* (10) 8. *deicide* (10) 9. *sentinels* (12) 10. *opaque* (12) 11. *domain* (12) 12. *abide* (13) 13. *enmities* (13) 14. *servitude* (13) 15. *nocturnal* (14)

THE WRITER'S AGENDA:

The author of this essay writes the kind of reminiscence that combines vivid imaginative description with far-ranging reflection on the meaning of the scenes and people described. Answer the following questions about how the essay takes shape:

1. How does the author in the opening paragraph create the *setting* for his childhood memories? Point out striking specific details and graphic, concrete words. Point out examples of striking imaginative comparisons, or figurative language. What for you is the unifying central idea or dominant impression in this paragraph?

2. On the occasion of his grandmother's death, Momaday briefly tells the story of his people. What to you is most instructive or most memorable about their history, their legends, and their religion? Show that his **point of view** is not that of a neutral outsider but that of a committed writer who identifies with and pays tribute to people who are his ancestors and represent his roots.

3. In the *portrait* of his grandmother that begins the last third of the essay, what details does the author use to make her real and distinctive to us as a person?

4. In his description of life at the grandmother's *house,* how does Momaday recreate the vanished past? What are some striking or vivid details? What for you is the unifying central idea or dominant impression? How does the author use the **contrast** between then and now to heighten the overall impression at which he aims?

5. How do the two concluding paragraphs take up again *earlier strands* of the essay? What is the symbolic significance of the cricket?

6. The author's style is rich in details and comments that may at times seem **paradoxical**—they may seem contradictory at first but begin to make sense on further thought. What is paradoxical about statements such as the following? How do they help the author avoid oversimplification or clichés?

a. Warfare for the Kiowas was pre-eminently a matter of disposition rather than of survival.

b. Some of them . . . carried the scars of old and cherished enmities.

c. Gossip was at once the mark and compensation of their servitude.

For discussion or writing:

1. In writing about the Native American past, Momaday deals with a subject that has often been obscured by prejudice, stereotypes, or neglect. What in this essay confirmed or reinforced familiar ideas? What for you was new or instructive?

2. In their search for roots, many Americans have in recent years written about the past nostalgically. They have idealized the history of their groups. How much in this essay is nostalgia for a vanished past? How much is meaningful or relevant as guidance for the future?

3. Use the author's description of life at his grandmother's house as a model for a childhood reminiscence or nostalgic re-creation of a scene from your own past.

4. Write a tribute to a person who, like the author's grandmother, represents a distinctive way of life. Write about someone you know well from close observation.

5. Describe a natural scene, including ample detail from patient first-hand observation. For instance, take a close look at a cliff, forest clearing, deserted beach, undeveloped lakefront, stretch of desert. Or describe a typical city scene, taking a close look at a parking lot, public square, major avenue, major intersection in a shopping area, main street, or the like. Aim at a unifying overall impression.

6. Use Momaday's account of the migration of the Kiowas as a model for an account of a journey or of moving from one part of the country to another. Use vivid concrete detail to make settings or stages real for your readers. Try to establish a clear pattern or to convey a sense of meaningful progression.

FOR FURTHER DISCUSSION AND WRITING: Leonard Michaels wrote the following short piece after a return visit to New York City, where he grew up. What is his view of life in the big city? Does his account seem unfair or biased to you? Why or why not? How does his view of city life compare with yours?

Leonard Michaels

New York, New York

1   MY MOTHER has four rooms with a balcony on the 16th floor of the Seward Park Project. Her windows look onto Grand Street and East Broadway. The park lies between these streets. Daylong it's wild with kids and pigeons. People sit on the benches under the trees, gossiping, watching the crowd that strolls by—mommas and babies, gangs of adolescents, women with shopping bags, men with newspapers. Nameless elements enter the park at night.

2   From my mother's balcony I could see the neighborhood where I grew up. The schools, the library, the stores, and many of the buildings are still there, but formerly Jewish streets are now Puerto Rican. The Forward Building is owned by Chinese investors. I could also follow the skyline, beginning at the Empire State Building, going west and south until stopped by the new, twin towers of the World Trade Center. They stand shoulder to shoulder like huge rectangular thugs.

3   I'd take morning coffee on the balcony when the sky was clear. Sometimes, it looked almost pure: and the complexity of Manhattan, downtown to midtown, seemed to strike up to the sky in one dazzling voice from a vast field of streets. Directly below, in the park, a group of men and women occasionally practiced the slow, dreamy motions of Chinese calisthenics. Kids always arrived early and started basketball games. Beyond the park the streets were soon quick and squeezed with traffic. Noise increased all day and then sirens became frequent—fire engines, police cars, ambulances—announcing the supernatural agonies of nighttime Manhattan.

My first night was buried in a hot, kosher meal of meats. Wrong for this African August, but correct for my psychological climate. I was home, the place I came from, to which mail is addressed "New York, New York," as if to the essence of the essence.   4

We sat in it after dinner—mother, wife, kids—sweating and familial, a body above the war, planning what to do. In fact, they planned. I was here on business and I'd already decided the important thing. I would not go even once into the subway. I wouldn't see trains decorated by sacred hysteria, or guns who pace from car to car to protect me from sudden death between stations, and I wouldn't read the sign that advises you to hurry into the front car if nobody is smiling.   5

Kafka, my favorite writer, loved the noise in the Paris Metro. He loved the sense of mysterious passage and the freedom from speech. Our subway is a different story; it is all about raging harassment through dingy, lunatic channels.   6

But I went into the subway. Taxis were expensive, they were too slow and they were also much too fast. The first one I rode in hit 40 m.p.h. near Chatham Square when a pothole received us and spit us out into the blazing emphysema. I glanced back. Apparently, the divider line had been painted into and out of the hole.   7

The next day, riding the F train, feeling like a Kafka, I witnessed an argument. One man wanted doors shut between cars and another didn't. It was hot and miserable in the train, but if he wanted the doors shut that seemed no reason to rise up against him full of dangerous threats. They stood eyeball to eyeball.   8

The night before we left New York, I couldn't sleep. I was on the balcony very early. The morning was cool. The city lay in quiet, hazy, blue light. When I glanced down into the park, I saw the body of a woman, lying on a bench. The police had roped off the area and thrown a sheet over her. She seemed to be naked. That evening I phoned my mother from California. She told me some facts: 26 years old; a heroin addict; she'd been stabbed. Then, in a sad apologetic tone, she said, "It has never happened before." She meant never in that park. She meant it is possible to mourn and to feel responsible for strangers.   9

Sirens, taxis, arguments—does New York have a coherent idea? A woman said to me, "Where anything is possible, everything is equivalent. New York is the only place I feel alive."   10

EXPERIENCE:
Roles People Play

The Common Theme: Autobiographical writing takes stock of the author's experience. It is different from a diary that merely chronicles events from day to day. Effective autobiography soon focuses on what truly mattered to the author. The writers in this unit deal with a common theme: As we grow up, trying to decide who we are, we are often strongly aware of the roles that we are expected to play. Often we find ourselves caught in a conflict between competing models of what we should be. Often we are caught in a conflict between an outward public role expected of us and the private person that is our real identity. In this unit, Lillian Hellman, in "An Only Child," writes about the two branches of her family that represented two different ways of looking at life. Jade Snow Wong, in "Fifth Chinese Daughter," is torn between the traditional ways of immigrant parents and the Americanized ways of school and the world outside. George Orwell, in "Shooting an Elephant," writes about the doubts and divided loyalties of the private person behind the façade of authority.

WRITER'S GUIDE 2:
Writing from Experience

Much writing hands on what the author has heard and read. But the roots of much truly effective writing are in what the writers know for themselves. Much writing that is truly worth reading grows out of the writer's own experience. We sense that the subject matters to the writer personally. Theoretical arguments come to life when the examples or the evidence presented make us feel: "This is something this writer has lived through. This is close to the writer's own life."

Writing that takes a close look at the writer's personal experience is called **autobiography**. Effective autobiographical writing covers some of the same ground as description: It creates a setting; it uses authentic detail to make places and people come to life before our eyes. But autobiography focuses on the actions and reactions of people. It tells us how people act and what they say, but especially also what they think and feel. The thoughts, feelings, and attitudes of the people involved play a major role. Autobiographical writing tells the story of events, but its central interest is in what the events meant to the writer.

In papers in which you draw on your personal experience, try to do justice to the five major dimensions of successful autobiographical writing:

(1) *Use vivid, authentic detail to recreate the setting.* Satisfy the readers who want to know: "Where are we?" Apply what you have learned in studying and practicing descriptive writing. In the autobiographical essays reprinted in this unit, setting plays a major role. Each essay takes us to places that helped shape the outlook or the personality of the author: a boarding house in New Orleans, the basement sweatshops of Chinatown in San Francisco, the wretched prisons and squalid "native" quarters of colonial Burma under British rule.

(2) *Make the people you write about real for your reader.* Satisfy the readers who want to know: "Who are these people?" The following capsule portrait from an autobiographical essay is packed with details about the author's father. It uses details that reveal character; we feel we are coming to know the father as a person:

> Six days a week he rose early, dressed, ate breakfast alone, put on his hat, and walked to his barbershop at 207 Henry Street on the Lower East Side of Manhattan, about half a mile from our apartment. He returned after dark. The family ate dinner together on Sundays and Jewish holidays. Mainly he ate alone. I don't remember him staying home from work because of illness or bad weather. He took few vacations, but once we spent a week in Miami and he tried to enjoy himself, wading

into the ocean, being brave, stepping, inch by inch, into the warm blue unpredictable immensity. Then he slipped. . . . He came up thrashing, struggling back to the beach on skinny white legs. "I nearly drowned," he said, very exhilarated. He never went into the water again. I think he preferred his barbershop to the natural world. He retired after thirty-five years, when his hands trembled too much for scissors and razors and angina made it impossible for him to stand up for long periods. Then he took walks in the neighborhood and carried a vial of whiskey in his shirt pocket. When pain stopped him in the street, he'd stand very still and sip his whiskey. A few times I stood beside him, as still as he, waiting for the pain to end, both of us speechless and frightened.

    —Leonard Michaels, "My Father's Life," *Esquire*

(3) *Give a dramatic account of key events.* Satisfy the readers who want to know: "What happened?" Select incidents that help us see how an issue arose in a concrete situation. If you write about an important conflict, show how it was acted out—in little incidents or in a major confrontation. If you want us to be aware of an important character trait, make it show in what the person did and said. Here is a revealing incident as told by a writer who knows how to dramatize everyday situations and events:

    I forget to give change to a middle-aged woman with bitter eyes. I charged her forty-five cents for a pound and a third of apples and she gave me half a dollar. Now she is demanding her nickel, and her eyes are narrower than the sides of dimes. She is a round-shouldered person, beaky and short—short-changed. In her stare at me, there is an entire judiciary system—accusation, trial, and conviction. "You give me my nickel, mister."

    "I'm sorry. I forgot. Here is your nickel."

    She does not believe my mistake a mistake. She walks away in a white huff. Now she stops, turns, glowers. She moves on. Twice more, as she departs from the market, she stops, turns, and stares angrily back. I watch her all the way to the curb.

    —John McPhee, "Giving Good Weight"

(4) *Do justice to feelings and attitudes.* Satisfy the readers who want to know: "How do these people think and feel?" In autobiographical writing, the external events are important, but just as important, or more so, is what happens in people's minds. Give a candid account of your own feelings and reactions. In the following passages, the author

vividly recalls standards and feelings that were part of the spirit of her favorite sport:

> There were important by-products of playing field hockey. We always congratulated the loser on having played well. We congratulated the winner on her superb work, whether we thought she cheated, or had an advantage of age or experience. I am still anguished when I hear my Brooklyn-bred husband scream at the children over the Monopoly board: "Hurrah, I win—ha-ha, you lose.". . . .
>
> I remember a girl named Karen with blood pouring down her face and onto her white middy blouse and a dark accusing hole where her front teeth had been. It is blurred in my mind whose stick was responsible, but I was close enough to feel guilt and fear and the excitement of both those emotions. It never occurred to me that a simple child's game, a ball playing, might not be worth a lifetime of false teeth.
>
> —Anne Roiphe, on field hockey, in *Ms.*

(5) *Aim at a unifying overall point.* Satisfy the readers who want to know: "Why is this important?" If you focus on a single important event, spell out what it meant to you or what you learned from the experience. If you discuss related experiences, make your readers see the common thread. Have a central question or key issue arise early in the paper. Concentrate on a unifying theme or concern.

The following passage from an autobiographical essay spells out a theme that we encounter in much American autobiography: Millions of young Americans have grown up with immigrant parents whose goal was to have their children become "Americanized" and live out the dream of success that had brought the parents across the sea. The author's father, who had come to this country from Puerto Rico, constantly exhorted his children to become educated and not to "end up like me":

> "You're all going to get good educations and good jobs," he'd tell us day after day. He meant that we were not going to follow in his stumbling footsteps. . . . We had to avoid his mistakes from the beginning; otherwise we'd end up like him: paying for his sins in the hotel kitchen, and at night in bed, unable to sleep because—there was that job of his. Job? He'd been better off tending anemic chickens in the old home village. He was paying, but we weren't going to; we were going to collect, and that, he said, was the reward he wanted out of life. We told Mami we wanted to go back to the Island, but she said "Muy

tarde," too late. We were americanos—not she, not Papi, but *we,* los hijos—and we'd just have to make the most of that situation.

—Edward Rivera, "La Situación," *New York*

Much autobiographical writing focuses from the beginning on things that really mattered to the writer. We then follow along as the author's conclusions take shape or as the meaning of what happened becomes clear. However, in a paper that aims at one major point, you may state your central idea as your **thesis** at the beginning of the paper. You then follow up by discussing in detail the experiences that were part of the same basic pattern. The following might be the introduction of an autobiographical student paper that is clearly focused on one major point:

Child Labor

THESIS: *Have I encountered the "work ethic"? I grew up with it.* To my family, work is a virtue, and play is a sin. My earliest memories of my mother include watching her work at a machine that punched holes in cards. For as long as I can remember, my father has been moonlighting and working on weekends. By the time I was in the fourth grade, my parents had me get up at six to deliver papers so I would learn "the value of a dollar."

To sum up: Autobiographical writing often appears under the heading of **narration**—it tells the story of events from the author's own life. But the central interest in autobiographical writing is in the *meaning* of the events. The key question for the writer is: "What have I learned from the experience? How has it affected me as a person?" Writing that draws directly on the author's personal experience often has a strength missing from more impersonal writing. People write with a special commitment when they try to make sense of what has happened to them, when they try to understand where they came from and who they are.

PREWRITING ACTIVITIES 2

1. Write a *personal résumé* that will introduce you to other people. Write a paragraph under each of the following headings:

◆ Roots (family; place or places where you grew up)

- ◆ Schooling (what kind of schools, best and worst subjects)

- ◆ Interests (reading, hobbies, sports, activities)

- ◆ Work (summer jobs, chores, regular employment)

Include some factual information, but concentrate mostly on what mattered to you as a person.

2. What are some of your earliest memories of people other than your parents? Who are some of the people who mattered to you most during your childhood years or your first years of school? Do some *free writing* about one or more of these people. Record events, images, or feelings as they come to mind. Write quickly, following the chain of associations as one remembered scene calls up another.

3. Start a *journal*. Two or three times a week, write about things that have happened, scenes you have observed, or people you have met. Record your candid impressions and reactions. Develop the habit of writing down in a rough preliminary form things that you might later use as material for more structured writing.

BACKGROUND: Talking about the sources of her own work, a famous American biographer said, "Every experience of life feeds the writer." Lillian Hellman (born 1907) is an American playwright whose life and whose work as a writer are difficult to separate. She was born in New Orleans but spent much of her childhood in New York. She went to college there and later went to work for a New York publishing house. In her twenties, she became a successful playwright for the Broadway stage, one of her best-known plays being *The Little Foxes*. Several of her plays were made into movies, and she wrote screenplays for additional films. Like many of her friends, she became a political activist, deeply involved in the struggle against fascism and in the internal battles of the American left. Her account of experiences during the thirties provided the basis for the movie *Julia*, starring Vanessa Redgrave and Jane Fonda. In 1969, Hellman published the autobiographical *An Unfinished Woman*, from which the following excerpt is taken.

Lillian Hellman
An Only Child

GUIDE TO READING: In reading the following autobiographical selection, ask yourself: "What are the questions about herself and about her childhood that the author is trying to answer?" We can tell what topics are important to her because she *dwells* on them. Pay special attention to what she tells us about the following topics: the two branches of her family, her relations with her mother and with her father, and the traits of her own personality that become evident as she looks back at her experiences as a child.

I WAS BORN in New Orleans to Julia Newhouse from Demopolis, 1 Alabama, who had fallen in love and stayed in love with Max Hellman, whose parents had come to New Orleans in the German 1845–1848 immigration to give birth to him and his two sisters. My mother's family, long before I was born, had moved from Demopolis to Cincinnati and then to New Orleans, both desirable cities, I guess, for three marriageable girls.

But I first remember them in a large New York apartment: my two 2 young and very pretty aunts; their taciturn, tight-faced brother; and the silent, powerful, severe woman, Sophie Newhouse, who was their mother, my grandmother. Her children, her servants, all of her relatives except her brother, Jake, were frightened of her, and so was I. Even as a small child I disliked myself for the fear and showed off against it.

3   The Newhouse apartment held the upper-middle-class trappings, in touch of things and in spirit of people, that never manage to be truly stylish. Heavy weather hung over the lovely oval rooms. True, there were parties for my aunts, but the parties, to a peeping child in the servants' hall, seemed so muted that I was long convinced that on fancy occasions grown people moved their lips without making sounds. In the days after the party one would hear exciting stories about the new suitors, but the suitors were never quite good enough, and the parties were, obviously, not good enough for those who might have been. Then there were the Sunday dinners, with great-uncles and -aunts sometimes in attendance, full of open ill will about who had the most money or who spent it too lavishly, who would inherit what, who had bought what rug that would last forever, who what jewel she would best have been without. It was a corporation meeting, with my grandmother unexpectedly in the position of vice-chairman. The chairman was her brother, Jake, the only human being to whom I ever saw her defer. Early, I told myself that was because he was richer than she was, and did something called managing her money. But that was too simple: He was a man of great force, given, as she was given, to breaking the spirit of people for the pleasure of the exercise. But he was also witty and rather worldly, seeing his own financial machinations as natural not only to his but to the country's benefit, and seeing that as comic. (I had only one real contact with my Uncle Jake: When I graduated from school at fifteen, he gave me a ring that I took to a Fifty-ninth Street hock shop; I got twenty-five dollars and bought books. I went immediately to tell him what I'd done, deciding, I think, that day that the break had to come. He stared at me for a long time, and then he laughed and said the words I later used in *The Little Foxes:* "So you've got spirit after all. Most of the rest of them are made of sugar water.")

4   But that New York apartment where we visited several times a week, the summer cottage where we went for a visit each year as the poor daughter and granddaughter, made me into an angry child and forever caused in me a wild extravagance mixed with respect for money and those who have it. The respectful periods were full of self-hatred, and during them I always made my worst mistakes. . . .

5   It was not unnatural that my first love went to my father's family. He and his two sisters were free, generous, funny. But as I made my mother's family all one color, I made my father's family too remarkable, and then turned both extreme judgments against my mother.

In fact, she was a sweet eccentric, the only middle-class woman I 6 have ever known who had not rejected the middle class—that would have been an act of will—but had skipped it altogether. She liked a simple life and simple people, and would have been happier, I think, if she had stayed in the backlands of Alabama riding wild on the horses she so often talked about, not so lifelong lonely for the black men and women who had taught her the only religion she ever knew. I didn't know what she was saying when she moved her lips in a Baptist church or a Catholic cathedral or, less often, in a synagogue, but it was obvious that God could be found anywhere, because several times a week we would stop in a church, any church, and she seemed to be at home in all of them.

But simple natures can also be complex, and that is difficult for a 7 child, who wants all grown people to be sharply one thing or another. I was puzzled and irritated by the passivity of my mother as it mixed with an unmovable stubbornness. (My father had not been considered a proper husband for a rich and pretty girl, but my mother's deep fear of her mother did not override her deep love for my father, although the same fear kept my two aunts from ever marrying and my uncle from marrying until after his mother's death.)

Mama seemed to do only what my father wanted, and yet we lived 8 the way my mother wanted us to live. She deeply wanted to keep my father and to please him, but no amount of protest from him could alter the strange quirks that Freud already knew about. Windows, doors, and stoves haunted her, and she would often stand before them for as long as half an hour, or leaving the house, would insist upon returning to it while we waited for her in any weather. And sad, middle-aged ladies would be brought home from a casual meeting on a park bench to fill the living room with woe: Plain tales of sickness, or poverty, or loneliness in the afternoon often led to their staying on for dinner with my bored father.

My mother's childbearing had been dangerously botched by a fash- 9 ionable doctor in New Orleans, and forever after she stood in fear of going through it again, and so I was an only child. (Twenty-one years later, when I was married and pregnant, she was as frightened for me, and unashamedly happy when I lost the child.) I was thirty-four years old, after two successful plays, and fourteen or fifteen years of heavy drinking in a nature that wasn't comfortable with anarchy, when a doctor told me about the lifelong troubles of an only child. Most certainly I needed a doctor to reveal for me the violence and disorder of my life, but I had always known about the powers of an only child. I was not meaner or more ungenerous or more unkind than other children, but I was off-balance in a world where I knew my grand importance to two other people who certainly loved me for myself, but who also liked to

use me against each other. I don't think they knew they did that, because most of it was affectionate teasing between them, but somehow I
knew early that my father's jokes about how much my mother's family
liked money, how her mother had crippled her own children, my
grandmother's desire to think of him—and me—as strange vagabonds
of no property value, were more than teasing. He wished to win me to
his side, and he did. He was a handsome man, witty, high-tempered,
proud, and, although I guessed very young I was not to be certain until
much later, with a number of other women in his life. Thus his attacks
on Mama's family were not always for the reasons claimed.

10   When I was about six years old, my father lost my mother's large
dowry. We moved to New York and were shabby poor until my father
finally settled for a life as a successful traveling salesman. It was in
those years that we went back to New Orleans to stay with my father's
sisters for six months each year. I was thus moved from school in New
York to school in New Orleans without care for the season or the quality of the school. This constant need for adjustment in two very different worlds made formal education into a kind of frantic tennis game,
sometimes played with children whose strokes had force and bril-
liance, sometimes with those who could barely hold the racket. Possibly it is the reason I never did well in school or in college, and why I
wanted to be left alone to read by myself. I had found, very early, that
any other test found me bounding with ease and grace over one fence
to fall on my face as I ran toward the next one.

11   There was a heavy fig tree on the lawn where the house turned the
corner into the side street, and to the front and sides of the fig tree
were three live oaks that hid the fig from my aunts' boardinghouse. I
suppose I was eight or nine before I discovered the pleasures of the fig
tree, and although I have lived in many houses since then, including a
few that I made for myself, I still think of it as my first and most beloved
home.

12   I learned early, in our strange life of living half in New York and
half in New Orleans, that I made my New Orleans teachers uncomfortable because I was too far ahead of my schoolmates, and my New York
teachers irritable because I was too far behind. But in New Orleans I
found a solution: I skipped school at least once a week and often twice,
knowing that nobody cared or would report my absence. On those days
I would set out for school done up in polished strapped shoes and a
prim hat against what was known as "the climate," carrying my books
and a little basket filled with delicious stuff my Aunt Jenny and Carrie,
the cook, had made for my school lunch. I would round the corner of
the side street, move on toward St. Charles Avenue, and sit on a bench
as if I were waiting for a streetcar until the boarders and the neighbors
had gone to work or settled down for the post-breakfast rest that all
Southern ladies thought necessary. Then I would run back to the fig

tree, dodging in and out of bushes to make sure the house had no dangers for me. The fig tree was heavy, solid, comfortable, and I had, through time, convinced myself that it wanted me, missed me when I was absent, and approved all the rigging I had done for the happy days I spent in its arms: I had made a sling to hold the school books, a pulley rope for my lunch basket, a hole for the bottle of afternoon cream-soda pop, a fishing pole and a smelly little bag of elderly bait, and a pillow embroidered with a picture of Henry Clay on a horse that I had stolen from Mrs. Stillman, one of my aunts' boarders; and I drove a proper nail to hold my dress and shoes to keep them neat for the return to the house.

It was in that tree that I learned to read, filled with the passions that can only come to the bookish, grasping, very young, bewildered by almost all of what I read, sweating in the attempt to understand a world of adults I fled from in real life but desperately wanted to join in books. (I did not connect the grown men and women in literature with the grown men and women I saw around me. They were, to me, another species.)   13

It was in the fig tree that I learned that anything alive in water was of enormous excitement to me. True, the water was gutter water and the fishing could hardly be called that: sometimes the things that swam in New Orleans gutters were not pretty, but I didn't know what was pretty, and I liked them all. After lunch—the men boarders returned for a large lunch and a siesta—the street would be safe again, with only the noise from Carrie and her helpers in the kitchen, and they could be counted on never to move past the back porch or the chicken coop. Then I would come down from my tree to sit on the side-street gutter with my pole and bait. Often I would catch a crab that had wandered in from the Gulf; more often I would catch my favorite, the crayfish, and sometimes I would, in that safe hour, have at least six of them for my basket. Then, about two thirty, when house and street would stir again, I would go back to my tree for another few hours of reading or dozing or having what I called the ill hour. It is too long ago for me to know why I thought the hour "ill," but certainly I did not mean sick. I think I meant an intimation of sadness, a first recognition that there was so much to understand that one might never find one's way, and the first signs, perhaps, that for a nature like mine, the way would not be easy. I cannot be sure that I felt all that then, although I can be sure that it was in the fig tree, a few years later, that I was first puzzled by the conflict which would haunt me, harm me, and benefit me the rest of my life: simply, the stubborn, relentless, driving desire to be alone when I wanted as it came into conflict with the desire not to be alone when I wanted not to be. I already guessed that other people wouldn't allow that, although, as an only child, I pretended for the rest of my life that they would and must allow it to me.   14

15   I liked my time in New Orleans much better than I liked our six
months' apartment life in New York. The life in my aunts' boardinghouse seemed remarkably rich. And what a strange lot my own family
was. My aunts Jenny and Hannah were both tall, large women, funny
and generous, who coming from a German, cultivated, genteel tradition had found they had to earn a living and earned it without complaint, although Jenny, the prettier and more complex, had frequent
outbursts of interesting temper. It was strange, I thought then, that my
mother, who so often irritated me, was treated by my aunts as if she
were a precious Chinese clay piece from a world they didn't know. And
in a sense, that was true: Her family was rich, she was small, delicately
made, and charming—she was a sturdy, brave woman, really, but it took
years to teach me that—and because my aunts loved my father very
much, they were good to my mother and protected her from the less
wellborn boarders. I don't think they understood—I did, by some kind
of child's malice—that my mother enjoyed the boarders and listened to
them with the sympathy Jenny couldn't afford. I suppose none of the
boarders were of great interest, but I was crazy about what I thought
went on behind their doors.

16   I was conscious that Mr. Stillman, a large, loose, good-looking man,
flirted with my mother and sang off-key. I knew that a boarder called
Collie, a too thin, unhappy-looking no-age man, worked in his uncle's
bank and was drunk every night. He was the favorite of the lady boarders, who didn't think he'd live very long. (They were wrong: Over twenty
years later, on a visit to my retired aunts, I met him in Galatoire's Restaurant looking just the same.) And there were two faded, sexy, giggly
sisters called Fizzy and Sarah, who pretended to love children and all
trees. I once overheard a fight between my mother and father in which
she accused him of liking Sarah. I thought that was undignified of my
mother and was pleased when my father laughed it off as untrue. He
was telling the truth about Sarah: He liked Fizzy, and the day I saw
them meet and get into a taxi in front of a restaurant on Jackson Avenue
was to stay with me for many years. I was in a black rage, filled with
fears I couldn't explain, with pity and contempt for my mother, with an
intense desire to follow my father and Fizzy to see whatever it was they
might be doing and to kill them for it. An hour later, I threw myself
from the top of the fig tree and broke my nose, although I did not know
I had broken a bone and was concerned only with the hideous pain.

17   I went immediately to Sophronia, who had been my nurse when I
was a small child before we moved, or half moved, to New York. She
worked now for people who lived in a large house a streetcar ride from
ours, and she took care of two little red-haired boys whom I hated with
pleasure in my wicked jealousy. Sophronia was the first and most certain love of my life. (Years later, when I was a dangerously rebellious
young girl, my father would say that if he had been able to afford So-

phronia through the years, I would have been under the only control I ever recognized.) She was a tall, handsome, light-tan woman—I still have many pictures of the brooding face—who was for me, as for so many other white Southern children, the one and certain anchor so needed for the young years, so forgotten after that. (It wasn't that way for us: We wrote and met as often as possible until she died when I was in my twenties, and the first salary check I ever earned she returned to me in the form of a gold chain.) The mother of the two red-haired boys didn't like my visits to Sophronia, and so I always arrived by the back door.

But Sophronia was not at home on the day of my fall. I sat on her kitchen steps crying and holding my face until the cook sent the upstairs maid to Audubon Park on a search for Sophronia. She came, running, I think for the first time in the majestic movements of her life, waving away the two redheads. She took me to her room and washed my face and prodded my nose and put her hand over my mouth when I screamed. She said we must go immediately to Dr. Fenner, but when I told her that I had thrown myself from the tree, she stopped talking about the doctor, bandaged my face, gave me a pill, put me on her bed, and lay down beside me. I told her about my father and Fizzy and fell asleep. When I woke up she said that she'd walk me home. On the way she told me that I must say nothing about Fizzy to anybody ever, and that if my nose still hurt in a few days I was only to say that I had fallen on the street and refuse to answer any questions about how I fell. A block from my aunts' house we sat down on the steps of the Baptist church. She looked sad, and I knew that I had displeased her. I touched her arm, which had always been between us a way of saying that I was sorry.

She said, "Don't go through life making trouble for people." 19

I said, "If I tell you I won't tell about Fizzy, then I won't tell." 20

She said, "Run home, now. Good-bye." 21

And it was to be good-bye for another year, because I had forgotten 22
that we were to leave for New York two days later, and when I telephoned to tell that to Sophronia, the woman she worked for said I wasn't to telephone again. In any case, I soon forgot about Fizzy, and when the bandage came off my nose—it looked different but not different enough—our New York doctor said that it would heal by itself, or whatever was the nonsense they believed in those days about broken bones.

 USING THE DICTIONARY: Much of this autobiographical selection deals with the author's reactions to other people. It expresses her thoughts and feelings about them, and it therefore often uses words that carry attitudes and judgments as well as objective, impersonal information. Dictionary definitions usually concentrate on what a word stands for or what it points to—its **denotation**. But a definition may also hint at the attitudes, favorable or unfavorable, that a word implies— its **connotations**. Check the following words in your dictionary. Pay special attention to any hints of favorable or unfavorable connotations: 1. *taciturn* (2) 2. *stylish* (3) 3. *lavish* (3) 4. *machinations* (3) 5. *eccentric* (5) 6. *passivity* (7) 7. *anarchy* (9) 8. *vagabond* (9) 9. *prim* (12) 10. *genteel* (15)

The writer's agenda:

This selection reads like the kind of leisurely autobiography that starts at the beginning ("I was born in New Orleans") and then brings in the author's early memories. However, the author soon focuses on a few topics that really matter to her. We become aware of major influences and central character traits that help explain what kind of person she grew up to be. Answer the following questions about the main points that the author focuses on in this autobiographical narrative:

1. Throughout her childhood, Lillian Hellman felt the need to adjust as necessary to "two different worlds." A major focus in this selection is the *contrast* between her mother's side of the family and her father's. Describe the mother's family and its New York setting. Provide capsule portraits of some of the central characters. (What are some of the labels the author applies to them? What are especially telling or revealing details?) What was the author's relationship to this setting? What were her feelings about these people?

2. The *father's side* of the family provides a strong contrast—a different and often opposite influence on the author's growing up. What different and contrasting influence was provided by the father's family and the New Orleans setting? Describe the father and the relatives on the father's side. (Discuss telling or revealing details and happenings.) Sum up the contrast between the two branches of the family, and the relationship between them.

3. What do we learn about the *author's mother* and the daughter's relationship with her? What was the mother's role or position in the conflict between the two branches of the family?

4. In the central part of the essay, the author focuses on her consciousness of being an only child, and on her frequent desire "to be left alone" to read and think. Discuss the *fig tree* as a central symbol in her private world of thoughts and feelings. Discuss details that help

give us a confidential inside look at the author as a private person.

5. Toward the end of this selection, the author says of herself that she grew up to be a "dangerously rebellious young girl." When do we first become aware of this *rebellious* side of her character? What other evidence or illustrations of this central character trait appear in this selection?

6. The **tone** of this selection is that of a writer taking *a candid look* at the past. The author talks freely, taking us into her confidence, holding little back. Point out passages or details that a less candid writer might have glossed over. (Where does her candor about her private feelings help us understand puzzling or strange surface behavior?)

For discussion or writing:

1. Where and how does this selection go counter to the familiar, nostalgic view of childhood as a happy, innocent time? What are major examples of mixed feelings or contradictory emotions?

2. How was the author affected by growing up as part of an old-fashioned "extended family" with many relatives forming an extended family group or clan? Have you encountered anything similar in your own observation or experience?

3. Is a person's character mainly the result of inherited traits and natural inclination, or is it determined in large part by formative influences during a person's upbringing or childhood? To what extent do you think the author's personality was shaped by her experiences as a child?

4. Prepare a portrait of a memorable person who played a major role in your life. Avoid general labels or generalized praise or blame. Use authentic details from personal experience to make the person come to life for your readers. Focus on what explains the person's influence on your life and personality.

5. How has your own family history or family background influenced you? Focus on a major influence or on key factors. Give a vivid, authentic account of people, situations, or events.

6. Prepare a candid self-portrait that concentrates on one major character trait that you think has helped shape your personality. If you can, show it as a common thread in several related experiences. Show how this side of your personality has affected what you do, how you act, or how you relate to other people.

BACKGROUND: Jade Snow Wong was born in 1922 as the daughter of Chinese immigrants. She graduated from Mills College and worked for the Navy during World War II. Like millions of young Americans, she had to chart her way between the old-country ways of home and the American ways of school or neighborhood. The record of her search for identity is her book *Fifth Chinese Daughter,* about her growing up in the traditional Chinatown of San Francisco. Many Chinese immigrants of her parents' generation had come to the American West to work as laborers building the railroads or as restaurant and laundry workers in the towns. They often maintained the strong tradition-al family unit of their homeland. People sought protection and justice in a clan that included many of their close relatives. People honored their parents and their ancestors; the upkeep of their ancestors' graves in the distant homeland was an important duty. Children were taught obedience and filial respect—the respect of a dutiful, grateful son or daughter for the parents. Like many young Americans, Wong had to chart her way between two cul-tures. The following excerpt from a longer essay follows a classic pattern of much autobiography: The author focuses on a key stage in the process of growing up. She traces the change from the unquestioning attitudes of child-hood days to the first assertion of independence during adolescence. The essay comes to a head with the first open conflict between the adolescent daughter and her parents.

Jade Snow Wong

Fifth Chinese Daughter

GUIDE TO READING: In reading the essay, pay special attention to how the contrast between two different styles of life takes shape. What are the corner-stones of the parents' traditional way of life? What are key differences be-tween the parents' ways and more familiar American ways? What are some early hints of dissatisfaction or of a critical attitude on the part of the daughter? What is the basic issue in the conflict between parents and daugh-ter, and what is the outcome?

1   FROM INFANCY to my sixteenth year, I was reared according to nineteenth-century ideals of Chinese womanhood. I was never left alone, though it was not unusual for me to feel lonely, while surround-

ed by a family of seven others, and often by ten (including bachelor cousins) at meals.

My father (who enjoyed our calling him Daddy in English) was the 2 unquestioned head of our household. He was not talkative, being preoccupied with his business affairs and with reading constantly otherwise. My mother was mistress of domestic affairs. Seldom did these two converse before their children, but we knew them to be a united front, and suspected that privately she both informed and influenced him about each child.

In order to support the family in America, Daddy tried various oc- 3 cupations—candy making, the ministry to which he was later ordained—but finally settled on manufacturing men's and children's denim garments. He leased sewing equipment, installed machines in a basement where rent was cheapest, and there he and his family lived and worked. There was no thought that dim, airless quarters were terrible conditions for living and working, or that child labor was unhealthful. The only goal was for all in the family to work, to save, and to become educated. It was possible, so it would be done.

My father, a meticulous bookkeeper, used only an abacus, a brush, 4 ink, and Chinese ledgers. Because of his newly learned ideals, he pioneered for the right of women to work. Concerned that they have economic independence, but not with the long hours of industrial home work, he went to shy housewives' apartments and taught them sewing.

My earliest memories of companionship with my father were as his 5 passenger in his red wheelbarrow, sharing space with the piles of bluejean materials he was delivering to a worker's home. He must have been forty. He was lean, tall, inevitably wearing blue overalls, rolled shirt sleeves, and high black kid shoes. In his pockets were numerous keys, tools, and pens. On such deliveries, I noticed that he always managed time to show a mother how to sew a difficult seam, or to help her repair a machine, or just to chat.

I observed from birth that living and working were inseparable. My 6 mother was short, sturdy, young looking, and took pride in her appearance. She was at her machine the minute housework was done, and she was the hardest-working seamstress, seldom pausing, working after I went to bed. The hum of sewing machines continued day and night, seven days a week. She knew that to have more than the four necessities, she must work and save. We knew that to overcome poverty, there were only two methods: working and education.

Having provided the setup for family industry, my father turned his 7 attention to our education. Ninety-five percent of the population in his native China had been illiterate. He knew that American public schools would take care of our English, but he had to nurture our Chinese knowledge. Only the Cantonese tongue was ever spoken by him or my mother. When the two oldest girls arrived from China, the schools of Chinatown received only boys. My father tutored his daughters each morning before breakfast. In the midst of a foreign environment, he clung to a combination of the familiar old standards and what was permissible in the newly learned Christian ideals.

8   My eldest brother was born in America, the only boy for fourteen years, and after him three daughters—another older sister, myself, and my younger sister. Then my younger brother, Paul, was born. That older brother, Lincoln, was cherished in the best Chinese tradition. He had his own room; he kept a German shepherd as his pet; he was tutored by a Chinese scholar; he was sent to private school for American classes. As a male Wong, he would be responsible some day for the preservation of and pilgrimages to ancestral graves—his privileges were his birthright. We girls were content with the unusual opportunities of working and attending two schools. By day, I attended American public school near our home. From 5:00 P.M. to 8:00 P.M. on five weekdays and from 9:00 A.M. to 12 noon on Saturdays, I attended the Chinese school. Classes numbered twenty to thirty students, and were taught by educated Chinese from China. We studied poetry, calligraphy, philosophy, literature, history, correspondence, religion, all by exacting memorization.

9   Daddy emphasized memory development; he could still recite fluently many lengthy lessons of his youth. Every evening after both schools, I'd sit by my father, often as he worked at his sewing machine, sing-songing my lessons above its hum. Sometimes I would stop to hold a light for him as he threaded the difficult holes of a specialty machine, such as one for bias bindings. After my Chinese lessons passed his approval, I was allowed to attend to American homework. I was made to feel luckier than other Chinese girls who didn't study Chinese, and also luckier than Western girls without a dual heritage.

10   There was little time for play, and toys were unknown to me. In any spare time, I was supplied with embroidery and sewing for my mother. The Chinese New Year, which by the old lunar calendar would fall sometime in late January or early February of the Western Christian calendar, was the most special time of the year, for then the machines stopped for three days. Mother would clean our living quarters very thoroughly, decorate the sitting room with flowering branches and fresh oranges, and arrange candied fruits or salty melon seeds for callers. All of us would be dressed in bright new clothes, and relatives or close friends, who came to call, would give each of us a red paper packet containing a good luck coin—usually a quarter. I remember how my classmates would gleefully talk of *their* receipts. But my mother made us give our money to her, for she said that she needed it to reciprocate to others.

Yet there was little reason for unhappiness. I was never hungry. 11
Though we had no milk, there was all the rice we wanted. We had hot
and cold running water—a rarity in Chinatown—as well as our own
bathtub. Our sheets were pieced from dishtowels, but we had sheets. I
was never neglected, for my mother and father were always at home.
During school vacation periods, I was taught to operate many types of
machines—tacking (for pockets), overlocking (for the raw edges of
seams), buttonhole, double seaming; and I learned all the stages in
producing a pair of jeans to its final inspection, folding, and tying in
bundles of a dozen pairs by size, ready for pickup. Denim jeans are
heavy—my shoulders ached often. My father set up a modest nickel-
and-dime piecework reward for me, which he recorded in my own
notebook, and paid me regularly.

My mother dutifully followed my father's leadership. She was ex- 12
tremely thrifty, but the thrifty need pennies to manage, and the old
world had denied her those. Upon arrival in the new world of San
Francisco, she accepted the elements her mate had selected to shape
her new life: domestic duties, seamstress work in the factory-home,
mothering each child in turn, church once a week, and occasional movies. Daddy frowned upon the community Chinese operas because of
their very late hours (they did not finish till past midnight) and their
mixed audiences.

Very early in my life, the manners of a traditional Chinese lady were 13
taught to me. How to hold a pair of chopsticks (palm up, not down);
how to hold a bowl of rice (one thumb on top, not resting in an open
palm); how to pass something to elders (with both hands, never one);
how to pour tea into the tiny, handleless porcelain cups (seven-eighths
full so that the top edge would be cool enough to hold); how to eat
from a center serving dish (only the piece in front of your place; never
pick around); not to talk at table, not to show up outside of one's room
without being fully dressed; not to be late, ever; not to be too playful—
in a hundred and one ways, we were molded to be trouble-free, unobtrusive, cooperative.

We were disciplined by first being told, and then by punishment if 14
we didn't remember. Punishment was instant and unceremonious. At
the table, it came as a sudden whack from Daddy's chopsticks. Away
from the table, punishment could be the elimination of a privilege or
the blow on our legs from a bundle of cane switches.

Only Daddy and Oldest Brother were allowed individual idiosyn- 15
crasies. Daughters were all expected to be of one standard. To allow
each one of many daughters to be different would have posed enormous problems of cost, energy, and attention. No one was shown physical affection. Such familiarity would have weakened my parents and
endangered the one-answer authoritative system. One standard from

past to present, whether in China or in San Francisco, was simpler to enforce. My parents never said "please" and "thank you" for any service or gift. In Chinese, both "please" and "thank you" can be literally translated as "I am not worthy" and naturally, no parent is going to say that about a service which should be their just due.

16   Traditional Chinese parents pit their children against a standard of perfection without regard to personality, individual ambitions, tolerance for human error, or exposure to the changing social scene. It never occurred to that kind of parent to be friends with their children on common ground.

17   During the Depression, my mother and father needed even more hours to work. Daddy had been shopping daily for groceries (we had no icebox) and my mother cooked. Now I was told to assume both those duties. My mother would give me fifty cents to buy enough fresh food for dinner and breakfast. In those years, twenty-five cents could buy a small chicken or three sanddabs, ten cents bought three bunches of green vegetables, and fifteen cents bought some meat to cook with these. After American school I rushed to the stores only a block or so away, returned and cleaned the foods, and cooked in a hurry in order to eat an early dinner and get to Chinese school on time. When I came home at 8:00 P.M., I took care of the dinner dishes before starting to do my homework. Saturdays and Sundays were for housecleaning and the family laundry, which I scrubbed on a board, using big galvanized buckets in our bathtub.

18   I had no sympathetic guidance as an eleven-year-old in my own reign in the kitchen, which lasted for four years. I finished junior high school, started high school, and continued studying Chinese. With the small earnings from summer work in my father's basement factory (we moved back to the basement during the Depression), I bought materials to sew my own clothes. But the routine of keeping house only to be dutiful, to avoid tongue or physical lashings, became exasperating. The tiny space which was the room for three sisters was confining. After I graduated from Chinese evening school, I began to look for part-time paying jobs as a mother's helper. Those jobs varied from cleaning house to baking a cake, amusing a naughty child to ironing shirts, but wearying, exhausting as they were, they meant money earned for myself.

19   As I advanced in American high school and worked at those jobs, I was gradually introduced to customs not of the Chinese world. American teachers were mostly kind. I remember my third-grade teacher's skipping me half a year. I remember my fourth-grade teacher—with whom I am still friendly. She was the first person to hold me to her physically and affectionately—because a baseball bat had been accidentally flung against my hand. I also remember that I was confused by

being held, since physical comfort had not been offered by my parents. I remember my junior high school principal, who skipped me half a grade and commended me before the school assembly, to my great embarrassment.

In contrast, Chinese schoolteachers acted as extensions of Chinese   20 parental discipline. There was a formal "disciplinarian dean" to apply the cane to wayward boys, and girls were not exempt either. A whisper during chapel was sufficient provocation to be called to the dean's office. No humor was exchanged; no praise or affection expressed by the teachers. They presented the lessons, and we had to learn to memorize all the words, orally, before the class. Then followed the written test, word for word. Without an alphabet, the Chinese language requires exact memorization. No originality or deviation was permitted and grading was severe. One word wrong during an examination could reduce a grade by 10 percent. It was the principle of learning by punishment.

Interest and praise, physical or oral, were rewards peculiar to the   21 American world. Even employers who were paying me thanked me for a service or complimented me on a meal well cooked, and sometimes helped me with extra dishes. Chinese often said that "foreigners" talked too much about too many personal things. My father used to tell me to think three times before saying anything, and if I said nothing, no one would say I was stupid. I perceived a difference between two worlds.

By the time I was graduating from high school, my parents had   22 done their best to produce an intelligent, obedient daughter, who would know more than the average Chinatown girl and should do better than average at a conventional job, her earnings brought home to them in repayment for their years of child support. Then, they hoped, she would marry a nice Chinese boy and make him a good wife, as well as an above-average mother for his children. Chinese custom used to decree that families should "introduce" chosen partners to each other's children. The groom's family should pay handsomely to the bride's family for rearing a well-bred daughter. They should also pay all bills for a glorious wedding banquet for several hundred guests. Then the bride's family could consider their job done. Their daughter belonged to the groom's family and must henceforth seek permission from all persons in his home before returning to her parents for a visit.

But having been set upon a new path, I did not oblige my parents   23 with the expected conventional ending. At fifteen, I had moved away from home to work for room and board and a salary of twenty dollars per month. Having found that I could subsist independently, I thought it regrettable to terminate my education. Upon graduating from high school at the age of sixteen, I asked my parents to assist me in college expenses. I pleaded with my father, for his years of encouraging me to be above mediocrity in both Chinese and American studies had made me wish for some undefined but brighter future.

24   My father was briefly adamant. He must conserve his resources for my oldest brother's medical training. Though I desired to continue on an above-average course, his material means were insufficient to support that ambition. He added that if I had the talent, I could provide for my own college education. When he had spoken, no discussion was expected. After his edict, no daughter questioned.

25   But this matter involved my whole future—it was not simply asking for permission to go to a night church meeting (forbidden also). Though for years I had accepted the authority of the one I honored most, his decision that night embittered me as nothing ever had. My oldest brother had so many privileges, had incurred unusual expenses for luxuries which were taken for granted as his birthright, yet these were part of a system I had accepted. Now I suddenly wondered at my father's interpretation of the Christian code: was it intended to discriminate against a girl after all, or was it simply convenient for my father's economics and cultural prejudice? Did a daughter have any right to expect more than a fate of obedience, according to the old Chinese standard? As long as I could remember, I had been told that a female followed three men during her lifetime: as a girl, her father; as a wife, her husband; as an old woman, her son.

26   My indignation mounted against that tradition and I decided then that my past could not determine my future. I knew that more education would prepare me for a different expectation than my other female schoolmates, few of whom were to complete a college degree. I, too, had my father's unshakable faith in the justice of God, and I shared his unconcern with popular opinion.

27   So I decided to enter junior college, now San Francisco's City College, because the fees were lowest. I lived at home and supported myself with an after-school job which required long hours of housework and cooking but paid me twenty dollars per month, of which I saved as much as possible. The thrills derived from reading and learning, in ways ranging from chemistry experiments to English compositions, from considering new ideas of sociology to the logic of Latin, convinced me that I had made a correct choice. I was kept in a state of perpetual mental excitement by new Western subjects and concepts and did not mind long hours of work and study. I also made new friends, which led to another painful incident with my parents, who had heretofore discouraged even girlhood friendships.

28   The college subject which had most jolted me was sociology. The instructor fired my mind with his interpretation of family relationships. As he explained to our class, it used to be an economic asset for Ameri-

can farming families to be large, since children were useful to perform agricultural chores. But this situation no longer applied and children should be regarded as individuals with their own rights. Unquestioning obedience should be replaced with parental understanding. So at sixteen, discontented as I was with my parents' apparent indifference to me, those words of my sociology professor gave voice to my sentiments. How old-fashioned was the dead-end attitude of my parents! How ignorant they were of modern thought and progress! The family unit had been China's strength for centuries, but it had also been her weakness, for corruption, nepotism, and greed were all justified in the name of the family's welfare. My new ideas festered; I longed to release them.

One afternoon on a Saturday, which was normally occupied with   29 my housework job, I was unexpectedly released by my employer, who was departing for a country weekend. It was a rare joy to have free time and I wanted to enjoy myself for a change. There had been a Chinese-American boy who shared some classes with me. Sometimes we had found each other walking to the same 8:00 A.M. class. He was not a special boyfriend, but I had enjoyed talking to him and had confided in him some of my problems. Impulsively, I telephoned him. I knew I must be breaking rules, and I felt shy and scared. At the same time, I was excited at this newly found forwardness, with nothing more purposeful than to suggest another walk together.

He understood my awkwardness and shared my anticipation. He   30 asked me to "dress up" for my first movie date. My clothes were limited but I changed to look more graceful in silk stockings and found a bright ribbon for my long black hair. Daddy watched, catching my mood, observing the dashing preparations. He asked me where I was going without his permission and with whom.

I refused to answer him. I thought of my rights! I thought he surely   31 would not try to understand. Thereupon Daddy thundered his displeasure and forbade my departure.

I found a new courage as I heard my voice announce calmly that I   32 was no longer a child, and if I could work my way through college, I would choose my own friends. It was my right as a person.

My mother heard the commotion and joined my father to face me;   33 both appeared shocked and incredulous. Daddy at once demanded the source of this unfilial, non-Chinese theory. And when I quoted my college professor, reminding him that he had always felt teachers should be revered, my father denounced that professor as a foreigner who was disregarding the superiority of our Chinese culture, with its sound family strength. My father did not spare me; I was condemned as an ingrate for echoing dishonorable opinions which should only be temporary whims, yet nonetheless inexcusable.

The scene was not yet over. I completed my proclamation to my   34 father, who had never allowed me to learn how to dance, by adding that I was attending a movie, unchaperoned, with a boy I met at college.

35   My startled father was sure that my reputation would be subject to whispered innuendos. I must be bent on disgracing the family name; I was ruining my future, for surely I would yield to temptation. My mother underscored him by saying that I hadn't any notion of the problems endured by parents of a young girl.

36   I would not give in. I reminded them that they and I were not in China, that I wasn't going out with just anybody but someone I trusted! Daddy gave a roar that no man could be trusted, but I devastated them in declaring that I wished the freedom to find my own answers.

37   Both parents were thoroughly angered, scolded me for being shameless, and predicted that I would some day tell them I was wrong. But I dimly perceived that they were conceding defeat and were perplexed at this breakdown of their training. I was too old to beat and too bold to intimidate.

 USING THE DICTIONARY: Word roots often help us' recognize, understand, and remember new words. The word *nepotism* has the Latin word for nephew in it; politicians or employers practice nepotism when they grant special privileges to relatives—for instance, to a nephew. What are the roots that help explain the following words from this essay? How does a shared root help explain the word itself and the related words that follow? 1. *calligraphy—orthography, stenography, stenographer* (8) 2. *philosophy—philanthropy* (8) 3. *unobtrusive—intrusion, intruder* (13) 4. *exasperating—asperity* (18) 5. *deviation—deviate, deflect* (20) 6. *edict—verdict, indictment* (24) 7. *impulsive—compulsive, repulsive* (29) 8. *incredulous—incredible* (33) 9. *filial—affiliation* (33) 10. *ingrate—gratitude* (33)

THE WRITER'S AGENDA:

To explain to herself the kind of person she is, the author of this essay looks back over the contradictory or opposed elements in her background. She weighs the influence of her traditional Chinese parents and the influence of "Western," or American, ways. Trace the major elements in her traditional upbringing and the role of new or different ideas.

1. Early in the essay, the author says, "I observed from birth that living and working were inseparable." Find the details that give sub-

stance to this general statement. Describe the setting and working conditions. Describe the *attitudes toward work* that were an important part of the author's upbringing.

2. In the end, the author challenges the traditional *authority of parents*. Where and what does she tell us about the traditional relationship between parents and children during her childhood years? What was expected of children? What manners was the author taught? What were traditional ideas of discipline? What were traditional attitudes toward giving praise and toward displays of affection?

3. The contrast between the traditional Chinese style of *education* and new or different American ways played a major part in the author's growing up. What were the traditional ways? Where and how did the author experience the new American ways?

4. Jade Snow Wong's parents had come from a *patriarchal society* where men had special privileges and where women played an inferior role. How did this tradition affect the author's life and that of her family? Where does she express her feelings about this tradition most strongly and most directly? (Had her parents moved *away* from the traditional definition of sex roles in any way?)

5. The high point, or **climax**, of this autobiographical narrative is the daughter's open *defiance* of her father's authority. What was the central issue? What were the thoughts that went through her mind? What strategy did she adopt during the confrontation with her parents, and what was the outcome?

6. The rebellion of a daughter or a son sometimes causes great bitterness and leaves deep scars. What is the **tone** of the author as she looks back over her experiences? Would you call her bitter or resentful? Does she show fondness or appreciation for her parents?

FOR DISCUSSION OR WRITING:

1. We often hear that the "work ethic" is part of the American tradition. Where have you encountered it, or where have you had a chance to observe it? Do you believe it is anchored in the experience of immigrants like Wong's parents?

2. Some people say that our society is overly permissive toward the young. To judge from your experience, how far has American society moved from the kind of parental authority and discipline that we observe in this essay?

3. A dual heritage or an exposure to two cultures is sometimes

seen as a problem, sometimes as an asset. From what the author has told us about her life, would you conclude that in her case the experience was an asset or a liability? Defend your answer.

4. Where have you observed or experienced the meeting of two cultures or of two different ways of life? In your own family or among your friends, have you been able to see the encounter or the merging of different traditions? Show the contrast in two or three areas—manners, customs, attitudes toward work, or the like.

5. Focus on a situation or an experience in which you have seen two different traditions or ways of life come into conflict. Describe and explain the clash between two different ways of doing things or of looking at life.

6. Write an essay whose title begins "In Defense of . . ." Fill in the word *Permissiveness, Authority,* or *Discipline* to complete the title. Use material from your own first-hand observation and experience.

BACKGROUND: George Orwell (1903–50), whose real name was Eric Blair, was a British socialist widely admired as one of the great masters of modern expository prose. Many of his essays and books are autobiographical; others reflect his sharp-eyed observations of what was happening in the world around him. He wrote at a time in European history when print and radio often seemed dominated by tired clichés, blatant propaganda, and self-serving lies. Orwell went against the tide by writing as an honest witness, telling the truth as he knew it from his own experience. He had been born in India as the son of English parents; his early political education took place when he served with the British Imperial Police in Burma, a country to the east of India that was then, like India, a British colony. He later fought in the Spanish Civil War with the republican, or loyalist, forces opposing the armies of the future fascist dictator, Franco. Two of his novels have been read by millions around the world: *Animal Farm* (1946), a biting satirical attack on Russian communism under Stalin; and *1984* (1949), which predicted a joyless totalitarian society of the future where every move and thought of a citizen would be watched by Big Brother.

George Orwell
Shooting an Elephant

GUIDE TO READING: This autobiographical essay takes an honest look at a *single central event* in order to explore its significance. As you read the essay, look for the answers to five basic questions: Where are we? What people are involved? What happens? What feelings or emotions do the events bring into play? What does it all mean to the author?

IN MOULMEIN, in Lower Burma, I was hated by large numbers of   1
people—the only time in my life that I have been important enough for
this to happen to me. I was subdivisional police officer of the town, and
in an aimless, petty kind of way anti-European feeling was very bitter.
No one had the guts to raise a riot, but if a European woman went
through the bazaars alone somebody would probably spit betel juice[1]

[1] [The betel (bē′tl) palm was a tree whose nuts and leaves were chewed as a stimulant in some parts of Asia.]

over her dress. As a police officer I was an obvious target and was baited whenever it seemed safe to do so. When a nimble Burman tripped me up on the football field and the referee (another Burman) looked the other way, the crowd yelled with hideous laughter. This happened more than once. In the end the sneering yellow faces of young men that met me everywhere, the insults hooted after me when I was at a safe distance, got badly on my nerves. The young Buddhist priests were the worst of all. There were several thousands of them in the town and none of them seemed to have anything to do except stand on street corners and jeer at Europeans.

2   All this was perplexing and upsetting. For at that time I had already made up my mind that imperialism was an evil thing and the sooner I chucked up my job and got out of it the better. Theoretically—and secretly, of course—I was all for the Burmese and all against their oppressors, the British. As for the job I was doing, I hated it more bitterly than I can perhaps make clear. In a job like that you see the dirty work of Empire at close quarters. The wretched prisoners huddling in the stinking cages of the lockups, the gray, cowed faces of the long-term convicts, the scarred buttocks of the men who had been flogged with bamboos—all these oppressed me with an intolerable sense of guilt. But I could get nothing into perspective. I was young and ill-educated and I had had to think out my problems in the utter silence that is imposed on every Englishman in the East. I did not even know that the British Empire is dying, still less did I know that it is a great deal better than the younger empires that are going to supplant it. All I knew was that I was stuck between my hatred of the empire I served and my rage against the evil-spirited little beasts who tried to make my job impossible. With one part of my mind I thought of the British Raj[2] as an unbreakable tyranny, as something clamped down, *in saecula saeculorum,*[3] upon the will of prostrate peoples; with another part I thought that the greatest joy in the world would be to drive a bayonet into a Buddhist priest's guts. Feelings like these are the normal by-products of imperialism; ask any Anglo-Indian official, if you can catch him off duty.

3   One day something happened which in a roundabout way was enlightening. It was a tiny incident in itself, but it gave me a better glimpse than I had had before of the real nature of imperialism—the real motives for which despotic governments act. Early one morning the subinspector at a police station the other end of town rang me up on the phone and said that an elephant was ravaging the bazaar. Would

---

[2] [Raj (räj) and rajah (rä′jə) are the words for "rule" and "ruler" in Hindi, one of the principal languages of India.]

[3] [a Latin phrase meaning "throughout the ages, forever and ever"]

I please come and do something about it? I did not know what I could do, but I wanted to see what was happening and I got onto a pony and started out. I took my rifle, an old .44 Winchester and much too small to kill an elephant, but I thought the noise might be useful *in terrorem.*[4] Various Burmans stopped me on the way and told me about the elephant's doings. It was not, of course, a wild elephant, but a tame one which had gone "must."[5] It had been chained up as tame elephants always are when their attack of "must" is due, but on the previous night it had broken its chain and escaped. Its mahout,[6] the only person who could manage it when it was in that state, had set out in pursuit, but he had taken the wrong direction and was now twelve hours' journey away, and in the morning the elephant had suddenly reappeared in the town. The Burmese population had no weapons and were quite helpless against it. It had already destroyed somebody's bamboo hut, killed a cow, and raided some fruit stalls and devoured the stock; also it had met the municipal rubbish van, and, when the driver jumped out and took to his heels, had turned the van over and inflicted violence upon it.

The Burmese subinspector and some Indian constables were waiting for me in the quarter where the elephant had been seen. It was a very poor quarter, a labyrinth of squalid bamboo huts, thatched with palm leaf, winding all over a steep hillside. I remember that it was a cloudy stuffy morning at the beginning of the rains. We began questioning the people as to where the elephant had gone, and, as usual, failed to get any definite information. That is invariably the case in the East; a story always sounds clear enough at a distance, but the nearer you get to the scene of events the vaguer it becomes. Some of the people said that the elephant had gone in one direction, some said that he had gone in another, some professed not even to have heard of any elephant. I had almost made up my mind that the whole story was a pack of lies, when we heard yells a little distance away. There was a loud, scandalized cry of "Go away, child! Go away this instant!" and an old woman with a switch in her hand came round the corner of a hut, violently shooing away a crowd of naked children. Some more women followed, clicking their tongues and exclaiming; evidently there was something there that the children ought not to have seen. I rounded the hut and saw a man's dead body sprawling in the mud. He was an Indian, a Dravidian[7] coolie, almost naked, and he could not have been

[4] [a Latin phrase meaning "to cause fright"]

[5] [a phase of sexual excitement and destructive frenzy]

[6] [A mahout (mə hout/) is a trainer and driver of an elephant used for work and transportation.]

[7] [Dravidians were a major ethnic group in southern India.]

dead many minutes. The people said that the elephant had come suddenly upon him round the corner of the hut, caught him with its trunk,
put its foot on his back, and ground him into the earth. This was the
rainy season and the ground was soft, and his face had scored a trench a
foot deep and a couple of yards long. He was lying on his belly with
arms crucified and head sharply twisted to one side. His face was
coated with mud, the eyes wide open, the teeth bared and grinning
with an expression of unendurable agony. (Never tell me, by the way,
that the dead look peaceful. Most of the corpses I have seen looked
devilish.) The friction of the great beast's foot had stripped the skin
from his back as neatly as one skins a rabbit. As soon as I saw the dead
man I sent an orderly to a friend's house nearby to borrow an elephant
rifle. I had already sent back the pony, not wanting it to go mad with
fright and throw me if it smelled the elephant.

5   The orderly came back in a few minutes with a rifle and five cartridges, and meanwhile some Burmans had arrived and told us that the
elephant was in the paddy fields below, only a few hundred yards away.
As I started forward practically the whole population of the quarter
flocked out of their houses and followed me. They had seen the rifle
and were all shouting excitedly that I was going to shoot the elephant.
They had not shown much interest in the elephant when he was merely
ravaging their homes, but it was different now that he was going to be
shot. It was a bit of fun to them, as it would be to an English crowd;
besides, they wanted the meat. It made me vaguely uneasy. I had no
intention of shooting the elephant—I had merely sent for the rifle to
defend myself if necessary—and it is always unnerving to have a crowd
following you. I marched down the hill, looking and feeling a fool,
with the rifle over my shoulder and an ever-growing army of people
jostling at my heels. At the bottom, when you got away from the huts,
there was a metaled road and beyond that a miry waste of paddy fields a
thousand yards across, not yet plowed but soggy from the first rains and
dotted with coarse grass. The elephant was standing eighty yards from
the road, his left side toward us. He took not the slightest notice of the
crowd. He was tearing up bunches of grass, beating them against his
knees to clean them, and stuffing them into his mouth.

6   I had halted on the road. As soon as I saw the elephant I knew with
perfect certainty that I ought not to shoot him. It is a serious matter to
shoot a working elephant—it is comparable to destroying a huge and
costly piece of machinery—and obviously one ought not to do it if it
can possibly be avoided. And at that distance, peacefully eating, the
elephant looked no more dangerous than a cow. I thought then and I
think now that his attack of "must" was already passing off; in which
case he would merely wander harmlessly about until the mahout came

back and caught him. Moreover, I did not in the least want to shoot him. I decided that I would watch him for a little while to make sure that he did not turn savage again, and then go home.

But at that moment I glanced round at the crowd that had followed [7] me. It was an immense crowd, two thousand at the least and growing every minute. It blocked the road for a long distance on either side. I looked at the sea of yellow faces above the garish clothes—faces all happy and excited over this bit of fun, all certain that the elephant was going to be shot. They were watching me as they would watch a conjurer about to perform a trick. They did not like me, but with the magical rifle in my hands I was momentarily worth watching. And suddenly I realized that I should have to shoot the elephant after all. The people expected it of me and I had got to do it; I could feel their two thousand wills pressing me forward, irresistibly. And it was at this moment, as I stood there with the rifle in my hands, that I first grasped the hollowness, the futility of the white man's dominion in the East. Here was I, the white man with his gun, standing in front of the unarmed native crowd—seemingly the leading actor of the piece; but in reality I was only an absurd puppet pushed to and fro by the will of those yellow faces behind. I perceived in this moment that when the white man turns tyrant it is his own freedom that he destroys. He becomes a sort of hollow, posing dummy, the conventionalized figure of a sahib. For it is the condition of his rule that he shall spend his life in trying to impress the "natives" and so in every crisis he has got to do what the "natives" expect of him. He wears a mask, and his face grows to fit it. I had got to shoot the elephant. I had committed myself to doing it when I sent for the rifle. A sahib has got to act like a sahib; he has got to appear resolute, to know his own mind and do definite things. To come all that way, rifle in hand, with two thousand people marching at my heels, and then to trail feebly away, having done nothing—no, that was impossible. The crowd would laugh at me. And my whole life, every white man's life in the East, was one long struggle not to be laughed at.

But I did not want to shoot the elephant. I watched him beating his [8] bunch of grass against his knees, with that preoccupied grandmotherly air that elephants have. It seemed to me that it would be murder to shoot him. At that age I was not squeamish about killing animals, but I had never shot an elephant and never wanted to. (Somehow it always seems worse to kill a *large* animal.) Besides, there was the beast's owner to be considered. Alive, the elephant was worth at least a hundred pounds; dead, he would only be worth the value of his tusks—five pounds, possibly. But I had got to act quickly. I turned to some experienced-looking Burmans who had been there when we arrived, and asked them how the elephant had been behaving. They all said the same thing: he took no notice of you if you left him alone, but he might charge if you went too close to him.

9   It was perfectly clear to me what I ought to do. I ought to walk up to within, say, twenty-five yards of the elephant and test his behavior. If he charged I could shoot; if he took no notice of me it would be safe to leave him until the mahout came back. But also I knew that I was going to do no such thing. I was a poor shot with a rifle and the ground was soft mud into which one would sink at every step. If the elephant charged and I missed him, I should have about as much chance as a toad under a steamroller. But even then I was not thinking particularly of my own skin, only the watchful yellow faces behind. For at that moment, with the crowd watching me, I was not afraid in the ordinary sense, as I would have been if I had been alone. A white man mustn't be frightened in front of "natives"; and so, in general, he isn't frightened. The sole thought in my mind was that if anything went wrong those two thousand Burmans would see me pursued, caught, trampled on, and reduced to a grinning corpse like that Indian up the hill. And if that happened it was quite probable that some of them would laugh. That would never do. There was only one alternative. I shoved the cartridges into the magazine and lay down on the road to get a better aim.

10   The crowd grew very still, and a deep, low, happy sigh, as of people who see the theater curtain go up at last, breathed from innumerable throats. They were going to have their bit of fun after all. The rifle was a beautiful German thing with cross-hair sights. I did not then know that in shooting an elephant one should shoot to cut an imaginary bar running from earhole to earhole. I ought therefore, as the elephant was sideways on, to have aimed straight at his earhole; actually I aimed several inches in front of this, thinking the brain would be further forward.

11   When I pulled the trigger I did not hear the bang or feel the kick— one never does when a shot goes home—but I heard the devilish roar of glee that went up from the crowd. In that instant, in too short a time, one would have thought, even for the bullet to get there, a mysterious, terrible change had come over the elephant. He neither stirred nor fell, but every line of his body had altered. He looked suddenly stricken, shrunken, immensely old, as though the frightful impact of the bullet had paralyzed him without knocking him down. At last, after what seemed a long time—it might have been five seconds, I dare say—he sagged flabbily to his knees. His mouth slobbered. An enormous senility seemed to have settled upon him. One could have imagined him thousands of years old. I fired again into the same spot. At the second shot he did not collapse but climbed with desperate slowness to his feet and stood weakly upright, with legs sagging and head drooping. I

fired a third time. That was the shot that did for him. You could see the agony of it jolt his whole body and knock the last remnant of strength from his legs. But in falling he seemed for a moment to rise, for as his hind legs collapsed beneath him he seemed to tower upwards like a huge rock toppling, his trunk reaching skyward like a tree. He trumpeted, for the first and only time. And then down he came, his belly toward me, with a crash that seemed to shake the ground even where I lay.

I got up. The Burmans were already racing past me across the mud.   12
It was obvious that the elephant would never rise again, but he was not dead. He was breathing very rhythmically with long rattling gasps, his great mound of a side painfully rising and falling. His mouth was wide open—I could see far down into caverns of pale pink throat. I waited a long time for him to die, but his breathing did not weaken. Finally I fired my two remaining shots into the spot where I thought his heart must be. The thick blood welled out of him like red velvet, but still he did not die. His body did not even jerk when the shots hit him; the tortured breathing continued without a pause. He was dying, very slowly and in great agony, but in some world remote from me where not even a bullet could damage him further. I felt that I had got to put an end to that dreadful noise. It seemed dreadful to see the great beast lying there, powerless to move and yet powerless to die, and not even to be able to finish him. I sent back for my small rifle and poured shot after shot into his heart and down his throat. They seemed to make no impression. The tortured gasps continued as steadily as the ticking of a clock.

In the end I could not stand it any longer and went away. I heard   13
later that it took him half an hour to die. Burmans were arriving with dahs[8] and baskets even before I left, and I was told they had stripped his body almost to the bones by the afternoon.

Afterwards, of course, there were endless discussions about the   14
shooting of the elephant. The owner was furious, but he was only an Indian and could do nothing. Besides, legally I had done the right thing, for a mad elephant has to be killed, like a mad dog, if its owner fails to control it. Among the Europeans opinion was divided. The older men said I was right, the younger men said it was a shame to shoot an elephant for killing a coolie, because an elephant was worth more than any Coringhee coolie. And afterwards I was very glad that the coolie had been killed; it put me legally in the right and it gave me a sufficient pretext for shooting the elephant. I often wondered whether any of the others grasped that I had done it solely to avoid looking like a fool.

---

[8] [large, heavy knives]

USING THE DICTIONARY: This essay deals with the days of British colonial rule in Asia and Africa. It uses a number of political terms as well as words that came into British English in the days of colonialism. What do the following words mean? From what language or region did they come into English? 1. *bazaar* (1) 2. *raj* (2) 3. *prostrate* (2) 4. *imperialism* (3) 5. *despotic* (3) 6. *constable* (4) 7. *coolie* (4) 8. *paddy* (5) 9. *dominion* (7) 10. *sahib* (7)

THE WRITER'S AGENDA:

This essay is a classic example of autobiographical writing focused on one central event. The author gives us a vivid, dramatic account of this incident, and he explains what the event meant to him—what he learned from the experience. Answer the following questions about his account of the event and about its meaning:

1. The two opening paragraphs *set the scene* by taking us to Burma in the later days of British colonialism. What do we learn from this introduction about the setting and the people? Point out striking details that help create the situation for the reader. Pay special attention to the contradictory feelings and attitudes described in these two paragraphs. (What makes the opening sentence effective as a means of getting the reader's attention? How does it set the tone for the rest of the essay?)

2. George Orwell is a master of effective **narration**. Study his account of the physical events leading up to the climactic shooting. Summarize what happens. What striking details help make the setting and the events real for the reader?

3. As we approach the climactic shooting, the author begins to focus on the *meaning* that the experience had for him. What were the contradictory thoughts and feelings that went through his mind? What were his thoughts about the public role he played as a representative of British rule? (What sentence or passage best sums up for you the central idea, thus serving as a possible **thesis** for the essay as a whole?)

4. We reach the dramatic high point or **climax** of the essay with the two paragraphs beginning "When I pulled the trigger . . ." Study this account of the effects of the shots on the elephant. What is the keynote or dominant impression in the first of these two paragraphs? What is it in the second? In each paragraph, trace the network of closely related words and details that all reinforce the same dominant impression. (Identify exceptionally concrete or expressive words that help us imagine the scene.)

5. How does the author wind up the essay in his **conclusion**? Does he restate his main point? (If so, how or where?) What added thoughts or considerations appear in the conclusion, and how are they related to the central thesis of the essay?

For discussion or writing:

1. Representatives of colonial rule have often been accused of callousness, insensitivity, or condescension. They have been accused of being unable to understand or feel sympathy for the oppressed. How would you judge the author in the light of these charges? (Discuss fully any possible pro and con.)

2. A test of a writer's candor is the willingness to give a frank account of inner doubts, divided loyalties, and unflattering truths. What role do these play in the essay as a whole? How do they affect your view of the author as a person?

3. Is it common for people in authority to feel the need to keep up a façade or to keep up a front? Where have you observed or encountered something similar?

4. People are sometimes intensely aware of the difference between a public role they play and their own private personality. Focus on such a difference or conflict in discussing your attempt to play a role like the following:

- a good member of a team
- a model employee
- a successful student
- a good scout
- a dutiful son or daughter
- a model churchgoer

5. Great autobiography often reveals the divided loyalties or conflicts of conscience experienced by people faced with conflicting demands on their allegiance. Discuss one such conflict that you believe is especially meaningful to members of your generation.

6. We like to think of ourselves as being on the right side or serving the good cause. Have you ever felt you were on the wrong side or were serving the wrong cause? Describe your experience, and discuss what you learned from it.

7. Write an autobiographical essay modeled on Orwell's "Shooting an Elephant." Focus on a single major incident or event that had a special meaning for you as a person.

FOR FURTHER DISCUSSION AND WRITING: This article was written by an associate dean of the Columbia University Graduate School of Journalism (and former Washington reporter) for the "My Turn" column of *Newsweek* magazine. Which features of the "small places" she describes are most attractive to you? Is the lifestyle she describes a realistic alternative for you or for people you know well? Why or why not?

Carolyn Lewis

A Different Drummer

1   MY TWO sons live lives starkly different from my own. They make their homes in small rural places, and theirs are lives of voluntary simplicity.

2   They have chosen work that gives service to others, requires no great competitiveness, and does no harm in the name of greater good. They share a singular lack of interest in accruing possessions. Their clothes would make Brooks Brothers shudder, and they drive automobiles that are both ancient and uncomely.

3   They till the earth around their modest houses to grow vegetables, trees, and flowers. They are entertained by shared festivities with neighbors, wives, and children. They have records for music, books for learning, and each lives close enough to the sea to enjoy the esthetic pleasures of blue vistas and open sky.

4   This curious phenomenon—of ambitious, competitive, urban parents spawning gentle, unambitious, country offspring—is not unique to my own experience. I observe it all around me and listen with amusement to the puzzled comments of middle-aged parents faced with this unexpected generational shift.

5   "We gave him everything, and he chooses to weave blankets in Maine," they say accusingly. Or, "We invested in Andover and Harvard, and he cuts trees in Oregon." The refrain is sorrowful, even embarrassed, as though our children have somehow turned against us by choosing to live in ways different from our own.

But I confess that every time I return to the big city after visiting my   6
children, I am haunted by a psychic malaise. I go through my days
comparing this with that, and more and more the *that* is looking better.

What my sons have is a world that is small enough to be readily   7
understood, where those responsible wear a human face. When I talk
about the big city where I live, in the only terms that can grasp its
enormity—about groups and studies, trends and polls—my sons smile
sweetly and speak of people who live around the corner, have specific
names and definitive problems. Theirs are flesh-and-blood realities instead of my pale, theoretical formulations. They remind me that the
collective humanity I measure and label is far less interesting and vital
than the individual who, mercifully, in the end will defy categorization.

When I ask him how he likes living in a town of 500 people three   8
hours away from the nearest large city, my son Peter says: "Just fine.
You see, I know who I am here."

That statement resonates in my brain. It's true; he has a definable   9
space to call his own. He has warming relationships with family and
neighbors. He has what E. F. Schumacher would call "good work."

On the other hand, he certainly cannot be labeled rich. His income   10
is hardly the kind that makes the GNP go into a tailspin. When the
sophisticated instruments of measurement are applied to his life—husband, wife, two children (family of four earning so much)—they mark
him low income.

I, by comparison, living in my overpriced city apartment, walking to   11
work past putrid sacks of street garbage, paying usurious taxes to local
and state governments I generally abhor, I am rated middle class. This
causes me to wonder, do the measurements make sense? Are we meas-
uring only that which is easily measured—the numbers on the money
chart—and ignoring values more central to the good life?

For my sons there is of course the rural bounty of fresh-grown vege-   12
tables, line-caught fish, and the shared riches of neighbors' orchards
and gardens. There is the unpaid baby-sitter for whose children my
daughter-in-law baby-sits in return, and neighbors who barter their
skills and labor. But more than that, how do you measure serenity?
Sense of self? The feeling that, in order to get ahead, you don't have to
trample on somebody else's skull?

I don't want to idealize life in small places. There are times when   13
the outside world intrudes brutally, as when the cost of gasoline goes
up or developers cast their eyes on untouched farmland. There are
cruelties, there is bigotry, there are all the many vices and meannesses
in small places that exist in large cities. Furthermore, it is harder to
ignore them when they cannot be banished psychologically to another
part of town or excused as the vagaries of alien groups—when they
have to be acknowledged as "part of us."

14   Nor do I want to belittle the opportunities for small decencies in cities—the eruptions of one-stranger-to-another caring that always surprise and delight. But these are, sadly, more exceptions than rules and are often overwhelmed by the awful corruptions and dangers that surround us.

15   In this society, where material riches and a certain notoriety are considered admirable achievements, it takes some courage to say, no thanks, not for me. The urban pleasures and delights—restaurants, museums, theater, crowds in the streets—continue to have an urgent seductiveness for many young people. For parents like myself, who strove to offer our children these opportunities and riches, it is hard to be reconciled to those same children spurning the offer and choosing otherwise.

16   Plainly, what my sons want and need is something different—something smaller, simpler, and more manageable. They march to a different drummer, searching for an ethic that recognizes limits, that scorns overbearing competition and what it does to human relations, and that says simply and gently, enough is enough.

17   Is my sons' solution to the complexity and seeming intractability of modern problems the answer for everyone? Of course not. Some of us have to stay in the cities, do what we can, fight when it is necessary, compete in order to survive. Maybe if we are diligent, we can make things a little better where we are.

18   But to choose small places, modest ambitions, and values that are tolerant and loving is surely an admirable alternative. It may in the end be the only alternative we have to an urban culture in which we have created so much ugliness, and where we seem to inflict so much pain on each other through neglect, selfishness, and failure of will.

POINTS OF VIEW:
Law and Disorder

The Common Theme: Law and order has long been a familiar rallying cry of editorial writers and candidates for public office. People of widely differing views seem to agree on the basic issue: Our society is becoming more violent and disordered, and no easy answers or quick solutions are in sight. The three essays in this unit present the points of view of writers who have thought about what the law can and cannot do to help bring about a more humane society. The essays are written by people with strong personal views, ready to take a stand— and, if necessary, to go against the tide. Stephen Darst, in "A Violent Majority," tells the story of his unsuccessful fight for a gun control law designed to lower the homicide rate in a large American city. Margaret Mead, in "We Need Taboos on Sex at Work," argues that new laws or legal remedies alone are not enough to change traditional patterns of behavior. A. S. Neill, in "Punishment Never Cures Anything," challenges conventional assumptions about crime and punishment.

WRITER'S GUIDE 3:
Supporting a Thesis

No one writes in a vacuum. Our opinions take shape in the give-and-take of discussion that goes on all around us. To write effectively, we have to learn to listen and read attentively. We have to learn to take in the opinions of others before we present our own. Much effective writing is part of a continuing dialogue: A question arises, and we feel we have at least part of the answer. Something we care about is misrepresented, and we want to set the record straight. We are ready to take a stand; we are ready to present our own point of view.

Much writing that is worth reading presents an informed opinion on a subject of common concern. The kind of statement that *sums up* the author's point of view is called a thesis. The thesis spells out the central idea of a paper. It provides the answer for the reader who wants to know: "What is the point? What are you trying to prove?" In a paper worth reading, the thesis is the result of your own honest thinking about the subject. To formulate an effective thesis, you have to add up what you know. You have to pull together what you have heard and read.

When you write a paper that presents and supports a central thesis, remember the following guidelines:

(1) *Focus on an issue of common concern.* A live issue is one that cannot simply be settled by announcements from on high or by appeals to what "everybody knows." People with a knowledge of the subject take different sides. They disagree not just from spite or ignorance but because they see things differently. They have come to the subject from different backgrounds and with different expectations. On many topics of current public debate, some people's minds may already be set in concrete, but many other people are not sure they have the right answer. They may be willing to listen to your arguments if they feel that they will learn something and that their right to make up their own minds will be respected.

A writer today should be able to find an audience for a serious discussion of issues like the following:

♦ Should the government take steps to reduce illegal immigration?

♦ Should private citizens be allowed to arm themselves for protection against criminals?

♦ Should people sign marriage contracts that spell out how domestic chores and child raising will be shared between the spouses?

♦ Should the government finance programs designed to create jobs?

♦ What should be done when parents object to books on high school reading lists or in high school libraries?

♦ Does the separation of church and state rule out school prayer or programs related to religious holidays?

♦ Does the constant presentation of brutal violence in movie and television entertainment help to create a brutal, callous society?

♦ Should Americans stress English as the single national language of instruction in the schools?

♦ What should be done to correct the disparity between the earnings of women and men?

(2) *Sum up your central idea as the thesis of your paper.* The thesis is a brief one-sentence or two-sentence statement of the answer you give to the basic question raised by your paper. It clearly and directly states your point of view on the issue. It satisfies the reader who wants to know: "What is the message? Where do you stand?" Do not use your thesis merely to set vague general directions for your paper: "We should look at *several factors* involved in prejudice" or "There are *many objections* to gun control." Use your thesis to take a definite stand:

TOO OPEN: Like many other minority students, I have had a variety of experiences with white friends.

POINTED: So-called liberals who befriend minority students are often fair-weather friends; on weekends and on social occasions, they are nowhere to be found.

TOO OPEN: Many serious questions have been raised about the ever-present violence in movies and on TV.

POINTED: The main objection to television and movie violence is that it makes killing seem swift and easy.

TOO OPEN: Much has been written in recent years about the attitude Americans have toward work.

POINTED: To judge from fashionable movies and books, many Americans today hate their work.

(3) *Use your introduction to lead directly into your central thesis.* At times, a writer will lead up to the main point indirectly or in stages. But an early statement of your thesis will focus your readers' attention and let them know what is at issue. The following might be the opening paragraph of an essay on careers open to women:

Introduction   When a bright young woman graduate started
looking for a job, why was the first question always:
"Can you type?" A history of prejudice lies behind
that question. Why are women thought of as secretaries, not administrators? Librarians and teachers, but
THESIS   not doctors and lawyers? *Because they are thought of
as different and inferior. The happy homemaker
and the contented darky are both stereotypes produced by prejudice.*
—Shirley Chisholm, "A Visiting Feminine Eye," *McCall's*

(4) *Support your thesis with relevant evidence or detailed examples.* A thesis serves as a promise to the reader. The implied promise is,
"This is what I believe, and I will show *why.*" Suppose a writer dis-
agrees with the conventional view that assumes a large gap between
highbrow and lowbrow art, between culture and "popular" culture.
When the writer asserts that this division is undesirable, and that art
should "speak to all of us," our natural reaction is to ask: "What makes
you think so?" We expect the writer to provide a set of convincing
examples like the following:

THESIS   *Whenever art was vital, it was always equally
popular with the ordinary person and the most re-
fined person.*

First   Had Greek drama and comedy meant nothing to
example   most citizens, the majority of the population would
(Greek   not have sat all day long entranced on hard stone
drama)   slabs, watching the events on the stage; nor would
the entire population have conferred prizes on the
winning dramatist. . . .

Second   The medieval pageants and mystery plays out of
example   which modern drama grew were popular entertain-
(later drama) ments, as were the plays of Shakespeare. . . .

Third   Michelangelo's David stood at the most public
example   place in Florence, embodying the people's vision
(Renaissance that tyranny must be overthrown, while it also re-
art)   lated to their religious vision, as it represented the
myth of David and Goliath. Everybody admired the
statue; it was simultaneously popular and great
art. . . .
—Bruno Bettelheim, "The Art of Moving Pictures,"
Harper's

(5) *Consider including in your thesis a clue to the organization of your paper.* A thesis can serve as a preview; it can sketch out a program for the rest of a paper. Suppose you have been asked to write about a term that echoes in much current political discussion. A thesis like the following can set the direction for the development of your paper:

> THESIS: *Exploitation is using others for personal advantage: Individuals exploit other human beings; stronger nations have always exploited weaker nations.*

This thesis statement makes us expect a paper that has two major parts. First, we are likely to find examples of *individual* exploitation:

> First category Today it is not unusual for adults to exploit children. Children are pushed into acting or modeling at a very young age by their parents. . . .

In the second part of the paper, we are likely to find examples of *nations* exploiting other nations:

> Second category In the history of modern imperialism, we see many examples of small, weak nations being invaded for their gold and diamonds, or exploited for their oil and other raw materials. . . .

(6) *Make your thesis the key to the unity of your paper as a whole.* Almost everything that is part of a well-focused paper helps to present, explain, support, and reinforce the writer's central idea. Suppose a writer is concerned about the failure of modern parents to set moral standards in the home. The following is a rough outline of an article that would follow the pattern of thesis–explanation–support–reinforcement.

> THESIS: *In home after home that I have visited, and in many classrooms, I have met children who not only are growing emotionally and intellectually but also are trying to make sense of the world morally.*

> Explanation *That is to say,* they are asking themselves and others about issues of fair play, justice, liberty, equality. Those last words are abstractions, of course—the stuff of college term papers. And there are, one has to repeat, those in psychology and psychiatry who would deny elementary-school children access to that "higher level" of moral reflection. . . .

> Examples In 1963, when I was studying school desegrega-

tion in the South, I had extended conversations with Black and white elementary-school children caught up in a dramatic moment of historical change. . . .

Restatement   Children need and long for words of moral advice, instruction, warning, as much as they need words of affirmation or criticism from their parents about other matters. They must learn how to dress and what to wear, how to eat and what to eat; and they must also learn how to behave under X or Y or Z conditions, and why.
—Robert Coles, "I Listen to My Parents," *Redbook*

To sum up: A thesis is a statement in need of support. In the rough-and-tumble of public debate, it is not enough to *have* an opinion. The key question we ask of a writer is: "What makes you think so?" The point of view you present in a paper must be founded in something. It must derive from an honest look at the issue. You are entitled to your opinion, but your readers will expect you to back it up with examples, statistics, case histories, expert testimony, and other kinds of support.

PREWRITING ACTIVITIES 3

1. Use *discovery frames* like the following to work up a subject in a systematic, organized way. Ask yourself questions that will help you discover what you already know about a topic. Suppose a topic asks you to express your views, or take a stand, on environmental pollution. For a preliminary collection of material, write detailed responses under all or most of the following headings:

I. *Common knowledge:* What is it that "everybody says" or "everybody knows" about this subject? What are some typical headlines? How frequently is pollution in the news? What would a reader find in recent newspaper or magazine articles on this subject?

II. *Personal experience:* Where have you yourself seen striking evidence of pollution? Is it an issue where you live? Where has it played a role in the lives or the work of people you know? What do you know about this topic from first-hand observation and experience?

III. *Long-range causes:* What are the basic causes of our current problems with pollution? What are the major long-range historical developments that explain our current dilemmas? Which in your opinion are the chief culprits (and which perhaps are merely scapegoats)?

IV. *Current efforts:* What has been done, or is being done, to clean up the environment? What are some recent successes or failures? What are major obstacles or hopeful signs?

V. *Future prospects:* What lies ahead? How optimistic or how pessimistic would your own personal forecast be, and why?

2. For an *opinion inventory,* write down your views on several subjects. Write freely and quickly, recording views, ideas, or reactions as they come to mind. Write on several of the following: law and order, the draft, corruption, pornography, affirmative action, nuclear power, political parties, drugs, race, war.

3. How good a listener are you? How often do you make the effort to understand fully the point of view of someone with whom you strongly *disagree?* Play the devil's advocate. Explain as fully and as fairly as you can an attitude, position, or point of view with which you strongly disagree.

BACKGROUND: Stephen Darst is a journalist who writes not as a detached, dispassionate reporter but as a concerned citizen personally involved in the issues of the day. In this article on gun control, he looks back on his own experience as a lawmaker at the grass-roots level. He takes us back to a period in our national life when public opinion on the issue of gun control had been aroused by dramatic examples of murderous violence: A few years earlier, in 1963, President John F. Kennedy had been killed with a mail-order rifle while riding through the streets of Dallas in an open limousine. In 1968, Martin Luther King, the eloquent leader of the civil rights movement of the sixties, was assassinated in Memphis. A few weeks later, President Kennedy's younger brother, Senator Robert Kennedy, running for the presidential nomination of his party, was gunned down in a Los Angeles hotel. As the author of the following article said, "If you couldn't pass a gun control bill then, you will never pass one."

Stephen Darst

A Violent Majority

GUIDE TO READING: In this magazine article, we become involved in an important issue as we study a *case history*. What do we learn as we study the workings of the lawmaking process at the local level, closest to the everyday lives of the citizen? Pay special attention to how the clash of different opinions and interests takes shape in this essay. As you read, outline in your mind the author's thinking about his bill, the sources of support for it, and the obstacles it encounters.

1   IN 1968 I WAS a member of the St. Louis Board of Aldermen. The aldermanic job was very undemanding, with only one meeting of the board per week, and occasional committee meetings, plus much fence-mending work back in the ward. All the aldermen had other jobs. Several were lawyers, a few undertakers, and an ungodly number were tavern owners. It was a local joke that when the clerk put his head in the door of the board chambers one day yelling, "Your tavern is on fire!" the chamber immediately emptied.

2   My outside job was newspaper reporting. Journalism was really a

much stranger occupation than embalming or saloon-keeping to combine with politicking, but there were some points where the two professions met. For example, the reading I did to keep abreast of issues was helpful in both fields. I read a wide variety of newspapers and magazines, filing away articles that might make future articles or speeches. In 1967 I read an article in the *Saturday Review* about a Philadelphia gun-control bill which had had a startling success in reducing firearms crimes in the City of Brotherly Love. I filed it away for possible reference.

The article would have remained safely filed away but for the fact 3 that shortly afterward I agreed to accept a student on sabbatical from Webster College in suburban St. Louis as my "administrative assistant." The idea was that she would work on fascinating political projects that would be far more instructive than anything she could learn in a poli-sci class.

The problem with my administrative assistant was that there was a 4 serious lack of fascinating practical political assignments. I began casting about for a project for her, and when I ran across the *Saturday Review* article on gun control it seemed promising. I told my assistant to round up gun-control legislation—the Philadelphia bill and any others of interest—with the idea that we might put together a composite bill which I would introduce in the Board of Aldermen.

In addition, we made a few phone calls to legislators in other cities 5 who had written gun-control bills. I called the president of the Philadelphia City Council, Paul D'Ortona, the man who had drafted and pushed through the bill which had received such glowing reviews in the *Saturday Review*. I was particularly concerned, I told him, about the role the National Rifle Association had played in opposing the Philadelphia bill.

"Don't be afraid of that crowd," Council President D'Ortona shot 6 back in a fearless voice. "They just make a lot of noise. They threatened to oppose me the next time I ran, but I got the bill through the Council and the next time I ran better than ever. The National Rifle Association is a paper tiger."

The firearms ordinances of the City Code of St. Louis were not 7 especially permissive, but there were enough loopholes to permit any madman or criminal to buy almost any kind of gun. So the first job was to plug the loopholes in the present law, especially through requirements for registration of guns and gun owners. By this time I was working with several lawyers to draft the new bill. As we took anything that looked valuable from the legislation which had been tried elsewhere, the bill gradually grew longer and tighter. For example, the old St. Louis law required police to check an applicant before issuing a permit for a handgun. But the police check was useless. There was no positive identification through fingerprinting or photographing, and there was

no check with FBI files in Washington or with other police depart-
ments across the country. An applicant could have committed mass
murder with a bazooka as long as he had done it outside the city limits
of St. Louis. Our bill demanded fingerprinting, photographing, and a
check against FBI records. Felons, chronic alcoholics, drug addicts,
and persons with histories of mental illness would be disqualified from
receiving a permit, and would not be able to buy or own any long gun
or handgun or ammunition. All guns had to be registered, even those
owned before passage of the bill. The maximum penalty was a year in
jail and a $500 fine for any violation. It was the toughest gun-control
bill in the United States.

8   A week later after it was drafted Dr. Martin Luther King, Jr., was
killed in Memphis. Several weeks after that, Sen. Robert Kennedy was
assassinated in Los Angeles. Both murders were accomplished, of
course, with firearms. The clamor for tighter gun-control laws was immediate, loud, and seemingly unappeasable. I threw my bill into the
legislative hopper within a few days of Kennedy's murder.

9   Several days later the *St. Louis Post-Dispatch* strongly recommend-
ed immediate passage of the bill. One alderman after another came up
to me in the chamber and told me it was high time we tightened our
gun-control laws and took guns out of the hands of these idiots, high
time we put these overarmed madmen in their place. The aldermen
were behind me to a man.

10   "Those hoosiers down in my ward are mad as hell about this bill
but I'm going to be with you when the time comes," one alderman
promised. "Every one of those bastards has a gun. When they aren't
shooting squirrels back home in Tennessee or Arkansas on the weekend, they're shooting each other up here in bars in my ward during the
week. None of them pays taxes in this city, and none of them votes
here. If they don't vote here, I don't owe them nothing. Screw those
hoosiers."

11   Seemingly, the bill was a shoo-in. But later, looking back on it all, I
came to the conclusion that the bill had been in trouble from the start.
The first problem was timing. The Board of Aldermen was in session for
only a few days after the gun-control bill was introduced before the
three-month summer recess began. The board was not scheduled for a
regular meeting until mid-September and the bill had to be read three
times before it could be voted on. So it was hard to see a vote before
October. Each passing day put that much distance between the assassi-
nations and the vote. And before the vote there had to be a public
hearing.

12   The public hearing was generally conceded to have been the wild-
est meeting in the history of the turn-of-the-century City Hall. When the
date for the hearing was set for a night in mid-August, the aldermen's

mailboxes began to fill with letters and notes and telegrams, an average of 500 per alderman, all in opposition to the bill.

On the appointed night, the hearing room filled up early with vociferous gun nuts. (Although in public debate we always went through the obligatory gestures of respect for our worthy, if temporarily benighted, opponents, in private we always thought and spoke of them as "gun nuts." They, in turn, referred to us, in public and private, as "bleeding hearts.")

"They're mean looking—that's the meanest-looking mob I've ever seen," Donald Gunn, the president of the Board of Aldermen, told me. The crowd looked not only furious but armed. "The first shot you hear, turn over that table we'll be sitting at," Gunn said. "It's made out of oak and it's thick, and if we can turn it over and get behind it we might be able to hold out through the shooting until the police can restore order."

The police were there not only to keep order but also to testify for the bill. Police are generally in favor of gun control, knowing that their own chances for survival amidst a citizenry armed to the teeth are not good. But the police department was among the few supporters. Speaker after speaker rose to denounce the bill, and by the end of the hearing I could feel a definite tide beginning to run against it.

"A cooling-off period," one alderman told me, "that's what we need. Give those people a couple of months to forget about this and your bill will breeze through."

The opposite happened. Even aldermen who had been strongly in favor of the bill began to have reservations. I tried to bring them around again through appeals to reason. One of my strongest appeals, I thought, had to do with a glaring weakness in the old bill. According to the St. Louis gun law then in force, the Sheriff of the City of St. Louis issued permits for handguns. One requirement stipulated by Sheriff Martin L. Tozer was that any wife wishing to buy a handgun had to produce a letter from her husband giving his permission. Husbands were not required to have similar letters from their wives. I pointed out this seeming inconsistency to one wavering alderman.

"What does it say there—women need their husband's permission?" the alderman asked. "Well, I should hope so. There's a lot of common sense to that. I mean what if the old lady gets it into her head to blow her old man's head off some night? With this regulation we've got Sheriff Tozer right there wanting to see that letter from the husband before he's going to issue the wife a permit to buy a gun to kill the old man with. Which the old man has gotta be crazy if he writes. Now I think that's a great idea, that letter from the husband. That stops a lot of bloodshed."

"But the husband doesn't need permission of the wife if he wants

13
14
15
16
17
18
19

to buy a gun," I pointed out. "Does that seem fair—the wife has to have the letter from the husband if she wants to buy a gun but not vice versa?"

20   "Yeah, that makes a lot of sense to my way of thinking," he said. "I can understand that perfectly. You wouldn't want to have to ask your wife's permission every time before you bought a gun for the protection of your home, would you?"

21   But wives should need letters from husbands? I asked.

22   "That's right, he said. He looked at me as if he were talking to a very small and very liberal child. "Say, I thought you were supposed to be trying to take guns away from dangerous persons? That's the idea, isn't it? But now you want to arm all the wives. That's the real gun control—putting pistols in the hands of every dizzy broad. You could get a lot of good men killed that way."

23   When I talked to the sheriff about the requirement, he pointed out that the state law gave him great leeway in these matters. Hauling out the statute book, he opened it to the section that dealt with the powers of the Office of Sheriff.

24   "It says that to buy a handgun you must be of good moral character and the sheriff must be satisfied that the issuance of the permit will not endanger the public safety," Sheriff Tozer said.

25   He stopped and looked at me piercingly to see if I appreciated the full nuances of the law.

26   "You will notice that it says 'the sheriff must be satisfied.' That means, in this case, myself. Sheriff Tozer must be satisfied. So I got to thinking about it one day and it occurred to me that more wives shoot their husbands than husbands shoot their wives. So I got the idea of requiring a letter from the husband before the wife can go out and buy a pistol. And I can tell you it's one of the best and most popular things I've ever done in this office, and I enforce it."

27   Tozer produced several pieces of paper—applications for handgun permits from wives who had failed to include the required letter from their husbands.

28   "Applications denied!" Sheriff Tozer said, shaking the flawed papers. A clerk in his office told me later that even when an application form from a wife did include the husband's letter, the sheriff frequently took it upon himself to put in a quiet phone call to see if the husband was in full possession of his faculties.

29   In addition to disarming the potentially dangerous wives of the city, the sheriff's regulations refused pistols to anyone who was not a duly registered voter. The official reason was the necessity of having some check on the address of the applicant, but the real reason, I suspected, was that the sheriff saw no reason to do a man the favor of permitting him to own a gun if the man could not return the favor by voting for the sheriff and his political allies.

Besides wives and unregistered citizens, easily the most under- 30
gunned segment of the population were the sex deviates. The statute
did not specify what crimes disqualified a person from purchasing a
pistol. Again, the sheriff was given broad discretion. Common sense
might have decreed that crimes of violence would be automatically
disqualifying, but such was not the case. Persons with violent crimes on
their records were often given permits for handguns. The sheriff came
down like a ton of bricks, however, when it came to persons with sex
crimes on their records.

"Any sexual pervert who attempts to arm himself in the City of St. 31
Louis will not get by the Office of the Sheriff," Tozer told me. "As long
as I am Sheriff of the City of St. Louis those deviates will not be roaming
the streets with guns."

With the sheriff standing as a first line of defense against poten- 32
tially bloodthirsty, trigger-happy degenerates, we were never troubled
in St. Louis with murderous shoot-outs between rival gangs of deviates.
What we were troubled with was a homicide rate among the citizens at
large that was unusually high. At about that time the FBI came out with
its annual crime statistics, statistics which put St. Louis at the top of the
list among the large cities of the country for murders per capita.

I thought that our soaring murder rate would be a good argument 33
for my bill, but at about this time the National Rifle Association stepped
up its campaign. I don't know why the NRA seemed a paper tiger to the
gun-control advocates of Philadelphia; in St. Louis its influence was
overpowering. A few days before my bill came up for a vote, the NRA
sent out a special bulletin giving the name, address, and phone number
of each alderman. Aldermen were deluged with calls and letters. Because I was the sponsor of the bill, I got no calls and only one letter, a
note from the White Citizens' Council of Greater St. Louis informing
me that, although it was their policy never to work for or against any
candidate, presumably preferring to concentrate their efforts on the
larger cause of intolerance in the abstract, they would be willing to
make an exception in my case and if I ever again filed for office they
would do everything in their power to bury me.

The day the bill was to be voted on, the gallery of the board cham- 34
ber was packed with gun nuts who beamed down benevolently as the
roll, one nay vote after another, was called. My vote came early so I was
able to record one aye for the great cause. I was certain mine was going
to be the only one. And then:

"Aye." 35

The clerk could not believe his ears. 36

"Would you repeat your vote, Alderman Martin?" 37

"Aye— I vote in favor of the bill—my vote is aye," Alderman Ted 38
Martin repeated. The roll call continued to a close, twenty-six nays and
two ayes, as I crossed the floor to thank Alderman Martin.

39   "You don't owe me any thanks," he said, shaking my hand. "I
didn't vote for that bill to do you a favor—I voted for that bill because
it's a good bill. I voted for that bill because it's the kind of bill we're
going to have to have in this town if we're ever going to reduce the
murder rate. And, last and most important, I voted for that bill because
I decided a couple of days ago that I was never going to run for office
again."

 USING THE DICTIONARY: Dictionaries list different meanings
or uses of a word in sets of numbered definitions. We have to
choose the definition that fits the **context** in which the word is
being used. For each of the following, choose the definition
that fits the way the word is used in this essay. (What are other
meanings or uses of some of these words?) 1. a *sabbatical*
leave (3) 2. a *composite* bill (4) 3. a firearms *ordinance* (7)
4. a public *clamor* (8) 5. the legislative *hopper* (8) 6. *obligatory* gestures of respect (13) 7. *reservations* about the bill
(17) 8. a *stipulated* requirement (17) 9. the *nuances* of the
law (25) 10. in possession of his *faculties* (28)

THE WRITER'S AGENDA:

In this essay, the author records his candid first-hand observation of
some of the forces that shape public opinion. Answer the following
questions about the clash of different points of view in this essay.

1. Gun control is an issue that has long been a familiar subject of
controversy. As *readers,* we do not approach the issue with a totally
open mind: We remember slogans, facts, statistics, arguments, or personal experiences that are in some way related to the topic. What, for
you, are associations, memories, attitudes, or arguments that the issue
brings to mind?

2. What were the aims and detailed provisions of the author's *proposed law?* How strong a case or how worthy a cause do you think he
was presenting to other people for their support?

3. During the various stages of the author's promotion of the bill,
what *sources of support* did he mobilize? Who supported him, and
why? (Were any of these sources of support predictable; were any
unexpected?)

4. As the author tried to rally faltering support for his bill, he concentrated with little success on a "glaring weakness" in the *old bill*

then in force. What was that weakness? What is the gist of his long discussions with a fellow alderman and with the sheriff? What did he learn from the experience?

5. In public debate, we are expected to show respect for people who *disagree* with us. Did either side in this controversy live up to this ideal standard? How did the author's opponents view him? How did he view them?

6. Although the author is serious about the basic issue, he treats it with a *lighter touch*. The humorous tone of the essay owes much to his use of **irony**. Our sense of irony makes us respond with a wry smile when something does not live up to our naive expectations or unrealistic standards. Point out several examples of this kind of irony in different parts of the essay.

For discussion or writing:

1. We know that the author has strong personal views, but to some extent he lets the events of his story speak for themselves. How would you sum up the point of what happened? What defeated him? Do you think the defeat was inevitable—a foregone conclusion? Why, or why not?

2. How widespread is crime or violence involving the use of guns? Read the issues of a major newspaper for about one week. Take stock of all news reports of relevant incidents. Prepare a report on the nature and extent of gun-related violence during one ordinary week. Sort your findings out into major categories.

3. Much of public debate on an issue like gun control uses familiar slogans and familiar arguments. Discuss such familiar slogans as "Guns don't kill people—people kill people" and "If guns are outlawed, only outlaws will have guns." How convincing or how effective are these slogans? What for you is the meaning of the often quoted Second Amendment to the Constitution: "A well-regulated militia being necessary to the security of a free state, the right of the people to keep and bear arms shall not be infringed"?

4. Go through back issues of a major newspaper or magazine to find an editorial or short article dealing with the issue of gun control. What is the point of view of the author? How does the author support that point of view? How do you react as a reader, and why? (If you can, bring a photocopy of the article to class.)

5. Some years ago, Marya Mannes, a widely read television and drama critic, accused the people responsible for American television

programs of a "wholesale preoccupation with killing by gun." The daily lesson for millions of young viewers, she said, was that hero and criminal were both "cowards who answered questions by pulling triggers." How much gun-related violence is there in current television programming? How is it presented? What attitudes does it reflect, or what lesson does it teach?

6. Prepare a paper in which you present and support your own point of view on the subject of gun control. State your own position as the thesis, or central idea, early in your paper. Support it with any relevant statistics, first-hand observation, personal experience, quoted authorities, or the like.

7. It it often said that the public tends to be apathetic about large-scale anonymous suffering and violence. But public opinion is aroused by single spectacular or sensational examples of crime or violence. People trying to influence public opinion use single spectacular cases to dramatize an issue. To judge from your own observation or reading, how true are these conclusions? Discuss several detailed examples.

BACKGROUND: Margaret Mead (1901–78) became famous as a young anthropologist who went to Samoa in 1925 to live with the islanders and study their way of life. The book she wrote about her experiences, *Coming of Age in Samoa,* became one of the most widely read books in the history of anthropology and was still the subject of scholarly debate fifty-five years after its publication in 1928. Mead grew up in New Jersey and Pennsylvania, moving frequently as required by the studies or teaching assignments of her parents. After studying at Columbia University, she ignored the advice of a famous fellow anthropologist and linguist to stay home and have children. Instead, she went on to years of field work studying the patterns of growing up of adolescent girls in cultures relatively untouched by Western civilization; she published a succession of widely read books ranging from *Growing Up in New Guinea* (1930) to *Male and Female* (1949). In the final years of her career, Mead wrote to provide young people with guidance through the challenges and confusions of our time. The essay that follows illustrates well how opinions take shape in the give-and-take of public discussion. Mead wrote this essay at a time when public discussion was focused on legal remedies to problems of sexual harassment and sexual discrimination. Her own experience as a student of human behavior made her conclude that new laws alone were not enough to change traditional cultural patterns.

Margaret Mead

We Need Taboos on Sex at Work

GUIDE TO READING: In the essay that follows, the author identifies the central problem and discusses a familiar suggested solution. She then presents her own solution, stating a strong personal point of view. As you read the essay, look for answers to the following questions: What is the problem, and how and where does she identify it? What are the possible solutions, and how are they different? What historical background does the author present to help us understand the issue? What does she do to help convince us?

1   WHAT SHOULD we—what can we—do about sexual harassment on the job?

2   During the century since the first "type writer"—that is, the first young woman clerk who had mastered the operation of the mechanical writing machine—entered a business office and initiated a whole new female-male work relationship, women have had to struggle with the problem of sexual harassment at work. And we still are at a loss as to how to cope with it successfully.

3   Certainly no one of us—young or old, single or married, attractive or homely, naive or socially skilled—has escaped entirely unscathed. True, actual sexual assaults—rape and seduction—have been less common in almost any work situation than fathers and brothers once feared and predicted. But who among us hasn't met the male kiss-and-tell office flirt, the pinching prankster, the man in search of party girls, or the man who makes sex a condition for job promotion? Who has not known the man who thinks no task is too tedious, unpleasant, or demeaning for his "girl" to do in or out of office hours, the gossipmonger and—perhaps most dangerous—the apparently friendly man who subtly undercuts every direction given by a woman, depreciates every plan she offers, and devalues her every accomplishment? Some women get discouraged and give up; most women learn to be wary. But as long as so many men use sex in so many ways as a weapon to keep down the women with whom they work, how can we develop mature, give-and-take working relationships?

4   As I see it, it isn't more laws that we need now, but new taboos.

5   Not every woman—and certainly not every man—realizes and acknowledges that the mid-1960s marked a watershed in the *legal* treatment of women in the working world. Beginning with the Equal Pay Act of 1963 and the Civil Rights Acts of 1964 (especially Title VII), legislation has been passed, executive orders have been issued, official guidelines have been established and decisions in a great many court cases have set forth a woman's right to be a first-class working citizen. Slowly but surely, using the new laws, women are making progress in their fight to gain what the law now so clearly defines as the right of every working person. And today almost half of all adult women are working persons.

6   But there are serious discrepancies. At home and at school we still bring up boys to respond to the presence of women in outmoded ways—to become men who cannot be trusted alone with a woman, who are angry and frustrated by having to treat a woman as an equal—either as a female with power who must be cajoled or as a female without power who can be coerced. But at the same time we are teaching our daughters to expect a very different working world, one in which both women and men are full participants.

7   In keeping with this goal, we are insistent that the rights women

have gained must be spelled out and that women use every legal device to ensure that new rules are formulated and translated into practice. Why, then, do I think that the new laws will not be sufficient to protect women—and men too, for that matter—from the problems of sexual harassment on the job? Why do I think we need new taboos?

I realize that this must sound strange to a generation of young 8 women who have felt the need to break and abandon taboos of many kinds—from taboos against the inappropriate use of four-letter words to taboos against petty pilfering; from taboos against the use of addictive drugs to taboos against the public display of the naked human body; from the taboo against the frank enjoyment of sex to the taboos against full sexual honesty.

In some circles it has even become fashionable to call incest ta- 9 boos—the taboo against sex with close family members other than husband and wife—out of date and unimportant. Yet incest taboos remain a vital part of any society. They insure that most children can grow up safe in the household, learn to trust, to be loved and to be sexually safe, unexploited and unmolested within the family.

When we examine how any society works, it becomes clear that it is 10 precisely the basic taboos—the deeply and intensely felt prohibitions against "unthinkable" behavior—that keep the social system in balance. Laws are an expression of principles concerning things we can and do think about, and they can be changed as our perception of the world changes. But a taboo, even against taking a human life, may or may not be formulated in legal terms in some societies; the taboo lies much deeper in our consciousness, and by prohibiting certain forms of behavior also affirms what we hold most precious in our human relationships. Taboos break down in periods of profound change and are re-created in new forms during periods of transition.

We are in such a period now. And like the family, the modern 11 business and the modern profession must develop incest taboos. If women are to work on an equal basis with men, with men supervising women in some cases and women supervising men in others, we have to develop decent sex mores in the whole working world.

In the past, when women entered the working world as factory 12 workers or clerks in shops, as typists or chorus girls, they entered at the bottom; their poverty and their need for the job were part of their helplessness. Like women in domestic service, they were very vulnerable to sexual advances and seduction by men in positions of power over them. But sex also presented a precarious ladder by which a girl just might climb to become the pampered mistress or even the wife of the boss, the producer, the important politician.

For a long time after women began to work away from home, peo- 13 ple made a sharp distinction between women who virtuously lived at home and limited "work" to voluntary efforts and other women who, lacking the support and protection of a father, brother, husband, or son, were constrained to work for money. Wage-earning women were sexually vulnerable, and it was generally believed that the woman who was raped probably deserved it and that the woman who was seduced probably had tempted the man. By leaving home, a woman did not merely move beyond the range of the laws that protected her there, but beyond the areas of living made safe by the force of taboos.

14   In the primitive societies in which I worked and lived as a young woman and as an older one, women who obeyed the accepted rules of behavior were not molested. But a woman who broke the rules—went out in the bush at night, worked alone in a distant garden or followed a lonely path without even a child companion—was asking for trouble. In general, women and men knew what was expected of them—until their lives were shaken up by change through the coming of strangers and the introduction of new kinds of work and new expectations. Then, along with other sorts of confusion, there was confusion about the sex relations of men and women. Cases of sex molestation, attack, and rape reflected the breakdown of traditional security.

15   Everywhere and at all times, societies have developed ways of stylizing relations between women and men. Though the rules might be cruel and exploitative, they defined with clarity the posture and gait, the costume and the conversation, that signaled a woman's compliance with the rules as well as the circumstances in which a woman defined herself as a whore. In our own society, when women first became nurses their costume, reminiscent of the dress of nuns, at once announced the virtue of their calling. When a young American woman went away from home to teach children in one of the thousands of one-room schoolhouses that abounded in the countryside, the local community took charge of her virtue. Sometimes the rules were broken—on purpose. But the rules that protected men as well as women were known and agreed upon.

16   Today, with our huge and restless mobility from country to city, from one city to another, from class to class and from one country to another, most of the subtle ways in which women and men related to each other in a more limited setting have broken down. And now a new element has entered into their working relations with the demands that women must be employed in unfamiliar occupations and at higher executive and professional levels. Almost without warning, and certainly without considering the necessity for working out new forms of acceptable behavior, men and women are confronting each other as colleagues with equal rights.

17   And suddenly there is an outburst of complaints from women who find themselves mistreated in ways to which they are quite unaccustomed, as well as complaints from women who have suddenly discovered that sexual harassment on the job no longer is part of the expected

life of a working woman. By banding together, organizing themselves and counseling one another, women are beginning to feel their strength and are making themselves heard, loud and clear, on the job, in the media and in the courts. Harassment on the job and wife beating at home have become part of our public consciousness.

Now, how to deal with the problems, the social discord and dissonance, in the relations between women and men? The complaints, the legal remedies and the support institutions developed by women all are part of the response to the new conception of women's rights. But I believe we need something much more pervasive, a climate of opinion that includes men as well as women, and that will affect not only adult relations and behavior on the job but also the expectations about the adult world that guide our children's progress into that world.   18

What we need, in fact, are new taboos that are appropriate to the new society we are struggling to create—taboos that will operate within the work setting as once they operated within the household. Neither men nor women should expect that sex can be used either to victimize women who need to keep their jobs or to keep women from advancement or to help men advance their own careers. A taboo enjoins. We need one that says clearly and unequivocally, "You don't make passes at or sleep with the people you work with."   19

This means that girls and boys will have to grow up together expecting and respecting a continuous relationship, in season and out, alone together or in a mixed group, that can withstand tension and relaxation, stimulation and frustration, frankness and reserve, without breaking down. It will have something of the relationship of brothers and sisters who have grown up safely within a household, but it also will be different. For where brother and sister have a lifelong relationship, women and men who work together may share many years or only a few weeks or days or even hours.   20

In the way in which societies do develop new ways of meeting new problems, I believe we are beginning to develop new ways of working together that carry with them appropriate taboos—new ways that allow women and men to work together effortlessly and to respect each other as persons.   21

The beginning was made not at work but in our insistence on coeducation in the earliest grades of school, and gradually at all levels. This has made it possible for women to have much greater freedom wherever they go—so much so that we take it almost wholly for granted. We know it is not always wholehearted, but it is a beginning we know well.   22

And now, in line with new attitudes toward sex and equality, many students have demanded, and obtained, coeducational dormitories. Their elders mistook this as a demand for freer sexual access; but student advocates said firmly that, as young men and women, they wanted   23 to meet under more natural circumstances and get to know one another as friends.

24   Today, wherever there is coeducation with a fairly even ratio between the sexes and several years' experience of living in coeducational dormitories, a quiet taboo is developing without the support of formal rules and regulations, fines or public exposure, praise or censure—a taboo against serious dating within the dormitory. Young women and young men who later will have to work side by side, in superordinate and subordinate relations as well as equals and members of a team, are finding their way toward a kind of harmony in which exploitative sex is set aside in favor of mutual concern, shared interests and, it seems to me, a new sense of friendship.

25   This is just a beginning, and one that is far from perfect. But one of the very good things is that women are discovering they can be frank and outspoken without being shrill, just as men are discovering there are pleasures in friendships without domination.

26   It is just a beginning, but students can set a style that will carry over into working relations in which skill, ability, and experience are the criteria by which persons are judged, and appreciation of a woman or a man as a whole person will deeply modify the exploitation and the anguish of sexual inequality. Laws and formal regulations and the protection given by the courts are necessary to establish and maintain institutional arrangements. But the commitment and acceptance that are implied by taboos are critical in the formation and protection of the most meaningful human relations.

USING THE DICTIONARY: Margaret Mead is resourceful in her choice of words with the right impact. Where they are appropriate, she uses strong words of praise or condemnation. Look up the following words, paying attention to special uses and connotations. 1. How are the words *unscathed* (3) and *scathing* related? 2. Where does the word *taboo* (4) come from, and what are its usual connotations? 3. How does your dictionary convey the negative connotations or unfavorable associations of *demeaning* (3), *cajole* (6), and *coerce* (6)? 4. How is the word *mores* (11) related to *moral* and *morality?* 5. What are "stylized" relations between men and women? (Where or how is the word *stylize* (15) usually employed?) 6. What does *virtue* (15) mean in Mead's references to teachers and nurses? What are other major current and earlier meanings of the word? 7. What are the literal or original meanings of *discord* (18) and *dissonance* (18)?

8. Does your dictionary cover the figurative meanings of the italicized words in "legal *remedies*" (18) and "*climate* of opinion" (18)? 9. What does your dictionary tell you about the origin, meaning, and connotations of *equivocal* (19)? 10. What is the difference between *pain* and *anguish* (26)?

THE WRITER'S AGENDA:

In this selection, the writer's central purpose shapes the organization and general strategy of a whole essay. The author sets out to give her own view of a problem that asks for a solution. She first identifies the problem. She then looks at one possible solution that is not the whole answer. She then presents the other solution that is the heart of her message. Trace the way she presents and supports her strong personal point of view.

1. The author starts with a key question that is answered by her essay as a whole. The answer is *summed up* in a central **thesis** that is stated early and becomes a program or preview for the rest of the essay. Restate the key question in your own words. Show how it is echoed and expanded in the introductory paragraphs. Point out the thesis sentence and the introductory phrase that signals its appearance.

2. When sexual harassment was first widely discussed, some observers complained that the term was vague, covering various kinds of behavior previously considered harmless or ordinary. In her **introduction**, the author briefly but pointedly tells us what she means by her key term. Discuss her examples. (Which are most telling or convincing?) Sum up her definition and use of the term *sexual harassment.*

3. Much of the first half of this essay develops the distinction summed up in its thesis sentence. The author starts with the more *familiar* or predictable of the two possible solutions to the central problem. What is that solution? What, according to Mead, are the obstacles in its path?

4. The general strategy of the author is to move from the familiar to the *unfamiliar,* from the expected to the new and difficult. Where does she start discussing her own alternative to reliance on legal answers? Why does she think that for many young women the notion of new "taboos" may be difficult to accept? (How does her mentioning of the "incest taboo" become relevant to the main trend of the argument?)

5. In the central part of the essay, Mead discusses the *historical background* for the current period of "profound change" and "transition." What were important results of women's entry into the "working

world"? How does the author's observation of rules or taboos in primitive societies help her explain our own past? How does she use women who worked as nurses and teachers as examples? What happens to taboos in the modern world, and with what results?

6. In several paragraphs that start the final third of the essay, the author *restates and expands* her central point about the need for new taboos in our modern world. (Point out several **transitional expressions** that signal the author's return from the past to the present.) What does she add here to our understanding of what "taboos" are and how they work? How does she use the precedent of coeducational dormitories as an instructive example and guide to the future?

7. Study the author's **conclusion**. Show how the two concluding sentences serve as a strong restatement of the author's main point. The final two or three paragraphs spell out the author's basic goals in strongly *idealistic or inspirational* terms. Point out phrases that seem especially important or eloquent to you.

8. What in this essay is the **tone** and implied attitude *toward men?* Is it hostile or conciliatory, harsh or understanding? Provide evidence from the essay.

FOR DISCUSSION OR WRITING:

1. What parts of Mead's essay can you relate to your own observation or experience? Where have you observed the older patterns or traditional sex roles that she describes? Where have you seen evidence of the changes or transitional patterns she traces?

2. In presenting her point of view, Mead has to overcome the usually negative associations or unfavorable connotations of the word *taboo*. Has the author convinced you of the need for new modern taboos?

3. We often hear it said that everyone has a right to be recognized and appreciated "as a person." Can you show that this phrase is more than a cliché? What does it or what should it mean in practice?

4. Many people feel that private personal relations are people's own business and should not be the concern of employers or institutions. Do you agree? In your opinion, should there be important exceptions to this rule?

5. In working toward a better future, some people put their faith in better laws. Other people put their faith in changes in people's attitudes. To you, which of the two choices seems more promising or more important? Explain and support your choice.

6. How much progress has there been toward equality of the sexes? Choose one major area: school, work, or home. Sum up your answer as the thesis early in your paper. Provide detailed examples to support your thesis.

ɔ: A basic issue for the concerned citizen is how a civilized
ɔuld use punishment to control delinquency and crime. Liberals
l that, in the past, discipline in the home and in school was often
ι⌐ They tend to feel that penal laws at one time were barbaric, with
capital punishment and long prison terms dealt out freely by judges with
little humanity or compassion. Conservatives tend to feel that our modern
society has become too lenient and permissive, with much crime going
unpunished and with violence out of control. A. S. Neill (1883–1973), the
author of the following article, was not the kind of writer who would help
readers find a safe middle ground between these opposing views. Part of a
tradition of radical reformers, he devoted a lifetime to a well-known educational experiment, the Summerhill School in Suffolk, in the southeast of
England. As a teacher in his native Scotland, he had begun to feel that
traditional school discipline stifled true learning and moral growth. The
Summerhill School, which he founded and directed, tried to deal with "problem students" in ways totally different from traditional methods. Neill championed his ideas in many books, including *Summerhill: A Radical Approach
to Child Rearing* (1960) and *Freedom—Not License!* (1966).

A. S. Neill

Punishment Never
Cures Anything

GUIDE TO READING: The author of this article strongly presents an individual
point of view. As you read the essay, pay special attention to statements that
emphatically sum up the key idea (or key ideas) of the essay. Divide the
body of the essay into three major sections as the author applies his ideas
about discipline and punishment to three major areas. Watch for the major
examples and arguments he uses to clarify and support his point of view.

1 THE USUAL defense of punishment is that it is intended to act as
a deterrent. I think that the deterrent argument is simply a rationalization. The motive for punishment is revenge—not deterrence. In the
home, punishment is a projection of anger. Father, having been put on

the mat by his boss, may come home and leather his little son for having spilled a half-glass of milk.

Punishment is hate. A woman who hits her child does not love that child. In the case of children, physical punishment is always cowardly; it's hitting someone who cannot hit back. The headmaster will not cane the school janitor when he is obviously a bit drunk, but he will cane the schoolboy whose breath smells of cigarettes. The school bully never hits someone bigger than himself.

The most horrifying thing about corporal punishment is that the children who receive it carry on the tradition when they themselves become parents. This, combined with the total lack of instruction in child care in our schools, perpetuates the hatred that makes our sick world. The violence of thugs has its roots in the spanking nursery. Happy free people do not beat their children. To a child, punishment means *I am not loved.* The worst female criminal in the world is the mother who says: "Mommy doesn't love you anymore." Punishment induces fear, and as any psychologist will tell you, fear lingers on, long after its first beginning.

Can a home or school do without punishment? My wife and I never punished Zoe, now twenty-four. Summerhill has its own system of punishment made by the general self-government meeting, without suggestion or interferences from any grown-up. Not once in fifty years has a school meeting suggested corporal punishment; not once has such a meeting punished a child for stealing; the group of peers only demanded that the value of the stolen article be repaid.

School laws at Summerhill are made by majority vote; and some of the laws have punishment attached to them. For example, if you ride another kid's bike without his permission, you pay him sixpence in compensation. If you break the bedtime law by staying up late, you are fined your breakfast cereal. (You can, however, stoke up on as much bread, butter, and jam as you like.) The punishments are nearly always in terms of money; but when an American pupil who gets too many dollars from home breaks a rule, he may be ordered to pick up any loose papers strewn on the grounds. No child takes offense at the punishment he is given, mainly because the punishment is impartial and impersonal.

Punishment in the home is a more difficult problem because there is more emotion in a home than there is in a school. If Tommy is fined by the Summerhill meeting, he has no hidden resentment. But if he is disciplined by his father at home, the Oedipus complex comes into the picture. Tommy has to repress his hate of Father.

In a home that encourages a system of self-regulation, punishment does not present a problem. I told Zoe not to play with my typewriter, and she told me to leave her toys alone. You can only have a free atmosphere in the home when fear is absent. Alas, in all countries, there is fear in many a home. You cannot have self-regulation when there is a lack of freedom and love. Instead, you will have defiance.

8   You have to say no to a child again and again, and if the noes have no effect, there is some deep cause. The child may feel: *You don't love me; I'll make you take notice of me; I'll smash a window.* The thought is not conscious, so the window is broken "accidentally."

9   In the home, continuous and indiscriminate punishment by deprivation is criminal. "You bad boy, you won't have your ice cream tonight."

10   I confess that I do not know the answer to the problem of crime and punishment. All I know is that punishment never cured anything. Homer Lane, in his Little Commonwealth for delinquents, showed that the only cure is approval. No child who is beaten for breaking his father's possessions can possibly feel that his dad approves of him. The question isn't: *Why does a child need punishment?* It is: *Why does a parent want to punish?*

11   And let us not be humbugs about it. If a problem boy tripped me up when I was carrying a bowl of soup, my natural reaction would be to cuff him hard. But I cannot recall any instance in which I reacted with sudden anger and violence. This is not to imply that I am a saint, but rather that problem children haven't had the desire to trip me up.

12   I am convinced that punishment does not cure; it only inhibits and suppresses violent emotions. Most of us will acknowledge the horrible repressed hate aroused by punishment. The old colonel who proudly cries, "Dammit, sir, I was beaten as a boy, and I am all the better for it," is a man who has remained a child.

13   One difficulty about home discipline is the age factor. You can tell a child of five not to touch the electric stove, but you cannot tell that to a child of eighteen months. But proper handling of the infant should not be a slap on the bottom. Good parents will try to have a home in which dangerous gadgets are out of a child's reach. I am convinced that a child can be reared without punishment—if parents really understand what the motives of the child really are, and if the parents are balanced people with an understanding of what is valuable and what is meretricious. The mother who makes her possessions more valuable than her child will possibly spank her child for breaking a cup. Of course, when Father breaks a cup it's an accident. Father is just too big to spank.

14   I am often asked the question: How can a mother deal with three small kids without punishing them when they destroy the furniture?

15   The answer is it depends on the particular mother. I recall a fisherwoman in Scotland in my boyhood days, a woman ignorant of all academic psychology. Because she was a placid motherly type, she never seemed to have to yell at her children. I never saw her hit any one of them. The Law makes the Crime, went the old adage; apparently, the parent, for the most part, creates or avoids a punishment situation.

A hating parent has hating children. Even if the corollary is not [16] entirely true that a loving parent has loving children, the chances are that a placid parent makes a placid home. But loving parents can have an unloving child, a fact that psychology in its present state of knowledge cannot explain. For one thing, we do not know enough about heredity; even if we did, we might not be able to do much about such a situation.

Clearly punishment for children is wrong. But what about adults? [17]

England is nominally a Christian country, but it sends men to a hell [18] of prison life for thirty years for robbery. The Law gives "life" to a murderer who is often a poor, mentally sick man of diminished responsibility. The barbarity of our prisons harks back to the Middle Ages. Alas, in a sick society the penal code must also be sick. It is evil to deprive a man of freedom, of love, and of sex; it is just a primitive revenge, an eye for an eye, a tooth for a tooth.

True, there must be some sort of confinement for people who are [19] dangerous to society—compulsive murderers, rapists, pathological thieves. But a sane civilization would not render their confinement one of misery and hopelessness. Some enlightened countries allow prisoners to be with their wives at weekends.

One cannot think of punishment without considering the causes of [20] crime. Take the case of the English teen-agers who, after their favorite side loses a football match, wreck trains, throw bottles, and kick referees. Summerhill pupils would never think of doing that, nor would most upper- and middle-class youths. Born in a mean street, in a home without culture, with no books, no good conversation, no music except pop, born into a home with perhaps a stupid, drunken father and a screaming, ignorant mother, what chance has a lad of turning out to be socially minded and pro-life? His only outlet for his emotion is his street-corner gang and his guilty, maybe sadistic, sex with girls of the same background. He sees wealth and extravagance all around him. The parking attendant has gone home, and a Jaguar is unattended. Come on, dames, let's go for a ride.

Boys like this have never had a positive emotion. They hate society [21] and they hate themselves. Compelled to attend school until fifteen, they are made to learn things that have no meaning to them, things they drop the moment they leave school. Maybe they had to read Shakespeare, Hardy,[1] and Tennyson[2] in school; but how many books by these authors would one find in the homes of a football crowd of seventy thousand?

[1] [Thomas Hardy (1840–1928), English novelist and poet, author of *The Mayor of Casterbridge*]

[2] [Alfred Lord Tennyson (1809–92), whose poems—"The Charge of the Light Brigade," "Ulysses"—were long part of the standard fare in British schoolbooks]

22   People who are treated as underlings become sheep. A system can fashion a society. And it is the System that fashions our underprivileged classes of crooks and destroyers. I am convinced that crime keeps increasing because wealth and privilege keep increasing. God is dead, and so far no one has taken his place. Hence, perhaps, the flight into drugs to find a haven of happiness that cannot be found in this mad world of profit and pollution.

23   Punishment is accepted as the only way to deal with the have-nots of life. The law makes the crime. In the Trobriand Islands, where sex was accepted as natural and free for all ages, Malinowski[3] could not find any evidence of sex crime. And there was none until the missionaries came. It is possible to run a primitive society without a penal code; why not a cultured society?

24   Criminals are sick; they should be patients, not prisoners. But I fear that very little is done in the way of curing them. In Britain, the number of offenders rises frighteningly every year. The prisons are overcrowded. The crooks are organized by clever men. I should guess that most cases of bank robberies, car stealing, and wage snatching escape the cops. Criminals take the risk of a long stretch in jail, and the threat of punishment does not deter them. Antisocial drives, of course, have their unconscious components, and no punishment can reach the unconscious.

25   In class, Tommy wrote *I have went*. His teacher made him stay behind and write *I have gone* a hundred times. Next morning, the teacher found fifty lines written by Tommy. The note attached said: "Dere Teacher, I am tired so I have went home."

26   And that is the case, too, of the tough lout on his motorbike who is fined $50 for kicking a peaceful citizen at a seaside resort. The punishment doesn't sink in, for deep repressions are not touched by any punishment. They cannot be reached. No, punishment is *not* a deterrent.

27   Come on, folks; let us be honest. We punish because we hate, and because we fear. We punish strikers and students because we fear them. Not one of the bigwigs in Washington goes out with a club to bludgeon a striker personally. Crowds are bludgeoned and shot at by fellow citizens in uniform.

28   What can be done about punishment is to abolish the kind of rich and poor that makes crime. But that isn't practical politics. Nor is it practical politics to abolish the insanity we call schooling or to abolish the beating of children in homes. Given this fearful world of crime and nuclear bombs and nationalistic fear and hate, I am afraid we cannot do very much in the way of substituting something more humane for punishment.

---

[3][Bronislaw Malinowski (1884–1942), Polish-born British anthropologist]

But I can dream. I can dream of being Home Secretary for Great 29
Britain. I'd begin by ordering all prisoners to be examined by skilled
psychiatrists. They would eliminate those who would never be likely
to commit a crime again—the man who in a moment of jealousy or in a
state of intoxication killed his wife; the weak, erring clerk who
pinched money from the company till; the motorist who got drunk and
killed two people; in short, the accidental lawbreaker. Possibly 75 percent of all prisoners could be let out of jail free, without danger to the
community.

The old lags—the recidivists, the sex criminals, nearly all incur- 30
able—would be housed in country estates with as normal a life as possible. They would have self-government, which is, in effect, group analysis. This works well with patients who are mentally disturbed. I saw
this in action in Henderson Hospital, Epsom, Surrey, and it seemed to
be the best way to help patients live together with good interpersonal
relationships. In his Little Commonwealth, Homer Lane showed how
splendidly self-government worked with youthful offenders. Under
self-government, tough delinquent boys and girls became social, constructive people. Alas, it was a demonstration that got lost.

The British official policy with delinquents is still based on hate— 31
making them move at the double, granting hardly any leisure, demanding obedience (the worst of the seven deadly virtues), administering
punishment. In short, wayward adolescents are treated with the very
attitudes that made them delinquent to begin with. Delinquents are
always deprived of love, and only love can save them.

But how can there be love in an institution with strict laws that 32
foster fear of authority? Hence my open prison would be founded on—
I'd better not use the word love—it is becoming a dirty four-letter
word—*approval,* approval meaning to be on the side of the sick
offender.

Years ago I read an American book about a prison warden who had 33
appointed a murderer, a lifer, as head of the shoemaking department.
The warden sent him out to study the latest machinery in factories. The
prisoner returned with a full report.

Said the warden: "Why didn't you slip off when you were free?"   34

The convict scratched his head. "Dunno, warden, I guess it was 35
because you trusted me."

The chances are that if the warden had said: "I trust you to return," 36
the prisoner would have gone off, for by so saying the warden would
have revealed that he did not trust him. If all prison wardens had that
man's humanity and good sense, prisons would not be the hell they are
today.

In Britain, there are a few prisons without bars. One seldom reads 37
of an escape from such jails.

38   My prisons would be self-governing by prisoners and staff. The general meetings would be group-therapy sessions. There would be some difficulties because many criminals are of low intelligence and low emotional development, and have what British law defines as diminished responsibility. (The man in the street might call it being dumb.) In my school, I found out long ago that even slightly retarded children could not govern themselves and had to be guided gently. An open prison for adults who were retarded would have to use kindly authority instead of self-government.

39   One of the most evil features of imprisonment is that it deprives inmates of a normal sex life. My prisoners would have their wives or lovers living in or coming in for weekends. Constant sex frustration must make thousands of prisoners hate society more than ever. The sex deprivation is, to me, clear proof that punishment stresses revenge.

40   We seem to classify our children, together with our crooks, as dangerous animals that must be controlled by the whip. Many of the "animals" who have come to Summerhill in the last fifty years came full of destruction and hate; it is because of this experience that I know that my plans for a sane prison would succeed.

41   Prison statistics like the following have appeared in the English press about the Borstal Boys (juvenile delinquents):

42   By 1969, 68% of boys released in 1966 had been reconvicted. Almost half went back to Borstal, or on to prison. Over 60% of men released from preventive detention or corrective training in 1966 had been reconvicted last year. Again about half were sent back to prison.

43   This is proof enough that treating criminals by methods that to them mean hate is just sheer madness and ignorance. But there must be a way in which humaneness can be applied instead of suppression. We hear so little of experiments in approval and sympathy; and we hear so much of the savage men made more savage by the savagery of society; men whose savagery is made permanent by the savagery of what we call Justice, and by that powerful weapon of the haves against the have-nots—Law and Order.

 USING THE DICTIONARY: The professional vocabulary of educators, lawyers, and psychologists makes extensive use of words derived from Greek and Latin roots. Look up the following words from this essay. Pay special attention to how a Greek or Latin root helps explain the meaning of a word. 1. *deterrent* (1) 2. *rationalization* (1) 3. *projection* (1) 4. *repress* (6) 5. *indiscriminate* (9) 6. *placid* (15) 7. *corollary* (16) 8. *nominally* (18) 9. *compulsive* (19) 10. *pathological* (19) 11. *extravagance* (20) 12. *recidivist* (30)

THE WRITER'S AGENDA:

The author of this article forcefully presents an unconventional or unpopular point of view. Answer the following questions about how he presents and supports his central thesis.

1. The author of this article believes in speaking out, in taking a stand. Many of his statements directly confront and challenge the reader. The following is a sampling of brief, pointed statements that present and drive home the author's point of view. Which of these make you say, "I agree"; which make you say, "I disagree"? *Why* do you agree or disagree? Which of these statements best sums up the author's central idea, or **thesis**? (Defend your choice.)

a. "The motive for punishment is revenge, not deterrence."

b. "Punishment is hate."

c. "Most of us will acknowledge the horrible repressed hate aroused by punishment."

d. "A hating parent has hating children."

e. "The barbarity of our prisons harks back to the Middle Ages."

f. "Criminals are sick; they should be patients, not prisoners."

g. "Delinquents are always deprived of love, and only love can save them."

2. To support his central thesis, the author looks at punishment in three major institutions: the school, the home, and the prison. Look at his discussion of the first major area: *discipline in schools.* What are the alternatives to punishment that he describes?

3. The author says that punishment *in the home* is "a more difficult problem" than punishment in school. Why? Explain and discuss the special problems or complications that he deals with in his discussion of home discipline.

4. Look at the author's discussion of *adult crime* in the third and final major section of this essay. What, according to him, are the causes of crime? What are his objections to the traditional treatment of crimi-

nals? What are his proposals for more humane treatment? Which of his examples or arguments in this section are to you most striking or thought-provoking, and why?

5. The author of this essay writes as an outspoken critic of society. He turns the tables on our conventional self-righteous ideas about justice and about law and order. Point out several passages that present an especially emphatic or telling indictment of society. How do you react to them as a reader?

FOR DISCUSSION OR WRITING:

1. Radical reformers are often accused of being dreamers or Utopians who are out of touch with the real world. Does the author of this essay recognize harsh realities? Where and how? Does he sound like an unrealistic dreamer to you? Where and why?

2. A. S. Neill throughout stresses the need for approval, for recognition, and for affection if children and young adults are going to become "social, constructive people." Do you agree that recognizing this need is of crucial importance? Do you agree that it is neglected in much of our traditional educational system or in our ways of dealing with "problem" citizens? (Support your answers with detailed reasons or examples.)

3. During the last ten years, there has been much discussion of the need for prison reform. Find three magazine articles on this topic that have been published in recent years. Choose articles that represent different points of view. Prepare a report in which you explain the point of view of each author. Discuss major arguments and examples that each author uses to support an individual point of view. (Quote key phrases or brief key passages from each article.)

4. Has our society become too permissive? Has there been a breakdown of "law and order"? Prepare a paper in which you state and support your own point of view. Narrow your general topic: Concentrate on one major area, one major cause, or one major remedy. Make your own view the central thesis of your paper, and support it with detailed arguments and examples.

5. The three authors is this unit—Darst, Mead, and Neill—each have a different perspective on the role of law in human society. Discuss their different perspectives. What do they expect from the law? What is their view of its basic functions and its limitations? (Use key phrases and brief quotations from the three essays.)

FOR FURTHER DISCUSSION AND WRITING: Charles McCabe was a newspaper columnist who often wrote about his Irish heritage and who watched the passing scene with wry humor. How do you react to this column? Of the points of view expressed by the letter writers, which is closest to your own? To judge from your own experience and observation, how ready are frustrated citizens to "take the law into their own hands"? Are we witnessing a return to vigilantism? Do you think it is justified?

Charles McCabe
Muggers and Morals

IT WAS, Suzanne Geller wrote to the *New York Times* on July 1, 1981, "one of those clear, comfortable days when it feels like the most exciting city street in the world on which to walk. I was stunned by what is frequently called 'an incident'—a very sad incident."

She was crossing south on 51st Street and heard a lot of shouting. She turned and saw two men fighting in the middle of the crosswalk. She was watching a mugging in progress. Several pedestrians "came to the rescue of the victim of a robbery attempt and forced the perpetrator to the ground.

"My respect for the responsible citizens was short-lived, as the would-be robber was held down, he was kicked, punched, stomped, and beaten. I watched in horror and heard myself scream, 'Stop beating him, stop!' Against the noise of the traffic and the ever-increasing mob, this was no more than a whisper. The attack was brief, and when the wounded man was pulled to his feet, the observers clapped and cheered.

"The hatred and anger and violence of the well-groomed 'responsible' citizens was more frightening than the attempted robbery. To observe the display of uncontrolled animal-like behavior of the attaché-case carriers and the support of the crowd left me feeling sick and ashamed."

5   Why the *Times* ran this letter is beyond me. Its effect, if not its
intention, was inflammatory. To express more sympathy for a mugger
than the people who prevented what Geller admitted was an "attempted robbery" is surely something new, even in New York on the
corner of 51st and Fifth. Hysterical protests frequently reach New York
city desks, but their publication is rather more the business of the afternoon *Post*, which specializes in sensationalism.

6   A week later the *Times* published three letters protesting Geller's
peculiar views. One was from an eyewitness to the incident, Edgar
Tafel. "A man in sneakers was darting between cars from the north side
of the street to the south side.

7   "Yes, two men dropped their attaché cases and grabbed the 'perpetrator' who was holding a gold chain. He tried to free himself, called
his captors filthy names, tried to strike them. They responded with their
fists.

8   "Two traffic officers went over to help, soon joined by a police
officer. All the time the captured man tried to break loose. It was then
that I heard . . . a female voice: 'Don't hurt him! Don't hit him!' The
other onlookers applauded the two men, who had by then returned the
gold chain to the woman who had been attacked."

9   Tafel concluded: "I think Suzanne Geller should have withheld
her tongue and pen."

10   Another correspondent, David M. Kaplan, wrote: ". . . The overzeal-
ousness of the passersby in this incident, which Miss Geller found
alarming, is far preferable to the old stereotype of New Yorkers' unwill-
ingness to become involved in such incidents."

11   A third writer, Fred Jacobs, said, ". . . what is 'sad' about this incident? Far sadder it would have been if nobody had done anything.

12   "And what is wrong with giving a little roughing up (she herself
says the attack was 'brief') to a crook when he is caught red-handed?
It's the only semblance of justice he will ever face. For the bad know
that in New York, if they are punished with any severity—if they are
punished at all—they are the exception, not the rule.

13   ". . . In fact, I kind of hope to find myself soon in a 'well-groomed
mob' like the one Miss Geller saw. Should I witness the original incident, why, I'd like to get in a few kicks myself."

PATTERNS FOR WRITING

HOW DOES good writing take shape? The first task of a writer is to work up the material for a substantial piece of writing. The second task is to *organize* it. To explore the subject, to collect a rich fund of promising material, is only the necessary first step. How does the material add up? What general conclusions does it justify? In what order should they be presented to the reader? A crucial second stage in the process of writing a paper is to develop a workable overall plan. Every writer has to learn to do the kind of thinking that gives shape to miscellaneous materials. As you work on your papers, learn to sort out materials that may at first seem contradictory or confusing. Set up priorities. Decide what points to take up in what order.

Part Two of this book focuses on the patterns that will give your writing its structure, its shape. Effective writers know how to choose (or adapt) from among familiar patterns of organization the one that will do justice to the topic at hand. They know how to choose the pattern that will serve the writer's purpose. The selections in this second part of this book will give you a chance to learn from how experienced writers work out the pattern that is right for the task at hand.

The patterns that you are going to study and practice will at first be fairly simple or predictable. They will become more complicated, or call for more thinking about strategy, as you go along:

4 ♦ PROCESS

Every writer has to learn to follow a process or a sequence of events in time. A good writer knows how to mark off major stages in a chain of events and how to do justice to one major step at a time. A good writer knows how to do justice to the essential details that are needed to make a procedure work.

5 ♦ COMPARISON AND CONTRAST

A good writer knows how to make us understand something by comparing it to what is similar and contrasting it with what is different. A good writer knows how to guide our choices by working out an instructive point-by-point comparison. Effective comparison and contrast line things up in such a way that we can see important connections and become aware of important distinctions.

6 ♦ CLASSIFICATION

One of the most basic organizing skills required of a writer is the ability to sort out a mass of material into major categories. When we start sorting our miscellaneous material, what goes together and why? Sometimes ready-made categories are built into the subject or come with the territory: lower class–middle class–upper class; single–married–divorced. More often, we have to set up our own categories or modify existing ones so that they will serve our present purpose.

7 ♦ CAUSE AND EFFECT

In much argument, we are tracing relationships between cause and effect. We explain a present situation by tracing the causes that produced it. We argue the merits of a proposal by showing what its consequences would be if adopted. We project current trends into the future by showing the results that similar causes will produce if they continue to operate. In many situations that require a choice among alternatives, we use cause-and-effect reasoning to guide the reader.

8 ♦ DEFINITION

A good writer knows how to keep an argument from bogging down in a dispute over words. When we define an important term, we map out the territory it covers; we set it off from other related or opposite terms. We may have to clarify a confusing term by tracing its history. We may have to look at several case histories to find a common denominator. An extended definition of a key term can clarify the reader's thinking on an important issue; it can provide a rallying point or imply a program for action.

9 ♦ PERSUASION

The test of effective writing is its ability to convince the reader. Our power of persuasion is put to the test when we need to enlist the reader's support, when we aim to change the reader's mind. An experienced writer knows how to work out the right strategy: how to tackle obstacles, or how to lead up to what is difficult or controversial. A good writer knows how to appeal to shared values, how to mobilize latent good will.

U N I T 4

PROCESS:
The Illusion of Progress

The Common Theme: For much of our century, most people believed that the general course of civilization was in the direction of material progress. Science was teaching us how to make things work; modern technology was putting the findings of science to work in the service of humanity. Modern machinery was freeing workers of backbreaking labor on farms and in factories. Improved sanitation and advances like vaccination were stamping out diseases. Spectacular advances in transportation and communication were shrinking distances between regions and between nations. In recent years, however, many people have had second thoughts about our traditional faith in progress. Modern technology, they claim, has set in motion processes that are out of control. Our heedless pursuit of progress is rapidly exhausting "finite" resources, polluting the planet, and breaking up age-old patterns of living. The writers in this unit examine some of the processes that are changing our lives in the name of progress. The topics range from what progress does to where and how we live ("Land Rush") to what it does to how people work and what they eat ("The Ruination of the Tomato").

WRITER'S GUIDE 4:
Tracing a Process

A well-written paper has a plan that the reader can follow. The paper is organized—the writer has sorted things out and laid them out in a pattern. One thing follows another in an order that makes sense. Develop your own ability to organize your writing by practicing some of the basic patterns that writers use over and over as they structure their material and lay it out for the reader.

One of the most basic patterns of organization is the pattern we use when we trace a process. We use this pattern to explain how something works or how it came to be. We can use it to give directions or instructions; a "how-to" paper might show readers how to bake their own bread, or how to grow their own vegetables, or how to build an award-winning kite. Or we can use the process pattern to reconstruct a chain of events that brought about a result we want to explain. A process paper might explain how beavers build their dams and thereby change the ecology of an area until they finally move on and start a similar cycle elsewhere.

Much practical, scientific, and historical writing helps the reader understand a subject by showing how one thing leads to another in a series of steps. Remember the following guidelines when writing a paper that traces a process:

(1) *Explain the purpose or the benefits of the process.* Keep your reader aware of the *why* as well as the *how.* The following might be the introduction to a paper about how to bake bread:

A Perfect Loaf of Bread

One step toward becoming a more self-sufficient person in our consumer society is learning how to bake old-fashioned homemade bread. Bread provides carbohydrates, a basic necessity in our diet. However, much of the bread sold in stores is filled with preservatives so that it can stay on the shelves longer without spoiling. Much of it has an unnatural bleached appearance. It often has the consistency and the taste of a sponge. If we want to reduce the amount of dubious chemicals and additives in our diet, we can start by baking our own bread from natural ingredients.

(2) *Provide all necessary details.* Provide the necessary information about supplies, ingredients, and tools. The following instructions for building a concrete walkway pay careful attention to the *why,* the *what,* and the *how:*

FIRST STAGE: Before actually mixing the cement, we need to
(Why)   block off the area where the concrete is to be placed.
This is the first step because a framework is needed
to hold the concrete in place right after the ingredi-
(What)   ents are mixed. The wood used for this frame should
be rot-resistant, like redwood or cedar. We will need
two 2 × 4s four feet long and two 2 × 4s two feet
long. . . .

(How)   We check the area for the walkway to see that the
ground is hard and free of debris. Then we position
the wood in a rectangle with the pieces of equal
length running parallel to each other. We nail the
sides together, making sure their top surfaces are
flush with the grade planned for the concrete. . . .

SECOND STAGE: Mixing the cement, sand, gravel, and water is a
(Why)   slow but important process. If we were to mix a
faulty batch of concrete, our patio would crack, or
our walkway might break apart. To mix the ingredi-
(What)   ents, we need a pail marked off to show gallons and
quarts; two shovels, one for mixing dry materials, the
other for blending wet materials; and a large flat surface to use as a mixing board. . . .

(How)   First we put about two shovelfuls of sand on the
mixing board and add one shovelful of cement. We
mix these with the "dry" shovel until no brown or
gray streaks remain. . . .

(3) *Explain the technical workings of things.* Whenever you are
dealing with something difficult or unusual, make clear what needs to
be done to make the process work. Study the amount of detailed technical explanation that the following passage provides to make us understand how a snake can swallow its prey:

FIRST STAGE: Imagine you are watching a hungry rattlesnake
(stalking)   stalk its prey in the Georgia woods on a moonless
fall night. Using its sense of smell and its infrared
equipment for night sight, the snake has picked up a
young gopher on the way home to its gopher hole.
The gopher is preoccupied with a pine cone and not
alert to danger. The rattler inches along the ground
until its night sight and heat perception tell it that it
is within striking range. . . .

SECOND STAGE: The snake slowly, quietly coils. In a fraction of a
(attacking)   second, it strikes with its fangs unsheathed, injects
the poison, and withdraws. . . .

THIRD STAGE: To get the gopher, four times the circumference
(devouring)   of the rattler's head, into its mouth and down its gul-
let is a challenging feat, since the reptile has no
claws for leverage or dismemberment. When it has
caught a frog or large mammal, the snake will swallow its meal headfirst. *Its jaws open in back as well
as in front* (human beings can open only the front
part), giving it tremendous stretch. It is actually able
to *unhinge its jaws and extend them around the victim's head.* Then the snake shifts from side to side,
*pulling itself over the dead rodent the way a stocking
slides over a leg as we pull on it.* . . .

FOURTH STAGE: When the gopher is finally a settled lump in its
(digesting)   stomach, the snake finds a safe place to rest and digest its meal, vomiting up the bones and fur later. . . .

(4) *Divide the process into major stages.* People who are good at
explaining things naturally divide a procedure or a sequence of events
into major stages. This clear division into steps or parts helps us see
the broad outlines of the process as a whole. At each point during the
process, it makes us feel that we know where we are. In a passage like
the one about the snake, we can easily find our bearings if the writer
clearly marks off the major steps: (1)stalking, (2) attacking, (3) devouring, (4) digesting. What might have seemed a confusing sequence of "one thing after another" falls into a pattern that makes
sense.

When we give instructions or directions, dividing a process clearly
into major steps helps us build our readers' confidence: They can feel
that they will be able to master one thing at a time. The following
might be the major stages for the paper on baking bread:

   I. Mixing the dough

   II. Letting the dough rise

   III. Baking the bread

The following might be the major stages of a paper on how to grow
a vegetable garden:

   I. Preparing the soil

   II. Planting

   III. Tending the growing plants

   IV. Harvesting

Help your readers find their bearings by providing an *overview* or preview of the major stages at the beginning of your paper. If necessary, summarize, or recapitulate, the major stages again at the end. The writer describing the natural process summarized in the following passages made sure the reader would have the basic one-two-three sequence firmly in mind:

OVERVIEW: A small beetle, the mimosa girdler, undertakes *three pieces of linked, sequential behavior:* finding a mimosa tree and climbing up the trunk and out to the end of a branch; cutting a longitudinal slit and laying within it five or six eggs; and crawling back on the limb and girdling it neatly down into the cambium [the layer between the wood and the bark]. . . .

SAMPLE STEP: *The third step* is an eight-to-ten-hour task of hard labor, from which the beetle gains no food for itself—only the certainty that the branch will promptly die and fall to the ground in the next brisk wind, thus enabling the larvae to hatch and grow in an abundance of dead wood. . . .

RECAPIT-
ULATION: The beetle's brain is only a few strings of neurons connected in a modest network, capable therefore of only *three tiny thoughts, coming into consciousness one after the other:* find the right tree; get up there and lay eggs in a slit; back up and spend the day killing the branch so the eggs can hatch.

—Lewis Thomas, "Debating the Unknowable," *Atlantic*

(5) *Use clear transitions to mark major stages or phases.* A **transition** provides the link or bridge that helps the reader move from one point to the next. The transitional phrases in the following excerpt help the reader move forward *in time* as the author identifies major phases in a historical process:

THESIS: *Asians have long encountered discrimination and exploitation in this country.* Indeed, many who have arrived in America in the last 150 years probably wished that they had stayed home.

FIRST STAGE: *During the 19th century,* thousands of poor Chinese workers were imported to this country to provide cheap labor for construction of the Western railroads. Serfs in all but name, they left a synonym in our language for exploited, underpaid workers: coolie labor. . . .

SECOND STAGE: *In later years,* sizable numbers of Japanese and Koreans went to the West Coast, mostly to work as farm laborers, although some eventually prospered in business and other fields. In 1924, amid emotional outcries about a "yellow peril," Congress passed the Alien Quota Act, which all but excluded Asians by setting numerical quotas restricting immigration almost exclusively to Europeans. . . .

THIRD STAGE: *After Pearl Harbor pushed the United States into World War II,* sentiment against Orientals intensified once again, and thousands of Japanese who lived on the West Coast were interned in prison camps. . . .

FOURTH STAGE: *In 1965, as a kind of an ancillary effect of the civil-rights movement,* Congress repealed the 1924 law, and racial quotas were abolished. . . .

—Robert Lindsay, "The New Asian Immigrants," *New York Times Magazine*

(5) *Explain technical terms that are likely to be unfamiliar to the outsider.* Any writer providing instructions or explanations has to ask: "How much does my reader already know?" Most people know what a monkey wrench is, but a true amateur might have to be told that it is a wrench with one fixed and one movable jaw, and with a screw used to adjust the movable jaw to make the wrench fit different sizes. Most people will have a general idea of what a laser is, but a writer discussing its use in eye surgery will feel the need to provide an exact technical description: A laser is a device that focuses, narrows, and amplifies a beam of light to turn it into an extremely concentrated and intense ray that can be used as a powerful tool and with microscopic precision.

Remember that the writer explaining a process generally writes as the expert or insider explaining things to the newcomer or outsider. A writer explaining how early photographers worked will have to make sure that the uninitiated reader understands terms like *emulsion, autochrome, negative,* and *transparency*—terms that the reader who merely pushes the button on an instant camera is not likely to have encountered.

(6) *Use comparisons or analogies to help explain what is difficult or unfamiliar.* We can often explain something by showing how it is similar to something the reader already knows. We can clarify a difficult process by showing how it resembles a simpler, easier-to-follow procedure. When an extended comparison fits well enough to apply to several related features, we call it an **analogy**. Here is the analogy that a well-

known science writer used to explain his point that we are *selective* in taking in the world around us—that our minds take in only what we are *geared* to observe:

> It's partly by studying examples of animal awareness that we come to understand more about the way the human mind works. We realize that, like other animals, we go around creating whatever the reality is that we perceive, with our own instruments, all the time. A frog, for example, has one kind of reality, which is a dark speck against a lighted background. Of course, the real "thought" that the frog has is of a fly, and if that speck doesn't move, or if it doesn't move in a flylike fashion, it doesn't get recorded in the frog's brain. He sees only the thing that he is designed to see. We might be in somewhat the same situation: we may have some things that we're designed with receptors to see and other things for which we just don't have receptors—yet, anyway.
>
> —Lewis Thomas, "Turning Points," *Quest*

To sum up: Writing that traces a process answers the question "What does it take to make this work?" Writing tracing a process focuses the writer's attention on what is needed, on what is essential. It trains a writer to trace something step by step, following it through the necessary stages in the right order. Process writing has to be methodical, and it may at times seem unexciting. However, it often has the compensating advantage of being honest, educational, and useful. It is hard to fake, and when it is well done, it leaves its readers with the feeling that they have learned something that is interesting or good to know.

PREWRITING ACTIVITIES 4

1. For *sentence practice,* write half a dozen sentences that each trace an activity or a process in considerable detail. Start with simple physical actions or events, but go on to larger patterns. Use the following as possible models:

a. A dirty long-haired young man in a faded army fatigue jacket, weary from walking, reached through the barbed-wire fence to pet a mud-covered jersey milk cow grazing in a field alongside the country road.

b. On an early January day in 1968, a volcanic eruption pushed some steaming rocks above the surface waters of the South Pacific, adding a new island to the remote Tonga Archipelago.

c. We begin as children; we mature; we leave the parental nest; we give birth to children who, in turn, grow up, leave and begin the process all over again. (Alvin Toffler)

2. Many of the things we do are so familiar to us that we do them almost unthinkingly or automatically. We become consciously aware of what is involved when we have to demonstrate to a complete new-comer how to do things right in every detail, step by step. Write fool-proof *how-to instructions* for someone totally unfamiliar with an every-day activity like the following: changing an automobile tire; doing a large pile of dinner dishes; cooking a hamburger; painting one's own room.

3. Much of what we do in our bureaucratic modern society requires that we go through a series of necessary steps in the right order. As helpfully as you can, explain the *procedure* for one of the following: admission to college, registering for courses, getting married, getting divorced, buying or selling a house.

BACKGROUND: Peter Meyer (born 1950) is a political writer who published a book about President Carter. He wrote the following article for *Harper's,* one of the country's oldest magazines of opinion. Whereas newsmagazines devote most of their space to reporting and interpreting the week's news, magazines like *Harper's* or the *Atlantic* often publish articles that take the longer view. Many such articles are "investigative journalism" in the best sense: They are based, like this article, on the patient sifting of "hundreds of pages of reports, documents, studies, and statistics" as well as on first-hand personal observation, interviews, and private talks. Unlike fashionable exposé journalists, Peter Meyer in this article does not try to expose to public view the shady dealings or private shortcomings of individuals. Instead, he tries to make us understand some of the often impersonal forces that are at work to change or condition our lives. In this article, he takes a critical look at a process of which the bulldozer has become the symbol: the transformation of traditional rural neighborhoods into suburban developments in the name of progress.

Peter Meyer

Land Rush

GUIDE TO READING: The author of this article uses a **case history** to dramatize an important issue. He gives a faithful, detailed account of one representative case that can teach us much about processes at work in other similar situations. As you read the essay, look for the answers to the following questions: What is the central issue? How does the process work that, according to the author, is typical of what has happened in many communities across the country? What, according to the author, is the general significance or larger meaning of what he has described?

ABOUT TWO years ago I witnessed for the first time an American event that in the past decade has become so saturated with meaning as to assume the significance of ritual. It was an early weekday evening in Salem, Oregon, a small but growing city like many others around the country. Downtown, in a local government building emptied of employees except for a janitor waxing and polishing the marble floor, ten or fifteen people were standing outside a small conference room, talking casually about their families, their work, their animals, and the weather. Among the group were a carpenter, a lawyer, a housewife or two, a farmer, an interior designer, a reporter, a jeweler, an electrician and his wife, and a student—as varied a group as could be found milling about the front doors of church on a Sunday morning. Some were devout believers, others only Sunday practitioners. But their devotion was to the same idol: property. The event was a land planning commission meeting convened by the three elders of the board, which was to decide whether to approve a proposed housing development on ten acres of wooded land just south of the city.

2   It was a raucous two-hour meeting, and it seemed that most of the participant-landowners, whose title claims ranged from as little as a quarter-acre residential lot to as much as thirty acres of farmland, opposed the development planned in their backyards. Toward the end of the session a gentleman farmer, prominent in the town as a jeweler, stood to state his objections. After a few minutes of kindly debate—the commissioners arguing that the proposed subdivision land was located within the established "urban growth boundary" and would be subdivided eventually anyway, and that, in any case, the owner had a right to use his property the way he saw fit; the longtime resident saying that that was all right as long as he would be left alone—the official behind the table decided to end the discussion. "Mr. Jackson," he said in an effort to summarize, "I don't think your property is really at issue here. It's a case of apples and oranges, and our board has to concern itself with the proposal at hand. But thank you very much for your comments."

3   The group waited for Jackson to take his seat. The gray-haired man, who had lived most of his seventy years on his eight acres of land, remained standing, rocking to and fro, his hands on the folding chair in front of him. Finally, with most of the eyes in the room now turned in his direction, Jackson blurted, "Hell! I'm not talking about apples *or* oranges! I'm talking about *bananas!*"

4   Stone-faced, Jackson slowly sat. His unexpected reply had prompted a burst of supportive applause and laughter from his neighbors, but it was only a symbolic victory. Several minutes later the three commissioners voted to approve the development.

5   A few months after that, the city council, on the recommendation of the planning commission, agreed to annex the property to the city, thus guaranteeing that the subdivision would be provided with sewer, water, and electrical lines and police and fire protection. Then, because of a state law that forbade "islands" of non-city land within city limits,

most of the property of owners who had fought against the development was automatically annexed to the city. Next came a flock of other developers, now assured of city services, knocking on the doors of once-irate residents, offering as much as $8,000 for an acre of land that—only months before—was worth $1,000 at best. The tax assessors came, too: not only would tax rates be higher—to pay for the added services the city was obliged to provide all of its residents—but the assessed value of the property would have to be adjusted to reflect the change in market value. Almost overnight, property taxes jumped wildly. One by one the residents, many of whom had owned their ten or twenty or thirty acres of green and wooded hillsides for a generation or more, sold. Those who didn't soon began receiving notices from the city asking for permission to cross their land with sewer or water lines to the new developments. If permission was refused, the city began "condemnation" proceedings to acquire an easement on, or title to, the land it needed. Legal fees soon became another major cost of owning the land. Meanwhile, earthmoving machines were leveling hillsides, bulldozers were uprooting trees, huge dump trucks were unloading their tons of gravel, steamrollers were packing the new asphalt streets and four-lane thoroughfares were being laid over old country roads in anticipation of the traffic.

I happened recently to meet one of the landowners who had early 6 on decided to subdivide his sixteen acres of orchard land. The man, a retired carpenter and part-time farmer, was riding his ancient caterpillar tractor, scratching away at the land owned by one of his neighbors— a man who for years had resolutely refused to sell his property to developers or make concessions to the city. When the farmer stepped down from his machine to say hello, I asked him why he was bulldozing land that wasn't his.

He bristled a bit. "The city owns this land," he said, "and this is 7 where the street into my subdivision is going to be."

Coincidentally, I had just seen the deed to the land, and it showed 8 that his neighbor owned it. I asked what he meant.

"Well, hell," he muttered, "the city gets what it wants anyway; and 9 they've already given permission for the street—yesterday. If they don't own it now, they will later. So what's the difference?" With that, he turned around, climbed back on his tractor, and continued his leveling.

In almost every section of the country these days at least half the 10 citizens in any given town or agency seem to be embroiled in a passionate land dispute. Over the past year, while sorting through hundreds of pages of reports, documents, studies, and statistics purporting to describe these arguments, I came to understand that they had as much to do with vivid myths and dreams as with the so-called facts of the matter.

The metaphor of the land (whether as Eden, homestead, utopia, farm, refuge, or fortress) still exerts a commanding force on the American imagination.

11   This is true even though nobody knows very much about what is happening to the land or who owns it or how much of it remains open to what kind of use and settlement. Some observations, however, can be made with a certain degree of confidence. In the decade between 1965 and 1975 the value of land of all kinds and descriptions increased at an average rate of 150 percent. During the same period the population increased by 11 percent, the consumer price index by 80 percent, and the divorce rate by 100 percent. It is possible that people were paying such high prices for land only for speculative reasons, because it provided them with a defense against inflation.

12   But I suspect that the prices also reflected a collective and unconscious fear that American land might be slipping away from beneath people's feet and that its loss entailed the defeat of the great national dream. Everywhere the courts were besieged with suits from people trying to retain their holdings against what they perceived as heavy odds. Last year as much as one-fifth of the American estate was being contested in courtrooms, in legislatures, before town councils and government commissions. Huge corporations were buying more land (not that they didn't already own a great deal), and many individuals were finding themselves helpless to correct what they saw as the wanton destruction of the environment—mountainsides clearcut of timber, water courses polluted with industrial wastes, hillsides scraped bare of soil. People aligning themselves with both the commercial and the environmental interests beseeched the government at every level (municipal, state, federal) to intercede on their behalf and to help them bring about the proper management of the public lands that they regarded as part of their private inheritance.

13   The clamoring of people with different visions of the landscape has resulted in what one federal official described as a decade of "quiet revolution." Responding to the many and contradictory appeals for justice, the federal government gradually has assumed the role of gardener and caretaker, not only for the 761 million acres that it already owned but for almost all of the 2.2 billion acres of America's vast estate. To the extent that this revolution has become known to people, it has encouraged yet another fear—that government itself will usurp the individual's right to own property. There is an irony in this worthy of a literature not yet written. Seeking to assert the inalienable right to hold property, it is possible that people have given their rights away. The unhappiness of the small landowners in Oregon testifies to the not only lingering but still powerful belief in the American dream; it also testifies to the bleak and melancholy possibility that the circumstances of modern America may no longer warrant holding to such a belief.

USING THE DICTIONARY: A. Look up the following words and explain how each might be used in a typical situation: 1. *raucous* (2) 2. *embroiled* (10) 3. *purport* (10) 4. *myth* (10) 5. *metaphor* (10) 6. *entail* (12) 7. *beseech* (12) 8. *intercede* (12) 9. *usurp* (13) B. Look up the following **technical terms** of special interest to people who own land: 10. *annex* (5) 11. *assess* (5) 12. *condemnation* (5) 13. *easement* (5) 14. *title* (5) 15. *deed* (8) 16. *speculative* (11) 17. *holdings* (12) 18. *estate* (12) 19. *contested* (12)

THE WRITER'S AGENDA:

The author of this article knows how to *dramatize an issue.* He is the kind of writer who translates abstract issues into dramatic happenings. He translates lifeless statistics into things that people do or that happen to people. Answer the following questions:

1. In the introductory paragraph, what does the author do to make the *setting and the people* real for the reader? Point out several details that tell the reader: "I was there." (The author compares the people at the planning commission meeting to "churchgoers." How many words can you find that follow up this **analogy**?)

2. In the paragraphs that describe the meeting of the commission, the *central issue* comes into focus. What is the central issue or central dispute? (How is Jackson a symbolic figure in this section? How is what happens to him at the meeting symbolic of what happens in this essay as a whole?)

3. After his initial account of the meeting, the author vividly describes the **process** that turns the countryside into a suburb. He shows us several *major stages* in the process, stressing how one thing leads to another. Outline this process as it is described by the author. Identify five or six major stages. (What are some striking details that help make the process real for the reader?)

4. The author follows his description of the process with a brief account of how he met the man riding the tractor. The author uses this brief story the way effective writers often use an **anecdote**—a brief account of an incident that at the same time helps them make or reinforce a point. What is the point of this anecdote?

5. In the final four paragraphs, the author moves from the specific case history to its more general meaning. What is "the great national dream" that he claims is threatened or defeated by current developments? (What are the "myths and dreams" about land that he claims are as important as the "so-called facts of the matter"? How would the land

be an "Eden"? What pictures and feelings does the word *homestead* bring to mind? How would the land be a "utopia" or a "refuge"? In what sense is each of these a **metaphor?**)

6. What, according to the author, are the large-scale current developments that threaten to defeat "the great national dream"?

FOR DISCUSSION OR WRITING:

1. Where we stand on an issue like the one raised in this essay depends on where our sympathies lie. It depends on our preferences, loyalties, likes and dislikes. Looking back over the essay, sum up the standards, preferences, expectations, or loyalties of the author. What labels, if any, would you attach to the outlook he represents?

2. In reading this essay, do you feel that there is another side to this story that the author leaves untold? If you had to defend the decision of the planning commission, for instance, what would you say? Explain and defend your arguments.

3. Have you been able to observe the change of a city, a neighborhood, or an area—for better or for worse? Describe the process. Identify several major stages.

4. Do you know well, or do you have a chance to study at first hand, a kind of construction or building that is a complex task? Explain to your reader a task like the following:

   ◆ how to build a house

   ◆ how to build a road

   ◆ how to dam a river

   ◆ how to build a bridge

   ◆ how to construct a high-rise office building

Describe the process. Identify several major stages. Explain technical terms and details unknown to the outsider.

5. Many people today try to learn skills that would make them more self-sufficient than the typical member of the consumer society. Give detailed instructions on how to do something like the following:

   ◆ how to bake your own bread

   ◆ how to grow vegetables in your own garden

   ◆ how to make clothes from the raw materials

Choose a task that would require your readers to do justice to several important stages.

6. Many industries today are implementing processes needed (or mandated by law) for environmental protection. Study one of these and explain it to readers with little technical background.

BACKGROUND: Joan Didion was born in Sacramento, California, in 1934 and was a student at the University of California at Berkeley. She went East to work for magazines like *Vogue, Saturday Evening Post,* and *Esquire;* many of her best magazine articles were collected in *Slouching Towards Bethlehem* (1968) and *The White Album* (1979). Her essays and several novels (*Play It As It Lays, A Book of Common Prayer, Run River*) made her widely known as a witty, sharp-eyed chronicler of what is freakish, plastic, eccentric, or absurd in American life. (She once said that her first writing experiments as a five-year-old revealed "a certain predilection for the extreme" that has dogged her into adult life.) Her essays on subjects like the hippie scene of the sixties helped create the popular stereotype of California as a garish lotusland where uprooted people practice bizarre rituals. However, she has also written nostalgically of the semi-rural California of her youth, with its summer droughts and winter floods, where she early learned that "the apparent ease of California life is an illusion." She once said about writers, "we live entirely" by imposing "a narrative line" upon disjointed images, by making up the ideas that will "freeze the shifting phantasmagoria which is our actual experience."

Joan Didion

Bureaucrats

GUIDE TO READING: The author of the following essay is a sharp-eyed observer who is good at explaining how things work—and why they often don't. As she takes us behind the scenes of a traffic control center, what do we learn about its inner workings? At the same time, what, according to the author, is wrong with how the center operates? What warnings about the electronic future are implied in her account?

1   THE CLOSED door upstairs at 120 South Spring Street in downtown Los Angeles is marked OPERATIONS CENTER. In the windowless room beyond the closed door a reverential hush prevails. From six A.M. until seven P.M. in this windowless room men sit at consoles watching a huge board flash colored lights. "There's the heart attack," someone will murmur, or "We're getting the gawk effect." 120 South Spring is the Los Angeles office of Caltrans, or the California Department of

Transportation, and the Operations Center is where Caltrans engineers monitor what they call "the 42-Mile Loop." The 42-Mile Loop is simply the rough triangle formed by the intersections of the Santa Monica, the San Diego and the Harbor freeways, and 42 miles represents less than ten percent of freeway mileage in Los Angeles County alone, but these particular 42 miles are regarded around 120 South Spring with a special veneration. The Loop is a "demonstration system," a phrase much favored by everyone at Caltrans, and is part of a "pilot project," another two words carrying totemic weight on South Spring.

The Loop has electronic sensors embedded every half-mile out 2 there in the pavement itself, each sensor counting the crossing cars every twenty seconds. The Loop has its own mind, a Xerox Sigma V computer which prints out, all day and night, twenty-second readings on what is and is not moving in each of the Loop's eight lanes. It is the Xerox Sigma V that makes the big board flash red when traffic out there drops below fifteen miles an hour. It is the Xerox Sigma V that tells the Operations crew when they have an "incident" out there. An "incident" is the heart attack on the San Diego, the jackknifed truck on the Harbor, the Camaro just now tearing out the Cyclone fence on the Santa Monica. "Out there" is where incidents happen. The windowless room at 120 South Spring is where incidents get "verified." "Incident verification" is turning on the closed-circuit TV on the console and watching the traffic slow down to see (this is "the gawk effect") where the Camaro tore out the fence.

As a matter of fact there is a certain closed-circuit aspect to the 3 entire mood of the Operations Center. "Verifying" the incident does not after all "prevent" the incident, which lends the enterprise a kind of tranced distance, and on the day recently when I visited 120 South Spring it took considerable effort to remember what I had come to talk about, which was that particular part of the Loop called the Santa Monica Freeway. The Santa Monica Freeway is 16.2 miles long, runs from the Pacific Ocean to downtown Los Angeles through what is referred to at Caltrans as "the East-West Corridor," carries more traffic every day than any other freeway in California, has what connoisseurs of freeways concede to be the most beautiful access ramps in the world, and appeared to have been transformed by Caltrans, during the several weeks before I went downtown to talk about it, into a 16.2-mile parking lot.

The problem seemed to be another Caltrans "demonstration," or 4 "pilot," a foray into bureaucratic terrorism they were calling "The Diamond Lane" in their promotional literature and "The Project" among themselves. That the promotional literature consisted largely of schedules for buses (or "Diamond Lane Expresses") and invitations to join a car pool via computer ("Commuter Computer") made clear not only the putative point of The Project, which was to encourage travel by car pool and bus, but also the actual point, which was to eradicate a central

Southern California illusion, that of individual mobility, without anyone really noticing. This had not exactly worked out. "FREEWAY FIASCO," the *Los Angeles Times* was headlining page-one stories. "THE DIAMOND LANE: ANOTHER BUST BY CALTRANS." "CALTRANS PILOT EFFORT ANOTHER IN LONG LIST OF FAILURES." "OFFICIAL DIAMOND LANE STANCE: LET THEM HOWL."

5   All "The Diamond Lane" theoretically involved was reserving the fast inside lanes on the Santa Monica for vehicles carrying three or more people, but in practice this meant that 25 percent of the freeway was reserved for 3 percent of the cars, and there were other odd wrinkles here and there suggesting that Caltrans had dedicated itself to making all movement around Los Angeles as arduous as possible. There was for example the matter of surface streets. A "surface street" is anything around Los Angeles that is not a freeway ("going surface" from one part of town to another is generally regarded as idiosyncratic), and surface streets do not fall directly within the Caltrans domain, but now the engineer in charge of surface streets was accusing Caltrans of threatening and intimidating him. It appeared that Caltrans wanted him to create a "confused and congested situation" on his surface streets, so as to force drivers back to the freeway, where they would meet a still more confused and congested situation and decide to stay home, or take a bus. "We are beginning a process of deliberately making it harder for drivers to use freeways," a Caltrans director had in fact said at a transit conference some months before. "We are prepared to endure considerable public outcry in order to pry John Q. Public out of his car. . . . I would emphasize that this is a political decision, and one that can be reversed if the public gets sufficiently enraged to throw us rascals out."

6   Of course this political decision was in the name of the greater good, was in the interests of "environmental improvement" and "conservation of resources," but even there the figures had about them a certain Caltrans opacity. The Santa Monica normally carried 240,000 cars and trucks every day. These 240,000 cars and trucks normally carried 260,000 people. What Caltrans described as its ultimate goal on the Santa Monica was to carry the same 260,000 people, "but in 7,800 fewer, or 232,200 vehicles." The figure "232,200" had a visionary precision to it that did not automatically create confidence, especially since the only effect so far had been to disrupt traffic throughout the Los Angeles basin, triple the number of daily accidents on the Santa Monica, prompt the initiation of two lawsuits against Caltrans, and cause large numbers of Los Angeles County residents to behave, most uncharacteristically, as an ignited and conscious proletariat. Citizen guerrillas splashed paint and scattered nails in the Diamond Lanes. Diamond Lane maintenance crews expressed fear of hurled objects. Down at 120 South Spring the

architects of the Diamond Lane had taken to regarding "the media" as the architects of their embarrassment, and Caltrans statements in the press had been cryptic and contradictory, reminiscent only of old communiqués out of Vietnam.

To understand what was going on it is perhaps necessary to have   7 participated in the freeway experience, which is the only secular communion Los Angeles has. Mere driving on the freeway is in no way the same as participating in it. Anyone can "drive" on the freeway, and many people with no vocation for it do, hesitating here and resisting there, losing the rhythm of the lane change, thinking about where they came from and where they are going. Actual participants think only about where they are. Actual participation requires a total surrender, a concentration so intense as to seem a kind of narcosis, a rapture-of-the-freeway. The mind goes clean. The rhythm takes over. A distortion of time occurs, the same distortion that characterizes the instant before an accident. It takes only a few seconds to get off the Santa Monica Freeway at National-Overland, which is a difficult exit requiring the driver to cross two new lanes of traffic streamed in from the San Diego Freeway, but those few seconds always seem to me the longest part of the trip. The moment is dangerous. The exhilaration is in doing it. "As you acquire the special skills involved," Reyner Banham observed in an extraordinary chapter about the freeways in his 1971 *Los Angeles: The Architecture of Four Ecologies,* "the freeways become a special way of being alive . . . the extreme concentration required in Los Angeles seems to bring on a state of heightened awareness that some locals find mystical."

Indeed some locals do, and some nonlocals too. Reducing the   8 number of lone souls careering around the East-West Corridor in a state of mechanized rapture may or may not have seemed socially desirable, but what it was definitely not going to seem was easy. "We're only seeing an initial period of unfamiliarity," I was assured the day I visited Caltrans. I was talking to a woman named Eleanor Wood and she was thoroughly and professionally grounded in the diction of "planning" and it did not seem likely that I could interest her in considering the freeway as regional mystery. "Any time you try to rearrange people's daily habits, they're apt to react impetuously. All this project requires is a certain rearrangement of people's daily planning. That's really all we want."

It occurred to me that a certain rearrangement of people's daily   9 planning might seem, in less rarefied air than is breathed at 120 South Spring, rather a great deal to want, but so impenetrable was the sense of higher social purpose there in the Operations Center that I did not express this reservation. Instead I changed the subject, mentioned an earlier "pilot project" on the Santa Monica: the big electronic message boards that Caltrans had installed a year or two before. The idea was that traffic information transmitted from the Santa Monica to the Xerox Sigma V could be translated, here in the Operations Center, into suggestions to the driver, and flashed right back out to the Santa Monica. This operation, in that it involved telling drivers electronically what they already knew empirically, had the rather spectral circularity that seemed to mark a great many Caltrans schemes, and I was interested in how Caltrans thought it worked.

10   "Actually the message boards were part of a larger pilot project," Mrs. Wood said. "An ongoing project in incident management. With the message boards we hoped to learn if motorists would modify their behavior according to what we told them on the boards."

11   I asked if the motorists had.

12   "Actually no," Mrs. Wood said finally. "They didn't react to the signs exactly as we'd hypothesized they would, no. *But*. If we'd *known* what the motorist would do . . . then we wouldn't have needed a pilot project in the first place, would we."

13   The circle seemed intact. Mrs. Wood and I smiled, and shook hands. I watched the big board until all lights turned green on the Santa Monica and then I left and drove home on it, all 16.2 miles of it. All the way I remembered that I was watched by the Xerox Sigma V. All the way the message boards gave me the number to call for CAR POOL INFO. As I left the freeway it occurred to me that they might have their own rapture down at 120 South Spring, and it could be called Perpetuating the Department. Today the California Highway Patrol reported that, during the first six weeks of the Diamond Lane, accidents on the Santa Monica, which normally range between 49 and 72 during a six-week period, totaled 204. Yesterday plans were announced to extend the Diamond Lane to other freeways at a cost of $42,500,000.

 USING THE DICTIONARY: To set the humorous **tone** of her essay, the author often uses solemn, impressive words for prosaic, everyday matters. She describes the prosaic matter of traffic control in terms that we might use in describing a religious experience, a battleground, or a problem in philosophy. What is the meaning of each of the following examples, and what is its usual frame of reference? 1. *reverential* (1) 2. *veneration* (1) 3. *totemic* (1) 4. *connoisseur* (3) 5. *foray* (4) 6. *putative* (4) 7. *fiasco* (4) 8. *idiosyncratic* (5) 9. *opacity* (6) 10. *proletariat* (6) 11. *secular* (7) 12. *narcosis* (7) 13. *empirically* (9) 14. *spectral* (9) 15. *hypothesize* (12)

THE WRITER'S AGENDA:

In this essay, the author reports on the operations of an agency in order to make us think about the electronic, bureaucratically controlled future that may lie ahead. How does she inform us? How does she make us think?

1. The first three paragraphs of this essay tell us about the nature and the task of the Caltrans Center. What do we learn about its task and about how it operates? Summarize the *factual information* that the author gives us in her introductory paragraphs.

2. In these same introductory paragraphs, the author creates the characteristic *atmosphere* or mood of the center, and she strongly suggests her personal attitude toward it. What is that atmosphere, and what is her attitude? What are key phrases or especially revealing details?

3. The central section and centerpiece of this essay is the author's account of the Diamond Lane *pilot project.* What was the aim? What was the procedure? What was the result?

4. From the beginning, the author shows her strongly *negative* attitude toward the experiment. Where and how? What are the deeper reasons for her negative attitude? What is the basis of her objections?

5. Throughout the essay but especially toward the end, Didion quotes people working at the center or reproduces the *terminology* used there. She often seems to use the statements or characteristic phrases of the people as evidence against them. Where and how?

6. Toward the end, the author mentions an earlier pilot project. How does she use it as a *parallel* or precedent?

7. The concluding paragraph illustrates well Didion's ability to let her observations and revealing details "speak for themselves." How does this conclusion *reinforce* the basic attitudes prevailing in her essay? How does it leave the reader with a fitting sense of satisfactory completion?

FOR DISCUSSION OR WRITING:

1. Joan Didion is a master of **irony**. She knows how to produce the wry disillusioned smile that is our reaction to the contrast between good intentions and unfortunate unintended results, or between what we expect of people and what they actually do. How pervasive is this irony in her essay? To what extent does it influence what she notices and how she describes it?

2. Didion entitles her essay "Bureaucrats" without using the word *bureaucrat* in the essay itself. What are familiar popular notions or stereotypes of bureaucrats and bureaucracy? How do they compare with the view of bureaucracy implied in this essay? Is there something to be said *in defense* of the bureaucrats she attacks?

3. Do you think that what the author describes in this essay is symbolic or prophetic of what awaits us in the future?

4. Critics of innovation for its own sake often complain that much over-elaborate or unnecessary technology is used without regard for what it does to people's lives. To judge from your own observation and experience, how true is this charge?

5. Detailed and convincing description of a workable process is often required when we present a suggested solution to a problem. Write a paper in which you first show that a current procedure is *not* working. Then present a better way of doing the same thing. Possible subjects are traffic control, teaching a foreign language, electing a President, rehabilitating convicted criminals, providing low-income housing, or curing addiction.

BACKGROUND: Mark Kramer (born in 1944 in New York City) was a student at Brandeis University and Columbia University. He became a farmer in western Massachusetts who wrote (and helped make a film) about living in the country and the "high human costs" of the changes in American agriculture. He says, "I write about people whose lives are tangled up with changing technology and new business structures." In the following article, published in the *Atlantic* in January 1980, he writes the history of the modern tomato— its change from a juicy and tasty item of locally grown produce to a tasteless, rubbery product that is grown, processed, and marketed on a large scale according to modern techniques. The tomato in this article becomes a symbol of what "progress" has meant for the people who produce and market food: "High-technology" and modern business practices combine in a highly complicated system that outsiders can no longer understand. Kramer is a critical observer who makes it his business to find out how things work. He provides the kind of **analysis** that we need to understand a complex subject. He knows how to take things apart into their components; he shows the workings of each part; and he shows how different processes combine or interact to feed into a common end result.

Mark Kramer

The Ruination of the Tomato

GUIDE TO READING: The author's aim in this article is to help us understand complicated processes by a patient tracing of how things work. Pay special attention to the way he analyzes several related processes: the harvesting of tomatoes in mechanized modern agriculture; the development of the new "improved" tomato wanted by modern growers; and the larger workings of the economic system of which the tomato business is a part.

SAGEBRUSH AND lizards rattle and whisper behind me. I stand in the moonlight, the hot desert at my back. It's tomato harvest time, 3 A.M. The moon is almost full and near to setting. Before me stretches the first lush tomato field to be taken this morning. The field is farmed by a company called Tejon Agricultural Partners, and lies three hours northeast of Los Angeles in the middle of the bleak, silvery drylands of California's San Joaquin Valley. Seven hundred sixty-six acres, more than a mile square of tomatoes—a shaggy, vegetable-green rug dappled with murky red dots, 105,708,000 ripe tomatoes lurking in the night. The field is large and absolutely level. It would take an hour and a half to walk around it. Yet, when I raise my eyes past the field to the much vaster valley floor, and to the mountains that loom farther out, the enormous crop is lost in a big flat world.

2   This harvest happens nearly without people. A hundred million tomatoes grown, irrigated, fed, sprayed, now taken, soon to be cooled, squashed, boiled, barreled, and held at the ready, then canned, shipped, sold, bought, and after being sold and bought a few more times, uncanned and dumped on pizza. And such is the magnitude of the vista, and the dearth of human presence, that it is easy to look elsewhere and put this routine thing out of mind. But that quality—of blandness overlaying a wondrous integration of technology, finances, personnel, and business systems—seems to be what the "future" has in store.

3   Three large tractors steam up the road toward me, headlights glaring, towing three thin-latticed towers which support floodlights. The tractors drag the towers into place around an assembly field, then hydraulic arms raise them to vertical. They illuminate a large, sandy work yard where equipment is gathering—fuel trucks, repair trucks, concession trucks, harvesters, tractor-trailers towing big open hoppers. Now small crews of Mexicans, their sunburns tinted light blue in the glare of the three searchlights, climb aboard the harvesters; shadowy drivers mount tractors and trucks. The night fills with the scent of diesel fumes and with the sound of large engines running evenly.

4   The six harvesting machines drift across the gray-green tomato-leaf sea. After a time, the distant ones come to look like steamboats afloat across a wide bay. The engine sounds are dispersed. A company foreman dashes past, tally sheets in hand. He stops nearby only long enough to deliver a one-liner. "We're knocking them out like Johnny-be-good," he says, punching the air slowly with his right fist. Then he runs off, laughing.

5   The nearest harvester draws steadily closer, moving in at about the speed of a slow amble, roaring as it comes. Up close, it looks like the aftermath of a collision between a grandstand and a San Francisco tram car. It's two stories high, rolls on wheels that don't seem large enough, astraddle a wide row of jumbled and unstaked tomato vines. It is not streamlined. Gangways, catwalks, gates, conveyors, roofs, and ladders are fastened all over the lumbering rig. As it closes in, its front end snuffles up whole tomato plants as surely as a hungry pig loose in a farmer's garden. Its hind end excretes a steady stream of stems and rejects. Between the ingestion and the elimination, fourteen laborers

face each other on long benches. They sit on either side of a conveyor that moves the new harvest rapidly past them. Their hands dart out and back as they sort through the red stream in front of them.

Watching them is like peering into the dining car of a passing train. 6 The folks aboard, though, are not dining but working hard for low wages, culling what is not quite fit for pizza sauce—the "greens," "molds," "mechanicals," and the odd tomato-sized clod of dirt which has gotten past the shakers and screens that tug tomato from vine and dump the harvest onto the conveyor.

The absorbing nature of the work is according to plan. The workers 7 aboard this tiny outpost of a tomato sauce factory are attempting to accomplish a chore at which they cannot possibly succeed, one designed in the near past by some anonymous practitioner of the new craft of *management*. As per cannery contract, each truckload of tomatoes must contain no more than 4 percent green tomatoes, 3 percent tomatoes suffering mechanical damage from the harvester, 1 percent tomatoes that have begun to mold, and .5 percent clods of dirt.

"The whole idea of this thing," a farm executive had explained 8 earlier in the day, "is to get as many tons as you can per hour. Now, the people culling on the machines strive to sort everything that's defective. But to us, that's as bad as them picking out too little. We're getting $40 to $47 a ton for tomatoes—a bad price this year—and each truckload is 50,000 pounds, 25 tons, 1100 bucks a load. If we're allowed 7 or 8 percent defective tomatoes in the load and we don't have 7 or 8 percent defective tomatoes in the load, we're giving away money. And what's worse, we're paying these guys to make the load too good. It's a double loss. Still, you can't say to your guys, 'Hey, leave 4 percent greens and 1 percent molds when you sort the tomatoes on that belt.' It's impossible. On most jobs you strive for perfection. They do. But you want to stop them just the right amount short of perfection—because the cannery will penalize you if your load goes over spec. So what you do is run the belt too fast, and sample the percentages in the output from each machine. If the load is too poor, we add another worker. If it's too good, we send someone home."

The workers converse as they ride the machine toward the edge of 9 the desert. Their lips move in an exaggerated manner, but they don't shout. The few workers still needed at harvest time have learned not to fight the machine. They speak under, rather than over, the din of the harvest. They chat, and their hands stay constantly in fast motion. . . . Just a few years ago, when harvesting of cannery tomatoes was still done by hand, ten times the labor was required on the same acreage to handle a harvest that yielded only a third of what growers expect these days. The transformation of the tomato industry has happened in the course of about twenty years.

Much has been written recently about this phenomenon, and with 10 good reason. The change has been dramatic, and is extreme. Tomatoes we remember from the past tasted rich, delicate, and juicy. Tomatoes hauled home in today's grocery bag taste bland, tough, and dry. The new taste is the taste of modern agriculture.

11   The ruination of the tomato was a complex procedure. It required cooperation from financial, engineering, marketing, scientific, and agricultural parties that used to go their separate ways more and cross paths with less intention. Now larger institutions control the money that consumers spend on tomatoes. It is no more possible to isolate a "cause" for this shift than it is possible to claim that it's the spark plugs that cause a car to run. However, we can at least peer at the intricate machinery that has taken away our tasty tomatoes and given us pale, scientific fruit.

12   Let us start then, somewhat arbitrarily, with processors of tomatoes, especially with the four canners—Del Monte, Heinz, Campbell, and Libby, McNeill & Libby—that sell 72 percent of the nation's tomato sauce. What has happened to the quality of tomatoes in general follows from developments in the cannery tomato trade.

13   The increasingly integrated processors have consolidated, shifted, and "reconceptualized" their plants. In the fast world of marketing processed tomatoes, the last thing executives want is to be caught with too many cans of pizza sauce, fancy grade, when the marketplace is starved for commercial catsup. What processors do nowadays is capture the tomatoes and process them until they are clean and dead, but still near enough to the head of the assembly line so they have not yet gone past the squeezer that issues tomato juice or the sluice gate leading to the spaghetti sauce vat, the paste vat, the aspic tank, or the cauldrons of anything in particular. The mashed stuff of tomato products is stored until demand is clear. Then it's processed the rest of the way. The new manufacturing concept is known in the trade as aseptic barreling, and it leads to success by means of procrastination.

14   The growers supplying the raw materials for these tightly controlled processors have contracted in advance of planting season for the sale of their crops. It's the only way to get in. At the same time, perhaps stimulated by this new guaranteed marketplace—or perhaps stimulating it—these surviving growers of tomatoes have greatly expanded the size of their planting. The interaction of large growers and large processors has thus crowded many smaller growers out of the marketplace, not because they can't grow tomatoes as cheaply as the big growers (they can) but because they can't provide large enough units of production to attract favorable contracts with any of the few canners in their area.

15   In turn, the increasing size of tomato-growing operations has encouraged and been encouraged by a number of developments in technology. Harvesters (which may have been the "cause" precipitating the

other changes in the system) have in large part replaced persons in the fields. But the new machines became practical only after the development of other technological components—especially new varieties of tomato bred for machine harvesting, and new chemicals that make machine harvesting economical.

What is remarkable about the tomato from the grower's point of 16 view is its rapid increase in popularity. In 1920, each American ate 18.1 pounds of tomato. These days we each eat 50.5 pounds of tomato. Half a million acres of cropland grow tomatoes, yielding nearly 9 million tons, worth over $900 million on the market. Today's California tomato acre yields 24 tons, while the same acre in 1960 yielded 17 tons and in 1940, 8 tons.

The increased consumption of tomatoes reflects changing eating 17 habits in general. Most food we eat nowadays is prepared, at least in part, somewhere other than in the home kitchen, and most of the increased demand for tomatoes is for processed products—catsup, sauce, juice, canned tomatoes, and paste for "homemade" sauce. In the 1920s, tomatoes were grown and canned commercially from coast to coast. Small canneries persisted into the 1950s.

Tomatoes were then a labor-intensive crop, requiring planting, 18 transplanting, staking, pruning. And, important in the tale of changing tomato technology, because tomatoes used to ripen a few at a time, each field required three or four forays by harvesting crews to recover successively ripening fruits. The forces that have changed the very nature of tomato-related genetics, farming practices, labor requirements, business configurations, and buying patterns started with the necessity, built so deeply into the structure of our economic system, for the constant perfection of capital utilization.

Some critics sometimes seem to imply that the new mechanization 19 is a conspiracy fostered by fat cats up top to make their own lives softer. But though there are, surely, greedy conspirators mixed in with the regular folks running tomato farms and tomato factories and tomato research facilities, the impulse for change at each stage of the tomato transformation—from the points of view of those effecting the change—is "the system." The system always pressures participants to *meet the competition.*

Even in the 1920s, more tomatoes were grown commercially for 20 processing than for fresh consumption, by a ratio of about two to one. Today the ratio has increased to about seven to one. Fifty years ago, California accounted for about an eighth of all tomatoes grown in America. Today, California grows about 85 percent of tomatoes. Yet as recently as fifteen years ago, California grew only about half the tomato crop. And fifteen years ago, the mechanical harvester first began to show up in the fields of the larger farms.

Before the harvester came, the average California planting was 21 about 45 acres. Today, plantings exceed 350 acres. Tomato production in California used to be centered in family farms around Merced. It has now shifted to the corporate farms of Kern County, where Tejon Agricultural Partners operates. Of the state's 4000 or so growers harvesting canning tomatoes in the late sixties, 85 percent have left the business since the mechanical harvester came around. Estimates of the number of part-time picking jobs lost go as high as 35,000.

22   The introduction of the harvester brought about other changes too. Processors thought that tomatoes ought to have more solid material, ought to be less acid, ought to be smaller. Engineers called for tomatoes that had tougher skins and were oblong so they wouldn't roll back down tilted conveyor belts. Larger growers, more able to substitute capital for labor, wanted more tonnage per acre, resistance to cracking from sudden growth spurts that follow irrigation, leaf shade for the fruit to prevent scalding by the hot sun, determinate plant varieties that grow only so high to keep those vines in rows, out of the flood irrigation ditches.

23   As geneticists selectively bred for these characteristics, they lost control of others. They bred for thickwalledness, less acidity, more uniform ripening, oblongness, leafiness, and high yield—and they could not also select for flavor. And while the geneticists worked on tomato characteristics, chemists were perfecting an aid of their own. Called ethylene, it is in fact also manufactured by tomato plants themselves. All in good time, it promotes reddening. Sprayed on a field of tomatoes that has reached a certain stage of maturity (about 15 percent of the field's tomatoes must have started to "jell"), the substance causes the plants to start the enzyme activity that induces redness. About half of the time a tomato spends between blossom and ripeness is spent at full size, merely growing red. (Tomatoes in the various stages of this ripening are called, in the trade, immature greens, mature greens, breakers, turnings, pinks, light reds, and reds.) Ethylene cuts this reddening time by a week or more and clears the field for its next use. It recovers investment sooner. Still more important, it complements the genetic work, producing plants with a determined and common ripening time so machines can harvest in a single pass. It guarantees precision for the growers. The large-scale manufacturing system that buys the partnership's tomatoes requires predictable results. On schedule, eight or ten or fourteen days after planes spray, the crop will be red and ready. The gas complements the work of the engineers, too, loosening the heretofore stubborn attachment of fruit and stem. It makes it easier for the new machines to shake the tomatoes free of the vines.

24   The result of this integrated system of tomato seed and tomato chemicals and tomato hardware and tomato know-how has been, of course, the reformation of tomato business.

According to a publication of the California Agrarian Action Project, a reform-oriented research group located at Davis (some of whose findings are reflected in this article), the effects of an emerging "low-grade oligopoly" in tomato processing are discoverable. Because of labor savings and increased efficiency of machine harvesting, the retail price of canned tomatoes should have dropped in the five years after the machines came into the field. Instead, it climbed 111 percent, and it did so in a period that saw the overall price of processed fruits and vegetables climb only 76 percent. 25

There are "social costs" to the reorganization of the tomato processing industry as well. The concentration of plants concentrates work opportunities formerly not only more plentiful but more dispersed in rural areas. It concentrates problems of herbicide, pesticide, and salinity pollution. 26

As the new age of canner tomato production has overpowered earlier systems of production, a kind of flexibility in tomato growing, which once worked strongly to the consumer's advantage, has been lost. The new high-technology tomato system involves substantial investment "up front" for seed, herbicides and pesticides, machinery, water, labor, and for the "management" of growing, marketing, and financing the crop. 27

Today the cannery tomato farmer has all but ceased to exist as a discrete and identifiable being. The organizations and structures that do what farmers once did operate as part and parcel of an economy functioning at a nearly incomprehensible level of integration. So much for the tasty tomato. 28

 USING THE DICTIONARY: How clear and helpful are the definitions that your dictionary provides for **technical terms** from the world of work? Report on how your dictionary handles the following: 1. *catwalk* (5) 2. *rig* (5) 3. *conveyor* (5) 4. *spec* (8) 5. *vat* (13) 6. *sluice* (13) 7. *aspic* (13) 8. *cauldron* (13) 9. *component* (15) 10. *labor-intensive* (18) 11. *configuration* (18) 12. *enzyme* (23) 13. *genetic* (23) 14. *herbicide* (26) 15. *salinity* (26)

THE WRITER'S AGENDA:

The author of this article tells us that the "ruination of the tomato" was a complex procedure. Answer the following questions about his analysis of the processes involved.

1. The author makes his subject real for us by a mixture of factual information and vivid, imaginative description. How does he *set the scene* in the introductory paragraph? Point out striking concrete details and imaginative comparisons. (What are some especially striking concrete details and imaginative comparisons *later* in the essay?)

2. Early in the second paragraph, the author gives us a one-sentence *overview* of the process that brings the tomato to the consumer's pizza. Sum up the process in your own words. Write a similar sentence summing up the process that brings the chicken, hamburger, or similar product to the paper plate of the consumer in a fast-food restaurant.

3. The author's account of the *tomato harvest* is an exceptionally graphic and vivid description of a process, with much use of concrete detail. How is the account organized—how does the author depart from straight chronological description? Divide his account of the operation into four or five major sections. Summarize and explain each as clearly and concretely as you can.

4. In tracing the history of the new "improved" tomato, the author analyzes several related developments that were part of a complex set of changes. Summarize the changes in several related areas: changes in *marketing* patterns; changing eating habits on the part of *consumers;* selective *breeding* of plants by geneticists; the development and use of new *chemicals.*

5. The author uses his analysis of the tomato industry to help us understand the larger workings of the *economic system.* What do we learn? Discuss his use of key terms such as *management,* the *system,* and *integration.*

6. In order to be accepted as an authority in a technical field, a writer has to provide solid facts and figures rather than superficial personal impressions. What use does the author make of *statistics?* Study and discuss several passages that use facts and figures.

For discussion or writing:

1. Mark Kramer writes about the changes that are the subject of his essay from a critical perspective. Although he does not agree with writers who see them as the result of a "conspiracy," he talks about the "social costs" of the changes he describes. What are these social costs? If you asked this author to summarize what is *wrong* with the modern "agribusiness" he describes, what do you think he would say? (Support your answer with evidence from the essay.)

2. Writers like the author of this essay are sometimes accused of

being unfair or hostile to business. Would you find the author guilty of this charge? (Defend your verdict.)

3. Analyze a complex traditional manufacturing process that involves several major stages or operations. For instance, describe and explain papermaking, the making of sugar, the printing of a daily newspaper, or the like.

4. Writers have often complained about modern "processed" foods giving us a product that is a far cry from the real thing. Investigate and describe the making of a modern processed product like processed cheese, potato chips, imitation ice cream, or the like.

5. Prepare a paper in which you bring your reader up to date on modern methods or modern techniques that have transformed an occupation or manufacturing process. Describe the modernized operation or process. Choose a subject like the operation of a modern chicken farm, an assembly line using robots, or another automated manufacturing system.

6. Both friendly and hostile critics of American education at times write about schools as if they were factories turning out a "product." Describe the process of education in American schools as you know them, using this basic analogy.

FOR FURTHER DISCUSSION AND WRITING: Ben Bova published this defense of technology in *Analog,* a magazine of "science fiction" and "science fact" in 1974. Modern technology, long boosted as humanity's hope for a future free from want, was increasingly under attack for endangering our survival. According to the author, why and how did modern technology develop? What role did it play in the history of human culture? To what extent do you agree or disagree with his arguments in its defense? Support or challenge his view, or weigh the two sides.

Ben Bova

In Defense of Technology

1   HOW AND why did technology become such a powerful force in human life?

2   Before there were human beings there was technology. Fossil remains of our predecessors dating from more than a million years ago show that our remote ancestors made tools out of pebbles and animal bones. And that's what technology is: toolmaking. The human animal doesn't have the speed of a horse, the fighting teeth of a chimpanzee, the wings of an eagle, the claws of a tiger, or the protective fleece of a sheep. But we have discovered (or invented) technology. We make tools, where other species make physiological adaptations. We have fire and all the energy-producing engines stemming from it. We travel faster than the horse, fly higher than the eagle, fight much more devastatingly than any predator, and protect our bodies with not only sheep's wool, but artificial fabrics as well.

3   One man alone can't kill a mammoth. But a handful of men, armed with nothing more sophisticated than stone-tipped spears and fire, apparently drove the mammoths into extinction. By the time the last glaciation dwindled, humankind was the supreme ruler of every land mass on Earth, except isolated Antarctica. And we ruled with fire, spear, awl, scraper: technology.

Instead of adapting physiologically to solve our survival problems, 4
we have adapted psychologically and sociologically. In the great glacia-
tions we now call the Ice Age, we didn't grow long shaggy coats of fur,
as did the mammoth. We invented *culture,* the adaptation of individuals that allows them to share their abilities and knowledge while mini-
mizing their weaknesses. The price we paid was to give up some measure of our individuality.

But how much? We are mammals. We aren't hatched from untend- 5
ed eggs, as the dinosaurs were. No human being can survive without
the company and care of another human being. Solitary adults are so
rare among us that hermits are an object of curiosity and humor.

The invention of culture depended on another human invention, 6
the greatest one of all history: speech. Other animals communicate
over limited ranges of data-sharing. A chimp, in the wild, can warn of
danger or give a show of friendship. Only humans—and perhaps dol-
phins—can discuss what communication is all about.

Technology is part and parcel of the human experience. To envi- 7
sion a human being without technology is to envision a dead naked
ape, not a happy noble savage. Anti-technologists have pointed out that
the powerful men of society have always used technology as a tool for
keeping their power and dominating the poor and the weak. Yes, just as
they have used superstition and sheer physical force. Over the long
run, however, technology has led to a broadening of human freedom, a
sharing of wealth and power among the common people, a leavening
of the power of the elite.

Certainly a man who belongs to a primitive hunting clan is not as 8
free to do what he wishes as he would be if he were a solitary hunter.
Yet solitary hunters die much more quickly than those who hunt in
groups. And a solitary human being misses many of the kinds of experience that make life worth living. We *are* mammals; we thrive in the
company of our fellow humans. There must be a balance, though: every
human psyche needs a degree of privacy, as well as companionship.

Modern technology is threatening our need for privacy. It can de- 9
humanize us, reduce us to statistics. But this is merely a short-range
problem. The long-range effect of modern technology will be to liberate us, allow us to be freer, more fully human. This is what technology
has always done for us; there's no reason to suspect that it won't continue this millennia-long trend.

Without technology, we would not have survived the Ice Age. If 10
technology had been stopped before the invention of steam power,
slavery would still be a major institution in all human societies. If technology had been stopped before the invention of the internal combustion engine, most of us would be working on farms from predawn to
dusk, and wondering if we'd survive through the next winter.

11   If technology is stopped now, most human beings will die. They are already dying in gruesome famines in Africa, mainly because our social institutions can't distribute food properly, and partly because our technology cannot yet control geophysical forces such as climate.

12   We will never go "beyond" technology. We may develop technologies that are nonpolluting, nonobtrusive, clean and quiet, and completely reliable. But we will no more forsake technology than we could grow the fangs of a rattlesnake.

U N I T 5

COMPARISON AND CONTRAST: Daily Rituals

The Common Theme: We like to think of ourselves as unique individuals who shape their own lives. But psychologists and other students of human behavior tell us that much of what we do fits into predictable patterns. At times, they write about us as if we were ants in a colony or bees in a hive, following predictable, programmed patterns of behavior. Much of what we do fits culturally conditioned patterns of behavior so natural to us that we are not consciously aware of them. We become aware of such patterns when we start to *compare.* Each of the essays in this unit asks us to compare and contrast two different patterns of behavior. Lewis Thomas asks us to compare the behavior of "social animals" like ants and bees with our own. Amy Gross asks us to compare the behavior of the "all-male" male with that of the androgynous male, who has left the macho image behind. Richard Rodriguez asks us to compare two somewhat different religious traditions that shaped the rituals of his childhood days.

WRITER'S GUIDE 5:
Comparison and Contrast

We compare and contrast two things to get a clear picture of similarities and differences. How are the two things alike? How are they different? Many occasions that require some organized thinking call for comparison and contrast. Car buyers, for example, compare prices, engines, interiors, gas mileage, and optional equipment. If they start asking themselves, "Why trade it in?" they may start comparing payments, cost of maintenance, and fuel costs for a new model with estimated cost of repairs and fuel costs of the old model they were about to trade in.

A paper requiring systematic comparison and contrast tests your ability to organize a substantial body of material. You will have to work out a pattern that helps the reader see the important connections. You will have to line things up in such a way that important similarities and differences stand out. Remember the following points about the *why* and *how* of papers devoted to comparison and contrast:

(1) *Use comparison and contrast to call attention, to make things stand out.* The basic function of comparison and contrast is to help open our eyes, to make us notice things that we might otherwise overlook. Suppose a writer wants to impress on us the fact that architects for two thousand years have imitated the architecture of ancient Greece. We will begin to get the point if we are first made to visualize the massive supporting columns and low gables of the ancient Greek temples and then the use of these features in buildings like the White House or the New York Stock Exchange. Or suppose a writer wants to show the drastic changes in architectural styles during the last century. We will get the point if we are first made to see the elaborately carved gables, towers, and cornices of a Victorian mansion and then the stark glass façade of a modern high rise.

Contrast especially is a great teacher. It often makes us notice and appreciate things that we would otherwise take for granted. The following are two key passages from a column about the author's return from a weekend trip to the country. By going from the friendly, warm small-town atmosphere of the holiday weekend to the suspicious, cold workaday world of city streets, we become more vividly aware of both:

(The rural community)   The weekend is over, and we drive down the country road from the cottage to the pier, passing out our last supply of waves. We wave at people walking and wave at people riding. We wave at people we know and wave at people who are strangers. . . . When we arrive at the pier, the boat is already crowded with the end-of-summer exodus. Island emigrants help each other stack cat carriers and lift bags onto the back of the boat. Crossing the water, everyone is patient with each other's dogs and children. . . .

(The city)   To ease my reentry into workaday life, I decide to walk the last mile home. I am left at a familiar, safe city corner and, yes, almost immediately, my accent changes. I begin to "speak" in the city's body language: neutral and wary. Suddenly conscious of my own adjustments, I notice how few eyes meet on this mile. Women do not look at men. Old people do not look at teenagers. Men do not smile at each other. People don't wave to strangers on these streets. They measure them.

A quarter of a mile from home, inevitably, I pass two young men who give their own obnoxious verbal greeting to every woman who crosses their stoop. . . .

—Ellen Goodman, "Wave of the Past," *Washington Post*

(2) *Use comparison and contrast to help explain.* We can use important similarities to help the reader go from the familiar to the unfamiliar. Then we can point to important differences to help explain what made the unfamiliar strange and new. In the following sample passage, the writer helps us visualize the musk-ox, at one time nearly extinct, by comparing it with its more familiar cousin, the bison, or buffalo:

A robust and shaggy animal, the musk-ox at first glance resembles a bison because of its humped shoulders and stocky build. Like the bison, it feeds on plants, but it is smaller, growing to about six feet in length and the height of a man's chest. Designed to thrive in the cold, the musk-ox has a coat so thick that it needs no barn to shelter it from Arctic blizzards. It retains body heat with two thicknesses of hair: an outer coat of long black hair that completely covers the animal except for the lips and nostrils, shedding the rain, and an inner coat of soft, gray-brown hair, called qiviut, that is so dense that neither cold nor moisture can penetrate it.

—Noel Vietmeyer, "The Return of the Musk-Ox," *Quest*

(3) *Use comparison and contrast to help the reader make choices.* Writers often compare things in order to guide our evaluation—to

show us which is preferable and why. A magazine article may provide a detailed comparison to make us choose mass transit over private cars, private health insurance over "socialized medicine," or coal-burning plants over nuclear reactors. The following excerpts focus on the advantages that an old familiar method of hauling loads has over more modern ones. Note the **thesis** that states the point of the comparison:

Time to Get a Horse

THESIS: Draft horses are back in fashion. *Work horses do some jobs better than tractors or trucks.* During a recent blizzard, the animal keepers at Chicago's Brookfield Zoo found that the only way to haul feed through the snow was using their team of Clydesdales. More and more farmers in Northern states are keeping a team on hand to sledge hay and manure in the winter: the horses plunge through belly-deep snow that bogs down tractors. There's no trouble getting them started in the morning and, best of all, farmers can raise the fuel right on the farm.

AREAS OF APPLICATION: (1) Forestry

In Oregon, Washington, and Montana, more and more horses are being used in forestry, especially in selective logging. The animals are gentle to the forest floor: within weeks there is no record that they were there, whereas years after a crawler tractor has passed through, the scars are often still visible. . . .

(2) Farming

All over the country, small farmers are finding it harder and harder to meet the cost of buying and operating gas-guzzling machinery designed for big acreage. Recent analysis of horse-powered Amish farms in Pennsylvania shows that consumption of fossil fuel is minuscule, and profitability is higher than on neighboring mechanized farms. . . .

(3) Special hauling

Horses also seem to have a future in special haulage: utility companies in Washington and some Southern states, for instance, use horses to pull electric and telephone cables through broken terrain where wheeled or tracked vehicles are difficult to operate. . . .

—Noel Vietmeyer, *Quest*

(4) *Line things up clearly for a point-by-point comparison.* To organize your comparison, you first have to line up possible similarities and

differences clearly in your own mind. Most often, you are likely to weigh *both* similarities and differences to show important common traits but also significant distinctions. To make sure the reader sees the important connections, you may decide to try a **point-by-point** comparison. You first identify perhaps three or four major areas or features where comparison would prove instructive. Then you take up each of these in turn. You proceed like a sales representative asking customers to compare two competing cars point by point—first the engines of both, then the interiors of both, then the warranties that accompany both.

An essay such as Jade Snow Wong's "Fifth Chinese Daughter," reprinted earlier in this book, provides material well suited for a point-by-point comparison. The author was raised in the strict Chinese tradition of her immigrant parents, but she slowly adopted contrasting Americanized ways. On some points, the two traditions are similar: The parents' unrelenting dedication to hard work has its parallel in the traditional American "work ethic." However, on other points, such as the methods of education, the two traditions are strikingly different. An outline for a point-by-point comparison might look like this:

Chinese Tradition and the American Way

THESIS: Jade Snow Wong was raised in the strict Chinese tradition but gradually adopted more modern American ways.

    I. The work ethic
      A. The traditional Chinese way
      B. The American way

   II. The authority of parents
      A. The traditional Chinese way
      B. The American way

  III. The methods of education
      A. The traditional Chinese way
      B. The American way

  IV. The different roles of men and women
      A. The traditional Chinese way
      B. The American way

(5) *Line things up clearly for a parallel-order comparison.* Sometimes we feel that tracing a comparison point by point would keep the reader from getting a coherent overall picture of each of the two things being compared. For instance, when comparing two people or two in-

stitutions, we may decide that we should do a separate portrait of each in order to do them justice. However, in order to help the reader make the necessary connections, we then try to take up the same or similar points in the same order. For example, a writer intrigued by the resemblances between a school and a jail might describe each institution separately but discuss major points in the same order: first, the role of the *authorities;* then, the duties of the *inmates;* finally, the system of *punishments and rewards.*

In such a **parallel-order** comparison, we must help the reader see the pattern and make the right connections at each point. A conclusion that summarizes the similarities or differences can help make sure that such a paper does not break into two separate halves, with the important links not apparent. The following is a sample outline of a paper comparing two characters from imaginative literature: the shrewd Odysseus (or Ulysses) of Homer's *Odyssey* and the glorious Achilles of Homer's *Iliad*—two of the most famous warriors of classical antiquity. Each half of the paper takes up key qualities of the traditional heroes in the same order: their fame as warriors, their eloquence as leaders, and their personal temperament.

The Fox and the Lion

THESIS: Odysseus and Achilles are both great traditional heroes, but Odysseus is closer to an ideal blending of brain and brawn.

  I. Odysseus as a traditional hero
  A. Great warrior (unsurpassed in archery)
  B. Eloquent speaker
  C. Shrewd counselor (carefully weighing the facts)
  D. Very human character (lover of good food and wine)

  II. Achilles as a traditional hero
  A. Great warrior
  B. Not a great speaker
  C. Impulsive person (insolent and resentful)
  D. Half divine (indifferent to food)

(6) *Group similarities and differences together in separate parts of your paper if this division seems the best strategy.* You may first want to show why two things seem superficially different but then go on to show underlying similarities. Or you may want to show that two things are superficially alike but then go on to show underlying differences.

Many writers have compared human beings to ants or have commented on the amazing almost-human working together of numberless ants or bees as part of one huge insect society. A writer following up such a comparison in detail might first make us aware of the surface resemblances between such insect societies and our own: In a big city, the masses of pedestrians hurrying to and fro may seem like the restlessly scurrying columns of ants; the teams of workers on a big construction job may seem like the restless worker bees busy in the hive. But in the second part of the essay, the writer may start to stress the qualities that make us human: our ability to move on and strike out on our own, or our capacity for taking on many different tasks and trying new and different ways.

Whatever overall plan you adopt, use the necessary links or **transitional expressions** that serve as signposts for the reader. We steer the reader toward similarities by words and phrases such as *like, similarly, in similar fashion.* We signal a contrast by such words and phrases as *however, whereas, by contrast, on the other hand.*

To sum up: Systematic comparison or contrast forces a writer to work out a clear overall strategy for a paper. It requires a writer to organize the material in such a way that important similarities or differences become clear to the reader. When well done, comparison and contrast can make us see important connections, alert us to important differences, and help us make important choices.

PREWRITING ACTIVITIES 5

1. The following passages are adapted from a description of New York City elementary schools of many years ago. For a *"Then-and-Now" contrast,* provide contrasting material from your own grade-school experience. Write a paragraph or two for each of the four headings.

   I. *The students:* Many students were the children of poor immigrants. Their parents spoke Italian or German or Yiddish at home. Often their parents and their "greenhorn" relatives knew little or no English. Though they worked in the sweatshops, many of these immigrants believed in America as a haven from persecution and as the land of opportunity. . . .

   II. *The teachers:* The teachers were almost all women. They wore long dresses with high lace collars and black, shiny, "pointy" shoes. They were all extraordinarily clean-looking. Most of them seemed to be called Miss McDonald. . . .

   III. *Goals:* Teachers often did not seem to like, let alone love, us students. But they taught us—firmly, thoroughly, and relentlessly. They did not ask or seem to care who their students were or where they came from. But the teachers knew what students were in school for—to become civilized, to be Americanized, to learn to read and write English. . . .

IV. *Tools:* The main teaching tool was the "reader," a collection of readings somewhat stuffy, stodgy, "noble," and, at times, mind-stretching. The "readers" were filled with "memory gems"—lines, phrases, and thoughts that echoed in the students' minds. . . .

2. A familiar figure in much modern literature is the alienated, frustrated, or lonely individual. Prepare a preliminary outline for a *parallel-order* comparison of two such figures. Choose characters from books you have read or from plays or movies you have seen. After each subheading in your outline, jot down some details that show what kind of detail you would use to develop each point.

3. For *sentence practice,* write half a dozen sentences that sum up an important contrast in a pointed, memorable form. Use the following sentences as possible models:

a. To err is human; to forgive, divine. (Alexander Pope)

b. To do good is noble; to teach others to do good is nobler, and no trouble. (Mark Twain)

c. The summer soldier and the sunshine patriot will, in this crisis, shrink from the service of his country, but he that stands it now deserves the love and thanks of man and woman. (Thomas Paine)

d. The practical person comes out of the house, sees the rain clouds, and goes back for an umbrella; the poetic person comes out of the house, says, "Look at those clouds!" and walks off into the rain.

Lewis Thomas

Ant City and Human Society

GUIDE TO READING: Lewis Thomas makes us study animal behavior for the light it throws on our behavior and our problems as human beings. The basic technique for this kind of study is **comparison and contrast**: We look at instructive similarities, but at the same time we keep important differences in mind. In reading this essay, pay special attention to the perspective the author sets up in the opening paragraph: What does the introduction make you expect—on what does it focus your attention as a reader? Then, as you read on, take stock of the similarities between insects and human beings, both considered as "social animals." At the same time, take stock of the differences that set them apart. What is the central difference that concerns the author?

1   NOT ALL social animals are social with the same degree of commitment. In some species, the members are so tied to each other and interdependent as to seem the loosely conjoined cells of a tissue. The social insects are like this. They move, and live all their lives, in a mass; a beehive is a spherical animal. In other species, less compulsively social, the members make their homes together, pool resources, travel in packs or schools, and share the food, but any single one can survive solitary, detached from the rest. Others are social only in the sense of being more or less congenial, meeting from time to time in committees, using social gatherings as *ad hoc* occasions for feeding and breeding. Some animals simply nod at each other in passing, never reaching even a first-name relationship.

2   It is not a simple thing to decide where we fit, for at one time or another in our lives we manage to organize in every imaginable social arrangement. We are as interdependent, especially in our cities, as bees or ants, yet we can detach if we wish and go live alone in the woods, in theory anyway. We feed and look after each other, constructing elaborate systems for this, even including vending machines to dispense ice cream in gas stations, but we also have numerous books to tell us how to live off the land. We cluster in family groups, but we tend, unpredictably, to turn on each other and fight as if we were different species. Collectively, we hanker to accumulate all the information in the universe and distribute it around among ourselves as though it were a kind of essential foodstuff, ant-fashion. (The faintest trace of real news in science has the action of a pheromone, lifting the hairs of workers in laboratories at the ends of the earth.) But each of us also builds a private store of his own secret knowledge and hides it away like untouchable treasure. We have names to label each as self, and we believe without reservation that this system of taxonomy will guarantee the entity, the absolute separateness of each of us, but the mechanism has no discernible function in the center of a crowded city; we are essentially nameless, most of our time.

3   Nobody wants to think that the rapidly expanding mass of mankind, spreading out over the surface of the earth, blackening the ground, bears any meaningful resemblance to the life of an anthill or hive. Who would consider for a moment that the more than 3 billion of us are a sort of stupendous animal when we become linked together? We are not mindless, nor is our day-to-day behavior coded out to the last detail by our genomes. Nor do we seem to be engaged together, compulsively, in any single, universal, stereotyped task analogous to the construction of a nest. If we were ever to put all our brains together in fact, to make a common mind the way the ants do, it would be an unthinkable thought, way over our heads.

4   Social animals tend to keep at a particular thing, generally some-

thing huge for their size; they work at it ceaselessly under genetic instructions and genetic compulsion, using it to house the species and protect it, assuring permanence.

There are, to be sure, superficial resemblances in some of the things we do together, like building glass and plastic cities on all the land and farming under the sea, or assembling in armies, or landing samples of ourselves on the moon, or sending memoranda into the next galaxy. We do these together without being quite sure why, but we can stop doing one thing and move to another whenever we like. We are not committed or bound by our genes to stick to one activity forever, like the wasps. Today's behavior is no more fixed than when we tumbled out over Europe to build cathedrals in the twelfth century. At that time we were convinced that it would go on forever, that this was the way to live, but it was not; indeed, most of us have already forgotten what it was all about. Anything we do in this transient, secondary social way, compulsively and with all our energies but only for a brief period of our history, cannot be counted as social behavior in the biological sense. If we can turn it on and off, on whims, it isn't likely that our genes are providing the detailed instructions. Constructing Chartres[1] was good for our minds, but we found that our lives went on, and it is no more likely that we will find survival in Rome plows or laser bombs, or rapid mass transport or a Mars lander, or solar power, or even synthetic protein. We do tend to improvise things like this as we go along, but it is clear that we can pick and choose.

For practical purposes, it would probably be best for us not to be biologically social, in the long run. Not that we have a choice, of course, or even a vote. It would not be good news to learn that we are all roped together intellectually, droning away at some featureless, genetically driven collective work, building something so immense that we can never see the outlines. It seems especially hard, even perilous, for this to be the burden of a species with the unique attribute of speech, and argument. Leave this kind of life to the insects and birds, and lesser mammals, and fish.

 Using the dictionary: How much help does your dictionary give you with *technical terms?* Compare the treatment of the following specialized terms in two college-level dictionaries. Which dictionary provides more help for the general reader? How or why? Check the following: 1. *ad hoc* (1)

---

[1] [The cathedral at Chartres, built between 1130 and 1260, is one of the most famous examples of medieval Gothic architecture.]

2. *pheromone* (2) 3. *taxonomy* (2) 4. *genome* (3) 5. *genetic* (4) 6. *gene* (5) 7. *species* (2) 8. *galaxy* (5) 9. *laser* (5) 10. *protein* (5)

THE WRITER'S AGENDA:

In order to make effective use of comparison and contrast, a writer has to be quick to notice both similarities and differences. The author of this essay makes us aware of striking similarities in the behavior of "social animals" and human beings. But his final aim is to show a key difference that sets social animals and human beings apart. Answer the following questions about how this author uses comparison and contrast:

1. An author tracing similarities has to decide which are merely superficial and which are more detailed *parallels* that can become instructive. As a preliminary exercise for a discussion of this essay, study the following excerpt from another comparison of insect life and human life by the same author. Find all the terms that seem borrowed from the sphere of human activity, human life, human history. Do any of these terms change their meanings when they are applied to insects rather than to people? Which seem to fit best? Which seem to have been stretched or modified most?

> . . . Think about the construction of the Hill by a colony of a million ants: each one working ceaselessly and compulsively to add perfection to his region of the structure without having the faintest notion of what is being constructed elsewhere, living out his brief life in a social enterprise that extends back into what is for him the deepest antiquity (ants die at the rate of 3–4 percent per day; in a month or so an entire generation vanishes, while the Hill can go on for sixty years or, given good years, forever), performing his work with infallible, undistracted skill in the midst of a confusion of others, all tumbling over each other to get the twigs and bits of earth aligned in precisely the right configurations for the warmth and ventilation of the eggs and larvae, but totally incapacitated by isolation.
>
> —Lewis Thomas, *The Lives of a Cell*

2. In the opening paragraph of the actual essay, the author distinguishes *four kinds* of "social animals." What are the four kinds, and what sets them apart? Show that the author prepares us from the beginning for the later comparison and contrast with human behavior. Point out and discuss the terms that are taken from the sphere of human life and here applied to animals.

3. In the second paragraph of the essay, the author begins to make us aware of some of the *surface similarities* between human beings and social animals. List and explain the similarities.

4. In the second paragraph of the essay, the author pairs the similarities between human and animal life with facts that point the opposite way. What are the *differences* that he mentions in this paragraph?

5. In the second half of this essay, the author closes in on what to him is the most important difference between the social animals and human society. Explain the *basic difference* in your own words. What are some of the key terms that the author uses to make the distinction? What are key examples that he uses to prove his point?

6. In the final paragraph, the author most clearly goes beyond scientific description to *judgments of value*. What are the judgments he makes here? Show how his attitudes and preferences are reflected in strongly **connotative** words that he uses in this conclusion.

7. Lewis Thomas is a writer who knows how to be serious without being glum. Point out passages or expressions in this essay that show his ability to provide a lighter touch.

For discussion or writing:

1. How basically alike or how fundamentally different we are when compared with our animal kindred has long been a subject of heated debate. On the basis of your own observation or previous reading, what similarities between the lives of ants or bees and human life seem most striking or fundamental to you?

2. What is the key feature that sets human beings apart from animals? Discuss some of the different possible answers to this question, or defend your own.   neo-cortex

3. Thomas says that not all social animals "are social with the same degree of commitment." Apply the same perspective to human beings. Choose two groups of people that you know well. Compare and contrast them on the basis of how social they are—how and how closely they interact with others. The two groups you choose could be age groups, religious or ethnic groups, occupational groups, or the like.

4. Choose two styles of living that you have had a chance to compare. For instance, choose city and suburban living, snow belt and sun belt living, boarding-school and day-student life, or army life and civilian life. Focus on three or four key features—do a clear *parallel-order* or *point-by-point* comparison.

5. Discuss two things that are superficially alike but yet *different* in one or more fundamental ways. For instance, discuss mechanization and automation, a school and a business, or kinship and marriage. Start with the surface similarities, and then close in on what is fundamentally different.

BACKGROUND: Amy Gross (born 1942) is a feature editor for *Vogue* who has written on women's issues and women's lives for publications including *Redbook* and the *New York Times*. She wrote the following essay for *Mademoiselle* in 1976. At the time, the term *androgyny* was first being widely used by feminist psychologists trying to overcome stereotyped traditional assumptions about masculine and feminine roles. Combining the Greek root words for "man" and "woman," the term *androgyny* reflects the assumption that members of both sexes combine in different degrees "male" and "female" psychological traits. In her article, Gross followed the lead of researchers exploring the implications of a "liberated sexual identity." She applauded the androgynous man as she reevaluated, from a woman's perspective, the meaning of masculine appeal.

Amy Gross

The Appeal of the Androgynous Man

GUIDE TO READING: The author discusses the "androgynous" man informally, using personal anecdote and humorous asides. What are the major features of the androgynous man that emerge from her discussion? What are the major points of contrast with the traditional "macho" image of the male? How does she buttress her personal impressions with references to psychological studies?

JAMES DEAN was my first androgynous man.[1] I figured I could talk to him. He was anguished and I was 12, so we had a lot in common. With only a few exceptions, all the men I have liked or loved have been a certain kind of man: a kind who doesn't play football or watch the games on Sunday, who doesn't tell dirty jokes featuring broads or

---

[1] [James Dean, who died young in an automobile accident, was the moody, gloomy hero of movies about rebellious, alienated youth.]

chicks, who is not contemptuous of conversations that are philosophically speculative, introspective, or otherwise foolish according to the
other kind of man. He is more self-amused, less inflated, more quirky,
vulnerable and responsive than the other sort (the other sort, I'm visualizing as the guys on TV who advertise deodorant in the locker room).
He is more like me than the other sort. He is what social scientists and
feminists would call androgynous: having the characteristics of both
male and female.

2   Now the first thing I want you to know about the androgynous man
is that he is neither effeminate nor hermaphroditic. All his primary and
secondary sexual characteristics are in order and I would say he's all-
man, but that is just what he is not. He is more than all-man.

3   The merely all-man man, for one thing, never walks to the grocery
store unless the little woman is away visiting her mother with the kids,
or is in the hospital having a kid, or there is no little woman. All-men
men don't know how to shop in a grocery store unless it is to buy a 6-pack
and some pretzels. Their ideas of nutrition expand beyond a 6-pack and
pretzels only to take in steak, potatoes, scotch or rye whiskey, and maybe a wad of cake or apple pie. All-men men have absolutely no taste in
food, art, books, movies, theatre, dance, how to live, what are good
questions, what is funny, or anything else I care about. It's not exactly
that the all-man's man is an uncouth illiterate. He may be educated,
well-mannered, and on a first-name basis with fine wines. One all-man
man I knew was a handsome individual who gave the impression of
being gentle, affectionate, and sensitive. He sat and ate dinner one
night while I was doing something endearingly feminine at the sink. At
one point, he mutely held up his glass to indicate in a primitive, even
ape-like, way his need for a refill. This was in 1967, before Women's
Liberation. Even so, I was disturbed. Not enough to break the glass over
his handsome head, not even enough to mutely indicate the where-
abouts of the refrigerator, but enough to remember that moment in all
its revelatory clarity. No androgynous man would ever brutishly expect
to be waited on without even a "please." (With a "please," maybe.)

4   The brute happened to be a doctor—not a hard hat—and, to all
appearances, couth. But he had bought the whole superman package,
complete with that fragile beast, the male ego. The androgynous man
arrives with a male ego too, but his is not as imperialistic. It doesn't
invade every area of his life and person. Most activities and thoughts
have nothing to do with masculinity or femininity. The androgynous
man knows this. The all-man man doesn't. He must keep a constant
guard against anything even vaguely feminine (*i.e.,* "sissy") rising up
in him. It must be a terrible strain.

5   Male chauvinism is an irritation, but the real problem I have with
the all-man man is that it's hard for me to talk to him. He's alien to me,

and for this I'm at least half to blame. As his interests have not carried him into the sissy, mine have never taken me very far into the typically masculine terrains of sports, business and finance, politics, cars, boats and machines. But blame or no blame, the reality is that it is almost as difficult for me to connect with him as it would be to link up with an Arab shepherd or Bolivian sandalmaker. There's a similar culture gap.

It seems to me that the most masculine men usually end up with the most feminine women. Maybe they like extreme polarity. I like polarity myself, but the poles have to be within earshot. As I've implied, I'm very big on talking. I fall in love for at least three hours with anyone who engages me in a real conversation. I'd rather a man point out a paragraph in a book—wanting to share it with me—than bring me flowers. I'd rather a man ask what I think than tell me I look pretty. (Women who are very pretty and accustomed to hearing that they are pretty may feel differently.) My experience is that all-men men read books I don't want to see paragraphs of, and don't really give a damn what I or any woman would think about most issues so long as she looks pretty. They have a very limited use for women. I suspect they don't really like us. The androgynous man likes women as much or as little as he likes anyone. 6

Another difference between the all-man man and the androgynous man is that the first is not a star in the creativity department. If your image of the creative male accessorizes him with a beret, smock and artist's palette, you will not believe the all-man man has been seriously short-changed. But if you allow as how creativity is a talent for freedom, associated with imagination, wit, empathy, unpredictability, and receptivity to new impressions and connections, then you will certainly pity the dull, thick-skinned, rigid fellow in whom creativity sets no fires. 7

Nor is the all-man man so hot when it comes to sensitivity. He may be true-blue in the trenches, but if you are troubled, you'd be wasting your time trying to milk comfort from the all-man man. 8

This is not blind prejudice. It is enlightened prejudice. My biases were confirmed recently by a psychologist named Sandra Lipsetz Bem, a professor at Stanford University. She brought to attention the fact that high masculinity in males (and high femininity in females) has been "consistently correlated with lower overall intelligence and lower creativity." Another psychologist, Donald W. MacKinnon, director of the Institute of Personality Assessment and Research at the University of California in Berkeley, found that "creative males give more expression to the feminine side of their nature than do less creative men . . . [They] score relatively high on femininity, and this despite the fact that, as a group, they do not present an effeminate appearance or give evidence of increased homosexual interests or experiences. Their elevated scores on femininity indicate rather an openness to their feelings and 9 emotions, a sensitive intellect and understanding self-awareness and wide-ranging interests including many which in the American culture are thought of as more feminine . . ."

10   Dr. Bem ran a series of experiments on college students who had been categorized as masculine, feminine, or androgynous. In three tests of the degree of nurturance—warmth and caring—the masculine men scored painfully low (painfully for anyone stuck with a masculine man, that is). In one of those experiments, all the students were asked to listen to a "troubled talker"—a person who was not neurotic but simply lonely, supposedly new in town and feeling like an outsider. The masculine men were the least supportive, responsive or humane. "They lacked the ability to express warmth, playfulness and concern," Bem concluded. (She's giving them the benefit of the doubt. It's possible the masculine men didn't express those qualities because they didn't possess them.)

11   The androgynous man, on the other hand, having been run through the same carnival of tests, "performs spectacularly. He shuns no behavior just because our culture happens to label it as female and his competence crosses both the instrumental [getting the job done, the problem solved] and the expressive [showing a concern for the welfare of others, the harmony of the group] domains. Thus, he stands firm in his opinion, he cuddles kittens and bounces babies and he has a sympathetic ear for someone in distress."

12   Well, a great mind, a sensitive and warm personality are fine in their place, but you are perhaps skeptical of the gut appeal of the androgynous man. As a friend, maybe, you'd like an androgynous man. For a sexual partner, though, you'd prefer a jock. There's no arguing chemistry, but consider the jock for a moment. He competes on the field, whatever his field is, and bed is just one more field to him: another opportunity to perform, another fray. Sensuality is for him candy to be doled out as lure. It is a ration whose flow is cut off at the exact point when it has served its purpose—namely, to elicit your willingness to work out on the field with him.

13   Highly masculine men need to believe their sexual appetite is far greater than a woman's (than a nice woman's). To them, females must be seduced. Seduction is a euphemism for a power play, a con job. It pits man against woman (or woman against man). The jock believes he must win you over, incite your body to rebel against your better judgment: in other words—conquer you.

14   The androgynous man is not your opponent but your teammate. He does not seduce: he invites. Sensuality is a pleasure for him. He's not quite so goal-oriented. And to conclude, I think I need only remind you here of his greater imagination, his wit and empathy, his unpredictability, and his receptivity to new impressions and connections.

USING THE DICTIONARY: What does each of the following terms mean in the context in which it is used in the essay? 1. *anguished* (1) 2. *speculative* (1) 3. *vulnerable* (1) 4. *effeminate* (2) 5. *uncouth* (3) 6. *revelatory* (3) 7. *imperialistic* (4) 8. *terrains* (5) 9. *empathy* (7) 10. *correlated* (9) 11. *supportive* (10) 12. *humane* (10) 13. *sensuality* (12) 14. *elicit* (12) 15. *incite* (13)

THE WRITER'S AGENDA:

The author uses comparison and contrast to explain and defend a strong personal preference. Answer the following questions about how she proceeds.

1. In the first five or six paragraphs, the author repeatedly makes us see what the androgynous man is like by showing us what he is *not*. What are the major *points of contrast* between the androgynous man and the stereotypical "all-man" man that emerge from these paragraphs? Can you fit them into some overall pattern?

2. In these early paragraphs, the author frequently forestalls *misunderstandings* or misconceptions. What are some examples?

3. How do the *research findings* cited by the author confirm her "biases"? What are the most striking or most important points that emerge from this part of the essay?

4. In her discussion of men as sexual partners, the author uses the athlete as an example of the highly masculine man. How and with what results does she use the imagery of *sports?*

5. Throughout the essay, the author cites as examples *concrete situations* or activities that put men to the test. As you look back over the essay, which of these do you remember best, or which do most to make the basic contrast clear?

FOR DISCUSSION OR WRITING:

1. Is there a single clue or a central trait that for you helps explain the basic contrast between the two types examined by the author? What for you is the most essential difference?

2. In Gross's essay, how much is merely personal preference? How much to you seems valid observation of general patterns of behavior? What in her essay reminds you of personal experience or observation?

3. Is there something to be said in defense of the "all-man" man?

4. Prepare an essay that would be the logical companion piece to the author's article: "The Appeal of the Androgynous Woman." Develop the contrast between her and a traditional "feminine" image.

5. Prepare a "Then-and-Now" paper in which you contrast the changing images of one of the following: a good mother (father); a successful marriage; the ideal male (or female) movie star; the ideal minister.

6. Has the androgynous ideal influenced the portrayal of men in movies or on television?

BACKGROUND: Richard Rodriguez (born 1944) grew up in Sacramento, California, as the son of Mexican immigrants. On his first day of school, he found himself in a class of white middle-class children in which he was the only Mexican-American, able to understand "some fifty stray English words." His widely praised autobiography, *Hunger of Memory* (1981), is the history of his education as a "disadvantaged" child who went on to become a scholarship student and a successful writer and lecturer. An English major in college, he studied English literature at prestigious places including Stanford, Berkeley, and the British Museum in London. A major theme of his book is the price of assimilation: his growing separation from the world of his parents and relatives; his gradual estrangement from the familiar, intimate Spanish of his childhood home as English, the "public" language of school and office, slowly became his primary language. In the early stages of learning English, Rodriguez says, he was "a listening child . . . wide-eyed with hearing." Like other bilingual, bicultural Americans, he remained an alert observer of the differences in people's ways of talking, their gestures, and their daily rituals—differences that provide us with clues to who and what they are. The selection printed here is from Chapter 3 of *Hunger of Memory*.

Richard Rodriguez
Children of Ceremony

GUIDE TO READING: In this essay, a writer with a sharp eye for contrasts traces distinctions that would escape a superficial observer. As he compares the Mexican-Catholic tradition of his parents with the Irish-Catholic tradition of his teachers, look for the common elements that made him feel at home in both. At the same time, look for the subtle differences that set them apart.

I REMEMBER my early Catholic schooling and recall an experience of religion very different from anything I have known since. Never since have I felt so much at home in the Church, so easy at mass. My grammar school years especially were the years when the great Church doors opened to enclose me, filling my day as I was certain the Church filled all time. Living in a community of shared faith, I enjoyed much more than mere social reenforcement of religious belief. Experienced continuously in public and private, Catholicism shaped my whole day. It framed my experience of eating and sleeping and washing; it named the season and the hour.

2   The sky was full then and the coming of spring was a religious event. I would awaken to the sound of garage doors creaking open and know without thinking that it was Friday and that my father was on his way to six-thirty mass. I saw, without bothering to notice, statues at home and at school of the Virgin and of Christ. I would write at the top of my arithmetic or history homework the initials *Jesus, Mary,* and *Joseph.* (All my homework was thus dedicated.) I felt the air was different, somehow still and more silent on Sundays and high feastdays. I felt lightened, transparent as sky, after confessing my sins to a priest. Schooldays were routinely divided by prayers said with classmates. I would not have forgotten to say grace before eating. And I would not have turned off the light next to my bed or fallen asleep without praying to God.

3   The institution of the Church stood an extraordinarily physical presence in my world. One block from the house was Sacred Heart Church. In the opposite direction, another block away, was Sacred Heart Grammar School, run by the Sisters of Mercy. And from our back-yard, I could see Mercy Hospital, Sacramento's only Catholic hospital. All day I would hear the sirens of death. Well before I was a student myself, I would watch the Catholic school kids walk by the front of the house, dressed in gray and red uniforms. From the front lawn I could see people on the steps of the church, coming out, dressed in black after funerals, or standing, the ladies in bright-colored dresses in front of the church after a wedding. When I first went to stores on errands for my mother, I could be seen by the golden-red statue of Christ, where it hovered over the main door of the church.

4   I was *un católico* before I was a Catholic. That is, I acquired my earliest sense of the Church—and my membership in it—through my parents' Mexican Catholicism. It was in Spanish that I first learned to pray. I recited family prayers—not from any book. And in those years when we felt alienated from *los gringos,* my family went across town every week to the wooden church of Our Lady of Guadalupe, which was decorated with yellow Christmas tree lights all year long.

5   Very early, however, the *gringo* church in our neighborhood began to superimpose itself on our family life. The first English-speaking din-ner guest at our house was a priest from Sacred Heart Church. I was about four years old at the time, so I retain only random details with which to remember the evening. But the visit was too important an event for me to forget. I remember how my mother dressed her four children in outfits it had taken her weeks to sew. I wore a white shirt and blue woolen shorts. (It was the first time I had been dressed up for

a stranger.) I remember hearing the priest's English laughter. (It was the first time I had heard such sounds in the house.) I remember that my mother served a *gringo* meat loaf and that I was too nervous or shy to look up more than two or three times to study the priest's jiggling layers of face. (Smoothly, he made believe that there was conversation.) After dinner we all went to the front room where the priest took a small book from his jacket to recite some prayers, consecrating our house and our family. He left a large picture of a sad-eyed Christ, exposing his punctured heart. (A caption below records the date of his visit and the imprimatur of Francis Cardinal Spellman.) That picture survives. Hanging prominently over the radio or, later, the television set in the front room, it has retained a position of prominence in all the houses my parents have lived in since. It has been one of the few permanent fixtures in the environment of my life. Visitors to our house doubtlessly noticed it when they entered the door—saw it immediately as the sign we were Catholics. But I saw the picture too often to pay it much heed.

I saw a picture of the Sacred Heart in the grammar school class- 6 room I entered two years after the priest's visit. The picture drew an important continuity between home and the classroom. When all else was different for me (as a scholarship boy) between the two worlds of my life, the Church provided an essential link. During my first months in school, I remember being struck by the fact that—although they worshipped in English—the nuns and my classmates shared my family's religion. The *gringos* were, in some way, like me, *católicos*. Gradually, however, with my assimilation in the schoolroom, I began to think of myself and my family as Catholics. The distinction blurred. At home and in class I heard about sin and Christ and Satan and the consoling presence of Mary the Virgin. It became one Catholic faith for me.

Only now do I trouble to notice what intricate differences sepa- 7 rated home Catholicism from classroom Catholicism. In school, religious instruction stressed that man was a sinner. Influenced, I suspect, by a bleak melancholic strain in Irish Catholicism, the nuns portrayed God as a judge. I was carefully taught the demands He placed upon me. In the third grade I could distinguish between venial and mortal sin. I knew—and was terrified to know—that there was one unforgivable sin (against the Holy Ghost): the sin of despair. I knew the crucial distinction between perfect and imperfect contrition. I could distinguish sins of commission from sins of omission. And I learned how important it was to be in a state of grace at the moment of death.

Death. (How much nearer it seemed to the boy than it seems to me 8 now.) Again and again the nuns would pull out the old stories of death-bed conversions; of Roman martyrdoms; of murdered African missionaries; of pious children dying of cancer to become tiny saints; of souls going immediately to heaven. We were taught how to baptize in case of emergency. I knew why some souls went to Limbo after the death of the body, and others went for a time to Purgatory, and why others went to heaven or hell—"forever and ever."

9 Among the assortment of possible sins to commit, sexual sins—the cherries—were certainly mentioned. With the first years of puberty, the last years of grammar school, we began hearing about "sins of the flesh." There were those special mornings when the priest would come over from church to take the boys to the cafeteria, while the nun remained with the girls—"the young ladies"—in the classroom. For fifty minutes the priest would talk about the dangers of masturbation or petting, and some friend of mine would turn carefully in his chair to smirk in my direction or somebody else would jab me in the back with a pencil.

10 Unlike others who have described their Catholic schooling, I do not remember the nuns or the priests to have been obsessed with sexual sins. Perhaps that says more about me or my Mexican Catholicism than it says about what actually went on in the classroom. I remember, in any case, that I would sometimes hear with irony warnings about sins of the flesh. When we were in eighth grade the priest told us how dangerous it was to look at our naked bodies, even while taking a bath—and I noticed that he made the remark directly under a near-naked figure of Christ on the cross.

11 The Church, in fact, excited more sexual wonderment than it repressed. I regarded with awe the "wedding ring" on a nun's finger, her black "wedding veil"—symbols of marriage to God. I would study pictures of martyrs—white-robed virgins fallen in death and the young, almost smiling, St. Sebastian, transfigured in pain. At Easter high mass I was dizzied by the mucous perfume of white flowers at the celebration of rebirth. At such moments, the Church touched alive some very private sexual excitement; it pronounced my sexuality important.

12 Sin remained, nevertheless. Confession was a regular part of my grammar school years. (One sought forgiveness through the ritual plea: "Bless me, father, for I have sinned. . . .") Sin—the distance separating man from God—sin that burdened a sorrowful Christ; sin remained. ("I have disobeyed my parents fourteen times . . . I have lied eight times . . . I am heartily sorry for having offended Thee. . . .") God the Father judged. But Christ the Son had interceded. I was forgiven each time I sought forgiveness. The priest murmured Latin words of forgiveness in the confessional box. And I would leave the dark.

13 In contrast to the Catholicism of school, the Mexican Catholicism of home was less concerned with man the sinner than with man the supplicant. God the Father was not so much a stern judge as One with the power to change our lives. My family turned to God not in guilt so

much as in need. We prayed for favors and at desperate times. I prayed for help in finding a quarter I had lost on my way home. I prayed with my family at times of illness and when my father was temporarily out of a job. And when there was death in the family, we prayed.

I remember my family's religion, and I hear the whispering voices 14 of women. For although men in my family went to church, women prayed most audibly. Whether by man or woman, however, God the Father was rarely addressed directly. There were intermediaries to carry one's petition to Him. My mother had her group of Mexican and South American saints and near-saints (persons moving toward canonization). She favored a black Brazilian priest who, she claimed, was especially efficacious. Above all mediators there was Mary, *Santa María,* the Mother. Whereas at school the primary mediator was Christ, at home that role was assumed by the Mexican Virgin, *Nuestra Señora de Guadalupe,* the focus of devotion and pride for Mexican Catholics. The Mexican Mary "honored our people," my mother would say. "She could have appeared to anyone in the whole world, but she appeared to a Mexican." Someone like us. And she appeared, I could see from her picture, as a young Indian maiden—dark just like me.

On her feastday in early December my family would go to the Mexi- 15 can church for a predawn high mass. The celebration would begin in the cold dark with a blare of trumpets imitating the cries of a cock. The Virgin's wavering statue on the shoulders of men would lead a procession into the warm yellow church. Often an usher would roughly separate me from my parents and pull me into a line of young children. (My mother nodded calmly when I looked back.) Sometimes alone, sometimes with my brother and sisters, I would find myself near the altar amid two or three hundred children, many of them dressed like Mexican cowboys and cowgirls. Sitting on the floor it was easier to see the congregation than the altar. So, as the mass progressed, my eye would wander through the crowd. Invariably, my attention settled on old women—mysterious supplicants in black—bent deep, their hands clasped tight to hold steady the attention of the Mexican Virgin, who was pictured high over the altar, astride a black moon.

The *gringo* Catholic church, a block from our house, was a very 16 different place. In the *gringo* church Mary's statue was relegated to a side altar, imaged there as a serene white lady who matter-of-factly squashed the Genesis serpent with her bare feet. (Very early I knew that I was supposed to believe that the shy Mexican Mary was the same as this European Mary triumphant.) In the *gringo* church the floors were made not of squeaky wood but of marble. And there was not the devotional clutter of so many pictures and statues and candle racks. "It doesn't feel like a church," my mother complained. But as it became our regular church, I grew to love its elegant simplicity: the formal march of its eight black pillars toward the altar; the Easter-egg-shaped sanctuary that arched high over the tabernacle; and the dim pink light suffused throughout on summer afternoons when I came in not to pray but to marvel at the cool calm.

17   The holy darkness of church never frightened me. It was never nighttime darkness. Religion at school and at church was never night-time religion like religion at home. Catholicism at home was shaped by the sounds of the "family rosary": tired voices repeating the syllables of the Hail Mary; our fingers inching forward on beads toward the point of beginning; my knees aching; the coming of sleep.

18   Religion at home was a religion of bedtime. Prayers before sleep-ing spoke of death coming during the night. It was then a religion of shadows. The last thing I'd see before closing my eyes would be the cheap statue of Mary aglow next to my bed.

19   But the dark at the foot of my bed billowed with malevolent shapes. Those nights when I'd shudder awake from a nightmare, I'd remember my grandmother's instruction to make a sign of the cross in the direc-tion of my window. (That way Satan would find his way barred.) Sitting up in bed, I'd aim the sign of the cross against the dim rectangle of light. Quickly, then, I'd say the Prayer to My Guardian Angel, which would enable me to fall back to sleep.

20   In time dawn came.

21   A child whose parents could not introduce him to books like *Grimm's Fairy Tales,* I was introduced to the spheres of enchantment by the nighttime Catholicism of demons and angels. The superstitious Catholicism of home provided a kind of proletarian fairy-tale world.

22   Satan was mentioned in the classroom. And depicted on the nuns' cartoon placards as bringing all his evil to bear on the temptation of nicely dressed boys and girls. In the morning's bright light and in the safe company of classmates, Satan never aroused very much terror. Around the time I was in fourth grade, moreover, religion classes be-came increasingly academic. I was introduced to that text familiar to generations of Catholic students, *The Baltimore Catechism.* It is a text organized by questions about the Catholic faith. (Who is God? What is Penance? What is Hope?)

23   Today's Catholic elementary schools attempt a less mechanical ap-proach to religious instruction. Students are taught—what I never had to be taught—that religion is not simply a matter of dogmas or theolog-ical truths; that religion involves a person's whole way of life. To make the point, emphasis has shifted from the theological to the ethical. Students are encouraged to consider social problems and responses to "practical" dilemmas in a modern world through which angels and devils no longer dance.

My schooling belonged to another time. *The Baltimore Catechism* 24 taught me to trust the authority of the Church. That was the central lesson conveyed through the experience of memorizing hundreds of questions and answers. I learned an answer like, God made us to know, love, and serve Him in this life, and to be happy with Him in the next. The answer was memorized *along with* the question (it belonged with the question), Why did God make us? I learned, in other words, question and answer together. Beyond what the answer literally stated, two things were thus communicated. First, the existence of a question implies the existence of an answer. (There are no stray questions.) And second, that my questions about religion had answers. (The Church knows.)

Not only in religion class was memory exercised. During those 25 years when I was memorizing the questions and answers of *The Baltimore Catechism,* I was also impressing on my memory the spelling of hundreds of words, grammar rules, division and multiplication tables. The nuns deeply trusted the role of memorization in learning. Not coincidentally, they were excellent teachers of basics. They would stand in front of the room for hours, drilling us over and over (5 times 5 . . . 5 times 9; *i* before *e* except after *c;* God made us to know, love, and serve Him in this world . . .). Stressing memorization, my teachers implied that education is largely a matter of acquiring knowledge already discovered. And they were right. For contrary to more progressive notions of learning, much that is learned in a classroom must be the already known; and much that is already known must be learned before a student can achieve truly independent thought.

Stressing memorization, the nuns assumed an important Catholic 26 bias. Stated positively, they believed that learning is a social activity; learning is a rite of passage into the group. (Remembrance is itself an activity that establishes a student's dependence upon and union with others.) Less defensibly, the nuns distrusted intellectual challenges to authority. In religion class especially, they would grow impatient with the relentlessly questioning student. When one nun told my parents that their youngest daughter had a "mind of her own," she meant the remark to be a negative criticism. And even though I was urged to read all that I could, several teachers were dismayed to learn that I had read the novels of Victor Hugo and Flaubert.[1] ("Those writers are on the Index, Richard.") With classmates I would hear the nuns' warning

[1] [Victor Hugo (1802–85), French author of *Les Miserables,* shocked some of his contemporaries with graphic descriptions of poverty and injustice. Gustave Flaubert (1821–80), French author of *Madame Bovary,* shocked some of his readers with his frank treatment of sexual frustration and adultery.]

about non-Catholic colleges, stories of Faustian Catholics falling victim to the foolish sin of intellectual pride.[2]

27   Trust the Church. It was the institution established by the instruction of Christ to his disciple: "Thou art Peter and upon this rock I will build. . . ." (How could Protestants not hear?) The nun drew her pointer to the chart in front of the classroom where the line of popes connected the name of St. Peter to that of Pope Pius XII. Trust the Church, the nun said. It was through the Church that God was best known.

 USING THE DICTIONARY: What is the meaning of the following terms in the context of religious instruction? 1. *consecrate* (5) 2. *imprimatur.* (5) 3. *venial* (7) 4. *contrition* (7) 5. *grace* (7) 6. *purgatory* (8) 7. *martyr* (11) 8. *supplicant* (13) 9. *canonization* (14) 10. *rosary* (17) 11. *catechism* (22) 12. *penance* (22) 13. *dogma* (23) 14. *Index* (26) 15. *disciple* (27)

THE WRITER'S AGENDA:

In this essay, the author studies major influences in his life that were in some ways different and yet fundamentally alike. Answer the following questions about the differences and similarities:

1. In the first three paragraphs, how does the author describe the *role of religion* in his early life? What are striking examples and revealing details? What is the implied contrast with the role religion plays in many people's lives today?

2. What major features does the author stress when he describes the *Irish Catholicism* that for him "provided an essential link" between the world of home and that of the classroom? What are distinctive preoccupations or characteristic trends?

3. When the author goes on to contrast the *Mexican Catholicism* of home with the Catholicism of school, what is the first major difference that he emphasizes? What related features or details help develop and reinforce it? What contrasts in the style or appearance of the two different kinds of churches does it explain?

---

[2] [Dr. Faustus is the legendary medieval scholar who sold his soul to the devil in return for magical powers. In two famous plays—Marlowe's *Dr. Faustus* (ca. 1589) and Goethe's *Faust* (1829)—he becomes the symbol of the questing human intellect trying to transcend human limitations in the search for knowledge and power.]

4. What dimension of his early religious experience does the author explore in his description of the *"night-time religion"* of his childhood years?

5. In the concluding paragraphs, the author discusses the *teaching* in the parochial schools of his youth. What essential connection does he show between the content and the methods of instruction? How does he contrast religious instruction then with more modern or more "progressive" approaches?

6. In much of his autobiography, Rodriguez explores the *mixed feelings* of the person whose loyalties are divided between different or conflicting traditions. In this excerpt, what evidence is there of his current attitude toward the religious experiences of his youth? Is there evidence of nostalgia, solidarity, irony, criticism, rejection?

FOR DISCUSSION OR WRITING:

1. What in this essay reminds you most strongly of what you know about a religious upbringing? What seemed most strange or unexpected?

2. How important are the differences in emphasis and behavior that the author traces between the two religious traditions? How are these differences likely to influence someone's personality?

3. Drawing on examples from this essay, how would you explain your view of the difference between religion and superstition, or between tradition and a personal, individual faith?

4. Many young people in recent years have turned to unconventional kinds of religious experience or affiliation. How do these differ from conventional or traditional forms of religion, and why?

5. Compare and contrast two traditions, institutions, or kinds of behavior that are similar or closely related and yet separated by important differences. Choose a pair like the following:

- parochial or other private schools and public schools

- American industry and Japanese industry

- Catholic and Protestant traditions in religion

- prejudices encountered by Hispanics and those encountered by blacks or another minority

- fraternities and sororities

- factories and schools

6. Often the contrasting architecture or layout of two places reflects or symbolizes differences in the attitudes or patterns of behavior of the people who live, work, or study there. Explore such a contrast, drawing on your own observation or experience.

FOR FURTHER DISCUSSION AND WRITING: Linguists engage in the systematic study of language. This short selection is from a linguist's study of the differences between women's talk and men's talk, ranging from lexical items (word choice) to syntactic relationships (sentence structure). What is the point of her comparison? Can you think of additional examples of similar differences? How far do you agree with the author's interpretation of her examples? Are there similar differences in gestures, manners, or social behavior?

Robin Lakoff

Talking like a Lady

W OMEN'S SPEECH differs from men's speech. . . . Aside from specific lexical items like color names, we find differences between the speech of women and that of men in the use of particles that grammarians often describe as "meaningless." There may be no referent for them, but they are far from meaningless: they define the social context of an utterance, indicate the relationship the speaker feels between himself and his addressee, between himself and what he is talking about.

As an experiment, one might present native speakers of standard American English with pairs of sentences, identical syntactically and in terms of referential lexical items, and differing merely in the choice of "meaningless" particle, and ask them which was spoken by a man, which a woman. Consider:

(1) *(a)* Oh dear, you've put the peanut butter in the refrigerator again.

(b) Shit, you've put the peanut butter in the refrigerator again.

It is safe to predict that people would classify the first sentence as part of "women's language," the second as "men's language." It is true that many self-respecting women are becoming able to use sentences like (1) *(b)* publicly without flinching, but this is a relatively recent development, and while perhaps the majority of Middle America might condone the use of *(b)* for men, they would still disapprove of its use by women. (It is of interest, by the way, to note that men's language is increasingly being used by women, but women's language is not being adopted by men, apart from those who reject the American masculine image [for example, homosexuals]. This is analogous to the fact that men's jobs are being sought by women, but few men are rushing to become housewives or secretaries. The language of the favored group, the group that holds the power, along with its nonlinguistic behavior, is generally adopted by the other group, not vice versa. In any event, it is a truism to state that the "stronger" expletives are reserved for men, and the "weaker" ones for women.)

4   Now we may ask what we mean by "stronger" and "weaker" expletives. (If these particles were indeed meaningless, none would be stronger than any other.) The difference between using "shit" (or "damn," or one of many others) as opposed to "oh dear," or "goodness," or "oh fudge" lies in how forcefully one says how one feels— perhaps, one might say, choice of particle is a function of how strongly one allows oneself to feel about something, so that the strength of an emotion conveyed in a sentence corresponds to the strength of the particle. Hence in a really serious situation, the use of "trivializing" (that is, "women's") particles constitutes a joke, or at any rate, is highly inappropriate. (In conformity with current linguistic practice, an asterisk (*) will be used to mark a sentence that is inappropriate in some sense, either because it is syntactically deviant or used in the wrong social context.)

(2) *(a)* *Oh fudge, my hair is on fire.

  (b) *Dear me, did he kidnap the baby?

5   As children, women are encouraged to be "little ladies." Little ladies don't scream as vociferously as little boys, and they are chastised more severely for throwing tantrums or showing temper: "high spirits" are expected and therefore tolerated in little boys; docility and resignation are the corresponding traits expected of little girls. Now, we tend to excuse a show of temper by a man where we would not excuse an identical tirade from a woman: women are allowed to fuss and complain, but only a man can bellow in rage. It is sometimes claimed that there is a biological basis for this behavior difference, though I don't believe conclusive evidence exists that the early differences in behavior that have been observed are not the results of very different treatment of babies of the two sexes from the beginning; but surely the use of different particles by men and women is a learned trait, merely mirroring nonlinguistic differences again, and again pointing out an ineq-

uity that exists between the treatment of men, and society's expectations of them, and the treatment of women. Allowing men stronger means of expression than are open to women further reinforces men's position of strength in the real world: for surely we listen with more attention the more strongly and forcefully someone expresses opinions, and a speaker unable—for whatever reason—to be forceful in stating his views is much less likely to be taken seriously. Ability to use strong particles like "shit" and "hell" is, of course, only incidental to the inequity that exists rather than its cause. But once again, apparently accidental linguistic usage suggests that women are denied equality partially for linguistic reasons, and that an examination of language points up precisely an area in which inequity exists. Further, if someone is allowed to show emotions, and consequently does, others may well be able to view him as a real individual in his own right, as they could not if he never showed emotion. Here again, then, the behavior a woman learns as "correct" prevents her from being taken seriously as an individual, and further is considered "correct" and necessary for a woman precisely because society does *not* consider her seriously as an individual.

U N I T 6

CLASSIFICATION:
Types and Stereotypes

The Common Theme: To find our way, we sort things and people out into categories. We put labels on people, classifying them with others of the same kind: introvert and extrovert; gifted, average, and retarded; workaholics, time servers, and dropouts. When such categories are carefully set up, they help us understand people, and they guide us in our dealings with them. But often such categories are too narrow, too one-sided, or unfair. Individuals complain that the labels we put on them do not do them justice; they feel misrepresented, nailed into a box. When does a representative type become a narrow or offensive stereotype? The writers in this group set up representative types. But they also question narrow stereotypes, like the ones Marya Mannes observed in television commercials.

WRITER'S GUIDE 6:
Division and Classification

The two most widely useful methods of organizing a paper are **division** and **classification**. We use these methods again and again to bring order into a mass of material. We use them to set up a strategy allowing us to take up one major part of our subject at a time.

Some subjects divide along already established lines. A brief guide describing American colleges to foreign students might take up in turn two-year colleges, four-year colleges, and graduate schools. But more often you as the writer will have to set up the categories that suit your purpose. You will have to sort out and classify—pigeonholing examples and details according to a system that you yourself have devised. When you ask how people define a "good education," you may decide that their definitions tend to be of three different kinds. Their views may fit under three major headings that reflect what different people consider most important:

 I. A subject-centered ideal of education
    (with the emphasis on a thorough grounding in an academic discipline like math, history, or literature)

 II. A teacher-centered ideal of education
    (with the emphasis on outstanding teachers who served as models or as inspiration)

 III. A student-centered ideal of education
    (with the emphasis on how students were recognized, encouraged, motivated, and made to realize their potential)

A clearly worked out scheme of division or classification will often organize a paper or an article as a whole. When organizing such a paper, remember the following guidelines:

(1) *Use ready-made lines of division when they suit your purpose.* Often major lines of division are already built into the subject matter, ready for use. A writer charting changing patterns of immigration will at first face a bewildering array of facts and figures. One way to sort these out might be to classify people who have come from abroad according to their legal status. In this case, major boundary lines are already established by law. The writer's scheme of classification might look like this:

A Nation of Immigrants

THESIS: As in earlier days, Americans today everywhere encounter representatives of a new wave of immigrants, legal and illegal.

    I. Temporary visitors (who are in the country legally for a limited time for study, visits, or travel)

    II. Illegal aliens (who have entered the country, or stayed on, without valid legal papers)

    III. Resident aliens (who have entered legally to work and live here but who are not, or not yet, U. S. citizens)

    IV. Naturalized U. S. citizens

However, for a different purpose a writer might sort out people coming to this country along different lines. A writer who is opposed to an increased flow of immigration might focus on what *entitles* people to immigrate:

    I. Traditional national quotas

    II. Marriage to U. S. citizens or close kinship

    III. Preferred occupational categories

    IV. Legalized illegal immigrants (through amnesties or in hardship cases, for instance)

(2) *Set up your own categories as needed or appropriate.* Often you will have to draw your own boundary lines, setting up major kinds. As you set up your scheme of classification, ask yourself: "How well do my categories accommodate the evidence? How effectively will they help my readers find their way?" A scheme like the following will be convincing if it seems to fit many (or all) of the examples that come to mind. The system of classification will work if it enables readers to pigeonhole many of the books about schools that they have read:

GENERAL   School novels may be divided and subdivided,
SCHEME: but the essential distinction—perhaps it is also the essential distinction among students—separates those that are proschool from those that are antischool.

FIRST CATEGORY: In proschool novels, school is the seat of order and
civilization, the clean well-lighted place where conventions are learned and values accepted . . . prizes
and demerits are justly given, the class has a top and
a bottom, and the Head, in his (or her) wisdom, separates the sheep from the goats. . . .

SECOND   Antischool novels assume that school is the
CATEGORY: place where we learn the conventions of oppression
and hypocrisy. . . . Antischool novels are written
from the point of view of the anarchic student, ever
hopeful that something deliciously awful will happen, that all the teachers, the bores, and the pillars
of the community will by some happy accident be
unveiled . . .
—Frances Taliaferro, "Blackboard Art," *Harper's*

(3) *Set up your major categories according to a consistent principle of classification.* Suppose you wanted to sort out the students at
your college into major kinds. You could classify them according to
their occupational goals, or according to how serious they are about
their studies, or according to their political outlook. Each line of investigation would enable you to set up groupings that would be part of the
same spectrum. If your principle of classification is political outlook,
for instance, your groupings might range from radical through moderate to ultraconservative. Confusion starts when your basic principle of
selection is not clear, or when you unexpectedly shift from one to the
other.

The writer's purpose will determine which of several possible criteria will provide the basic principle of selection. In his autobiography,
Theodore H. White, known for his chronicles of presidential campaigns, at one point writes about the pecking order among students
during his days at Harvard University. He accordingly organizes this
section of the book according to the students' *social class.* He shows
how their social origins determined the opportunities open to them
and channeled them into characteristic pursuits and activities:

THESIS: Students divide themselves by their own dis-
The general   criminations in every generation, and the group I ran
scheme   with had a neat system of classification. Harvard, my
own group held, was divided into three groups—
white men, gray men, and meatballs. I belonged to
the meatballs, by self-classification.

FIRST GROUP:
The
"aristocracy"

White men were youngsters of great name; my own class held a Boston Saltonstall, a New York Straus, a Chicago Marshall Field, two Roosevelts (John and Kermit), a Joseph P. Kennedy, Jr. The upper classes had another Roosevelt (Franklin, Jr.), a Rockefeller (David, with whom I shared a tutor in my sophomore year), a Morgan, and New York and Boston names of a dozen different fashionable pedigrees. Students of such names had automobiles; they went to Boston deb parties, football games, the June crew race against Yale; they belonged to clubs. . . .

SECOND GROUP:
The solid
middle class

Between white men above and meatballs at the bottom came the gray men. The gray men were mostly public high school boys, sturdy sons of America's middle class. They went out for football and baseball, manned the *Crimson* and the *Lampoon,* ran for class committees and, later in life, for school committees and political office. They came neither of the aristocracy nor of the deserving poor, as did most meatballs and scholarship boys. . . .

THIRD GROUP:
The "mobile
lower middle
classes"

Meatballs were usually day students or scholarship students. We were at Harvard not to enjoy the games, the girls, the burlesque shows of the Old Howard, the companionship, the elms, the turning leaves of fall, the grassy banks of the Charles. We had come to get the Harvard badge, which says "Veritas," but really means a job somewhere in the future, in some bureaucracy, in some institution, in some school, laboratory, university, or law firm.

—"Growing Up in the Land of Promise," *Atlantic*

(4) *Base your classification on a combination of related criteria when they clearly serve your purpose.* Often several related factors work together to help us sort out people or things into categories. A marketing study, for instance, might set up the following four major groups of consumers:

I. Late teens

II. College students

III. Working singles

IV. Young marrieds

This scheme roughly follows chronological order, but age is only one of the factors that shape the buying habits of each group, and in strictly chronological terms the categories overlap. Other factors, such as occupational and marital status, combine with age level to determine the buying patterns of each category. College students, for instance, are as a group relatively young (and often active and in good health). They are often single (but with strong remaining ties to home and parents). A consumer's profile of the typical college student would show the combined effect of these factors:

♦ (Living habits) They spend much money on snacks, milk, and orange juice; they are seldom seen in expensive or pretentious restaurants.

♦ (Activities) They are buyers of sports equipment; they own, on the average, three pairs of shoes used in active sports.

♦ (Family status) They are away from home and, as a result, are travelers; in the last twelve months, 34 percent of them bought traveler's checks. On the average, they make six long-distance calls a month during the school year.

(5) *Develop each category with relevant examples and convincing details.* In a paper about stereotypes perpetuated by the media, a black student wrote about stereotypical images of blacks found in movies and on television. He set up three major categories, proceeding in roughly chronological order from the loyal Negro servants of *Gone with the Wind* to today's athletic superstars:

  I. Stereotypes concerning social class
     (tendency to appear in menial occupations, as gardeners, servants, and the like)

 II. Stereotypes concerning lifestyle
     (natural inclination toward music and dancing)

III. Stereotypes concerning athletic ability
     (tendency to excel in physical rather than intellectual or creative pursuits)

The following paragraph contains the kind of detailed example needed for each of these categories.

Many of the stereotypes we see in the area of athletics are not openly offensive but nevertheless damaging. Many sports announcers consciously or unconsciously reinforce subtle stereotypes. *For example,* a black running back may fake out the defense and run for a touchdown. The announcer will compliment the black player on his superb "instinct." This term implies that the running back did not have to think—he just had to take the ball and run and let his "natural rhythm" take him into the end zone.

To convince your readers that your categories are valid, you will have to make sure that your examples will not seem like isolated instances but will indeed seem representative. Often a mix of several examples briefly surveyed or summarized and then one or two followed up in detail will best do the job.

(6) *Use transitions to show the logical relationships between your categories.* Provide the logical links that show how your categories fit into the larger picture you are sketching out. Avoid lame transitions like "*Another* common stereotype is . . . " or "We should *also* mention that . . . " In a paper about stereotypes, use transitions that show how each category fits into your overall plan. Are you going from the crude and obvious to the more subtle? Are you looking at contradictory or opposed images—perhaps in order to look later for a common thread? Provide the necessary signals for your reader:

> *At one extreme,* we see the handsome, macho young single who wears designer jeans, drives a fast car, and is pursued by beautiful women . . .

> *At the opposite extreme,* we see the clumsy young husband who is displayed hopelessly attempting to make waffles while his son, after patiently waiting, says, "Why don't you make them like Mom does?"

Look at the transitional phrases at the beginning of each major section in the following discussion of television commercials:

Father Knows Best

THESIS: Television commercials continue to distinguish between "woman's work" and a "man-sized job."

FIRST CATEGORY: *On the one hand,* women seem to sell most of
(One clear-cut the products helping their sisters to maintain and
extreme) sanitize "home sweet home." Women in commercials are busy wiping noses, dishes, floors, and toilet bowls. . . .

SECOND   *On the other hand,* television commercials use
CATEGORY: men to sell what is big and important. From tires and
(Opposite   airline tickets to insurance, legal services, and in-
clear-cut   vestments, males generally sell the things that matter
extreme)   in the outside world. . . .

THIRD   *Admittedly,* current commercials are beginning
CATEGORY: to show men and women together, sharing work and
(In-between   sharing domestic responsibilities. Often, however,
area)   while both he and she may go off to work, it is still
               she who makes and serves the coffee. . . .

To sum up: Organizing a paper often means breaking up a subject
into its major parts or sorting material out into major kinds. A crucial
part of your planning for a paper will often be to construct an outline
that sets up major divisions or major categories. Ask yourself: Do the
dividing lines do justice to the subject matter? Do your categories serve
your purpose? Have you made the overall plan clear enough for the
reader?

PREWRITING ACTIVITIES 6

1. Many *widely used schemes* of classification channel our thinking
almost without our being consciously aware of them. Choose one of the
following schemes. For each of the three or four subheadings, write
down associations, details, or images as they come to mind. Write
quickly. Try to work up a rich fund of material for use in class discussion of the usefulness and limitations of the system of classification you
have chosen. Write on one of the following:

   a. upper class–middle class–lower class

   b. urban–suburban–rural

   c. child–adolescent–adult–the elderly

   d. right wing–moderate–left wing

   e. single–married–divorced

2. *Stereotypes* trigger automatic, unthinking associations. For several of the following, write down ideas, memories, and associations that
the term brings to mind. Use each term as a trigger word: Write quickly,
without stopping to think. Then go back to *one* of these for a closer
look. Look at the reality behind the stereotype, drawing on your observation, experience, and reading. Possible choices:

- the military
- Southern sheriff
- Latin lover
- blonde
- Asians

- Arabs
- natural rhythm
- politician
- football player
- psychiatrist

3. Set up a scheme of classification that would help you classify *friends and acquaintances.* For instance, you may want to set up three or four categories on a scale from introvert to extrovert, or from serious student to casual student. Describe and illustrate each category.

Ellen Goodman and
Sam Keen
Three Portraits

(1)

Ellen Goodman

The Company Man

HE WORKED himself to death, finally and precisely, at 3:00 A.M. 1
Sunday morning.

The obituary didn't say that, of course. It said that he died of a 2
coronary thrombosis—I think that was it—but everyone among his
friends and acquaintances knew it instantly. He was a perfect Type A, a
workaholic, a classic, they said to each other and shook their heads—
and thought for five or ten minutes about the way they lived.

This man who worked himself to death finally and precisely at 3:00 3
A.M. Sunday morning—on his day off—was fifty-one years old and a
vice-president. He was, however, one of six vice-presidents, and one of
three who might conceivably—if the president died or retired soon
enough—have moved to the top spot. Phil knew that.

He worked six days a week, five of them until eight or nine at night, 4
during a time when his own company had begun the four-day week for
everyone but the executives. He worked like the Important People. He
had no outside "extracurricular interests," unless, of course, you think
about a monthly golf game that way. To Phil, it was work. He always ate
egg salad sandwiches at his desk. He was, of course, overweight, by 20
or 25 pounds. He thought it was okay, though, because he didn't
smoke.

On Saturdays, Phil wore a sports jacket to the office instead of a 5
suit, because it was the weekend.

He had a lot of people working for him, maybe sixty, and most of 6
them liked him most of the time. Three of them will be seriously considered for his job. The obituary didn't mention that.

But it did list his "survivors" quite accurately. He is survived by his 7
wife, Helen, forty-eight years old, a good woman of no particular mar-
ketable skills, who worked in an office before marrying and mothering.
She had, according to her daughter, given up trying to compete with
his work years ago, when the children were small. A company friend
said, "I know how much you will miss him." And she answered, "I
already have."

"Missing him all these years," she must have given up part of her- 8
self which had cared too much for the man. She would be "well taken
care of."

His "dearly beloved" eldest of the "dearly beloved" children is a 9
hard-working executive in a manufacturing firm down South. In the day
and a half before the funeral, he went around the neighborhood re-

searching his father, asking the neighbors what he was like. They were embarrassed.

10   His second child is a girl, who is twenty-four and newly married. She lives near her mother and they are close, but whenever she was alone with her father, in a car driving somewhere, they had nothing to say to each other.

11   The youngest is twenty, a boy, a high-school graduate who has spent the last couple of years, like a lot of his friends, doing enough odd jobs to stay in grass and food. He was the one who tried to grab at his father, and tried to mean enough to him to keep the man at home. He was his father's favorite. Over the last two years, Phil stayed up nights worrying about the boy.

12   The boy once said, "My father and I only board here."

13   At the funeral, the sixty-year-old company president told the forty-eight-year-old widow that the fifty-one-year-old deceased had meant much to the company and would be missed and would be hard to replace. The widow didn't look him in the eye. She was afraid he would read her bitterness and, after all, she would need him to straighten out the finances—the stock options and all that.

14   Phil was overweight and nervous and worked too hard. If he wasn't at the office, he was worried about it. Phil was a Type A, a heart-attack natural. You could have picked him out in a minute from a lineup.

15   So when he finally worked himself to death, at precisely 3:00 A.M. Sunday morning, no one was really surprised.

16   By 5:00 P.M. the afternoon of the funeral, the company president had begun, discreetly of course, with care and taste, to make inquiries about his replacement. One of three men. He asked around: "Who's been working the hardest?"

(2)

Ellen Goodman

Superworkingmom or Superdrudge?

17   THERE WEREN'T any stunning revelations in the news last week. The Bureau of Labor reported that the wage gap between men and women was on the increase, while a *Newsweek* cover story analyzed the fact that the numbers gap between working men and women was on the decrease.

No, there were no stunning bulletins. The monkey-in-the-middle of 18 all this change was again described as the average employed mother who is not only working more and earning less, but bearing the full load of family care. In short, the only equality she's won after a decade of personal and social upheaval is with the working mothers of Russia.

Many of the back-to-work women are still apologizing for changing 19 the rules of the mating game as they were writ back in 1955. They are doing penance by "doing it all," or "juggling" as the magazines put it so cutely. They read cheerleading articles that say, "You, too, Dora Daring, can manage a home and job, can keep your roots blond, your children squeaky clean and have their permission slips signed on time if only you learn a few organizing tricks!"

But one thing that is apparent is that the younger women of Amer- 20 ica aren't buying it. Superworkingmom looks more like Superdrudge to them.

A generation ago, young women felt that they had to choose be- 21 tween being a housewife and a career woman. Today's young women often feel their choice is between Superdrudge or not mothering at all. Most of the college women I have talked with look upon motherhood as The End. When you talk about having babies, they stare at you.

The "best and the brightest" women in their twenties not only have 22 a horror of being housewives but a dread of getting on that working-mother treadmill.

Still, they may not be seeing the whole story. Both of the main 23 pieces in the *Newsweek* article ended on the note, "Men may well have to spend more time running the house and raising the children." But that isn't future-think. It's happening right now in the bumper crop of two-parent working families bearing their first child in their thirties.

Many of those men already found out that they would have to share 24 the kids if they wanted them. These days, there is a new version of the old play, *Lysistrata*.[1] In this one, child-bearing-age women—especially those with high aspirations—are simply rejecting pregnancy until they get some assurances of partnership parenting.

For a while, it looked as if this generation would simply choose to 25 be "child-free." But now it appears that they have charted a new trend.

Many of these couples discuss everything short of college tuition 26 for the kids before they conceive them. Because of the hesitations of women, the burden of proof has often been shifted onto the men.

It is often the men in their thirties who are pushed to really "de- 27 cide" if they want to raise, not just "have" children. One friend quizzed

---

[1][Aristophanes' comedy *Lysistrata* was first performed in Athens in 411 B.C. In the play, the women of Athens refuse to sleep with their husbands in order to force them to make peace with Sparta.]

her husband as if she were an Internal Revenue agent: "Will you get up in the middle of the night? Will you stay home half the time when the kids are sick? Who will call for the sitter?"

28   As her husband recalls, "She was sure that the minute we had a child, she would have two jobs and I would be sitting in the living room waiting for din-din."

29   But, in fact, these couples have gone into parenting differently and seem to offer the most appealing shared life pattern to emerge slowly out of the morass of guilt and conflict in changing expectations.

30   They may well be the cutting edge of a massive change in the life cycle. By the thirties, after all, many of us have settled some of the issues of personal confidence and professional competence. Many are ready to make compromises, or simply ready to raise children.

31   In any case the first-time thirties parents seem better prepared for the pressures and ready to share them. The thing that seems to surprise them is the pleasure. They are enjoying kids, not just crisply coping. No one seems to have warned them about that.

(3)

Sam Keen

A New Breed

32   JAY, A CARPENTER who has worked for me on several occasions, is a barrel of a man, stout as an oak log. Though not yet thirty years old, his convictions are well seasoned; he is true to the grain of his own wood. On good days he shows up for work between 9 and 10 a.m. If it is raining, or his dog needs to go to the veterinarian, or he has promised to help a friend, or there is an exhibit of Zen art at the museum, he may not get here at all. As yet he hasn't called to say the day is too beautiful to spend working. But I wouldn't be surprised if he did. When he arrives, he unwraps his bundles of Japanese woodworking tools, removes the fine saws and chisels from their mahogany cases, puts some shakuhachi flute music on his tape deck, and begins methodically to sculpt the elaborate joints in the beams that will form the structure of the studio we are building. He works slowly, pausing to watch a hawk circle overhead, to tell a joke, to savor the smell of the wood. Occasion-

ally I try to hurry him. "That looks close enough, Jay," I say. "May as well take the time to do it right the first time," he replies and goes on working at his own pace. After several days he announces that the beams are ready to be hoisted into place. We lift and tug and push. Notch joins notch. Tongue slips into groove. The puzzle fits together. We sigh with relief. A satisfying day.

Some would say Jay is an underachiever, a dropout, that he lacks 33 ambition. A college graduate with honors in football, he works sporadically, for carpenter's wages. He has no pension, no health insurance, no fringe benefits. He drives an old truck and lives in a funky neighborhood near the industrial district of Oakland. When he doesn't need money, he tends his garden, writes poetry, paints, and studies Japanese and wood joinery. "I get by," he says. "It doesn't make any sense to sell your soul for security and have no time left to do the things you love."

I say Jay is one of a new breed of Americans who are refusing to 34 make work the central value in their lives. These light-hearted rebels have paused to consider the lilies of the field (executive coronaries and the pollution of the Love Canal) and have decided neither to toil nor to spin. They are turning everything upside down and calling into question the traditional, orthodox virtues of the Protestant work ethic and American dream. They are inventing new "life-styles," forging new myths and visions of the good life, new definitions of happiness.

The rebellion is directed *against* the long-reigning secular theol- 35 ogy of work that is best summed up in the words of Ayn Rand, whose popular philosophy romanticized capitalism and sanctified selfishness: ". . . your work is the process of achieving your values . . . your body is a machine, but your mind is its driver . . . your work is the purpose of your life, and you must speed past any killer who assumes the right to stop you . . . any value you might find outside your work, any other loyalty or love, can be only travelers you choose to share your journey with and must be travelers going on their own power in the same direction."² The rebels reject the sacred symbol $ and refuse to judge the worth of their lives by the economic equivalent of the Last Judgment— The Bottom Line. Disillusioned with the ideal of Progress, they are no longer willing to sacrifice present happiness for the promise of future economic security. In short, they have declared: the great God Work is dead.

---

²[Ayn Rand (1905–82), Russian-born advocate of a philosophy of competitiveness and self-reliance, wrote *The Fountainhead* (1943) and *Atlas Shrugged* (1957).]

USING THE DICTIONARY: Columnists like Ellen Goodman are trend-watchers who look out not only for new ideas but also for the new expressions and "buzzwords" that we use to talk about them. Check your dictionary for the following expressions that have become widely used. Then choose three of them that are not treated in your dictionary or treated very briefly. For each, write a short paragraph explaining its meaning, implications, and typical uses. Check the following: 1. *workaholic* (2) 2. *stock option* (13) 3. *parenting* (24) 4. *cutting edge* (30) 5. *coping* (31) 6. *underachiever* (33) 7. *dropout* (33) 8. *lifestyle* (34) 9. *work ethic* (34) 10. *bottom line* (35)

THE WRITER'S AGENDA:

Many readers read the work of columnists like Ellen Goodman with a sense of recognition. Frequently, a column makes them say, "Yes, I have seen this kind of person myself" or "Yes, I have experienced the same thing." Study the way these two authors sketch out types that many of their readers will recognize as representative of general trends.

1. Goodman gives us a vivid dramatized account of what she considers a typical "company man." What are the features that for her make the person representative of a widespread type? Describe the person's role in the company, his work habits, and his relationship with his family. What other points are an important or revealing part of the picture?

2. What are the key features in Goodman's portrait of the "average employed mother"? What guidance does she provide for the future in her discussion of choices or *alternatives* facing young women?

3. Sam Keen assembles characteristic details that help define a person representing "a new breed of Americans." What are the most important or striking of these details? What are the major points he makes when tracing the *contrast* with "orthodox" or traditional values?

4. Writers with a lively sense of **irony** are quick to notice the contrast between what is and what should be. Our sense of irony makes us react with bitter amusement or with a wry smile when people fail to live up to expectations—whether our own or those of society. Find and discuss several examples of this kind of irony in this group of selections.

FOR DISCUSSION OR WRITING:

1. What in these three selections do you recognize as typical or representative? Turning to your own experience, discuss examples or observations that would bear out the general descriptions given by the two authors.

2. Whenever we describe something as typical, we run the risk of giving a one-sided or oversimplified picture. Where in these three selections do you feel there is a danger of oversimplification or exaggeration? (Defend your answer.)

3. How do the types of workers described in these selections fit into a more general picture of Americans at work? How large or how limited a part do these types play in the larger picture? Prepare your *own* portrait of one major type that is not included in these brief portraits.

4. Do a close-up of a representative person. Choose a type that you know well from personal observation or experience. Possible types are the unemployed teenager, the person running a small store or other business, the career woman, the high school principal. Model your portrait of the type on one of the portraits you have read.

5. Set up your own classification of several representative types of workers. Identify and describe several major categories or types. Use one or a combination of the following as the basis of your classification: the kind of work they do, the attitude toward work, and the role work plays in their lives. For instance, on the basis of different attitudes toward work, major types might range from people considering their work a calling or vocation (ministers, missionaries) to people disliking their work and working strictly to make a living. Give detailed examples.

6. Immigrant or minority groups differ in how completely they have become submerged in the "mainstream" culture. In different degrees, members of immigrant or minority groups maintain a separate identity, with their own ways and cultural traditions. Set up a system of classification based on the degree of assimilation. Identify and describe three or four major types or categories. Show how they differ in their attitude toward and relationship with mainstream American culture. Draw on examples from your own observation, experience, and reading.

BACKGROUND: Marya Mannes was born in 1904 in New York City. She worked as writer and editor for publications including *Vogue, The Reporter, McCall's* and the *New York Times*. She became widely known as a television critic who vigorously condemned the failure of the medium to live up to its educational and cultural potential. In addition to her role as a television critic with high standards, she wrote as a playwright, feature editor, radio scriptwriter, drama critic, and author of satirical verse. In 1961, she published *The New York I Know*, a "fierce, loving, and critical" portrait of her native New York City. Her autobiographical *Out of My Time* appeared in 1971. Her work is that of a true professional, combining sharp-eyed observation, outspoken advocacy of her convictions, and satirical bite. She was an early critic of the "gigantic dosage of violence" in television entertainment. In the following article, first published in 1970, she took aim at another target that has since attracted the attention of many writers: the stereotyping of women in television commercials.

Marya Mannes

Television: The Splitting Image

GUIDE TO READING: Pay special attention to how this author *sorted out* the constant stream of images in television commercials. What recurrent types did she identify—types of people that appeared in commercials again and again? What examples did she give to make each type real? What were her objections to each of the major types she described? How does she relate her discussion of stereotyping in commercials to larger issues raised by the role of television in our society? How have things changed?

1   A BRIDE WHO looks scarcely fourteen whispers, "Oh, Mom, I'm so *happy!"* while a doting family adjusts her gown and veil and a male voice croons softly, "A woman is a harder thing to be than a man. She has more feelings to feel." The mitigation of these excesses, it appears, is a feminine deodorant called Secret, which allows our bride to approach the altar with security as well as emotion.

A successful actor turned pitchman bestows his attention on a lady 2
with two suitcases, which prompt him to ask her whether she has been
on a journey. "No," she says, or words to that effect, as she opens the
suitcases. "My two boys bring back their soiled clothes every weekend
from college for me to wash." And she goes into the familiar litany of
grease, chocolate, mud, coffee, and fruit-juice stains, which presumably
record the life of the average American male from two to fifty. The actor
compliments her on this happy device to bring her boys home every
week and hands her a box of Biz, because "Biz *is* better."

Two women with stony faces meet cart to cart in a supermarket as 3
one takes a jar of peanut butter off a shelf. When the other asks her in a
voice of nitric acid why she takes that brand, the first snaps, "Because
I'm choosy for my family!" The two then break into delightful smiles as
Number Two makes Number One taste Jif for "mothers who are
choosy."

If you have not come across these dramatic interludes, it is because 4
you are not at home during the day and do not watch daytime television. It also means that your intestinal tract is spared from severe assaults, your credibility unstrained. Or, for that matter, you may look at
commercials like these every day and manage either to ignore them or
find nothing—given the fact of advertising—wrong with them. In that
case, you are either so brainwashed or so innocent that you remain
unaware of what this daily infusion may have done and is doing to an
entire people as the long-accepted adjunct of free enterprise and support of "free" television.

"Given the fact" and "long-accepted" are the key words here. Only 5
socialists, communists, idealists (or the BBC) fail to realize that a mass
television system cannot exist without the support of sponsors, that the
massive cost of maintaining it as a free service cannot be met without
the massive income from selling products. You have only to read of the
unending struggle to provide financial support for public, noncommer-
cial television for further evidence.

Besides, aren't commercials in the public interest? Don't they help 6
you choose what to buy? Don't they provide needed breaks from programming? Aren't many of them brilliantly done, and some of them
funny?

Tick off the yeses and what have you left? You have, I venture to 7
submit, these intangible but possibly high costs: the diminution of human worth, the infusion and hardening of social attitudes no longer
valid or desirable, pervasive discontent, and psychic fragmentation.

Should anyone wonder why deception is not an included detri- 8
ment, I suggest that our public is so conditioned to promotion as a way
of life, whether in art or politics or products, that elements of exaggeration or distortion are taken for granted. Nobody really believes that a

certain shampoo will get a certain swain, or that an unclogged sinus can make a man a swinger. People are merely prepared to hope it will.

9   But the diminution of human worth is much more subtle and just as pervasive. In the guise of what they consider comedy, the producers of television commercials have created a loathsome gallery of men and women patterned, presumably, on Mr. and Mrs. America. Women liberationists have a major target in the commercial image of woman flashed hourly and daily to the vast majority. There are, indeed, only four kinds of females in this relentless sales procession: the gorgeous teen-age swinger with bouncing locks; the young mother teaching her baby girl the right soap for skin care; the middle-aged housewife with a voice like a power saw; and the old lady with dentures and irregularity. All these women, to be sure, exist. But between the swinging sex object and the constipated granny there are millions of females rarely shown in commercials. These are—married or single—intelligent, sensitive women who bring charm to their homes, who work at jobs as well as lend grace to their marriage, who support themselves, who have talents or hobbies or commitments, or who are skilled at their professions.

10   We are left with the full-time housewife in all her whining glory: obsessed with whiter wash, moister cakes, shinier floors, cleaner children, softer diapers, and greaseless fried chicken. In the rare instances when these ladies are not in the kitchen, at the washing machine, or waiting on hubby, they are buying beauty shops (fantasy, see?) to take home so that their hair will have more body. Or out at the supermarket being choosy.

11   If they were attractive in their obsessions, they might be bearable. But they are not. They are pushy, loud-mouthed, stupid, and—of all things now—bereft of sexuality. Presumably, the argument in the tenets of advertising is that once a woman marries she changes overnight from plaything to floor-waxer.

12   To be fair, men make an equivalent transition in commercials. The swinging male with the mod hair and the beautiful chick turns inevitably into the paunchy slob who chokes on his wife's cake. You will notice, however, that the voice urging the viewer to buy the product is nearly always male: gentle, wise, helpful, seductive. And the visible presence telling the housewife how to get shinier floors and whiter wash and lovelier hair is almost invariably a man: the Svengali in modern dress, the Trilby (if only she were!), his willing object.[1]

13   Woman, in short, is consumer first and human being fourth. A wife and mother who stays home all day buys a lot more than a woman who lives alone or who—married or single—has a job. The young girl bent on marriage is the next most susceptible consumer. It is entirely understandable, then, that the potential buyers of detergents, foods, polishes,

---

[1] [Svengali is the evil hypnotist in the novel *Trilby* (1894) by George du Maurier.]

toothpastes, pills, and housewares are the housewives, and that the sex object spends most of *her* money on cosmetics, hair lotions, soaps, mouthwashes, and soft drinks.

Here we come, of course, to the youngest class of consumers, the 14 swinging teen-agers so beloved by advertisers keen on telling them (and us) that they've "got a lot to live, and Pepsi's got a lot to give." This affords a chance to show a squirming, leaping, jiggling group of beautiful kids having a very loud high on rock and—of all things—soda pop. One of commercial TV's most dubious achievements, in fact, is the reinforcement of the self-adulation characteristic of the young as a group.

As for the aging female citizen, the less shown of her the better. 15 She is useful for ailments, but since she buys very little of anything, not having a husband or any children to feed or house to keep, nor—of course—sex appeal to burnish, society and commercials have little place for her. The same is true, to be sure, of older men, who are handy for Bosses with Bad Breath or Doctors with Remedies. Yet, on the whole, men hold up better than women at any age—in life or on television. Lines on their faces are marks of distinction, while on women they are signatures of decay.

There is no question, in any case, that television commercials (and 16 many of the entertainment programs, notably the soap serials that are part of the selling package) reinforce, like an insistent drill, the assumption that a woman's function is that of wife, mother, and servant of men: the inevitable sequel to her earlier function as sex object and swinger.

At a time when more and more women are at long last learning to 17 reject these assumptions as archaic and demeaning, and to grow into individual human beings with a wide option of lives to live, the sellers of the nation are bent upon reinforcing the ancient pattern. They know only too well that by beaming their message to the Consumer Queen they can justify her existence as the housebound Mrs. America: dumber than dumb, whiter than white.

The conditioning starts very early: with the girl child who wants the 18 skin Ivory soap has reputedly given her mother, with the nine-year-old who brings back a cake of Camay instead of the male deodorant her father wanted. (When she confesses that she bought it so she could be "feminine," her father hugs her, and, with the voice of a child-molester, whispers, "My little girl is growing up on me, huh.") And then, before long, comes the teenaged bride who "has feelings to feel."

It is the little boys who dream of wings, in an airplane commercial; 19 who grow up (with fewer cavities) into the doers. Their little sisters turn into *Cosmopolitan* girls, who in turn become housewives furious that their neighbors' wash is cleaner than theirs.

There is good reason to suspect that this manic obsession with 20 cleanliness, fostered, quite naturally, by the giant soap and detergent interests, may bear some responsibility for the cultivated sloppiness of so many of the young in their clothing as well as in their chosen hide-outs. The compulsive housewife who spends more time washing and vacuuming and polishing her possessions than communicating to, or stimulating her children creates a kind of sterility that the young would instinctively reject. The impeccably tidy home, the impeccably tidy lawn are—in a very real sense—unnatural and confining.

21   Yet the commercials confront us with broods of happy children, some of whom—believe it or not—notice the new fresh smell their clean, white sweatshirts exhale thanks to Mom's new "softener."

22   Who are, one cannot help but ask, the writers who manage to combine the sales of products with the selling-out of human dreams and dignity? Who people this cosmos of commercials with dolts and fools and shrews and narcissists? Who know so much about quirks and mannerisms and ailments and so little about life? So much about presumed wants and so little about crying needs?

23   Do they not know, these extremely clever creators of commercials, what they could do for their audience even while they exploit and entertain them? How they could raise the levels of manners and attitudes while they sell their wares? Or do they really share the worm's-eye view of mass communication that sees, and addresses, only the lowest common denominator?

24   It can be argued that commercials are taken too seriously, that their function is merely to amuse, engage, and sell, and that they do this brilliantly. If that were all to this wheedling of millions, well and good. But it is not. There are two more fallouts from this chronic sales explosion that cannot be measured but that at least can be expected. One has to do with the continual celebration of youth at the expense of maturity. In commercials only the young have access to beauty, sex, and joy in life. What do older women feel, day after day, when love is the exclusive possession of a teenage girl with a bobbing mantle of hair? What older man would not covet her in restless impotence?

25   The constant reminder of what is inaccessible must inevitably produce a subterranean but real discontent, just as the continual sight of things and places beyond reach has eaten deeply into the ghetto soul. If we are constantly presented with what we are not or cannot have, the dislocation deepens, contentment vanishes, and frustration reigns. Even for the substantially secure, there is always a better thing, a better way, to buy. That none of these things makes a better life may be consciously acknowledged, but still the desire lodges in the spirit, nagging and pulling.

26   This kind of fragmentation works in potent ways above and beyond the mere fact of program interruption, which is much of the time more

of a blessing than a curse, especially in those rare instances when the commercial is deft and funny: the soft and subtle sell. Its overall curse, due to the large number of commercials in each hour, is that it reduces the attention span of a people already so conditioned to constant change and distraction that they cannot tolerate continuity in print or on the air.

Specifically, commercial interruption is most damaging during that 27 10 percent of programming (a charitable estimate) most important to the mind and spirit of a people: news and public affairs, and drama.

To many (and among these are network news producers), commer- 28 cials have no place or business during the vital process of informing the public. There is something obscene about a newscaster pausing to introduce a deodorant or shampoo commercial between an airplane crash and a body count. It is more than an interruption; it tends to reduce news to a form of running entertainment, to smudge the edges of reality by treating death or disaster or diplomacy on the same level as household appliances or a new gasoline.

Enormous amounts of time, money, and talent go into commer- 29 cials. Technically they are often brilliant and innovative, the product not only of the new skills and devices but of imaginative minds. A few of them are both funny and endearing.

Among the enlightened sponsors, moreover, are some who manage 30 to combine an image of their corporation and their products with accuracy and restraint.

What has to happen to mass medium advertisers as a whole, and 31 especially on TV, is a totally new approach to their function not only as sellers but as social influencers. They have the same obligation as the broadcast medium itself: not only to entertain but to reflect, not only to reflect but to enlarge public consciousness and human stature.

This may be a tall order, but it is a vital one at a time when Ameri- 32 cans have ceased to know who they are and where they are going, and when all the multiple forces acting upon them are daily diminishing their sense of their own value and purpose in life, when social upheaval and social fragmentation have destroyed old patterns, and when survival depends on new ones.

If we continue to see ourselves as the advertisers see us, we have 33 no place to go. Nor, I might add, has commercial broadcasting itself.

 USING THE DICTIONARY: Marya Mannes uses many words with strong negative **connotations**. Explain what is unflattering about each italicized word in the following phrases. Check unfamiliar words in your dictionary. 1. a *doting* family (1)

2. a male voice *croons* (1) 3. an actor turned *pitchman* (2)
4. a familiar *litany* (2) 5. a *dubious* achievement (14) 6. *self-adulation* of the young (14) 7. *archaic* and *demeaning* assumptions (17) 8. a *manic* obsession (20) 9. a kind of *sterility* (20) 10. *dolts . . . shrews* and *narcissists* (21) 11. *quirks* and *mannerisms* (21) 12. this *wheedling* (23) 13. restless *impotence* (23) 14. the *dislocation* deepens (24)

THE WRITER'S AGENDA:

To many jaded viewers, commercials on television mean merely one pleading or cajoling sales message after the other. The author of this article wanted to make us *pay attention.* She did so by focusing on several recurring types who people these commercials and who together add up to a revealing pattern.

1. What is the author's central **thesis?** Sum up and explain the major charges that she brings against television commercials in this article. What does she mean by the "hardening of social attitudes no longer valid or desirable"? What does she mean by the "diminution of human worth"?

2. The author has classified the women who appear in television commercials under *four major headings.* What are the four major types? Describe each type, drawing on concrete details the author provides in different parts of the article.

3. What, according to the author, makes each of these types a damaging misrepresentation or stereotype? What are her *objections* to each? Where does she most forcefully or most directly champion the truths misrepresented by these stereotypes?

4. The author is determined to be fair in her account of how *men* are represented in commercials. She tries to give the kind of balanced account that would reassure readers suspicious of one-sided or exaggerated charges. On the one hand, what negative or stereotyped images of men does she find in commercials? On the other hand, what features of commercials make men appear in superior traditional roles?

5. In several paragraphs toward the end of her introduction, and again in her concluding paragraphs, Mannes discusses some of the *larger issues* raised by the role television plays in our lives. What are some of these issues? What are the standards she applies or the goals she sets for television as a medium? (Does she have anything good to say about the medium as she observed it?)

6. Mannes has a gift for **satire**—she knows how to use cruel humor as a weapon in attacking things she deplores. She has a gift for the memorable concrete phrase or image with a strong satirical touch ("the worm's-eye view of mass communication"). Find and discuss a few striking examples.

FOR DISCUSSION OR WRITING:

1. Compare the image of women projected in current television commercials with the situation described by the author. Do the stereotypes she describes survive? Where and how? Has there been progress toward a more balanced or truthful picture of women in commercials and advertising? Where and how? (Give detailed examples.)

2. What stereotypes about women, other than those observed by Mannes in commercials, exist in our society? How and where are they kept alive? Identify three or four major stereotypes and give detailed examples for each. (What are their probable causes or origins? What harm do they do? What are possible remedies?)

3. Do the media, and especially movies and television, keep alive stereotypes about men? Sort out and classify prevailing male stereotypes. Limit yourself to several major types and give detailed examples for each.

4. How much truth is there in the stereotype? Of the many groups in our society that are misrepresented by stereotypes, choose one that you know well from personal observation or experience. Write a paper that "talks back" to the stereotype—or that shows to what extent the stereotype may be true. In the first half of your paper, explore the prevailing stereotype as it is promoted by jokes and stories, movies and television, or other means. In the second half, draw on your own observation of or experience with the group. Try to show the reality that is obscured or misrepresented by the stereotype. Choose from groups like the following: a. (social or occupational groups) members of motorcycle clubs, politicians, "schoolmarms," police officers, athletes, "good ole boys," sales representatives b. (ethnic or regional groups) the Irish, Texans, Italians, Germans, Asians, Mexicans, Jews, native Americans, Arabs.

5. Like Mannes, many television critics see on television much that appeals to the "lowest common denominator." Set up a system of classification for shows that in your judgment fall under this general heading. Describe and illustrate fully three or four major types.

BACKGROUND: Paul Fussell is a widely published teacher of literature and a frequent contributor to national journals. He was born in 1924 in Pasadena, California, and was educated at Pomona College and Harvard University. He became a professor of English at Rutgers University and published on subjects including Walt Whitman and Samuel Johnson. Toward the end of World War II, he served with an American infantry unit in France. In 1975, he published *The Great War in Modern Memory,* which he dedicated to an American sergeant killed next to him in France in March 1945. The book deals with the British experience on the Western Front during the earlier war, from 1914 to 1918. It records the disillusionment of a generation of writers, many of them killed in the war, whose legacy was an abiding distrust of the people who had described war as the "great adventure," in which brave comrades vanquish the base foe. In the article that follows, first published in *Harper's,* Fussell looks with the trained eye of the cultural historian at a peacetime ritual: the Indianapolis 500, the annual motor racing classic.

Paul Fussell

Speedway

GUIDE TO READING: In this essay, the author deals with two related problems of classification. In much of the essay, he discusses the Indianapolis race in relation to the *social status* of the spectators. He places spectators for sports events on a spectrum ranging from upper class (absent at Indy) through middle class to lower class (the "proles," or proletarians). However, he also examines automobile racing in relation to *other spectator sports* like rodeo or bullfighting. As you read the essay, identify the key criteria he uses in setting apart types of spectators and types of sports.

1   In 1982, THE violent death of driver Gordon Smiley at Indianapolis in May, only a week after the violent death of driver Gilles Villeneuve in Belgium, started a cascade of objections to motor racing, most of them based on the assumption that human beings are rational creatures, despite evidence to the contrary. In *Time,* Tom Callahan deplored the whole Indy enterprise: "Some 450,000 people," he wrote,

"will perch or picnic at the Speedway on Sunday. Nobody knows how many of them are ghouls spreading their blankets beside a bad intersection." This reprehension of ghoulishness was attended by four gruesome color photographs intended specifically to gratify the ghoul in all of us. At the same time, Frank Deford was setting off his anti-Indy blast in *Sports Illustrated,* finding the race not a sport but a mere hustling of automotive products ("The drivers at Indy look much less like athletes than like a lot of congested billboards"). He concluded that among the spectators lurk a significant number of "barbarians." George Vecsey, in the sports pages of *The New York Times,* suggested that the Indy race is becoming too dangerous to be regarded as a sport. "I can see accidents," he said, "on the Long Island Expressway."

Were these people right? Is the Indy 500 a sporting event, or is it something else? And if something else, is it evil or benign? 2

Although the automotive industry moved to Detroit early in this 3 century, Indianapolis is still a motor city, swarming with car washes and auto-parts stores, and the sign on the road into town from the airport, WELCOME TO INDIANAPOLIS: CROSSROADS OF AMERICA, seems to imply that you're entering a place best reached by car. Here, nobody walks. One day I walked two and a half miles along Sixteenth Street to the Speedway, and in that one hour found myself literally the only person not in an automobile. Returning a few hours later, I was still the only walker, with the exception of a man who accosted me and tried to borrow sixty-two cents.

To a Northeasterner, Indianapolis seems at first to be a strangely 4 retrograde repository of piety and patriotism. When I arrived, an editorial in the only paper in town was raising a populist voice in a call for school prayer, and a front-page box offered "Today's Prayer," just above "Today's Chuckle." After a short sojourn in Indianapolis one is no longer surprised at the imperious sign in the store window, GO TO CHURCH SUNDAY. Catholics wishing to arrive at the race very early Sunday morning, like everyone else, have their needs taken care of by the Archdiocese of Indianapolis, which has ruled that they may fulfill their holy Sunday obligation "by attending Mass the evening before." Driving to the Speedway, the motorist passes a billboard advertising (of course) cars, but shouting also GOD BLESS AMERICA. At the Speedway, even at qualifying trials weeks before the race, the national anthem is played at every opportunity, and the official program offers odd, vainglorious ads like one inserted by the International Association of Machinists and Aerospace Workers: "PRIDE—Pride helped build America into the greatest nation on earth."

"Naptown" is what many locals call Indianapolis, and it does seem 5 a somnolent place. As I experienced the slowness of the Indianapolis pace—every transaction seems to drag on interminably, every delay welcomed with friendly patience—I began to wonder whether speed and danger were not celebrated there one day a year just for the sheer relief and the novelty of it, just because on all other days life was so safe and predictable and slow. But friendly as well, it must be said. Ron Dorson, an authority on the anthropology of Indy, observes that although "in most public social settings . . . it is considered socially deviant for strangers to approach one another," at the Speedway things are different. There, "it becomes perfectly acceptable to engage total strangers in conversation about lap times, automotive technology, Speedway management, or race-driver intrigue." There's something of pioneer individualism lingering in this friendliness, and on race Sunday, when you see the infield crowded with campers, tents, trailers, and "recreational vehicles," their occupants cooking and drawing water and cosseting children and making love in the friendliest fashion, you realize what the Indy setting really is: it's an early-nineteenth-century American pioneer campsite surrounded, as if fortuitously, by an early-twentieth-century two-and-a-half-mile track. And you almost begin to wonder if it's not the camping out, that primeval American ceremony of innocence, rather than the race and its hazards, that has drawn these crowds here.

6   I'd say the people can be divided into three social classes: the middles, who on race day tend, in homage to the checkered flag, to dress all in black and white and who sit in reserved seats; the high proles, who watch standing or lolling in the infield, especially at the turns, "where the action is"; and the uglies, the overadvertised, black-leathered, beer-sodden, pot-headed occupiers of that muddy stretch of ground in the infield at the first turn, known as the Snake Pit. These are the ones who, when girls pass, spiritlessly hold up signs reading SHOW US YOUR T—S. The uglies are sometimes taken to be the essence of Indy, and they are the people who, I think, Frank Deford has in mind when he speaks of "barbarians." But they are not the significant Indy audience. The middle class is, all those people arriving at the Speedway in cars bearing Purdue and Indiana State stickers.

7   The middles are privileged to participate in an exclusive social event, the classy pit promenade. Beginning three hours before the start, anyone who can wangle a pit pass strolls slowly up and down in the space between the pits and the track proper, all dressed up and watched enviously, he imagines, by some tens of thousands of his social inferiors in the stands. On race morning in Indianapolis this is the stylish place to be, a place where one wouldn't dare show oneself unshaven or in dirty clothes. Many spandy-clean black-and-white getups are to be seen there, including trousers with two-inch black-and-white squares. Even though the social tone is compromised a bit by the presence of representatives of the press (that's how I got there), the thing struck me as comparable with some of the great snob social operations

of the world, like appearing in or near the royal box at Ascot or nodding to well-dressed friends while strolling slowly down the Champs Elysées.[1] But this promenade was for middle-class people. The upper-middle class is not to be found at Indy. If you're the sort of person drawn to Forest Hills, or the Test Matches at Lord's, or the Americas Cup Races at Newport, you're not likely to be seen at the Speedway.[2]

From the outset, devotees of auto racing have felt anxieties about   8 its place on the class-status ladder. Is motor racing on a par with cockfighting and mud wrestling, or up there with football and perhaps even badminton? The surprise registered by an Indianapolis paper after the 1912 race speaks volumes, socially: "There has been no better-mannered gathering in Indianapolis. . . . There was no pushing, no crowding, no profanity, no discourtesies." When the Chief Steward issues the portentous injunction, "Gentlemen, start your engines," we may feel that the first word insists a bit too much. Presumably, if women drivers were to become a regular feature in the Indy, the formula would have to include "Ladies and . . ." Janet Guthrie, who has been on the premises (she was until 1982 the only woman to participate—three times), says: "I think that racing's image needs all the help it can get. It has traditionally been a lowbrow image."

The sense that racing will naturally sink prole-ward unless rigor-   9 ously disciplined is what one takes away from a reading of the rule book promulgated by the United States Auto Club, the official supervisor of Indy racing. Cars are not to bear "undignified names," "improper language or conduct" is forbidden, and everything must be neat and clean at all times, just the way a gentleman would want it: "*Appearance:* cars, crews, and all pit personnel whose appearance detracts from the character of the program may be excluded."

A similar aspiration to respectability seems to be partially responsi-   10 ble for euphemisms that abound at Indy. Just as the self-conscious middle class may remark that someone has "passed away" (sometimes "over"), the Indy public-address announcer will inform the spectators that "We have a fatality." Instead of saying there's been a terrible smash-up on the third turn, he'll say, "We have a yellow light." A car never hits the wall, it "gets into" it, or even "kisses" it, and speakers aspiring to even greater tastefulness might observe that the driver has "visited Cement City." Driver Danny Ongais, badly injured in a crash in 1981, spoke of it not as the crash or even the accident but as "the incident." Everywhere there is the gentleman's feeling that if you pre-

[1] [Ascot Heath is the site of famous traditional horse races in England; the *Champs Elysées* is the name of the fashionable avenue in the center of Paris.]

[2] [Forest Hills, on Long Island, is associated with tennis; Lord's, in London, with cricket; and Newport with yacht races.]

tend something has not happened, it has not. Thus the rule prohibiting cars to add oil during a race. Adding oil would publicly acknowledge, as racing journalist Terry Reed points out, "that a car is blowing (or leaking) its original supply on the track, making the course even more hazardous." Almost immediately after Gordon Smiley's body nauseatingly stained the wall, it was repainted, white and pure. Now his tire marks on the third turn run oddly into a clean expanse of white.

11   As Danny Ongais's indirection suggests, there are psychological as well as social reasons for all this euphemism. Racing is deadly dangerous, especially now that speeds around 200 miles an hour are the rule, which makes more true than ever Jackie Stewart's point: "Motor racing will always be dangerous because you are always going too fast for things around you." At eleven in the morning of May 22, 1982, the third day of qualifying at Indy, I entered the Speedway through an underpass running beneath the track itself and for the first time heard those cars screaming by just overhead. They give off not just an almost unbearable sudden noise, but shocking heat and concussion as well. In their appalling whoosh is the quintessential menace of the Machine. Not even an observer feels entirely safe at the Speedway, and indeed the spectators are in literal danger all the time—from hurtling machines, tires, and fragments, and from the deadly methanol fuel, which burns with a scarcely visible flame, consuming ears and fingers before onlookers are even aware that the victim's on fire. No wonder "13" is, by USAC edict, never used in car numbering.

12   Obviously there's much more going on here than is commonly imagined by the "Eastern press," and there's certainly more going on than an overpowering desire to see someone killed. There is a powerful and, in my view, benign element of ritual purgation about Indy, and the things purged are precisely such impurities as vulgarity, greed, snobbery, and sadism.

13   The events just preceding the race, presented always in the same order and with the same deliberate, ample timing, are enough to hint at this ritual element. It is a Sunday morning, a time once appropriated for rituals of purgation. When I asked why the race was run on Sunday despite protests from the local Baptists about profaning the Sabbath, and the inconvenience of closed liquor stores, I was told that Monday, a holiday, was always available as a rain date. But the race seems to gravitate to Sunday for deeper reasons.

14   We've entered the Speedway very early, at 7:00 or 8:00 in the morning, although the crazies will have poured in, already blotto on beer and clad in T-shirts proclaiming the wearer TOO DRUNK TO F—K, when the gates open at 5:00. We're all anticipating the hour of start, 11:00, the hour when, formerly, church services began. By 9:30 virtually everyone involved in the unvarying prestart ceremonies is in place. At 9:45, as—

I'm quoting the official program—"the Purdue University Band plays 'On the Banks of the Wabash,'" the cars, still inert, silent, dead things, a threat to no one, are pushed by hand from the pits to their starting positions on the too narrow track, where they are formed up in eleven rows of a viciously hazardous but thoroughly traditional three-abreast arrangement. At 10:34 the Chief Steward makes a stately circuit in the pace car, inspecting the track for impurities one last time. At 10:44, all rise: "The Star-Spangled Banner." At 10:47, heads bowed for the invocation, delivered by a local divine, who prays for a safe race and reminds us of the dead of all our wars—and of all past Indys. One minute later "Taps." It is Memorial Day, one suddenly remembers. Two minutes after "Taps," the band plays, quite slowly, "Back Home Again in Indiana."

As with a great many contemporary experiences, the meaning of 15 Indy is elusive because it won't fit familiar schemes of classification. The rationalist, trying to make sense of its competitive elements, concludes that news about it belongs on the sports page. But then Warner Wolf, the TV sports commentator, appalled by the destruction of Villeneuve and Smiley, argues that racing's not a sport at all and indignantly defames it as merely a thing about machines. Although there probably is a legitimate sport called "motor sport," indulged in largely by amateurs, Wolf is right in perceiving that what takes place at Indy is not a sport. The true nature of Indy is in its resemblance to other rituals in which wild, menacing, nonhuman things are tamed.

I'm thinking of the rodeo and the bullfight. Subduing beasts that, 16 unsubdued, would threaten man—that's the ritual of rodeo, and, with some additional deepening of the irrational element, of the bullfight as well. Just like at Indy, you can get hurt trying to subdue wild horses, killed trying to dominate bulls. Warner Wolf is also right when he notes that Indy is a thing about machines, but it's about machines only the way rodeos would be about broncos if no one were there to break them and bullfights about *toros* if no *toreros* were there to command them.[3] Indy enacts the ritual taming and dominating of machines, emphasizing the crucial distinction between man and machine, the one soft and vulnerable but quick with courage and resource, the other hard and threatening but cold and stupid. The cars are at Indy so that the drivers can be shown to be capable of dominating them, and the wonder and glory of the dominators is the point. Indy is thus a great Sunday-morning proclamation of human dignity, and no number of discarded chicken bones or trampled beer cans can change that. Like former Sunday-morning rituals, Indy insists that people are worth being saved.

Do some people, regardless, come to see drivers killed? Probably, 17

---

[3] [*Toro* and *torero* are Spanish for "bull" and "bullfighter."]

but as irrelevant a tiny number of the sick as those who enjoy seeing a bullfight ruined by the bullfighter's being gored. If you see someone die at Indy, you are seeing that the machine has won, and that's opposed to everything the ritual is saying. A longtime student of the race, Sam Posey, seems to get the point when he addresses the pleasure spectators take in identifying themselves with the driver-tamer of the machine. When things go wrong and the crowd sees a driver killed, he says, "They are terribly shocked and extremely depressed. They wish they had not been there." What the spectator wants to see—needs to see?—is the machine crashing, disintegrating, wheels flying off, and in the end the man springing out and waving "I'm okay." "Because that's the moment of the greatest thrill," says Posey. "That's when man has conquered the machine. The machine has bitten back, but the man jumps out laughing and therefore the spectator's dream of immortality is confirmed." Immortality: hence, value, and value much longer lasting than the value conferred on congeries of steel, aluminum, and rubber by the mere age of the machine.

 USING THE DICTIONARY: Although occasionally using informal words (*crazies, blotto*), the author generally draws on a **formal** vocabulary, often using words that we seldom hear in casual conversation. For which of the following examples can you find a simple everyday equivalent? For which of them is it hard to find a simple substitute, and why? 1. *cascade* (1) 2. *accost* (3) 3. *retrograde* (4) 4. *repository* (4) 5. *populist* (4) 6. *sojourn* (4) 7. *imperious* (4) 8. *vainglorious* (4) 9. *somnolent* (5) 10. *deviant* (5) 11. *cosset* (5) 12. *fortuitous* (5) 13. *primeval* (5) 14. *quintessential* (11) 15. *edict* (11) 16. *purgation* (12) 17. *divine* (n.) (14) 18. *elusive* (15) 19. *rationalist* (15) 20. *congeries* (17)

THE WRITER'S AGENDA:

The author of this article takes issue with people who are too quick to pigeonhole an event like the Indianapolis race according to ready-made categories. Drawing on his detailed observation of the race and the spectators, he shows us how he classifies the event according to the kind of audience it attracts and according to its symbolic meaning as entertainment.

1. Paul Fussell uses his introduction to identify *stereotypes* about the race and its spectators that his article will seek to correct. What are these stereotypes?

2. After the author asks his central question about the nature of the Indy 500 event, he uses the next three paragraphs to create the *setting*—from the city itself to the infield encampment at the race track. What are the three or four key qualities of the American "heartland" atmosphere that he stresses here? What are striking examples or illustrations?

3. In his account of the actual events at the race, the author concentrates on a central part of his thesis—the *middle-class* nature and appeal of the proceedings. What evidence does he use, and how convincing is it?

4. How does he use the "uglies" for *contrast*?

5. When discussing the danger to drivers and spectators, Fussell begins to explore the *symbolic meaning* of the race. What is his explanation, and how does it counter familiar misconceptions or criticisms? How does he use the contrast with rodeos or bullfights to support his point?

6. In his discussion of the race as a *ritual,* the author does not just examine the physical events but pays close attention to the use of language, music, and the like. Discuss examples.

FOR DISCUSSION OR WRITING:

1. How convincing is Fussell's defense of the race against the charge of "ghoulish violence"? How convincing is his claim that the race is a "great Sunday-morning proclamation of human dignity"?

2. The label *middle-class* is often applied to American popular culture and the American way of life by both hostile and friendly observers. How representative is what Fussell describes of middle-class values? How dominant or widespread are middle-class values and attitudes in American life?

3. Set up a system of classification that classifies sports according to the social status of the typical spectator or participant. For instance, describe upper-class, middle-class, and lower-class sports. Use convincing, detailed examples.

4. Set up a system of classification for sports according to the nature of the opponent or the nature of the challenge faced by the competitor. For instance, describe and illustrate

a. contests involving human competitors and animals

b. contests involving human competitors and machines

c. contests among human competitors

d. contests that pit human competitors against themselves

5. Set up a system of classification for public entertainments or spectacles in general. Classify them according to a major principle, or according to a combination of closely related ones.

6. In your opinion, are there sports that affirm human dignity and others that tend to lower or debase it? Argue your position, using detailed examples.

FOR FURTHER DISCUSSION AND WRITING: Arthur Ashe was one of the first black athletes to gain an international reputation in tennis, until then often considered a sport reserved for the leisured white upper middle class. He won the first United States Open championship as an amateur in 1968. He won the Wimbledon tournament in England in 1975. The article reprinted here was first published in the *New York Times*. How persuasive is the article? How widespread and how damaging are the stereotypes the author describes? To what extent do you agree or disagree with him, and why?

Arthur Ashe

A Black Athlete Looks at Education

SINCE MY sophomore year at UCLA, I have become convinced   1
that we blacks spend too much time on the playing fields and too little time in the libraries. Consider these facts: for the major professional sports of hockey, football, basketball, baseball, golf, tennis and boxing, there are roughly only 3170 major league positions available (attributing 200 positions to golf, 200 to tennis and 100 to boxing). And the annual turnover is small.

There must be some way to assure that those who try but don't   2
make it to pro sports don't wind up on street corners or in unemployment lines. Unfortunately, our most widely recognized role models are athletes and entertainers—"runnin'" and "jumpin'" and "singin'" and dancin'."

Our greatest heroes of the century have been athletes—Jack John-   3
son, Joe Louis, and Muhammad Ali. Racial and economic discrimination forced us to channel our energies into athletics and entertainment. These were the ways out of the ghetto, the ways to get that Cadillac, those regular shoes, that cashmere sport coat.

Somehow, parents must instill a desire for learning alongside the   4 desire to be Walt Frazier. Why not start by sending black professional athletes into high schools to explain the facts of life?

5   I have often addressed high school audiences and my message is always the same: "For every hour you spend on the athletic field, spend two in the library. Even if you make it as a pro athlete, your career will be over by the time you are 35. You will need that diploma."

6   Have these pro athletes explain what happens if you break a leg, get a sore arm, have one bad year or don't make the cut for five or six tournaments. Explain to them the star system, wherein for every star earning millions there are six or seven others making $15,000 or $20,000 or $30,000. Invite a bench-warmer or a guy who didn't make it. Ask him if he sleeps every night. Ask him whether he was graduated. Ask him what he would do if he became disabled tomorrow. Ask him where his old high school athletic buddies are.

7   We have been on the same roads—sports and entertainment—too long. We need to pull over, fill up at the library and speed away to Congress and the Supreme Court, the unions and the business world.

8   I'll never forget how proud my grandmother was when I graduated from UCLA. Never mind the Davis Cup. Never mind the Wimbledon title. To this day, she still doesn't know what those names mean. What mattered to her was that of her more than thirty children and grandchildren, I was the first to be graduated from college, and a famous college at that. Somehow, that made up for all those floors she scrubbed all those years.

CAUSE AND EFFECT:
Projections

The Common Theme: Much of the serious thinking we do is devoted to the systematic study of cause and effect. The first modern scientists defined science as the study of consequences: If we study the causes of disease, malnutrition, or crop failure, we can then change our ways accordingly to bring about different and more beneficial effects. Much serious writing analyzes the causes that explain current trends; it projects these trends into the future in order to recommend action needed to change or prevent the predicted results. Cause-and-effect thinking dominates writing on technical subjects, where to understand something typically means to know the causes that bring it about. But much writing on nontechnical subjects tries to apply cause-and-effect thinking to social or economic concerns in order to affect our decisions about the future. The writers in this unit write about subjects ranging from pesticides to the future of the family. But all three writers make us ask similar questions: "What are the causes of current trends? What will the results be if current trends continue? What would we have to do to bring about different results?"

WRITER'S GUIDE 7:
Analyzing Causes and Effects

In a structured argument, one thing follows from the other. We take the reader along step by logical step. When we are really serious about a subject, or when the conclusions to be drawn seem especially important, we may want to leave little to the reader's goodwill or personal preference. We try to lay the subject out in such a way that a rational person, looking at the matter coolly and objectively, will reach the same logical conclusions that we did.

One important kind of systematic, step-by-step reasoning is the analysis of causes and effects. Cause-and-effect thinking is built into much of the reasoning that helps us understand our world and enables us to function in it. The basic purpose of cause-and-effect reasoning is to explain *why:* We trace the causes of something to show why it came about, to show why things are as they are. Analyzing causes and their effects helps us understand what happened in the past, but at the same time it provides guidance for the future. When we understand the causes of something, we can change our behavior in order to produce different or more desirable effects. The following paragraph about a marathon swimmer's training describes the effects of the training. At the same time it shows what someone else would have to do to achieve similar results:

> I have been working on swimming since I was ten, four hours a day or more, every day, skipping the greater part of my social life. . . . What I do is analogous to other long-distance competitions: running, cycling, rowing, those sports where training time far exceeds actual competition time. But swimming burns more calories per minute than anything else. The lungs, heart and muscles must all be working at peak efficiency for this sport, which doesn't require brute strength but rather the strength of endurance. I can do a thousand sit-ups in the wink of an eye—and I never do sit-ups on a regular basis. I've run the mile in 5:15, not exactly Olympic caliber, but better than most women can do. My lung capacity is six-point-one liters, greater than that of a lot of football players. My heartbeat is forty-seven or forty-eight when I am at rest, compared to the normal seventy-two for other people. A conditioned athlete usually has a heartbeat of sixty plus. These characteristics are not due to genetics—I attained them by swimming hour after hour, year after year.
>
> —Diana Nyad, "Mind over Water"

Systematic analysis of cause and effect may provide the basic structure for a single paragraph or for a paper as a whole. The following guidelines chart major possible strategies for papers that focus on causes and their results:

(1) *Trace a chain of cause and effect.* Much cause-and-effect writing traces a sequence of events, showing not only how it happened but also why. The writer makes sure to include each necessary development that triggered the next stage or phase in the sequence. The basic model for such cause-and-effect writing is provided by science writers who reconstruct the causes at work in a chain of events like the following:

> The earth breathes, in a certain sense. . . . There may have been cycles of oxygen production and carbon dioxide consumption, depending on relative abundances of plant and animal life. . . . An overwhelming richness of vegetation *may have caused* the level of oxygen to rise above today's concentration, with a corresponding depletion of carbon dioxide. Such a drop in carbon dioxide *may have impaired* the "greenhouse" property of the atmosphere, which holds in the solar heat otherwise lost by radiation from the earth's surface. The fall in temperature *would in turn have shut off* much of living, and, in a long sigh, the level of oxygen may have dropped by 90 per cent. Berkner speculates that this is what happened to the great reptiles; their size may have been all right for a richly oxygenated atmosphere, but they had the bad luck to run out of air.
>
> —Lewis Thomas, *The Lives of a Cell*

Much writing about social and cultural trends traces similar cause-and-effect relationships to explain human behavior and human motives. Notice the **transitions** in the following paragraph, which signal major links in a chain of causes. The **topic sentence**, or statement of the key idea, sums up the basic cause-and-effect relationship:

TOPIC SENTENCE:	*The hostility toward work that has developed in this generation comes largely from sons of fathers who were workaholics.* The fathers of today's mid-
Root cause:	dle-class children lived through and were wounded by the great Depression. Anyone who grew up in the 1940's lives with the fear that the tide of prosperity might recede again, as it did in 1931, and then there
Second link:	would be no jobs. *As a result,* most of the men who have risen to middle-management positions devoted themselves to their work and their corporations with
Third link:	religious zeal: the job was the center of their lives. *And so* a generation of sons and daughters identify "work" as the villain who took Daddy away from

them and returned him tired and used-up at the end of the day. A thousand times in the average middle-class home a child eager to play with Daddy was told, "Not now, Daddy's tired" or "Daddy has to go to work." "Work" was the excuse that covered a multitude of sins.

—Sam Keen, "Lovers vs. Workers," *Quest*

(2) *Trace the varied consequences of a single major cause.* Often cause-and-effect writing shows the repercussions of an important change or a crucial historical development. For instance, the dramatic rise in the price of oil in the seventies had far-reaching effects on the way we live, ranging from larger heating bills and smaller automobiles to colder offices and a return to coal as a source of energy. Here is an example of how an article might focus on a single root cause and then show its far-reaching effects:

The Car Explosion

The number of cars and trucks in the country rose by 2.2 million annually in the decade of the 1950's and by 3.7 million a year in the 1960's. In the last decade it rose by 4.4 million a year—or five times as fast as the population. The car explosion expressed in those figures represents perhaps the dominant social event in the country. It explains why it has been so hard to frame an energy program; to clear up traffic, polluted air, and court dockets; and—most important of all—to do anything about the inner cities and their down-and-out populations.

THESIS: *The car is probably the foremost example of a technological innovation which developed, as it spread, vast and largely unforeseen social consequences.*

First result: Immediately there was the matter of *traffic congestion.* . . .

Second result: *Pollution* of the air by car fumes, though first denied by the car companies, was later proved by scientists in California. . . .

Third result: *Court dockets* became so crowded with accident cases that about a decade ago relief was sought through no-fault insurance. . . .

Fourth result: The oil shortage and growing dependence on foreign sources for oil highlighted the role of the car as a consumer of an increasingly *scarce natural re-source.* . . .

Fifth result: Probably the least well-perceived consequence of the car is its impact on the *center cities.* . . .

The following two paragraphs develop the last of these five points. Notice the emphasis on cause-and-effect relationships:

> *Probably the least well-perceived consequence of the car is its impact on the center cities.* But basically it is the car which makes possible suburban living, and the relocation of industry to fringes of town. More and more of the white middle class moves to the suburbs and the cities become increasingly dominated by the black and brown minorities. More and more industry also moves to the suburbs leaving fewer and fewer jobs available downtown.
>
> Thus there is set in motion the downward spiral which has overtaken most central cities in the North and the Midwest, and is beginning to be felt in the South and West as well. As the local population declines in education and income, expenses for schools, welfare, and crime go up. But the tax base goes down, and the cities are plunged into crisis—a crisis inextricably linked with the rise of the car and growth of the suburbs.
>
> —Joseph Kraft, "Washington Insight"

(3) *Recognize a range of possible contributing causes.* Often several causes work together to produce a combined result. A writer may still want to close in on the most important one of these causes, or the one that could most easily be changed or corrected to help solve a problem. However, readers become wary of *oversimplification.* They need to see evidence that the writer is aware of the different possible causes that may be contributing to the same result. The following excerpts might represent an introductory survey of possible causes, but they could also provide the outline for a paper as a whole:

Cause 1: Some say there is so much violence in our nation simply because there are *too many of us*—the census strangling the senses. . . .

Cause 2: Some say it's because we have become *too permissive*—failing to understand that when anything goes, everything may go. . . .

Cause 3: Some say it's because violence is an *entertainment* for jaded appetites—part of the side show of

our time—perhaps not arranged but certainly exploited by television and the other media to keep
their profits high. . . .

Cause 4:   Some say violence is *big business,* that crime
does pay—handsomely. . . .

Cause 5:   Some say that violence is merely a crude form of
redistribution of wealth. . . .
—Bess Myerson, "As American as Apple Pie," *Redbook*

Concentrating on a single chief cause and ignoring other factors
leads to familiar kinds of shortcut thinking. The first of these is **scape-**
goating: Confronted with a problem, we like to identify a single cause
and make it the culprit. Much scapegoat thinking sets up a single, easily reached target for our anger. When students can't read, newspapers
and parents like to blame the teachers. The teachers chosen as scapegoats are likely to point to other factors: Reading ability varies statisti-
cally with the income level of the parents; students are kept from books
by jazzed-up visual entertainment; their peer culture and society at
large place little value on books and book learning. The opposite kind
of shortcut thinking is the search for the **panacea:** We look for a single
(and preferably cheap) remedy for complicated ills.

A special kind of shortcut thinking confuses *after* and *because.* The
post hoc fallacy (from the Latin for "after this") makes us jump to
conclusions when events follow each other closely in time. Harassing
phone calls start after a hostile-looking neighbor moves in across the
street. A wet, cold summer follows the eruption of a volcano. Cause and
effect? Or merely a hunch that would have to be confirmed by some
substantial evidence?

(4) *Go beyond surface appearances to trace underlying causes.*
When we take a serious look at a subject, we go beyond surface impressions to identify those factors that do not meet the eye. In much modern journalism, such probing is done in the spirit of **exposé.** The journalist aggressively seeks out the hidden causes and ulterior motives
behind official explanations. However, probing the underlying causes
often simply helps us to understand an issue and chart a future course,
rather than to place the blame. The following might be the outline of a
magazine article helping us understand a complex issue:

The Open Door

FAMILIAR VIEW: We usually think of our immigration policies as
↓   inspired by high-minded, idealistic motives. We hear
                      speakers say that we are all immigrants or the chil-

OPPOSED
THESIS:

dren of immigrants. We quote the familiar lines about the huddled masses of the old continent seeking refuge in the New World. However, *the real reasons for continuing large-scale immigration are often less flattering and more down-to-earth.* . . .

First cause:

Much support for immigration is motivated by *selfish interests.* In the words of one observer, "The primary selfish interest in unimpeded immigration is the desire of employers for cheap labor, particularly in industries and trades that offer degrading work. In the past, one wave of foreigners after another was brought into the U.S. to work at wretched jobs for wretched wages. . . ."

Second cause:

Much support for continued immigration is motivated by *practical political considerations.* In the past, rabid opponents of immigration used to warn that the country was being overrun by foreigners of supposedly inferior genetic stock. As a result, today the politician who votes to restrict immigration is likely to be accused of prejudice, bigotry, isolationism, and racism. . . .

Third cause:

Much illegal immigration is made possible by our traditional American *distaste for police-state methods.* We would need an army of immigration officers to seal off our coasts and our borders. We would need a national system of I.D. cards and fingerprinting to keep illegal aliens out of jobs. . . .

(5) *Weigh the consequences of alternative courses of action.* Many of our everyday decisions are the result of our asking ourselves: "What will happen if I follow course A? What will happen if I follow course B?" Often a structured argument will weigh different possible courses of action in order to make us choose the most promising or least painful one. Often the writer will proceed by **eliminating alternatives** in order to lead up to the remaining logical choice.

The following might be the outline of a paper weighing alternatives. Under each major heading, the writer would present arguments pro and con, examining first favorable and then unfavorable effects:

Our Crowded Jails

THESIS:

Ironically, at a time when public opinion is clamoring for stiffer sentences, courts and prison officials are looking for ways to keep or move more people out of our overcrowded jails.

   I. More use of plea bargaining
     A. Favorable results
     B. Unfavorable results

  II. Lowering bail requirements
     A. Statistics in support
     B. Important cautions

 III. Granting earlier paroles
     A. Desirable results
     B. Undesirable results

 IV. Leniency for "victimless" crimes
     A. Arguments in favor
     B. Predictable opposition

To sum up: The purpose of a structured argument is to convince the reader, to carry the reader along step by step. A well-argued piece of writing makes the reader say at each important step: "Yes, I can see the connection. I can see how you got from here to there." Often, the most important links in an argument are relationships between cause and effect. When analyzing causes and effects, we have to make sure not to take too much for granted. We have to show the actual workings of causes and their effects in convincing detail. We have to be alert to different possible causes contributing to the same result. We have to play down personal preferences and emotional reactions in order to do justice to the subject at hand.

PREWRITING ACTIVITIES 7

1. The following excerpts identify possible reasons for a high drop-out rate for students from one population group. Study these excerpts. Then do your own preliminary survey of four or five major *possible causes* of a similar situation that you have studied or observed. Fill in observations, details, facts, or figures for each cause you identify. Choose a situation like the following: high unemployment among one population group; success of foreign imports in a specific field; weight problems; high divorce rates; drug abuse among young people; inflation; growth of teenage gangs.

Strangers in Their Own Land

Possible cause 1:
Mexican Americans have a higher dropout rate than any other comparable group in the nation. One of the principal reasons for the high dropout rate of Mexican Americans has been simply that Mexican American youngsters *tend to be over age in grade levels.* By the time they get to the point where they are able to function in English and do the required first-grade work, they should chronologically be in the second grade. . . .

Possible cause 2:
There is no doubt that the high dropout rate of Mexican Americans is directly linked to *tests and measurements.* Of the many Mexican American children who were found to be over age in grade levels in a study at Arizona State University, their median performance on most tests was about one standard deviation below the Anglo groups. . . .

Possible cause 3:
Not only do Mexican American children enter school at a measurable disadvantage, but the disadvantage becomes more pronounced as they move up through the grades. With such factors reinforcing the *"failure-syndrome" and "negative self-concept,"* little wonder that Mexican American youngsters leave school in such great numbers. . . .

Possible cause 4:
The *lack of emphasis on education in the home* cannot be considered a significant factor in the high dropout rate of Mexican Americans. Studies have concluded that there is little difference between Mexican American families and other families in the emphasis on education. . . .
—Philip D. Ortego, "A Need for Bilingual Education," in *The Chicanos*

2. For *paragraph practice,* write a paragraph about the causes behind a current problem on your campus or in your neighborhood. In the first half of your paragraph, examine an apparent, alleged, or official reason. In the second half of your paragraph, examine what you consider the real reason or the deeper cause.

BACKGROUND: Rachel L. Carson (1907–64) was a dedicated scientist with a gift for sharing not only scientific knowledge but also her fascination with the beauty and mystery of nature. She studied biology at the Pennsylvania College for Women and continued her work as a biologist at Johns Hopkins University in Baltimore and at the Marine Biological Laboratory at Woods Hole, Massachusetts. She instructed and delighted many readers with her books about the "mystery and meaning of the sea": *The Sea Around Us* (which won the National Book Award in 1951), *Under the Sea Wind,* and *The Edge of the Sea.* Her classic *Silent Spring* (1962) predicted a future in which our remaining wildlife had been destroyed by the heedless use of pesticides; it became a call to arms in the crusade to save the environment. Her chief target was DDT, a powerful insecticide that had been spectacularly successful against such scourges as malaria, carried by mosquitoes. However, DDT was eventually banned because of the poisonous concentrations built up as the chemical traveled up the food chain through insects to birds and mammals. Carson helped bring about a general change in outlook that led from the heedless exploitation of natural resources to a new respect for the workings of nature and "that essential unity that binds life to the earth." The following essay is part of chapter 2 of *Silent Spring.*

Rachel Carson
Our War Against Nature

GUIDE TO READING: From its beginnings, the aim of science has been to understand natural causes and their effects. Scientists can then put this understanding to work in order to produce results beneficial to humanity. But in recent years, much attention has focused on the unexpected or harmful results that are the *unintended* by-products of human interference in the workings of nature. In reading this essay, pay special attention to the cause-and-effect relationships traced by the author—those that are part of the workings of nature, and those that result from human intervention.

IT TOOK hundreds of millions of years to produce the life that now inhabits the earth—eons of time in which that developing and evolving and diversifying life reached a state of adjustment and balance with its surroundings. The environment, rigorously shaping and directing the life it supported, contained elements that were hostile as well as supporting. Certain rocks gave out dangerous radiation; even within the light of the sun, from which all life draws its energy, there were short-wave radiations with power to injure. Given time—time not in years but in millennia—life adjusts, and a balance has been reached. For time is the essential ingredient; but in the modern world there is no time.

The rapidity of change and the speed with which new situations are created follow the impetuous and heedless pace of man rather than the deliberate pace of nature. Radiation is no longer merely the background radiation of rocks, the bombardment of cosmic rays, the ultraviolet of the sun that have existed before there was any life on earth; radiation is now the unnatural creation of man's tampering with the atom. The chemicals to which life is asked to make its adjustment are no longer merely the calcium and silica and copper and all the rest of the minerals washed out of the rocks and carried in rivers to the sea; they are the synthetic creations of man's inventive mind, brewed in laboratories, and having no counterparts in nature.

To adjust to these chemicals would require time on the scale that is nature's; it would require not merely the years of a man's life but the life of generations. And even this, were it by some miracle possible, would be futile, for the new chemicals come from our laboratories in an endless stream; almost five hundred annually find their way into actual use in the United States alone. The figure is staggering and its implications are not easily grasped—500 new chemicals to which the bodies of men and animals are required somehow to adapt each year, chemicals totally outside the limits of biologic experience.

Among them are many that are used in our war against nature. Since the mid-1940's over 200 basic chemicals have been created for use in killing insects, weeds, rodents, and other organisms described in the modern vernacular as "pests"; and they are sold under several thousand different brand names.

These sprays, dusts, and aerosols are now applied almost universally to farms, gardens, forests, and homes—nonselective chemicals that have the power to kill every insect, the "good" and the "bad," to still the song of birds and the leaping of fish in the streams, to coat the leaves with a deadly film, and to linger on in soil—all this though the intended target may be only a few weeds or insects. Can anyone believe it is possible to lay down such a barrage of poisons on the surface of the earth without making it unfit for all life? They should not be called "insecticides," but "biocides."

6   The whole process of spraying seems caught up in an endless spiral. Since DDT was released for civilian use, a process of escalation has been going on in which ever more toxic materials must be found. This has happened because insects, in a triumphant vindication of Darwin's principle of the survival of the fittest, have evolved super races immune to the particular insecticide used, hence a deadlier one has always to be developed—and then a deadlier one than that. It has happened also because destructive insects often undergo a "flareback," or resurgence, after spraying, in numbers greater than before. Thus the chemical war is never won, and all life is caught in its violent crossfire.

7   Along with the possibility of extinction by nuclear war, the central problem of our age has therefore become the contamination of our total environment with such substances of incredible potential for harm—substances that accumulate in the tissues of plants and animals and even penetrate the germ cells to shatter or alter the very material of heredity upon which the shape of the future depends.

8   Some would-be architects of our future look toward a time when it will be possible to alter the human germ plasm by design. But we may easily be doing so now by inadvertence, for many chemicals, like radiation, bring about gene mutations. It is ironic to think that man might determine his own future by something so seemingly trivial as the choice of an insect spray.

9   All this has been risked—for what? Future historians may well be amazed by our distorted sense of proportion. How could intelligent beings seek to control a few unwanted species by a method that contaminated the entire environment and brought the threat of disease and death even to their own kind? Yet this is precisely what we have done. We have done it, moreover, for reasons that collapse the moment we examine them. We are told that the enormous and expanding use of pesticides is necessary to maintain farm production. Yet is our real problem not one of *overproduction?* Our farms, despite measures to remove acreages from production and to pay farmers *not* to produce, have yielded such a staggering excess of crops that the American taxpayer by 1962 is paying out more than one billion dollars a year as the total carrying cost of the surplus-food storage program. And is the situation helped when one branch of the Agriculture Department tries to reduce production while another states, as it did in 1958, "It is believed generally that reduction of crop acreages under provisions of the Soil Bank will stimulate interest in use of chemicals to obtain maximum production on the land retained in crops."

10   All this is not to say there is no insect problem and no need of control. I am saying, rather, that control must be geared to realities, not to mythical situations, and that methods employed must be such that they do not destroy us along with the insects.

The problem whose attempted solution has brought such a train of disaster in its wake is an accompaniment of our modern way of life. Long before the age of man, insects inhabited the earth—a group of extraordinarily varied and adaptable beings. Over the course of time a small percentage of the more than half a million species of insects have come into conflict with human welfare in two principal ways: as competitors for the food supply and as carriers of human disease.

Disease-carrying insects become important where human beings are crowded together, especially under conditions where sanitation is poor, as in time of natural disaster or war or in situations of extreme poverty and deprivation. Then control of some sort becomes necessary. It is a sobering fact, however, that the method of massive chemical control has had only limited success, and also threatens to worsen the very conditions it is intended to curb.

Under primitive agricultural conditions the farmer had few insect problems. These arose with the intensification of agriculture—the devotion of immense acreages to a single crop. Such a system set the stage for explosive increases in specific insect populations. Single-crop farming does not take advantage of the principles by which nature works; it is agriculture as an engineer might conceive it to be. Nature has introduced great variety into the landscape, but man has displayed a passion for simplifying it. Thus we undo the built-in checks and balances by which nature holds the species within bounds. One important natural check is a limit on the amount of suitable habitat for each species. Obviously then, an insect that lives on wheat can build up its population to much higher levels on a farm devoted to wheat than on one in which wheat is intermingled with other crops to which the insect is not adapted.

The same thing happens in other situations. A generation or more ago, the towns of large areas of the United States lined their streets with the noble elm tree. Now the beauty they hopefully created is threatened with complete destruction as disease sweeps through the elms, carried by a beetle that would have only limited chance to build up large populations and to spread from tree to tree if the elms were only occasional trees in a richly diversified planting.

Another factor in the modern insect problem is one that must be viewed against a background of geologic and human history: the spreading of thousands of different kinds of organisms from their native homes to invade new territories. This worldwide migration has been studied and graphically described by the British ecologist Charles Elton in his book *The Ecology of Invasions*. During the Cretaceous Period, some hundred million years ago, flooding seas cut many land bridges between continents and living things found themselves confined in what Elton calls "colossal separate nature reserves." There, isolated from others of their kind, they developed many new species. When some of the land masses were joined again, about 15 million years ago, these species began to move out into new territories—a movement that is not only still in progress but is now receiving considerable assistance from man.

16 The importation of plants is the primary agent in the modern spread of species, for animals have almost invariably gone along with the plants, quarantine being a comparatively recent and not completely effective innovation. The United States Office of Plant Introduction alone has introduced almost 200,000 species and varieties of plants from all over the world. Nearly half of the 180 or so major insect enemies of plants in the United States are accidental imports from abroad, and most of them have come as hitchhikers on plants.

17 In new territory, out of reach of the restraining hand of the natural enemies that kept down its numbers in its native land, an invading plant or animal is able to become enormously abundant. Thus it is no accident that our most troublesome insects are introduced species.

18 These invasions, both the naturally occurring and those dependent on human assistance, are likely to continue indefinitely. Quarantine and massive chemical campaigns are only extremely expensive ways of buying time. We are faced, according to Dr. Elton, "with a life-and-death need not just to find new technological means of suppressing this plant or that animal"; instead we need the basic knowledge of animal populations and their relations to their surroundings that will "promote an even balance and damp down the explosive power of outbreaks and new invasions."

19 Much of the necessary knowledge is now available but we do not use it. We train ecologists in our universities and even employ them in our governmental agencies but we seldom take their advice. We allow the chemical death rain to fall as though there were no alternative, whereas in fact there are many, and our ingenuity could soon discover many more if given opportunity.

20 It is not my contention that chemical insecticides must never be used. I do contend that we have put poisonous and biologically potent chemicals indiscriminately into the hands of persons largely or wholly ignorant of their potentials for harm. We have subjected enormous numbers of people to contact with these poisons, without their consent and often without their knowledge. If the Bill of Rights contains no guarantee that a citizen shall be secure against lethal poisons distributed either by private individuals or by public officials, it is surely only because our forefathers, despite their considerable wisdom and foresight, could conceive of no such problem.

21 I contend, furthermore, that we have allowed these chemicals to be used with little or no advance investigation of their effect on soil, wa-

ter, wildlife, and man himself. Future generations are unlikely to condone our lack of prudent concern for the integrity of the natural world that supports all life.

 USING THE DICTIONARY: Check the following specialized or technical terms: 1. *eon* (1) 2. *millennium* (1) 3. *bombardment* (2) 4. *silica* (2) 5. *toxic* (6) 6. *resurgence* (6) 7. *plasm* (8) 8. *mutation* (13) 9. *habitat* (13) 10. *Cretaceous* (15)

THE WRITER'S AGENDA:

In this essay, the author raises a voice of warning: She projects the "shape of the future" on the basis of what has happened in the past and of what is happening now. Answer the following questions:

1. In the introductory paragraphs, Rachel Carson sets up the basic *contrast* between the workings of nature and the effects of human intervention. What are the crucial differences? What are her key examples?

2. Throughout this essay, the author reiterates, or insistently repeats, her central **thesis**: Grave dangers face us from the *inadvertent results* of chains of events that human beings have set in motion. Where does she first state her thesis? At what other points in the essay do you find emphatic or eloquent restatements of her central idea?

3. According to the author, what causes the "endless spiral," or *escalation,* in the use of pesticides?

4. The expanding use of pesticides is often justified by urgent *need.* How does the author deal with this justification?

5. In a central portion of this essay, the author traces our current insect problems to our human tampering with the "built-in" *checks and balances* of nature. What are her three key examples? Explain the causes and effects at work in each case.

6. Toward the end of her essay, the author strongly implies that *alternatives* exist to the massive use of pesticides. To judge from what you have read in this essay, what are they?

FOR DISCUSSION OR WRITING:

1. In the controversies that followed the publication of *Silent Spring,* environmentalists have been variously labeled "one-sided,"

"biased," "unrealistic," and "alarmist." Does this essay by Carson seem to you objective or biased, balanced or exaggerated? Where and how?

2. Plagues and blights figure prominently in the earliest written records going back to biblical times. Choose one that has recently been in the news: the gypsy moth, elm disease, pigeons, rats, cockroaches, the medfly, or the like. Investigate the cause-and-effect relationships involved in its appearance and in efforts to combat it.

3. Carson said in *Silent Spring* that "only within the moment of time represented by the present century" has one species—ours—acquired the power to alter the nature of our world. Investigate the cause-and-effect relationships involved in one prominent example of this power: acid rain, dust bowls, "dead" lakes, the growth of deserts, or the like.

4. The American biologist Garrett Hardin formulated "Hardin's Law," which says: "You can never do merely one thing." In recent years, public opinion has become vividly aware of the *unintended* consequences or undesirable side effects of well-intentioned actions and projects. Writers with a strong sense of irony have shown the unexpected or undesirable results of well-meant efforts, from prohibition and abortion laws to the volunteer army and foreign aid. Focus on one major area, such as law, foreign policy, or medicine. Discuss examples (or one extended example) of good intentions followed by unintended consequences.

5. Pundits ponder the underlying causes of social trends that seem merely faddish on the surface. Examine the underlying causes of one of the following:

- current passing fads

- the spread of cults

- popularity of presidential candidates

- changing sexual mores

BACKGROUND: Garrett Hardin (born 1915 in Dallas, Texas) is the author of numerous books and articles on "human ecology"—the study of how human life is sustained on this planet. He completed his doctoral work in biology at Stanford University in 1941. He was on the faculty of the University of California at Santa Barbara for many years, and he has lectured at many other universities. His writings, including the widely reprinted article "The Tragedy of the Commons," attack the conventional American self-image of good intentions and philanthropy around the world as sentimental and misguided. Hardin represents a new kind of conservative intellectual trying to counter the views of the "guilt-ridden," "conscience-stricken" humanitarian liberal with a more "hard-nosed" view of America's interests as a nation. The essay reprinted here was published as part of a longer article in *Psychology Today*.

Garrett Hardin

Lifeboat Ethics

GUIDE TO READING: The question that Hardin repeatedly makes us ponder in this essay is: "If we choose one course over another, what will be the consequences of our actions?" As you read the essay, ask yourself: "What are the well-intentioned proposals that the author argues against in this essay? How does he repeatedly trace a chain of cause and effect to the predicted consequences in order to make us reject the proposals?"

ENVIRONMENTALISTS USE the metaphor of the earth as a 1 "spaceship" in trying to persuade countries, industries and people to stop wasting and polluting our natural resources. Since we all share life on this planet, they argue, no single person or institution has the right to destroy, waste, or use more than a fair share of its resources.

But does everyone on earth have an equal right to an equal share of 2 its resources? The spaceship metaphor can be dangerous when used by misguided idealists to justify suicidal policies for sharing our resources through uncontrolled immigration and foreign aid. In their enthusiastic but unrealistic generosity, they confuse the ethics of a spaceship with those of a lifeboat.

3   A true spaceship would have to be under the control of a captain, since no ship could possibly survive if its course were determined by committee. Spaceship Earth certainly has no captain; the United Nations is merely a toothless tiger, with little power to enforce any policy upon its bickering members.

4   If we divide the world crudely into rich nations and poor nations, two thirds of them are desperately poor, and only one third comparatively rich, with the United States the wealthiest of all. Metaphorically each rich nation can be seen as a lifeboat full of comparatively rich people. In the ocean outside each lifeboat swim the poor of the world, who would like to get in, or at least to share some of the wealth. What should the lifeboat passengers do?

5   First, we must recognize the limited capacity of any lifeboat. For example, a nation's land has a limited capacity to support a population and as the current energy crisis has shown us, in some ways we have already exceeded the carrying capacity of our land. So here we sit, say 50 people in our lifeboat. To be generous, let us assume it has room for 10 more, making a total capacity of 60. Suppose the 50 of us in the lifeboat see 100 others swimming in the water outside, begging for admission to our boat or for handouts. We have several options: we may be tempted to try to live by the Christian ideal of being "our brother's keeper," or by the Marxist ideal of "to each according to his needs." Since the needs of all in the water are the same, and since they can all be seen as "our brothers," we could take them all into our boat, making a total of 150 in a boat designed for 60. The boat swamps; everyone drowns. Complete justice, complete catastrophe.

6   Since the boat has an unused excess capacity of 10 more passengers, we could admit just 10 more to it. But which 10 do we let in? How do we choose? Do we pick the best 10, the neediest 10, "first come, first served"? And what do we say to the 90 we exclude? If we do let an extra 10 into our lifeboat, we will have lost our "safety factor," an engineering principle of critical importance. For example, if we don't leave room for excess capacity as a safety factor in our country's agriculture, a new plant disease or a bad change in the weather could have disastrous consequences.

7   Suppose we decide to preserve our small safety factor and admit no more to the lifeboat. Our survival is then possible, although we shall have to be constantly on guard against boarding parties.

8   While this last solution clearly offers the only means of our survival, it is morally abhorrent to many people. Some say they feel guilty about their good luck. My reply is simple: "Get out and yield your place to others." This may solve the problem of the guilt-ridden person's conscience, but it does not change the ethics of the lifeboat. The needy person to whom the guilt-ridden person yields his place will not him-

self feel guilty about his good luck. If he did, he would not climb aboard. The net result of conscience-stricken people giving up their unjustly held seats is the elimination of that sort of conscience from the lifeboat. *if you want to share - do it on your own*

This is the basic metaphor within which we must work out our solutions. Let us now enrich the image, step by step, with substantive additions from the real world, a world that must solve real and pressing problems of overpopulation and hunger. 9

The harsh ethics of the lifeboat become even harsher when we consider the reproductive differences between the rich nations and the poor nations. The people inside the lifeboats are doubling in numbers every 87 years; those swimming around outside are doubling, on the average, every 35 years, more than twice as fast as the rich. And since the world's resources are dwindling, the difference in prosperity between the rich and the poor can only increase. 10 *facts*

As of 1973, the U.S. had a population of 210 million people, who were increasing by 0.8 percent per year. Outside our lifeboat, let us imagine another 210 million people (say the combined populations of Colombia, Ecuador, Venezuela, Morocco, Pakistan, Thailand, and the Philippines), increasing at a rate of 3.3 percent per year. Put differently, the doubling time for this aggregate population was 21 years, compared to 87 years for the U.S. 11

Now suppose the U.S. agreed to pool its resources with those seven countries, with everyone receiving an equal share. Initially the ratio of Americans to non-Americans in this model would be one-to-one. But consider what the ratio would be after 87 years, by which time the Americans would have doubled to a population of 420 million. By then, doubling every 21 years, the other group would have swollen to 354 billion. Each American would have to share the available resources with more than eight people. 12 *based on evidence*

But, one could argue, this discussion assumes that current population trends will continue, and they may not. Quite so. Most likely the rate of population increase will decline much faster in the U.S. than it will in the other countries, and there does not seem to be much we can do about it. In sharing with "each according to his needs," we must recognize that needs are determined by population size, which is determined by the rate of reproduction, which at present is regarded as a sovereign right of every nation, poor or not. This being so, the philanthropic load created by the sharing ethic of the spaceship can only increase. 13 *philanthropy*

The fundamental error of spaceship ethics, and the sharing it requires, is that it leads to what I call "the tragedy of the commons." Under a system of private property, people who own property recognize their responsibility to care for it, for if they don't they will eventu- 14

E.

"commons" third argument

ally suffer. A farmer, for instance, will allow no more cattle in a pasture than its carrying capacity justifies. If he overloads it, erosion sets in, weeds take over, and he loses the use of the pasture.

15   If a pasture becomes a commons open to all, the right of each to use it may not be matched by a corresponding responsibility to protect it. Asking everyone to use it with discretion will hardly do, for the considerate herdsman who refrains from overloading the commons suffers more than a selfish one who says his needs are greater. If everyone would restrain himself, all would be well; but it takes only one less than everyone to ruin a system of voluntary restraint. In a crowded world of less than perfect human beings, mutual ruin is inevitable if there are no controls. This is the tragedy of the commons.

16   One of the major tasks of education today should be the creation of such an acute awareness of the dangers of the commons that people will recognize its many varieties. For example, the air and water have become polluted because they are treated as commons. Further growth in the population or per-capita conversion of natural resources into pollutants will only make the problem worse. The same holds true for the fish of the oceans. Fishing fleets have nearly disappeared in many parts of the world; technological improvements in the art of fishing are hastening the day of complete ruin. Only the replacement of the system of the commons with a responsible system of control will save the land, air, water and oceanic fisheries.

17   In recent years there has been a push to create a new commons called a World Food Bank, an international depository of food reserves to which nations would contribute according to their abilities and from which they would draw according to their needs. This humanitarian proposal received support from many liberal international groups, and from such prominent citizens as Margaret Mead, the U.N. Secretary General, and Senator Edward Kennedy.

18   A world food bank appeals powerfully to our humanitarian impulses. But before we rush ahead with such a plan, let us ask if such a program would actually do more good than harm, not only momentarily but also in the long run. Those who propose a food bank usually refer to a current "emergency" or "crisis" in terms of world food supply. But what is an emergency? Although they may be infrequent and sudden, everyone knows that emergencies will occur from time to time. A well-run family, company, organization or country prepares for the likelihood of accidents and emergencies. It expects them, it budgets for them, it saves for them.

19   What happens if some organizations or countries budget for accidents and others do not? If each country is solely responsible for its own well-being, poorly managed ones will suffer. But they can learn from experience. They may mend their ways, and learn to budget for

infrequent but certain emergencies. For example, the weather varies from year to year, and periodic crop failures are certain. A wise and competent government saves out of the production of the good years in anticipation of bad years to come. Joseph taught this policy to Pharaoh in Egypt more than 2,000 years ago. Yet the great majority of the governments in the world today do not follow such a policy. They lack either the wisdom or the competence, or both. Should those nations that do manage to put something aside be forced to come to the rescue each time an emergency occurs among the poor nations?

"But it isn't their fault!" some kind-hearted liberals argue. "How can we blame the poor people who are caught in an emergency? Why must they suffer for the sins of their governments?" The concept of blame is simply not relevant here. The real question is, what are the operational consequences of establishing a world food bank? If it is open to every country every time a need develops, slovenly rulers will not be motivated to take Joseph's advice. Someone will always come to their aid. Some countries will deposit food in the world food bank, and others will withdraw it. There will be almost no overlap. As a result of such solutions to food shortage emergencies, the poor countries will not learn to mend their ways, and will suffer progressively greater emergencies as their populations grow.

On the average, poor countries undergo a 2.5 percent increase in population each year; rich countries, about 0.6 percent. Only rich countries have anything in the way of food reserves set aside, and even they do not have as much as they should. Poor countries have none. If poor countries received no food from the outside, the rate of their population growth would be periodically checked by crop failures and famines. But if they can always draw on a world food bank in time of need, their population can continue to grow unchecked, and so will their "need" for aid. In the short run, a world food bank may diminish that need, but in the long run it actually increases the need without limit.

Without some system of worldwide food sharing, the proportion of people in the rich and poor nations might eventually stabilize. The overpopulated poor countries would decrease in numbers while the rich countries that had room for more people would increase. But with a well-meaning system of sharing, such as a world food bank, the growth differential between the rich and the poor countries will not only persist, it will increase. Because of the higher rate of population growth in the poor countries of the world, 88 percent of today's children are born poor, and only 12 percent rich. Year by year the ratio becomes worse as the fast-reproducing poor outnumber the slow-reproducing rich.

A world food bank is thus a commons in disguise. People will have more motivation to draw from it than to add to any common store. The less provident and less able will multiply at the expense of the abler and more provident, bringing eventual ruin upon all who share in the commons. Besides, any system of "sharing" that amounts to foreign aid from the rich nations to the poor nations will carry the taint of charity, which will contribute little to the world peace so devoutly desired by those who support the idea of a world food bank.

24   As past U.S. foreign-aid programs have amply and depressingly demonstrated, international charity frequently inspires mistrust and antagonism rather than gratitude on the part of the recipient nation.

25   The modern approach to foreign aid stresses the export of technology and advice, rather than money and food. As an ancient Chinese proverb goes: "Give a man a fish and he will eat for a day; teach him how to fish and he will eat for the rest of his days." Acting on this advice, the Rockefeller and Ford Foundations have financed a number of programs for improving agriculture in the hungry nations. Known as the "Green Revolution," these programs have led to the development of "miracle rice" and "miracle wheat," new strains that offer bigger harvests and greater resistance to crop damage.

26   Whether or not the Green Revolution can increase food production as much as its champions claim is a debatable but possibly irrelevant point. Those who support this well-intended humanitarian effort should first consider some of the fundamentals of human ecology. Ironically, one man who did was the late Alan Gregg, a vice president of the Rockefeller Foundation. Two decades ago he expressed strong doubts about the wisdom of such attempts to increase food production. He likened the growth and spread of humanity over the surface of the earth to the spread of cancer in the human body, remarking that "cancerous growths demand food, but, as far as I know, they have never been cured by getting it."

27   Every human born constitutes a draft on all aspects of the environment: food, air, water, forests, beaches, wildlife, scenery and solitude. Food can, perhaps, be significantly increased to meet a growing demand. But what about clean beaches, unspoiled forests, and solitude? If we satisfy a growing population's need for food, we necessarily decrease its per capita supply of the other resources needed by people.

28   India, for example, now has a population of 600 million, which increases by 15 million each year. This population already puts a huge load on a relatively impoverished environment. The country's forests are now only a small fraction of what they were three centuries ago, and floods and erosion continually destroy the insufficient farmland that remains. Every one of the 15 million new lives added to India's population puts an additional burden on the environment, and increases the economic and social costs of crowding. However humanitarian our in-

tent, every Indian life saved through medical or nutritional assistance from abroad diminishes the quality of life for those who remain, and for subsequent generations. If rich countries make it possible, through foreign aid, for 600 million Indians to swell to 1.2 billion in a mere 28 years, as their current growth rate threatens, will future generations of Indians thank us for hastening the destruction of their environment? Will our good intentions be sufficient excuse for the consequences of our actions?

Without a true world government to control reproduction and the use of available resources, the sharing ethic of the spaceship is impossible. For the foreseeable future, our survival demands that we govern our actions by the ethics of a lifeboat, harsh though they may be. Posterity will be satisfied with nothing less.

USING THE DICTIONARY: Garrett Hardin frequently translates his arguments into graphic, concrete language. Check examples of a more formal, more impersonal vocabulary: 1. *ethics* (2) 2. *abhorrent* (8) 3. *substantive* (9) 4. *reproductive* (10) 5. *aggregate* (11) 6. *ratio* (12) 7. *sovereign* (13) 8. *philanthropic* (13) 9. *discretion* (15) 10. *antagonism* (24)

THE WRITER'S AGENDA:

The author's method in this essay is to trace in detail several imaginative comparisons, or metaphors, that can guide our thinking about the ethics of survival on our crowded planet. Each metaphor makes us think in a different way about important causes and their effects. Answer the following questions about how the author structures his argument:

1. *"Spaceship Earth"* became a widely echoed slogan of the environmental movement. What are its implications? On what grounds does Hardin in the introductory paragraphs reject it in favor of his own competing metaphor of the lifeboat?

2. In much of the early part of the essay, the author uses the *lifeboat analogy* as the basic metaphor "within which we must work out our solutions." If we follow the logic of the lifeboat analogy, what, according to the author, are our basic options and their consequences?

3. How does Hardin interpret the statistics concerning *population growth* that he presents when applying the lifeboat image to conditions in the "real world"? Summarize and explain his projections.

4. In the latter half of the essay, Hardin introduces his second key analogy—the *commons*. What is its history or original context? What psychological mechanisms or cause-and-effect relationships is it meant to dramatize for the reader? What modern examples of its workings does Hardin examine?

5. Hardin's discussion of the *"Green Revolution"* takes his basic argument an important step further. How?

6. "Protecting the environment" and safeguarding "the quality of life" are familiar aims of the "well-intentioned" *liberals* whose proposals Hardin generally opposes or rejects. In his concluding paragraphs, how does he appropriate these aims for his own purposes?

7. Hardin relies mainly on the logic of his arguments to sway the reader. However, he also freely uses strong **connotative** language to express disapproval or ridicule. Explain how expressions like the following are meant to steer the reactions of the reader: "misguided idealists," "toothless tiger," "boarding parties," "guilt-ridden person," "conscience-stricken people," "kind-hearted idealists," "spread of cancer."

FOR DISCUSSION OR WRITING:

1. How valid or convincing do the three basic survival metaphors seem to you—the spaceship, the lifeboat, the commons? Argue for the most convincing and against the least convincing of these metaphors.

2. People who agree with Hardin tend to pride themselves on their "realism" or "pragmatism." Their opponents often accuse them of "cynicism" or callousness. To you, is Hardin a realist or a cynic? (Defend your answer.)

3. The point of view that Hardin adopts in this essay is that of the rich nations as against the poor. Look at his arguments from the *other* side of the line that divides the rich and the poor.

4. Do you agree with Hardin's arguments in part? Prepare a "Yes, but" paper in which you show to what extent you agree and disagree.

5. Choose a local or national issue that presents officials or the voters with a choice among different courses of action. Prepare a paper in which you examine different options and their consequences. Choose an issue that you have had a chance to study or investigate. Possible choices:

   ♦ welfare policy

   ♦ rent control

- the draft and its alternatives
- the legal drinking age
- publicly financed abortions
- objectionable books in high school libraries

6. Examine the implications and possible limitations of a key metaphor that has played a role in much political discussion. Possible examples include the "arms race," the "cold war," the "iron curtain," the "family of nations," "brotherhood," "sisterhood," the "melting pot," the "sexual revolution," the "silent majority," the "taxpayers' revolt."

BACKGROUND: Michael Novak (born 1933), a native of western Pennsylvania, is a teacher and writer with strong conservative views. He has made the influence of his ideas felt as a professor of philosophy and religious studies, as a government consultant, and as a syndicated columnist. He has written numerous articles and books about the changing Catholic church and about Catholic life in America. His book *The Rise of the Unmeltable Ethnics* (1972) played a major role in the ethnic revival of the seventies that led many Americans to revise their conventional "melting-pot" theories about American culture. Novak and others claimed that the "white ethnics"—such as the descendants of Irish, Italian, Polish, or Czech immigrants—had often found their own background or experience ignored in the schools, in the media, or in traditional American literature. In the name of assimilation, official mainstream culture—White Anglo-Saxon Protestant—had tried to force a superficial, illiberal homogeneity on millions of Americans with cultural roots and group loyalties of their own. Novak and other advocates of new cultural pluralism felt special ties to writers like Jimmy Breslin, writing about the New York Irish, or Mike Royko, writing about the Polish-American community in Chicago. In the essay reprinted here, Novak champions a cause close to the heart of many representatives of the "white ethnics"—often predominantly Catholic, and often strong defenders of the traditional family.

Michael Novak

The Family Out of Favor

GUIDE TO READING: In coming to the defense of an embattled institution, Novak traces major causes that combine to produce powerful social trends. As you read the essay, sort out and outline the causes and effects he surveys under two major headings: According to the author, what are the major causes that have been at work to weaken the traditional family unit? As a result, what benefits and traditional values are in danger of being lost?

1   RECENTLY A FRIEND of mine told me the following anecdote. At lunch in a restaurant, he had mentioned that he and his wife intended to have a second child soon. His listener registered the words, stood,

and reached out his hand with unmistakable fervor: "You are making a political statement. Congratulations!"

We live in lucky times. So many, so varied, and so aggressive are the antifamily sentiments in our society that brave souls may now have (for the first time in centuries) the pleasure of discovering for themselves the importance of the family. Choosing to have a family used to be uninteresting. It is, today, an act of intelligence and courage. To love family life, to see in family life the most potent moral, intellectual, and political cell in the body politic is to be marked today as a heretic. ²

Orthodoxy is usually enforced by an economic system. Our own system, postindustrial capitalism, plays an ambivalent role with respect to the family. On the one hand, capitalism demands hard work, competition, sacrifice, saving, and rational decision-making. On the other, it stresses liberty and encourages hedonism. ³

Now the great corporations (as well as the universities, the political professions, the foundations, the great newspapers and publishing empires, and the film industry) diminish the moral and economic importance of the family. They demand travel and frequent change of residence. Teasing the heart with glittering entertainment and gratifying the demands of ambition, they dissolve attachments and loyalties. Husbands and wives live in isolation from each other. Children of the upwardly mobile are almost as abandoned, emotionally, as the children of the ghetto. The lives of husbands, wives, and children do not mesh, are not engaged, seem merely thrown together. There is enough money. There is too much emotional space. It is easier to leave town than to pretend that one's lives truly matter to each other. (I remember the tenth anniversary party of a foreign office of a major newsmagazine; none of its members was married to his spouse of ten years before.) At an advanced stage capitalism imparts enormous centrifugal forces to the souls of those who have most internalized its values; and these forces shear marriages and families apart. ⁴

To insist, in the face of such forces, that marriage and family still express our highest moral ideals is to awaken hostility and opposition. For many, marriage has been a bitter disappointment. They long to be free of it and also of the guilt they feel, a residual guilt which they have put to sleep and do not want awakened. They loathe marriage. They celebrate its demise. Each sign of weakness in the institution exonerates them of personal failure. ⁵

Urban industrial life is not designed to assist families. Expressways divide neighborhoods and parishes. Small family bakeries, cheese shops, and candy stores are boarded up. Social engineers plan for sewers, power lines, access roads, but not for the cultural ecology which allows families of different histories and structures to flower and prosper. The workplace is not designed with family needs in mind; neither are working hours. ⁶

7   Yet, clearly, the family is the seedbed of economic skills, money habits, attitudes toward work, and the arts of financial independence. The family is a stronger agency of educational success than the school. The family is a stronger teacher of the religious imagination than the church. Political and social planning in a wise social order begin with the axiom *What strengthens the family strengthens society.* Highly paid, mobile, and restless professionals may disdain the family (having been nurtured by its strengths), but those whom other agencies desert have only one institution in which to find essential nourishment.

8   The role of a father, a mother, and of children with respect to them, is the absolutely critical center of social force. Even when poverty and disorientation strike, as over the generations they so often do, it is family strength that most defends individuals against alienation, lassitude, or despair. The world around the family is fundamentally unjust. The state and its agents, and the economic system and its agencies, are never fully to be trusted. One could not trust them in Eastern Europe, in Sicily, or in Ireland—and one cannot trust them here. One unforgettable law has been learned painfully through all the oppressions, disasters, and injustices of the last thousand years: *if things go well with the family, life is worth living; when the family falters, life falls apart.*

9   These words, I know, go against the conventional grain. In America, we seem to look to the state for every form of social assistance. Immigrant Jews and Catholics have for fifty years supported progressive legislation in favor of federal social programs: for minimum wage, Social Security, Medicare, civil rights. Yet dignity, for most immigrant peoples, resides first of all in family strength. Along with Southern blacks, Appalachians, Latins, and Indians, most immigrants to America are family people. Indeed, virtually all Americans, outside our professional classes, are family people.

10   As for the media, outrageous myths blow breezily about. Everyone says that divorces are multiplying. They are. But the figures hide as much as they reveal. Some 66 percent of all husbands and wives stick together until death do them part. In addition, the death that "parts" a marriage comes far later now than it did in any previous era. Faithful spouses stay together for a longer span of years than ever. For centuries, the average age of death was, for a female, say, thirty-two, and, for a male, thirty-eight. That so many modern marriages carry a far longer span of years with a certain grace is an unprecedented tribute to the institution.

11   Finally, aggressive sentiments against marriage are usually expressed today in the name of "freedom," "openness," "play," or "serious commitment to a career." Marriage is pictured as a form of imprisonment, oppression, boredom, and chafing hindrance. Not all these accusations are wrong; but the superstition surrounding them is.

Before one can speak intelligently of marriage, one must discuss 12
the superstition that blocks our vision. We lack the courage nowadays
to live by creeds, or to state our doctrines clearly (even to ourselves).
Our highest moral principle is flexibility. Guided by sentiments we are
embarrassed to put into words, we support them not by argument but
by their trendiness.

The central idea of our foggy way of life, however, seems unambig- 13
uous enough. It is that life is solitary and brief, and that its aim is self-
fulfillment. Total mastery over one's surroundings, control over the
disposition of one's time—these are necessary conditions for self-
fulfillment. ("Stand not in my way.") Autonomy we understand to mean
protection of our inner kingdom—protection around the self from in-
trusions of chance, irrationality, necessity, and other persons. ("My self,
my castle.") In such a vision of the self, marriage is merely an alliance.
It entails as minimal an abridgment of inner privacy as one partner or
the other may allow. Children are not a welcome responsibility, for to
have children is, plainly, to cease being a child oneself.

For the modern temper, great dreads here arise. Sanity, we think, 14
consists in centering upon the only self one has. Surrender self-control,
surrender happiness. And so we keep the other out. We then maintain
our belief in our unselfishness by laboring for "humanity"—for women,
the oppressed, the Third World, or some other needy group. The solitary self needs distant collectivities to witness to its altruism. It has a
passionate need to love humankind. It cannot give itself to a spouse or
children. "Individual people" seek happiness through concentration
upon themselves, although perhaps for the sake of service to others.
Most television cops, detectives, cowboys, and doctors are of this tribe.
The "family people" define themselves through belonging to others:
spouse, children, parents, siblings, nieces, cousins, and the rest. For
the family people, to be human is to be, so to speak, molecular. I am
not solely I. I am husband, father, son, brother, uncle, cousin; I am a
family network.

There is, beyond the simplicities of half-hour television, a gritty 15
realism in family life. Outside the family, we choose our own friends,
like-minded folk whose intellectual and cultural passions resemble
ours. Inside the family, however, divergent passions, intellections, and
frustrations slam and batter us. Families today bring together professions, occupations, social classes, and sometimes regional, ethnic, or
religious differences. Family life may remain in the United States the
last stronghold of genuine cosmopolitanism and harsh, truthful differences.

For a thousand years, the family was the one institution the peoples 16
of Eastern and Southern Europe, the Irish, and others could trust. The
family constitutes their political, economic, and educational strength.

The public schools of the United States failing them, they reached into their families and created an astonishingly successful system of parochial schools. Hardly literate, poor, and diffident peoples, they achieved something of an educational miracle. Economically, the Jews, the Greeks, the Lebanese established one another in as many small businesses as they could open. The Italians, the Poles, the Slovaks, the Croatians gave each other economic help amounting to two or three thousands of dollars a year per family. Cousin Joe did the electrical work; Pete fixed cars; Emil helped paint the house; aunts and uncles and grandparents canned foods, minded the children; fathers in their spare time built playrooms, boats, and other luxuries in the basements of row houses.

17   The family network was also a political force in precinct, ward, or district. People of the upper classes could pass on to their children advantages of inheritance, admission to exclusive schools, and high-level contacts. Children of the immigrants also made their families the primary networks of economic and political strength. Kinship is a primary reality in many unions and in all urban political "machines." Mothers and fathers instructed their children simultaneously, "Don't trust anybody," and "The family will never let you down."

18   In contemporary conditions, of course, these old family methods and styles have atrophied. There is no way of going back to the past. (Not everything about the past, in any case, was attractive.) Education media help children to become sophisticated about everything but the essentials: love, fidelity, childbearing, mutual help, care for parents and the elderly. Almost everything about mobile, impersonal, distancing life in the United States—tax policies, real-estate policies, the demands of the corporations, and even the demands of modern political forms—makes it difficult for families that feel ancient moral obligations to care for their aged, their mentally disturbed, their retarded, their needy.

19   It is difficult to believe that the state is a better instrument for satisfying such human needs than the family. If parents do not keep after the children to do their schoolwork, can the large, consolidated school educate? Some have great faith in state services: in orphanages, child-care centers, schools, job-training programs, and nursing homes. Some want the state to become one large centralized family. Such faith taxes credulity. Much of the popular resistance to federal child care arises from distrust of social workers and childhood engineers who would be agents of state power. Families need help in child care, but many distrust the state and the social-work establishment.

20   An economic order that would make the family the basic unit of social policy would touch every citizen at the nerve center of daily life. The family is the primary teacher of moral development. In the strug-

gles and conflicts of marital life, husbands and wives learn the realism and adult practicalities of love. Through the love, stability, discipline, and laughter of parents and siblings, children learn that reality accepts them, welcomes them, invites their willingness to take risks. The family nourishes "basic trust." From this spring creativity, psychic energy, social dynamism. If infants are injured here, not all the institutions of society can put them back together.

Economic and educational disciplines are learned only in the home and, if not there, hardly at all. Discipline in black families has been traditionally severe, very like that in white working-class families. Survival has depended on family discipline. Working-class people, white and black, cannot count on having their way; most of the time they have to be docile, agreeable, and efficient. Otherwise, they are fired. They cannot quit their jobs too often; otherwise their employment record shows instability. Blacks as well as whites survive by such rules, as long as authority in the home is strong. From here, some find the base for their mobility, up and out. Without a guiding hand, however, the temptations to work a little, quit, enjoy oneself, then work a little, are too much encouraged by one's peers on the street. *Either* the home, *or* the street: This is the moral choice. Liberals too seldom think about the economic values of strong family life; they neglect their own source of strength, and legislate for others what would never have worked for themselves.

 USING THE DICTIONARY: In discussing major social trends, Michael Novak uses many terms that label ideas and attitudes. Check ten of the following in your dictionary: 1. *fervor* (1) 2. *heretic* (2) 3. *orthodoxy* (3) 4. *ambivalent* (3) 5. *hedonism* (3) 6. *residual* (5) 7. *exonerate* (5) 8. *alienation* (8) 9. *lassitude* (8) 10. *myth* (10) 11. *autonomy* (13) 12. *altruism* (14) 13. *cosmopolitanism* (15) 14. *fidelity* (18) 15. *dynamism* (20)

THE WRITER'S AGENDA:

Novak's aim in this essay is twofold: to trace the causes that work against the traditional family, and to speak up in defense of the benefits and traditional values that are being lost as a result. Answer the following questions:

1. How does the *introduction* lead up to and spell out the central thesis hinted at in the title?

2. Early in the essay, Novak discusses *two basic causes* that work against the traditional family—an "upwardly mobile" lifestyle and the conditions of "urban industrial life." What are the cause-and-effect relationships that he traces here? Explain them as fully as you can.

3. In the central portion of the essay, the author discusses *myths and superstitions* that reinforce our modern tendency to be "individual people" rather than "family people." What are the ideas and attitudes he attacks here? What are their sources?

4. Much of the author's idealized description of family life centers on the *ethnic family.* How does he define it? What does he say about its history? What does he say about its psychological, educational, economic, and political role? (Quote some of the statements that seem to you most provocative or persuasive.)

5. In his concluding paragraphs, Novak rejects two kinds of *substitute family*—the "state" and the "street." How does he contrast their roles with that of the family?

FOR DISCUSSION OR WRITING:

1. Where in his essay does the author come closest to something you yourself have observed or experienced? From his account, select one limited generalization concerning one of the benefits of or threats to the traditional family. Test it against your own observation or experience. Show why you agree or disagree.

2. Is the traditional family doomed? In your judgment, what causes are working for it or against it? What factors shape the thinking of people in your own generation about marriage and family?

3. Novak says that the "family nourishes basic trust. . . . If infants are injured here, not all the institutions of society can put them back together." Have you seen the cause-and-effect relationship he describes here at work? Test his generalization against what you know from your own observation or experience.

4. Novak describes approvingly the attitude of people who distrust and resist the expansion of government services in such areas as child care, job training, or nursing homes. Explain his position, and defend your own stand on this issue. Why do you agree or disagree?

5. Prepare a paper in which you discuss major causes for a social, cultural, or economic trend that you have studied or read about. Choose a topic like the following:

+ a low birthrate
+ the decline of the automobile industry
+ large-scale unemployment
+ the plight of the inner city
+ high divorce rates
+ the search for roots

FOR FURTHER DISCUSSION AND WRITING: George Will is a widely read columnist. He wrote this column at a time when boxing and football, two of the country's favorite spectator sports, were under attack for the violence they permit and glorify. What are his arguments against boxing? (Does he seem biased or one-sided?) What are his projections concerning the future of boxing and similar sports? Do you agree or disagree with the author, and why?

George Will

The Barbarity of Boxing

1   FOR 150 YEARS people have been savoring Macauley's judgment that the Puritans hated bearbaiting not because it gave pain to the bear but because it gave pleasure to the spectators. However, there are moments, and this is one, for blurting out the truth: The Puritans were right. The pain to the bear was not a matter of moral indifference, but the pleasure of the spectators was sufficient reason for abolishing that entertainment.

2   Now another boxer has been beaten to death. The brain injury he suffered was worse than the injury the loser in a boxing match is supposed to suffer. It is hard to calibrate such things—how hard an opponent's brain should be banged against the inside of his cranium—in the heat of battle.

3   From time immemorial, in immemorial ways, men have been fighting for the entertainment of other men. Perhaps in a serene, temperate society boxing would be banned along with other blood sports—if, in such a society, the question would even arise. But a step toward the extinction of boxing is understanding why that is desirable. One reason is the physical injury done to young men. But a sufficient reason is the quality of the pleasure boxing often gives to spectators.

4   There is no denying that boxing like other, better sports, can exemplify excellence. Boxing demands bravery and, when done well, is beautiful in the way that any exercise of finely honed physical talents

is. Furthermore, many sports are dangerous. But boxing is the sport that has as its object the infliction of pain and injury. Its crowning achievement is the infliction of serious trauma on the brain. The euphemism for boxing is "the art of self-defense." No. A rose is a rose is a rose, and a user fee is a revenue enhancer is a tax increase, and boxing is aggression.

It is probable that there will be a rising rate of spinal cord injuries 5 and deaths in football. The force of defense players (a function of weight and speed) is increasing even faster than the force of ball carriers and receivers. As a coach once said, football is not a contact sport— dancing is a contact sport—football is a collision sport. The human body, especially the knee and spine, is not suited to that. But football can be made safer by equipment improvements and rules changes such as those proscribing certain kinds of blocks. Boxing is fundamentally impervious to reform.

It will be said that if two consenting adults want to batter each 6 other for the amusement of paying adults, the essential niceties have been satisfied, "consent" being almost the only nicety of a liberal society. But from Plato on, political philosophers have taken entertainments seriously and have believed the law should, too. They have because a society is judged by the kind of citizens it produces, and some entertainments are coarsening. Good government and the good life depend on good values and passions, and some entertainments are inimical to these.

Such an argument cuts no ice in a society where the decayed public 7 philosophy teaches that the pursuit of happiness is a right sovereign over all other considerations; that "happiness" and "pleasure" are synonyms, and that there is no hierarchy of values against which to measure particular appetites. Besides, some persons will say, with reason, that a society in which the entertainment menu includes topless lady mud wrestlers is a society past worrying about.

Sports besides boxing attract persons who want their unworthy pas- 8 sions stirred, including a lust for blood. I remember Memorial Day in the Middle West in the 1950s, when all roads led to the Indianapolis Speedway, where too many fans went to drink Falstaff beer and hope for a crash. But boxing is in a class by itself.

Richard Hoffer of the *Los Angeles Times* remembers the death of 9 Johnny Owen, a young 118-pound bantamweight who died before he had fulfilled his modest ambition of buying a hardware store back home in Wales. Hoffer remembers that "Owen was put in a coma by a single punch, carried out of the Olympic (arena) under a hail of beer cups, some of which were filled with urine."

The law cannot prudently move far in advance of mass taste, so 10 boxing cannot be outlawed. But in a world in which many barbarities are unavoidable, perhaps it is not too much to hope that some of the optional sorts will be outgrown.

U N I T 8

DEFINITION:
Weighty Words

The Common Theme: Words channel much of our thinking. They direct us, inspire us, and discourage us. Often an important decision hinges on how we interpret a key term. What is "censorship," and what is merely the legitimate exercise of parents' rights or a school board's duty? When should a "juvenile" offender be tried as an "adult"? Lawyers debate what constitutes "negligence," "discrimination," or "insanity." The essays in this unit are by writers who give important words due weight. They know how to take a vague term and map out essential areas that are part of its meaning. They know how to take a traditional term and give it a new contemporary significance.

-+

WRITER'S GUIDE 8:
Writing to Define

Arguments over issues easily turn into disputes over words. Sooner or later, when we argue an important issue, someone is likely to say: "What do you mean by equal opportunity?" or "What do you mean by reverse discrimination?" Reading an editorial or article, we often want to ask: "Where do we draw the line?" Where do we draw the "poverty line"? Is creationism a "science"? Is nudity "obscene"? Many controversies hinge on what we mean by an important term.

Often the key words in an argument need exact definition. When we define a term, we mark off the territory it covers. We explain what it takes in and what it leaves out. Many important terms cover a territory whose boundaries are not clearly marked. They overlap with other related terms. They have a *range* of meanings, and they are pushed this way and that by different users for their own purposes. Careful definition of key terms helps our readers to see clearly what they are asked to agree with or what course of action they are asked to follow.

Often a writer will clarify an important word in passing, as needed in the course of an explanation or argument. We can often define a limited technical term in a sentence or in a phrase:

Air bags—*cushions that inflate on impact to protect passengers in a crash*—have been the subject of hotly debated experiments.

Almost every island has developed species that are endemic— that is, *they are peculiar to it alone and are duplicated nowhere else on earth.* (Rachel Carson)

Unfortunately, few of the terms that become the bone of contention in an argument are limited in this fashion. Terms like *censorship* or *discrimination* are "umbrella terms"; in the words of one observer, they provide a tent to cover "a large and active circus." To clarify such a term, the writer will often have to provide an **extended definition** that answers questions like the following: Why is this term important? What is its basic or most commonly agreed-upon meaning? What are typical examples of its use? What are borderline situations? Where do we draw the line?

Remember the following guidelines when writing a paper whose major purpose is to define an important term:

(1) *To sum up your definition, place the term in a general category and then specify what sets it apart.* A summary following this

traditional format is called a **formal definition**. It works like a road atlas that directs us first to a general area and then narrows it down by more specific coordinates. The format of a formal definition can be adapted to a wide range of words, from narrow technical terms to large abstractions:

TERM	GENERAL CLASS	SPECIFICS
A zebra is	a swift horselike animal	with dark stripes on a white or tawny body.
Entitlements are	federal benefits	for which people qualify automatically, by virtue of their age, income, or occupation.
Prejudice is	thinking ill of individuals	merely because of their membership in a group.
Democracy is	a form of government	that allows people to elect their representatives and encourages the free expression of political views.

A well worked-out formal definition provides efficient directions to what the term covers. By placing the term in a general class, like "a form of government," we already effectively direct attention to the general area where the question of definition is likely to arise. By giving the specifics (or "differentiae"), we spell out the requirements that make a given government eligible for the label.

An extended definition will often start with such a summary and then develop its implications in detail. In the following example, the writer spells out the full meaning of a definition of "entitlements" that focuses on a single key criterion: The benefits are *automatic;* the government is legally obligated to provide them to all who are eligible.

Entitlements

FORMAL
DEFINITION:

Neither liberals nor conservatives have yet devised a confident approach to that portion of federal spending known as "entitlements." *Entitlements, sometimes called "payments to individuals," are technically defined as benefits for which people qualify automatically, by virtue of their age or income or occupation.* Social Security is such an entitlement, by far the largest. So are medical programs

Key examples:

such as Medicare and Medicaid, civil-service and military pensions, unemployment insurance and price-support payments for farmers. . . .

Contrast: If the Congress appropriates $2 billion to build a dam or a highway, it can be confident that no more than $2 billion may legally be spent. But when it authorizes extended unemployment benefits, or a different reimbursement formula under Medicare, it can set no limit on the money that will ultimately flow from the Treasury, since *the government is legally obligated to provide benefits to anyone who* can prove that he is eligible. . . .

Common mis- The "entitlement problem" is often thought of
understanding: as a "welfare problem." To a trivial extent, it is: most federal programs for the needy, including the classic welfare program, AFDC (Aid to Families with Dependent Children), do fall within the entitlement budget. But they make up a small part of the whole. Only a sixth of all the money spent on entitlements is for programs that are "means-tested," or aimed at the poor, and those programs are the slowest-growing part of the entitlements budget. . . .

—James Fallows, "Entitlements," *Atlantic*

In arguments dealing with human behavior or with political trends, important terms can seldom be reduced to a single test criterion. Often, an informative definition has to specify several major requirements that *combine* to mark off what a term covers. A systematic examination of the major criteria may provide the framework for a paper or an article as a whole. The following might be the outline of an extended definition of *colonialism:*

The End of Empire

FORMAL   *Colonialism is the systematic domination and*
DEFINITION: *exploitation—military, economic, and cultural—of one country by another.* Classic colonialism followed military conquest and was marked by several distinguishing features. . . .

KEY CRITERIA: *First,* the imperial mother country controlled the colonial economy. It used the colony as a source of raw materials and as a market for finished goods. . . .

Second, the mother country controlled the currency of the colony and imposed taxes or tariffs. . . .

Third, the mother country maintained military control of the colony, raising colonial troops to be used in the service of the mother country. . . .

Fourth, the mother country imposed its language upon the subject people, as in the case of Portuguese in Brazil, Spanish in most of the rest of South America, or English and French in many parts of Africa.

Careful wording of a definition makes sure that it accurately reflects what a term takes in and what it leaves out. For instance, sociologists have begun to use the term *underclass* to describe a new social class of the chronically unemployed urban poor, including large numbers of high school dropouts and single mothers on welfare, many of them the victims of racism and of the falling demand for unskilled factory labor. The definition of the term would have to be worded in such a way that it *excludes* people who work regularly but are poor because they are poorly paid, or an older class of rural poor less reliant on welfare support.

(2) *Show what the word means in practice.* Verbal definitions remain lifeless and abstract unless they are followed up with vivid, convincing examples. A discussion of *literacy* will remain academic in the bad sense of the word unless we look at actual people and the tasks that face them or the skills they need. The term *welfare mentality* will remain a mere catchword unless we look at actual people on welfare—the way they live and make ends meet. One basic ground plan for a definition paper is to start with a general definition and then apply it to a range of detailed examples.

Here is an outline for an extended definition that presents a general definition as the initial thesis and then shows how it applies in several important examples of current interest:

Censors and the Schools

DEFINITION:　　Censorship is interference by officials, organizations, or individuals that employs threats, reprisals, legal means, or force to hamper the free expression of ideas.

I. "Obscene" books in high school libraries

II. The battle of the dictionaries

III. The controversy over evolution

Many words that sound good—*rehabilitation, equal opportunity*—easily remain empty promises. We have to give concrete examples of how they will be implemented. To give concrete meaning to such a term, we usually have to ask: "Where can we see it in action? How can we bring it about?" For example, many people in recent years have talked about the need for "high standards" in our schools. What does raising standards mean in practice? To make an article on this subject worth reading, the writer would have to ask questions like the following:

♦ What subjects are we going to stress?

♦ How high are we going to peg our expectations?

♦ How are we going to translate high standards into high achievement?

♦ In what ways are we going to encourage or reward the gifted?

♦ What are we going to do about low achievers or people who fall short?

(3) *With difficult or debatable terms, study test cases in order to arrive at a common denominator.* An important political or legal term may have become so entangled in controversy that we feel the need to start over from the beginning. To find solid common ground, we may want to ask our readers to look first of all at several situations where the word clearly applies. We can then ask: "What do these situations have in common?"

In much recent controversy, for instance, the word *insanity* seems to have been stretched beyond its commonsense meaning. Editorial writers deplore an "insanity defense" that is used to clear people charged with what seem deliberately planned acts, proceeding from more or less intelligible motives. Radical psychiatrists charge that modern society itself is "insane," forcing truly sane people to withdraw into a private world of their own. What is a basic definition of insanity that would provide some common basis for discussion?

The following is a simplified outline of a magazine article that sets out *in search of* a widely acceptable, widely applicable common meaning:

Going Crazy

There are "crazy people on the street" in all our cities, I suppose—angry black war veterans sniping from a hotel rooftop in New Orleans, shaven-headed girls with knives prowling the hills above Los Angeles—but New York, being the biggest and most anarchic and most enraged of all cities, seems at times to have a lunatic on every block. In some the lunacy is quite harmless. I once knew a man in a threadbare tweed coat, ornamented by an American flag at the lapel, whose only occupation was to board the Forty-second Street crosstown bus and preach the Gospel in a thick Swedish accent until the driver ejected him for not paying his fare. . . .

(Informal introductory example)

EXTENDED CASE HISTORY 1:

Emanuel Plaitakis was talking about a young man named Steve Cloud, of 92-41 190th Street, Jamaica, Queens, who went crazy at 10:30 on the morning of October 18, 1973. Plaitakis had just finished a cup of coffee in Deli City, right next to the Empire State Building, and he was wheeling himself out onto Thirty-fourth Street when he saw "one of those crazy people," later identified as Cloud, "walking up and down without any reason." Cloud approached Plaitakis, as though to ask him a question, but turned instead to an old man standing nearby, Harry Spector. Cloud asked him how to get to Eighth Avenue. "Before I could reply," Spector said later, "he pulled out a gun and started shooting.". . .

EXTENDED CASE HISTORY 2:

To Bellevue the city's ambulances bring its tired, its poor, its huddled masses and wretched refuse. During the course of my researches I visited it on several occasions, always depressed by the way its corridors echoed with sadness and fear. One morning I noticed behind the admissions desk a young Puerto Rican who tugged and strained against the white cloth tapes that held his wrists and ankles to a wheeled stretcher. . . .

EXTENDED CASE HISTORY 3:

Michael Mooney, Jr., was there early in 1973, and he had a vision. He is a husky youth of twenty-one with large blue eyes and moderately long reddish-brown hair. He had dropped out of Harvard to become a musician—he plays the piano, guitar, saxophone, and bass—but he grew increasingly subject to fits of paranoia. He became convinced that people could hear this thoughts. He heard voices demanding to know whether he was, as he puts it, in or out of society. . . .

(Brief
personal
experience
leading up to)
GENERAL
DEFINITION:

... During that moment, however, I think that I was standing on the border of what we call insanity. *The main symptoms were all there: a breakdown in the machinery of perception, or a breakdown in the rational mind's ability to receive and combine perceptions and to make judgments from them. And a sense of helplessness ... and panic. ...* That world where the mad live is not so remote. Most of us come near it at one time or another, even if only for a moment. It is, in some ways, like the chaotic world that we inhabit in our dreams, for there, night after night, we all go mad.

—Otto Friedrich, "Going Crazy," *Harper's*

An article following this pattern reverses the familiar pattern that starts with a general claim as its thesis and then provides support. Instead, it *leads up to* a thesis that is the result of a common search shared by writer and reader. We call a pattern of thought or writing that funnels material into a final conclusion an **inductive** pattern. The inductive pattern presents examples first, generalizations last. It makes special claims on the attention and patience of the reader, but it can produce lasting conviction when well done.

(4) *Explore the different uses of a term.* Often the meaning of a term shifts with the area where it is used, or with the purposes of the people using it. We can clear up apparent contradictions by showing why and how the same term means different things to different people. For instance, we could organize a paper exploring the uses of the term *insanity* by looking at the meanings of the term in different contexts:

I. COMMONSENSE DEFINITION—guiding many people's personal reactions:
Insanity means mental illness that causes wildly erratic behavior and renders people incapable of caring for themselves as well as dangerous to others.

II. MEDICAL DEFINITION—serving as a framework for treatment or therapy:
Insanity is a derangement or disease of the mind occurring usually as a specific disorder (like schizophrenia), not to be confused with mental retardation or different forms of neurosis.

III. LEGAL DEFINITION—serving as a guide in fixing legal responsibility:

> Insanity is an impairment of the mental faculties rendering a person unable to enter into legal contracts or relationships or to assume responsibility for illegal acts.

IV. STATISTICIAN'S DEFINITION—making possible the gathering of figures that can help guide legislators and others:
The narrowest definition of mental illness might limit the concept to people who actually enter a mental hospital for treatment—somewhat over half a million Americans every year.

(5) *Use comparison and contrast with closely related terms to mark off the boundaries of a term.* To help define something new, we often show how it differs from something familiar. A writer trying to define the "superhero" of much current fantasy literature and popular entertainment may emphasize the contrast with the traditional heroes of folklore and history:

TRADITIONAL: A hero is a human being who through discipline, bravery, determination, and perhaps divine assistance accomplishes seemingly incredible feats. Heroes generally must be good and serve a good cause, though sometimes brave and generous men in the service of an evil cause are deemed to be heroes— usually tragic but noble figures. Thus Robert E. Lee is honored by most of those who disapproved the cause of the South. . . .

NEW: A superhero, *by contrast,* is not a real human being, but a fantasy creature—Superman, Batman, Captain Marvel, Wonder Woman, *et al.* Superheroes, unlike the heroes of Greek mythology, have no Achilles' heel. Superman himself is vulnerable to the mineral kryptonite, but of course he will never be killed by it—unlike the great Achilles. Unlike the more traditional heroes of folklore and of reality, modern superheroes have no moral context. They are generally in the service of "good" and against "evil," of course. But the good that they serve is undefined. . . .
—Harold O. J. Brown, "Superman on the Screen," *Christianity Today*

A writer will often establish the boundaries of a term by marking it off from several of its closest cousins or look-alikes. For instance, *affec-*

tion, passion, and *infatuation* appear as near synonyms of *love;* they stand for something closely related but not exactly the same. By showing how each is different, a writer could mark off the boundaries of "true love."

(6) *Trace the history of a term to clarify its changing meanings.* Terms like *anarchist, pacifism, liberal,* or *democracy* are likely to remain confusing unless we clarify their historical roots and discuss some of the major historical developments in which they played a role. Even with fairly limited technical terms, historical information may be a major part of a basic definition:

> The "grandfather clause" is a legal term *originally applied* to passages in some Southern states' constitutions that exempted from voter literacy and property requirements anyone whose ancestors had voted before 1867 (i.e., white people). *Today,* the term "grandfather clause" is used to describe any legal provision that exempts people from some change in the rules simply because they got there first.
> —Michael Kinsley, "The Grandfather Clause Society," *Harper's*

Inspirational words and those that are part of the fighting words or slogans of historical movements change their associations as times and circumstances change. A writer may trace the history of such a term in order to *redefine* it for our times:

REVOLUTIONARY
FIRST STAGE:

The development of a sense of patriotism was a strong unifying force during our Revolution and its insecure aftermath. Defined then and now as "love of country," patriotism was an extremely important motivating force with which to confront foreign threats to the young nation. It was no happenstance that *The Star Spangled Banner* was composed during the War of 1812 when the Redcoats were not only coming but already here. . . .

EXPANSIONIST
SECOND STAGE:

As the United States moved into the 20th century and became a world power, far-flung alliances and wars fought thousands of miles away stretched the boundaries of patriotism. "Making the world safe for democracy" was the grandiose way Woodrow Wilson put it. At other times and places (such as Latin America) it became distorted into "jingoism." . . .

MODERN
THIRD STAGE:

World War II was the last war that all Americans fought with conviction. Thereafter, when "bombs bursting in air" would be atomic bombs, world war

> became a suicidal risk. . . . Wars that could be so fi-
> nal and so swift lost their glamour even for the most
> militaristically minded. When we became the most
> powerful nation on earth, the old insecurity that
> made patriotism into a conditioned reflex of "my
> country right or wrong" should have given way to a
> thinking process; as expressed by Carl Schurz: "Our
> country . . . when right, to be kept right. When
> wrong, to be put right." . . .
> —Ralph Nader, "We Need a New Kind of Patriotism," *Life*

To sum up: Careful definition of important words helps us say what we mean. Much misunderstanding is brought on by words that have different meanings for different people. Much controversy is caused by words whose meanings have begun to shift and whose exact bearings have to be specified. Without definition, many impressive or inspirational words that roll smoothly off the tongue remain just words. Careful definition of key terms helps us clarify our own thinking. It helps us keep an argument focused on the issues. It helps us make our readers see where we stand.

PREWRITING ACTIVITIES 8

1. The media constantly supply us with new *buzz words* for developments and trends. Choose two or three of the following, and write a paragraph about each. Provide as accurate and helpful a definition as you can. Choose from the following:

+ no-fault divorce

+ single-parent family

+ ethnic revival

+ freedom of information

+ the volunteer army

+ white flight

+ reverse discrimination

+ the Moral Majority

+ gentrification

+ the underclass

+ mainstreaming

2. Do a preliminary inventory of material for an extended definition of a term that has played or is playing an important role in American political life. Choose a term like *segregation, feminism, dissent,
patronage, due process, corruption, the Jewish vote, welfare state.* Fill
in material under all or most of the following headings:

 I. *Surface meaning* (What common associations or misconceptions cluster around the term?)

 II. *Historical roots* (For instance, what are the roots of segregation in the history of slavery and abolition? What are famous names in the history of dissent?)

 III. *Media coverage* (For instance, when is the last time you
have seen segregation play a major role in news coverage?)

 IV. *Personal experience* (Where in your own life or in the
lives of relatives and friends has segregation or dissent or
the welfare state become more than a distant abstraction?)

 V. *Related or contrasting terms* (In defining *feminism,* what
use would you make of related terms like *suffragist, wom-
en's rights, emancipation, women's liberation?*)

 VI. *Common denominator* (What to you are key elements or
dimensions of the term to which a definition would have
to do justice?)

3. Each of the following *model sentences* clarifies or brings into
focus an important term. Study the model sentences and the student-
written imitations. For each model, write an imitation of your own that
clarifies or brings into focus an important term. Follow the pattern or
structure of the original sentence as closely as you can.

MODEL 1:   Economy is the art of making the most of life.
(George Bernard Shaw)

IMITATION: Procrastination is the action of avoiding today's mistakes by putting them off until tomorrow.

MODEL 2:   Courage is not the absence of fear; it is the control
over fear. (Dickie Chapelle)

IMITATION: Positive thinking is not the absence of negative
thoughts; it is the control over negative thoughts.

MODEL 3:   Love is as necessary to human beings as food and
shelter. (Aldous Huxley)

IMITATION: Attention is as essential to children as are clothes and shoes.

MODEL 4: Marriage, like many other institutions, brings restrictions as well as benefits.

IMITATION: Idealism, like other philosophies, produces hope as well as despair.

MODEL 5: What makes democratic politics different from most other professions is that, occasionally, the politician has a duty to risk his job by performing it conscientiously. (George F. Will)

IMITATION: What makes women different from men is that often a woman is able to reach a better decision by adding the human factor to cold facts.

BACKGROUND: Susannah Lessard worked as an editor for *The Washington Monthly* and became a staff writer for *The New Yorker*. She writes reflective pieces about the current American scene and American values, on subjects ranging from Oyster Bay, Long Island, to the architecture of skyscrapers, which she examined in an article called "The Towers of Light." She wrote the following definition of "conservatism" as part of a longer article called "Civility, Community, Humor: The Conservatism We Need," which was published in *The Washington Monthly* in 1973. Like many other commentators at the time, she was writing to explain a general swing "to the right" in America. Her definition helps us understand a general conservative trend in American politics and morals, shown in examples ranging from "back to basics" in the schools to a backlash against "permissive" personal morality. This short selection illustrates well the basic function of a successful definition: The author takes us from the mere word *conservative* to the role that powerful conservative attitudes play in our lives. She clears up the possible confusions that might have resulted from the frequent use of the word as a catchall label or as a superficial term of disapproval. She maps out what the word stands for: attitudes that play a major role in shaping people's thoughts and actions.

Susannah Lessard

The Real Conservatism

GUIDE TO READING: This definition systematically maps out essential elements that combine to make up a conservative outlook. What are the key elements in the definition? What are the major areas to which the author applies the term? What related terms or near synonyms help us understand the term? What opposite or contrasting terms does the author use to set the conservative outlook off from rival or competing attitudes?

1   ONE AUTUMN Saturday afternoon I was listening to the radio when the station switched to the Dartmouth–Harvard game. The game had not begun, and the announcer was rambling on about the nip in the air, the autumn colors, past games, this year's players, their names and hometowns—a seminostalgic discourse that, despite an aversion

for football talk, I found unexpectedly moving. Autumn, a new crop of players, New England: The world was on a steady keel after all. I could not remember having felt that quiet sense of cycle, of ongoing life and the past floating so serenely to the surface, in a long time.

That morning, anyway, I felt like a conservative. 2

I am not a conservative. I think the government not only should try 3 to, but can, improve life for its citizens; yet for the first time I've begun to understand the value of tradition, both for the counterpoint it can provide to the Left and for the different perspective it offers on the drift rightward of the electorate.

Two elementary attitudes underlie the conservative tradition. The 4 first is a passionate sense of the need to conserve—the land, the culture, the institutions, codes of behavior—and to revere and protect those elements that constitute "civilization." The conservative looks to the enduring values of the past—to holding on to what we've got—in forming his political positions, rather than to alluring, idealistic visions of what the future could be.

The second attitude is a cautious view of raw democracy, or direct 5 representational government. The conservative believes firmly in the rights of minorities and those institutions that protect minorities from the whims of the majority, such as the Supreme Court—an elite, appointed body—and the Constitution, particularly the First Amendment. The concern behind this attitude is less for racial, ethnic or religious groups than for intellectual minorities—the educated elite—to which conservatives have always belonged.

These institutions that restrain the mass will are precious in the 6 conservative view, not just because they protect the few from being trampled by the many, but also because they protect the majority from its own mistakes. This awareness that the majority can often be wrong (so easily forgotten by social crusaders) produces a mental habit. Conservatives tend to be automatically uncomfortable with any idea or trend that smacks of mob psychology—anything that gains a swift and wide popularity—to the point of appearing to enjoy embracing unpopular positions and dropping wet blankets on the emotional political moods to which this country is prone.

An outgrowth of these attitudes—and one with particular value—is 7 the humor that the skeptical turn of the conservative mind can bring to bear on the confused, disaster-prone but unreservedly grand schemes for the betterment of mankind, which the quixotic and too often humorless liberal is forever earnestly pressing to perpetrate.

 USING THE DICTIONARY: A simple synonym, like *dislike* for *aversion,* can give us a quick guide to the meaning of a word. However, to use a word well, we usually have to know

more. Select five of the following. How much do you learn
from your dictionary about the history of each word, its range
of meaning or major uses, and possible overtones or associations? 1. *counterpoint* (3) 2. *code* (4) 3. *elite* (5) 4. *mob* (6)
5. *crusader* (6) 6. *skeptical* (7) 7. *quixotic* (7)

THE WRITER'S AGENDA:

The author of this definition in a very short space maps out an
important term. Answer the following questions about how she proceeds:

1. This selection starts with a *personal anecdote* that effectively
links a mere word to concrete experience. What are the major elements
that help create the **mood** of this introduction? What to you is the central clue to the conservative temperament that the author provides
here?

2. Of the two basic conservative attitudes that Lessard enumerates,
the first is the more *conventional* or familiar, and the closest to the
literal meaning of the word. What is the key element here? What are
major areas to which it applies? What examples would you give to show
what this part of the definition means in practice?

3. In going on to a second fundamental conservative attitude, the
author clears up a *misunderstanding* that might arise from her reference to the "rights of minorities." Why would this misunderstanding
arise? How does she clear it up?

4. Much of the second half of this definition deals with *practical*
political implications of conservative attitudes. What, according to the
author, is the conservative attitude toward "raw democracy" and "mob
psychology"? What are its practical political results?

5. Early in her definition, the author starts to *contrast* conservatism
with its liberal counterpoint. Where and how? How does the concluding paragraph round out the contrast between the two opposed terms?

FOR DISCUSSION OR WRITING:

1. What part of the author's definition do you find most convincing? What part do you question, and why?

2. Prepare your own one-sentence definitions of several of the key
terms used in this essay: *conservative, liberal, elite, raw democracy,
mob psychology.* Compare your definitions with those prepared by your
classmates. (Your instructor may ask you to choose one of these terms
for a paragraph-length definition.)

3. Discuss major synonyms and related terms that cluster around the word *conservative* in this selection: *tradition, values, culture, civilization.* How are they related? Where do we encounter them? How are they typically used? For what purposes?

4. Where have you seen evidence of a general "conservative" trend in our society? Provide your own working definition of *conservative,* and discuss striking examples. Or identify an important countertrend. Provide a definition and detailed examples.

5. Many arguments hinge on distinctions between related words. Prepare a paper in which you answer one of the following questions: When does a "conservative" become a "reactionary"? When does a "liberal" become a "radical"? When does an "authoritarian" government become "totalitarian"?

6. Using Lessard's definition as a model, prepare your own extended definition of a term often used by critical observers of American culture. Choose one: *sentimentality, sensationalism, materialism, permissiveness,* or *optimism.* Provide a definition and detailed examples. Mark the term off from other related or opposite terms as needed.

BACKGROUND: Jane Howard (born 1935) is a journalist who became known for her books about the changing American scene. She was born in Springfield, Illinois, and attended the University of Michigan. She went to work and live in New York City, working for *Life* magazine first as a reporter and later as editor and staff writer. Her books include *A Different Woman* (1973) and her widely reviewed *Families* (1978), from which the following article was adapted for publication in the *Atlantic* magazine. Unlike trend watchers who merely chart changing patterns of American life, Howard points new directions for readers who are looking for guidance in a time of shifting values. She helps us adapt old concepts or ways of thinking to changing circumstances in changing times.

Jane Howard

In Search of the Good Family

GUIDE TO READING: In this essay, the author sets out to give new meaning to an old familiar term. Why does she feel the need to redefine the word? What synonyms, near synonyms, and other related terms does she bring in, and how are they related to her central term? As she maps out the area covered by her central term, what part of the territory is familiar? What part of the territory is new or strange?

1   CALL IT a clan, call it a network, call it a tribe, call it a family. Whatever you call it, whoever you are, you need one. You need one because you are human. You didn't come from nowhere. Before you, around you, and presumably after you, too, there are others. Some of these others must matter a lot—to you, and if you are very lucky, to one another. Their welfare must be nearly as important to you as your own. Even if you live alone, even if your solitude is elected and ebullient, you still cannot do without a clan or a tribe.

2   The trouble with the clans and tribes many of us were born into is not that they consist of meddlesome ogres but that they are too far

away. In emergencies we rush across continents and if need be oceans to their sides, as they do to ours. Maybe we even make a habit of seeing them, once or twice a year, for the sheer pleasure of it. But blood ties seldom dictate our addresses. Our blood kin are often too remote to ease us from our Tuesdays to our Wednesdays. For this we must rely on our families of friends. If our relatives are not, do not wish to be, or for whatever reasons cannot be our friends, then by some complex alchemy we must try to transform our friends into our relatives. If blood and roots don't do the job, then we must look to water and branches, and sort ourselves into new constellations, new families.

These new families, to borrow the terminology of an African tribe (the Bangwa of the Cameroons), may consist either of friends of the road, ascribed by chance, or friends of the heart, achieved by choice. Ascribed friends are those we happen to go to school with, work with, or live near. They know where we went last weekend and whether we still have a cold. Just being around gives them a provisional importance in our lives, and us in theirs. Maybe they will still matter to us when we or they move away; quite likely they won't. Six months or two years will probably erase us from each other's thoughts, unless by some chance they and we have become friends of the heart.

Wishing to be friends, as Aristotle[1] wrote, is quick work, but friendship is a slowly ripening fruit. An ancient proverb he quotes in his *Ethics* had it that you cannot know a man until you and he together have eaten a peck of salt. Now a peck, a quarter of a bushel, is quite a lot of salt—more, perhaps, than most pairs of people ever have occasion to share. We must try though. We must sit together at as many tables as we can. We must steer each other through enough seasons and weathers so that sooner or later it crosses our minds that one of us, God knows which or with what sorrow, must one day mourn the other.

We must devise new ways, or revive old ones, to equip ourselves with kinfolk. Maybe such an impulse prompted whoever ordered the cake I saw in my neighborhood bakery to have it frosted to say "HAPPY BIRTHDAY SURROGATE." I like to think that this cake was decorated not for a judge but for someone's surrogate mother or surrogate brother: loathsome jargon, but admirable sentiment. If you didn't conceive me or if we didn't grow up in the same house, we can still be related, if we decide we ought to be. It is never too late, I like to hope, to augment our families in ways nature neglected to do. It is never too late to choose new clans.

The best-chosen clans, like the best friendships and the best blood families, endure by accumulating a history solid enough to suggest a future. But clans that don't last have merit too. We can lament them but

---

[1][ancient Greek philosopher (384–322 B.C.), whose *Nicomachean Ethics* includes friendship among the key virtues that contribute to the good life]

we shouldn't deride them. Better an ephemeral clan or tribe than none at all. A few of my life's most tribally joyous times, in fact, have been spent with people whom I have yet to see again. This saddens me, as it may them too, but dwelling overlong on such sadness does no good. A more fertile exercise is to think back on those times and try to figure out what made them, for all their brevity, so stirring. What can such times teach us about forming new and more lasting tribes in the future?

7   New tribes and clans can no more be willed into existence, of course, than any other good thing can. We keep trying, though. To try, with gritted teeth and girded loins, is after all American. That is what the two Helens and I were talking about the day we had lunch in a room way up in a high-rise motel near the Kansas City airport. We had lunch there at the end of a two-day conference on families. The two Helens were social scientists, but I liked them even so, among other reasons because they both objected to that motel's coffee shop even more than I did. One of the Helens, from Virginia, disliked it so much that she had brought along homemade whole wheat bread, sesame butter, and honey from her parents' farm in South Dakota, where she had visited before the conference. Her picnic was the best thing that happened, to me at least, those whole two days.

8   "If you're voluntarily childless and alone," said the other Helen, who was from Pennsylvania by way of Puerto Rico, "it gets harder and harder with the passage of time. It's stressful. That's why you need support systems." I had been hearing quite a bit of talk about "support systems." The term is not among my favorites, but I can understand its currency. Whatever "support systems" may be, the need for them is clearly urgent, and not just in this country. Are there not thriving "mega-families" of as many as three hundred people in Scandinavia? Have not the Japanese for years had an honored, enduring—if perhaps by our standards rather rigid—custom of adopting nonrelatives to fill gaps in their families? Should we not applaud and maybe imitate such ingenuity?

9   And consider our own Unitarians. From Santa Barbara to Boston they have been earnestly dividing their congregations into arbitrary "extended families" whose members are bound to act like each other's relatives. Kurt Vonnegut, Jr.[2] plays with a similar train of thought in his fictional *Slapstick*. In that book every newborn baby is assigned a randomly chosen middle name, like Uranium or Daffodil or Raspberry. These middle names are connected with hyphens to numbers between one and twenty, and any two people who have the same middle name are automatically related. This is all to the good, the author thinks,

---

[2][American novelist, master of satire and fantasy, who wrote *Slaughterhouse Five* (1969) and many other books]

because "human beings need all the relatives they can get—as possible donors or receivers not of love but of common decency." He envisions these extended families as "one of the four greatest inventions by Americans," the others being *Robert's Rules of Order,* the Bill of Rights, and the principles of Alcoholics Anonymous.

This charming notion might even work, if it weren't so arbitrary.   10
Already each of us is born into one family not of our choosing. If we're going to devise new ones, we might as well have the luxury of picking the members ourselves. Clever picking might result in new families whose benefits would surpass or at least equal those of the old. As a member in reasonable standing of six or seven tribes in addition to the one I was born to, I have been trying to figure which characteristics are common to both kinds of families.

1) Good families have a chief, or a heroine, or a founder—someone   11
around whom others cluster, whose achievements, as the Yiddish word has it, let them *kvell,*[3] and whose example spurs them on to like feats. Some blood dynasties produce such figures regularly; others languish for as many as five generations between demigods, wondering with each new pregnancy whether this, at last, might be the messianic baby who will redeem them. Look, is there not something gubernatorial about her footstep, or musical about the way he bangs with his spoon on his cup? All clans, of all kinds, need such a figure now and then. Sometimes clans based on water rather than blood harbor several such personages at one time.

2) Good families have a switchboard operator—someone who can-   12
not help but keep track of what all the others are up to, who plays Houston Mission Control to everyone else's Apollo. This role is assumed rather than assigned. The person who volunteers for it often has the instincts of an archivist, and feels driven to keep scrapbooks and photograph albums up to date, so that the clan can see proof of its own continuity.

3) Good families are much to all their members, but everything to   13
none. Good families are fortresses with many windows and doors to the outer world. The blood clans I feel most drawn to were founded by parents who are nearly as devoted to what they do outside as they are to each other and their children. Their curiosity and passion are contagious. Everybody, where they live, is busy. Paint is spattered on eyeglasses. Mud lurks under fingernails. Person-to-person calls come in the middle of the night from Tokyo and Brussels. Catcher's mitts, ballet slippers, overdue library books, and other signs of extrafamilial concerns are everywhere.

---

[3] [Leo Rosten, in *The Joys of Yiddish,* defines *kvell* as "beam with immense pride and pleasure . . . doting with conspicuous pride."]

14   4) Good families are hospitable. Knowing that hosts need guests as much as guests need hosts, they are generous with honorary memberships for friends, whom they urge to come early and often and to stay late. Such clans exude a vivid sense of surrounding rings of relatives, neighbors, teachers, students, and godparents, any of whom at any time might break or slide into the inner circle. Inside that circle a wholesome, tacit emotional feudalism develops: you give me protection, I'll give you fealty. Such pacts begin with, but soon go far beyond, the jolly exchange of pie at Thanksgiving or cake on a birthday. They mean that you can ask me to supervise your children for the fortnight you will be in the hospital, and that however inconvenient this might be for me, I shall manage to do so. It means I can phone you on what for me is a dreary, wretched Sunday afternoon and for you is the eve of a deadline, knowing you will tell me to come right over, if only to watch you type. It means we need not dissemble. ("To yield to seeming," as Martin Buber wrote, "is man's essential cowardice, to resist it is his essential courage . . . one must at times pay dearly for life lived from the being, but it is never too dear.")[4]

15   5) Good families deal squarely with direness. Pity the tribe that doesn't have, and cherish, at least one flamboyant eccentric. Pity too the one that supposes it can avoid for long the woes to which all flesh is heir. Lunacy, bankruptcy, suicide, and other unthinkable fates sooner or later afflict the noblest of clans with an undertow of gloom. Family life is a set of givens, someone once told me, and it takes courage to see certain givens as blessings rather than as curses. It surely does. Contradictions and inconsistencies are givens, too. So is the battle against what the Oregon patriarch Kenneth Babbs calls malarkey. "There's always malarkey lurking, bubbles in the cesspool, fetid bubbles that pop and smell. But I don't put up with malarkey, between my stepkids and my natural ones or anywhere else in the family."

16   6) Good families prize their rituals. Nothing welds a family more than these. Rituals are vital especially for clans without histories, because they evoke a past, imply a future, and hint at continuity. No line is the seder service at Passover reassures more that the last: "Next year in Jerusalem!" A clan becomes more of a clan each time it gathers to observe a fixed ritual (Christmas, birthdays, Thanksgiving, and so on), grieves at a funeral (anyone may come to most funerals; those who do declare their tribalness), and devises a new rite of its own. Equinox breakfasts can be at least as welding as Memorial Day parades. Several of my colleagues and I used to meet for lunch every Pearl Harbor Day, preferably to eat some politically neutral fare like smorgasbord, to "for-

---

[4][Martin Buber (1878–1965) was an Austrian-born Israeli philosopher and theologian.]

give" our only ancestrally Japanese friend, Irene Kubota Neves. For that
and other things we became, and remain, a sort of family . . .

7) Good families are affectionate. This of course is a matter of style. 17
I know clans whose members greet each other with gingerly hand-
shakes or, in what pass for kisses, with hurried brushes of jawbones, as
if the object were to touch not the lips but the ears. I don't see how
such people manage. "The tribe that does not hug," as someone who
has been part of many *ad hoc* families recently wrote to me, "is no tribe
at all. More and more I realize that everybody, regardless of age, needs
to be hugged and comforted in a brotherly or sisterly way now and
then. Preferably now."

8) Good families have a sense of place, which these days is not 18
achieved easily. As Susanne Langer wrote in 1957, "Most people have
no home that is a symbol of their childhood, not even a definite memory of one place to serve that purpose . . . all the old symbols are gone."
Once I asked a roomful of supper guests if anyone felt a strong pull to
any certain spot on the face of the earth. Everyone was silent, except for
a visitor from Bavaria. The rest of us seemed to know all too well what
Walker Percy means in *The Moviegoer* when he tells of the "genie-soul
of a place, which every place has or else is not a place [and which]
wherever you go, you must meet and master or else be met and mastered." All that meeting and mastering saps plenty of strength. It also
underscores our need for tribal bases of the sort which soaring real
estate taxes and splintering families have made all but obsolete.

So what are we to do, those of us whose habit and pleasure and 19
doom is our tendency, as a Georgia lady put it, to "fly off at every other
whipstitch"? Think in terms of movable feasts, that's what. Live here,
wherever here may be, as if we were going to belong here for the rest of
our lives. Learn to hallow whatever ground we happen to stand on or
land on. Like medieval knights who took their tapestries along on Cru-
sades, like modern Afghanis with their yurts, we must pack such totems
and icons as we can to make short-term quarters feel like home. Pil-
lows, small rugs, watercolors can dispel much of the chilling anonymity
of a motel room or sublet apartment. When we can, we should live in
rooms with stoves or fireplaces or at least candlelight. The ancient saying is still true: Extinguished hearth, extinguished family.

Round tables help too, and as a friend of mine once put it, so do 20
"too many comfortable chairs, with surfaces to put feet on, arranged so
as to encourage a maximum of eye contact." Such rooms inspire good
talk, of which good clans can never have enough.

9) Good families, not just the blood kind, find some way to connect 21
with posterity. "To forge a link in the humble chain of being, encir-
cling heirs to ancestors," as Michael Novak has written, "is to walk
within a circle of magic as primitive as humans knew in caves." He is

talking of course about babies, feeling them leap in wombs, giving them suck. Parenthood, however, is a state which some miss by chance and others by design, and a vocation to which not all are called. Some of us, like the novelist Richard P. Brickner, look on as others "name their children and their children in turn name their own lives, devising their own flags from their parents' cloth." What are we who lack children to do? Build houses? Plant trees? Write books or symphonies or laws? Perhaps, but even if we do these things, there should be children on the sidelines if not at the center of our lives.

22   It is a sadly impoverished tribe that does not allow access to, and make much of, some children. Not too much, of course; it has truly been said that never in history have so many educated people devoted so much attention to so few children. Attention, in excess, can turn to fawning, which isn't much better than neglect. Still, if we don't regularly see and talk to and laugh with people who can expect to outlive us by twenty years or so, we had better get busy and find some.

23   10) Good families also honor their elders. The wider the age range, the stronger the tribe. Jean-Paul Sartre[5] and Margaret Mead, to name two spectacularly confident former children, have both remarked on the central importance of grandparents in their own early lives. Grandparents are now in much more abundant supply than they were a generation or two ago, when old age was more rare. If actual grandparents are not at hand, no family should have too hard a time finding substitute ones to whom to pay unfeigned homage. The Soviet Union's enchantment with day-care centers, I have heard, stems at least in part from the state's eagerness to keep children away from their presumably subversive grandparents. Let that be a lesson to clans based on interest as well as to those based on genes.

 USING THE DICTIONARY: In her **allusions** to other cultures and other periods in history, Jane Howard uses many terms that have come into English from other languages. Check ten of the following. What language or part of the world does the word come from? 1. *alchemy* (2) 2. *constellation* (2) 3. *dynasty* (11) 4. *demigod* (11) 5. *messianic* (11) 6. *feudalism* (14) 7. *fealty* (14) 8. *flamboyant* (15) 9. *patriarch* (15) 10. *seder* (16) 11. *genie* (18) 12. *smorgasbord* (16) 13. *yurt* (17) 14. *totem* (17) 15. *icon* (17)

---

[5] [leading French philosopher, novelist, playwright, and political activist of the post-World War II period, who helped popularize the philosophy of existentialism]

THE WRITER'S AGENDA:

The author of this article sets out to give a contemporary meaning to a traditional concept. Answer the following questions about how she redefines her key term:

1. Where does the author first sum up her *redefinition* of the central term as the **thesis** of her essay? What does she say about the need for redefining the term? Later in the first five or six paragraphs, find several sentences that reiterate—restate, explain, reinforce—her central thesis.

2. In guiding us to the territory covered by her central term, the author brings in many *related terms* that cluster around the central concept. Discuss some of the traditional terms she uses: the term *family* itself and related terms like *clan, tribe, kin, dynasty, godparents, patriarch.* What are their meanings, familiar associations, typical but also extended uses? What are the implications or historical associations of familiar metaphors like *blood* and *roots?* What are the origins and implications of more modern terms like *network, surrogate mother, support system, extended family?*

3. Among the characteristics of good families listed by the author, select the three or four that to you seem *most basic* or most essential. What does the author say about them? Why do they seem especially important to you? Where or how have you observed them in action?

4. Among the characteristics of good families listed by the author, select those that seem to you most surprising—*least conventional* or least predictable. What does the author say about them? Does she make their inclusion plausible?

5. How successful is the author in showing what her ideas mean *in practice?* Discuss some of the examples, anecdotes, precedents, or parallels that for you are most helpful or most convincing.

FOR DISCUSSION OR WRITING:

1. Make your own list of the essential characteristics of "good families." Rearrange the order of those listed by Howard to reflect your own priorities. What characteristics would you add, and why? Which would you delete?

2. Terms like *family* and *marriage* change their meanings as legal boundaries and attitudes shift. What would you include in an extended definition of marriage as an institution? (Does it require legal or official

certification? Does it have to be sanctified by a religious rite? Does it have to be with someone of the other sex? What are its key responsibilities or obligations?)

3. Public discussion or controversy often focuses on terms that need redefinition as times change and as new questions or problems arise. Prepare a paper in which you define such a term, using detailed examples. Choose one:

- rehabilitation as a goal of the penal system
- the right to privacy
- pornography and community standards
- patriotism in today's world

4. Write an extended definition of the ideal family, or of true friendship, or of true love. If needed, set your key term off from other related or opposed terms.

5. Howard makes us reconsider some familiar human needs or key elements in people's lives. Prepare a paper in which you explore one of the following:

- the importance of ritual or ceremony in our lives
- the differences in how people show affection
- traditions of hospitality
- the way we treat or think of elders

BACKGROUND: On May 6, 1954, the British medical student Roger Bannister (born 1929) became the first person in history to run the mile in less than four minutes. After retiring from international athletics, he became a prominent neurologist. He has continued his involvement with sports, however, chairing the British Sports Council (1971–75) and, since 1976, serving as president of the International Council for Sport and Physical Recreation, an advisory body to UNESCO. In *The Four-Minute Mile,* the account of his extraordinary accomplishment, Bannister said, "We run, not because we think it is doing us good, but because we enjoy it and cannot help ourselves." Running "gives a man or woman the chance to bring out power that might otherwise remain locked away inside." In the following essay, he describes the increasingly important role he believes sports play in our lives. The essay appeared in a different form in *Sports Illustrated* and was reprinted from *The Four-Minute Mile* in *The Runner* magazine for October 1981.

Sir Roger Bannister
The Pursuit of Excellence

GUIDE TO READING: In this essay, the author maps out what sports has meant to him personally and what it ideally should mean in our lives. As you read the essay, outline the different dimensions of sports that the author explores, from the physical and technical to the psychological and political. What attention does he pay to the "darker, less promising side" of sports?

W HY DID we ever try to break the four-minute-mile barrier in 1954? Fifty-eight years had passed since the revival of the Olympic Games in 1896, and athletes had been edging toward this goal, the simple act of putting one foot after another faster than anyone had done before. Partly it was the time we lived in; the 1950s was an age of exploration and attempts to smash physical barriers in a world liberated from war, a world in which we were no longer soldiers, or bombed, or rationed. My first unsuccessful world-record bid was in 1953, the year Queen Elizabeth II was crowned and Everest scaled. But the world was not yet navigated by a single-handed nonstop sailor and the moon landing only dreamed of.

2   Chris Brasher, Chris Chataway and I, all of us at Oxford University, seemed more privileged than we actually were. We were labeled young "Elizabethans," possessing more than a touch of single-mindedness, optimism, and that now unfashionable quality, patriotism. Breaking world athletic records offered us an opportunity for intensely personal achievement. Pindar, the Greek poet, captured this idea when he wrote in 500 B.C., "Yet that man is happy and poets sing of him who conquers with hand and swift foot and strength."

3   After the four-minute mile, I ran almost daily for the next twenty years, but I never competed again. Astonishment at that decision would have been quickly allayed if the questioner had glimpsed my life. As an intern at St. Mary's Hospital in London, I looked after some 50 "beds," a round-the-clock schedule which allowed only a few snatched hours of sleep. It was a punishing (and since much-revised) make-or-break initiation to a teaching-hospital training for a consultant physician, but also an enormously rich and enthralling experience. Medicine, and neurology in particular—the teasing, endless puzzle of how the brain controls our every thought and activity—has captivated me to this day.

4   Since 1954, there has been a revolution in athletic training. Instead of working out for half an hour five days a week, athletes now run for up to three hours a day over two sessions. As a result of this longer, harder training and faster synthetic tracks, the world mile record has been lowered by several great athletes, whom I have enjoyed meeting and watching in action. Herb Elliott of Australia took the largest slice, lowering the record by 2.7 seconds to 3:54.5 in 1958. Peter Snell of New Zealand, probably a stronger miler than Elliott, brought the record to 3:54.1 in 1964. But I rate Jim Ryun of the United States as the most talented natural runner, though he was not the best competitor. Ryun was only 19 when he ran 3:51.3. His achievement was partially due to altitude training, a technique which athletes stumbled upon when faced with the prospect of the 1968 Mexico City Olympics to be held in the thin air at 7,500 feet. In 1967 Ryun went to a training camp at 7,400 feet. Then twice within six weeks he raced at sea level and lowered world records on each occasion. Unfortunately, this preparation was to no avail in the Olympics. Ryun was beaten in the final—altitude wrecked any predictability of performance.

5   Filbert Bayi of Tanzania brought the record down to 3:51 in 1975. He illustrates a second factor in distance record breaking: the advantage of dwelling at high altitudes. Even while one sleeps, the body is training to transport oxygen efficiently from the thin air to the muscles.

6   Like Snell, another great miler of the past two decades, John Walker, comes from New Zealand, which has a healthy antipodean Anglo-

Saxon tradition of sport. He brought the record below 3:50 (3:49.4) in 1975, but his Montreal Olympic gold medal in the 1,500 was somewhat devalued by Bayi's withdrawal from the race, robbed of his chance by African politicians using their athletes as pawns in the political battle against apartheid.

Just when we were beginning to believe that progress would come   7 only from runners with massive physiques like that of Cuba's Alberto Juantorena, two slightly built British runners, Sebastian Coe and Steve Ovett, set new mile world records in 1979 and 1980, respectively. The apparent ease with which both ran is a promise of still more records to come. (The women's mile record was broken in 1980 by Mary Decker of the United States—she ran it in 4:21.7 minutes.) With nearly 1,000 million Chinese and more than 600 million Indians waiting in the wings and about to enter the world sports stage, I foresee a continuous and steady progress in athletic record breaking. A 3:30 mile by the turn of the century is not impossible, provided that some harmony still prevails in our uneasy world and the sheer stupidity of political chicanery is held at bay.

Sport at its best means striving for excellence, international cooper-   8 ation and an inventive technical genius in elevating further what is, in essence, play within complex rules. But there is a darker, less promising side. Progress that brings the use of medical science to aid the injured athlete or advise the marathon runner on diet and training also brings knowledge of drugs that extend unfairly and dangerously the limits of performance, like evils released from a Pandora's box. The battle against drugs is not a short, sharp skirmish, but will be a long, drawn-out campaign. It needs continuing administrative and pharmacological resources to introduce on a world scale even more sophisticated tests against the few pharmacologists and doctors who are prepared to prostitute their knowledge to gain illegal advantage for their teams.

I am always bombarded with questions about amateurism. Since   9 Avery Brundage's retirement, the International Olympic Committee (IOC) has changed its position on amateurism and now permits almost any broken-time financial compensation the international governing bodies approve as reasonable. This applies in Western democracies as well as socialist Eastern states. I do not quarrel with any of this. Of course it is fairer than the old-fashioned system. But the ability to pay what amounts to a living wage to athletes depends on the economic wealth of the country and the importance it attaches to sporting success and prestige. At present, a promising Third World athlete who wants to participate in sport full time might as well whistle in the wind unless other abilities lead to teaching physical education. Financial compensation is a step toward equality of opportunity for all, and a reduction in the double-dealing into which athletes have been unwillingly drawn, but it would be healthy if a certain code of moderation could be hammered out. My blood freezes at the thought of athletics becoming one frenetic big-money deal as corrupting for the player as the onlooker. And I must add a warning: Time and again I have noticed that a runner who forsook a part-time job to spend every waking hour on sport was rewarded with a marked deterioration of performance caused by hypochondria and staleness. It may be that some stimulus is necessary to counterbalance the concentration on physical perfection. In 1979 Sebastian Coe broke his world records just after an enforced absence from training due to illness and exams.

10   More disturbing than the passing of amateurism are the dangers of the increasing size of international events such as the Olympics. This brings commercial exploitation (whose running shoes are worn on the rostrum?) and abuse by pressure groups seeking a platform with a ready-made television audience of hundreds of millions.

11   Despite the problems that threaten the Games, I remain an enthusiastic and hopeful Olympian, though the content and siting of the Games may need drastic changes. My participation in the Helsinki Olympics in 1952 was a high point of my career—even though I finished in fourth place. The six Olympic Games I have attended and watched since then have left me with memories of pathos and drama far above the petty ordinariness of so much of life.

12   In all the avalanche of criticism of international sport, it is often forgotten that every athlete who participates becomes a bulwark back in his own country against accepting complete lies about another nation. Once you have competed on the track and queued for food and joked in the shower room you can no longer be persuaded that a foreigner has two horns and a forked tail. In this sense, sporting exchanges are a great hope for the world, and it is in the deepest interest of the world for them to continue.

13   The revolution that has taken place in top-level sport in the last 20 years has been mirrored by another dramatic change. In the early '60s the British Sports Council examined ways of getting people to take part in sport. Sports facilities in Western democracies have always been the Cinderella of public spending and have been left to local clubs, often sadly impoverished. In Britain it was hardly surprising that there were so few aspiring athletes, with only half a dozen adequate running tracks in existence and sixty per cent of the swimming pools, having been built in Victorian times, linked with the idea of cleanliness rather than healthy recreation. Almost all our schools had fine facilities and compulsory games. So just why did adult participation wither away to a feeble ten per cent? Great urban conglomerations and our changeable climate often made the use of playing fields unattractive, but sociologi-

cal research showed that the vast majority of people yearned to use
their leisure more actively.

We promoted the indoor sports center—a multipurpose building   14
able to cater to 22 sports and often including a swimming pool. Simple
restaurants, stage facilities, and nurseries filled out the picture, making
our council's rallying cry of "Sport for All" a reality. The moment one
town opened a center and people flocked in, neighboring mayors and
city governments vied with each other to open similar sporting halls.
During my tenure as chairman of the council we saw the number of
centers leap from 20 to 400. We tried to persuade the larger schools to
share their sports facilities with the public in the evenings and on
school holidays. Where this happened there was an encouraging drop
in incidence of vandalism and petty crimes because it proved such a
boon to youngsters cooped up in cities.

Doctors, perhaps, have become too negative, saying no to food,   15
smoking, and alcohol. Now is the time to say a massive "yes" to positive health. The message now is running, not tranquilizers; tennis, not
heart attacks; sports clubs with friends, not psychotherapy groups. I
have always been reluctant to dragoon people into boring fitness rou-
tines; I have always wanted them to choose activities they find exciting.
The heartwarming spontaneity with which Americans grip a good new
idea and put it into practice should be a lesson to the rest of the world.
Even at noncompetitive levels, running, or jogging, has swept America,
becoming the only healthful addiction I know. It now attracts some 30
million Americans who not only feel better, but will also probably live
longer. Doubtless there are jogging bores, and some other fashion may
in time supplant recreational running, but nothing can detract from this
remarkable revolution in approach to physical activity. Stemming at
first from fear of coronary heart disease, it is now mainly sustained—
and this is the important fact—because it is enjoyable for its own sake.
Though an ankle injury in 1975 stopped my daily running, I ride my
bicycle and still enjoy the sense of muscles used and happily tired, the
sense of lungs stretched and a heart made to reach down for some of its
reserves.

There is no doubt that "Sport for All" is a twentieth-century move-   16
ment of real significance. Other mass movements have oppressed
where they intended to liberate. This movement liberates because it
has an essentially individual basis. The choice of speed, route, distance, or company is entirely yours. Instead of running, you may prefer
knocking an innocent ball with a piece of wood or metal or gut. Whatever the choice, it rests in freedom, echoing passion and needs that
have primitive, evolutionary significance and which to our peril we
have too often dismissed as uncivilized and immature. The experience

of the past 25 years has only served to reinforce my belief in the courage and infinite resourcefulness of athletes the world over. This augurs well for the future.

 USING THE DICTIONARY: Which of the following words would you have to check in your dictionary? How clear or helpful is the dictionary definition for each of the words you have to look up? 1. *Elizabethan* (2) 2. *allay* (3) 3. *enthrall* (3) 4. *antipodean* (6) 5. *apartheid* (6) 6. *chicanery* (7) 7. *pharmacological* (8) 8. *frenetic* (9) 9. *hypochondria* (9) 10. *rostrum* (10) 11. *pathos* (11) 12. *queue* (12) 13. *vie* (14) 14. *dragoon* (15) 15. *augur* (16)

THE WRITER'S AGENDA:

In this essay, the author explores the full range and implications of a term that has played a central role in his life. Answer the following questions about the meaning that the term *sports* has for the author.

1. How do the two introductory paragraphs set the **tone** for the rest of the essay? What do we learn about the setting and the *frame of mind* of Bannister and his competitors at the time of his major exploit?

2. In what light does the *autobiographical* information in the third paragraph put the author's discussion of sports in the rest of the essay?

3. Where in the essay does the author sum up his own *definition* of sports? What parts of it does he develop at some length in this essay; what part or parts does he seem to take for granted?

4. In the author's insider's or expert's account of the achievements of *later runners,* what do we learn about important physical or technical factors? (What other factors play a role?)

5. In a central section of the essay, Bannister faces up to familiar *problems or issues* related to the "darker side" of sports. What is his stand on drug use, amateurism, and commercialism?

6. In the final third of the essay, Bannister discusses the role of sports in international relations and what he considers positive developments in national sports in Britain and the United States. What are the major *political and personal* benefits of sports that he discusses here?

7. What are some of the things that make the last paragraph a strong *conclusion?*

FOR DISCUSSION OR WRITING:

1. How effective or persuasive is Bannister as a champion of the role of sports in our lives? What in his essay was for you most impressive or persuasive? What least?

2. Critics of American sports often paint a less idealized picture than Bannister does in this article. What are some of their major criticisms? To judge from your own personal observation or experience, how justified are these criticisms?

3. For you, how good a symbol of excellence or achievement in general is excellence or achievement in sports?

4. Write an extended definition of sports, using or modifying as necessary Bannister's description of it as "play within complex rules."

5. Write an extended definition of one of the following: true amateurism; commercialism in today's sports; the Olympic spirit; true professionalism.

6. Write a paper in which you support or question the ideal of "Sport for All."

7. For some years, equal support or recognition for women's sports has been a widely discussed issue. Write a paper in which you explore the full implications of this goal.

FOR FURTHER DISCUSSION AND WRITING: The following selection is from a publication designed to help teachers deal with censorship. What is the main point the authors make, and how well do they support it? What are their definitions—stated or implied—of *censorship, intellectual freedom,* and *obscenity?* Does this selection change or confirm your own thoughts about censorship? How or why?

Lee Burress and
Edward B. Jenkinson

Censorship Attacks
Good Books

1   CENSORSHIP ATTACKS good books, not poor books. One of the interesting characteristics of the current tensions between the schools and some parents is that the complaints involve generally very good materials. Although the term "obscene" is used quite frequently in complaints by parents about such books as are listed below, it is very doubtful if these books are, in fact, legally obscene.

2   No case is known to us of any books selected for use in the public schools that were held by a court to be obscene. In discussions between parents and teachers, it would be wise to restrict the word "obscene" to those works that have in fact been declared "obscene" by a court. Outside a court decision, the word is meaningless; what it most often means is that the user of the term finds the questioned work objectionable or repellent.

3   An examination of five surveys of objections to learning materials in the schools made between 1965 and 1981 show that some 600 book titles were the objects of complaint. Of these, approximately 22 appeared most often. The 22 most frequently cited titles are the following:

1. *The Catcher in the Rye,* J. D. Salinger
2. *The Grapes of Wrath,* John Steinbeck
3. *Of Mice and Men,* John Steinbeck

4. *Nineteen Eighty-Four,* George Orwell
5. *Lord of the Flies,* William Golding
6. *Go Ask Alice,* Anonymous
7. *Black Like Me,* John Griffin
8. *Brave New World,* Aldous Huxley
9. *To Kill a Mockingbird,* Harper Lee
10. *One Day in the Life of Ivan Denisovich,* Alexander Solzhenitsyn
11. *Love Story,* Erich Segal
12. *Manchild in the Promised Land,* Claude Brown
13. *One Flew Over the Cuckoo's Nest,* Ken Kesey
14. *The Scarlet Letter,* Nathaniel Hawthorne
15. *The Adventures of Huckleberry Finn,* Mark Twain
16. *Forever,* Judy Blume
17. *The Learning Tree,* Gordon Parks
18. *A Separate Peace,* John Knowles
19. *The Diary of a Young Girl,* Anne Frank
20. *Deliverance,* James Dickey
21. *The Good Earth,* Pearl S. Buck
22. *Slaughterhouse Five,* Kurt Vonnegut, Jr.

This list would be regarded by most teachers or librarians as a rea- 4
sonable sample of some of the best or most relevant writers of the
recent past. It should be noted that the list is largely composed of
American writers of the twentieth century. The conflicts between some
parents and schools involve the best learning materials, not the poorest.

A similar conclusion may be made concerning the periodicals that 5
are the objects of complaint. *Time, Newsweek, U.S. News and World
Report,* and *Sports Illustrated* are the periodicals most often objected
to, or removed. Notice that the schools do not select *Playboy* or other
similar magazines.

Another illustration of this point is that the five dictionaries recently 6
objected to in Texas are widely regarded by teachers as the best dictionaries available.

Intellectual freedom in the classrooms of the nation's schools is 7
not used for the poorest of material or for any books or films that a
court has found obscene. Instead, it is being used for films and books
that are among the most popular, that are translated into many foreign
languages, that deal with important human concerns, and that have
received serious and complimentary treatment from literary critics and
other writers.

UNIT 9

PERSUASION:
Unpopular Truths

The Common Theme: What does it take to make people face unwelcome truths? Ancient stories tell us about kings who punished messengers bringing them bad news. In our time, advertisers and political candidates, afraid to let us know the facts, gloss over unpleasant realities and tell us what we want to hear. However, one test of a truly persuasive writer is the ability to make us confront issues that we would rather evade. To make us change our ways, a writer must be able to overcome our resistance—our reluctance to face up to realities that we would prefer to ignore. The authors in this unit remind us of issues often hidden from us by a cloud of wishful thinking. They write with the force and single-mindedness of writers who aim at a change of attitude, or a change of heart.

WRITER'S GUIDE 9:
The Strategies of Persuasion

Persuasion is the art of changing the reader's mind. A persuasive writer knows how to overcome opposition and how to build support. When we write to persuade, we ask the reader to support a cause, to agree to a course of action, or to stop opposing something to which we are committed. We aim at a definite change in the reader's plans or attitudes. We may be aiming at a definite practical result—a vote, a contribution, or a sale.

To produce results, a persuasive writer has to have a sense of how the audience will react. A large part of the task is knowing what *not* to do—not to do things that will raise the defenses (or the hackles) of readers. Many readers have built up a resistance to persuasive writing that transparently serves the personal goals or private aims of the writer. They resist advertising and propaganda that too brazenly attempt to put something over on the audience. In order to reach intelligent, educated readers, you will have to respect their judgment. You will have to appeal to common interests or shared values. Your readers will want to feel that they are changing their minds for a good reason or for good cause.

What are some of the strategies of persuasion that will work with a critical reader? What are some of the pitfalls that the writer has to avoid? Remember the following guidelines when trying to make your writing more persuasive:

(1) *Make yourself heard.* In order to change people's minds, we must get their attention. To overcome indifference or break through the crust of apathy, we must first get a hearing. We must know how and when to speak up, how to make ourselves heard.

It is true that at times we will need to be diplomatic. We may have to prepare the ground. We may want to approach a booby-trapped subject like abortion or the draft very cautiously. But finally a persuasive writer must be able to make a strong plea. Truly persuasive writing cannot afford to sound lame or routine. Important points must receive proper **emphasis**; the writer must know how to give full weight to what truly matters.

The authors of the following excerpts know how to state key points emphatically. They know how to make essential points stand out. They present clear choices; they issue clear challenges. They know how to sum up important ideas in memorable form—we will remember these ideas and ponder them as they sink in:

Unjust laws exist: Shall we be content to obey them; or shall we endeavor to amend them, and obey them until we have succeeded; or shall we transgress them at once? (Henry David Thoreau)

The time to look upon the Mexican American as the poor, uneducated, tortilla-eating peon who is the victim of some fate stemming from Quetzalcoatl's disapproval is over. Mexican Americans are descendants of a proud race. As Americans they deserve their rightful place in the American sun. (Philip D. Ortego)

Women predominate in the lower-paying, menial, unrewarding, dead-end jobs, and when they do reach better positions, they are invariably paid less than a man gets for the same job. (Shirley Chisholm)

As you write or revise a persuasive paper, ask yourself: Can I point to a passage of the paper that sums up my central message or major plea in a quotable, memorable form? What can I do to highlight it or give it additional force?

(2) *Know how to use language that brings the readers' emotions into play and appeals to their basic values.* It is true that a persuasive writer must know how to present facts that objective readers can verify. But a writer who wants to influence people's opinions and actions cannot afford to remain neutral and detached, pondering the pros and cons with folded arms. Effective persuasive writing makes strategic use of emotive or connotative language—language that triggers the right attitudes and steers the readers' emotions. **Emotive language** does not merely describe or report; it shows where the writer stands. A writer attacking the traditional big-car policy of American auto makers will not simply refer to "big, powerful cars" but more likely to "road locomotives," "gas guzzlers," "American behemoths," "postwar dinosaurs," or "the world's biggest compacts."

The following passage is from a review of a book about "the dark side of the saga of the American West." It does not simply report on the contents of the book; rather, the language used by the reviewer is the language of a writer who is taking sides:

We cannot simply feel a distant guilt about past *massacres,* land *expropriations* and cultural *annihilations.* We are part of the persisting *assault* on the dignity, property and life of our original native population.

We are General Custer. Though we no longer dress in the uniform of the cavalry or carry Gatling guns, we continue to employ the weapons of law and power to deny American Indians what rightfully should be theirs. Our giant corporations *ravage* their land in search of minerals; our confused Government policy on the status of reservations *deprives* Indians of both real and genuine participation in American political life; our continuing racial *discrimination* against native Americans—both on and off the reservation—denies them the most basic tools for survival.

> —Alan M. Dershowitz, "Agents and Indians," *New York Times Book Review*

The language used by the reviewer carries strong **connotations**; it conveys strong negative and positive attitudes. Words like *massacre, assault,* and *ravage* carry strong condemnation; they are part of the language of accusation or indictment. Words like *dignity, rightful,* and *survival* carry strong approval; they appeal solemnly to shared basic values. The historical parallel ("We are General Custer") is fraught with powerful negative associations.

Language charged with strong emotions is a double-edged weapon. It can arouse powerful feelings of solidarity and common purpose in an audience that is already more than half-convinced. Strong charges and passionate appeals may work well with an "in-group" audience that is more than half-ready to follow the author's lead. However, strong language can easily seem inflammatory and prejudiced to the uncommitted. It may alienate fair-minded readers, and it may inflame the opposition. Avoid personal abuse: terms like *peacenik, do-gooder, redneck,* or *fem-libber* are insults that suggest a narrow-minded inability to take the views of others seriously. Labels like *socialism, fascism, collectivism,* or *communism* have been abused too often by people who make sweeping charges.

(3) *Know how to dramatize dry facts.* To be persuasive, writers must know how to bring issues to life. They must know how to highlight facts and select striking evidence. They must know how to present examples that will stir sympathy or indignation. Know how to support your main points with a variety of vivid, dramatic material:

♦ A striking *example* like the following can effectively bring an issue into focus:

> Recently a woman filed a lawsuit because she had slipped into a grave while attending a funeral; after being stuck for half an hour looking up at a coffin suspended overhead, she suffered nightmares, for which the court awarded her $400,000 in damages. In no other country would she have been given the time of day for anything so ridiculous. Nowhere else have personal irresponsibility and the refusal to accept the unavoidable

risks of life become so institutionalized that lawyers get their 30 percent regardless, and insurance pays for everything.
—Patrick Bogan, "The $310 Million Paranoia Subsidy," *Harper's*

♦ Striking *statistics,* strategically used, may help impress a previously indifferent reader:

The smiling brown face sandwiched between mortarboard and high-necked dark gown is becoming the educational exception, more and more. At rates even worse than in the days of overt discrimination, the American school system is rejecting the Hispanic student. Now, only 55 percent of our Latino youth are graduating from high school. Only 21 percent are entering college. Only 8 percent are completing a four-year curriculum.
—Cecilia Preciado Burciaga, "Voices," *Nuestro*

♦ Telling *comparisons* can impress the true meaning of facts and figures on readers who have become jaded or blasé. A writer said about the sum of three million dollars spent on the trial of a would-be assassin of a President:

Three million dollars would pay the cost to the federal government of 2,380,952 free school lunches for poor children, at $1.26 per lunch. If a similar amount were spent to decide the guilt or innocence of each of the more than 20,000 persons charged with murder or manslaughter and the more than 150,000 charged with using firearms in aggravated assaults in the United States every year, it would add up to more than $500 billion.
—Stuart Taylor, Jr., "Too Much Justice," *Harper's*

♦ Revealing *contrasts* can help the writer steer the reader's attention in the desired direction:

Over 10,000 people are killed with handguns every year in the United States. Other civilized countries with proper gun control laws, such as Britain and Japan, consider forty deaths a year by handguns excessive. The exact figures on those killed by handguns in a recent year were Great Britain, 8; Japan, 48; Canada, 52; West Germany, 42; and the United States, 10,728.

(4) *Work out an effective overall plan.* Often the basic strategy of a persuasive writer is to go from the simple to the difficult—from what is easy to accept to what is hard to believe. In order to be persuasive, we will often first try to find *common ground* with our readers. We will try to strengthen their trust in our good sense and good faith. Having put our readers in an assenting, receptive mood, we can then hope to take them with us as we go on to the difficult or the new.

In a famous lecture reprinted at the end of this book, the American historian Barbara Tuchman set out to counteract the widespread modern pessimism about humanity's potential for good or evil. She assumed that a modern audience would tend to be suspicious of human motives. It would be skeptical about our human capacity for dedication and achievement. It would see in much of history a record of violence and corruption. To restore our faith in human nature, Tuchman started her lecture by reminding us of achievements that we are least likely to question: the glories of art and music; the work of builders and architects; the courage and determination of explorers. Only then did she go on to the area that many modern readers find disillusioning or demoralizing—political history.

The following partial outline proceeds from the widely agreed-upon to the sometimes-overlooked:

Humanity's Better Moments

◆ the *exploits of seafarers and explorers* from the Vikings to the explorers of the North American continent

◆ the *glories of painters and architects*

◆ the *benefits of modern medicine*

◆ the *politics of reform,* with the abolitionist movement in England and the United States as an outstanding example

◆ the *struggle for liberty,* from the Jews fighting the Romans under the leadership of the Maccabees to the American colonists risking their property and their lives

(5) *Use an extended case history when it is the best means of proving your point.* A writer may decide that the best way to prove charges of discrimination or to alert us to the dangers of pollution is to examine one famous case in point in relentless detail. The more earnestly or painstakingly the story is told, the harder it will be for reluctant readers to brush off the author's charges as superficial or opinionated.

The outline of a magazine article on a famous case of environmental pollution may look somewhat like this:

Love Canal and the Poisoning of America

I. Innocent beginnings
   (An unfinished canal, left from a period of growth and

boosterism, is used as a chemical dump and then filled in; homes and a school are built on or near the site.)

II. First hints of trouble
(Foul-smelling substances are found in backyards and basements; skin rashes and suspicious ailments plague children and adults.)

III. The refusal to believe
(Public officials and corporate officers belittle charges and evade responsibility.)

IV. The emerging truth
(Determined sleuthing reveals the truth as isolated incidents become part of a pattern and the extent of the disaster becomes clear.)

V. Belated remedies
(Half-hearted or belated remedies are applied as victims organize and lawsuits proliferate.)

(6) *Challenge your opposition.* Writers aiming at effective persuasion often find that it is not enough to advance their own cause. They have to counteract opposing arguments. They have to head off rival claims to the reader's allegiance or support. To be persuasive, you will often have to make it your business to know competing proposals or rival claims—and to refute or discredit them if you can.

To help your own position prevail, you may have to do the following:

♦ Show *weaknesses* or contradictions in your opponents' proposals:

Any prayer used in a school would have to be composed by a committee and made innocuous enough to satisfy all the different religious groups that make up the population of this republic. Catholics, Protestants, Jews, Buddhists, Moslems, and all the others would have to agree that the language is not propaganda for the opposition. Thus, no mention of Yahweh, Jesus, Buddha, or Mahomet would be possible; we would have some lame-brained little homily with a muttered reference to God.
—Pete Hamill, "Prayers for the Past," *San Francisco Chronicle*

Censorship can, and often does, lead into absurdity, though not often slapstick absurdity like that of the New Jersey legisla-

ture in the 1960s when it enacted a subsequently vetoed anti-obscenity bill so explicit that it was deemed too dirty to be read in the legislative chambers without clearing out the public first.
—*Time*

♦ Counteract *myths* or wishful thinking by citing contrary facts:

We never had a country in which every schoolchild said his prayers in a classroom every day. A study made in 1960 by Richard B. Dierenfield of Macalaster College in St. Paul, Minn., showed that 91 percent of Western school systems and 74 percent in the Midwest never had school prayers. There were prayers in Southern schools and schools in the Northeast, but 50 percent of all American public schools had no prayers at all.
—Pete Hamill, "Prayers"

♦ Point out *conflicts of interest* or ulterior motives:

In our system of jurisprudence anyone can sue anyone else for practically anything. The real question is, "Can I sue and win?" Increasingly, the answer to that question is—no. Too often litigation *works only to the economic advantage of the attorneys. The more protracted the litigation, the more hours are spent and the more fees are generated.* By tacit agreement in the profession, litigation is usually conducted with the old bury-them-in-paperwork sleight of hand. . . . Abraham Lincoln said, "A lawyer's time is *his stock in trade.*" Lawyers today work hard at ensuring a bullish market for that stock.
—Stanley J. Lieberman, "A No-Lose Proposition," *Newsweek*

Remember, however, that personal attacks often backfire. When you are tempted to belittle and ridicule the opposition, remember the standards of the fair-minded reader. Avoid the appearance of a mere **ad hominem** attack—an attack aimed "at the person" and sidestepping or evading the issues.

(7) *Keep after your reader.* Effective persuasive writers often impress us by their single-minded pursuit of their goal. They know that it is not easy to make people change their minds, let alone bring about a change of heart. They know how to concentrate on the task at hand, keeping up a barrage of arguments and appeals. Their basic technique is not so much repetition as *reiteration*—reinforcement of the same basic idea in a variety of ways.

The following are excerpts from an article designed to persuade the reader that drastic reforms are needed in our system of criminal justice. The author keeps up a barrage of statistics, quotations from authorities on crime, striking extreme examples, attacks on opposing views, and the like.

Why the Justice System Fails

Statistics

... When a suspect is apprehended, the chances of his getting punished are slim. In New York State each year there are some 130,000 felony arrests; approximately 8,000 people go to prison. There are 94,000 felony arrests in New York City; 5,000 to 6,000 serve time. A study of the District of Columbia came up with a similar picture. Of those arrested for armed robbery, less than one-quarter went to prison. More than 6,000 aggravated assaults were reported; 116 people were put away....

Authority

Detroit Deputy Police Chief James Bannon believes that trial delays work against the victim. "The judge doesn't see the hysterical, distraught victim. He sees a person who comes into court after several months or years who is totally different. He sees a defendant that bears no relationship to what he appeared to be at the time of the crime...."

Extreme case

Procedural concerns can cause delays, and in rare cases defendants' rights can be carried to absurd extremes. California Attorney General George Deukmejian tells of Willie Edward Level, who was convicted of beating a Bakersfield College woman student to death with a table leg. Level was informed of his right to remain silent and/or have an attorney present (the *Miranda* ruling). He waived these rights and confessed the murder. Yet the California Court of Appeals threw out the conviction because Level had asked to speak to his mother at the time of his arrest and had not been permitted to; had he been able to do so, it was argued, he might not have made his confession....

Opposition discredited

Until recently few juvenile courts admitted there was such a thing as a bad boy, restricting their vision of youthful offenders to memories of Father Flanagan's Boys Town or to Judge Tom Clark's quaint view that "every boy, in his heart, would rather steal

second base than an automobile." In fact, there are
several boys these days who would prefer to kill the
umpire, and who have done so, only to receive light
sentences or none at all. . . .
—Roger Rosenblatt, *Time*

To sum up: In persuasive writing, the reader's response is the writer's central concern. Persuasion is effective when the reader decides to support a cause, or to agree to a course of action, or to change an attitude. To write persuasively, you have to develop a sense of how your audience is likely to respond to what you say. You have to be able to make a strong plea, using strong language where appropriate to dramatize needs or to express strong feelings. But you also have to be able to approach a subject cautiously, leading up gradually to something difficult or controversial. The more emphatic your writing becomes, the closer you will move to the line where statement becomes overstatement, or where strong assertion turns into exaggeration. An independent and experienced reader resents being pushed or manipulated. The art of writing persuasively is the art of making a strong plea without alienating the intelligent, fair-minded reader.

PREWRITING ACTIVITIES 9

1. The following paragraph is from a review of a book about Eugene Debs, an early hero of the American labor movement. Point out all features that make this passage different from an objective report. Show how the writer appeals to the reader's sympathy or to shared values. Then do research for, and write, a similar passage about a person you consider admirable or outstanding.

On Christmas Day 1921, a tall, thin 66-year-old man began
to walk through the empty yard of the federal penitentiary in
Atlanta—free after serving two years and nine months for de-
nouncing World War I and the government's prosecution of its
opponents. ("While there is a lower class, I am in it," he said at
his sentencing; "while there is a criminal element, I am of it;
while there is a soul in prison, I am not free.") As his emaciated
figure became visible from behind the bars of the main building, 2,300 inmates broke into a thunderous cheer. Slowly the
old man turned, his gaunt face streaming with tears, and raised
his arms in a symbolic embrace. Three days later, in Terre
Haute, Indiana, 25,000 people welcomed him home, as men
who had vied for the honor pulled him from the depot to his

house in the same wagon that had carried him over the same
route on his return from prison after the Pullman Strike of 1894.
—William H. Harbaugh, "Radical Democrat," *The New
Republic*

2. Record your candid reactions to both of the following passages.
Explain or defend your reactions in some detail. How persuasive is
each writer? Then compare your reactions with those of your classmates
and discuss differences in the reactions of different readers.

In view of our society's callous unconcern for existing children who are, in fact, unwanted, it is hard to listen tolerantly to
the hypocritical cant which defends the "rights" of minute
cells of human tissue which have had the mischance to be fer-
tilized. Despite the dramatic gains of genetics in recent years,
there will probably always be human beings misshapen in
mind or body because of heredity, accident, disease, war, famine, or the lack of loving nurture. To them, a humane people
owes the kind of support and rehabilitative effort which is now
no more than a utopian dream. Surely it is a form of madness to
insist on adding to this still-unaccepted burden responsibility
for thousands of children, rejected even before they are born.
—Marion K. Sanders, "The Right Not to Be Born," *Harper's*

For decades, one of Detroit's major advertising ploys was to
market its products as instruments of violence. During the entire postwar period, in fact, Detroit's marketing strategy was not
to sell automobiles as sensible family transportation, as one
might expect in a reasonably civilized society, but as vehicles
of mayhem and destruction. What's in a name? In Detroit's case,
plenty. Because over the years, as an auto writer once observed,
the very names Detroit managers gave to their cars reveal quite
plainly the industry's appeal to motives of violence and aggression. Consider the Oldsmobile *Cutlass,* the Buick *Le Sabre,* the
Plymouth *Fury,* the Plymouth *Barracuda,* the Chevrolet Cor-
vette *Stingray,* the Ford Mustang *Cobra,* the American Motors
Matador, the Mercury *Lynx,* Mercury *Bobcat,* and Mercury *Cou-
gar*—killers all. . . . The theme of violence in these names has a
cunning economic logic behind it. As we now know, Detroit
management's guiding theology during the postwar era was:
big car, big profit; small car, small profit. And what better way
to sell big, powerful cars than to link them in the public's mind
with the libidinal release of destructive impulses?
—Howell Raines, "Snarling Cars," *The New Republic*

3. Study the following brief report on a familiar controversy. Then write a strong plea designed to persuade ordinary motorists either to support or oppose a compulsory safety device, such as air bags or self-buckling seat belts.

Should the government require that new cars be equipped with air bags—cushions that inflate on impact to protect passengers in a crash? Like nuclear power, this is an issue where reasonable minds may differ, but reasonable minds are hard to find. To Ralph Nader, airbags have provided a litmus test of political virtue ever since the last Corvair rolled off the assembly line in the mid-Sixties. Nader bitterly denounced his protégée Joan Claybrook for not immediately requiring the devices when she was director of highway safety for Jimmy Carter. Opponents of airbags see them as the prime example of statist meddling. *Car and Driver,* a magazine for auto enthusiasts, refers to Nader and Claybrook as "Safety Nazis."

—"Harper's Journal," *Harper's*

BACKGROUND: Fern Kupfer was born in the Bronx, New York, in 1946 and graduated from a college of the State University of New York. After moving to Iowa, she did graduate work at Iowa State University and taught in a community college. In 1982, she published *Before and After Zachariah,* in her words, "a personal narrative about what happens to a family, and to a marriage, when a damaged child is born." She has written for *Redbook* and *Newsweek* and has been praised for her outspokenness and honesty in dealing with a subject often shrouded in euphemisms and taboos. Zachariah was the Kupfers' second child, severely brain-damaged from birth and deteriorating in spite of the best available help.

Fern Kupfer

Institution Is Not a Dirty Word

GUIDE TO READING: The author of this article champions an unpopular point of view. She tries to change her readers' minds on an emotion-laden subject. What is her strategy? What does she do to counteract the widely accepted opposing view? What does she do defend and advance her own?

uses stereotypical view

I WATCHED Phil Donahue recently. He had on mothers of handi- 1
capped children who talked about the pain and blessing of having a
"special" child. As the mother of a severely handicapped six-year-old
boy who cannot sit, who cannot walk, who will be in diapers all of his
days, I understand the pain. The blessing part continues to elude me— *clue to thesis*
notwithstanding the kind and caring people we've met through this
tragedy.

What really makes my jaws clench, though, is the use of the word 2
"special." The idea that our damaged children are "special," and that
we as parents were somehow picked for the role, is one of the myths
that come with the territory. It's reinforced by the popular media,
which present us with heartwarming images of retarded people who
marry, of quadriplegics who fly airplanes, of those fortunate few who

struggle out of comas to teach us about the meaning of courage and love. I like these stories myself. But, of course, inspirational tales are only one side of the story. The other side deals with the daily care of a family member who might need more than many normal families can give. Parents who endure with silent stoicism or chin-up good humor are greeted with kudos and applause. "I don't know how you do it," the well-wishers say, not realizing, or course, that no one has a choice in this matter. No one would consciously choose to have a child anything less than healthy and normal. The other truth is not spoken aloud: "Thank God, it's not me."

3   One mother on the Donahue show talked about how difficult it was to care for her severely brain-damaged daughter, but in the end, she said serenely, "She gives much more than she takes from our family." And no, she would never institutionalize her child. She would never "put her away." For "she is my child," the woman firmly concluded as the audience clapped in approval. "I would never give her up."

4   Everyone always says how awful the institutions are. Don't they have bars on the windows and children lying neglected in crowded wards? Aren't all the workers sadists, taking direction from the legendary Big Nurse? Indeed, isn't institutionalizing a child tantamount to locking him away? Signing him out of your life forever? Isn't it proof of your failure as a parent—one who couldn't quite measure up and love your child, no matter what?

5   No, to all of the above. And love is beside the point.

6   Our child Zachariah has not lived at home for almost four years. I knew when we placed him, sorry as I was, that this was the right decision, for his care precluded any semblance of normal family life for the rest of us. I do not think that we "gave him up," although he is cared for daily by nurses, caseworkers, teachers and therapists, rather than by his mother and father. When we come to visit him at his "residential facility," a place housing 50 severely physically and mentally handicapped youngsters, we usually see him being held and rocked by a foster grandma who has spent the better part of the afternoon singing him nursery rhymes. I do not feel that we have "put him away." Perhaps it is just a question of language. I told another mother who was going through the difficult decision regarding placement for her retarded child, "Think of it as going to boarding school rather than institutionalization." Maybe euphemisms help ease the pain a little bit. But I've also seen enough to know that institution need not be a dirty word.

7   The media still relish those institution horror stories: a page-one photo of a retarded girl who was repeatedly molested by the janitor on night duty. Oh, the newspapers have a field day with something like that. And that is how it should be, I suppose. To protect against institutional abuse we need critical reporters with sharpened pencils and a

give specific examples if possible.

keen investigative eye. But there are other scenes from the institution as well. I've seen a young caseworker talk lovingly as she changed the diapers of a teen-age boy. I've watched as an aide put red ribbons into the ponytail of a cerebral-palsied woman, wipe away the drool and kiss her on the cheek. When we bring Zach back to his facility after a visit home, the workers welcome him with hugs and notice if we gave him a haircut or a new shirt.

The reporters don't make news out of that simple stuff. It doesn't 8 mesh with the anti-institutional bias prevalent in the last few years, or the tendency to canonize the handicapped and their accomplishments. This anti-institutional trend has some very frightening ramifications. We force mental patients out into the real world of cheap welfare ho- tels and call it "community placement." We parole youthful offenders because "jails are such dangerous places to be," making our city streets dangerous places for the law-abiding. We heap enormous guilt on the families that need, for their own survival, to put their no-longer-competent elderly in that dreaded last stop: the nursing home.

doublespeak

deals strongly with credit opposition

Another danger is that in a time of economic distress for all of us, 9 funds could be cut for human-service programs under the guise of anti-institutionalization. We must make sure, before we close the doors of those "awful" institutions, that we have alternative facilities to care for the clientele. The humanitarians who tell us how terrible institutions are should be wary lest they become unwilling bedfellows to conserva-tive politicians who want to walk a tight fiscal line. It takes a lot of money to run institutions. No politician is going to say he's against the handicapped, but he can talk in sanctimonious terms about efforts to preserve the family unit, about families remaining independent and self-sufficient. Translated, this means, "You got your troubles, I got mine."

Most retarded people do not belong in institutions any more than 10 most people over 65 belong in nursing homes. What we need are op-tions and alternatives for a heterogeneous population. We need group homes and halfway houses and government subsidies to families who choose to care for dependent members at home. We need accessible housing for independent handicapped people; we need to pay enough to foster-care families to show that a good home is worth paying for. We need institutions. And it shouldn't have to be a dirty word.

thesis

USING THE DICTIONARY: Explain ten of the following terms. Which of them have emotional associations or overtones? 1. *myth* (2) 2. *quadriplegic* (2) 3. *stoicism* (2) 4. *kudos* (2) 5. *Big Nurse* (4) 6. *tantamount* (4) 7. *semblance* (6) 8. *eu-*

phemism (6) 9. *canonize* (8) 10. *law-abiding* (8) 11. *clientele* (9) 12. *humanitarian* (9) 13. *sanctimonious* (9) 14. *heterogeneous* (10) 15. *halfway house* (10)

THE WRITER'S AGENDA:

The author of this article attempts to steer her reader's emotions. She takes on the difficult task of changing the reader's attitudes on an emotion-laden subject. Study her strategy as a persuasive writer:

1. In order to prepare the reader for an unpopular point of view, the author first attacks *currently fashionable* attitudes. How are expressions like the following meant to influence the reader: "myths," "heart-warming images," "inspirational tales," "chin-up good humor," "horror stories"? According to the author, how do the media treat the subject of the handicapped, and what are her objections?

2. The author's overall strategy is to *lead up* to an unpopular point of view. Where does she first raise the issue of institutionalization, and how? Where and how does she first state her own point of view?

3. In the central part of the article, the author matches her own *personal experience* against the "myths" and images projected by the media. Where and how?

4. In several paragraphs toward the end of her essay, the author makes charges that serve to *discredit* those who represent the current "anti-institutional" trend. What examples does she cite of ironic contradictions and ulterior motives?

5. How does the author's conclusion appeal to readers who like to find not just grievances or complaints but *positive suggestions* and workable solutions?

6. In the last paragraph, the author's language becomes assertive and insistent. What features of *sentence style* help produce this effect?

FOR DISCUSSION OR WRITING:

1. Has this article in any way changed your mind? Why or why not? Where is the author most persuasive? Where least?

2. What has been your own experience with the central issue raised by this article? What is it like to be handicapped, or to help people cope with their handicaps?

3. Have you yourself encountered evidence of a current "anti-insti-

tutional" bias in our society? What causes it? How does it show? To what degree is it justified?

4. Is it true that the media tend to treat the subject of the handicapped in an upbeat or inspirational fashion? What other subjects do the media tend to treat inspirationally?

5. Write a persuasive paper championing an unpopular view or one that many people do not share. Choose a debatable question or controversial issue: school prayer, divorce, homosexuality, police brutality, pornography, "Moonies." Try to persuade an audience whose views differ from your own.

BACKGROUND: Sabine R. Ulibarri (born in 1919 in Sante Fe) is a professor of Modern Languages at the University of New Mexico in Albuquerque and has published in both Spanish and English. His books include *La Fragua sin Fuego* and *Tierra Amarilla,* a collection of stories. In the lecture reprinted here, Ulibarri speaks up as a defender of the cultural and linguistic heritage of Spanish-speaking Americans of the Southwest. Like other bilingual, bicultural Hispanic Americans, he raises the issue of schooling for minority children that serves their needs poorly or not at all. Like other advocates of bilingual education, he indicts traditional school programs and teachers ill-prepared to teach children with a culture and language different from their own. For many such children, who did not feel "different" in the safety of their own homes, school brought, in the words of a writer from Arizona, "the first inkling of what the other side expected of us, and it was a rough awakening."

Sabine R. Ulibarri

The Education of José Pérez

GUIDE TO READING: The author of this article goes counter to the familiar melting-pot theory of American culture. He thus goes counter to what most members of the Anglo majority would want to hear. What does he do to persuade people who are likely to be committed to a different point of view? How persuasive is his account of the central problem? How persuasive are his suggested solutions?

1   IN THE beginning was the Word. And the Word was made flesh. It was so in the beginning, and it is so today. The language, the Word, carries within it the history, the culture, the traditions, the very life of a people, the flesh. Language is people. We cannot even conceive of a people without a language, or a language without a people. The two are one and the same. To know one is to know the other.

2   Consider this dual unity, this single quality: a people and their

language, in danger of coming apart. This threatened split has become a national problem. A wedge has been driven between the Hispano and his language. As a result the Hispano is floundering in confusion, and his language is dying on the vine. A dynamic and aggressive Anglo culture has come between him and his past and is uprooting him from the soil, cutting him off from his ancestors, separating him from his own culture. Very little is being done to facilitate his transition from the culture of his ancestors, whose voice is silent, to the culture of the majority, whose voice makes his laws and determines his destiny. As his language fades, the Hispano's identity with a history, with a tradition, with a culture, becomes more nebulous with each passing day. His identity as an Anglo is not yet in sight. There is no assurance that such an identity is possible, or even desirable. In terms of the national interest, our greatest natural resources are our human differences, and it behooves us to cultivate those differences. It is one thing to homogenize milk; it is quite another thing to homogenize the citizenry. It would appear, therefore, that loyal, productive, and effective Hispano citizens, proud of what they are and what they have to give, have more to offer their country than a de-hispanized, disoriented Anglo with a dark skin, a mispronounced name, and a guilty conscience to boot.

From the standpoint of the preservation of our natural resources, every attempt must be made to save the Spanish language. It is the instrument that will make the English language available to the Spanish-speaking child through well-trained bilingual teachers. The voice of America must be multilingual if it is to be understood around the world. The best bilinguals in Spanish and English are coming out of the Spanish-speaking Southwest. This human resource, which our government and industry are utilizing most effectively, must not be allowed to dry up. For better or for worse our destiny is inextricably interwoven with the destiny of our Spanish-speaking friends to the south.

If we wish to hold on to the cultural heritage of the Southwest, we must preserve the Spanish language. If the language goes, the culture goes with it. This is precisely the spiritual crisis of the minorities of the United States. They are losing their native languages, and with the language they are losing a certain consciousness of their own existence. They are losing something of their vital polarity, something of their identity. They find themselves somewhat uprooted, somewhat disoriented. A manner of being, a way of life, forged slowly since the beginning of history, is lost with the loss of the language. Until a new consciousness, a new manner of being, is forged through and by the newly acquired language, these minorities will remain somewhat disoriented.

It is a matter of language. It is a matter of economics. It is a matter of rural versus urban societies. Hispano children speak Spanish. Most of them are poor. Many of them live in the country. Many have recently moved to the city. Consequently, they are predestined to failure, frustration, and academic fatigue in our national public schools.

6   Our Hispano child, José Pérez, begins with a handicap the very first day he shows up in the first grade. English is the language of the classroom. He speaks no English, or he speaks inadequate English. The whole program is designed to make him an Anglo. He doesn't want to become an Anglo, or he doesn't know how. He comes from a father-dominated home and finds himself in a female-dominated classroom. The Anglo concepts and values that govern and prevail are unintelligible to him. In all likelihood he comes from a low social and economic class, and there he is in an Anglo middle-class environment. Much too frequently he is fresh out of the country, and the city in general, and the school in particular, might just as well be on another planet. He probably feels very uncomfortable and self-conscious in the unfamiliar clothes he's wearing. He looks about him. The teacher, far from representing a mother image, must seem to him a remote and awe-inspiring creature. The children around him, so friendly with one another and so much at ease, look at him with suspicion. There is nothing in the atmosphere from which he can draw any comfort. Everything he sees is foreign. The climate of sound is confusing and frightening. The Hispano kid finds himself in a hostile environment indeed. He will never, ever, forget this day, and this day will influence everything he does from then on. So the very first day in school, before he comes up to bat, he has two strikes against him. Before the coin is tossed, he has a penalty of a hundred yards against him. He has to be something very special, a star, a hero, in order to win.

7   Amazingly enough, he does much better in the primary grades than one would expect. It is later when he gets into deep trouble. In the primary grades the language of the classroom is primarily what the linguists call "sign language," that is, the kind of language a dog would understand: "stand up," "sit down," "go to the blackboard," "open your books," "let's sing." The Hispano kid falls behind in the first grade, but not too much; his intuition and native intelligence keep him afloat.

8   Each successive year he falls farther behind, and as time goes on, as the language becomes more abstract and more transparent, the gap of deficiency becomes wider and wider—until he becomes a drop-out. We hear a great deal about the high school drop-out. We are going to hear more and more about the university drop-out. Imagine if you will the young Hispano with his high school diploma in his hot little hand who appears at the university. He's highly motivated, eager, and full of illusions. He has been more successful than most. His family is very

proud of him. He is going to be a somebody. Then comes the shock. He finds out. He doesn't know how to read! His teachers never taught him how to read. How could they? They didn't know Spanish. They didn't understand his culture. No teacher can teach a second language effectively without knowing the native language of her students and understanding their culture. So the kid is suspended. No one can blame him if he feels cheated, betrayed, and frustrated. He earned that high school diploma in good faith, and he put in more than the normal effort to earn it. And a valuable asset to our society is lost in anger and despair.

Education is the answer. School boards, school administrators, and 9 teachers must stop wringing their hands, or looking the other way, hoping the problems will vanish. They must face the issue and seek educational and social solutions. Admittedly, the problem is bigger than they are. Let them confess it. Then let them find the answers and the advice they need, outside the college of education if that is where they are to be found. Hispano parents must learn to place their confidence and cooperation in the schools. Employers must be educated too. They must find out that discrimination is detrimental to them and to the nation they profess to serve.

Above all, Hispanos should be educated in their own culture, their 10 own history, their own contribution to the lifestream of their country. American citizens of Jewish descent who are aware of their own culture will give more to themselves, to their people, and to the United States than those who are not. An Hispano who doesn't speak Spanish must choke on his chile. But before anyone can be proud of being an Hispano or a Jew, or anything else, one must be proud of being a human being. This is not easy in the poverty puddles in which many Hispanos exist on a subhuman level, according to American standards, with their grace, dignity and pride eroded by more than a hundred years of privation, denial, and dishonor. This nation can certainly give these people the tools and materials with which they can build themselves a ladder, and the dream that will make it worthwhile, with which to climb to a better and brighter *mañana.* If they've got the stuff, they'll make it, and they'll be the better for it, and the United States will be the richer because of it. In the name of the Virgin Guadalupana or a Cristo de Velásquez, don't offer them an elevator! The Statue of Liberty, the Constitution of the United States, and the great American dream promise opportunity to compete, the chance to challenge, the hope to cope with the imponderables of our times and circumstances.

And we must educate the child! We must begin with the first-grader. 11 Let us catch him before the traumatic first day in the first grade. Let us give him a preschool orientation where we work him in slowly with toys, games, puzzles, and songs into the new fabric that is going to be the pattern of his life. Let this happen with other children like him and a teacher that looks like his mother, his aunt, or his grandmother, and who speaks his language. Let us decorate his classroom with things he can identify and provide him with coloring books with people and events he can recognize.

12   In the first grade, and throughout the primary grades, let us give him instruction in both Spanish and English. Since he is, in most cases, illiterate, the printed word is as far off as the stars on the dark side of the moon to him. The printed word in English is practically null and void, since it often does not look at all like the spoken word. The Spanish printed word, however, is written exactly as it sounds, and thus is not nearly as remote. So, from a pedagogical standpoint, it makes sense to introduce the little learner to the concept of print and writing through a system of symbols he can understand. This is relatively easy because the spoken language with which the child is familiar corresponds point for point with the symbols that appear on the printed page. Once he accepts the idea of silent and visual communication, he can be eased into a similar experience in English. The teacher, it goes without saying, must know both languages perfectly. It would help tremendously if the child could have the same teacher for the first three years. English, of course, should be taught as a second language by a teacher who knows the score. This kind of approach would give the Hispano child a status he sorely needs. Furthermore, it would give him the sweet taste of success. Success in one area can cast a glow that will illuminate other areas.

13   As this Hispano child progresses through school, cultural content should infiltrate his program: the history of the conquest and colonization of the new world; the conquest and colonization of his state; the heroes of Spain and Spanish America. All of these will give him money to spend in the world's fair, will make him a person to be considered in the social arena that is so important to big and little people. In the process, Hispanic culture and all it has to enrich our Anglo-American culture will endure, aesthetically, practically, and vitally.

 USING THE DICTIONARY: Check the following words. For each, find and explain a related word that uses the same root (example: *bilingual—linguist*). 1. *multilingual* (3) 2. *polarity* (4) 3. *predestined* (5) 4. *detrimental* (9) 5. *privation* (10) 6. *imponderables* (10) 7. *traumatic* (11) 8. *pedagogical* (12) 9. *colonization* (13) 10. *aesthetic* (13)

THE WRITER'S AGENDA:

The author of this essay relies on the persuasive force of strong assertion as he offers emphatic support for an unpopular cause. Study what he does to persuade the audience as he proceeds from his account of the problem to his proposals for its solution.

1. In his introductory paragraph, the author discusses language in strongly inspirational terms. What is the central **allusion** he uses? How persuasive or effective is it for you as a reader?

2. In the paragraphs that follow the introduction, Ulibarri presents the *general issue* and the basic options he sees in vivid, dramatic terms. What is his stand on the basic issue? What is his view of the alternatives? What arguments or appeals does he use in these paragraphs to sway the reader?

3. As he narrows his focus to the specific issue of the Hispanic child's education, the author stresses the crucial *contrasts* that make the child's first day of school traumatic. What are these contrasts? How real or important do they seem to you?

4. What *pattern* does the author trace as he follows the imaginary Hispanic child from the primary grades to college? How plausible or predictable do the stages in the process seem to you?

5. In the final third of the essay, the author presents and supports his *answers* to the questions he has raised. What are his concrete suggestions or proposals, and how feasible or persuasive do they seem? What are supporting arguments he uses, and how effective are they?

6. What passages in this essay seem to you especially *eloquent* or charged with emotion? To what values do they appeal? How do they use language with strong emotional associations? (Where and how does the author make effective or striking use of figurative language or imaginative comparisons?)

FOR DISCUSSION OR WRITING:

1. How familiar are you with the vocabulary and the slogans used in many discussions of the issues raised in this essay? Explore and discuss the meanings, associations, uses, and implications of terms like the following: *Hispanic, Latin, Anglo, Chicano, pocho, la raza.*

2. In recent years, many observers have charged that in a traditional school setting many children from minority groups are "predestined

to failure." Discuss this charge in the light of your own observation and experience.

3. In your opinion, how much recognition or allowance should there be in American schools for cultural and linguistic diversity? Make your arguments persuasive for an audience committed to a different point of view.

4. Do you know well or do you belong to a group that has had to defend its right to be different? Plead the cause of the group to an audience of outsiders, or plead the need for conformity to members of the group.

BACKGROUND: Martin Luther King, Jr. (1929–68) was born in Atlanta, Georgia, and became a Baptist minister like his father. He was the pastor of the Dexter Avenue Baptist Church in Montgomery, Alabama, when a black woman challenged the back-of-the-bus rule of the city's bus system. King organized the successful 381-day boycott of the segregated transit system that marked the birth of the modern civil rights movement, of which he became the acknowledged leader. He founded the Southern Christian Leadership Conference in 1957. Millions were stirred by broadcasts of his sermons and embraced the philosophy of nonviolent revolution that he preached in books like *Letter from Birmingham Jail* (1963) and *Why We Can't Wait* (1964). The movement he led helped bring about the 1964 Civil Rights Act and the 1965 Voting Rights Act. His eloquence and his example inspired a new generation of black leaders, from Andrew Young, who became U. S. ambassador to the United Nations and later mayor of Atlanta, to Julian Bond, Shirley Chisholm, and Jesse Jackson. King was jailed many times, spied on by government agents, stabbed and reviled; he was finally struck down by the bullet of an assassin in Memphis on April 4, 1968. "I Have a Dream" is the speech he gave in Washington, D.C., in August 1963 after he led a march of 200,000 people to commemorate the one hundredth anniversary of Lincoln's proclamation freeing the slaves.

Martin Luther King, Jr.
I Have a Dream

GUIDE TO READING: King's eloquence gave hope and a new sense of dignity to millions of angry and disillusioned black people while at the same time it stirred the conscience of many members of the defensive or complacent white majority. Where in this speech is he speaking most directly to his black followers? Where is he speaking most directly to the white majority? Where does he appeal most strongly to shared or common values?

FIVE SCORE years ago, a great American, in whose symbolic shadow we stand, signed the Emancipation Proclamation. This momentous decree came as a great beacon light of hope to millions of Negro slaves who had been seared in the flames of withering injustice. It came as a joyous daybreak to end the long night of captivity.

2   But one hundred years later, we must face the tragic fact that the Negro is still not free. One hundred years later, the life of the Negro is still sadly crippled by the manacles of segregation and the chains of discrimination. One hundred years later, the Negro lives on a lonely island of poverty in the midst of a vast ocean of material prosperity. One hundred years later, the Negro is still languishing in the corners of American society and finds himself an exile in his own land. So we have come here today to dramatize an appalling condition.

3   In a sense we have come to our nation's capital to cash a check. When the architects of our republic wrote the magnificent words of the Constitution and the Declaration of Independence, they were signing a promissory note to which every American was to fall heir. This note was a promise that all men would be guaranteed the unalienable rights of life, liberty, and the pursuit of happiness.

4   It is obvious today that America has defaulted on this promissory note insofar as her citizens of color are concerned. Instead of honoring this sacred obligation, America has given the Negro people a bad check; a check which has come back marked "insufficient funds." But we refuse to believe that the bank of justice is bankrupt. We refuse to believe that there are insufficient funds in the great vaults of opportunity of this nation. So we have come to cash this check—a check that will give us upon demand the riches of freedom and the security of justice. We have also come to this hallowed spot to remind America of the fierce urgency of *now*. This is no time to engage in the luxury of cooling off or to take the tranquilizing drugs of gradualism. *Now* is the time to make real the promises of Democracy. *Now* is the time to rise from the dark and desolate valley of segregation to the sunlit path of racial justice. *Now* is the time to open the doors of opportunity to all of God's children. *Now* is the time to lift our nation from the quicksands of racial injustice to the solid rock of brotherhood.

5   It would be fatal for the nation to overlook the urgency of the moment and to underestimate the determination of the Negro. This sweltering summer of the Negro's legitimate discontent will not pass until there is an invigorating autumn of freedom and equality. 1963 is not an end, but a beginning. Those who hope that the Negro needed to blow off steam and will now be content will have a rude awakening if the nation returns to business as usual. There will be neither rest nor tranquility in America until the Negro is granted his citizenship rights. The whirlwinds of revolt will continue to shake the foundations of our nation until the bright day of justice emerges.

6   But there is something that I must say to my people who stand on the warm threshold which leads into the palace of justice. In the pro-

cess of gaining our rightful place we must not be guilty of wrongful deeds. Let us not seek to satisfy our thirst for freedom by drinking from the cup of bitterness and hatred. We must forever conduct our struggle on the high plane of dignity and discipline. We must not allow our creative protest to degenerate into physical violence. Again and again we must rise to the majestic heights of meeting physical force with soul force. The marvelous new militancy which has engulfed the Negro community must not lead us to a distrust of all white people, for many of our white brothers, as evidenced by their presence here today, have come to realize that their destiny is tied up with our destiny and their freedom is inextricably bound to our freedom. We cannot walk alone.

And as we walk, we must make the pledge that we shall march 7 ahead. We cannot turn back. There are those who are asking the devotees of civil rights, "When will you be satisfied?" We can never be satisfied as long as the Negro is the victim of the unspeakable horrors of police brutality. We can never be satisfied as long as our bodies, heavy with the fatigue of travel, cannot gain lodging in the motels of the highways and the hotels of the cities. We cannot be satisfied as long as the Negro's basic mobility is from a smaller ghetto to a larger one. We can never be satisfied as long as a Negro in Mississippi cannot vote and a Negro in New York believes he has nothing for which to vote. No, no, we are not satisfied, and will not be satisfied until justice rolls down like waters and righteousness like a mighty stream.

I am not unmindful that some of you have come here out of great 8 trials and tribulations. Some of you have come fresh from narrow jail cells. Some of you have come from areas where your quest for freedom left you battered by the storms of persecution and staggered by the winds of police brutality. You have been the veterans of creative suffering. Continue to work with the faith that unearned suffering is redemptive.

Go back to Mississippi, go back to Alabama, go back to South Carolina, go back to Georgia, go back to Louisiana, go back to the slums and ghettos of our northern cities, knowing that somehow this situation can and will be changed. Let us not wallow in the valley of despair.

I say to you today, my friends, that in spite of the difficulties and 10 frustrations of the moment I still have a dream. It is a dream deeply rooted in the American dream.

I have a dream that one day this nation will rise up and live out the 11 true meaning of its creed: "We hold these truths to be self-evident; that all men are created equal."

I have a dream that one day on the red hills of Georgia the sons of 12 former slaves and the sons of former slaveowners will be able to sit down together at the table of brotherhood.

I have a dream that one day even the state of Mississippi, a desert 13 state sweltering with the heat of injustice and oppression, will be transformed into an oasis of freedom and justice.

14   I have a dream that my four little children will one day live in a nation where they will not be judged by the color of their skin but by the content of their character.

15   I have a dream today.

16   I have a dream that one day the state of Alabama, whose governor's lips are presently dripping with the words of interposition and nullification, will be transformed into a situation where little black boys and black girls will be able to join hands with little white boys and white girls and walk together as sisters and brothers.

17   I have a dream today.

18   I have a dream that one day every valley shall be exalted, every hill and mountain shall be made low, the rough places will be made plain, and the crooked places will be made straight, and the glory of the Lord shall be revealed, and all flesh shall see it together.

19   This is our hope. This is the faith with which I return to the South. With this faith we will be able to hew out of the mountain of despair a stone of hope. With this faith we will be able to transform the jangling discords of our nation into a beautiful symphony of brotherhood. With this faith we will be able to work together, to pray together, to struggle together, to go to jail together, to stand up for freedom together, knowing that we will be free one day.

20   This will be the day when all of God's children will be able to sing with new meaning

> My country, 'tis of thee,
> Sweet land of liberty,
>   Of thee I sing:
> Land where my fathers died,
> Land of the pilgrims' pride,
> From every mountain-side
>   Let freedom ring.

21   And if America is to be a great nation this must become true. So let freedom ring from the prodigious hilltops of New Hampshire. Let freedom ring from the mighty mountains of New York. Let freedom ring from the heightening Alleghenies of Pennsylvania!

22   Let freedom ring from the snowcapped Rockies of Colorado!

23   Let freedom ring from the curvaceous peaks of California!

24   But not only that; let freedom ring from Stone Mountain of Georgia!

25   Let freedom ring from Lookout Mountain of Tennessee!

26   Let freedom ring from every hill and molehill of Mississippi. From every mountainside, let freedom ring.

When we let freedom ring, when we let it ring from every village   27
and every hamlet, from every state and every city, we will be able to
speed up that day when all of God's children, black men and white
men, Jews and Gentiles, Protestants and Catholics, will be able to join
hands and sing in the words of the old Negro spiritual, "Free at last!
free at last! thank God almighty, we are free at last!"

 USING THE DICTIONARY: King uses a number of terms that
have played a major role in *American history* or politics.
How does your dictionary define each of the following? For
two or three of these, write a one-paragraph definition that
sums up what the term has meant in American life. 1. *emancipation* (1) 2. *segregation* (2) 3. *gradualism* (4) 4. *brotherhood* (4) 5. *militancy* (6) 6. *civil rights* (7) 7. *police brutality*
(7) 8. *the American dream* (10) 9. *interposition* (16) 10. *nullification* (16)

THE WRITER'S AGENDA:

In writing this famous speech, Martin Luther King had a double
aim: to mobilize the aspirations of the black community, and to appeal
to the conscience of white Americans. Answer the following questions
about the sources of his eloquence and its uses in this selection.

1. Examine the speaker's use of vivid **figurative** language to dramatize the evil of racism and to give emotional force to his appeals:

a. Point out and discuss several striking imaginative comparisons
(for instance, the "tranquilizing drugs of gradualism"). What is
their emotional or inspirational appeal?

b. Point out and discuss examples of imaginative comparisons that
are **antithetical**—lined up as balanced opposites (daybreak/night,
island/ocean). What is their appeal or effect?

c. As an example of a *sustained* or extended **metaphor**, examine
the bad-check analogy in the fourth paragraph. How is it carried
through into related details? What is its persuasive effect?

2. King appeals to *shared values* by quoting from or alluding to
famous American historical documents, the Bible, and Negro spirituals
(as well as Shakespeare, adapting his "the winter of our discontent").
What are some striking examples? What do you think is their effect on
the audience?

3. King took a stand different from that of other vocal representatives of the *black community.* Where does he speak most directly to "my people"? What warnings or cautions does he address to them? Where does he most forcefully give voice to their grievances?

4. In what parts of the speech does King address himself most directly to the *white majority?* What warnings does he address to them? In your judgment, how or where does he appeal most effectively to their consciences?

5. In the second half of his speech, King makes extensive use of **emphatic repetition** as a traditional oratorical device. Examine his repetition of words and phrases as well as his use of parallel sentence structure. What makes his use of repetition varied, emphatic, and eloquent rather than merely monotonous?

FOR DISCUSSION OR WRITING:

1. King said in this speech that his dream of the future was "a dream deeply rooted in the American dream." What did he mean? In your judgment, what is the persuasive force of this way of formulating the aspirations of the black minority?

2. King preached nonviolent revolution, adapting the philosophy of nonviolence taught by Gandhi in India during the struggle for independence from British rule. Argue for or against nonviolence as a means of social reform or political revolution. Make your arguments persuasive for a skeptical or reluctant audience.

3. In his speech, King addressed himself to members of America's minorities who were able to vote but who believed they had "nothing for which to vote." In our society today, what is the power of the right to vote? Make your argument persuasive for a skeptical audience.

4. Since King's death, various initiatives or efforts designed to combat segregation have been much debated: affirmative action, racial quotas, busing, and the like. Argue for or against one such major initiative, trying to persuade a skeptical or hostile audience.

5. What has done most to shape your own views of racial tension, racial prejudice, or discrimination? Examine the role of major influences or crucial experiences on your thinking. What has been the role of books, television, movies? Give a vivid account of experiences that had a major impact on you.

6. Many observers feel that apathy has to a large extent replaced

the moral fervor of the early days of the civil rights movement. Examine some current editorials or short articles that deal with social issues or social injustice. How persuasive are they? Do they seem too bland, conciliatory, or uninvolved?

FOR FURTHER DISCUSSION AND WRITING: Since Judy Syfers published her satirical "I Want a Wife" in *Ms.* magazine in December 1971, it has become a widely reprinted classic of feminist writing. What, according to the author, are major advantages men traditionally derive from marriage? What are major injustices suffered by women? Which of her points are most persuasive for you? Which least? Prepare a paper of your own, using as a title "I Don't Want a Wife," "I Want a Husband," "I Want to Be Single," "I Want to Be a Wife," or some other variation that best reflects your own perspective.

Judy Syfers

I Want a Wife

1   I BELONG to that classification of people known as wives. I am A Wife. And, not altogether incidentally, I am a mother.

2   Not too long ago a male friend of mine appeared on the scene fresh from a recent divorce. He had one child, who is, of course, with his ex-wife. He is looking for another wife. As I thought about him while I was ironing one evening, it suddenly occurred to me that I, too, would like to have a wife. Why do I want a wife?

3   I would like to go back to school so that I can become economically independent, support myself, and, if need be, support those dependent upon me. I want a wife who will work and send me to school. And while I am going to school I want a wife to take care of my children. I want a wife to keep track of the children's doctor and dentist appointments. And to keep track of mine, too. I want a wife to make sure my children eat properly and are kept clean. I want a wife who will wash the children's clothes and keep them mended. I want a wife who is a good nurturant attendant to my children, who arranges for their schooling, makes sure that they have an adequate social life with their peers, takes them to the park, the zoo, etc. I want a wife who takes care of the children when they are sick, a wife who arranges to be around when the children need special care, because, of course, I cannot miss class-

es at school. My wife must arrange to lose time at work and not lose the job. It may mean a small cut in my wife's income from time to time, but I guess I can tolerate that. Needless to say, my wife will arrange and pay for the care of the children while my wife is working.

I want a wife who will take care of *my* physical needs. I want a wife   4
who will keep my house clean. A wife who will pick up after my children, a wife who will pick up after me. I want a wife who will keep clothes clean, ironed, mended, replaced when need be, and who will see to it that my personal things are kept in their proper place so that I can find what I need the minute I need it. I want a wife who cooks the meals, a wife who is a *good* cook. I want a wife who will plan the menus, do the necessary grocery shopping, prepare the meals, serve them pleasantly, and then do the cleaning up while I do my studying. I want a wife who will care for me when I am sick and sympathize with my pain and loss of time from school. I want a wife to go along when our family takes a vacation so that someone can continue to care for me and my children when I need a rest and change of scene.

I want a wife who will not bother me with rambling complaints   5
about a wife's duties. But I want a wife who will listen to me when I feel the need to explain a rather difficult point I have come across in my course of studies. And I want a wife who will type my papers for me when I have written them.

I want a wife who will take care of the details of my social life.   6
When my wife and I are invited out by my friends, I want a wife who will take care of the babysitting arrangements. When I meet people at school that I like and want to entertain, I want a wife who will have the house clean, will prepare a special meal, serve it to me and my friends, and not interrupt when I talk about things that interest me and my friends. I want a wife who will have arranged that the children are fed and ready for bed before my guests arrive so that the children do not bother us. I want a wife who takes care of the needs of my guests so that they feel comfortable, who makes sure that they have an ashtray, that they are passed the hors d'oeuvres, that they are offered a second helping of the food, that their wine glasses are replenished when necessary, that their coffee is served to them as they like it. And I want a wife who knows that sometimes I need a night out by myself.

I want a wife who is sensitive to my sexual needs, a wife who makes   7
love passionately and eagerly when I feel like it, a wife who makes sure that I am satisfied. And, of course, I want a wife who will not demand sexual attention when I am not in the mood for it. I want a wife who assumes the complete responsibility for birth control, because I do not want more children. I want a wife who will remain sexually faithful to me so that I do not have to clutter up my intellectual life with jealousies. And I want a wife who understands that *my* sexual needs may

entail more than strict adherence to monogamy. I must, after all, be able to relate to people as fully as possible.

8   If, by chance, I find another person more suitable as a wife than the wife I already have, I want the liberty to replace my present wife with another one. Naturally, I will expect a fresh, new life; my wife will take the children and be solely responsible for them so that I am left free.

9   When I am through with school and have a job, I want my wife to quit working and remain at home so that my wife can more fully and completely take care of a wife's duties.

10   My God, who *wouldn't* want a wife?

P A R T

T H R E E

AUDIENCES FOR
WRITING

WE WRITE to be read. An effective writer has learned to look at writing through the reader's eyes. In writing, but especially also in revising a paper, we ask ourselves: "What does it take to attract and hold the reader's attention? How do we make a reader see the purpose and the direction of a paper? What does the reader need to have explained? What is needed to make a reader follow the steps in an argument? When we write for a particular audience, what common background can we assume? What shared interests and common values will work in our favor; what predictable resistance are we likely to encounter?"

This third part of the book asks you to think about the needs and expectations of audiences for different kinds of writing. Many of the writers in this section have a large loyal following. They know how to satisfy their readers' curiosity. They know how to honor their readers' standards and preferences; they know how to appeal to shared values. They know how to inform, please, entertain, and inspire readers.

The readings in Part Three appear under the following headings:

10 ✦ SCIENCE

A basic task of every writer is to shed light on the subject. The writers in this unit know how to make what is new or difficult accessible to the curious reader. Writing about science or technology, they write as experts sharing information and ideas with a lay audience. We can learn from them how an effective writer serves the reader's needs— how to explain what is different, how to lay out a technical subject in an intelligible pattern, how to use the parallels and analogies that will relate difficult concepts to the world of familiar experience.

11 ♦ MEDIA

People who write successfully about American popular culture know how to reckon with the attitudes of the audience. They do not just report and catalog; they bring into play attitudes ranging from nostalgia and amusement to bitter, slashing wit. Movie critics, media historians, and observers of the passing scene have to gauge how serious or how entertaining the audience expects their writing to be. They often develop a personal style that is at the right point along the spectrum from the solemn and earnest to the casual or jazzy and sensational. Much colorful writing about popular culture reminds us that a large segment of the reading public turns to writers who not only inform or argue but also know how to please, provoke, shock, or entertain.

12 ♦ HISTORY

The writers in this unit make us ponder the past in order to provide guidance or warnings for the future. Even more so than other readers, an audience seriously interested in historical subjects is likely to be wary of mere superficial opinion. When we look for the lessons of recent history, we turn to the testimony of the committed participant or to the writer who has seriously studied the record and weighed the evidence. Serious writing on historical subjects shows the writer's respect for the possible doubts of the audience and for its sense of fairness. We learn from such writing how to draw on the testimony of committed witnesses, how to weigh conflicting evidence, and how to do justice to a range of relevant sources.

13 ♦ CLASSIC ESSAYS

A piece of writing becomes a classic when it outlasts its limited role in a particular time and place because it speaks to many different readers. The writers in this unit write for an imaginary ideal educated reader. Their writing shows what they believe their audience to be capable of when it is at its best. They expect us to be sensitive to shades of meaning and to distinctions that do not meet the naked eye. They respect our intelligence; they trust in our basic goodwill; they appeal to our better selves. They trust that we will take the time to read an essay with pleasure, responding to the rhythms of an eloquent passage, remembering something that was well said.

U N I T 1 0

SCIENCE:
The Larger Public

The Common Theme: What does it take to communicate scientific information to the general reader? The technology that science has created and the theories it has constructed shape in many ways how we live and what we think. But although science reaches everywhere into our lives, the advance of specialized scientific knowledge has far outstripped the science education of the ordinary citizen. Much of what goes on in science is a mystery to anyone outside a small group of highly trained specialists, united by a special kind of dedication to and absorption in their work. When a writer tries to bridge the gap between the specialist and the general public, the needs and limitations of the audience become a central concern. The writers in this unit know how to present scientific or technical information to the newcomer or the outsider. The third of the essays is by a writer who knows how to explain scientific ideas but who often at the same time makes us think about how modern science shapes our attitudes toward life.

WRITER'S GUIDE 10:
Writing to Inform

The first duty of a writer is to shed light on the subject. The more technical the subject, the more the task of enlightening the reader may become the writer's chief concern. Much writing on topics in science, technology, or medicine aims to make expert knowledge understandable to the general reader. The writer sets out to serve the *needs of the audience.* To make us understand the subject, the writer presents essential facts, explains what is new or difficult, and shows important connections. We judge such writing by how successfully it makes technical information accessible to the newcomer or the outsider.

In much informative writing, the writer serves as a guide whose task it is to do justice to the subject at hand. Such writing has to be **objective**. It concentrates on showing and explaining what is "out there." It plays down personal, subjective thoughts, feelings, and preferences (although it often reflects the author's fascination with or commitment to the subject). Observe the following guidelines when writing papers whose major purpose is to inform and explain:

(1) *Show your respect for observable facts.* It is true that much informative or technical writing deals with the interpretation of facts, with theories constructed from data that have been collected. But the audience needs to have confidence in the person doing the interpreting. One way to build this confidence is to show that theories are rooted in the observable facts they are designed to explain.

Reassure readers who want to know: On what kind of observation are these data based? How could this statement be verified? Whenever possible, show your capacity for patient first-hand observation, as did the author of the following passage:

> Once, years ago, I saw red blood cells whip, one by one, through the capillaries in a goldfish's transparent tail. The goldfish was etherized. Its head lay in a wad of wet cotton wool; its tail lay on a tray under a dissecting microscope. . . . The red blood cells in the goldfish's tail streamed and coursed through narrow channels invisible save for glistening threads of thickness in the general translucency. They never wavered or slowed or ceased flowing. . . . They streamed redly around, up, and on, one by one, more, and more, without end.
> —Annie Dillard, *Pilgrim at Tinker Creek*

Readers who look for authoritative information like to feel that the authorities they trust make a habit of taking a look for themselves. In areas where readers are likely to be wary of glib secondhand theories, try to direct their attention to things they can observe or verify for themselves.

(2) *Include essential information.* Ask yourself: "What does the reader need to know? What essential parts does the reader need to know in order to understand the larger whole? What basic steps does the reader have to trace in order to see how a process works?" Give your reader the answers to the basic fact-finding questions: What? Where? When? How? Why?

The following description of comets provides in a brief space much essential information about what they are, when and where they are observed, and how they behave and why:

(Where is it found?)	Edmund Halley (1656–1742) was the first to state that comets are members of the solar system, traveling in elliptical orbits. Billions of comets continually circle the sun like a halo at distances of over 10 billion miles. Occasionally one is "kicked" out of its track by the gravitational attraction of a star or planet. It may then be wrenched into a new smaller orbit which makes it travel into the interior of the solar system, looping around the sun. . . .
(What is it made up of?)	A comet is merely an accumulation of frozen gases and grit, no more than a few miles in diameter, with a density much less than that of water. . . .
(How does it work?)	Off by itself in space, a comet has no tail. But when it approaches the sun, solar energy vaporizes its outer layers to form a swollen head and then drives some of this material away to form a tail of incandescence pointing out toward space. . . .
(What is striking evidence or a striking example?)	The Great Comet of 1843 had a tail that streamed out more than 500 million miles. . . .

Doubtless much more could be and has been said about comets. But this passage goes far toward explaining to readers what they basically want to know—why comets appear in the sky when they do, and what causes the fiery streaming tail that has awed and frightened people through the ages.

(3) *Build on what is familiar.* Go from the simple to the difficult.

Authors who write about technical subjects and yet reach large audiences know how to start from reassuring everyday knowledge. They constantly return to it for comparison and illustration. Here is one of the most widely read current science writers writing about the atom. Note the many homely, everyday references and comparisons:

> To make an apple pie, you need wheat, apples, a pinch of this and that, and the heat of the oven. The ingredients are made of molecules—sugar, say, or water. The molecules, in turn, are made of atoms—carbon, oxygen, hydrogen and a few others. . . . Suppose you *take an apple pie and cut it in half; take one of the two pieces, cut it in half;* and, in the spirit of Democritus, continue. How many cuts before you are down to a single atom? The answer is about *ninety successive cuts.* Of course, no knife could be sharp enough, the pie is too crumbly, and the atom would in any case be too small to see unaided.
>
> A typical atom has *a kind of cloud* of electrons on the outside. . . . Electrons determine the chemical properties of the atom—*the glitter of gold, the cold feel of iron, the crystal structure of the carbon diamond.* Deep inside the atom, hidden far beneath the electron cloud, is the nucleus, generally composed of positively charged protons and electrically neutral neutrons. Atoms are very small—one hundred million of them end to end would be *as large as the tip of your little finger.* But the nucleus is a hundred thousand times smaller still, which is part of the reason it took so long to be discovered. Nevertheless, most of the mass of an atom is in its nucleus; the electrons are by comparison just *clouds of moving fluff.*
>
> —Carl Sagan, *Cosmos*

Here is another famous science writer talking about the protein molecules that are the basic building blocks of our bodies. Again, although the information becomes technical, everyday comparisons help us see what it means in terms that we can understand:

> To begin with, proteins consist of large molecules. Even a protein molecule of only average size is made up of a conglomeration of perhaps four hundred thousand atoms. *In comparison, a water molecule is made up of three atoms and a molecule of table sugar of forty-five atoms.*
>
> Atoms within the protein molecule are arranged in combinations called amino acids, each of which is made up of anywhere from ten to thirty atoms. The amino acids are strung together, *like beads in a necklace,* to form a protein molecule. . . .

The interesting thing is that if two protein molecules are made up of the same number of the same types of amino acids, they will *still* be different if the order in which those amino acids occur in the chain differs. It is *as if you were to make a necklace out of twenty beads—five red, five yellow, five blue, and five green. Depending on the order in which you arranged them you could* make *twelve billion different patterns.*
—Isaac Asimov, *Is Anyone There?*

(4) *Proceed in a systematic fashion.* The less familiar the subject is to the reader, the more the writer has to be sure to cover essential parts of the subject in a clear, step-by-step order. The more difficult the subject, the less room there is for backtrackings and distractions. If the reader is to "get things straight," information has to be laid out in a straightforward, methodical fashion, providing a clear path for the reader to follow.

As a result, writing whose main aim is to inform is usually more rigorously organized than other kinds. The businesslike, systematic, step-by-step development is a signal to readers that they need to pay *attention*: If they blink, they might miss an important step. Often, the writer will be tracing a chain of events that will not make sense if important links are left out. An example of such a chain is the pattern of human metabolism—the sequence of chemical reactions by which the body breaks down food to form energy and build tissue.

Even when the writer is not tracing a step-by-step process or a chain of cause and effect, informative writing usually has the kind of systematic forward movement in which the different stages are not really optional. Instead, one step leads to and helps us understand another. For instance, a writer may trace the same principle through several related applications. In the following excerpt, the writer shows the same basic reaction at work in three different examples. But he does so in order to *lead up* from familiar ones to one that is less familiar and especially important:

GENERAL
PRINCIPAL:
First example
(vaccination)

The body builds up special defensive proteins (antibodies) that react with foreign molecules and neutralize them. This is one of its best defenses against invading bacteria and viruses. Once someone has formed an antibody against the measles virus, he is immune to further attacks. . . .

Second example
(allergies)

A negative instance of the same use of proteins is the fact that the body may also accidentally become sensitive to foreign substances that are fairly harmless in themselves; to the proteins of certain types of pollen, for instance, or to certain types of food. A person will in such a case suffer from hay fever or food allergy. . . .

Third example (rejection of grafts)   A particular antibody can always distinguish between a foreign substance and the molecules present in the body it belongs to. If an antibody can distinguish between two proteins, those two proteins must in some way be different. That being so, no two human beings, except for identical twins, can have proteins that are completely alike. The proof of this is that a skin graft will fail unless it is taken from another part of the patient's own body, or, at furthest remove, from the body of his identical twin, if he is lucky enough to have one.

—Isaac Asimov, *Is Anyone There?*

(5) *Explain necessary technical terms.* We cannot say much about a complex subject like body chemistry without using technical terms, any more than an auto mechanic can function efficiently without using terms like *carburetor, differential, valve,* and *gasket.* However, we have to remember what it takes to make specialized terms meaningful for the newcomer or the learner. Technical terms become an obvious problem when they are used to impress and befuddle the outsider. But they also become a barrier when they are used too freely and unthinkingly by the insider too familiar with them to think of them as a hurdle.

Select those technical terms that are clearly useful or necessary; make sure to explain them and illustrate their use. Whenever possible, present one new term at a time and give it a chance to sink in. All of the detail provided in the following passage helps to give meaning to the term *ecosystem* that appears at the end:

When three or four termites are collected together in a chamber they wander about aimlessly, but when more termites are added, they begin to build. It is the presence of other termites, in sufficient numbers at close quarters, that produces the work: they pick up each other's fecal pellets and stack them in neat columns, and when the columns are precisely the right height, the termites reach across and turn the perfect arches that form the foundation of the termitarium. No single termite knows how to do any of this, but as soon as there are enough termites gathered together they become flawless architects, sensing their distances from each other although blind, building an immensely complicated structure with its own air-conditioning and humidity control. They work their lives away in this *ecosystem* built by themselves.

— Lewis Thomas, "Debating the Unknowable," *Atlantic*

The following passage defines the term *conjunction* as used by astronomers and illustrates its use:

In addition to Venus, there are four other planets visible to the naked eye—Mercury, Mars, Jupiter, and Saturn. During their movements across the sky, two planets may sometimes appear to pass very close to one another—though in reality, of course, they are millions of miles apart. Such occurrences are called *conjunctions;* on occasion they may be so close that the planets cannot be separated by the naked eye. This happened for Mars and Venus on October 4, 1953, when for a short while the two planets appeared to be fused together to give a single star. Such a spectacle is rare enough to be very striking, and the great astronomer Johannes Kepler devoted much time to proving that the Star of Bethlehem was a special conjunction of Jupiter and Saturn.

— Arthur C. Clarke, *Report on Planet Three*

A writer introducing several important technical terms at a time must make a special effort to provide enough commonsense description to keep the terms clear:

The heart has four chambers—two atria and two ventricles—and four valves, two of which control the flow of blood from atrium to ventricle, and two of which control the pumping of the blood from the ventricles out into the arteries. The atria—the two chambers at the top of the heart—are *little more than reservoirs* for blood returning via the veins to the heart. They collect blood returned to the heart from the body and lungs, and deliver it to the heart's larger active chamber below. The first set of valves simply insures that the blood *flows only one way,* from the atria to the ventricles. The ventricles are *the blood pumps* that do the true work of the heart. These two larger chambers contract forcefully to pump the blood to the lungs and throughout the body.

In employing technical terms and categories, a writer has to be clearly aware of the needs and possible limitations of the audience. In practice, writers assume in their readers varying degrees of previous preparation for and interest in the subject. At one extreme are the authors of watered-down popularizations that are superficially entertaining but contain little solid information. At the opposite extreme are narrow specialists unable to talk about their specialty in plain English. In between are the authors who write for an educated lay audience— educated enough to have some grounding in science and technology, and educated enough to want to understand and learn.

Here, for instance, is Rachel Carson writing about tiny one-celled organisms of the ocean in her classic *The Sea Around Us:*

> Over great areas of the temperate oceans the sea floor is largely covered with the remains of unicellular creatures known as the foraminifera, of which the most abundant genus is Globigerina. The shells of Globigerina may be recognized in very ancient sediments as well as in modern ones, but over the ages the species have varied. Knowing this, we can date approximately the deposits in which they occur. But always they have been simple animals, living in an intricately sculptured shell of carbonate of lime, the whole so small you would need a microscope to see its details.

The author of this passage trusts her readers to know (or to make out) a technical term like *unicellular* (she has used *one-celled* earlier in the book). She expects her readers to have studied enough biology to know the difference between the more general *genus* and the more limited *species.* She expects them to recognize the scientist's need for exact identification and not be put off by exact labels like *foraminifera* and *Globigerina.* However, many of the more general passages in her book are written in beautifully clear nontechnical language:

> As the years passed, and the centuries, and the millions of years, the stream of life grew more and more complex. From simple, one-celled creatures, others that were aggregations of specialized cells arose, and then creatures with organs for feeding, digesting, breathing, reproducing. Sponges grew on the rocky bottom of the sea's edge and coral animals built their habitations in warm, clear waters. Jellyfish swam and drifted in the sea. Worms evolved, and starfish, and hard-shelled creatures with many-jointed legs.

To sum up: Practice in informative writing is good training for writers who otherwise might tend to take too much for granted. Trying to explain a technical subject to the nonspecialist, we learn to pay attention to the legitimate needs and expectations of the reader. We learn something about the difficulties of trying to say what we mean, but also about the satisfaction that comes from reaching an audience.

PREWRITING ACTIVITIES 10

1. For *paragraph practice,* write a paragraph that will explain a basic scientific principle or concept to a high school student with little background in science. Include essential technical details, but make sure they become clear through explanation, comparison, analogy, or the like. Choose a topic like the following: gravity, electricity, magnetism, combustion, leverage, inertia, friction.

2. For *a lay audience,* explain the advantages of an advanced camera over a simple one, of a diesel engine over an ordinary engine, of jet propulsion over propeller engines, or the like.

3. Do *a preliminary collection* of possibly useful material for a paper on automation and robots. Set up several major categories, such as personal experience; fictional treatments in books, television, or movies; and current reading about developments in industry.

BACKGROUND: Isaac Asimov (born 1920) is one of this country's leading authors of factual science writing as well as of science fiction. He came to New York City from Russia with his immigrant parents when he was three years old. He went to high school in Brooklyn, and he graduated from Columbia University with a degree in chemistry when he was nineteen. He became a professor of biochemistry at the Boston University School of Medicine but soon started to devote most of his time to writing. "From an early age," he says, "I had known I was a writer." As a boy, Asimov had become fascinated with early science fiction magazines such as *Amazing Stories* when his father would not let him read gory dime-store novels. He started his own career as a writer by publishing science fiction on topics including robots, time travel, and life on other planets. Many of his over 160 books, however, are nonfiction, explaining topics "on the frontiers of science" to the general reader. He says about his work as a science writer: "I can read a dozen dull books and make one interesting book out of them. I'm on fire to explain, and happiest when it's something reasonably intricate which I can make clear step by step."

Isaac Asimov

Nuclear Fusion

GUIDE TO READING: Discussions of nuclear energy have run the gamut from glowing predictions of a future of cheap energy to warnings of ecological disaster. How much technical knowledge does the general reader need to form a judgment on some of the issues involved? As you read Asimov's essay, pay special attention to how he sizes up the needs of the reader. What, in the judgment of the author, does the nonspecialist need to know and to have explained? What familiar or everyday knowledge does the author build on? Which points become clear to you; which remain confusing, and why?

1   THE WORLD faces a crisis that may destroy civilization in our own lifetime. It is usually referred to as an energy crisis, but it isn't. It is an oil crisis. The earth's oil wells may begin to run dry in 30 years, and without oil it would seem that the industrial world will clank to a

grinding halt and that there will be no way in which the teeming population of the world could be supported.

Yet who says oil is the only source of energy? It is, at present, the 2 most convenient source; at present, the most versatile. Matters do not, however, have to stay in the present.

The early decades of the 21st century may see oil supplies at a 3 useless trickle and yet find energy plentiful and electricity coursing through the nerves and veins of industry. With plentiful, unending electricity, we could even manufacture our own oil to fill indispensable needs: Electricity can break down water to hydrogen and oxygen; the oxygen can be discarded, and the hydrogen can be combined with carbon dioxide from the air to form gasoline. The gasoline can then be burned and will combine with the discarded oxygen to form water and carbon dioxide again.

Nothing will be used up but electricity, and the electricity can 4 come from the greatest and most copious source of energy on our planet —the hydrogen in seawater. That hydrogen represents the great ark in which humanity can ride out the oil shortage that now threatens to overwhelm us and come to rest finally on the quiet uplands of energy plenty.

There is a catch. The ark is not yet quite within reach. Our hands 5 still grope for it, but we cannot yet squeeze the energy out of hydrogen.

The simplest way of getting energy out of hydrogen is to combine it 6 with oxygen—to let it burn and deliver heat. Such a process, however, involves merely the outermost fringe of the hydrogen atom and delivers only a tiny fraction of the energy store available at its compact "nucleus."

Something other than hydrogen-burning—something much more 7 dramatic—takes place at the center of the sun. Under enormous gravitational pressures, the substance at the sun's core is squeezed together, raising the temperature there to a colossal 15 million degrees Centigrade (24 million degrees Fahrenheit).

At such pressures and temperatures, the very atoms of matter smash 8 to pieces. Their outer shells break away and expose the tiny nuclei at the center, which then drive into each other at thousands of miles per second and sometimes stick. When hydrogen nuclei stick together to form the slightly larger nuclei of helium atoms, the process is called "hydrogen fusion."

Every second, 650 million tons of hydrogen are fusing into 645.5 9 million tons of helium at the sun's center. This process produces energy. Each missing 4.6 million tons per second represents the energy that pours out of the sun in all directions. A very small fraction is intercepted by the earth, and on that energy all life is supported.

Though it takes an incredible amount of hydrogen fusion each second to support the sun, there is so much hydrogen in that giant object 10 that, even after some 5 billion years, it is still mostly hydrogen. The sun can continue to produce energy for perhaps 7 billion more years before its fusion mechanism begins to falter.

11   Can we somehow take advantage of this process on earth?

12   The trouble is we can't duplicate the conditions at the center of the sun in the proper way. To begin with, we need enormous temperatures. One way of achieving such temperatures is to explode an "atomic bomb" that is powered by uranium fission. For just a brief period of time, temperatures in the millions of degrees are produced at the center of that explosion. If hydrogen in some appropriate form is present there, it will fuse. The result is that the atomic bomb becomes the trigger for the greater blast of a "hydrogen bomb."

13   Naturally, we can't run the world by exploding hydrogen bombs. We want *controlled* fusion—the kind that produces energy a little bit at a time in usable, nondestructive quantities.

14   One way would be to start with a small quantity of hydrogen and heat it until it fuses. There would only be a small amount of energy produced. This could be bled away while the new hydrogen is added to the mix to undergo fusion in its turn.

15   Heating hydrogen to the required temperature isn't easy, but it can be done by electric currents or by pumping in energetic subatomic particles. The trouble is that hydrogen expands as it's heated, and its atoms drift irretrievably away in all directions. We must hold the hydrogen in place while it is being heated. But how? The sun holds its hydrogen in place with its enormous gravitational field, but we can't imitate the sun's gravity on earth.

16   Nor can we force the hydrogen to remain in place by keeping it in a container. The heat might cause the container to vaporize. On the other hand, if we kept the container cool while the hydrogen heated up, the hydrogen would lose heat again upon contact with the cool container.

17   One possibility is to use a magnetic field. A magnetic field is not matter and is neither hot nor cold. As the hydrogen is heated, its atoms break down to electrically charged fragments, and these are repelled by the magnetic field. The fragments can't break through the magnetic field and must stay in place.

18   The problem is designing a magnetic field of the proper shape and intensity that will remain stable and not spring a leak. It's not an easy job. Scientists in the U.S., Great Britain and the Soviet Union have been working at it for nearly 30 years. The best device proposed thus far is the "tokamak," first developed in the Soviet Union.

19   But even a tokamak won't do the job for ordinary hydrogen. In the center of the sun, a temperature of 15 million degrees Centigrade is sufficient because the hydrogen is squeezed together very densely. On earth we must work with much thinner gas, and that requires still

higher temperatures. Fortunately, there is a kind of hydrogen easier to fuse called deuterium. Only one out of every 6500 hydrogen atoms is deuterium, but even so there is enough in each gallon of seawater to equal the energy supplied by burning 300 gallons of gasoline. Since there are 3.6 quintillion gallons of seawater on earth, there is enough deuterium to last billions of years at the present rate of energy use.

The temperature required can be lowered further if a still-rarer 20 kind of hydrogen called tritium is added to the deuterium. Tritium is radioactive and hardly occurs in nature, but it can be manufactured in the laboratory. If a quantity of deuterium–tritium mixture is made dense enough, heated hot enough and kept in confinement long enough, it will fuse. There are well-worked-out figures for what is needed for all three conditions, and scientists have been edging toward the critical combination. Recent work with tokamaks at Princeton University and the Massachusetts Institute of Technology has confirmed that fusion induced by magnetic confinement is a real possibility— once a better tokamak can be built. But this, experts say, is still many years away.

But magnetic confinement isn't the only route to fusion power. It's 21 only needed when the hydrogen is heated slowly and would therefore expand and drift away while it is being heated.

Suppose the hydrogen were heated very rapidly. It might then 22 reach fusion temperature so rapidly that the hydrogen has no time to expand before it starts fusing. That's what happens in a hydrogen bomb. The uranium fission develops its high temperature so rapidly that any hydrogen present fuses before it can scatter.

We can't use a fission bomb for controlled fusion, however. Some 23 other way must be found to raise the temperature very rapidly. One way is to make use of a laser. Lasers, first developed in 1960, produce light in a very tight beam. The total energy may not be unusually great, but the beam can be focused on such a microscopic point that the concentrated energy raises the temperature at the point to millions of degrees in a fraction of a second.

Imagine a mixture of deuterium and tritium inside a tiny, thin- 24 walled glass bubble. If the bubble is struck simultaneously by a number of laser beams from different directions, the heating takes place all around the outer skin of the bubble. What expansion there is forces the gas upward. The inner portion of the bubble goes way up in density, further up in temperature, and begins to fuse.

We can imagine bubble after bubble dropping into position and 25 being fused by accurately timed bursts of laser light. Work is underway at the University of California's Lawrence Livermore Laboratory to determine the feasibility of laser fusion.

Of course, it takes considerable energy to keep the lasers going, 26 and they are expensive devices. Simpler and more efficient might be beams of high-energy subatomic particles such as electrons. We still haven't reached controlled fusion in this fashion either. Larger, more reliable lasers are needed—or more powerful electron beams.

27   Still, at the rate we are going now, it seems that sometime before the mid-1980s, one or the other of the methods—magnetic fields, lasers or electron beams—will work. Perhaps all three will work.

28   And how exciting that would be. We have atomic power now in the form of uranium fission, but hydrogen fusion would be much better:

29   ♦ Fission uses uranium and plutonium as fuel—rare metals that are hard to get and handle. Fusion uses hydrogen, easy to obtain and handle.

30   ♦ Fission must work with large quantities of uranium or plutonium, so runaway reactions can take place by accident and cause damage. Fusion works with tiny quantities of hydrogen at one time, so even runaway fusions would produce only a small pop.

31   ♦ Fission produces radioactive ash, which can be extremely dangerous and may not be disposed of safely. Fusion produces helium, which is completely safe; plus neutrons and tritium, which can be used up as fast as they are produced.

32   ♦ Finally, fission only produces a 10th as much energy as fusion, weight for weight.

33   Of course, even after we finally attain controlled fusion in the laboratory, it may take as long as 30 years to translate that into large fusion-power stations. There may be many engineering difficulties between a small demonstration that pleases scientists and a large, reliable supply that runs the world.

34   It may well be 2020, then, before we are a fusion society. It would be wise to conserve oil supplies and to substitute other energy sources (coal, shale, wind, flowing water, tides, hot springs, and so on) to keep us going until fusion can take over. And we might also strive to develop solar energy, making use of the nuclear fusion power that already exists and that we call the sun.

 USING THE DICTIONARY: How much help does your dictionary give you with basic scientific terms? Select ten such terms from this essay and check them in your dictionary. For each, prepare a one-sentence definition for the general reader.

THE WRITER'S AGENDA:

In explaining a specialized subject to a general audience, the author proceeds in a very systematic fashion: He starts from a familiar problem, presents his own solution, and then systematically examines the difficulties that need to be overcome if the solution is to work. Answer the following questions about how he presents and explains technical information for the general reader:

1. The author uses his introduction to correct a *misconception* about the problem to be solved. What is the misconception, and how does he correct it?

2. In the paragraphs that follow the introduction, the author sketches out his own hopeful perspective for the future. As clearly as you can, explain to a person with little background in physics and chemistry the two basic *processes* involved: how we can make gasoline from water, and how the sun generates energy from hydrogen. (What imaginative comparisons or figures of speech help set the positive, optimistic tone for this section of the essay?)

3. The central portion of the essay systematically surveys the *difficulties* and the possible solutions that we have to consider when trying to duplicate on earth the way the sun produces energy. Outline and explain these for the nonspecialist. (Draw on the concrete expressive language and everyday comparisons used by the author.)

4. Toward the end of his essay, Isaac Asimov summarizes the *advantages* nuclear fusion would have when compared with nuclear fission. What are these advantages? Outline them and explain them to the nonspecialist as clearly as you can.

5. The essay concludes with some final *cautions* or warnings. What are they?

6. When you read this essay as a nonspecialist reader, what parts became especially clear for you, and why? What parts remained difficult or confusing, and why?

FOR DISCUSSION OR WRITING:

1. In most Western countries, there is now strong opposition to nuclear power. What are the sources of that opposition? What forms does it take?

2. Do you think Asimov's essay would reassure or otherwise influence readers opposed to nuclear energy? Why or why not?

3. Fears about the safety of nuclear installations come to a head on occasions like the Three Mile Island accident or the licensing of the Diablo Canyon nuclear plant in California. Study and present some basic technical information that would help a voter understand some of the safety issues involved.

4. At times the media present alarming reports on such topics as public health hazards or the dangers of mind control or genetic manipulation. Do research on one such topic, and use the results to enlighten readers who lack the technical or scientific background to understand the complex issues involved. Investigate a topic like the following:

♦ splicing of genes

♦ biochemical causes of mental illness

♦ harmful side effects of a medication or therapy

♦ health hazards caused by asbestos or another widely used material

5. Is there enough emphasis on science education and science literacy to prepare the United States adequately for the needs of the future? To judge from your own observation, how much do the schools and the media do to promote a basic understanding of science on the part of the general public?

BACKGROUND: Ed Edelson (born 1932) lives in Jamaica, New York, and is the science editor of the New York *Daily News*. A graduate of New York University and a Sloan-Rockefeller fellow in the Advanced Science Writing Program, he formerly served as president of the National Association of Science Writers. In addition to magazine articles, Edelson has written numerous books on science, including *Healers in Uniform, Visions of Tomorrow,* and, recently, *Who Goes There?,* a study of the search for extraterrestrial intelligence. In the article reprinted here, Edelson writes as the kind of popularizer whom we turn to when new developments in technology seem to outstrip our ability to understand them and adjust to them. Ready or not, we find that computers are transforming the way we learn, bank, do business, keep records, and spend our leisure time. Afraid to be left behind as a new generation grows up with "computer literacy," we turn to writers who can translate advanced technical information into reassuring everyday terms for a general audience.

Ed Edelson

Smart Computers— Now They Speak Our Language

GUIDE TO READING: In this essay, the author discusses two contrasting approaches to the development of computers that respond to instructions in ordinary English. What is the basic principle on which each contrasting system is based? What key terms does the author have to define for us? What examples or illustrations does he use? (For you as the reader, what becomes especially clear; what stays difficult or confusing?)

IN FRONT of just *any* computer I wriggle a bit when asked to make it do something meaningful. But this time, in front of a new *smart* computer, I'm confident. 1

"When did Fred join us?" I typed on the keyboard, asking the hulk 2 to search its electronic files for a specific piece of data. The response on the CRT display:

3   1. WHEN DID SOMEONE JOIN THE COMPANY?
4   2. WHEN DID X JOIN THE HUMAN RACE?
5   3. WHEN DID X JOIN THE HOMO SAPIENS?
6   I had to be more specific, so I typed "3"—and got Fred's birthday.

7   Who's Fred? He's really just a fictitious name stored in a demonstration computer program. But what makes him so important is that I could get his data without knowing any formal computer language. My question was in plain English; my answer came back in the same understandable way.

8   Anyone who has struggled with BASIC or any other computer language knows just how revolutionary this plain-talk computing can be. Suddenly, the computer isn't something to be approached warily and only after special training; it's a helpful companion you can chat with almost conversationally.

9   The people who have developed these "user-friendly" natural-language programs think the future belongs to them. To find out just what that future may be like, I had two hands-on demonstrations of plain-English computing—one in Albuquerque, N.M.; the other in Waltham, Mass., just outside Boston. The two systems are as far apart philosophically as they are geographically.

10   The Waltham company, Artificial Intelligence Corporation, has a program called Intellect. It make a rigorous analysis of every sentence you enter to understand its meaning.

The Albuquerque company, Excalibur Technologies Corporation, has Savvy. It works by transforming your statements into three-dimensional patterns and comparing them with those representing previous statements. Savvy doesn't really understand what you're saying—in a sense, it intuits the answer.

11   The difference between the way these programs "think" is similar to the way our own brains work—the left-brain/right-brain theory. Nobel prize winner Roger Sperry found that the two halves of our brain have distinctly different ways of operating. The left brain processes information through analysis and logic; cold, mathematical reasoning prevails. The right side, however, finds an answer by using creativity, intuition, and imagination.

12   It was this left-brain/right-brain theory that gave James Dowe III the idea for Savvy in 1979, when he was associate director of the University of New Mexico computing center.

13   A friend sent him a copy of a book called *The Origin of Consciousness in the Breakdown of the Bicameral Mind*, by Julian Jaynes, a Princeton psychologist. It was Dowe's first exposure to the left-brain/right-brain difference, and that, he says, "got me to think that the con-

ventional way of having computers understand plain language by rigorous analysis ['computational linguistics,' to use the formal term] wasn't good enough."

The result was Savvy, from Excalibur Technologies—a company   14
tucked away in a shopping center near Albuquerque's Old Town. Its sneakers-and-jeans atmosphere makes it seem more like a research lab than an office.

As the youthful-looking, 39-year-old Dowe explains, Savvy takes the   15
intuitive approach. It assigns a weighting factor—a number—to each letter as it is typed. The letter "A" may be a "1," for example, a "B" equal to "2," and so on. As the letters are entered, a sort of bar graph is produced—words in a sentence create a pattern. The pattern becomes a mathematical representation of the sentence. Being a city boy, I compared the pattern to the New York skyline. Dowe, a country boy at heart, calls it a "terrain."

"Given this terrain, how does it compare with past terrains?" said   16
Dowe. "Now it's a problem of matching terrains, not analyzing words. If Savvy has seen the terrain before, it will solve the problem exactly. If not, it will give the closest fit."

The idea of using pattern analysis to understand ordinary language   17
has been around for years. "What you do is create a conceptual mathematical space," says Gary Hendrix of the Machine Intelligence Corporation in Palo Alto, Calif. "Then you try to locate the meanings of sentences by locating features on this space. Things are related in meaning if they are close in these dimensions."

But most people in the field have dropped the idea because, they   18
claim, they simply couldn't fit enough patterns into a computer's memory to make the method useful. Dowe, however, says that Savvy has a way of packing more patterns into a relatively small amount of computer memory, and it has a fast way of matching them with the incoming patterns. How? "We prefer to keep that a trade secret," Dowe said curtly.

To show some of what Savvy can do, Dowe sat me down at a computer   19
terminal. Its memory contained simulated payroll information for a small company with nine workers. It wasn't a highly realistic demonstration, for a couple of reasons. First, the Savvy program was on a disc, which meant that it worked rather slowly. The machine would stop and "think" for 10 or 15 seconds after I typed a question. Second, I was encouraged to word my questions in a way that would fool the program—to show how it handles unusual requests.

My first try—getting Fred's birth date—was successful, but I also   20
got some idea of the chinks in Savvy's armor. When I typed in, "What will we pay out to workers next month?" the answer was, GOSH, I DON'T KNOW THIS EMPLOYEE. When I typed in "How mny people are on the payroll?" I was told to leave the typo uncorrected as a test.

Savvy gave four possibilities, none of which applied precisely.

21   "That sort of problem is potentially manageable," says Howard Morgan, a professor of decisions sciences at the University of Pennsylvania, who has been keeping tabs on Savvy. But it demonstrates an essential weakness in pattern analysis.

22   "The major question is how much basic dictionary can they build in about applications so the kind of failure you experienced can be handled," Morgan said. "If 'workers' had been entered as one of the concepts before, the system would have understood."

23   The problem is how far you can get with a system that works on the computer equivalent of intuition, said Morgan. "They're taking a shortcut, and the shortcut is getting them a very useful level of performance. But they admit their system doesn't have any deep-level understanding. They're saying it can be useful without any understanding."

24   Still, knowing Savvy's limitations, Morgan was impressed enough to buy a few hundred shares of Excalibur stock after seeing a demonstration. And after its experts looked over Savvy for months, the Microdata Corporation, McDonnell Douglas's computer subsidiary, agreed last December to buy one million shares of Excalibur stock, pumping as much as $6 million into the company.

25   One reason for the enthusiasm is another Savvy capability that Dowe demonstrated. "Tell it what you want to do," he said, "and it will write the programs for you." As I watched, Dowe instructed Savvy to set up a file on customers of a mythical corporation—names, addresses, and so on. Savvy, acting on its own, then produced a series of programs for handling the customer data. It even displayed the programs so you could make detailed changes in them.

26   If you believe Dowe, Savvy is going to put most computer programmers out of business. In years to come, anyone will be able to sit down at a computer and have programs written to order by Savvy, with no technical expertise needed.

27   Harrison Miller, a farmer-entrepreneur who works out of the unlikely locality of Waterproof, La., believes it. He set up American Business Computers to market Savvy. "It's not just a pipe dream. I'm totally committed to the prospect that anyone can learn programming on a mail-order basis. I've never had a lesson in computer language in my life, and I can take Savvy and do anything I can think through. It's an equalizer. It makes me the equal of anyone with a degree in computer sciences."

28   If you fly north and east to Massachusetts, you'll find a colder climate about Savvy. "It's an interesting toy, an adult game," says Jerrold M. Diesenroth, sales director for Artificial Intelligence. "They have in no way attacked the root problem. They've taken a limited technique and come up with a partial solution."

Far from a shopping-center storefront, Artificial Intelligence is in   29
one of the newly sprouted office buildings just off Route 128. Here,
three-piece suits set the all-businesslike tone. Makers of Intellect, they
have taken the analytical approach to the left-brain/right-brain theory.

Larry Harris started with the thought that a program has to have full   30
understanding of what it's told in order to be useful. "Take something
as simple as the word 'and,' " Harris said. "It has surprisingly ambiguous meanings.

"If you're doing a data-base query and you ask for the names of all   31
employees who are married and live in New York, you're asking for
things that are members of two sets. That's a search intersection. If you
ask for data on the men's department and the women's department,
you're asking for a union of two sets. If you ask for the names of employees who make between $20,000 and $30,000, you're asking for a
range selection. That's three different meanings for the word 'and.' "
He adds, "The intelligence of a pattern-recognition system ends as
soon as it says, 'I recognize the word "and." ' "

Harris began developing Intellect in the 1970's, when he was still   32
in his twenties. (He's 34 now.) He took his degree at Cornell in artificial intelligence—the science of getting machines to do thinking
tasks—and went on to the computer-sciences department at Dartmouth. There he worked on natural-language understanding—getting
computers to comprehend ordinary English—and data-base query, ex-
tracting information from the data stored in a computer's memory.

It was natural to apply one subject to the other and develop a natu-   33
ral-language program that would allow people to get information from
a data base. It wasn't a new idea; plenty of computer companies saw
there was money to be made from a program that gave executives simple, instant access to computerized information. But the way Harris
went about making the idea work was unique.

The basic principle of his approach is simple. When a question is   34
typed into a terminal, the program first looks up the meanings of the
words. If the question is "How many workers are on the payroll?" for
example, the program looks up the meaning of "workers" and "payroll" in an electronic dictionary. Then it parses the sentence, analyzing
it grammatically: "Are" is a verb, "workers" and "payroll" are nouns,
and so on. When it understands the question, it gets the answer from
the data base.

Put that way, it sounds simple. But Intellect works only because it   35
contains an enormous amount of information—information about the
meaning of specific words, information about English grammar, information about the ways in which people can bend or break grammatical
rules, information about colloquialisms and slang. Think back to the
school days when your English teacher made you take a sentence apart,
listing every word by part of speech and function, and you'll have a

good idea of what Intellect does. It uses the accumulated body of knowledge about the English language to grasp exactly what it's being told.

36   Most efforts to make such a system work have failed because natural language isn't as simple as it seems. The human brain can sort out meanings that baffle a computer program. To take a simple example, "How many cars are green?" asks for a color, while "How many cars are Fords?" asks for a manufacturer. A basic problem in developing a program is to devise an electronic dictionary that would include all the meanings of all the words that the program would encounter. Such dictionaries tend to be so big and cumbersome that the program has only limited value.

37   Harris's solution was to organize the data into categories. The category in which a word is listed provides many of the definitions (replacing the need for every word to have its own specific definition). "Green" is listed in the data base under colors, for example, while "Ford" is listed under auto manufacturers. By devising a way for the program to extract such information from the data base, based on its category, Harris kept the dictionary to a manageable size.

38   It wasn't as simple as it sounds, of course. "We spent five years and $10 million writing this program," Jerrold Diesenroth said. The details are carefully guarded proprietary secrets.

39   There's an air of sleek prosperity in the offices of Artificial Intelligence. Diesenroth happily ticked off the names of Intellect users: Chase Manhattan Bank, Ford, Boeing, Xerox, Du Pont, and more. They're paying from $40,000 to over $60,000 to have the use of Intellect.

40   When I had my demonstration, I could see why. Intellect easily answered such questions as "How many women in the Western region were over quota last year?"—and from a data base that included hundreds of names and lots of other information. It can also go on to answer casually worded follow-up questions: "Where do they live?" or "How long have they been with the company?" Ask Intellect, "Give me a bar graph showing actual sales by division and our estimates," and it will do so in seconds.

41   This sophisticated, expensive approach seems a far cry from the world of personal computers that Savvy hopes to conquer. At the moment, Intellect can be run only on mainframe computers, the giants that are used by very large enterprises, and it's expensive. But Harris and Diesenroth say it's just a matter of time before Intellect is available for smaller businesses and then for the personal-computer market. "We're negotiating right now with manufacturers who make minis," Harris said, referring to the office-sized computers that are becoming commonplace in small businesses.

How long before Intellect is available for microcomputers, the kind   42
you can take home with you? "A fairly long time," Harris said. How
long? A thoughtful look came over him, and I expected to hear something about the year 2000. "Maybe three to five years," he said finally.

About the only thing that Dowe and Harris agree upon is that voice-   43
pattern recognition will someday provide the next major step in computer communication: Instead of typing a command, you'll just speak it
and the computer will understand. Speech recognition is one of the
toughest challenges for a computer program—given the variety of accents, grammatical mistakes, and general sloppiness of any "human"
language. What we say and how we say it may defy logical analysis, but
it can yield to pattern-recognition techniques. Harris sees a voice-
recognition system as the front end of a rigorously analytical natural-
language computer program such as Intellect. Dowe sees it as a logical
extension of a pattern-recognition program such as Savvy. Neither of
them doubts that the natural-language revolution is happening.

 USING THE DICTIONARY: Like much of the language of science
and technology, our current high-tech vocabulary draws on a
familiar common stock of Greek and Latin roots. Check the
origins of the following examples, and explain the connection between the earliest meanings and current uses. 1. *computer* (1) 2. *electronic* (2) 3. *data* (2) 4. *intelligence* (10)
5. *simulated* (19) 6. *disc* (19) 7. *micro-* (24) 8. *circuit* (27)
9. *intersection* (31) 10. *mini-* (41)

THE WRITER'S AGENDA:

The author's task in this essay is to make clear what before was
mysterious and bewildering to many of his readers. Answer the following questions about how he tries to satisfy the needs of his audience.

1. In the introductory paragraphs, the author several times alludes
to his typical discomfort or to previous *struggles* when dealing with
computers. What effect are these allusions meant to have on his audience? How do they lead up to the main point he wants to make about
the new plain-language computers?

2. The right-brain/left-brain theory assigns familiar analytical and
mathematical reasoning to the left hemisphere of the brain. What *right-
brain* functions do the developers of Savvy try to build on or simulate?
What key terms and key examples does the author use to help us understand what he means by "intuition" here?

3. Explain to the outsider the contrasting *analytical approach* to plain-language computers employed by the developers at Artificial Intelligence. (What does "parsing" mean? What makes the word *and* ambiguous—what distinctions must the computer make to handle different uses of the word? What problems are illustrated by the pair of contrasting questions about cars?)

4. Where in this essay is the "anyone can . . ." kind of optimism that is often seen in promoters of new technology strongest? Where do possible *doubts* or reservations come through most strongly?

5. For many observers, the computer, like much modern technology, is forbiddingly *impersonal* or even inhuman. What does the author do to personalize and humanize his account of the new technologies?

FOR DISCUSSION AND WRITING:

1. What has been your own experience with computers? What do they do? What problems do they cause? What changes do they bring about in people's lives?

2. "Computer literacy" is becoming a buzzword in our society. Everyone, many people contend, must have a basic vocabulary and understanding of computer technology. Interview an expert on this subject, perhaps a professor in the computer science department of your school, about what concepts or operations he or she feels are fundamental to achieving computer literacy. Explain these to a readership generally unfamiliar with the world of computers.

3. Explain the advantages of replacing a specific manual or mechanical operation with a computerized one. Write for an audience that is familiar with the task or operation but largely unfamiliar with computers. For instance, argue the advantages of a word processor over a typewriter, or of a computerized accounting system over manual bookkeeping.

4. The left-brain/right-brain theory has been much publicized lately. Read two or three newspaper or magazine articles on this subject. Explain some of the basic principles and implications to a lay audience.

5. A cherished possession of the Smithsonian Institution is a letter one of the Wright brothers wrote trying to show the feasibility of human flight. Choose a similar moment or situation in the history of science and technology. Predict and explain an important future advance to a skeptical contemporary audience.

BACKGROUND: Loren Eiseley (1907–77) was born in Nebraska. He majored in anthropology and English at the University of Nebraska and taught anthropology at Oberlin College and at the University of Pennsylvania. His book *The Immense Journey* (1957) found a large audience among readers who deplored the split of our modern civilization into "two cultures": the intellectual tradition of scientists and engineers, on the one hand, and the cultural tradition of artists and imaginative writers, on the other. His admirers found in him the rare combination of a scientist and a person who could write imaginatively and passionately about the meaning of the long journey from the earliest forms of life to the emergence of the human spirit. His other books include *The Unexpected Universe, The Night Country, All the Strange Hours,* and *The Star Thrower.* He once said "We cannot in one lifetime see all that we would like to see or learn all we hunger to know."

Loren Eiseley

The Bird and the Machine

GUIDE TO READING: In this essay, the author many years later recalls an incident that then inspires a series of reflections. He never forgot the birds that play a central role in his story: a young hawk that he captured and released while on an assignment as a young naturalist, and its mate. What symbolic role do these birds come to play in the author's discussion of our modern technological civilization? What other objects and forms of life play a symbolic role in this essay?

I SUPPOSE their little bones have years ago been lost among the 1 stones and winds of those high glacial pastures. I suppose their feathers blew eventually into the piles of tumbleweed beneath the straggling cattle fences and rotted there in the mountain snows, along with dead steers and all the other things that drift to an end in the corners of the wire. I do not quite know why I should be thinking of birds over the *New York Times* at breakfast, particularly the birds of my youth half a continent away. It is a funny thing what the brain will do with memories and how it will treasure them and finally bring them into odd juxtapositions with other things, as though it wanted to make a design, or get some meaning out of them, whether you want it or not, or even see it.

2   It used to seem marvelous to me, but I read now that there are machines that can do these things in a small way, machines that can crawl about like animals, and that it may not be long now until they do more things—maybe even make themselves—I saw that piece in the *Times* just now. And then they will, maybe—well, who knows—but you read about it more and more with no one making any protest, and already they can add better than we and reach up and hear things through the dark and finger the guns over the night sky.

3   This is the new world that I read about at breakfast. This is the world that confronts me in my biological books and journals, until there are times when I sit quietly in my chair and try to hear the little purr of the cogs in my head and the tubes flaring and dying as the messages go through them and the circuits snap shut or open. This is the great age, make no mistake about it; the robot has been born somewhat appropriately along with the atom bomb, and the brain they say now is just another type of more complicated feedback system. The engineers have its basic principles worked out; it's mechanical, you know; nothing to get superstitious about; and man can always improve on nature once he gets the idea. Well, he's got it all right and that's why, I guess, that I sit here in my chair, with the article crunched in my hand, remembering those two birds and that blue mountain sunlight. There is another magazine article on my desk that reads, "Machines Are Getting Smarter Every Day." I don't deny it, but I'll still stick with the birds. It's life I believe in, not machines.

4   Maybe you don't believe there is any difference. A skeleton is all joints and pulleys, I'll admit. And when a man was in his simpler stages of machine building in the eighteenth century, he quickly saw the resemblances. "What," wrote Hobbes, "is the heart but a spring, and the nerves but so many strings, and the joints but so many wheels, giving motion to the whole body?"[1] Tinkering about in their shops it was inevitable in the end that men would see the world as a huge machine "subdivided into an infinite number of lesser machines."

5   The idea took on with a vengeance. Little automatons toured the country—dolls controlled by clockwork. Clocks described as little

---

[1][In his *Leviathan* (1651), the British philosopher Thomas Hobbes attempted a systematic analysis of psychology and politics in mechanistic terms, proceeding from the assumption that all life was "matter in motion."]

worlds were taken on tours by their designers. They were made up of moving figures, shifting scenes, and other remarkable devices. The life of the cell was unknown. Man, whether he was conceived as possessing a soul or not, moved and jerked about like these tiny puppets. A human being thought of himself in terms of his own tools and implements. He had been fashioned like the puppets he produced and was only a more clever model made by a greater designer.

Then in the nineteenth century, the cell was discovered, and the 6 single machine in its turn was found to be the product of millions of infinitesimal machines—the cells. Now, finally, the cell itself dissolves away into an abstract chemical machine, and that into some intangible, inexpressible flow of energy. The secret seems to lurk all about, the wheels get smaller and smaller, and they turn more rapidly, but when you try to seize it the life is gone—and so, by popular definition, some would say that life was never there in the first place. The wheels and the cogs are the secret and we can make them better in time—machines that will run faster and more accurately than real mice to real cheese.

I have no doubt it can be done, though a mouse harvesting seeds 7 on an autumn thistle is to me a fine sight and more complicated, I think, in his multiform activity than a machine "mouse" running a maze. Also, I like to think of the possible shape of the future brooding in mice, just as it brooded once in a rather ordinary mousy insectivore who became a man. It leaves a nice finite indeterminate sense of wonder that even an electronic brain hasn't got, because you know perfectly well that if the electronic brain changes, it will be because of something man has done to it. But what man will do to himself he doesn't really know. A certain scale of time and a ghostly intangible thing called change are ticking in him. Powers and potentialities like the oak in the seed, or a red and awful ruin. Either way, it's impressive; and the mouse has it, too. Or those birds, I'll never forget those birds—yet before I measured their significance, I learned the lesson of time first of all. I was young then and left alone in a great desert—part of an expedition that had scattered its men over several hundred miles in order to carry on research more effectively. I learned there that time is a series of planes existing superficially in the same universe. The tempo is a human illusion, a subjective clock ticking in our own kind of protoplasm.

As the long months passed, I began to live on the slower planes and 8 to observe more readily what passed for life there. I sauntered, I passed more and more slowly up and down the canyons in the dry baking heat of midsummer. I slumbered for long hours in the shade of huge brown boulders that had gathered in tilted companies out on the flats. I had forgotten the world of men and the world had forgotten me. Now and then I found a skull in the canyons, and these justified my remaining there. I took a serene cold interest in these discoveries. I had come, like many a naturalist before me, to view life with a wary and subdued attention. I had grown to take pleasure in the divested bone.

9   I sat once on a high ridge that fell away before me into a waste of sand dunes. I sat through hours of a long afternoon. Finally, as I glanced beside my boot an indistinct configuration caught my eye. It was a coiled rattlesnake, a big one. How long he had sat with me I do not know. I had not frightened him. We were both locked in the sleep-walking tempo of the earlier world, baking in the same high air and sunshine. Perhaps he had been there when I came. He slept on as I left, his coils, so ill-discerned by me, dissolving once more among the stones and gravel from which I had barely made him out.

10   Another time I got on a higher ridge, among some tough little wind-warped pines half covered over with sand in a basinlike depression that caught everything carried by the air up to those heights. There were a few thin bones of birds, some cracked shells of indeterminable age, and the knotty fingers of pine roots bulged out of shape from their long and agonizing grasp upon the crevices of the rock. I lay under the pines in the sparse shade and went to sleep once more.

11   It grew cold finally, for autumn was in the air by then, and the few things that lived thereabouts were sinking down into an even chillier scale of time. In the moments between sleeping and waking I saw the roots about me and slowly, slowly, a foot in what seemed many centuries, I moved my sleep-stiffened hands over the scaling bark and lifted my numbed face after the vanishing sun. I was a great awkward thing of knots and aching limbs, trapped up there in some long, patient endurance that involved the necessity of putting living fingers into rock and by slow, aching expansion bursting those rocks asunder. I suppose, so thin and slow was the time of my pulse by then, that I might have stayed on to drift still deeper into the lower cadences of the frost, or the crystalline life that glistens pebbles, or shines in a snowflake, or dreams in the meteoric iron between the worlds.

12   It was a dim descent, but time was present in it. Somewhere far down in that scale the notion struck me that one might come the other way. Not many months thereafter I joined some colleagues heading higher into a remote windy tableland where huge bones were reputed to protrude like boulders from the turf. I had drowsed with reptiles and moved with the century-long pulse of trees; now, lethargically, I was climbing back up some invisible ladder of quickening hours. There had been talk of birds in connection with my duties. Birds are intense, fast-living creatures—reptiles, I suppose one might say, that have escaped out of the heavy sleep of time, transformed fairy creatures danc-

ing over sunlit meadows. It is a youthful fancy, no doubt, but because of something that happened up there among the escarpments of that range, it remains with me a lifelong impression. I can never bear to see a bird imprisoned.

We came into that valley through the trailing mists of a spring 13 night. It was a place that looked as though it might never have known the foot of man, but our scouts had been ahead of us and we knew all about the abandoned cabin of stone that lay far up on one hillside. It had been built in the land rush of the last century and then lost to the cattlemen again as the marginal soils failed to take to the plow.

There were spots like this all over that country. Lost graves marked 14 by unlettered stones and old corroding rim-fire cartridge cases lying where somebody had made a stand among the boulders that rimmed the valley. They are all that remain of the range wars; the men are under the stones now. I could see our cavalcade winding in and out through the mist below us: torches, the reflection of the truck lights on our collecting tins, and the far-off bumping of a loose dinosaur thigh bone in the bottom of a trailer. I stood on a rock a moment looking down and thinking what it cost in money and equipment to capture the past.

We had, in addition, instructions to lay hands on the present. The 15 word had come through to get them alive—birds, reptiles, anything. A zoo somewhere abroad needed restocking. It was one of those reciprocal matters in which science involves itself. Maybe our museum needed a stray ostrich egg and this was the payoff. Anyhow, my job was to help capture some birds and that was why I was there before the trucks.

The cabin had not been occupied for years. We intended to clean it 16 out and live in it, but there were holes in the roof and the birds had come in and were roosting in the rafters. You could depend on it in a place like this where everything blew away, and even a bird needed some place out of the weather and away from the coyotes. A cabin going back to nature in a wild place draws them till they come in, listening at the eaves, I imagine, pecking softly among the shingles till they find a hole, and then suddenly the place is theirs and man is forgotten.

Sometimes of late years I find myself thinking the most beautiful 17 sight in the world might be the birds taking over New York after the last man has run away to the hills. I will never live to see it, of course, but I know just how it will sound because I've lived up high and I know the sort of watch birds keep on us. I've listened to sparrows tapping tentatively on the outside of air conditioners when they thought no one was listening, and I know how other birds test the vibrations that come up to them through the television aerials.

"Is he gone?" they ask, and the vibrations come up from below, 18 "Not yet, not yet."

19   Well, to come back, I got the door open softly and I had the spot-light all ready to turn on and blind whatever birds there were so they couldn't see to get out through the roof. I had a short piece of ladder to put against the far wall where there was a shelf on which I expected to make the biggest haul. I had all the information I needed, just like any skilled assassin. I pushed the door open, the hinges squeaking only a little. A bird or two stirred—I could hear them—but nothing flew and there was a faint starlight through the holes in the roof.

20   I padded across the floor, got the ladder up and the light ready, and slithered up the ladder till my head and arms were over the shelf. Everything was dark as pitch except for the starlight at the little place back of the shelf near the eaves. With the light to blind them, they'd never make it. I had them. I reached my arm carefully over in order to be ready to seize whatever was there and I put the flash on the edge of the shelf where it would stand by itself when I turned it on. That way I'd be able to use both hands.

21   Everything worked perfectly except for one detail—I didn't know what kind of birds were there. I never thought about it at all, and it wouldn't have mattered if I had. My orders were to get something inter-esting. I snapped on the flash and sure enough there was a great beat-ing and feathers flying, but instead of my having them, they, or rather he, had me. He had my hand, that is, and for a small hawk not much bigger than my fist he was doing all right. I heard him give one short metallic cry when the light went on and my hand descended on the bird beside him; after that he was busy with his claws and his beak was sunk in my thumb. In the struggle I knocked the lamp over on the shelf, and his mate got her sight back and whisked neatly through the hole in the roof and off among the stars outside. It all happened in fifteen seconds and you might think I would have fallen down the ladder, but no, I had a professional assassin's reputation to keep up, and the bird, of course, made the mistake of thinking the hand was the enemy and not the eyes behind it. He chewed my thumb up pretty effectively and lacerated my hand with his claws, but in the end I got him, having two hands to work with.

22   He was a sparrow hawk and a fine young male in the prime of life. I was sorry not to catch the pair of them, but as I dripped blood and folded his wings carefully, holding him by the back so that he couldn't strike again, I had to admit the two of them might have been more than I could have handled under the circumstances. The little fellow had saved his mate by diverting me, and that was that. He was born to it and made no outcry now, resting in my hand hopelessly but peering toward me in the shadows behind the lamp with a fierce, almost indifferent glance. He neither gave nor expected mercy and something out of the high air passed from him to me, stirring a faint embarrassment.

23   I quit looking into that eye and managed to get my huge carcass

with its fist full of prey back down the ladder. I put the bird in a box too
small to allow him to injure himself by struggle and walked out to
welcome the arriving trucks. It had been a long day, and camp still to
make in the darkness. In the morning that bird would be just another
episode. He would go back with the bones in the truck to a small cage
in a city where he would spend the rest of his life. And a good thing,
too. I sucked my aching thumb and spat out some blood. An assassin
has to get used to these things. I had a professional reputation to
keep up.

In the morning, with the change that comes on suddenly in that   24
high country, the mist that had hovered below us in the valley was
gone. The sky was a deep blue, and one could see for miles over the
high outcroppings of stone. I was up early and brought the box in
which the little hawk was imprisoned out onto the grass where I was
building a cage. A wind as cool as a mountain spring ran over the grass
and stirred my hair. It was a fine day to be alive. I looked up and all
around and at the hole in the cabin roof out of which the other little
hawk had fled. There was no sign of her anywhere that I could see.

"Probably in the next county by now," I thought cynically, but   25
before beginning work I decided I'd have a look at my last night's
capture.

Secretively, I looked again all around the camp and up and down   26
and opened the box. I got him right out in my hand with his wings
folded properly and I was careful not to startle him. He lay limp in my
grasp and I could feel his heart pound under the feathers but he only
looked beyond me and up.

I saw him look that last look away beyond me into a sky so full of   27
light that I could not follow his gaze. The little breeze flowed over me
again, and nearby a mountain aspen shook all its tiny leaves. I suppose
I must have had an idea then of what I was going to do, but I never let it
come up into consciousness. I just reached over and laid the hawk on
the grass.

He lay there a long minute without hope, unmoving, his eyes still'   28
fixed on that blue vault above him. It must have been that he was
already so far away in heart that he never felt the release from my hand.
He never even stood. He just lay with his breast against the grass.

In the next second after that long minute he was gone. Like a flicker   29
of light, he had vanished with my eyes full on him but without actually
seeing even a premonitory wing beat. He was gone straight into that
towering emptiness of light and crystal that my eyes could scarcely bear
to penetrate. For another long moment there was silence. I could not
see him. The light was too intense. Then from far up somewhere a cry
came ringing down.

I was young then and had seen little of the world, but when I heard   30 that cry my heart turned over. It was not the cry of the hawk I had captured; for, by shifting my position against the sun, I was now seeing farther up. Straight out of the sun's eye, where she must have been soaring restlessly above us for untold hours, hurtled his mate. And from far up, ringing from peak to peak of the summits over us, came a cry of such unutterable and ecstatic joy that it sounds down across the years and tingles among the cups on my quiet breakfast table.

31   I saw them both now. He was rising fast to meet her. They met in a great soaring gyre that turned to a whirling circle and a dance of wings. Once more, just once, their two voices, joined in a harsh wild medley of question and response, struck and echoed against the pinnacles of the valley. Then they were gone forever somewhere into those upper regions beyond the eyes of men.

32   I am older now, and sleep less, and have seen most of what there is to see and am not very much impressed any more, I suppose, by anything. "What Next in the Attributes of Machines?" my morning headline runs. "It Might Be the Power to Reproduce Themselves."

33   I lay the paper down and across my mind a phrase floats insinuatingly: "It does not seem that there is anything in the construction, constituents, or behavior of the human being which it is essentially impossible for science to duplicate and synthesize. On the other hand . . ."

34   All over the city the cogs in the hard, bright mechanisms have begun to turn. Figures move through computers, names are spelled out, a thoughtful machine selects the fingerprints of a wanted criminal from an array of thousands. In the laboratory an electronic mouse runs swiftly through a maze toward the cheese it can neither taste nor enjoy. On the second run it does better than a living mouse.

35   "On the other hand . . ." Ah, my mind takes up, on the other hand the machine does not bleed, ache, hang for hours in the empty sky in a torment of hope to learn the fate of another machine, nor does it cry out with joy nor dance in the air with the fierce passion of a bird. Far off, over a distance greater than space, that remote cry from the heart of heaven makes a faint buzzing among my breakfast dishes and passes on and away.

 USING THE DICTIONARY: The author's vocabulary ranges from scientific terms to terms with literary or poetic associations. Which of the following would you have to look up? 1. *glacial* (1) 2. *juxtaposition* (1) 3. *infinitesimal* (6) 4. *intangible* (6) 5. *insectivore* (7) 6. *tempo* (7) 7. *protoplasm* (7) 8. *divest* (8) 9. *configuration* (9) 10. *crevice* (10) 11. *cadence* (11)

12. *crystalline* (11) 13. *lethargic* (12) 14. *escarpment* (12)
15. *cavalcade* (14) 16. *lacerate* (21) 17. *premonitory* (29)
18. *gyre* (31) 19. *pinnacle* (31) 20. *array* (34)

THE WRITER'S AGENDA:

The author presents his ideas to us as a series of informal, leisurely reflections at the breakfast table. But as he shares his thoughts and memories with us, we become aware that they are focused on a key issue and that they support a central, passionately held conviction. Answer the following questions about how the essay takes shape and how it supports its central thesis:

1. In the first half dozen paragraphs of this essay, the author presents his view of the brave new world of *modern technology,* a view he sums up in his central **thesis**: "It's life I believe in, not machines." How does he describe the modern attitudes from which he dissents? How does he trace their historical roots? What use does he make of symbols like the clock and the mouse?

2. A key metaphor in much of Loren Eiseley's writing is the "scale" of life—the place of each living being in the *chain of evolution* that stretches through endless centuries into the distant past. In this essay, what happens during his "descent into time" before he tells the story of the birds? What stage on the scale of life is represented by the pine?

3. What are striking details in the story of the two birds? How does it show the author's *fellow feeling* for the creatures of the wild and his tendency to take their side against their human enemy? What phrases are especially charged with the emotions that the experience inspired in the author?

4. As the author returns to the original issue in his conclusion, how does the story of the two birds help him clinch his point? How does his conclusion echo details or ideas from earlier in the essay?

5. Many readers have admired Eiseley for combining the careful, systematic observation of the scientist with the passion and sense of wonder of the poet. In what passages in this essay does he seem to you most the scientist? In what passages does he seem to you most the poet?

FOR DISCUSSION OR WRITING:

1. What does nature mean to this author? What is his relation to the natural world? How does his relationship with nature compare with

that of other advocates of a close relationship with the natural world or a "return to nature"?

2. We are often told that what animal life we observe as modern civilized human beings is too tamed, too domesticated, or too vestigial to give us a true sense of what life in the wild was like before the triumph of human civilization. To judge from your own observation, how true is this charge?

3. Since earliest time, people have chosen animals or plants as symbols of what meaning life had for them. Prepare a paper in which you discuss some possible symbols of life that are especially meaningful for you.

4. Choose two central symbols that for you best sum up the contrast or the rivalry between the living and the mechanical, or between the organic and the technological. Choose a pair like the bird and the machine, or like the mouse and the clock. Discuss fully the implications of the symbols you have chosen.

5. How wide is the gap between the "two cultures"? Prepare a paper in which you explain the world of the engineer to the artist, the world of the artist to the scientist, or the like.

6. Eiseley was fascinated with the slow emergence of the human spirit or the human soul during the long journey of our animal-like ancestors "from the dark borders of the ancient forest into which our footprints vanish." Have you encountered different views of what is most essential or most permanent in our common heritage from the distant past? Which is closest to your own view, and why?

FOR FURTHER DISCUSSION AND WRITING: Lewis Thomas, the widely read biologist, published this tribute to social scientists as part of an article he wrote
for the *Atlantic* magazine in 1981. His key example is the work of comparative linguists who traced the common origin of the Indo-European languages.
These range from Sanskrit, an ancient religious language of India, to most
modern European languages, including Spanish and English. In what ways is
the concept of evolution, as applied here to language, similar to the concept
of evolution in biology, as developed by Darwin and others? How much is
the theory of evolution today part of the general public's background in
science? How widely is it known or accepted? What challenges to it exist
today, and how serious are they?

Lewis Thomas

Language and
Evolution

THE SOCIAL scientists are in the hardest business of all—trying   1
to understand how humanity works. They are caught up in debates all
over town; everything they touch turns out to be one of society's nerve
endings, eliciting outrage and cries of pain. Wait until they begin coming close to the bone. They surely will someday, provided they can
continue to attract enough bright people—fascinated by humanity, un-
afraid of big numbers, and skeptical of questionnaires—and provided
the government does not starve them out of business, as is now being
tried in Washington. Politicians do not like pain, not even wincing, and
they have some fear of what the social scientists may be thinking about
thinking for the future.

The social scientists are themselves too modest about the history of   2
their endeavor, tending to display only the matters under scrutiny today
in economics, sociology, and psychology, for example—never boast-
ing, as they might, about one of the greatest of all scientific advances in
our comprehension of humanity, for which they could be claiming

credit. I refer to the marvelous accomplishments of the nineteenth-century comparative linguists. When the scientific method is working at its best, it succeeds in revealing the connection between things in nature that seem at first totally unrelated to each other. Long before the time when the biologists, led by Darwin and Wallace, were constructing the tree of evolution and the origin of species, the linguists were hard at work on the evolution of language. After beginning in 1786 with Sir William Jones and his inspired hunch that the remarkable similarities among Sanskrit, Greek, and Latin meant, in his words, that these three languages must "have sprung from some common source, which, perhaps, no longer exists," the new science of comparative grammar took off in 1816 with Franz Bopp's classic work "On the conjugational system of the Sanskrit language in comparison with that of the Greek, Latin, Persian and Germanic languages"—a piece of work equivalent, in its scope and in its power to explain, to the best of nineteenth-century biology. The common Indo-European ancestry of English, Germanic, Slavic, Greek, Latin, Baltic, Indic, Iranian, Hittite, and Anatolian tongues, and the meticulous scholarship connecting them was a tour de force for research—science at its best, and social science at that.

3   It is nice to know that a common language, perhaps 20,000 years ago, had a root word for the earth which turned, much later, into the technical term for the complex polymers that make up the connective tissues of the soil: humus and what are called the humic acids. There is a strangeness, though, in the emergence from the same root of words such as "human" and "humane," and "humble." It comes as something of a shock to realize that the root for words such as "miracle" and "marvel" meant, originally, "to smile," and that from the single root *sa* were constructed, in the descendant tongues, three cognate words, "satisfied," "satiated," and "sadness." How is it possible for a species to show so much wisdom in its most collective of all behaviors—the making and constant changing of language—and at the same time be so habitually folly-prone in the building of nation–states? Modern linguistics has moved into new areas of inquiry as specialized and inaccessible for most laymen (including me) as particle physics; I cannot guess where linguistics will come out, but it is surely aimed at scientific comprehension, and its problem—human language—is as crucial to the species as any other field I can think of, including molecular genetics.

MEDIA:
The Popular Imagination

The Common Theme: For many years, critics ignored or deplored the world of American popular culture. Television was the great "wasteland"; Hollywood movies appealed to the "lowest common denominator." "Mass culture" and true culture were kept in separate compartments. But gradually over the years popular culture has gained an ambiguous kind of scholarly and critical respectability. Screen comedy of the silent-film era has been resurrected in countless retrospectives. Critics have found in the early Westerns and in TV series like *Star Trek* myths that are a basic part of the American heritage and a part of our "collective unconscious" as a nation. Much current writing about the mass media and American popular culture reflects a paradoxical mixture of fascination and irony. The writers in this unit write about American mass culture with the mixture of nostalgia and ridicule shared by many readers who have gone beyond it but never really left it behind.

WRITER'S GUIDE 11:
Formal and Informal Language

Serious written English is more **formal** than casual speech. The words and sentences of formal writing are our signals to the audience that we want our ideas to be taken seriously. To write effectively, we must be able to shift from the language of informal talk to the language of serious writing. Serious here does not mean stuffy, pompous, or pretentious. Formal writing at its best is clear and vigorous. By calling it "formal," we mean that we have chosen the words and put together the sentences with care, so that they will be worth the reader's serious attention.

Look at the use of formal written English in the following example of serious expository writing—writing that conveys information and ideas:

> The volume of solid matter discharged annually into the world's waters amounts to over sixty-five cubic miles—equivalent to a mountain with twenty-thousand-foot vertical sides and a flat top of over sixteen square miles. This includes so much sewage that bathing in many lakes, including even the Lake of Geneva, and on numerous sea beaches has become either disgusting, dangerous to health, or both. Our vaunted Affluent Society is rapidly turning into an Effluent Society. Meanwhile, rubbish dumps and used automobiles are polluting the land; automobile exhausts, domestic smoke, and industrial fumes are polluting the air; and pesticides and herbicides are killing off our birds, our wild flowers, and our butterflies. The net result is that nature is being wounded, the environment desecrated, and the world's resources of enjoyment and interest demolished or destroyed.
>
> —Julian Huxley, *The Crisis in Man's Destiny*

This passage uses many words that are more accurate, demanding, or technical than words we would use in talking about today's lunch or tomorrow's party: *discharged, cubic, equivalent, vertical, vaunted, herbicide, effluent.* However, many other words in this passage are simple, unadorned words that have been part of our common language for many centuries: *lakes, beaches, smoke, birds, flowers, butterflies.* The words that carry the author's conclusions or judgments are blunt and straightforward: *disgusting, net result, dangerous, destroyed.* There is a playful, lighter touch that keeps the writing from becoming pompous or too solemn (the "affluent society" is turning into the "effluent" society).

The art of writing effective formal English is to write plain English with the care and with the respect for words that will repay the serious reader's attention. The following guidelines will help you use formal English effectively in your own writing:

(1) *Use the full range of a formal, educated vocabulary.* Formal written English uses more of the language than ordinary casual speech. It chooses from a wide range the words that carry the right information or have the right shade of meaning. In much casual talk, too many mental blanks are filled in with all-purpose words like *great, wonderful, awful, terrific,* or *really funny.* A well-stocked vocabulary allows us to use words that are accurate and informative. Often these words have a history or associations that make them fit especially well.

In each of the following pairs, the first word adds something to the meaning of a simpler or more common synonym:

terse—brief:	*Brief* just means short; *terse* means short but to the point, without any flourish or show of emotion.
indignation—anger:	Indignation is a righteous anger, anger caused by some wrong or injustice.
concoct—make up:	When we concoct a story, we do more than just make it up. We make it up with some effort, often with a devious intention, and often with somewhat outlandish or weird results.

A well-stocked vocabulary allows us to choose words with the right **connotations**—words we use because of the attitudes they suggest and the associations they carry. The right word will create the right associations in the reader's mind:

archaic:	An archaic mode of transportation would be to ride a horse down a freeway.
sterile:	The phrase "a sterile environment" brings to mind something cold, whitewashed, and devoid of imperfections, not allowing anything spontaneous or irregular to grow.

(2) *Avoid trite informal language.* In a serious discussion of issues, avoid informal words that would create an unintended folksy, humorous, or facetious effect. Avoid informal expressions that unintentionally suggest an amused or belittling attitude: "have a fit" for "get angry"; "spring from jail" instead of "release"; "pack them in" instead of "fill the hall."

The informal words and expressions in the following pairs have a definite casual, conversational flavor:

INFORMAL	FORMAL	INFORMAL	FORMAL
creepy	frightening	kidding	teasing
chintzy	cheap	stuck up	conceited
folks	relatives	mad	angry
fake	forged	takeoff	parody
come-on	invitation	hassle	difficulty
sloppy	untidy	shape up	improve
broke	penniless	show-off	exhibitionist

Informal English uses many abbreviations that can suggest hurry or indifference: *prof, math, econ.* The bane of an excessively informal style is often its reliance on tired familiar expressions, or **clichés**. Avoid the many tired sayings that come to us ready-made and really throw no light on the specific topic at hand: "light at the end of the tunnel"; "a new ballgame"; "takes all kinds"; "you can't win them all"; "one of those days." We have heard such expressions too often from people who were not making the effort to take a fresh, honest look.

(3) *Use informal language selectively only when it suits your subject or when you aim at a humorous or ironic tone.* When writing casually about amusing sidelights of our everyday lives, we do not want to appear solemn. When writing about the more entertaining or colorful side of popular culture, a critic may deliberately use selected informal language to help set a humorous tone—to suggest a half-amused, half-serious attitude.

Pauline Kael, considered by many the country's best movie critic, writes about movies as the insider who is not awed by her subject and who is often in turns brash, cutting, and amusing. She writes about the greats of movie history in a half-amused, half-serious style that makes selective, deliberate use of informal language:

- "a man who couldn't marry her without *messes* and scandal"

- "a *spunky,* funny, beautiful girl"

- "the public in general *got wise*"

- "*fell for* one of the *dumbest* smart *con tricks* of all time"

- "the public can *swallow* just so much"

Tom Wolfe, author of *The Right Stuff,* has made a career of writing about the more sensational or freakish fringes of American life; he uses **slang** to create a deliberately jazzy, disrespectful effect. Slang is *extremely* informal; it is more aggressively unconventional and disre-

spectful than ordinary informal language. New slang is often colorful and pointed (*flaky, hang loose, put-down, spaced out*). However,
it soon wears out from constant repetition, and it often becomes
crude and insulting. In writing about the hard-drinking, fast-driving,
rough-talking test pilots from among whom America's astronauts were
selected, Wolfe uses a jazzy, slangy style to shock and entertain the
reader:

> . . . staggered, *bawled,* and sang . . . like a *jerk* . . . like a *zom-
> bie* . . . get more *wasted* or else more quietly *fried* . . . cheap PX
> *booze* . . . *barreling* down the highway . . . *chalked it up* to
> youth . . . *slapping* oxygen tank cones on their faces . . . *revved
> up* with adrenalin.

In examples such as these, informal language or slang is used deliberately to create a highly personal, characteristic style. In ordinary
prose, highly informal language is usually limited to selected expressions used for a deliberately humorous or satirical effect:

> Conservatives tend to be automatically uncomfortable with any
> idea or trend that smacks of mob psychology . . . to the point of
> *dropping wet blankets* on the emotional political moods to
> which this country is prone. (Susannah Lessard)

> I know of one *gifted crackpot* who used to be employed gain-
> fully in the fields of humor and satire, who has taken a solemn
> pledge not to write anything funny or light-hearted . . . again
> till things get straightened out in the world. (E. B. White)

(4) *Avoid the loosely-strung-together sentences of informal speech
in serious writing.* Sentences like the following preserve the informal,
loosely constructed effect of the spoken sentence. With parts strung
together with weak links like *and* or *and then,* they read as if the
author were still thinking while writing them. He was still adding details as they came to mind:

> INFORMAL: It seemed that every fighter jock thought himself
>   an ace driver, and he would do anything to obtain a
>   hot car, especially a sports car, *and* the drunker he
>   was, the more convinced he would be about his driv-
>   ing skills, as if the right stuff, being indivisible, car-
>   ried over into any enterprise whatsoever, under any
>   conditions. (Tom Wolfe)

> INFORMAL: Every young fighter jock knew the feeling of get-

ting two or three hours' sleep *and then* waking up at
5:30 a.m. and having a few cups of coffee, a few cigarettes, *and then* carting his poor quivering liver out
to the field for another day of flying. (Tom Wolfe)

By contrast, the sentences of formal writing are more deliberate,
more carefully planned. They make use of devices like **parallel** structure, which require the author to fit many different details into a carefully constructed overall pattern. The following sentence is from the
introduction to a book about the wildlife of Sequoia National Park:

> PARALLEL: Even hardened adults must read it at *their own
> risk—the risk* of being seized with an overwhelming
> desire *to hear* the wind in the treetops and *to smell*
> the incense of the forest . . . *to hear* the evening
> songs of birds, *to see* the bats come out at dusk, and
> *to share* with the creatures of the wilderness the ad-
> ventures of the night. (Robert C. Miller)

The following passage has the clear focus and systematic, determined forward movement of effective formal English. The short, emphatic opening sentence states the main point. The sentences that follow up the main point make use of parallel structure to line up related
ideas in similar grammatical form: "We want . . . . We refuse . . . " Opposed ideas are presented as carefully balanced opposites: "The *large
family* is no more *a blessing*/than the *childless couple* is *a crime.*" The
general effect is that of a passage that was carefully worked out rather
than of a passage that just grew:

> Society forgets that not all women are naturally maternal. . . .
> all of us must know by now that the large family is no more a
> blessing than the childless couple is a crime. In fact, the wom-
> an who is a copious breeder is doing infinitely more harm than
> good to this suffocating planet and its crowded broods. The
> rest of us really want more men in our lives, not fewer. We want
> their comradeship at work as well as their company at home.
> We refuse a life that forces us to live ten hours of every week-
> day confined to the company of children and women.
> —Marya Mannes, "How Men Will Benefit from the Women's
> Power Revolution," *Midwest*

(5) *Revise usages or constructions associated with informal English.* Constructions like the following are part of natural, idiomatic

English, but they carry a strong **colloquial**—that is, casually conversational—flavor:

because . . . does not mean

> INFORMAL: *Because* Jack Anderson said it *does not necessarily mean* it is not so. (William F. Buckley)

> FORMAL: *That* her opponent was dishonest *does not mean* she was a saint.

is when

> INFORMAL: Nepotism *is when* people give jobs or promotions to close relatives.

> FORMAL: Nepotism *is the practice of* giving jobs or promotions to close relatives.

like as conjunction (used with its own subject and verb)

> INFORMAL: They acted *like* the accident had been my fault.

> FORMAL: They acted *as if* the accident had been my fault.

informal *you* (unless in instructions or advice to the reader)

> INFORMAL: When *you* live on a dirt road, *you* can always tell when a car is coming; first *you* see the dust trails, and then *you* hear the engine.

> FORMAL: *People* who live on a dirt road can always tell when a car is coming.

(6) *Avoid pretentious pseudo-formal language and jargon.* Much bad writing results when people who try to avoid excessive informality go to the opposite extreme. **Jargon** is language that dresses up simple or ordinary matters in scientific-sounding words. Do not try to impress your readers by using words like *factor, aspect, hypothesize, interrelationship, parameter, maximize, preadolescence.*

Here is Ellen Goodman making fun of the psychological jargon some people use in talking about their personal lives:

> A relationship, unlike a love affair, is something which is carefully negotiated to be "self-actualizing" and "growth-oriented" and "nonbinding." It is written along the lines of the model approved by the National Mental Health Association. It

is then signed by two consenting adults who are too embarrassed to tell their friends that they've fallen in love.

In truth, one never falls into a relationship. One is too mature, healthy, sensible and dreary for that. Rather, one enters a
relationship as if it were a law firm.

—Ellen Goodman, "Sinking the Relationship," *Close to Home*

Rather than using overly technical language where it is out of
place, effective writers know how to use vivid, everyday language to
make technical matters clear to the ordinary reader. Look at the vivid,
imaginative comparison in the following sentence as an example:

Nearly half of the 180 or so major insect enemies of plants in
the United States are accidental imports from abroad, and most
of them have come as *hitchhikers* on plants. (Rachel Carson)

To sum up: Formal English, effectively used, shows that you are
taking your subject and your reader seriously. In serious written
English, we avoid informal expressions that would make our writing
sound too casual, too trite, or too disrespectful. On the other hand,
effective formal writing is not cut off from everyday speech. It draws on
much of common language but goes *beyond* it. Depending on the subject and on the writer's intention, it may use selected informal expression for the lighter touch or for special effect.

PREWRITING ACTIVITIES 11

1. For sentence practice, write a series of one-sentence *capsule
plots* for recent or well-remembered movies and television shows. Pack
each sentence with characteristic detail or telling information. Divide
your capsule plots into two sets: In the first set, use **formal** language to
describe serious films or programs (or those that you want the reader to
take seriously). In the second set, use more **informal** language for
shows with humorous intent or shows that you want to put in a humorous light. Study the following sentences as possible models:

(Formal language)

a. A stranded reptilelike alien, befriended by human children, escapes from the planet Earth by salvaging parts from a toy chest in
order to make a radio transmitter.

b. Sir Thomas More, a man of high position, with the respect of his peers and the friendship of his king, is brought to disgrace, ruin, and even execution by his inability to abandon his conscience.

c. Clint Eastwood, never allowing his jaws to move while talking, portrays the man with no name, who killed for a fistful of dollars in the Old West.

d. Diana Ross, in *Lady Sings the Blues,* portrayed Billie Holiday's upbringing in Harlem, success in entertainment as a jazz singer, and tragic downfall from drinking and drugs.

(Informal language)

e. Gaining tremendous strength from eating spinach, a runty one-eyed sailor no longer puts up with the pummelings he receives from a big brute.

f. A hypochondriac photographer and a sloppy sportswriter sharing an apartment get on each other's nerves as the original "odd couple."

g. Meggie, poor kinfolk living on her rich aunt's sheep ranch, falls in love with a handsome young priest and dreams that one day he will kick the habit, so to speak, and tie the knot.

2. Study the following brief, pointed movie review from *The New Yorker.* Look at the way it combines information, evaluation, and entertainment. Write a similar brief review in which you can include plot essentials, key thematic or symbolic elements, and amusing sidelights.

Planet of the Apes

This is one of the liveliest science-fiction fantasies ever to come out of Hollywood. The writing, by Michael Wilson and Rod Serling, who adapted Pierre Boulle's novel *Monkey Planet,* is often fancy-ironic in the old school of poetic disillusion, but the construction is first-rate. An American astronaut finds himself in the future, on a planet run by apes; the audience is rushed along with this hero, who keeps going as fast as possible to avoid being castrated or lobotomized. All this wouldn't be so forceful or so funny if it weren't for the use of Charlton Heston in the role. With his perfect, lean-hipped, powerful body, Heston is a godlike hero; built for strength, he's an archetype of what makes Americans win. He doesn't play a nice guy; he's harsh and hostile, self-centered and hot-tempered. Yet we don't hate him, because he's so magnetically strong; he represents American power—and he has the profile of an eagle. He is the perfect American Adam for this black-comedy entertainment. The director, Franklin Schaffner, has thought out the action in terms of the wide screen, and he uses space and distance dramatically. The makeup (there is said to be a million dollars' worth) and the costuming of the actors playing the apes are rather witty, and the apes have a wonderful nervous, hopping walk. The best little hopper is Kim Hunter, as an ape lady doctor; she somehow manages to give a distinctive, charming performance in this makeup. (With Roddy McDowall, Maurice Evans, James Whitmore, James Daly, and Linda Harrison.) The movie spun off four sequels and a TV series.

3.   Authors who write on American popular culture often aim at a snappy, jazzy, or otherwise unconventional style, reflecting a half-serious, half-amused attitude toward their subject. Study the following short sample passages. Select one of them as the model for an imitation or parody.

a. Blackmail. Abortion. Teenage runaways. Drug addiction. Rape. Lies up the wazoo. And that's not even a good day. On a good day, college dorms will echo with screams:
    "Don't do it, Luke!"
    "Erica, how *could* you?"
Once the domain of grandmothers, housewives, and night-shift nurses, soap operas have now become the national campus pastime. But consider their content. It's not reality. It's not comedy. It's a relentlessly oppressive world tainted by horrible audio, cheap sets, lugubrious pacing and an excess of Farrah Fawcett hair. These assets notwithstanding, and not to mention the *real* sex, drugs, and alcohol readily available on campus, you'd think college students wouldn't require massive doses of soap operas to make it through the afternoon. But they do.
    —Lisa Birnbach, "The Daze of Our Lives," *Rolling Stone*

b. The center was not holding. It was a country of bankruptcy notices and public-auction announcements and commonplace reports of casual killings and misplaced children and abandoned homes and vandals who misspelled even the four-letter words they scrawled. It was a country in which families routinely disappeared, trailing bad checks and repossession papers. Adolescents drifted from city to torn city, sloughing off both the past and the future as snakes shed their skins, children who were never taught and would never now learn the games that had held the society together. People were missing. Children were missing. Parents were missing. Those left behind filed desultory missing-persons reports, then moved on themselves.

—Joan Didion, *Slouching Towards Bethlehem*

c. Combat had its own infinite series of tests, and one of the greatest sins was "chattering" or "jabbering" on the radio. The combat frequency was to be kept clear of all but strategically essential messages, and all unenlightening comments were regarded as evidence of funk, of the wrong stuff. A Navy pilot (in legend, at any rate) began shouting, "I've got a MiG at zero! A MiG at zero!"—meaning that it had maneuvered in behind him and was locked in on his tail. An irritated voice cut in and said, "Shut up and die like an aviator." One had to be a Navy pilot to appreciate the final nuance. A good Navy pilot was a real *aviator;* in the Air Force they merely had pilots and not precisely the proper stuff.

—Tom Wolfe, *The Right Stuff*

James Thurber

The Secret Life of Walter Mitty

GUIDE TO READING: The hero of this story drifts back and forth between fantasy and reality. What is the content of Walter Mitty's fantasy life? What contrast does it offer to his everyday reality?

1   "WE'RE GOING through!" The Commander's voice was like thin ice breaking. He wore his full-dress uniform, with the heavily braided white cap pulled down rakishly over one cold gray eye. "We can't make it, sir. It's spoiling for a hurricane, if you ask me." "I'm not asking you, Lieutenant Berg," said the Commander. "Throw on the power lights! Rev her up to 8,500! We're going through!" The pounding of the cylinders increased; ta-pocketa-pocketa-pocketa-*pocketa-pocketa.* The Commander stared at the ice forming on the pilot window. He walked over and twisted a row of complicated dials. "Switch on No. 8

auxiliary!" he shouted. "Switch on No. 8 auxiliary!" repeated Lieutenant Berg. "Full strength in No. 3 turret!" shouted the Commander. "Full strength in No. 3 turret!" The crew, bending to their various tasks in the huge, hurtling eight-engined Navy hydroplane, looked at each other and grinned. "The Old Man'll get us through," they said to one another. "The Old Man ain't afraid of anything!"

"Not so fast! You're driving too fast!" said Mrs. Mitty. "What are you driving so fast for?" 2

"Hmm?" said Walter Mitty. He looked at his wife, in the seat beside him, with shocked astonishment. She seemed grossly unfamiliar, like a strange woman who had yelled at him in a crowd. "You were up to fifty-five," she said. "You know I don't like to go more than forty. You were up to fifty-five." Walter Mitty drove on toward Waterbury in silence, the roaring of the SN-202 through the worst storm in twenty years of Navy flying fading in the remote, intimate airways of his mind. "You're tensed up again," said Mrs. Mitty. "It's one of your days. I wish you'd let Dr. Renshaw look you over." 3

Walter Mitty stopped the car in front of the building where his wife went to have her hair done. "Remember to get those overshoes while I'm having my hair done," she said. "I don't need overshoes," said Mitty. She put her mirror back into her bag. "We've been all through that," she said, getting out of the car. "You're not a young man any longer." He raced the engine a little. "Why don't you wear your gloves? Have you lost your gloves?" Walter Mitty reached in a pocket and brought out the gloves. He put them on, but after she had turned and gone into the building and he had driven on to a red light, he took them off again. "Pick it up, brother!" snapped a cop as the light changed, and Mitty hastily pulled on his gloves and lurched ahead. He drove around the streets aimlessly for a time, and then he drove past the hospital on his way to the parking lot. 4

..."It's the millionaire banker, Wellington McMillan," said the pretty nurse. "Yes?" said Walter Mitty, removing his gloves slowly. "Who has the case?" "Dr. Renshaw and Dr. Benbow, but there are two specialists here, Dr. Remington from New York and Dr. Pritchard-Mitford from London. He flew over." A door opened down a long, cool corridor and Dr. Renshaw came out. He looked distraught and haggard. "Hello, Mitty," he said. "We're having the devil's own time with McMillan, the millionaire banker and close personal friend of Roosevelt. Obstreosis of the ductal tract. Tertiary. Wish you'd take a look at him." "Glad to," said Mitty. 5

In the operating room there were whispered introductions: "Dr. Remington, Dr. Mitty. Dr. Pritchard-Mitford, Dr. Mitty." "I've read your book on streptothricosis," said Pritchard-Mitford, shaking hands. "A brilliant performance, sir." "Thank you," said Walter Mitty. "Didn't 6 know you were in the States, Mitty," grumbled Remington. "Coals to Newcastle, bringing Mitford and me up here for a tertiary." "You are very kind," said Mitty. A huge, complicated machine, connected to the operating table, with many tubes and wires, began at this moment to go pocketa-pocketa-pocketa. "The new anaesthetizer is giving way!" shouted an interne. "There is no one in the East who knows how to fix it!" "Quiet, man!" said Mitty, in a low, cool voice. He sprang to the machine, which was now going pocketa-pocketa-queep-pocketa-queep. He began fingering delicately a row of glistening dials. "Give me a fountain pen!" he snapped. Someone handed him a fountain pen. He pulled a faulty piston out of the machine and inserted the pen in its place. "That will hold for ten minutes," he said. "Get on with the operation." A nurse hurried over and whispered to Renshaw, and Mitty saw the man turn pale. "Coreopsis has set in," said Renshaw nervously. "If you would take over, Mitty?" Mitty looked at him and at the craven figure of Benbow, who drank, and at the grave, uncertain faces of the two great specialists. "If you wish," he said. They slipped a white gown on him; he adjusted a mask and drew on thin gloves; nurses handed him shining . . .

7   "Back it up, Mac! Look out for that Buick!" Walter Mitty jammed on the brakes. "Wrong lane, Mac," said the parking-lot attendant, looking at Mitty closely. "Gee. Yeh," muttered Mitty. He began cautiously to back out of the lane marked "Exit Only." "Leave her sit there," said the attendant. "I'll put her away." Mitty got out of the car. "Hey, better leave the key." "Oh," said Mitty, handing the man the ignition key. The attendant vaulted into the car, backed it up with insolent skill, and put it where it belonged.

8   They're so cocky, thought Walter Mitty, walking along Main Street; they think they know everything. Once he had tried to take his chains off, outside New Milford, and he had got them wound around the axles. A man had had to come out in a wrecking car and unwind them, a young, grinning garageman. Since then Mrs. Mitty always made him drive to a garage to have the chains taken off. The next time, he thought, I'll wear my right arm in a sling; they won't grin at me then. I'll have my right arm in a sling and they'll see I couldn't possibly take the chains off myself. He kicked at the slush on the sidewalk. "Over-shoes," he said to himself, and he began looking for a shoe store.

9   When he came out into the street again, with the overshoes in a box under his arm, Walter Mitty began to wonder what the other thing was his wife had told him to get. She had told him twice before they set out from their house for Waterbury. In a way he hated these weekly trips to town—he was always getting something wrong. Kleenex, he thought, Squibb's, razor blades? No. Toothpaste, toothbrush, bicarbonate, carbo-rundum, initiative and referendum? He gave up. But she would remem-

ber it. "Where's that what's-its-name?" she would ask. "Don't tell me you forgot the what's-its-name." A newsboy went by shouting something about the Waterbury trial.

. . . "Perhaps this will refresh your memory." The District Attorney 10 suddenly thrust a heavy automatic at the quiet figure on the witness stand. "Have you ever seen this before?" Walter Mitty took the gun and examined it expertly. "This is my Webley-Vickers 50.80," he said calmly. An excited buzz ran around the courtroom. The Judge rapped for order. "You are a crack shot with any sort of firearms, I believe?" said the District Attorney, insinuatingly. "Objection!" shouted Mitty's attorney. "We have shown that the defendant could not have fired the shot. We have shown that he wore his right arm in a sling on the night of the fourteenth of July." Walter Mitty raised his hand briefly and the bickering attorneys were stilled. "With any known make of gun," he said evenly, "I could have killed Gregory Fitzhurst at three hundred feet *with my left hand.*" Pandemonium broke loose in the courtroom. A woman's scream rose above the bedlam and suddenly a lovely, dark-haired girl was in Walter Mitty's arms. The District Attorney struck at her savagely. Without rising from his chair, Mitty let the man have it on the point of the chin. "You miserable cur!"

"Puppy biscuit," said Walter Mitty. He stopped walking and the 11 buildings of Waterbury rose up out of the misty courtroom and surrounded him again. A woman who was passing laughed. "He said 'Puppy biscuit,'" she said to her companion. "That man said 'Puppy biscuit' to himself." Walter Mitty hurried on. He went into an A & P, not the first one he came to but a smaller one farther up the street. "I want some biscuit for small, young dogs," he said to the clerk. "Any special brand, sir?" The greatest pistol shot in the world thought a moment. "It says 'Puppies Bark for It' on the box," said Walter Mitty.

His wife would be through at the hairdresser's in fifteen minutes, 12 Mitty saw in looking at his watch, unless they had trouble drying it; sometimes they had trouble drying it. She didn't like to get to the hotel first; she would want him to be there waiting for her as usual. He found a big leather chair in the lobby, facing a window, and he put the overshoes and the puppy biscuit on the floor beside it. He picked up an old copy of *Liberty* and sank down into the chair. "Can Germany Conquer the World Through the Air?" Walter Mitty looked at the pictures of bombing planes and of ruined streets.

. . . "The cannonading has got the wind up in young Raleigh, sir," 13 said the sergeant. Captain Mitty looked up at him through tousled hair. "Get him to bed," he said wearily, "with the others. I'll fly alone." "But you can't, sir," said the sergeant anxiously. "It takes two men to handle that bomber and the Archies are pounding hell out of the air. Von Richtman's circus is between here and Saulier." "Somebody's got to get the ammunition dump," said Mitty. "I'm going over. Spot of brandy?" He poured a drink for the sergeant and one for himself. War thundered and whined around the dugout and battered at the door. There was a rending of wood, and splinters flew through the room. "A bit of a near thing," said Captain Mitty carelessly. "The box barrage is closing in," said the sergeant. "We only live once, Sergeant," said Mitty, with his faint, fleeting smile. "Or do we?" He poured another brandy and tossed it off. "I never see a man could hold his brandy like you, sir," said the sergeant. "Begging your pardon, sir." Captain Mitty stood up and strapped on his huge Webley-Vickers automatic. "It's forty kilometers through Hell, sir," said the sergeant. Mitty finished one last brandy. "After all," he said softly, "what isn't?" The pounding of the cannon increased; there was the rat-tat-tatting of machine guns, and from somewhere came the menacing pocketa-pocketa-pocketa of the new flame-throwers. Walter Mitty walked to the door of the dugout humming, "Auprès de Ma Blonde."[1] He turned and waved to the sergeant. "Cheerio!" he said. . . .

14   Something struck his shoulder. "I've been looking all over this hotel for you," said Mrs. Mitty. "Why do you have to hide in this old chair? How did you expect me to find you?" "Things close in," said Walter Mitty vaguely. "What?" Mrs. Mitty said. "Did you get the what's-its-name? The puppy biscuit? What's in that box?" "Overshoes," said Mitty. "Couldn't you have put them on in the store?" "I was thinking," said Walter Mitty. "Does it ever occur to you that I am sometimes thinking?" She looked at him. "I'm going to take your temperature when I get you home," she said.

15   They went out through the revolving doors that made a faintly derisive whistling sound when you pushed them. It was two blocks to the parking lot. At the drugstore on the corner she said, "Wait here for me. I forgot something. I won't be a minute." She was more than a minute. Walter Mitty lighted a cigarette. It began to rain, rain with sleet in it. He stood up against the wall of the drugstore, smoking. . . . He put his shoulders back and his heels together. "Keep the handkerchief," said Walter Mitty scornfully. He took one last drag on his cigarette and snapped it away. Then, with that faint, fleeting smile playing about his lips, he faced the firing squad; erect and motionless, proud and disdainful. Walter Mitty the Undefeated, inscrutable to the last.

 USING THE DICTIONARY: The impressive vocabulary of Mitty's daydreams helps set up the comic contrast with his everyday world of petty informal talk. Check the meaning and origin

[1] [a French song of World War I vintage]

of the following: 1. *turret* (1) 2. *distraught* (5) 3. *craven* (6) 4. *insinuating* (10) 5. *pandemonium* (10) 6. *bedlam* (10) 7. *cannonading* (13) 8. *fleeting* (15) 9. *derisive* (15) 10. *inscrutable* (15)

THE WRITER'S AGENDA:

Some writers look for humor in what is weird, zany, grotesque, far out. James Thurber found a rich source of humor in what is laughable in familiar everyday patterns of human behavior. Answer the following questions about the appeal of his brand of humor.

1. Walter Mitty's daydreams are reminiscent of the Hollywood movies of the thirties and forties. Which of the episodes seem especially *familiar?* What are typical situations? What details remind us of familiar stereotypes or clichés?

2. What, if any, is the *common thread* of Walter Mitty's fantasies?

3. Much of the humor in this piece derives from the *contrast* between the roles Walter Mitty plays in his daydreams and the role he plays in real life. What are some striking examples of this comic contrast?

4. Walter Mitty became a kind of *folk hero* to a generation of readers. What is the secret of his appeal? What is the relationship between Walter Mitty and the reader?

5. Thurber delights in little unexpected *humorous touches* and satirical jabs. What are some examples in this story?

FOR DISCUSSION OR WRITING:

1. Holden Caulfield said in *The Catcher in the Rye,* "The movies . . . they ruin you." Define the kind of escape entertainment that is the subject of this story, identifying its key features. Is it harmful? Is it beneficial? Does it serve a basic need?

2. What daydreams did traditional Hollywood movies offer to women?

3. Look at current popular movies or television shows that offer escape or fantasy to the viewers. What fantasies are being acted out in them? Concentrate on two or three major types and discuss detailed examples.

4. We frequently hear calls for more realism or more maturity in movies or television dramas. Define what one of these terms means for you, and discuss outstanding examples.

5. Discuss a kind of escape literature that you know well—for example, detective novels, historical novels, or science fiction. What does it show about its intended audience? What expectations does it cater to; what standards is it designed to meet?

6. Write a daydream, or sequence of daydreams, of your own, Walter-Mitty style.

BACKGROUND: Tom Wolfe (born 1931) started his career with a doctorate in American studies from Yale. He went on to work as a journalist for *The Washington Post* and started to publish articles in *Esquire, New York* magazine, and other publications. He became legendary as the inventor of the "New Journalism," a freewheeling, flamboyant, disrespectful, razzle-dazzle style of reportage that abandoned the reporter's conventional stance of detachment and objectivity. Instead, Wolfe plunged his readers into a stream of images, striking details, and snatches of conversation to make them imagine themselves as participants, sharing in the immediacy and excitement of the experience described. He became a leading chronicler of American popular culture, often seeming mesmerized by its surface glitter and zaniness but also looking for the deeper symbolic significance of trends and fads like the demolition derby, rock concerts, surfers, pot, the "me" generation, and radical chic. His colorful prose was collected in a succession of books, including *The Kandy-Kolored Tangerine-Flake Streamline Baby* (1965), *The Electric Kool-Aid Acid Test* (1968), *Radical Chic and Mau-Mauing the Flak Catchers* (1970), *The Painted Word* (1975), and *From Bauhaus to Our House* (1981). In 1981, Wolfe published *The Right Stuff*, a runaway bestseller about the astronauts of Project Mercury, America's first program for manned spacecraft. In the excerpt reprinted here, Wolfe describes the flight training of future astronauts early in their career.

Tom Wolfe

The Right Stuff

GUIDE TO READING: This excerpt from Wolfe's book illustrates the image building or myth making that is a major function of American popular journalism and popular entertainment. What is "the right stuff"? How does Wolfe use example and contrast to show us the meaning of his central term? What is his attitude toward the people he describes and the mystique they represent?

A YOUNG MAN might go into military flight training believing that he was entering some sort of technical school in which he was simply going to acquire a certain set of skills. Instead, he found himself all at once enclosed in a fraternity. And in this fraternity, even though it was military, men were not rated by their outward rank as ensigns, lieutenants, commanders, or whatever. No, herein the world was divided into those who had it and those who did not. This quality, this *it,* was never named, however, nor was it talked about in any way.

2   As to just what this ineffable quality was . . . well, it obviously involved bravery. But it was not bravery in the simple sense of being willing to risk your life. The idea seemed to be that any fool could do that, if that was all that was required, just as any fool could throw away his life in the process. No, the idea here (in the all-enclosing fraternity) seemed to be that a man should have the ability to go up in a hurtling piece of machinery and put his hide on the line and then have the moxie, the reflexes, the experience, the coolness, to pull it back in the last yawning moment—and then to go up again *the next day,* and the next day, and every next day, even if the series should prove infinite— and, ultimately, in its best expression, do so in a cause that means something to thousands, to a people, a nation, to humanity, to God. Nor was there *a test* to show whether or not a pilot had this righteous quality. There was, instead, a seemingly infinite series of tests. A career in flying was like climbing one of those ancient Babylonian pyramids made up of a dizzy progression of steps and ledges, a ziggurat, a pyramid extraordinarily high and steep; and the idea was to prove at every foot of the way up that pyramid that you were one of the elected and anointed ones who had *the right stuff* and could move higher and higher and even—ultimately, God willing, one day—that you might be able to join that special few at the very top, that elite who had the capacity to bring tears to men's eyes, the very Brotherhood of the Right Stuff itself.

3   None of this was to be mentioned, and yet it was acted out in a way that a young man could not fail to understand. When a new flight (i.e., a class) of trainees arrived at Pensacola, they were brought into an auditorium for a little lecture. An officer would tell them: "Take a look at the man on either side of you." Quite a few actually swiveled their heads this way and that, in the interest of appearing diligent. Then the officer would say: "One of the three of you is not going to make it!"— meaning, not get his wings. That was the opening theme, the *motif* of primary training. We already know that one-third of you do not have the right stuff—it only remains to find out who.

4   Furthermore, that was the way it turned out. At every level in one's progress up that staggeringly high pyramid, the world was once more divided into those men who had the right stuff to continue the climb and those who had to be *left behind* in the most obvious way. Some were eliminated in the course of the opening classroom work, as either not smart enough or not hardworking enough, and were left behind.

Then came the basic flight instruction, in single-engine, propeller-driven trainers, and a few more—even though the military tried to make this stage easy—were washed out and left behind. Then came more demanding levels, one after the other, formation flying, instrument flying, jet training, all-weather flying, gunnery, and at each level more were washed out and left behind. By this point easily a third of the original candidates had been, indeed, eliminated . . . from the ranks of those who might prove to have the right stuff.

In the Navy, in addition to the stages that Air Force trainees went through, the neophyte always had waiting for him, out in the ocean, a certain grim gray slab; namely, the deck of an aircraft carrier; and with it perhaps the most difficult routine in military flying, carrier landings. He was shown films about it, he heard lectures about it, and he knew that carrier landings were hazardous. He first practiced touching down on the shape of a flight deck painted on an airfield. He was instructed to touch down and gun right off. This was safe enough—the shape didn't move, at least—but it could do terrible things to, let us say, the gyroscope of the soul. *That shape!—it's so damned small!* And more candidates were washed out and left behind. Then came the day, without warning, when those who remained were sent out over the ocean for the first of many days of reckoning with the slab. The first day was always a clear day with little wind and a calm sea. The carrier was so steady that it seemed, from up there in the air, to be resting on pilings, and the candidate usually made his first carrier landing successfully, with relief and even *élan.* Many young candidates looked like terrific aviators up to that very point—and it was not until they were actually standing on the carrier deck that they first began to wonder if they had the proper stuff, after all. In the training film the flight deck was a grand piece of gray geometry, perilous, to be sure, but an amazing abstract shape as one looks down upon it on the screen. And yet once the newcomer's two feet were on it . . . *Geometry*—my God, man, this is a . . . *skillet!* It *heaved,* it moved up and down underneath his feet, it pitched up, it pitched down, it rolled to port (this great beast *rolled!*) and it rolled to starboard, as the ship moved into the wind and, therefore, into the waves, and the wind kept sweeping across, sixty feet up in the air out in the open sea, and there were no railings whatsoever. This was a *skillet!*—a frying pan!—a short-order grill!—not gray but black, smeared with skid marks from one end to the other and glistening with pools of hydraulic fluid and the occasional jet-fuel slick, all of it still hot, sticky, greasy, runny, virulent from God knows what traumas—still ablaze!—consumed in detonations, explosions, flames, combustion, roars, shrieks, whines, blasts, horrible shudders, fracturing impacts, as little men in screaming red and yellow and purple and green shirts with black Mickey Mouse helmets over their ears skittered about on the surface as if for their very lives (you've said it now!), hooking fighter planes onto the catapult shuttles so that they can explode their after-burners and be slung off the deck in a red-mad fury with a *kaboom!* that pounds through the entire deck—a procedure that seems absolutely controlled, orderly, sublime, however, compared to what he is about to watch as aircraft return to the ship for what is known in the engineering stoicisms of the military as "recovery and arrest." To say that an F-4 was coming back onto this heaving barbecue from out of the sky at a speed of 135 knots . . . that might have been the truth in the training lecture, but it did not begin to get across the idea of what the newcomer saw from the deck itself, because it created the notion that perhaps the plane was gliding in. On the deck one knew differently! As the aircraft came closer and the carrier heaved on into the waves and the plane's speed did not diminish and the deck did not grow steady—indeed, it pitched up and down five or ten feet per greasy heave—one experienced a neural alarm that no lecture could have prepared him for: This is not an *airplane* coming toward me, it is a brick with some poor sonofabitch riding it *(someone much like myself!)*, and it is not *gliding,* it is *falling,* a fifty-thousand-pound brick, headed not for a stripe on the deck but for *me*—and with a horrible *smash!* it hits the skillet, and with a blur of momentum as big as a freight train's it hurtles toward the far end of the deck—another blinding storm!—another roar as the pilot pushes the throttle up to full military power and another smear of rubber screams out over the skillet—and this is nominal!—quite okay!— for a wire stretched across the deck has grabbed the hook on the end of the plane as it hit the deck tail down, and the smash was the rest of the fifteen-ton brute slamming onto the deck, as it tripped up, so that it is now straining against the wire at full throttle, in case it hadn't held and the plane had "boltered" off the end of the deck and had to struggle up into the air again. And already the Mickey Mouse helmets are running toward the fiery monster . . .

6   And the candidate, looking on, begins to *feel* that great heaving sun-blazing deathboard of a deck wallowing in his own vestibular system—and suddenly he finds himself backed up against his own limits. He ends up going to the flight surgeon with so-called conversion symptoms. Overnight he develops blurred vision or numbness in his hands and feet or sinusitis so severe that he cannot tolerate changes in altitude. On one level the symptom is real. He really cannot see too well or use his fingers or stand the pain. But somewhere in his subconscious he knows it is a plea and a beg-off; he shows not the slightest concern (the flight surgeon notes) that the condition might be permanent and affect him in whatever life awaits him outside the arena of the right stuff.

7   Those who remained, those who qualified for carrier duty—and

even more so those who later on qualified for *night* carrier duty—
began to feel a bit like Gideon's warriors. *So many have been left
behind!* The young warriors were now treated to a deathly sweet and
quite unmentionable sight. They could gaze at length upon the
crushed and wilted pariahs who had washed out. They could inspect
those who did not have that righteous stuff.

The military did not have very merciful instincts. Rather than pack-   8
ing up these poor souls and sending them home, the Navy, like the Air
Force and the Marines, would try to make use of them in some other
role, such as flight controller. So the washout has to keep taking classes
with the rest of his group, even though he can no longer touch an
airplane. He sits there in the classes staring at sheets of paper with
cataracts of sheer human mortification over his eyes while the rest steal
looks at him . . . this man reduced to an ant, this untouchable, this poor
sonofabitch. And in what test had he been found wanting? Why, it
seemed to be nothing less than *manhood* itself. Naturally, this was
never mentioned, either. Yet there it was. *Manliness, manhood, manly
courage* . . . there was something ancient, primordial, irresistible about
the challenge of this stuff, no matter what a sophisticated and rational
age one might think he lived in.

Perhaps because it could not be talked about, the subject began to   9
take on superstitious and even mystical outlines. A man either had it or
he didn't! There was no such thing as having *most* of it. Moreover, it
could blow at any seam. One day a man would be ascending the pyramid at a terrific clip, and the next—bingo!—he would reach his own
limits in the most unexpected way. Conrad and Schirra met an Air Force
pilot who had had a great pal at Tyndall Air Force Base in Florida. This
man had been the budding ace of the training class; he had flown the
hottest fighter-style trainer, the T-38, like a dream; and then he began
the routine step of being checked out in the T-33. The T-33 was not
nearly as hot an aircraft as the T-38; it was essentially the old P-80 jet
fighter. It had an exceedingly small cockpit. The pilot could barely
move his shoulders. It was the sort of airplane of which everybody said,
"You don't get into it, you *wear* it." Once inside a T-33 cockpit this
man, this budding ace, developed claustrophobia of the most paralyz-
ing sort. He tried everything to overcome it. He even went to a psychiatrist, which was a serious mistake for a military officer if his superiors
learned of it. But nothing worked. He was shifted over to flying jet
transports, such as the C-135. Very demanding and necessary aircraft
they were, too, and he was still spoken of as an excellent pilot. But as
everyone knew—and, again, it was never explained in so many words—
only those who were assigned to fighter squadrons, the "fighter jocks,"
as they called each other with a self-satisfied irony, remained in the
true fraternity. Those assigned to transports were not humiliated like

washouts—*somebody* had to fly those planes—nevertheless, they, too, had been *left behind* for lack of the right stuff.

10   Or a man could go for a routine physical one fine day, feeling like a million dollars, and be grounded for *fallen arches.* It happened!—just like that! (And try raising them.) Or for breaking his wrist and losing only *part* of its mobility. Or for a minor deterioration of eyesight, or for any of hundreds of reasons that would make no difference to a man in an ordinary occupation. As a result all fighter jocks began looking upon doctors as their natural enemies. Going to see a flight surgeon was a no-gain proposition; a pilot could only hold his own or lose in the doctor's office. To be grounded for a medical reason was no humiliation, looked at objectively. But it was a humiliation, nonetheless!—for it meant you no longer had that indefinable, unutterable, integral stuff.

 USING THE DICTIONARY: Wolfe likes to dazzle his readers with a vocabulary ranging from slang (*moxie, washed out*) to allusions to distant history. What is the meaning and the source of each of the following examples? 1. *ineffable* (2) 2. *ziggurat* (2) 3. *anointed* (2) 4. *motif* (3) 5. *neophyte* (5) 6. *gyroscope* (5) 7. *élan* (5) 8. *virulent* (5) 9. *stoicism* (5) 10. *Gideon* (7) 11. *pariah* (7) 12. *mortification* (8) 13. *primordial* (8) 14. *mystical* (9) 15. *claustrophobia* (9)

THE WRITER'S AGENDA:

Tom Wolfe writes a highly charged prose that seems designed to dazzle, shock, impress, and entertain the reader. Answer the following questions about how he achieves these results in this selection.

1.   In the introductory paragraph, the author in a variety of ways alerts us to expect more than a literal-minded, uninitiated, unimaginative observer would see. How does he establish an *insider's* perspective; how does he create an air of mystery and importance?

2.   Though the author repeatedly says that "the right stuff" is indefinable and unutterable, he does define *key qualities* that are involved. What are they? How and where does he deal with them?

3.   Wolfe's dramatic account of *carrier landings* is a spectacular example of his colorful, emotion-charged kind of "action writing." How does he use his tools as a writer to create the desired dramatic effect? How does he use point of view, striking details, vivid language, striking comparisons? (Select two or three of the most striking sentences to read out loud.)

4. How does the final third of the essay drive home the idea of the *exclusiveness,* the select quality, of the group?

5. Wolfe often writes satirically, with a quick eye for what is cheap, gaudy, pretentious, or contradictory. What is his own *attitude* toward the trainees and the program they go through? Are we as readers expected to admire or glorify the people who have "the right stuff"? (Do *you* admire them? Why or why not?)

FOR DISCUSSION OR WRITING:

1. One of the oldest myths perpetuated by American popular entertainment is that of the lone rugged individual, facing danger and adventure. How do the space cowboys of popular science fiction use or adapt this myth? Is Wolfe's mystique of "the right stuff" in the same tradition?

2. At a time when women are joining the ranks of pilots and astronauts, is Wolfe's mystique of "manliness, manhood, manly courage" becoming obsolete?

3. The American tradition teaches us to believe in the worth of ordinary individuals, yet we are often asked to admire members of a highly competitive élite, like Wolfe's astronauts. Are these two tendencies opposed or contradictory? Which do you think is the stronger influence in American life?

4. Prepare a paper in which you explain what would be "the right stuff" for some other profession or calling: minister, teacher, lawyer, social worker, nurse, sales representative, or the like.

5. The astronauts became celebrities, with extensive media coverage of their private lives, personalities, and beliefs. What is the role of celebrities in the world of American media? What is their influence, or what needs do they serve? Are there different kinds?

6. Do a reportage in the Tom Wolfe style of some scene that is part of American popular culture: the rodeo, the gambling casino, the small-town parade, a prizefight, a beauty contest, or the like.

7. To judge from American popular entertainment, what are our current folk heroes? Are there several major recurrent types?

BACKGROUND: Pauline Kael was born in 1919 in a small farming community in northern California and did some of her earliest movie reviews for a listener-supported radio station in Berkeley. She grew up as part of a generation for whom Hollywood movies were the great folk art of the twentieth century. As she says in the selection that follows, she had the kind of memory that made her remember movies "in almost terrifying detail." She became one of the country's most influential movie critics, whose reviews in *The New Yorker* could rescue a movie from obscurity. Her movie criticism was collected in *I Lost It at the Movies* (1965), *Kiss Kiss Bang Bang* (1968), *Deeper into the Movies* (1973), and *When the Lights Go Down* (1980). One of her best-known pieces is "Raising Kane," a long account of the making of *Citizen Kane,* one of the great legendary Hollywood movies of the forties. First shown in 1941, it is admired by filmmakers for its technical mastery and kept alive by movie buffs as a cult movie. Its producer, Orson Welles, was an ambitious wonder-boy actor and director already notorious for his *War of the Worlds* radio broadcast, which his panicked listeners had taken for an actual report of a Martian invasion. *Citizen Kane* was an exposé, in the muckraking tradition, of William Randolph Hearst, reactionary press lord and king of yellow journalism, who held court in his imitation castle at San Simeon in California and hobnobbed with Presidents, screen stars, artists, and writers. Hearst fought the movie with threats, boycotts, and harassment. *Time* called it Hollywood's "greatest creation"; *Newsweek* called Welles, who played the press tycoon, "the best actor in the history of acting." In the movie, Hearst, thinly disguised, became "Citizen Kane"; Marion Davies, the Hollywood star who was Hearst's protégée, became Susan Alexander. Herman Mankiewicz, legendary alcoholic and "sacred monster" of the Hollywood era, wrote the script.

Pauline Kael

The Mass Audience
and *Citizen Kane*

GUIDE TO READING: In this excerpt from "Raising Kane," Kael focuses on the images that the mass media create for their popular audience. What do these images do to the people whom they supposedly represent? Study her account of the motives and effects of the publicity that Hearst created for the screen star whose career he sponsored. Study her account of how the movie catered to the expectations of the popular audience, how it followed the conventions of "popular melodrama."

ONE CAN sometimes hurt one's enemies, but that's nothing com- 1 pared to what one can do to one's friends. Marion Davies, living in the style of the royal courtesans with a man who couldn't marry her without messes and scandal (his wife, Millicent, had become a Catholic, and she had also given him five sons), was an easy target. Hearst and Louella Parsons had set her up for it, and she became the victim of *Citizen Kane.* In her best roles, Marion Davies was a spunky, funny, beautiful girl, and that's apparently what she *was* and why Hearst adored her. But, in his adoration, he insisted that the Hearst press over-publicize her and overpraise her constantly, and the public in general got wise. A typical Davies film would open with the theater ventilating system pouring attar of roses at the audience, or the theater would be specially redecorated, sometimes featuring posters that famous popular artists had done of her in the costumes of the picture. Charity functions of which she was the queen would be splashed all over the society pages, and the movie would be reviewed under eight-column head-lines. In the news section, Mayor Hylan of New York would be saying, *"When Knighthood Was in Flower* is unquestionably the greatest pic-ture I have even seen. . . . No person can afford to miss this great screen masterpiece," or *"Little Old New York* is unquestionably the greatest screen epic I have ever looked upon, and Marion Davies is the most versatile screen star ever cast in any part. The wide range of her stellar acting is something to marvel at. . . . Every man, woman and child in New York City ought to see this splendid picture. . . . I must pay my tribute to the geniuses in all lines who created such a masterpiece."

When the toadying and praise were already sickening, Hearst fell 2 for one of the dumbest smart con tricks of all time: A young movie reviewer named Louella O. Parsons, working for the *New York Tele-graph* for $110 a week, wrote a column saying that although Marion Davies' movies were properly publicized, the star herself wasn't publi-cized *enough.* Hearst fell for it and hired Parsons at $250 a week, and she began her profitable lifework of praising (and destroying) Marion Davies. Some of Davies' costume spectacles weren't bad—and she was generally charming in them—but the pictures didn't have to be bad for all the corrupt drumbeaters to turn the public's stomach. Other ac-tresses were pushed to stardom and were accepted. . . . Marion Davies had more talent than most of the reigning queens, but Hearst and Louella were too ostentatious, and they never let up. There was a steady march of headlines ("Marion Davies' Greatest Film Opens Tonight"); there were too many charity balls. The public can swallow just so much: her seventy-five-thousand-dollar fourteen-room mobile "bungalow" on the M-G-M lot, O.K.; the special carpet for alighting, no. Her pictures had to be forced on exhibitors, and Hearst spent so much on them that even when they did well, the cost frequently couldn't be recovered. One of his biographers reports a friend's saying to Hearst, "There's money in the movies," and Hearst's replying, "Yes. Mine."

3   Marion Davies was born in 1897, and, as a teen-ager, went right from the convent to the musical-comedy stage, where she put in two years as a dancer before Ziegfeld "glorified" her in the "Ziegfeld Follies of 1916." That was where William Randolph Hearst, already in his mid-fifties, spotted her. It is said, and may even be true, that he attended the "Follies" every night for eight weeks, buying two tickets— one for himself and the other for his hat—just "to gaze upon her." It is almost certainly true that from then "to the day of his death," as Adela Rogers St. Johns put it, "he wanted to know every minute where she was." Marion Davies entered movies in 1917, with *Runaway Romany,* which she also wrote, and then she began that really strange, unparalleled movie career. She had starred in about fifty pictures by the time she retired, in 1937—all under Hearst's aegis, and under his close personal supervision. (Leading men were afraid to kiss her; Hearst was always watching.) The pictures were all expensively produced, and most of them were financial failures. Marion Davies was a mimic and a parodist and a very original sort of comedienne, but though Hearst liked her to make him laugh at home, he wanted her to be a romantic maiden in the movies, and—what was irreconcilable with her talent— dignified. Like Susan, she was tutored, and he spent incredible sums on movies that would be the perfect setting for her. He appears to have been sincerely infatuated with her in old-fashioned, sentimental, ladylike roles; he loved to see her in ruffles on garden swings. But actresses didn't become public favorites in roles like those, and even if they could get by with them sometimes, they needed startling changes of pace to stay in public favor, and Hearst wouldn't let Marion Davies do anything "sordid."

4   To judge by what those who worked with her have said, she was thoroughly unpretentious, and was depressed by Hearst's taste in roles for her. She finally broke out of the costume cycle in the late twenties and did some funny pictures: *The Red Mill* (which Fatty Arbuckle, whom Hearst the moralizer had helped ruin, directed, under his new, satirical pseudonym, Will B. Goodrich), *The Fair Coed,* my childhood favorite *The Patsy,* and others. But even when she played in a slapstick parody of Gloria Swanson's career (*Show People,* in 1928), Hearst wouldn't let her do a custard-pie sequence, despite her own pleas and

those of the director, King Vidor, and the writer, Laurence Stallings. (King Vidor has described the conference that Louis B. Mayer called so that Vidor could make his case to Hearst for the plot necessity of the pie. "Presently, the great man rose and in a high-pitched voice said, 'King's right. But I'm right, too—because I'm not going to let Marion be hit in the face with a pie.'") She wanted to play Sadie Thompson in *Rain,* but he wouldn't hear of it, and the role went to Gloria Swanson (and made her a star all over again). When Marion Davies should have been playing hard-boiled, good-hearted blondes, Hearst's idea of a role for her was Elizabeth Barrett Browning in *The Barretts of Wimpole Street.*[1] When Thalberg reserved that one for *his* lady, Norma Shearer, Hearst, in 1934, indignantly left M-G-M and took his money and his "Cosmopolitan Pictures" label over to Warner Brothers. (The editors of his newspapers were instructed never again to mention Norma Shearer in print.) It was a long blighted career for an actress who might very well have become a big star on her own, and she finally recognized that with Hearst's help it was hopeless. By the time *Citizen Kane* came out, she had been in retirement for four years, but the sickening publicity had gone grinding on relentlessly, and, among the audiences at *Kane,* probably even those who remembered her as the charming, giddy comedienne of the late twenties no longer trusted their memories.

Mankiewicz, catering to the public, gave it the empty, stupid, no-talent blonde it wanted—the "confidential" backstairs view of the great gracious lady featured in the Hearst press. It was, though perhaps partly inadvertently, a much worse betrayal than if he'd made Susan more like Davies, because movie audiences assumed that Davies was a pathetic whiner like Susan Alexander, and Marion Davies was nailed to the cross of harmless stupidity and nothingness, which in high places is the worst joke of all.

Right from the start of movies, it was a convention that the rich were vulgarly acquisitive but were lonely and miserable and incapable of giving or receiving love. As a mass medium, movies have always soothed and consoled the public with the theme that the rich can buy everything except what counts—love. (The convention remains, having absorbed the *Dolce Vita* variation that the rich use each other sexually because they are incapable of love.) It was consistent with this popular view of the emptiness of the lives of the rich to make Susan Alexander a cartoon character; the movie reduces Hearst's love affair to an infatuation for a silly, ordinary nothing of a girl, as if everything in his life were synthetic, his passion vacuous, and the object of it a cipher. What

[1][The play is based on the love story of two famous British nineteenth-century poets, Robert Browning and his wife, Elizabeth Barrett, author of *Sonnets from the Portuguese* ("How do I love thee? Let me count the ways . . .").]

happened in Hearst's life was far more interesting: he took a beautiful, warm-hearted girl and made her the best-known kept woman in America and the butt of an infinity of dirty jokes, and he did it out of love and the blindness of love.

7   *Citizen Kane,* however, employs the simplification, so convenient to melodrama, that there is a unity between a man's private life and his public one. This simplification has enabled ambitious bad writers to make reputations as thinkers, and in the movies of the forties it was given a superficial plausibility by popular Freudianism. Hideous character defects traceable to childhood traumas explained just about anything the authors disapproved of. Mankiewicz certainly knew better, but as a screenwriter he dealt in ideas that had popular appeal. Hearst was a notorious anti-union, pro-Nazi Red-baiter, so Kane must have a miserable deformed childhood. He must be *wrecked* in infancy. It was a movie convention going back to silents that when you did a bio or a thesis picture you started with the principal characters as children and showed them to be miniature versions of their later characters. This convention almost invariably pleased audiences, because it also demonstrated the magic of movies—the kids so extraordinarily resembled the adult actors they would turn into. And it wasn't just makeup—they really did, having been searched out for that resemblance. (This is *possible* in theater, but it's rarely feasible.) That rather old-fashioned view of the predestination of character from childhood needed only a small injection of popular Freudianism to pass for new, and if you tucked in a trauma, you took care of the motivation for the later events. Since nothing very bad had happened to Hearst, Mankiewicz drew upon Little Orson Annie. He *orphaned* Kane, and used that to explain Hearst's career. (And, as Welles directed it, there's more real emotion and pain in the childhood separation sequence than in all the rest of the movie.)

8   Thus Kane was emotionally stunted. Offering personal emptiness as the explanation of Hearst's career really doesn't do much but feed the complacency of those liberals who are eager to believe that conservatives are "sick" (which is also how conservatives tend to see liberals). Liberals were willing to see this hollow-man explanation of Hearst as something much deeper than a cliché of popular melodrama, though the film's explaining his attempts to win public office and his empire-building and his art collecting by the childhood loss of maternal love is as unilluminating as the conservative conceit that Marx was a revolutionary because he hated his father. The point of the film becomes the cliché irony that although Hearst has everything materially, he has nothing humanly.

9   Quite by chance, I saw William Randolph Hearst once, when I was about nineteen. It was Father's Day, which sometimes falls on my birth-

day, and my escort bumped me into him on the dance floor. I can't remember whether it was at the Palace Hotel in San Francisco or at the St. Francis, and I can't remember the year, though it was probably 1938. But I remember Hearst in almost terrifying detail, with the kind of memory I generally have only for movies. He was dinner-dancing, just like us, except that his table was a large one. He was seated with Marion Davies and his sons with their wives or dates; obviously, it was a kind of family celebration. I had read the then current *Hearst, Lord of San Simeon* and Ferdinand Lundberg's *Imperial Hearst,* and probably almost everything else that was available about him, and I remember thinking, as I watched him, of Charles A. Beard's preface to the Lundberg book—that deliberately cruel premature "Farewell to William Randolph Hearst," with its tone of "He will depart loved by few and respected by none whose respect is worthy of respect. . . . None will be proud to do honor to his memory," and so on. You don't expect to bump into a man on the dance floor after you've been reading that sort of thing about him. It was like stumbling onto Caligula, and Hearst looked like a Roman emperor mixing with the commoners on a night out.[2] He was a huge man—six feet four or five—and he was old and heavy, and he moved slowly about the dance floor with *her.* He seemed like some prehistoric monster gliding among the couples, quietly majestic, towering over everyone; he had little, odd eyes, like a whale's, and they looked pulled down, sinking into his cheeks. Maybe I had just never seen anybody so massive and dignified and old *dancing,* and maybe it was that plus who he was, but I've never seen anyone else who seemed to incarnate power and solemnity as he did; he was frightening and he was impressive, almost as if he were wearing ceremonial robes of office. When he danced with Marion Davies, he was indifferent to everything else. They looked isolated and entranced together; this slow, huge dinosaur clung to the frowzy-looking aging blonde in what seemed to be a ritual performance. Joined together, they were as alone as the young dancing couple in the sky with diamonds in *Yellow Submarine.* Maybe they *were* that couple a few decades later, for they had an extraordinary romance—one that lasted thirty-two years—and they certainly had the diamonds (or *had* had them). He seemed unbelievably old to me that night, when he was probably about seventy-five; they were still together when he died, in 1951, at the age of eighty-eight.

The private pattern that was devised as a correlative (and possible 10
explanation) of Hearst's public role was false. Hearst didn't have any (recorded) early traumas. Marion Davies did have talent, and they were an extraordinarily devoted pair; far from leaving him, when he faced

---

[2][Caligula (12–41 A.D.) was a Roman emperor notorious for his excesses.]

bankruptcy she gave him her money and jewels and real estate, and even borrowed money to enable him to keep his newspapers. He was well loved, and *still* he was a dangerous demagogue. And, despite what Charles A. Beard said and what Dos Passos said, and despite the way Mankiewicz presented him in *Citizen Kane,* and all the rest, Hearst and his consort were hardly lonely, with all those writers around, and movie stars and directors, and Shaw, and Winston Churchill, and weekend parties with Marion Davies spiking teetotaller Calvin Coolidge's fruit punch (though only with liquor that came from fruit). Even Mrs. Luce came.[3] The pictures of Hearst on the walls at Time-Life might show him as an octopus, but who could resist an invitation? Nor did Hearst lose his attraction or his friends after he lost his *big* money. After San Simeon was stripped of its silver treasures, which were sold at auction in the thirties, the regal-party weekends were finished, but he still entertained, if less lavishly, at his smaller houses. Dos Passos played the same game as *Citizen Kane* when he wrote of Hearst "amid the relaxing adulations of screenstars, admen, screenwriters, publicitymen, columnists, millionaire editors"—suggesting that Hearst was surrounded by third-raters and sycophantic hirelings.[4] But the lists and the photographs of Hearst's guests tell another story. He had the one great, dazzling court of the first half of the twentieth century, and the statesmen and kings, the queens and duchesses at his table were as authentic as the writers and wits and great movie stars and directors. When one considers who even those screenwriters were, it's not surprising that Hearst wanted their company. Harold Ross must have wondered what drew his old friends there, for he came, too, escorted by Robert Benchley.

11   It is both a limitation and *in the nature of the appeal* of popular art that it constructs false, easy patterns. Like the blind-beggar-for-luck, *Kane* has a primitive appeal that is implicit in the conception. It tells the audience that fate or destiny or God or childhood trauma has already taken revenge on the wicked—that if the rich man had a good time he has suffered remorse, or, better still, that he hasn't really enjoyed himself at all. Before Mankiewicz began writing the script, he talked about what a great love story it would be—but who would buy tickets for a movie about a rich, powerful tycoon who also found true love?

---

[3] [Famous names from the world of publishing listed here as among Hearst's guests include Clare Boothe Luce, the playwright and wife of the founder of *Life* and *Time.* Harold Ross and Robert Benchley, mentioned later, were associated with *The New Yorker.*]

[4] [John Dos Passos (1869–1970), American depression-era novelist, included in his panoramic trilogy *U.S.A.* (1930–36) satirical portraits of the high and mighty.]

USING THE DICTIONARY: Pauline Kael's style appeals to readers who admire writers able to use the *whole range* of language—from the formal and sophisticated to the informal and popular. A. How does your dictionary label or deal with the following examples of **informal** language? 1. *get wise* (1) 2. *toady* (2) 3. *fall for* (2) 4. *dumb* (2) 5. *con trick* (2) 6. *swallow* (in the sense of "accept") (2) 7. *hard-boiled* (4) 8. *whiner* (5) 9. *bio* (7) 10. *kids* (7)

B. What is the meaning and origin of the following examples of **formal** language? 11. *courtesan* (1) 12. *attar* (1) 13. *stellar* (1) 14. *aegis* (3) 15. *parodist* (3) 16. *comedienne* (3) 17. *pseudonym* (4) 18. *cipher* (6) 19. *predestination* (7) 20. *trauma* (7) 21. *conceit* (8) 22. *incarnate* (9) 23. *correlative* (10) 24. *demagogue* (10) 25. *sycophantic* (10)

C. What are the sources of the following **allusions**? 26. *Freudian* (7) 27. *Little Orphan Annie* (7) 28. *Red-baiter* (8) 29. *Caligula* (9) 30. *Coolidge* (10).

THE WRITER'S AGENDA:

Pauline Kael writes as the knowing insider. She writes for readers who want the "inside story"—readers who are not taken in by surface effects and who are not swayed by simple partisan loyalties. She appeals strongly to her readers' sense of **irony**: She describes surface appearances, good intentions, and comfortable clichés and then contrasts them with the underlying realities, with disillusioning but also comic effect.

1. **A paradox** is a contradiction that we begin to understand upon further thought. Study Kael's account of the publicity engineered by Hearst for Marion Davies and of how he guided her career. How does Kael's account illustrate the paradox of *good intentions* and the unintended results we may achieve? Where or how does she sum up the paradox?

2. How does the author steer the *reactions of her readers* in this opening section of the essay? Where do her sympathies lie? Discuss striking examples of emotive or connotative language. Point out comic or disrespectful touches that appeal to the reader's sense of irony.

3. Kael writes as the insider, with much name-dropping—much **allusion** to names that read like a *Who's Who* of the early Hollywood era. Which of the following names still mean something to the general reader today? (Your instructor may ask you to do some biographical research on one of these.)

- Louella Parsons, gossip columnist

- Florence Ziegfeld, music-hall producer

- Fatty Arbuckle, center of a notorious Hollywood scandal

- Gloria Swanson, screen star

- King Vidor, Hollywood director

- Louis B. Mayer, legendary movie mogul

- Clare Boothe Luce, playwright and publisher

- Harold Ross, *New Yorker* editor

4.   Having introduced us to the real people on whose lives the movie was based, Kael in the second part of her essay turns to the *images* that the producer and director of the movie created of them on the screen. How, according to her, did the movie make its central characters conform to Hollywood conventions and to the clichés of "popular melodrama"? What was the role of "popular Freudianism"?

5.   What does the author's *personal memory* of Hearst and Davies add to her account? What details or phrases for you do most to set the **tone** of this part of the essay? What is its effect on the reader?

6.   The conclusion of the essay restates the author's central **thesis**. Where and how? Sum up how the rest of this essay has led up to and helped support her final point.

FOR DISCUSSION AND WRITING:

1.   For Kael, the central irony of *Citizen Kane* was that Hearst, who had trained a generation of reporters to "betray *anyone* for a story," became at last the victim of his own style of journalism." Show what she meant.

2.   What kind of person would be an ideal imaginary reader for Kael's essay? What would be the person's background, attitudes, expectations, taste? To what extent do *you* meet these qualifications?

3.   Do the conventions and clichés that Kael describes in this essay survive in the mass media today?

4.   Does the tradition of the **exposé**, of personal attack and exposure, survive in the mass media today? Examine prominent examples in detail.

5.   Movie reviewers and television critics often explore the relationship between image and reality. Study the treatment of this issue in

a group of reviews of Vietnam war movies, or of movie or television treatments of the Holocaust.

6. Do research on one of the great legendary early movies to answer the question: What was the secret of its audience appeal? What does it show about the tastes or expectations of the movie-going public? Choose a movie like *Birth of a Nation, Battleship Potemkin, The Jazz Singer, Ben Hur, Modern Times, Gone with the Wind, The Wizard of Oz,* or *The Blue Angel.*

For further discussion and writing: S. J. Perelman (1904–79) was a humorist who wrote for the Marx Brothers and for *The New Yorker* and whose zany commentaries on American popular culture were collected in many books. What advertisers' techniques are Perelman's targets in this parody? Do they survive in current television commercials, or have they been replaced by others? What would your aim and approach be in your own updated parody of current advertising? Or, what would you say in defense of the kind of advertising Perelman satirizes here?

S. J. Perelman

Choc-Nugs Are
Loaded with Energy

Scene: The combination cellar and playroom of the Bradley home in Pelham Manor. Mr. and Mrs. Bradley and their two children, Bobby and Susie, are grouped about their new automatic oil burner. They are all in faultless evening dress, including Rover, the family Airedale.

1 **Bobby:** Oh, Moms, I'm so glad you and Dads decided to install a Genfeedco automatic oil burner and air conditioner with the new self-ventilating screen flaps plus finger control! It is noiseless, cuts down heating bills, and makes the air we breathe richer in vita-ray particles!

2 **Susie:** Think of it! Actual experiments performed by trained engineers under filtered water prove that certain injurious poisons formerly found in cellars are actually cut down to thirty-four percent by switching to a Genfeedco!

3 **Mr. Bradley:** *(tonelessly)* Well, I suppose anything's better than a heap of slag at this end of the cellar.

4 **Mrs. Bradley:** Yes, and thanks to Buckleboard, the new triple-ply, satin-smooth, dirt-resisting wall plastic, we now have an ugly little playroom where we can sit and loathe each other in the evening.

Bobby: Hooray for Buckleboard! Since Dads made this feedbin into a playroom, no more hanging around the livery stable with questionable acquaintances! 5

Mr. Bradley: Yes, we now have a livery stable right in our own home. The initial expense was brutal, but the money only gathered two and a half per centum in the bank. 6

Bobby and Susie: *(munching candy bars)* Hooray! Hooray for this new taste sensation! 7

Mrs. Bradley: Harvey, I'm worried about the children. Don't you think they have too much energy? 8

Susie: Choc-Nugs are just *loaded* with energy, Moms! These crackly nuggets of purest Peruvian cocoa, speckled with full-flavored, rain-washed nut meats, call forth a chorus of "Yums" from every wide-awake girl and boy! 9

Bobby: In Mexico it's "Viva el Choc-Nugo!" but in America it's "Hooray for Choc-Nugs!" Any way you pronounce it, it is pronounced "Goodylicious" by millions of eager, happy candy-lovers! 10

Mr. Bradley: I see that I have fathered a couple of Yahoos. . . . Bobby, answer the door. 11

Bobby: Had we installed a set of Zings, the new electric chime, it would not be necessary for callers to wait outside in the rain and sleet. . . . 12

Mr. Bradley: Answer the door or I will knock your block off, you little saw-toothed ape. *(Bobby goes to door, admits Mr. and Mrs. Fletcher and their three children, attired in long balbriggan underwear. General greetings.)* 13

Mrs. Fletcher: Don't mind us, Verna, we just dropped in to sneer at your towels. *(unfolding a towel)* My, they're so absorbent and fluffy, aren't they? You know, they're made of selected fibers culled from high-grade flat-tailed Montana sheep subject to rigid inspection by qualified sheep inspectors. 14

Mrs. Bradley: *(listlessly)* They fall apart in two days, but we got tired of using blotters. 15

Mrs. Fletcher: Verna, I think it's about time you and I had a heart-to-heart talk about your skin. You're as rough and scaly as an old piece of birch bark. 16

Mrs. Bradley: I know; it's my own fault. I neglected my usual beauty cocktail. 17

Mrs. Fletcher: Skins, you know, are divided into three types—cameo, butterscotch, and mock nutria. Yours defies classification. 18

Mrs. Bradley: *(miserably)* Oh, how can I win back my Prince Charming? 19

Mrs. Fletcher: Why not follow the example of glamorous Mrs. Barney Kessler, socially prominent matron of the Main Line? 20

Mrs. Bradley: What does she do? 21

Mrs. Fletcher: Each morning, on rising, she scrubs her skin with an 22 ordinary sink-brush. Then she gently pats in any good brand of vanishing cream until Kessler disappears to his office.

23 **Mrs. Bradley**: And then?

24 **Mrs. Fletcher**: I can't remember, but she's got a complexion like a young girl.

25 **Mr. Fletcher**: Say, Harvey, make this test for yourself. Do some brands of pipe tobacco irritate your tongue, cause your eyeballs to capsize in your head? Then pack your old briar with velvety Pocahontas Mixture and know true smoke-ease. After all, you have to put something into your pipe. You can't just sit there like a bump on a log.

26 **Mr. Bradley**: I get along all right smoking old leaves from my lawn.

27 **Mr. Fletcher**: Yes, but look at the fancy tin these people give you. Remember that five hundred of these tins and a fifty-word essay on "Early Kentish Brass Rubbings" entitle you to the Pocahontas Mixture vacation offer, whereby you retire at sixty with most of your faculties impaired.

28 **Mrs. Fletcher**: Er—Fred, don't you think it's time we. . .

29 **Mr. Fletcher**: Now, Harriet, don't interrupt. Can't you see I'm talking to Harvey Bradley?

30 **Mrs. Fletcher**: *(timidly)* I know, but there seems to be about two feet of water in this cellar and it's rising steadily.

31 **Mr. Bradley**: *(sheepishly)* I guess I should have specified Sumwenco Super-Annealed Brass Pipe throughout. My contractor warned me at the time.

32 **Mr. Fletcher**: *(bailing like mad with his tin)* Well, this is a pretty how-do-you-do.

33 **Mrs. Bradley**: *(comfortably)* At least, whatever else happens, under the Central American Mutual Perpetual Amortizational Group Insurance Plan our loved ones need not be reduced to penury.

34 **Mrs. Fletcher**: What good is that? Our loved ones are right here with us!

35 **Mr. Bradley**: *(mildly)* You don't tell me.

36 **Mrs. Bradley**: I always say the added protection is worth the difference, don't you, Harvey? *(She pats her husband's shoulder reassuringly as they all drown like rats in a trap.)*

U N I T   1 2

HISTORY:
Common Causes

The Common Theme: We expect writing on historical subjects to rise above partisan propaganda. We expect it to rise above the passions of the moment to get at a more objective and more lasting truth. Nevertheless, much writing on historical subjects aims at an audience that is expected to share the writer's commitments or basic goals. The people we turn to for eyewitness reports of historic events are often not detached observers but people who were involved. They are often setting down for the record something that had for them an intense personal meaning. Other writers look back at past events to reaffirm a sense of common purpose, to relive moments when they experienced the sense of solidarity that comes from a shared commitment to a common cause. Other writers write about the past in order to raise voices of warning, trying to make us learn the lessons taught by past experience. The writers in this unit are committed writers who expect the audience to identify with a common cause.

+——————— WRITER'S GUIDE 12: ———————+
Using and Documenting Sources

How does a writer become an authority on a subject? We consider a writer an authority who has made a careful study of a subject, has explored its history, is familiar with different approaches, and can give balanced, considered answers to difficult questions. We feel confident that the writer has turned for information to people who should know or who have made the effort to find out. We feel that the writer has taken seriously views different from his or her own and has explored the pros and cons of open issues.

Authoritative writing is at the opposite end of the spectrum from writing that relies on the author's own superficial impressions or preconceived opinions. The author knows how to draw on different sources of information and ideas. When we want to stake out a claim as an authority on a subject, we will often follow the conventions of a **documented** paper—a paper that draws on a variety of sources and clearly identifies these for the reader.

Whether in a short research report or in a full-length research paper, we follow the conventions of the documented paper when the origin of our facts, the credibility of our information, and the validity of our judgments are major issues. In a documented paper, we clearly mark all quoted material. We clearly show the sources of facts or opinions borrowed or adapted from other writers. We give exact information about the who, what, where, and when of published material in **footnotes** (or end notes), and often again in a final **bibliography** (an alphabetical list of sources).

Remember the following guidelines when writing a documented paper based on your systematic study of a range of relevant material:

(1) *Clearly identify your sources.* When you draw on a variety of printed sources, make clear to your readers who said what. Provide clear answers to questions like the following: "How do we know this? Where does this material come from? Who said this—when and where?"

The following examples show how Langston Hughes identifies sources in different parts of his biography of Harriet Tubman:

Early biography	A number of books have been written about her. The first one, *Scenes in the Life of Harriet Tubman,* by Sarah H. Bradford, appeared in 1869. . . .
Contemporary historian	And at the great public meetings of the North, as the Negro historian William Wells Brown wrote in

1854, "all who frequented anti-slavery conventions, lectures, picnics, and fairs, could not fail to have seen a black woman of medium size, . . ."

Contemporary newspaper report

As reported by the Boston *Commonwealth*, for July 10, 1863, they "under the guidance of a black woman, dashed into the enemy's country, struck a bold and effective blow, destroying millions of dollars' worth of commissary stores, . . ."

—Langston Hughes, "Harriet Tubman, the Moses of Her People"

The following examples show how the author of a research paper on censorship might identify sources of information:

Authoritative study

Efforts to ban books in public libraries and schools doubled in number during this decade, as author L. C. Woods documents in *A Decade of Censorship in America: The Threat to Classrooms and Libraries*. . . .

Authoritative professional organization

The upsurge in book banning continues, one reason being that some two hundred local, state, and national organizations now take part in skirmishes over the contents of books circulating under public auspices. The American Library Association, which has been reporting an almost annual increase in censorship pressures, has just totaled up the score for the past year. . . .

(2) *Use a variety of techniques for reproducing material from your sources.* As you read and take notes, identify the material that you are going to adapt for your own use. Remember the most basic rule: Identify as a quotation anything that you copy verbatim, word for word, from a printed source. Identify clearly the origin of information and ideas that you put in your own words, so that you can later give credit where it is due.

Make flexible, varied use of different ways of adapting material— ranging from extended direct quotation to a brief summary of an author's argument in your own words:

DIRECT QUOTATION—Quote word for word to make your account of what others have said authentic. Quote directly to show that you have gone to the actual source and studied it at first hand. However, use direct quotation selectively. Do not merely copy long, undigested, unevaluated passages. Quote a whole sentence or short passage when it sums up well an important idea, or when it shows well the author's stand on a controversial point. Similarly, quote verbatim when a statement shows well the spirit or tone of something you have read—when it shows well the author's indignation, wit, or gift for words. *Excerpt* longer passages when it seems especially important to reproduce ideas or arguments in the actual words used by the original author.

Study different uses of **direct quotation** in the following examples. (The raised footnote numerals would direct the reader to a note for the facts of publication and page numbers.)

♦ The following two passages quote the positions taken by two different authorities on a *debatable point.* The first shows the standard way of quoting a complete, self-contained short statement. (A colon could replace the comma that precedes the quotation.) The second passage shows the use of selected quoted phrases that become part of a larger sentence. (The person quoting has added an explanation to the quotation in square brackets.)

> William Labov, a noted linguist, once said about the use of black English, "It is the goal of most black Americans to acquire full control of the standard language without giving up their own culture."[1]

> James Baldwin once defended black English by saying it had added "vitality to the language," and even went so far as to label it a language in its own right, saying, "Language [i.e., black English] is a political instrument" and a "vivid and crucial key to identity."[2]

♦ The quotation in the following passage spells out a *central idea* in exceptionally graphic, vivid terms. (The person quoting has shortened the quotation and used three dots—an **ellipsis**—to show the omission.)

> In his 1973 attack on judicial sentencing, *Criminal Sentences: Law Without Order,* the distinguished federal judge Marvin E. Frankel claimed that in "the great majority of federal criminal cases . . . a defendant who comes up for sentencing has no way of knowing or reliably predicting whether he will walk out of the courtroom on probation, be locked up for a term of years that may consume the rest of his life, or something in between."[7]

♦ The following passage quotes a key section of a *legal document* used to justify an official decision:

Anticipating a protest against the dictionaries, Texas Education Commissioner Marlin Brockette stated that no works should be purchased that "present material which would cause embarrassing situations or interfere in the learning atmosphere in the classroom."[11] By quoting that section of the Texas textbook adoption proclamation, the commissioner justified the removal of five dictionaries from the purchase list. . . .

♦ The following passage reproduces as a **block quotation**—set off from the text, *no* quotation marks—a passage that shows the *characteristic language* of advocates of censorship:

Several organizations hailed the removal of the dictionaries from the Texas list as a major victory. Educational Research Analysts, which bills itself as the "nation's largest textbook review clearing house," noted:

God gave parents a number of victories. In Texas alone, the State Textbook Committee did a good job of selecting the best of the available books. Then, the State Commissioner of Education removed ten books, including the dictionaries with vulgar language and unreasonable definitions.[8]

♦ The following passage illustrates the way short, apt quotations are used to lend an *authentic touch* to much biographical and historical writing:

Encouraged by her sister-in-law to "write something that would make the whole nation feel what an accursed thing slavery is,"[4] Stowe began drawing from long-stored memories of her experience living in Cincinnati's "Little Africa" to write *Uncle Tom's Cabin.* While caring for her seven children, doing laundry, baking bread, mending clothes, and teaching a group of young women, she seized every odd moment to scribble her story on whatever was at hand, often brown wrapping paper. Eighteen months later, in 1852, Stowe's labors resulted in the publication of the book Lincoln said "made the big war."

—Judy Mednick, "The Right to Write," *California English*

SUMMARY AND PARAPHRASE—A paper drawing on several sources becomes unwieldy (and unreadable) when one long quotation merely follows another. Try not to quote big chunks of undigested material. Excerpt, summarize, explain. Anticipate the questions of the reader who asks: "What part of this is important? What am I supposed to make of this? Why is this in here?" Often you will **paraphrase** material—put it in your own words. This way you show that you have made the material your own. You can emphasize what is most important; you can condense and explain the material at the same time.

Here are some examples of how authors summarize or paraphrase material from their sources. Remember that in a documented paper summarized or paraphrased material will also have to be footnoted and credited to its source.

♦ A writer will often summarize *facts and figures* without direct quotation:

> Most writers have not led easy or comfortable lives. A recent survey of P.E.N., the international writers' organization, found that the annual median income from writing was $4,700, with 68 percent making under $10,000.[4]

♦ In the following passage, a writer summarizes a *researcher's findings*. Note that key terms taken directly from the original study appear in quotation marks:

> There is what Harvard psychologist Robert Rosenthal once called the "Pygmalion effect." In his now-classic study, he told teachers that certain randomly selected elementary school children were "intellectual bloomers" and would show great intellectual gains in the coming year. Sure enough, those children did indeed show gains compared with children not labeled "bloomers."[6]

♦ The following excerpts show how a writer has outlined for his readers major *steps in an argument* (in this case, arguments against the abolition of capital punishment):

> The case for abolition is popularly known. The other case less so, and (without wholeheartedly endorsing it) I give it as it was given recently to the Committee of the Judiciary of the House of Representatives by Professor Ernest van den Haag. . . . Mr. van den Haag, a professor of social philosophy at New York University, ambushed the most popular arguments of the abolitionists, taking no prisoners:
>
> (1) The business about the poor and the black suffering excessively from capital punishment is no argument against capital punishment. It is an argument against the *administration* of justice, not against the penalty. . . .
>
> (2) The argument that the death penalty is "unusual" is

circular. Capital punishment continues on the books of a majority of states, the people continue to sanction the concept of
capital punishment, and indeed capital sentences are routinely
handed down. What has made capital punishment "unusual" is
that the courts and, primarily, governors have intervened in the
process so as to collaborate in the frustration of the execution
of the law. . . .

(3) Capital punishment is cruel. That is a historical judgment. But the Constitution suggests that what must be pro-
scribed as cruel is (a) a particularly painful way of inflicting
death, or (b) a particularly undeserved death; and the death
penalty, as such, offends neither of these criteria. . . .

—William F. Buckley, Jr., *Execution Eve and Other
Contemporary Ballads*

(3) *Aim at a fair and balanced treatment of your sources.* Even
when you refer to a source only briefly, you are responsible for not
misrepresenting the author's intentions or point of view. Quote from
others as you would have them quote from you: Do not take a quotation
out of context. When you argue with an author's opinions at length, or
when you evaluate an author's claims or contribution, fair treatment of
your source becomes a major issue.

Show that you are the kind of reader who can be trusted to give a
balanced accounting of what others have said. Show that you have identified an author's point of view, that you have traced the major steps in
an argument, and that you have noted key examples. When you disagree, do not just dismiss or brush off unwelcome data or an opposing
view. Do not seem to be pouncing on a single weak link in an extended
argument. You show that you take opposing views seriously when you
present counterexamples and careful counterarguments of your own.

The following examples show how writers try to do justice to a
major source, regardless of whether they agree with it. Notice the mix
of summary, paraphrase, and direct quotation in the following discussion of a book:

Source identified	It is instructive to go back to the late 1950s and read *Seventeen* magazine, or *Mademoiselle,* or such an etiquette book as *On Becoming a Woman,* by Mary McGee Williams and Irene Kane, which went through 17 printings and sold hundreds of thousands of copies.
MAIN IDEA	Throughout the book, the assumption reigned that marriage and motherhood were every woman's sole destiny and reason for existence. The book con-

Key example

Quoted title

Key example
with quote

Key quote

tained lists of things girls were supposed to do to please their adolescent dates. There was no suggestion that the boy had to please the girl. She was supposed to steer the conversation toward automobile engines, baseball, and such subjects, and defer to his interests and knowledge. A typical chapter is called "It's Not Too Soon to Dream of Marriage."

The image of the desirable girl was almost entirely a passive one. Under no circumstances was a girl to phone a boy and ask him out. "In dating, like dancing," we read, "a boy likes to take the lead: a girl's role, traditionally, is to follow." On a dinner date, the girl was supposed to tell the boy her choices and he would tell the waiter.

Chastity was also a constant theme. "Boys," we read, "will only respect you if you say no."

—Jeffrey Hart, "The 1950's," *National Review*

The following example shows how a writer combines summary or explanation of a historical study with an evaluation of its importance, going on to register partial disagreement with its findings:

Conventional
account

New finding

Outline of
major sections

Partial dissent

Michael Bliss, a historian at the University of Toronto, has investigated the university's most famous achievement, the discovery of insulin in 1922. According to the conventional account, insulin was discovered by two neophyte medical researchers, Frederick Banting and Charles Best. They succeeded where others failed, goes this version, because . . .

By reconstructing the course of the experiments day by day and dog by dog, Bliss has provided an intriguing vignette of the process of discovery at work. Perhaps his most remarkable finding is that almost everything Banting and Best did was probably wrong. . . .

Bliss's careful study delineates the different contributions made by the four leading players in the discovery. Banting, the central character. . . .

It's possible to disagree, however, with Bliss's contention that the Nobel Foundation was right to give its award to Macleod and Banting alone. . . .

—Nicholas Wade, "A Scientific Quest,"
The New Republic

(4) *Establish fruitful connections between your different sources.*

When we seriously explore a range of sources, we find it impossible to adopt ready-made conclusions, presenting them in a familiar pattern. Instead, we encounter different points of view, authorities drawing on different sources of information, confident assertions clashing with strongly voiced doubts. Our task is to find areas of agreement and disagreement. Our challenge is to weigh differing testimony and to reconcile conflicting views.

In a paragraph like the following, a writer brings together evidence and testimony from several different sources to support a *general conclusion:*

General point   American women who were successful writers often had to overcome incredible opposition and discouragement. When Phillis Wheatley, a freed Negro slave, published her *Poems on Various Subjects, Religious and Moral,* there was widespread skepticism about her being the true author. She was subjected to a public examination to test her knowledge

First source   of the Bible and of Latin and Greek. Her examiners signed a document, included in the 1773 edition of her poems, which concluded that "Phillis, a young Negro girl, who but a few years since was brought an uncultivated barbarian from Africa" was qualified to

Second source   have written the poems.[11] Louisa May Alcott, the author of *Little Women,* became a published playwright at 16, but only because, in her own words, "a certain editor labored under the delusion that the

Third source   writer was a man."[12] In her autobiography, *The Living of Charlotte Perkins Gilman,* the author describes a consultation with a nerve specialist who told her to end all intellectual activity, never to "touch pen, brush, or pencil," as long as she lived.[13]

Often our task is to line up *conflicting* views for comparison and contrast. For instance, we may find that authorities on the subject of prison reform differ widely on the nature and practicality of rehabilitation as an aim of imprisonment. The conclusions we reach as we weigh their conflicting testimony will help determine our general strategy. Perhaps we will first present the views of those who set up rehabilitation as the central goal of a humane correctional system. We will quote reports on promising experiments in helping convicts find a new self-identity or a new direction in life. We will show how idealistic proponents of reform see the benefits to the individuals concerned and to society at large.

However, we may then decide to give equal or more weight to the testimony of disillusioned observers. Merely by giving them the last word, we may already be tipping the balance in favor of a more "hard-nosed" realistic view. We may quote statistics on "repeaters" or "hard-core criminals" that dampen hopes for large-scale change. We may give space to skeptical accounts of "utopian" experimental programs.

Even more so than an ordinary expository paper, a paper drawing on a variety of sources needs a well-worked-out agenda that becomes clear to the reader early. The paper needs a clear overall plan that could be presented as a formal outline. It needs the transitional expressions and other links that take the reader from "on the one hand" to "on the other hand."

(5) *Document your sources fully to demonstrate your good faith as a writer.* Documented writing, whether on historical, political, or scientific subjects, has a "glass-house" effect: Readers are free to inspect the evidence. They are welcome to *verify* information—to go to the original sources and see for themselves. Documentation provides all necessary information about the *who, what, where,* and *when* of the sources consulted by the author.

FOOTNOTES—Footnotes (now usually **end notes** in typed manuscripts) give basic facts of publication, including the full name of the author and full title of the publication if these have not been given in the actual text of the paper. Study the following sampling of standard notes, directing the reader to the specific pages of the publications cited:

(Magazine article)

[2] Valerie Brooks, "Dancing Toward the Light," Saturday Review, March-Apr. 1983, p. 21.

(Magazine article with volume number—pages numbered consecutively during the year)

[7] Jake Page, "Inside the Sacred Hopi Homeland," National Geographic, 162 (Nov. 1982), 613.

(Newspaper article—unsigned)

[11] "Tiny Chip Could Revolutionize Electronic Age," San Francisco Examiner, 8 May 1983, Sec. E, p. 11.

(Book)

[4] Paul Fussell, The Great War and Modern Memory (New York: Oxford Univ. Press, 1975), p. 87.

(Book with subtitle)

[3] Barbara W. Tuchman, A Distant Mirror: The Calamitous 14th Century (New York: Ballantine, 1978), pp. 103-14.

(First and abbreviated second reference to a book)

[12] Aram Saroyan, Last Rites: The Death of William Saroyan (New York: William Morrow, 1982), p. 17.

[14] Saroyan, Rites, p. 77.

(Book edited or translated by other than original author)

[8] Toni Cade, ed., The Black Woman: An Anthology (New York: New American Library, 1970), p. 101.

[5] Bertolt Brecht, Mother Courage and Her Children, trans. Eric Bentley (New York: Grove Press, 1966), p. 25.

(Part of a collection)

[15] Roy Newquist, "Interview with Doris Lessing," in Woman as Writer, ed. Jeannette L. Webber and Joan Grumman (Boston: Houghton Mifflin, 1978), p. 82.

(Book that is one of several volumes)

[6] G. M. Trevelyan, History of England (Garden City, N.Y.: Doubleday, 1956), II, 81.

(Book in a new or revised edition)

[19] James M. McCrimmon, Writing with a Purpose, 7th ed. (Boston: Houghton Mifflin, 1980), p. 4.

BIBLIOGRAPHY—A bibliography is a list of sources arranged in alphabetical order. The typical entry starts with the last name of an author, or with the title in the case of an unsigned or anonymous article. Indenting and punctuation differ from those of footnotes. Inclusive page numbers replace specific page references for articles or other parts of larger publications. Sample entries:

(Magazine article)

Brooks, Valerie.   "Dancing Toward the Light."   Saturday Review,

     March-Apr. 1983, pp. 20-22.

(Magazine article with volume number)

Page, Jake.   "Inside the Sacred Hopi Homeland."   National

     Geographic, 162 (Nov. 1982), 607-29.

(Newspaper article—unsigned)

"Tiny Chip Could Revolutionize Electronic Age."   San Fran-

     cisco Examiner, 8 May 1983, Sec. E, pp. 11-12.

(Book)

Fussell, Paul.   The Great War and Modern Memory.   New York:

     Oxford Univ. Press, 1975.

(Book with subtitle)

Tuchman, Barbara W.   A Distant Mirror: The Calamitous 14th

     Century.   New York: Ballantine, 1978.

(Book edited or translated by other than original author)

Cade, Toni, ed.   The Black Woman: An Anthology. New York: New

     American Library, 1970.

Brecht, Bertolt.   Mother Courage and Her Children.   Trans.

     Eric Bentley.   New York: Grove Press, 1966.

(Part of a collection)

Newquist, Roy. "Interview with Doris Lessing." In <u>Woman as</u>

    <u>Writer</u>. Ed. Jeannette L. Webber and Joan Grumman.

    Boston: Houghton Mifflin, 1978.

(Book that is one of several volumes)

Trevelyan, G. M. <u>History of England</u>. Vol. II. Garden City,

    N.Y.: Doubleday, 1956.

(Book in a new or revised edition)

McCrimmon, James M. <u>Writing with a Purpose</u>. 7th ed. Boston:

    Houghton Mifflin, 1980.

Note: A bibliography is not always limited to sources a writer has actually cited. It may include additional sources for further reading or more detailed research.

To sum up: An authoritative study of a subject often draws on a variety of relevant sources. It brings in facts and figures from reliable studies. It weighs the conflicting opinions of experts. It may quote from current sources to show the range of popular opinion; it may piece together testimony from different sources to reconstruct historical events. When you draw on the work of other writers, you have to learn to choose material and put it to good use. You have to convince your audience that you have been a fair-minded, responsive reader. You have to show clearly your indebtedness to others, and you have to identify your sources in such a way that your readers can check them and see for themselves.

PREWRITING ACTIVITIES 12

1. The following brief passages are by writers who turn to the past in order to help us understand the issues and problems of the present. On the basis of these samples, what preliminary estimate would you form of their value as sources? What would you judge to be each writer's background, point of view, and purpose? How informative and how reliable would you expect the writing of each to be? How well ground-

ed would you expect each author's opinions to be in a knowledge of historical fact?

a. During the Grant administration, the grafting in the Indian appropriations was at its height, first in contract letting (pants that went to pieces like blotting paper in water, sugar that was half sand) and then through actual thievery by both the contractors and the agency employees. The resultant starvation fell with particular weight upon the Northern Cheyennes, always stepchildren of the hungry Sioux agency. Now they were thrust upon the most shaming dependence of all—upon the hospitality of their relatives, the Southern Cheyennes, with a cut below the appropriations that those people had last year just for themselves. But they were all helpless, as all the western tribes were helpless. Congress knew this and took the occasion to grow economical, cutting appropriations far below treaty stipulations, and with much encouragement from army contractors, who made millions out of all the starvation flights of 1877 and 1878.

—Mari Sandoz, *Cheyenne Autumn*

b. It is still women—about three million volunteers—who do most of this work in the American political world. The best any of them can hope for is the honor of being district or county vice-chairman, a kind of separate-but-equal position with which a woman is rewarded for years of faithful envelope stuffing and card-party organizing. In such a job, she gets a number of free trips to state and sometimes national meetings and conventions, where her role is supposed to be to vote the way her male chairman votes. When I tried to break out of that role in 1963 and run for the New York State Assembly seat from Brooklyn's Bedford-Stuyvesant, the resistance was bitter. From the start of that campaign, I faced undisguised hostility because of my sex.

But it was four years later, when I ran for Congress, that the question of my sex became a major issue. Among members of my own party, closed meetings were held to discuss ways of stopping me. My opponent, the famous civil-rights leader James Farmer, tried to project a black, masculine image; he toured the neighborhood with sound trucks filled with young men wearing Afro haircuts, dashikis, and beards. While the television crews ignored me, they were not aware of a very important statistic, which both I and my campaign manager, Wesley MacD. Holder, knew. In my district there are 2.5 wom-

en for every man registered to vote. And those women are organized—in PTAs, church societies, card clubs, and other social
and service groups. I went to them and asked their help.

—Shirley Chisholm, "A Visiting Feminine Eye," *McCall's*

   c. The Mexican-American can*not* relate to the eastern sea-
board experience of the "founding fathers," the bases of which
are *England and northern Europe.* Mexican-Americans, because of their Indian heritage, are *indigenous* to their area. Up
to 1821 their history is the *colonial history of the Spanish Empire;* from 1821 to 1848 it becomes the history of the Mexican
nation, Mexico having achieved independence from Spain in
1821. From 1848 to the present time the history of the Mexican
people is unique: their cultural and social history having been
a bi-cultural experience differentiates the Mexican-Americans
from the Mexicans raised *south* of the border.

   Furthermore, in terms of political history, the Mexican-
Americans have had little to say; and, except as spectators, they
have not been permitted to become involved in the building of
the political history of the United States of America. What has
occurred has been affected by the fact that the border set up
under the Treaty of Guadalupe-Hidalgo (and later changed
somewhat by the Gadsden Purchase) has been but a *political*
border and not a *cultural* border.

   The movement of the people north from Mexico has continued to be more a *migration* than an *immigration.* The border has been and continues to be a very nebulous and mythical
one, especially as it relates to the social and cultural makeup,
for the continued migration north from Mexico has invalidated
the border as a cultural one. . . . No other group within the political or continental limits of the United States has received
the continued reinforcement of those elements that make for a
distinct people and culture (e.g., food, language, traditions,
music, etc.).

—Feliciano Rivera, "Toward a History of the Mexican-American," *A Guideline for the Study of the Mexican-American*

   2. Consulting the card catalog, the *Reader's Guide,* the *Book Review Digest,* or other sources, locate three articles and books that take
stock of the American involvement in Vietnam. Study each article (or
selected chapter from a book). Prepare a brief report on the perspective
adopted by each author, the nature of the writer's involvement, the
scope and purpose of the work, and the use of sources or personal
experience. Include several representative and instructive quotations
from each of the three works.

BACKGROUND: Maya Angelou (born 1928) has become widely known during her career as dancer, actress, teacher, writer, director, and producer. In her autobiographical *I Know Why the Caged Bird Sings* (1970), she told the story of her growing up as a Southern black girl determined to "defy the odds." She was born in St. Louis and spent much of her childhood in Stamps, Arkansas, where she attended a segregated school and where her grandmother had a general merchandising store that at the same time served as a social center for the black people living there. Angelou became a successful dancer and actress, and she performed in the musical *Porgy and Bess* when it was sponsored by the State Department on a twenty-two-nation tour. She worked for a time with Martin Luther King, Jr., for the Southern Christian Leadership Conference. She has written plays and screenplays and directed a television series on Africa. She has traveled widely, and she wrote newspaper columns while living in Ghana and Egypt. Her later autobiographical books include *Gather Together in My Name* (1974) and *The Heart of a Woman* (1981). In the following selection from *I Know Why the Caged Bird Sings,* the author has left the South to live in California with her mother. The situation confronting her tests her determination to overcome the traditional barriers in a young black woman's path.

Maya Angelou

Step Forward in the Car, Please

GUIDE TO READING: Angelou uses a single autobiographical episode to make her readers see and understand historical patterns of discrimination that might otherwise have remained hearsay and sociological abstraction. What actually happens in this selection—what are the "bare facts"? How does the author interpret what happens—what to her is the meaning of the experience? How does she expect her audience to react?

MY ROOM had all the cheeriness of a dungeon and the appeal of a tomb. It was going to be impossible to stay there, but leaving held no attraction for me, either. The answer came to me with the suddenness of a collision. I would go to work. Mother wouldn't be difficult to convince; after all, in school I was a year ahead of my grade and Mother was a firm believer in self-sufficiency. In fact, she's be pleased to think that I had that much gumption, that much of her in my character. (She liked to speak of herself as the original "do-it-yourself girl.")

Once I had settled on getting a job, all that remained was to decide which kind of job I was most fitted for. My intellectual pride had kept me from selecting typing, shorthand, or filing as subjects in school, so office work was ruled out. War plants and shipyards demanded birth certificates, and mine would reveal me to be fifteen, and ineligible for work. So the well-paying defense jobs were also out. Women had replaced men on the streetcars as conductors and motormen, and the thought of sailing up and down the hills of San Francisco in a dark-blue uniform, with a money changer at my belt, caught my fancy.

Mother was as easy as I had anticipated. The world was moving so fast, so much money was being made, so many people were dying in Guam, and Germany, that hordes of strangers became good friends overnight. Life was cheap and death entirely free. How could she have the time to think about my academic career?

To her question of what I planned to do, I replied that I would get a job on the streetcars. She rejected the proposal with: "They don't accept colored people on the streetcars."

I would like to claim an immediate fury which was followed by the noble determination to break the restricting tradition. But the truth is, my first reaction was one of disappointment. I'd pictured myself, dressed in a neat blue serge suit, my money changer swinging jauntily at my waist, and a cheery smile for the passengers which would make their own work day brighter.

From disappointment, I gradually ascended the emotional ladder to haughty indignation, and finally to that state of stubbornness where the mind is locked like the jaws of an enraged bulldog.

I would go to work on the streetcars and wear a blue serge suit. Mother gave me her support with one of her usual terse asides, "That's what you want to do? Then nothing beats a trial but a failure. Give it everything you've got. I've told you many times, 'Can't Do is like Don't Care.' Neither of them has a home."

Translated, that meant there was nothing a person can't do, and there should be nothing a human being didn't care about. It was the most positive encouragement I could have hoped for.

In the offices of the Market Street Railway Company, the receptionist seemed as surprised to see me there as I was surprised to find the interior dingy and drab. Somehow I had expected waxed surfaces and carpeted floors. If I had met no resistance, I might have decided against working for such a poor-mouth-looking concern. As it was, I explained that I had come to see about a job. She asked, was I sent by an agency, and when I replied that I was not, she told me they were only accepting applicants from agencies.

10   The classified pages of the morning papers had listed advertisements for motorettes and conductorettes and I reminded her of that. She gave me a face full of astonishment that my suspicious nature would not accept.

11   "I am applying for the job listed in this morning's *Chronicle* and I'd like to be presented to your personnel manager." While I spoke in supercilious accents, and looked at the room as if I had an oil well in my own backyard, my armpits were being pricked by millions of hot pointed needles. She saw her escape and dived into it.

12   "He's out. He's out for the day. You might call him tomorrow and if he's in, I'm sure you can see him." Then she swiveled her chair around on its rusty screws and with that I was supposed to be dismissed.

13   "May I ask his name?"

14   She half turned, acting surprised to find me still there.

15   "His name? Whose name?"

16   "Your personal manager."

17   We were firmly joined in the hypocrisy to play out the scene.

18   "The personnel manager? Oh, he's Mr. Cooper, but I'm not sure you'll find him here tomorrow. He's. . . Oh, but you can try."

19   "Thank you."

20   "You're welcome."

21   And I was out of the musty room and into the even mustier lobby. In the street I saw the receptionist and myself going faithfully through paces that were stale with familiarity, although I had never encountered that kind of situation before and, probably, neither had she. We were like actors who, knowing the play by heart, were still able to cry afresh over the old tragedies and laugh spontaneously at the comic situations.

22   The miserable little encounter had nothing to do with me, the me of me, any more than it had to do with that silly clerk. The incident was a recurring dream concocted years before by whites, and it eternally came back to haunt us all. The secretary and I were like people in a scene where, because of harm done by one ancestor to another, we were bound to duel to the death. (Also because the play must end somewhere.)

23   I went further than forgiving the clerk; I accepted her as a fellow victim of the same puppeteer.

24   On the streetcar, I put my fare into the box and the conductorette

looked at me with the usual hard eyes of white contempt. "Move into the car, please move on in the car." She patted her money changer.

Her Southern nasal accent sliced my meditation and I looked deep   25 into my thoughts. All lies, all comfortable lies. The receptionist was not innocent and neither was I. The whole charade we had played out in that waiting room had directly to do with me, black, and her, white.

I wouldn't move into the streetcar but stood on the ledge over the   26 conductor, glaring. My mind shouted so energetically that the announcement made my veins stand out, and my mouth tighten into a prune.

I WOULD HAVE THE JOB. I WOULD BE A CONDUCTORETTE   27 AND SLING A FULL MONEY CHANGER FROM MY BELT. I WOULD.

The next three weeks were a honeycomb of determination with   28 apertures for the days to go in and out. The Negro organizations to whom I appealed for support bounced me back and forth like a shuttlecock on a badminton court. Why did I insist on that particular job? Openings were going begging that paid nearly twice the money. The minor officials with whom I was able to win an audience thought me mad. Possibly I was.

Downtown San Francisco became alien and cold, and the streets I   29 had loved in a personal familiarity were unknown lanes that twisted with malicious intent. My trips to the streetcar office were of the frequency of a person on salary. The struggle expanded. I was no longer in conflict only with the Market Street Railway but with the marble lobby of the building which housed its offices, and elevators and their operators.

During this period of strain Mother and I began our first steps on   30 the long path toward mutual adult admiration. She never asked for reports and I didn't offer any details. But every morning she made breakfast, gave me carfare and lunch money, as if I were going to work. She comprehended that in the struggle lies the joy. That I was no glory seeker was obvious to her, and that I had to exhaust every possibility before giving in was also clear.

On my way out of the house one morning she said, "Life is going to   31 give you just what you put in it. Put your whole heart in everything you do, and pray, then you can wait." Another time she reminded me that "God helps those who help themselves." She had a store of aphorisms which she dished out as the occasion demanded. Strangely, as bored as I was with clichés, her inflection gave them something new, and set me thinking for a little while at least. Later when asked how I got my job, I was never able to say exactly. I only knew that one day, which was tiresomely like all the others before it, I sat in the Railway office, waiting to be interviewed. The receptionist called me to her desk and shuffled a bundle of paper to me. They were job application forms. She said they had to be filled out in triplicate. I had little time to wonder if I had won or not, for the standard questions reminded me of the necessity for lying. How old was I? List my previous jobs, starting from the last held and go backward to the first. How much money did I earn, and why did I leave the position? Give two references (not relatives). I kept my face blank (an old art) and wrote quickly the fable of Marguerite Johnson, aged nineteen, former companion and driver for Mrs. Annie Henderson (a White Lady) in Stamps, Arkansas.

32   I was given blood tests, aptitude tests, and physical coordination tests, then on a blissful day I was hired as the first Negro on the San Francisco streetcars.

33   Mother gave me the money to have my blue serge suit tailored, and I learned to fill out work cards, operate the money changer and punch transfers. The time crowded together and at an End of Days I was swinging on the back of the rackety trolley, smiling sweetly and persuading my charges to "step forward in the car, please."

34   For one whole semester the streetcars and I shimmied up and scooted down the sheer hills of San Francisco. I lost some of my need for the black ghetto's shielding-sponge quality, as I clanged and cleared my way down Market Street, with its honky-tonk homes for homeless sailors, past the quiet retreat of Golden Gate Park and along closed undwelled-in-looking dwellings of the Sunset District.

35   My work shifts were split so haphazardly that it was easy to believe that my superiors had chosen them maliciously. Upon mentioning my suspicions to Mother, she said, "Don't you worry about it. You ask for what you want, and you pay for what you get. And I'm going to show you that it ain't no trouble when you pack double."

36   She stayed awake to drive me out to the car barn at four-thirty in the mornings, or to pick me up when I was relieved just before dawn. Her awareness of life's perils convinced her that while I would be safe on the public conveyances, she "wasn't about to trust a taxi driver with her baby."

37   When the spring classes began, I resumed my commitment with formal education. I was so much wiser and older, so much more independent, with a bank account and clothes that I had bought for myself, that I was sure I had learned and earned the magic formula which would make me a part of the life my contemporaries led.

38   Not a bit of it. Within weeks, I realized that my schoolmates and I were on paths moving away from each other. They were concerned and excited over the approaching football games. They concentrated great interest on who was worthy of being student body president, and when the metal bands would be removed from their teeth, while I remembered conducting a streetcar in the uneven hours of the morning.

USING THE DICTIONARY: **Synonyms** are often near-synonyms. They overlap to an extent; a large *part* of the territory they cover is the same. In each of the following pairs of synonyms, the second word is the one used by the author. Check it in your dictionary. What does the word *add* to the meaning it shares with the synonym? 1. *prison—dungeon* (1) 2. *self-confidence—self-sufficiency* (1) 3. *unqualified—ineligible* (2) 4. *anger—indignation* (6) 5. *brief—terse* (7) 6. *superior—supercilious* (11) 7. *make up—concoct* (22) 8. *acting—charade* (25) 9. *strange—alien* (28)

THE WRITER'S AGENDA:

Maya Angelou's eyewitness account brings historical patterns of segregation and discrimination to life for her readers. The people in her account act out an old familiar story like characters playing their roles in an old familiar play. Answer the following questions:

1. What would be a dry, impersonal *factual summary* of the events, limited to the undisputed "bare facts"?

2. People often find it hard to *prove* charges of prejudice or discrimination. What do we learn in this selection about the excuses, roundabout ways, or subterfuges through which prejudice works?

3. What evidence is there in this account that the author is trying to be an honest witness, giving a *candid* account of her own contradictory reactions and mixed feelings? Discuss her reactions to and her explanations or rationalizations for what happens.

4. What are some of the things that give Angelou's writing its *inspirational* quality? What reminds us that she is not a dispassionate outside observer but a committed participant?

5. What is the *audience* today for the kind of writing that this selection represents? (Is it true that many people are tired of hearing about the problems of the past? Is it true that many people today prefer not to be always identified as members of a "minority"? Do you think white readers or members of other groups would imagine themselves in the author's shoes? Would their reaction be defensive or hostile?)

FOR DISCUSSION OR WRITING:

1. Is the kind of discrimination that Angelou encountered in her youth a thing of the past? Or do similar patterns of discrimination exist

in our society today? (Support your answer with detailed evidence from your observation, experience, or reading.)

2. Northerners are often accused of a smug, superior attitude toward historical patterns of race relations in the South. Teachers or intellectuals often pride themselves on their enlightened attitudes on questions of segregation or discrimination. Is it true that attitudes on questions of segregation or discrimination differ from region to region, group to group, situation to situation, social class to social class?

3. We are sometimes told that exploring the history of discrimination in the United States is "divisive." In order to promote racial harmony, we should look toward the future rather than the past. Is there something to be said for this point of view?

4. Recent decades have seen many efforts aimed at counteracting historical patterns of segregation in American society. How successful were these efforts? What were their goals and methods? Assume that you are preparing a documented paper on a topic like the following: equal opportunity legislation, open admissions programs, busing as a means of desegregating schools, Head Start or compensatory educational programs. As a preliminary exercise, use the *Reader's Guide* (and other periodical indexes if you wish) to find two magazine articles on one such topic. Choose articles that reach different conclusions or represent different points of view. For each article, prepare four or five sample **note cards**. Use a range of different note-taking techniques: direct quotation, partial paraphrase, summary of information.

5. In recent years, publishers have started to compensate for years of neglect by publishing much biographical material on outstanding representatives of minority groups. Assume that you are preparing a biographical paper devoted to one such figure. Using the card catalog and periodical indexes, prepare a short **bibliography** of promising sources. Follow conventional bibliography format. Include six or more items. (If possible, include one or more book-length biographical or autobiographical sources.) Choose a figure from the following list, or choose your own outstanding representative of a minority group:

César Chavez	Paul Robeson
Maya Angelou	José Antonio Villareal
N. Scott Momaday	Piri Thomas
James Weldon Johnson	Leontyne Price
Lorraine Hansberry	Marian Anderson
Richard Wright	Martin Luther King
Langston Hughes	Mahalia Jackson
Maxine Hong Kingston	James Baldwin

Simon J. Ortiz
Alice Walker
Harriet Tubman
Frederick Douglass
W. E. Burghardt DuBois

Alex Haley
Thurgood Marshall
Shirley Chisholm
Cicely Tyson
Ralph Ellison

BACKGROUND: William Strickland is a professor of political science at the University of Massachusetts at Amherst. He has served as vice-president of the Institute of the Black World (IBW) in Atlanta. In the article that follows, he invokes the names of black leaders who helped shape the thinking of black writers and scholars of his generation: Frederick Douglass, abolitionist and former slave, whose *The Life and Times of Frederick Douglass* was first published in 1881; W. E. Burghardt DuBois, who had written his doctoral dissertation at Harvard on *The Suppression of the African Slave Trade* and whose *The Souls of Black Folk* was first published in 1903; Malcolm X, whose *Autobiography,* written with Alex Haley, appeared in 1965; and Martin Luther King. This article was written twenty-five years after the famous *Brown v. Board of Education* decision in 1954, in which the U.S. Supreme Court ruled that racial segregation in the public schools was unconstitutional. This decision overturned the "separate but equal" doctrine that had been used to justify separate schools for white and black pupils during much of the century. Strickland's article was published in *The Black Scholar* in 1979. The notes that follow this article are those used by the author to identify his sources.

William Strickland

The Road Since *Brown*: The Americanization of the Race

GUIDE TO READING: What is the meaning of the *Brown* decision for the author as he looks back over a shared history of struggle and achievement? What is the basis of his criticism as he looks at what has happened to the civil rights movement since? What sources does he use, and how, to create a sense of a shared history and a common commitment or purpose?

1   ANY RETROSPECTIVE look at the *Brown* decision must also be a retrospective look at the black struggle which produced *Brown*—and then was forever changed by it. And the story of that linkage properly

begins not in Washington, D.C. in 1954, but in Clarendon County, South Carolina in 1949 with a minister-teacher named Joseph Albert DeLaine. It was Reverend J. A. DeLaine who rallied the black community of Clarendon to file suit against the racial discrimination of the Clarendon county public schools. And it was that South Carolina suit, consolidated with others from Delaware, Virginia, Kansas and Washington, D.C. by a consortium of attorneys headed by the NAACP's chief counsel, Thurgood Marshall, which was placed on the docket of the Supreme Court as *Oliver Brown et al v. Board of Education of Topeka.*

The *Brown* case, therefore, represents the legal dimension of the   2
black struggle against school segregation in the South. But this legal dimension should always be traced back to its real and nonlegal origins, to the life and death confrontation between black and white which the courtroom adversary relationship only faintly symbolizes. White retaliation against Reverend DeLaine, for example, illustrates what black plaintiffs had to endure:

> Before it was over, they fired him from the little schoolhouse at which he had taught for ten years. And they fired his wife and two of his sisters and a niece. And they sued him on trumped-up charges and convicted him in a kangaroo court and left him with a judgment that denied him credit from any bank. And they burned his home to the ground while the fire department stood around watching the flames consume the night. And they stoned the church at which he pastored. And fired shotgun shells at him out of the dark. But he was not Job and so he fired back and called the police who did not come and kept not coming. Then he fled, driving north at 85 miles an hour until he was across the state line. Soon after, they burned his church to the ground and charged him, for having shot back that night, with felonious assault with a deadly weapon, and so he became an official fugitive from justice. In time the governor of the state announced that they would not prosecute this minister who had caused all the trouble and said of him: Good riddance.[1]

And that was only part of the price paid for *Brown.*

In remembering *Brown* today, we must avoid the error of discon-   3
necting the decision from the struggle that made it all possible. For, at bottom, *Brown* was the result of "the willingness of black men and women to risk their jobs and land to sign affidavits, to challenge southern white officials, to place their seemingly frail lives against the entire weight of the South and the nation. It was this courage, determination and strength which finally *forced*... (emphasis mine) ... consider-

ation of the black demand that the white-controlled separate but un-
equal facilities be done away with."[2]

4   In fact, decisive as it was, black resistance was not the sole political
factor that contributed to the Supreme Court's decision re *Brown.* Cold
war politics was also a prime consideration. Thus, in arguing the Eisen-
hower administration's position before the court, then Attorney General Herbert Brownell urged the justices to be mindful of America's image abroad. He asked that "the separate but equal doctrine be stricken
down . . . (because) . . . it furnishes grist for the communist propaganda mills, and it raises doubt, even among friendly nations, as to the
intensity of our devotion to the democratic faith."[3]

5   In the decades since *Brown,* these less flattering realities have
been submerged under a mythology more self-serving to the system.
Instead of acknowledging the developments, domestic and international, which gave rise to the *Brown* decision, there has been an effort to
extol the white court and, by extension, the American legal system.
Such advocates neglect the fact that it was this same legal system which
made outlaws of freedom-fighters like Reverend DeLaine and which
legitimized the southern caste structure against which blacks were re-
belling in the first place. So, in recollecting the achievements of
Brown, we need to be conscious of the ways in which racism has
shrouded much of its essential meaning—conscious of the ways in
which our history has been expropriated in this instance, just as in past
instances the system has expropriated our labor and our lives.

6   But criticism of this kind is much more the perspective of the present than the past. On May 17, 1954, when the decision was announced,
most black people felt that the country, represented by its Supreme
Court, had joined our freedom struggle. It seemed a new era, one in
which America, like God, had come over to our side. (What was new, of
course, was that never before had we—who had been enslaved by law;
discriminated against by law; rendered landless, homeless, and lifeless
by law—ever had our cause so championed by American Law.) This
unexpected support had an immense psychological impact upon black
people. It seemed to affirm the moral tide of the struggle, and, consequently, it encouraged people to join the movement and push it beyond the merely legal frontiers.

7   So these mid-fifties were not times for looking gift administration
horses in the mouth. Black America took the Warren decision at its full
moral face value, jubilant that the American dream seemed to be coming true for blacks at last. It was a time of innocence and belief.

8   For it was our beliefs which made us strong and confident of ourselves, our struggle and our future. Indeed, the struggle was *about* and
for that future. And the future of the race for which these sacrifices and
many more were to be made was nothing more—but also nothing

less—than black children. That is the bedrock essence of *Brown*. It symbolized the determination of one generation that those who were to come after it would not be scarred and stunted by the racism of American society as they had been. People laid down their lives so that black children would not be denied.

Nor was this solely a southern commitment. James Baldwin, writing   9 to his fifteen-year-old nephew ten years after *Brown,* expressed the same concern from the vantage point of the black urban North:

> ... This innocent country set you down in a ghetto in which, in fact, it intended that you should perish ... You were born where you were born and faced the future that you faced because you were black and *for no other reason* ... (emphasis in original) ... The limits of your ambition were, thus, expected to be set forever. You were born into a society which spelled out with brutal clarity, and in as many ways as possible, that you were a worthless human being. You were not expected to aspire to excellence: you were expected to make peace with mediocrity.[4]

But "making peace with mediocrity" was precisely what black people, North and South, refused to do any longer. Instead, they rejected the constraints imposed upon them and moved to create a new black future.

Looking back then on the movement that produced *Brown,* it   10 seems self-evident that the source of our sacrifice and our determination was our commitment to one another, our ties to one another, our sense of racial kinship that was anchored in, but also transcended, specific ties of blood. We had imperfect but prevailing unity then between young and old, literate and illiterate, lawyer and layman, male and female, preachers and parishioners, fathers and daughters, sons and mothers. All were part of the upsurge that we called "the movement" and that is so difficult now to describe for those who were not there.

Many commentators have remarked on the differences between   11 those movement days and now. There are differences, but these differences are as much *in us* as *in the times.* We are different. Much less of a people; much more of a heterogeneous mass. Some call this progress. I call it the Americanization of the race. For the sense of community which one associates with the movement years is not simply romantic recollection. It *was* there, and it was detected by the more sensitive observers ... even the white ones.

Pat Watters, for instance, a former reporter and editor for the *Atlan-*   12 *ta Journal,* encountered this quality in Albany, Georgia, and he tried to describe it as best he could:

Why was it that most of America was unable to perceive and understand the real meaning of the movement? . . . This is the central question of my preoccupation with the movement; I return again and again to it and always find the same answer. That what I saw and felt that first day in Albany and through the years of the movement was *extra-cultural, beyond the normal limits of American culture* . . . that my inarticulateness back then and all the failure of the media and even art to convey what was happening in the movement can be accounted for in terms of this extra-cultural quality, because *the culture defines how those in it perceive reality* and their repertoire of response; that the culture also makes such definitions for itself and thereby limits alternatives for the way it will continue its shaping of itself and the people who live in it; that the southern movement, *in pushing beyond these limits, held forth alternatives which the culture was incapable of accepting and which, therefore, it actively resisted.*[5] (emphasis mine)

13   Of course, what Pat Watters calls *the* "culture" is really only white culture. It was white culture which found the press and substance of the black movement so antithetical to its own values that it resisted the movement "actively" and sometimes to the death. *We* were the unacceptable alternative, the other path America refused to follow or acknowledge. That was the essence of *Brown* and the essence of the whole movement: a challenge, not simply to the institutions of injustice, but also to the cultural heart of the nation.

14   What was the difference between black culture and white? Ours used to be both moral *and* materialist. (We are, after all, both black and American.) Theirs was only materialist. Throughout our history, the source of black strength has been that we approached America from a higher level of social and ethical criticism. That is the meaning of Du-Bois, Robeson, Martin, Douglass, Malcolm, et al. Our courage was wrapped in the conviction that we were right, and that conviction fortified black people to face dogs and guns and ropes and rapes for the cause. That is what made the movement, at its best, a movement of, by and for the people, a movement beyond egocentrism and beyond self-infatuation. Indeed, the movement was the people's art, their mode of expression, self-discovery and affirmation. That is what Pat Watters saw and marveled at and realized that it was somehow alien to the America that he knew:

Sometimes, covering events, crisis in the onward sweep of the southern Negro movement during its early, greatest days, I would lie in my motel bed, half asleep, half yet with senses heightened, and hear all night the echo in my mind of the singing in the church, that incomparable music. . . . *I can remember the feeling of being in the presence of something different in America, something awesomely portentous.* . . .[6] (emphasis mine)

Watters was right, of course. We were a singing people. We sang about our beliefs, and our beliefs inspired our songs. We sang, mostly, about our God and our freedom . . . "Woke up this morning with my mind stayed on Jesus . . . Woke up this morning with my mind stayed on freedom. . . . " It was all the same, and in that connection lay our moral edge. For if we were God's children, then none of these earthly devils could, finally, turn us around. Isn't that what ties together *Reverend* Oliver Brown, father of Linda, and *Reverend* J. A. DeLaine, good shepherd of his Clarendon County flock? They symbolize the two traditions, religion and struggle, which are inextricably bound up in the history of the race—traditions which we have now largely abandoned. Yet it was exactly in those traditions that our moral strength was to be found and it is their loss that accounts for much of our floundering today.

It takes no great genius to trace the gains of the recent past—now rapidly being reclaimed by white society—to the black struggle which created them. But we do not often consider how that movement was based on the social and political culture of black people. Where would Martin's dream have come from if not from the religious depths of black culture? And where would Malcolm's formidable debating style have come from if it had not been honed in the street culture of black Boston and Harlem? At the bottom of whatever political and economic progress we have made in recent history lies the question of black culture, the body of common assumptions, beliefs and traditions which clarify a people's identity and make possible its effective struggle for power. But when a people's culture erodes, where does its vision come from?

There is something different about the modern black man and woman. We are now rootless in a way we have never been before. We are individuals in new and unprecedented ways; more influenced, in some quarters, by sexual rather than racial identity; ignorant of our history; unthinking of our future; spoiled and mindless like the America we have come so much to resemble. But a people who believes that its history is irrelevant is a people on its way, at the very least, to cultural extinction.

The road since *Brown,* then, I would argue, has been a road from clarity to unclarity; from struggle to self-indulgence; from caring about

one another, especially the children, to indifference to all things outside ourselves. This is in contrast to the movement which was not an
organization but a community. Some called it "the beloved community." The destruction of that sense of community has produced this new
and pernicious individualism which characterizes present-day black
America. The race has never before been so fragmented without caring
about its fragmentation, never before so cut off from its past or so careless about its future. That is how much we have changed since the days
of *Brown* when we took responsibility ourselves for the continuity of
our history.

19   Reverend DeLaine and the others were simply being true to our
oldest tradition: seeking after freedom. They took it up, husbanded it
with their lives, and then passed it on to the new generation. And that
generation of high school and college students of the freedom rides
and sit-ins of the 1960s "were not really so new; for many of them were
the same children who had first run the gauntlets in the school struggles half a decade before." [7]

20   It was thus the children of *Brown* who took up the gauntlet, who
"confronted segregation and racism in all of its public bastions . . . in
the schools, restaurants, department stores, churches, swimming pools,
motels, bus and train depots and toilets. These students, some in their
early teens, *were about business, the struggle of their people,* and they
moved to seize and affirm black rights to all public facilities with their
own hands. Everywhere they wrote new definitions of black freedom
with their blood and scars. *Acting on behalf of all black people,* they
purchased a new access to the society we had helped to build." [8] (emphasis mine)

21   Some group, some element, in some region, has always heretofore
taken up the task of "acting in behalf of all black people." Sometimes
this was done formally, as a sacred trust; other times, as a dimly perceived obligation that simply overtook one in the living out of one's
everyday life. Always, though, there were some—enough—to take up
the fight in and for their time. But the ability to keep this tradition alive
rested upon one granite foundation: a cross-generational agreement
upon the meaning of our history and our experience in America. Now
this agreement is in tatters, and so is the tradition of black struggle
which was its offspring.

22   In the past, there were black schools, black churches and black
families to transmit the history which informed the sense of struggle.
Moreover, there was always the system itself, with its signs and symbols,
its atrocities and hypocrisies, to keep ever before us the fact that we
were a people set apart. Nowadays, however, with the disappearance of
the visible institutional structures of discrimination and segregation,

the task of transmitting information, of waking people up to reality, of preserving culture, of decoding untruths, is infinitely more difficult.

Who are we today, and where should we be going? No clear answers to these questions come from the black institutions of yesteryear. Now television, that is to say, America, has taken over the education of our young people, so that where blacks once spoke, as corny as it was, of "racial uplift," we now speak of "getting over." But this is an amoral concept. One gets over any way one can. Thus a curious inversion has taken place. The method now used to combat (make it, survive) in America is no longer ours, but America's own: unscrupulousness. But once one starts down that road, it cannot be contained within black/white relations alone. Lack of principles seeps over into our own cultural space, contaminating and poisoning relations which must be solid and honest to ensure the legitimate preservation—not to mention the prevailing—of the race. This concern, however, implies that *we as a people still feel the need to fight America, not for selfish ends, but because we believe that the American way is the western way of death.* [23]

Whether that will or belief is still in us is one of the key questions pressing against us out of the history of *Brown*. For if the material basis of our morality has been our experience as victims of racism, and our ties to the black church, land and folkways of the South, then where will the new moral center of black people come from as we become an even more Americanized people? [24]

It is ironic that one of the unforeseen consequences of *Brown* has been that the responsibility for the socialization of the race has passed over from our hands to the system's. I would argue, therefore, that the essence of the contemporary crisis, invisible but nevertheless real, lies precisely in the loss or enervation of our quintessential traditions of black history, red memory, and revolt. [25]

Notes

[1] Richard Kluger, *Simple Justice* (New York: Knopf, 1976), p. 3.

[2] Vincent Harding, "The Black Wedge in America: Struggle, Crisis and Hope, 1955–1975," *Black Scholar,* 7 (Dec. 1975), 29.

[3] John Hope Franklin, *From Slavery to Freedom: A History of American Negroes* (New York: Knopf, 1967), p. 556.

[4] James Baldwin, *The Fire Next Time* (New York: Dial, 1963), p. 21.

[5] Pat Watters, *Down-to Now* (New York: Pantheon, 1971), pp. 10–11.

[6] Watters, p. 3.

[7] Harding, p. 36.

[8] Harding, p. 37.

USING THE DICTIONARY: The author uses a number of **legal terms** or terms that have special uses or implications in a court of law. Explain how the following would be used in the discussion of legal matters current or past: 1. *consortium* (1) 2. *counsel* (1) 3. *docket* (1) 4. *adversary* (2) 5. *plaintiff* (2) 6. *felony* (2) 7. *prosecute* (2) 8. *affidavit* (3) 9. *caste* (5) 10. *expropriate* (5)

THE WRITER'S AGENDA:

The author uses the past to recall common sources of inspiration and to set up a standard by which to judge the present. Answer the following questions about the way he links the present and the past:

1. In his "retrospective look" at the *struggle* that led to the *Brown* decision, what for you are especially striking or significant details? Where does his account seem most objective or factual? Where does he most strongly appeal to a shared sense of commitment?

2. What account does William Strickland give of the *motives* or the dynamics of the legal system that produced the *Brown* decision? What is his view of American justice?

3. What is Strickland's *criticism* of "the Americanization of the race"? What assumptions does he make about the nature of the white majority culture?

4. Of the *sources* the author quotes, which for you add most to the authenticity and impact of his article? For what purposes does he use them, and how? (What is the contribution of the **block quotations** that he uses at strategic points?)

5. In the *concluding* paragraphs, what is the author's answer to his central question: "Who are we today, and where should we be going?"

FOR DISCUSSION OR WRITING:

1. What kind of reader would be the ideal audience for this article? How successful do you think the author is in creating a sense of solidarity in black readers? Do you think a white audience would be alienated or feel left out?

2. Discuss the author's claim that the *Brown* case was "a challenge, not simply to the institutions of injustice, but also to the cultural heart of the nation."

3. The author condemns the "pernicious individualism which characterizes present-day black America." Do you think his criticism is fair or justified?

4. Find a publication by one of the black leaders mentioned or cited in this article: W. E. B. DuBois, Frederick Douglass, Malcolm X, Martin Luther King, James Baldwin. Find a publication that throws light on the author's view of what it means to be black in white America or of what the future holds for black people. Prepare eight to ten note cards with material you could use in reporting on the author's point of view. Use a variety of techniques: quotation, paraphrase, summary.

5. Research another famous court case or legal battle that in the minds of many observers raised fundamental moral or political issues. Prepare a preliminary bibliography of six or more sources on one of the following: the Dreyfus case, the Salem witch trials, the Scopes trial, Sacco and Vanzetti, the Nuremberg trials, the Eichmann case, the Watergate hearings, the trial of Julius and Ethel Rosenberg, the Moscow purge trials, the Bakke case.

BACKGROUND: Jonathan Schell (born in New York in 1943) has been for many years a writer for *The New Yorker*. In 1976, he published *The Time of Illusion,* a study of the Nixon Presidency that has been described as likely to become "one of the classic accounts of the Vietnam-Watergate era." In 1982, Schell published a series of three long, painstakingly researched articles that challenged public apathy concerning the threat of nuclear war. He attacked the widespread refusal to think about the threat of a nuclear holocaust that could mean not only the end of modern civilization but the biological destruction of humanity. Schell said that the bare statistics about bomb yields and probable secondary effects tell us nothing about the human reality of nuclear destruction: "We seek a human truth and come up with a handful of figures." To give his readers a glimpse of that human truth, Schell in the following excerpt turns to the testimony of the survivors of the bombing of Hiroshima on August 6, 1945. Originally published in *The New Yorker,* Schell's articles were reprinted as a book (*The Fate of the Earth,* 1982) that stirred heated debate among friendly and hostile critics and succeeded in forcing us "to confront head on the nuclear peril in which we all find ourselves" (*The New York Times*).

Jonathan Schell

What Happened at Hiroshima

GUIDE TO READING: The following account brings together eyewitness accounts from different published sources. Why has the author chosen the quotations he presents? What does each contribute to the selection as a whole? What is the overall pattern in which the author has arranged these quoted materials? How well do they serve his overall purpose?

1   ON AUGUST 6, 1945, at 8:16 A.M., a fission bomb with a yield of twelve and a half kilotons was detonated about nineteen hundred feet above the central section of Hiroshima. By present-day standards, the bomb was a small one, and in today's arsenals it would be classed

among the merely tactical weapons. Nevertheless, it was large enough to transform a city of some three hundred and forty thousand people into hell in the space of a few seconds. "It is no exaggeration," the authors of *Hiroshima and Nagasaki* tell us, "to say that the whole city was ruined instantaneously." In that instant, tens of thousands of people were burned, blasted, and crushed to death. Other tens of thousands suffered injuries of every description or were doomed to die of radiation sickness. The center of the city was flattened, and every part of the city was damaged. The trunks of bamboo trees as far away as five miles from ground zero—the point on the ground directly under the center of the explosion—were charred. Almost half the trees within a mile and a quarter were knocked down. Windows nearly seventeen miles away were broken. Half an hour after the blast, fires set by the thermal pulse and by the collapse of the buildings began to coalesce into a firestorm, which lasted for six hours. Starting about 9 A.M. and lasting until late afternoon, a "black rain" generated by the bomb (otherwise, the day was fair) fell on the western portions of the city, carrying radioactive fallout from the blast to the ground. For four hours at midday, a violent whirlwind, born of the strange meteorological conditions produced by the explosion, further devastated the city. The number of people who were killed outright or who died of their injuries over the next three months is estimated to be a hundred and thirty thousand. Sixty-eight per cent of the buildings in the city were either completely destroyed or damaged beyond repair, and the center of the city was turned into a flat, rubble-strewn plain dotted with the ruins of a few of the sturdier buildings.

In the minutes after the detonation, the day grew dark, as heavy clouds of dust and smoke filled the air. A whole city had fallen in a moment, and in and under its ruins were its people. Among those still living, most were injured, and of these most were burned or had in some way been battered or had suffered both kinds of injury. Those within a mile and a quarter of ground zero had also been subjected to intense nuclear radiation, often in lethal doses. When people revived enough from their unconsciousness or shock to see what was happening around them, they found that where a second before there had been a city getting ready to go about its daily business on a peaceful, warm August morning, now there was a heap of debris and corpses and a stunned mass of injured humanity. But at first, as they awakened and tried to find their bearings in the gathering darkness, many felt cut off and alone. In a recent volume of recollections by survivors called *Unforgettable Fire,* in which the effects of the bombing are rendered in drawings as well as in words, Mrs. Haruko Ogasawara, a young girl on that August morning, recalls that she was at first knocked unconscious. She goes on to write:

3   How many seconds or minutes had passed I could not tell, but, regaining consciousness, I found myself lying on the ground covered with pieces of wood. When I stood up in a frantic effort to look around, there was darkness. Terribly frightened, I thought I was alone in a world of death, and groped for any light. My fear was so great I did not think anyone would truly understand. When I came to my senses, I found my clothes in shreds, and I was without my wooden sandals.

4   Soon cries of pain and cries for help from the wounded filled the air. Survivors heard the voices of their families and their friends calling out in the gloom. Mrs. Ogasawara writes:

5   Suddenly, I wondered what had happened to my mother and sister. My mother was then forty-five, and my sister five years old. When the darkness began to fade, I found that there was nothing around me. My house, the next door neighbor's house, and the next had all vanished. I was standing amid the ruins of my house. No one was around. It was quiet, very quiet—an eerie moment. I discovered my mother in a water tank. She had fainted. Crying out, "Mama, Mama," I shook her to bring her back to her senses. After coming to, my mother began to shout madly for my sister: "Eiko! Eiko!"

6   I wonder how much time had passed when there were cries of searches. Children were calling their parents' names, and parents were calling the names of their children. We were calling desperately for my sister and listening for her voice and looking to see her. Suddenly, Mother cried "Oh Eiko!" Four or five meters away, my sister's head was sticking out and was calling my mother. . . . Mother and I worked desperately to remove the plaster and pillars and pulled her out with great effort. Her body had turned purple from the bruises, and her arm was so badly wounded that we could have placed two fingers in the wound.

7   Others were less fortunate in their searches and rescue attempts. In *Unforgettable Fire,* a housewife describes a scene she saw:

8   A mother, driven half-mad while looking for her child, was calling his name. At last she found him. His head looked like a boiled octopus. His eyes were half-closed, and his mouth was white, pursed, and swollen.

9   Throughout the city, parents were discovering their wounded or dead children, and children were discovering their wounded or dead parents. Kikuno Segawa recalls seeing a little girl with her dead mother:

A woman who looked like an expectant mother was dead.   10
At her side, a girl of about three years of age brought some
water in an empty can she had found. She was trying to let her
mother drink from it.

The sight of people in extremities of suffering was ubiquitous.   11
Kinzo Nishida recalls:

> While taking my severely wounded wife out to the river-   12
> bank by the side of the hill of Nakahiro-machi, I was horrified,
> indeed, at the sight of a stark naked man standing in the rain
> with his eyeball in his palm. He looked to be in great pain, but
> there was nothing that I could do for him.

Many people were astonished by the sheer sudden absence of the   13
known world. The writer Yoko Ota later wrote:

> I just could not understand why our surroundings had   14
> changed so greatly in one instant. . . . I thought it might have
> been something which had nothing to do with the war—the
> collapse of the earth, which it was said would take place at the
> end of the world, and which I had read about as a child.

And a history professor who looked back at the city after the explo-   15
sion remarked later, "I saw that Hiroshima had disappeared."

As the fires sprang up in the ruins, many people, having found   16
injured family members and friends, were now forced to abandon them
to the flames or to lose their own lives in the firestorm. Those who left
children, husbands, wives, friends, and strangers to burn often found
these experiences the most awful of the entire ordeal. Mikio Inoue
describes how one man, a professor, came to abandon his wife:

> It was when I crossed Miyuki Bridge that I saw Professor   17
> Takenaka, standing at the foot of the bridge. He was almost
> naked, wearing nothing but shorts, and he had a ball of rice in
> his right hand. Beyond the streetcar line, the northern area was
> covered by red fire burning against the sky. Far away from the
> line, Ote-machi was also a sea of fire.
>
> That day, Professor Takenaka had not gone to Hiroshima   18
> University, and the A-bomb exploded when he was at home. He
> tried to rescue his wife, who was trapped under a roofbeam, but
> all his efforts were in vain. The fire was threatening him also.
> His wife pleaded, "Run away, dear!" He was forced to desert
> his wife and escape from the fire. He was now at the foot of
> Miyuki Bridge.
>
> But I wonder how he came to hold that ball of rice in his   19
> hand. His naked figure, standing there before the flames with

that ball of rice, looked to me as a symbol of the modest hopes of human beings.

20   In *Hiroshima,* John Hersey describes the flight of a group of German priests and their Japanese colleagues through a burning section of the city:

21   The street was cluttered with parts of houses that had slid into it, and with fallen telephone poles and wires. From every second or third house came the voices of people buried and abandoned, who invariably screamed, with formal politeness, *"Tasukete kure!* Help, if you please!" The priests recognized several ruins from which these cries came as the homes of friends, but because of the fire it was too late to help.

21   And thus it happened that throughout Hiroshima all the ties of affection and respect that join human beings to one another were being pulled and rent by the spreading firestorm. Soon processions of the injured—processions of a kind that had never been seen before in history—began to file away from the center of the city toward its outskirts. Most of the people suffered from burns, which had often blackened their skin or caused it to sag off them. A grocer who joined one of these processions has described them in an interview with Robert Jay Lifton which appears in his book *Death in Life:*

22   They held their arms bent [forward] . . . and their skin—not only on their hands but on their faces and bodies, too—hung down . . . . If there had been only one or two such people . . . perhaps I would not have had such a strong impression. But wherever I walked, I met these people . . . . Many of them died along the road. I can still picture them in my mind—like walking ghosts. They didn't look like people of this world.

23   The grocer also recalls that because of people's injuries "you couldn't tell whether you were looking at them from in front or in back." People found it impossible to recognize one another. A woman who at the time was a girl of thirteen, and suffered disfiguring burns on her face, has recalled, "My face was so distorted and changed that people couldn't tell who I was. After a while I could call others' names but they couldn't recognize me." In addition to being injured, many people were vomiting—an early symptom of radiation sickness. For many, horrifying and unreal events occurred in a chaotic jumble. In *Unforgettable Fire,* Torako Hironaka enumerates some of the things that she remembers:

1. Some burned work-clothes.
2. People crying for help with their heads, shoulders, or

the soles of their feet injured by fragments of broken window glass. Glass fragments were scattered everywhere.

3. [A woman] crying, saying "Aigo! Aigo!" (a Korean expression of sorrow).

4. A burning pine tree.

5. A naked woman.

6. Naked girls crying, "Stupid America!"

7. I was crouching in a puddle, for fear of being shot by a machine gun. My breasts were torn.

8. Burned down electric power lines.

9. A telephone pole had burned and fallen down.

10. A field of watermelons.

11. A dead horse.

12. What with dead cats, pigs, and people, it was just a hell on earth.

Physical collapse brought emotional and spiritual collapse with it. 24 The survivors were, on the whole, listless and stupefied. After the escapes, and the failures to escape, from the firestorm, a silence fell over the city and its remaining population. People suffered and died without speaking or otherwise making a sound. The processions of the injured, too, were soundless. Dr. Michihiko Hachiya has written in his book *Hiroshima Diary:*

Those who were able walked silently toward the suburbs in 25 the distant hills, their spirits broken, their initiative gone. When asked whence they had come, they pointed to the city and said, "That way," and when asked where they were going, pointed away from the city and said, "This way." They were so broken and confused that they moved and behaved like automatons.

Their reactions had astonished outsiders, who reported 26 with amazement the spectacle of long files of people holding stolidly to a narrow, rough path when close by was a smooth, easy road going in the same direction. The outsiders could not grasp the fact that they were witnessing the exodus of a people who walked in the realm of dreams.

Those who were still capable of action often acted in an absurd or 27 an insane way. Some of them energetically pursued tasks that had made sense in the intact Hiroshima of a few minutes before but were now utterly inappropriate. Hersey relates that the German priests were bent on bringing to safety a suitcase, containing diocesan accounts and a sum of money, that they had rescued from the fire and were carrying around with them through the burning city. And Dr. Lifton describes a young soldier's punctilious efforts to find and preserve the ashes of a burned military code book while people around him were screaming for help. Other people simply lost their minds. For example, when the German priests were escaping from the firestorm, one of them, Father Wilhelm Kleinsorge, carried on his back a Mr. Fukai, who kept saying that he wanted to remain where he was. When Father Kleinsorge finally put Mr. Fukai down, he started running. Hersey writes:

28   Father Kleinsorge shouted to a dozen soldiers, who were standing by the bridge, to stop him. As Father Kleinsorge started back to get Mr. Fukai, Father LaSalle called out, "Hurry! Don't waste time!" So Father Kleinsorge just requested the soldiers to take care of Mr. Fukai. They said they would, but the little, broken man got away from them, and the last the priests could see of him, he was running back toward the fire.

29   In the weeks after the bombing, many survivors began to notice the appearance of petechiae—small spots caused by hemorrhages—on their skin. These usually signalled the onset of the critical stage of radiation sickness. In the first stage, the victims characteristically vomited repeatedly, ran a fever, and developed an abnormal thirst. (The cry "Water! Water!" was one of the few sounds often heard in Hiroshima on the day of the bombing.) Then, after a few hours or days, there was a deceptively hopeful period of remission of symptoms, called the latency period, which lasted from about a week to about four weeks. Radiation attacks the reproductive function of cells, and those that reproduce most frequently are therefore the most vulnerable. Among these are the bone-marrow cells, which are responsible for the production of blood cells. During the latency period, the count of white blood cells, which are instrumental in fighting infections, and the count of platelets, which are instrumental in clotting, drop precipitously, so the body is poorly defended against infection and is liable to hemorrhaging. In the third, and final, stage, which may last for several weeks, the victim's hair may fall out and he may suffer from diarrhea and may bleed from the intestines, the mouth, or other parts of the body, and in the end he will either recover or die. Because the fireball of the Hiroshima bomb did not touch the ground, very little ground material was mixed with the fission products of the bomb, and therefore very little local fallout was generated. (What fallout there was descended in the black rain.) Therefore, the fatalities from radiation sickness were probably all caused by the initial nuclear radiation, and since this affected only people within a radius of a mile and a quarter of ground zero, most of the people who received lethal doses were killed more quickly by the thermal pulse and the blast wave. Thus, Hiroshima did not experience the mass radiation sickness that can be expected if a weapon is ground-

burst. Since the Nagasaki bomb was also burst in the air, the effect of widespread lethal fallout on large areas, causing the death by radiation sickness of whole populations in the hours, days, and weeks after the blast, is a form of nuclear horror that the world has not experienced.

In the months and years following the bombing of Hiroshima, after 30 radiation sickness had run its course and most of the injured had either died of their wounds or recovered from them, the inhabitants of the city began to learn that the exposure to radiation they had experienced would bring about a wide variety of illnesses, many of them lethal, throughout the lifetimes of those who had been exposed. An early sign that the harm from radiation was not restricted to radiation sickness came in the months immediately following the bombing, when people found that their reproductive organs had been temporarily harmed, with men experiencing sterility and women experiencing abnormalities in their menstrual cycles. Then, over the years, other illnesses, including cataracts of the eye and leukemia and other forms of cancer, began to appear in larger than normally expected numbers among the exposed population. In all these illnesses, correlations have been found between nearness to the explosion and incidence of the disease. Also, fetuses exposed to the bomb's radiation in utero exhibited abnormalities and developmental retardation. Those exposed within the mile-and-a-quarter radius were seven times as likely as unexposed fetuses to die in utero, and were also seven times as likely to die at birth or in infancy. Surviving children who were exposed in utero tended to be shorter and lighter than other children, and were more often mentally retarded. One of the most serious abnormalities caused by exposure to the bomb's radiation was microcephaly—abnormal smallness of the head, which is often accompanied by mental retardation. In one study, thirty-three cases of microcephaly were found among a hundred and sixty-nine children exposed in utero.

What happened at Hiroshima was less than a millionth part of a 31 holocaust at present levels of world nuclear armament. The more than millionfold difference amounts to more than a difference in magnitude; it is also a difference in kind. The authors of *Hiroshima and Nagasaki* observe that "an atomic bomb's massive destruction and indiscriminate slaughter involves the sweeping breakdown of all order and existence—in a word, the collapse of society itself," and that therefore "the essence of atomic destruction lies in the totality of its impact on man and society." This is true also of a holocaust, of course, except that the totalities in question are now not single cities but nations, ecosystems, and the earth's ecosphere. Yet with the exception of fallout, which was relatively light at Hiroshima and Nagasaki (because both the bombs were air-burst), the immediate devastation caused by today's bombs would be of a sort similar to the devastation in those cities. The immediate effects of a twenty-megaton bomb are not different in kind from those of a twelve-and-a-half-kiloton bomb; they are only more extensive. (The proportions of the effects do change greatly with yield, however. In small bombs, the effects of the initial nuclear radiation are important, because it strikes areas in which people might otherwise have remained alive, but in larger bombs—ones in the megaton range—the consequences of the initial nuclear radiation, whose range does not increase very much with yield, are negligible, because it strikes areas in which everyone will have already been burned or blasted to death.) In bursts of both weapons, for instance, there is a radius within which the thermal pulse can ignite newspapers: for the twelve-and-a-half-kiloton weapon, it is a little over two miles; for the twenty-megaton weapon, it is twenty-five miles. (Since there is no inherent limit on the size of a nuclear weapon, these figures can be increased indefinitely, subject only to the limitations imposed by the technical capacities of the bomb builder—and of the earth's capacity to absorb the blast. The Soviet Union, which has shown a liking for sheer size in so many of its undertakings, once detonated a sixty-megaton bomb.) Therefore, while the total effect of a holocaust is qualitatively different from the total effect of a single bomb, the experience of individual people in a holocaust would be, in the short term (and again excepting the presence of lethal fallout wherever the bombs were ground-burst), very much like the experience of individual people in Hiroshima. The Hiroshima people's experience, accordingly, is of much more than historical interest. It is a picture of what our whole world is always poised to become—a backdrop of scarcely imaginable horror lying just behind the surface of our normal life, and capable of breaking through into that normal life at any second. Whether we choose to think about it or not, it is an omnipresent, inescapable truth about our lives today that at every single moment each one of us may suddenly became the deranged mother looking for her burned child; the professor with the ball of rice in his hand whose wife has just told him "Run away, dear!" and died in the fires; Mr. Fukai running back into the firestorm; the naked man standing on the blasted plain that was his city, holding his eyeball in his hand; or, more likely, one of millions of corpses. For whatever our "modest hopes" as human beings may be, every one of them can be nullified by a nuclear holocaust.

 USING THE DICTIONARY: How up to date is your dictionary? What help, if any, does it give you with terms like the following? 1. *kiloton* (1) 2. *tactical weapons* (1) 3. *ground zero*

(1) 4. *thermal pulse* (1) 5. *fallout* (1) 6. *radiation* (1) 7. *holocaust* (17) 8. *megaton* (17) 9. *ecosphere* (17) 10. *ecosystem* (17)

THE WRITER'S AGENDA:

In this account, the author tries to put the unspeakable into words. Study the pattern that takes shape as he uses the survivors' testimony to recreate the physical and psychological impact of the events for his readers.

1. In the first paragraph, the author provides *facts and figures* about the explosion and its immediate results. Which of these would you include in a short "bare-facts" summary? Which of the facts and details included in this paragraph do most to make the catastrophe real in the reader's mind? Which sentence best sums up the author's central point?

2. The first seven or eight extensive quotations describe the *aftermath* of the explosion as experienced by the survivors. Why did the author choose these quotations from the many available ones? Are there any common threads in these survivors' testimonies?

3. In several paragraphs in the middle of the essay, the author tries to sum up the *emotional or psychological* impact that the nightmare events had on the survivors. What are some of his generalizations, and how are they supported?

4. Jonathan Schell begins the last third of this excerpt by discussing the *aftereffects* of the bombing. What are some details that make this section read more like matter-of-fact reporting than other parts of the essay? Why do you think the author chose to make this section more "factual" than earlier sections?

5. In the final paragraph, the author tries to sum up the human meaning of what happened in Hiroshima. What sentence for you best sums up his **thesis**?

6. An effective **conclusion** often comes full circle by taking up or pointing back to something the author introduced earlier in the essay. How does Schell's conclusion fit this pattern? What is its effect on the reader?

FOR DISCUSSION OR WRITING:

1. Several reviewers of Schell's books commented on our "compelling urge to forget" horrible truths, on our tendency to resist reminders

of unpleasant facts. What was your reaction as a reader as you read this selection? Did it change your thinking about Hiroshima or about the threat of nuclear war? What was your attitude toward the author and what he was trying to do?

2. To judge from your observation and reading, what are major attitudes, expectations, or rationalizations current in our society regarding the threat of nuclear war?

3. In their treatment of recent history, the mass media—movies, television, popular nonfiction books—reflect changing attitudes and intellectual fashions. Attitudes may change from remembrance to neglect, from condemnation to rehabilitation. Discuss the treatment in the media of a topic like the following: the Russian Revolution, the Holocaust, Pearl Harbor, Vietnam, Hitler, World War II, World War I. Discuss detailed examples.

4. Find full bibliographical information for as many of Schell's sources as you can. Prepare a Hiroshima bibliography, using these and other relevant sources that you encounter. (Include Schell's own work.) Be sure to check for author cards and title cards in the card catalog of your library. Use conventional bibliography format.

5. Prepare a bibliography for another topic from the annals of inhumanity: Auschwitz, My Lai, Cambodia, Andersonville, or other.

6. Have you had a chance to listen to, or do you have a chance to interview, eyewitnesses of some upheaval in recent history? Report and interpret the testimony of participants—veterans, refugees, survivors.

FOR FURTHER DISCUSSION AND WRITING: Mary Wollstonecraft (1759–97) was an early champion of women's rights. Virginia Woolf said of her that she was "in revolt all her life—against tyranny, against law, against convention" and that her life was "an attempt to make human conventions conform more closely to human needs." Wollstonecraft published her *Vindication of the Rights of Woman* in England in 1792. The American War of Independence and the French Revolution had overturned traditional institutions. Revolutionaries like Tom Paine, drawing on ideas of French intellectuals like Rousseau, were proclaiming a new order based on "Rights of Man." What are Wollstonecraft's main arguments in this excerpt? Does she anticipate arguments of modern advocates of women's rights? To what extent have attitudes and conventions changed? How much closer is modern society to Wollstonecraft's ideals?

Mary Wollstonecraft
The Rights of Woman

MEN COMPLAIN, and with reason, of the follies and caprices of our sex, when they do not keenly satirize our headstrong passions and grovelling vices. Behold, I should answer, the natural effect of ignorance! The mind will ever be unstable that has only prejudices to rest on, and the current will run with destructive fury when there are no barriers to break its force. Women are told from their infancy, and taught by the example of their mothers, that a little knowledge of human weakness, justly termed cunning, softness of temper, outward obedience, and a scrupulous attention to a puerile kind of propriety, will obtain for them the protection of man; and should they be beautiful, every thing else is needless, for at least twenty years of their lives. . . .

The most perfect education, in my opinion, is such an exercise of the understanding as is best calculated to strenghten the body and form the heart. Or, in other words, to enable the individual to attain such habits of virtue as will render it independent. In fact, it is a farce to call any being virtuous whose virtues do not result from the exercise of its own reason. This was Rousseau's opinion respecting men. I extend it to women and confidently assert that they have been drawn out of their sphere by false refinement, and not by an endeavor to acquire masculine qualities. Still the regal homage which they receive is so intoxicating that till the manners of the times are changed and formed on more reasonable principles, it may be impossible to convince them that the illegitimate power, which they obtain by degrading themselves, is a curse, and that they must return to nature and equality if they wish to secure the placid satisfaction that unsophisticated affections impart. But for this epoch we must wait—wait, perhaps, till kings and nobles, enlightened by reason, and, preferring the real dignity of man to childish state, throw off their gaudy hereditary trappings; and if then women do not resign the arbitrary power of beauty, they will prove that they have *less* mind than man. . . .

3   How much more respectable is the woman who earns her own bread by fulfilling any duty than the most accomplished beauty! Beauty did I say? So sensible am I of the beauty of moral loveliness, or the harmonious propriety that attunes the passions of a well-regulated mind, that I blush at making the comparison. Yet I sigh to think how few women aim at attaining this respectability by withdrawing from the giddy whirl of pleasure, or the indolent calm that stupefies the good sort of women it sucks in.

4   Proud of their weakness, however, they must always be protected, guarded from care and all the rough toils that dignify the mind. If this be the fiat of fate, if they will make themselves insignificant and contemptible, sweetly to waste "life away," let them not expect to be valued when their beauty fades, for it is the fate of the fairest flowers to be admired and pulled to pieces by the careless hand that plucked them. In how many ways do I wish, from the purest benevolence, to impress this truth on my sex! Yet I fear that they will not listen to a truth that dear-bought experience has brought home to many an agitated bosom, nor willingly resign the privileges of rank and sex for the privileges of humanity, to which those have no claim who do not discharge its duties.

5   Those writers are particularly useful, in my opinion, who make man feel for man, independent of the station he fills, or the drapery of factitious sentiments. I then would fain convince reasonable men of the importance of some of my remarks, and prevail on them to weigh dispassionately the whole tenor of my observations. I appeal to their understandings, and as a fellow creature claim, in the name of my sex, some interest in their hearts. I entreat them to assist to emancipate their companion, to make her a help meet for them!

6   Would men but generously snap our chains and be content with rational fellowship instead of slavish obedience, they would find us more observant daughters, more affectionate sisters, more faithful wives, more reasonable mothers—in a word, better citizens. We should then love them with true affection, because we should learn to respect ourselves.

U N I T   1 3

CLASSIC ESSAYS:
The Ideal Reader

The Common Theme: Today's bestsellers, we are often told, are written according to formula. They give the audience "what it wants"; they are conceived or commissioned by people who study the audience and exploit its weaknesses. This unit brings together classics of expository prose whose authors write according to the opposite principle. They write for an imaginary ideal reader—a reader, who, in the words of Virginia Woolf, becomes the author's "fellow-worker and accomplice." The authors in this unit differ widely in background or historical context. They range from George Eliot and Jonathan Swift to George Orwell and E. B. White. But these writers share a common faith in the reader's understanding and goodwill. They trust us as readers to appreciate shades of meaning, to think seriously about things that matter, and to use our imagination to look at familiar subjects in a new light. They cater to the highest common denominator; their essays show what they expect us as readers to be capable of when we are at our best.

WRITER'S GUIDE 13:
╈ ────────────────────────── ╈
The Elements of Style

Writing that has style carries its meaning exceptionally well. It makes things clear that were murky or confused. It gives us things to remember and to quote. It is a pleasure to read.

When writing has style, we read it with the pleasure that comes from seeing something difficult done well. The writer has learned to do skillfully and gracefully what people at first do laboriously, as if holding the pencil with both hands. Writing that has style is for readers who take pleasure in the right words, in the sentence that makes them feel like saying, "Well put!" or "Well said!" When writing lacks style, language becomes a barrier; reading becomes a series of false starts, detours, backtrackings, and delays.

Part of our pleasure in reading good writing comes from the *individual* style of an author. In reading someone like Mark Twain, we seem to hear the author's personal voice. We come to recognize the wit or the eloquence that is an author's trademark. But many features or elements of an effective style are found over and over in good prose. To make your own writing more readable and more effective, remember the following guidelines:

(1) *Speak your mind.* "Effectiveness of assertion," said the British playwright and essayist George Bernard Shaw, is the beginning and end of style. A basic test of effective style is our ability to speak up and make ourselves heard. Many successful writers reached a large audience not because they catered to popular opinion but because they knew how to take a stand. They knew how to go on record with their own strongly felt views. They knew how to make what matters stand out. We remember emphatic statements like the following:

> When a sixth of the population of a nation which has undertaken to be the refuge of liberty are slaves, . . . I think that it is not too soon for honest men to rebel and revolutionize. (Henry David Thoreau)

> Official war propaganda, with its disgusting hypocrisy and self-righteousness, tends to make thinking people sympathize with the enemy. (George Orwell)

> A society that thinks the choice between ways of living is just a choice between equally eligible "life-styles" turns universities into academic cafeterias offering junk food for the mind. (George F. Will)

The quality of strength lined with tenderness is an unbeatable combination, as are intelligence and necessity when unblunted by formal education. (Maya Angelou)

(2) *Use accurate words.* The right word does not merely give us "the general idea"; it gives us the right shade of meaning. A large vocabulary enables the writer to choose the word that carries just the right meaning and the right attitude. A good writer is fascinated by words—their history and their uses. As one writer said in objecting to overly "mechanical" words like *tools* or *retooling* when used about schools and education:

> A "tool" is an instrument of manual or mechanical operation, a machine for shaping metal, wood or other inanimate matter. One shapes, forms, or finishes with a *tool.* It is used, relating to human affairs, in a highly derogatory sense, as of a person used to accomplish another's ends; a dupe; a tyrant's *tool.* Used as a verb, it means to equip a plant or industry (for volume production, for instance). . . . But what are the "tools" with which one equips, shapes, forms or finishes a child, a youth, a human character, a human mind? (Dorothy Thompson)

Writers who care about words expect their readers to appreciate distinctions like the following:

> The way to be *safe* is never to be *secure.* (Benjamin Franklin)

> Rage cannot be *hidden;* it can only be *dissembled.* (James Baldwin)

> For the gifted young woman today, such a life . . . is not a *destiny* but a *fate.* (Mary McCarthy)

Such differences are partly in the **denotations** of words—what the words point to. But they are often also in the **connotations** of words—the attitudes or judgments they imply. A person who *toils* carries more of a burden than one who merely *works,* and makes more of a claim to our sympathy. A person who *squanders* an inheritance does so more recklessly and foolishly than one who *wastes* it. A *sword* suggests valor; a *dagger* suggests treachery. Often a single well-chosen word carries information and attitudes more effectively than a roundabout explanation.

(3) *Translate the abstract into the concrete.* Relate general ideas to

the world of sights and sounds. When we state general ideas, we necessarily abstract, or "draw away" from specific people and events. We move away from specifics in order to formulate something that is true for many different situations. But good writers never move away too far or for too long from what we can see and hear, what we can imagine and visualize. They resist "mere abstractions"—general words that have been cut loose from their roots in concrete reality. They have a knack of stating even general ideas in such a way that we can see what they mean in practice or in people's lives.

Passages like the following reassure us that, to their authors, words are not just words. The writers easily and naturally relate their general ideas to the world of everyday experience:

> The West begins *where the annual rainfall drops below twenty inches*. (Bernard DeVoto)

> The only natural force over which we have any control out here is water, and that only recently. In my memory California summers were characterized by *the coughing of the pipes that meant the well was dry*, and California winters by *all-night watches on rivers about to crest*, by *sandbagging*, by *dynamite on the levees and flooding on the first floor*. (Joan Didion)

Here is E. B. White writing about "freedom" at a time when fascism was on the march in Europe:

> In this land the citizens are still invited . . . to talk politics with their neighbors without wondering whether the secret police are listening, to exchange ideas as well as goods, to kid the government when it needs kidding, and to read real news of real events instead of phony news manufactured by a paid agent of the state.

(4) *Use fresh figurative language to call up the right images and feelings*. Use imaginative comparisons that will create vivid images in the reader's mind and bring the right feelings and attitudes into play. The language of literal-minded people easily becomes gray and monotonous. Effective figurative language makes prose come to life. It makes readers take a fresh look; it appeals to their emotions as well as to their minds.

When the imaginative comparison, or figure of speech, is clearly presented as a comparison (introduced by words such as *like, as,* and *as if*), we call it a **simile:**

An abode without birds is *like meat without seasoning.*

His son spent money *as if he were trying to see the bottom of the mint.* (Alice Walker)

Prose consists less and less of words chosen for their meaning, and more and more of phrases tacked together *like the sections of a prefabricated henhouse.* (George Orwell)

When a writer talks about something as if it actually were the thing to which it is being compared, we call the imaginative comparison a **metaphor**:

I kept wishing that he would talk about himself, hoping to *break through the wall of rhetoric.* (Joan Didion)

Everyone is *a moon* and has *a dark side which he never shows to anybody.* (Mark Twain)

A riot is *the language of the unheard.* (Martin Luther King)

Phrases like "a not unjustifiable assumption" are a constant temptation, *a packet of aspirins always at one's elbow.* (George Orwell)

A sustained or extended metaphor follows the same basic comparison through into several related details:

In the midst of *this chopping sea of civilized life,* such are *the clouds and storms and quicksands* . . . that a man has to live, if he would not *founder and go to the bottom* and not *make his port* at all, by dead reckoning, and he must be a great calculator indeed who succeeds. (Henry David Thoreau)

Metaphors wear out. When we hear them over and over, they become merely a tired, secondhand way of stating a familiar idea. We can tell that metaphors no longer call up a vivid image when we find two combined in a mixed cliché. ("Young people today will have to *roll up their sleeves* if they want to *take their places at the banquet of life.*" "Today's teenagers have never been taught to *put the shoulder to the wheel* and *strike while the iron is hot.*") Avoid **mixed metaphors** that show you are no longer paying attention to the images your figurative expressions call up in the reader's mind:

CONSISTENT: There are a thousand *hacking away at the branches* of evil to one who is *striking at the root.* (Thoreau)

MIXED: The potential for disaster was there; only a *spark plug* was needed to *unleash* these tragic events.

A theme topic that might *die on its feet* in the wrong circumstances may *catch fire* when assigned at the right time.

The *long arm* of federal tyranny is reaching out to *crush us under its boot.*

(5) *Make full use of the varied resources of the English sentence.* A short, pointed sentence sums up. It is easy to remember and to quote:

As long as possible live free and uncommitted. (Thoreau)

Economy is the art of making the most of life. (G. B. Shaw)

Punctuality is the thief of time. (Oscar Wilde)

A long, elaborate sentence can follow through; it can explain and persuade; it can drive home a point; it can fill in a wealth of authentic detail:

The mild-mannered man who turns into a bear behind the wheel of a car—i.e., who finds in the power of the automobile a vehicle for the release of his inhibitions—is part of American folklore. (Tom Wolfe)

The effect was exactly what one expects that many simultaneous crashes to produce: the unmistakable tympany of automobiles colliding and cheap-gauge sheet metal buckling; front ends folding together at the same cockeyed angles police photographs of nighttime wreck scenes capture so well on grainy paper; smoke pouring from under the hoods and hanging over the infield like a howitzer cloud; a few of the surviving cars lurching eccentrically on bent axles. (Tom Wolfe on demolition derbies)

Study the way the first-rate writers use the short, pointed sentence to sum up a key point and then follow up with a more elaborate sentence that explains or provides details:

SHORT: | The great enemy of clear language is insincerity.
LONG: | When there is a gap between one's real and one's declared aims, one turns as it were instinctively to long words and exhausted idioms, like a cuttlefish squirting out ink. (George Orwell)

A good writer has an ear for how a well-built sentence sounds. Many well-balanced sentences owe their rhythm to the way related ideas have been lined up in similar grammatical form. Such lining up of related sentence elements is called **parallel structure**:

It is about time we realize that many women make
  better teachers than mothers,
  better actresses than wives,
  better diplomats than cooks. (Marya Mannes)

I have always felt sorry for people afraid
  of feeling,
  of sentimentality,
  of emotion,
who *conceal* what they feel
and *are unable* to weep with their whole heart.
  (Golda Meir)

Other sentences owe their rhythm to the balanced lining up of opposites. We call such a lining up of clear-cut opposites an **antithesis**. Here are examples of such antithetical balance:

Scientists have to be interested in *things,*
  not *persons.* (Marie Curie)

We have exchanged *being known in small communities*
  for *being anonymous in huge populations.*
  (Ellen Goodman)

(6) *Use humor and irony for their leavening effect.* When you write on a serious subject, you want to assure your readers that you take your subject and your audience seriously. But when writing becomes *too* serious, it can easily become humorless and forbidding. An occasional humorous or ironic touch will assure your readers that they are listening to a human being. Assure your readers that you can see yourself and your subject in perspective. Show them that you can see the humorous

side of familiar human predicaments.

One way a writer can steer away from deadly seriousness is to use occasional touches of verbal humor, or **word play**:

> The *settlement* of America had its origin in the *unsettlement* of Europe. (Lewis Mumford)

> The trouble with the *profit system* has always been that it was highly *unprofitable* to most people. The profits went to the few; the work went to the many. (E. B. White)

A writer with a lively sense of **irony** will keep prose from getting dull by pointing up revealing contradictions:

> Individualism is the belief that we should all paddle our own canoes, *especially on the high seas.*

> Progress is anything *turning on and off by itself.*
>   (Arthur Miller)

A writer with a sharp wit will surprise us by giving an unexpected twist to a familiar phrase or a familiar pious sentiment:

> To do good is noble; to teach others to do good is nobler, and no trouble. (Mark Twain)

To sum up: Writers with a sense of style have learned to look at their own writing through the reader's eyes—to listen to it with a reader's ears. Their feeling for words tells them whether the words they choose will make things clear for the reader or befog the subject. Their ear for sentences tells them whether a sentence will read well. Putting themselves in the reader's place, they sense when their writing becomes too solemn and plodding—or too chummy and frivolous. Good writing shows the writer's faith in the reader's ability to know the difference.

PREWRITING ACTIVITIES 13

1. For *sentence practice,* select two or three sentences in each of the following categories as model sentences. Write sentences that use your own subject matter but that imitate the style of the original as

closely as possible. Choose your model sentences from the following sections of this Writer's Guide:

   a. emphatic sentences—section (1)

   b. figurative sentences—section (4)

   c. short, pointed sentences—section (5)

   d. sentences with parallel structure—section (5)

   e. antithetical sentences—section (5)

   f. sentences with an ironic or humorous touch—section (6)

2. A favorite *stylistic exercise* for essayists has been the traditional "informal essay." It is often whimsical in its choice of a topic and leisurely and humorous in style. However, it often has serious undertones as it reveals to the reader the writer's personality or view of life. Write one or two paragraphs on a subject that allows you to be half serious and half humorous. Make your paragraphs a half-serious defense of something that some people may criticize but that to many people is not a serious issue: dirt roads, pigeons, cheerleaders, fast-food restaurants, low riders, T-shirt messages.

BACKGROUND: Marian Evans (1819–80), whose pen name was George Eliot, is one of the great nineteenth-century British novelists. Her books have been read by millions of readers around the world. She reached the large reading public of Victorian England with popular successes like *Adam Bede* (1859), *The Mill on the Floss* (1860), and *Silas Marner* (1860). Many critics consider her novel *Middlemarch* (1871–72) one of the truly great books of her century. Marian Evans was an independent, unconventional woman at a time when an unconventional professional or personal life incurred the wrath of the guardians of public morality. Her father had been the manager of a country estate, and her writing often reminds her readers of the simple pleasures of her childhood in the countryside. She had had a strong religious upbringing, but like many of her contemporaries she developed strong intellectual doubts. Her first published book was a translation of a German scholarly study designed to separate the truth about the "historical" Jesus from religious tradition. She lived for many years in a common-law marriage with George Henry Lewes, a well-known writer and critic, who was married and unable to obtain a legal divorce. This relationship scandalized many of her friends and led to an irreparable break with her family. Evans was a leading figure of nineteenth-century realism; her aim was to bring out the best in people such as they are. The following essay appeared as her introduction to the second part of *Adam Bede*. She here turns to her audience to explain her goals as a writer.

Marian Evans (George Eliot)

The Beauty of the Commonplace

GUIDE TO READING: What kind of person would Evans consider an ideal reader? In this essay, she argues with the expectations that many readers bring to fiction, and she sets up her own contrasting goals. Pay special attention to how she defines the two contrasting kinds of beauty that she sees in both art and literature. Pay special attention to the examples she uses to illustrate each.

MY STRONGEST effort is to give a faithful account of men and things as they have mirrored themselves in my mind. The mirror is doubtless defective. The outlines will sometimes be disturbed, the reflection faint or confused, but I feel as much bound to tell you as precisely as I can what that reflection is, as if I were in the witness box narrating my experience on oath. . . . Perhaps you will say, "Do improve the facts a little. Make them accord more with those correct views which it is our privilege to possess. The world is not just what we like. Do touch it up with a tasteful pencil, and make believe it is not quite such a mixed entangled affair. Let all people who hold unexceptionable opinions act unexceptionably. Let your most faulty characters always be on the wrong side, and your virtuous ones on the right. Then we shall see at a glance whom we are to condemn, and whom we are to approve. . . ."

But, my good friend, what will you do then with your fellow parishioner who opposes your husband in the vestry? With your newly appointed vicar, whose style of preaching you find painfully below that of his regretted predecessor? With the honest servant who worries your soul with her one failing? With your neighbor, Mrs. Green, who was really kind to you in your last illness, but has said several ill-natured things about you since your convalescence?—nay, with your excellent husband himself, who has other irritating habits besides that of not wiping his shoes? These fellow mortals, every one, must be accepted as they are. You can neither straighten their noses, nor brighten their wit, nor rectify their dispositions, and it is these people—amongst whom your life is passed—that it is needful you should tolerate, pity, and love. It is these more or less ugly, stupid, inconsistent people, whose movements of goodness you should be able to admire—for whom you should cherish all possible hopes, all possible patience. And I would not, even if I had the choice, be the clever novelist who could create a world so much better than this, in which we get up in the morning to do our daily work, that you would be likely to turn a harder, colder eye on the dusty streets and the common green fields—on the real breathing men and women, who can be chilled by your indifference or injured by your prejudice; who can be cheered and helped onward by your fellow feeling, your forbearance, your outspoken, brave justice.

So I am content to tell my simple story, without trying to make things seem better than they were; dreading nothing, indeed, but falsity, which, in spite of one's best efforts, there is reason to dread. Falsehood is easy, truth so difficult. The pencil is conscious of a delightful facility in drawing a griffin[1]—the larger the claws, and the larger the wings, the better; but that marvelous facility which we mistook for ge-

---

[1] [a mythological beast, half lion, half eagle]

nius is apt to forsake us when we want to draw a real unexaggerated lion. Examine your words well, and you will find that even when you have no motive to be false, it is a hard thing to say the exact truth, even about your own immediate feelings—much harder than to say something fine about them which is *not* the exact truth.

4   It is for this rare, precious quality of truthfulness that I delight in many Dutch paintings, which lofty-minded people despise. I find a source of delicious sympathy in these faithful pictures of a monotonous homely existence, which has been the fate of so many more among my fellow mortals than a life of pomp or of absolute indigence, of tragic suffering or of world-stirring actions. I turn, without shrinking, from cloudborne angels, from prophets, sibyls,[2] and heroic warriors, to an old woman bending over her flowerpot, or eating her solitary dinner, while the noonday light, softened perhaps by a screen of leaves, falls on her cap, and just touches the rim of her spinning wheel, and her stone jug, and all those cheap common things which are the precious necessaries of life to her. Or I turn to that village wedding, kept between four brown walls, where an awkward bridegroom opens the dance with a high-shouldered, broad-faced bride, while elderly and middle-aged friends look on, with very irregular noses and lips, and probably with quart-pots in their hands, but with an expression of unmistakable contentment and goodwill. "Foh!" says my idealistic friend, "what vulgar details! What good is there in taking all these pains to give an exact likeness of old women and clowns? What a low phase of life!—what clumsy, ugly people!"

5   But bless us, things may be lovable that are not altogether handsome, I hope? I am not at all sure that the majority of the human race have not been ugly, and even among those "lords of their kind," the British, squat figures, ill-shapen nostrils, and dingy complexions are not startling exceptions. Yet there is a great deal of family love amongst us. I have a friend or two whose class of features is such that the Apollo curl on the summit of their brows would be decidedly trying. Yet to my certain knowledge tender hearts have beaten for them, and their miniatures—flattering, but still not lovely—are kissed in secret by motherly lips. I have seen many an excellent matron, who could never in her best days have been handsome, and yet she had a packet of yellow love letters in a private drawer, and sweet children showered kisses on her sallow cheeks. And I believe there have been plenty of young heroes, of middle stature and feeble beards, who have felt quite sure they could never love anything more insignificant than a Diana,[3] and yet

[2] [wise women with the gifts of prophecy]

[3] [the Latin name of Artemis, the Greek goddess of chastity, often painted as a beautiful huntress]

have found themselves in middle life happily settled with a wife who waddles. Yes! thank God; human feeling is like the mighty rivers that bless the earth: it does not wait for beauty—it flows with resistless force and brings beauty with it.

All honor and reverence to the divine beauty of form! Let us culti- 6 vate it to the utmost in men, women, and children—in our gardens and in our houses. But let us love that other beauty too, which lies in no secret of proportion, but in the secret of deep human sympathy. Paint us an angel, if you can, with a floating violet robe, and a face paled by the celestial light. Paint us yet oftener a Madonna, turning her mild face upward and opening her arms to welcome the divine glory. But do not impose on us any rules which shall banish from the region of Art those old women scraping carrots with their work-worn hands, those heavy clowns taking holiday in a dingy pothouse, those rounded backs and weather-beaten faces that have bent over the spade and done the rough work of the world—those homes with their tin pans, their brown pitchers, their rough curs, and their clusters of onions. In this world there are so many of these common coarse people, who have no picturesque sentimental wretchedness! It is so needful we should remember their existence, else we may happen to leave them quite out of our religion and philosophy, and frame lofty theories which only fit a world of extremes. Therefore let art always remind us of them; therefore let us always have men ready to give the loving pains of a life to the faithful representing of commonplace things—men who see beauty in these commonplace things, and delight in showing how the light of heaven falls on them. There are few prophets in the world, few sublimely beautiful women, few heroes. I can't afford to give all my love and reverence to such rarities. I want a great deal of those feelings for my everyday fellow men, especially for the few in the foreground of the great multitude whose faces I know, whose hands I touch, for whom I have to make way with kindly courtesy. Neither are picturesque lazzaroni[4] or romantic criminals half so frequent as your common laborer, who gets his own bread, and eats it vulgarly but creditably with his own pocketknife. It is more needful that I should have a fiber of sympathy connecting me with that citizen who weighs out my sugar in a vilely assorted cravat and waistcoat than with the handsomest rascal in red scarf and green feathers—more needful that my heart should swell with loving admiration at some trait of gentle goodness in the faulty people who sit at the same hearth with me, or in the clergyman of my own parish . . . than at the deeds of heroes whom I shall never know except by hearsay.

---

[4] [homeless beggars formerly associated with the streets of Naples]

USING THE DICTIONARY: Marian Evans uses various words and meanings that were more current in her nineteenth-century English setting than they are today. Check the following examples in your dictionary. Are any of the words or meanings labeled old-fashioned or archaic? 1. *unexceptionable* (1) 2. *vicar* (2) 3. *vestry* (2) 4. *griffin* (3) 5. *indigence* (4) 6. *miniature* (5) 7. *clown* (6) 8. *picturesque* (6) 9. *cravat* (6) 10. *hearth* (6)

THE WRITER'S AGENDA:

Evans did not consider it her task simply to satisfy the expectations of her audience. Instead, like other exceptionally effective writers, she to some extent created her own audience by bringing into play capacities for thought and feeling that her readers might not have realized they had. Study the arguments she uses to help the people who are her audience to become more thoughtful readers.

1. In the first three paragraphs, the author makes her basic distinction between "truth" and "falsity" in a writer's work. Which sentence in these paragraphs for you best sums up her **thesis**? What is the key difference between the two opposed kinds of writing? Which of her examples for you best illustrates her point? What is her central objection to "falsehood"?

2. In these early paragraphs, Evans in turn compares writing to a mirror, to the testimony of a witness in court, and to a pencil drawing. Explain how each of these **metaphors** would guide or influence our view of the writer's task.

3. In the three long paragraphs that end the essay, Evans defines two different *kinds of beauty*—the kind cherished by her "idealistic" friends and the kind her idealistic friends find "vulgar" and uninspiring. What are the essential differences between the two kinds? Which of her examples are most striking or persuasive?

4. In discussion of art and literature, what would be some of the more conventional meanings and associations of the *heroic,* the *picturesque,* the *sentimental,* the *sublime,* and the *romantic?* What objections or unfavorable associations does the author bring in to help change the connotations that these terms have for her audience?

FOR DISCUSSION OR WRITING:

1. What to you would be a widely accepted definition of "idealism"? What do you think would be a widely accepted definition of

"realism"? Where would you place Evans on a scale ranging from one of these poles to the other?

2. Which of the two kinds of beauty that the author describes is to you truly beautiful? Defend your choice. Provide your own examples.

3. Compare and contrast two kinds of painting or sculpture that reflect different ideals of the artist's task. Describe key examples in vivid detail.

4. What is the role or justification of ugliness in the fine arts? Discuss detailed examples.

E. B. White

Once More to the Lake

GUIDE TO READING: This essay is a classic record of a writer's journey in search of the past. On the surface, it is the story of a week's camping trip to a lake remembered from childhood days. But the true purpose of the author is to relive bygone events, to revisit places long remembered, to recapture the mood of childhood summers when "the sun shone endlessly, day after day." What is he looking for? What does he find?

1   ONE SUMMER, along about 1904, my father rented a camp on a lake in Maine and took us all there for the month of August. We all got ringworm from some kittens and had to rub Pond's Extract on our arms and legs night and morning, and my father rolled over in a canoe with all his clothes on; but outside of that the vacation was a success and

from then on none of us ever thought there was any place in the world like that lake in Maine. We returned summer after summer—always on August 1st for one month. I have since become a salt-water man, but sometimes in summer there are days when the restlessness of the tides and the fearful cold of the sea water and the incessant wind which blows across the afternoon and into the evening make me wish for the placidity of a lake in the woods. A few weeks ago this feeling got so strong I bought myself a couple of bass hooks and a spinner and returned to the lake where we used to go, for a week's fishing and to revisit old haunts.

I took along my son, who had never had any fresh water up his nose ² and who had seen lily pads only from train windows. On the journey over to the lake I began to wonder what it would be like. I wondered how time would have marred this unique, this holy spot—the coves and streams, the hills that the sun set behind, the camps and the paths behind the camps. I was sure that the tarred road would have found it out and I wondered in what other ways it would be desolated. It is strange how much you can remember about places like that once you allow your mind to return into the grooves which lead back. You remember one thing, and that suddenly reminds you of another thing. I guess I remembered clearest of all the early mornings, when the lake was cool and motionless, remembered how the bedroom smelled of the lumber it was made of and of the wet woods whose scent entered through the screen. The partitions in the camp were thin and did not extend clear to the top of the rooms, and as I was always the first up I would dress softly so as not to wake the others, and sneak out into the sweet outdoors and start out in the canoe, keeping close along the shore in the long shadows of the pines. I remembered being very careful never to rub my paddle against the gunwale for fear of disturbing the stillness of the cathedral.

The lake had never been what you would call a wild lake. There ³ were cottages sprinkled around the shores, and it was in farming country although the shores of the lake were quite heavily wooded. Some of the cottages were owned by nearby farmers, and you would live at the shore and eat your meals at the farmhouse. That's what our family did. But although it wasn't wild, it was a fairly large and undisturbed lake and there were places in it which, to a child at least, seemed infinitely remote and primeval.

I was right about the tar: it led to within half a mile of the shore. ⁴ But when I got back there, with my boy, and we settled into a camp near a farmhouse and into the kind of summertime I had known, I could tell that it was going to be pretty much the same as it had been before—I knew it, lying in bed the first morning, smelling the bedroom, and hearing the boy sneak quietly out and go off along the shore in a boat. I began to sustain the illusion that he was I, and therefore, by simple transposition, that I was my father. This sensation persisted, kept cropping up all the time we were there. It was not an entirely new feeling, but in this setting it grew much stronger. I seemed to be living a dual existence. I would be in the middle of some simple act, I would be picking up a bait box or laying down a table fork, or I would be saying something, and suddenly it would be not I but my father who was saying the words or making the gesture. It gave me a creepy sensation.

5   We went fishing the first morning. I felt the same damp moss covering the worms in the bait can, and saw the dragonfly alight on the tip of my rod as it hovered a few inches from the surface of the water. It was the arrival of this fly that convinced me beyond any doubt that everything was as it always had been, that the years were a mirage and there had been no years. The small waves were the same, chucking the rowboat under the chin as we fished at anchor, and the boat was the same boat, the same color green and the ribs broken in the same places, and under the floor-boards the same fresh-water leaving and débris—the dead helgramite, the wisps of moss, the rusty discarded fishhook, the dried blood from yesterday's catch. We stared silently at the tips of our rods, at the dragonflies that came and went. I lowered the tip of mine into the water, tentatively, pensively dislodging the fly, which darted two feet away, poised, darted two feet back, and came to rest again a little farther up the rod. There had been no years between the ducking of this dragonfly and the other one—the one that was part of memory. I looked at the boy, who was silently watching his fly, and it was my hands that held his rod, my eyes watching. I felt dizzy and didn't know which rod I was at the end of.

6   We caught two bass, hauling them in briskly as though they were mackerel, pulling them over the side of the boat in a businesslike manner without any landing net, and stunning them with a blow on the back of the head. When we got back for a swim before lunch, the lake was exactly where we had left it, the same number of inches from the dock, and there was only the merest suggestion of a breeze. This seemed an utterly enchanted sea, this lake you could leave to its own devices for a few hours and come back to, and find that it had not stirred, this constant and trustworthy body of water. In the shallows, the dark, water-soaked sticks and twigs, smooth and old, were undulating in clusters on the bottom against the clean ribbed sand, and the track of the mussel was plain. A school of minnows swam by, each minnow with its small individual shadow, doubling the attendance, so clear and sharp in the sunlight. Some of the other campers were in swimming, along the shore, one of them with a cake of soap, and the water felt thin and clear and unsubstantial. Over the years there had been this person with the cake of soap, this cultist, and here he was. There had been no years.

Up to the farmhouse to dinner through the teeming, dusty field, 7
the road under our sneakers was only a two-track road. The middle
track was missing, the one with the marks of the hooves and the
splotches of dried, flaky manure. There had always been three tracks to
choose from in choosing which track to walk in; now the choice was
narrowed down to two. For a moment I missed terribly the middle
alternative. But the way led past the tennis court, and something about
the way it lay there in the sun reassured me; the tape had loosened
along the backline, the alleys were green with plantains and other
weeds, and the net (installed in June and removed in September)
sagged in the dry noon, and the whole place steamed with midday heat
and hunger and emptiness. There was a choice of pie for dessert, and
one was blueberry and one was apple, and the waitresses were the same
country girls, there having been no passage of time, only the illusion of
it as in a dropped curtain—the waitresses were still fifteen; their hair
had been washed, that was the only difference—they had been to the
movies and seen the pretty girls with the clean hair.

Summertime, oh summertime, pattern of life indelible, the fade- 8
proof lake, the woods unshatterable, the pasture with the sweetfern and
the juniper forever and ever, summer without end; this was the background, and the life along the shore was the design, the cottagers with
their innocent and tranquil design, their tiny docks with the flagpole
and the American flag floating against the white clouds in the blue sky,
the little paths over the roots of the trees leading from camp to camp
and the paths leading back to the outhouses and the can of lime for
sprinkling, and at the souvenir counters at the store the miniature
birch-bark canoes and the post cards that showed things looking a little
better than they looked. This was the American family at play, escaping
the city heat, wondering whether the newcomers in the camp at the
head of the cove were "common" or "nice," wondering whether it was
true that the people who drove up for Sunday dinner at the farmhouse
were turned away because there wasn't enough chicken.

It seemed to me, as I kept remembering all this, that those times 9
and those summers had been infinitely precious and worth saving.
There had been jollity and peace and goodness. The arriving (at the
beginning of August) had been so big a business in itself, at the railway
station the farm wagon drawn up, the first smell of the pine-laden air,
the first glimpse of the smiling farmer, and the great importance of the
trunks and your father's enormous authority in such matters, and the
feel of the wagon under you for the long ten-mile haul, and at the top
of the last long hill catching the first view of the lake after eleven
months of not seeing this cherished body of water. The shouts and
cries of the other campers when they saw you, and the trunks to be
unpacked, to give up their rich burden. (Arriving was less exciting
nowadays, when you sneaked up in your car and parked it under a tree

near the camp and took out the bags and in five minutes it was all over, no fuss, no loud wonderful fuss about trunks.)

10   Peace and goodness and jollity. The only thing that was wrong now, really, was the sound of the place, an unfamiliar nervous sound of the outboard motors. This was the note that jarred, the one thing that would sometimes break the illusion and set the years moving. In those other summertimes all motors were inboard; and when they were at a little distance, the noise they made was a sedative, an ingredient of summer sleep. They were one-cylinder and two-cylinder engines, and some were make-and-break and some were jump-spark, but they all made a sleepy sound across the lake. The one-lungers throbbed and fluttered, and the twin-cylinder ones purred and purred, and that was a quiet sound too. But now the campers all had outboards. In the daytime, in the hot mornings, these motors made a petulant, irritable sound; at night, in the still evening when the afterglow lit the water, they whined about one's ears like mosquitoes. My boy loved our rented outboard, and his great desire was to achieve singlehanded mastery over it, and authority, and he soon learned the trick of choking it a little (but not too much), and the adjustment of the needle valve. Watching him I would remember the things you could do with the old one-cylinder engine with the heavy flywheel, how you could have it eating out of your hand if you got really close to it spiritually. Motor boats in those days didn't have clutches, and you would make a landing by shutting off the motor at the proper time and coasting in with a dead rudder. But there was a way of reversing them, if you learned the trick, by cutting the switch and putting it on again exactly on the final dying revolution of the flywheel, so that it would kick back against compression and begin reversing. Approaching a dock in a strong following breeze, it was difficult to slow up sufficiently by the ordinary coasting method, and if a boy felt he had complete mastery over his motor, he was tempted to keep it running beyond its time and then reverse it a few feet from the dock. It took a cool nerve, because if you threw the switch a twentieth of a second too soon you would catch the flywheel when it still had speed enough to go up past center, and the boat would leap ahead, charging bull-fashion at the dock.

11   We had a good week at the camp. The bass were biting well and the sun shone endlessly, day after day. We would be tired at night and lie down in the accumulated heat of the little bedrooms after the long hot day and the breeze would stir almost imperceptibly outside and the smell of the swamp drift in through the rusty screens. Sleep would come easily and in the morning the red squirrel would be on the roof, tapping out his gay routine. I kept remembering everything, lying in bed in the mornings—the small steamboat that had a long rounded stern like the lip of a Ubangi, and how quietly she ran on the moon-

light sails, when the older boys played their mandolins and the girls sang and we ate doughnuts dipped in sugar, and how sweet the music was on the water in the shining night, and what it had felt like to think about girls then. After breakfast we would go up to the store and the things were in the same place—the minnows in a bottle, the plugs and spinners disarranged and pawed over by the youngsters from the boys' camp, the fig newtons and the Beeman's gum. Outside, the road was tarred and cars stood in front of the store. Inside, all was just as it had always been, except there was more Coca Cola and not so much Moxie and root beer and birch beer and sarsaparilla. We would walk out with a bottle of pop apiece and sometimes the pop would backfire up our noses and hurt. We explored the streams, quietly, where the turtles slid off the sunny logs and dug their way into the soft bottom; and we lay on the town wharf and fed worms to the tame bass. Everywhere we went I had trouble making out which was I, the one walking at my side, the one walking in my pants.

One afternoon while we were there at that lake a thunderstorm 12 came up. It was like the revival of an old melodrama that I had seen long ago with childish awe. The second-act climax of the drama of the electrical disturbance over a lake in America had not changed in any important respect. This was the big scene, still the big scene. The whole thing was so familiar, the first feeling of oppression and heat and a general air around camp of not wanting to go very far away. In mid-afternoon (it was all the same) a curious darkening of the sky, and a lull in everything that had made life tick; and then the way the boats suddenly swung the other way at their moorings with the coming of a breeze out of the new quarter, and the premonitory rumble. Then the kettle drum, then the snare, then the bass drum and cymbals, then crackling light against the dark, and the gods grinning and licking their chops in the hills. Afterward the calm, the rain steadily rustling in the calm lake, the return of light and hope and spirits, and the campers running out in joy and relief to go swimming in the rain, their bright cries perpetuating the deathless joke about how they were getting simply drenched, and the children screaming with delight at the new sensation of bathing in the rain, and the joke about getting drenched linking the generations in a strong indestructible chain. And the comedian who waded in carrying an umbrella.

When the others went swimming my son said he was going in too. 13 He pulled his dripping trunks from the line where they had hung all through the shower, and wrung them out. Languidly, and with no thought of going in, I watched him, his hard little body, skinny and bare, saw him wince slightly as he pulled up around his vitals the small, soggy, icy garment. As he buckled the swollen belt suddenly my groin felt the chill of death.

USING THE DICTIONARY: A. White knows how to make scenes and events real for his readers. For example, he calls things by their right names. Which of the following do you need to check in your dictionary, and what help does it provide? 1. *spinner* (1) 2. *gunwale* (2) 3. *helgramite* (5) 4. *mussel* (6) 5. *plantain* (7) 6. *sweetfern* (8) 7. *juniper* (8) 8. *fly-wheel* (10) 9. *snare* (12) 10. *cymbals* (12)

B. The unity of mood in this essay is reflected in a network of **synonyms** and related terms. There are many words that echo or reinforce the central theme—the quiet, the calm, the peace that make the lake a precious place for the author. Check the following words as necessary. Explain how they cluster around or relate to the central theme. 11. *placidity* (1) 12. *remote* (3) 13. *primeval* (3) 14. *pensive* (5) 15. *tranquil* (8) 16. *indelible* (8) 17. *sedative* (10) 18. *perpetuate* (12) 19. *indestructible* (12) 20. *languid* (13)

THE WRITER'S AGENDA:

White wrote this essay for an audience used to the New England tradition of **understatement**. Although he turns serious or even solemn at many points in the essay, he uses touches of dry humor to keep from becoming too emotional. Study the way this classic **informal essay** maintains a light or humorous tone while yet conveying ideas and feelings that are basic to the author's outlook on life.

1. What humorous details does the author use in the introductory paragraph to help set the **informal** tone of the essay? Point out humorous touches or amusing details later in the essay that help the author maintain an informal, understated tone.

2. The author says, "You remember one thing, and that suddenly reminds you of another thing." Describe some of the passages that are most clearly nostalgic memories of the *distant past*. Point out striking concrete details that help make these scenes real for the reader.

3. The author is at first divided between the wish to relive something "infinitely precious" to him and the fear that "time would have marred" the lake of his childhood memories. What are some of the things that have *changed?*

4. The high points of this essay occur where *past and present* blend—where the author discovers that "everything was as it had always been." Quote several other passages restating the same central idea. Describe key passages that support this main idea: the fishing, the

farmhouse dinner, the thunderstorm. Point out details that make them real and that help create the prevailing mood.

5. How does the presence of his *son* help the author bridge the gulf between the present and the past? What is the significance of the ending? (Defend your interpretation.)

6. White is a master stylist who knows how to choose the right words for the sights and sounds, and for the mood and feelings, that he is trying to convey. He frequently uses **figurative** language—imaginative comparisons that not only create vivid pictures in our minds but at the same time bring into play the right attitudes and emotions. Many of these comparisons are **metaphors**: They describe one thing as if it were the other to which it is being compared. In the early morning calm of the cool and motionless lake, he is afraid that the noise of a paddle would disturb "the stillness of the *cathedral.*" Later, the small waves are "*chucking* the rowboat *under the chin.*" Each minnow in a school swimming by had its own individual shadow, "doubling the *attendance.*"

Find all uses of figurative language in the passage describing the thunderstorm, in the last but one paragraph of the essay. Pay special attention to *sustained* metaphors—comparisons followed up through several related details.

FOR DISCUSSION OR WRITING:

1. Many readers feel that memories like those described in this essay give people spiritual nourishment and help them keep their sanity. To other readers, these memories may seem like an escape from unpleasant reality. Which of these views is closer to your own reaction, and why?

2. A high point of White's essay is the thunderstorm on a summer afternoon, which he describes as the reenactment of a familiar age-old drama and which he traces through its familiar accustomed stages. Write your own description of a similar age-old natural event running its course—a blizzard, the first big rainstorm of a rainy season, a hurricane, or the like.

3. Write an informal essay about a place, person, or event from the past whose memory continues to play a role in your thoughts or in your life.

4. One test of a classic is that it often makes a time and a place come to life unforgettably for its audience, sometimes making the setting seem more real than the readers' memories of their own past. Write

an essay in which you write as an imaginary visitor to one such well-remembered setting from your own reading.

5. Some of the sentences in White's essay are relatively informal. They have a conversational tone, like the sentences of a person speaking to us in a relaxed, casual way. Other sentences in the essay become more solemn or eloquent. They often follow up or build up an idea with a series of **parallel** elements—sentence parts of the same or of a similar kind. For each of the following examples, write a similar sentence on a subject of your own choice. Try to come as close as you can to the structure of the model sentence.

a. I wondered how time would have marred this unique,
   this holy spot—
   the coves and streams,
   the hills that the sun set behind,
   the camps and the paths behind the camps.

b. We caught two bass,
   hauling them in briskly as though they were mackerel,
   pulling them over the side of the boat in a businesslike
   manner without any landing net,
   and stunning them with a blow on the back of the head.

c. We explored the streams, quietly,
   where the turtles slid off the sunny logs
   and dug their way into the soft bottom;
   and we lay on the town wharf
   and fed worms to the tame bass.

BACKGROUND: Jonathan Swift (1667–1745), the author of *Gulliver's Travels*, is one of the great masters of satire in world literature. He aimed his biting wit at targets including religious fanaticism, political corruption, and war. Swift was born of English parents in Dublin, Ireland, at a time when Ireland was under English rule. Much of the wealth produced by Irish tenant farmers went to "absentee landlords." Religious divisions aggravated political conflicts: The Irish, then as now, were predominantly Catholic ("Papists," or followers of the Pope, in the language of the time). Their British rulers were Protestant, with the Church of England as the established or official state church. (Swift calls it "Episcopal," that is, guided by bishops.) Members of a third major religious group, the more extreme or more radical Protestants (dissenters or Puritans), were, like Catholics, barred from public office. As a young man, Swift was active in party politics in England, eventually siding with the Tories, traditionally the strongest supporters of the British monarchy and of the Church of England. He made a living as a clergyman and became Dean of St. Patrick's Cathedral in Dublin after his return to Ireland. In his famous "Modest Proposal" (1729), he aimed his slashing satire at the oppression and exploitation of the Irish under English rule. His goal was to stir his readers out of their complacency, to arouse their capacity for indignation. Swift wrote for an audience that he considered capable of "common sense and reason" but whose better inclinations were often corrupted by greed and hypocrisy. His mission as a writer was to bring out in his readers their buried sense of decency, to sharpen their blunted fellow feeling for suffering humanity, and to inspire in them contempt for callousness and greed.

Jonathan Swift

A Modest Proposal

GUIDE TO READING: Swift is a master of verbal **irony.** He often achieves his comic effects by saying the opposite of what he thinks—and wants us as the audience to think. As you read the essay, pay special attention to the difference between what he means and what he says. Where is he serious? Where is he mock-serious or ironic?

1   It is a melancholy object to those who walk through this great town or travel in the country, when they see the streets, the roads, and cabin doors crowded with beggars of the female sex, followed by three, four, or six children, all in rags and importuning every passenger for an alms. These mothers, instead of being able to work for their honest livelihood, are forced to employ all their time in strolling to beg sustenance for their helpless infants, who, as they grow up, either turn thieves for want of work, or leave their dear native country to fight for the Pretender in Spain,[1] or sell themselves to the Barbadoes.[2]

2   I think it is agreed by all parties that this prodigious number of children in the arms, or on the backs, or at the heels of their mothers, and frequently of their fathers, is in the present deplorable state of the kingdom a very great additional grievance; and therefore whoever could find out a fair, cheap, and easy method of making these children sound, useful members of the commonwealth would deserve so well of the public as to have his statue set up for a preserver of the nation.

3   But my intention is very far from being confined to provide only for the children of professed beggars; it is of a much greater extent, and shall take in the whole number of infants at a certain age who are born of parents in effect as little able to support them as those who demand our charity in the streets.

4   As to my own part, having turned my thoughts for many years upon this important subject, and maturely weighed the several schemes of other projectors, I have always found them grossly mistaken in their computation. It is true, a child just dropped from its dam may be supported by her milk for a solar year, with little other nourishment; at most not above the value of two shillings, which the mother may certainly get, or the value in scraps, by her lawful occupation of begging; and it is exactly at one year old that I propose to provide for them in such a manner as instead of being a charge upon their parents or the parish, or wanting food and raiment for the rest of their lives, they shall on the contrary contribute to the feeding, and partly to the clothing, of many thousands.

5   There is likewise another great advantage in my scheme, that it will prevent those voluntary abortions, and that horrid practice of women murdering their bastard children, alas, too frequent among us, sacrificing the poor innocent babes, I doubt, more to avoid the expense than

[1][The people of England had forced the last Stuart king, James II, from the British throne because of his pro-Catholic leanings. A son of James II was still a threat to the current monarch as a "Pretender" to the throne, claiming it as his rightful inheritance in alliance with such Catholic powers as Spain and with strong support from Irish Catholics.]

[2][Many poor Irish were emigrating to Barbados and other British colonies in the West Indies.]

the shame, which would move tears and pity in the most savage and inhuman breast.

The number of souls in this kingdom being usually reckoned one 6 million and a half, of these I calculate there may be about two hundred thousand couples whose wives are breeders; from which number I subtract thirty thousand couples who are able to maintain their own children, although I apprehend there cannot be so many under the present distresses of the kingdom; but this being granted, there will remain an hundred and seventy thousand breeders. I again subtract fifty thousand for those women who miscarry, or whose children die by accident or disease within the year. There only remain an hundred and twenty thousand children of poor parents annually born. The question therefore is how this number shall be reared and provided for, which, as I have already said, under the present situation of affairs, is utterly impossible by all the methods hitherto proposed. For we can neither employ them in handicraft or agriculture; we neither build houses (I mean in the country) nor cultivate land. They can very seldom pick up a livelihood by stealing till they arrive at six years old, except where they are of towardly parts,[3] although I confess they learn the rudiments much earlier, during which time they can however be looked upon only as probationers, as I have been informed by a principal gentleman in the county of Cavan, who protested to me that he never knew above one or two instances under the age of six, even in a part of the kingdom so renowned for the quickest proficiency in that art.

I am assured by our merchants that a boy or a girl before twelve 7 years old is no salable commodity; and even when they come to this age they will not yield above three pounds, or three pounds and half a crown at most on the Exchange; which cannot turn to account either to the parents or the kingdom, the charge of nutriment and rags having been at least four times that value.

I shall now therefore humbly propose my own thoughts, which I 8 hope will not be liable to the least objection.

I have been assured by a very knowing American of my acquain- 9 tance in London, that a young healthy child well nursed is at a year old a most delicious, nourishing, and wholesome food, whether stewed, roasted, baked, or boiled; and I make no doubt that it will equally serve in a fricassee or a ragout.[4]

I do therefore humbly offer it to public consideration that of the 10 hundred and twenty thousand children, already computed, twenty thousand may be reserved for breed, whereof only one fourth part to be males, which is more than we allow to sheep, black cattle, or swine;

[3][especially promising]

[4][French names for kinds of meat stew]

and my reason is that these children are seldom the fruits of marriage, a circumstance not much regarded by our savages, therefore one male will be sufficient to serve four females. That the remaining hundred thousand may at a year old be offered in sale to the persons of quality and fortune through the kingdom, always advising the mother to let them suck plentifully in the last month, so as to render them plump and fat for a good table. A child will make two dishes at an entertainment for friends; and when the family dines alone, the fore or hind quarter will make a reasonable dish, and seasoned with a little pepper or salt will be very good boiled on the fourth day, especially in winter.

11   I have reckoned upon a medium that a child just born will weigh twelve pounds, and in a solar year if tolerably nursed increaseth to twenty-eight pounds.

12   I grant this food will be somewhat dear, and therefore very proper for landlords, who, as they have already devoured most of the parents, seem to have the best title to the children.

13   Infant's flesh will be in season throughout the year, but more plentiful in March, and a little before and after. For we are told by a grave author, an eminent French physician, that fish being a prolific diet, there are more children born in Roman Catholic countries about nine months after Lent than at any other season; therefore, reckoning a year after Lent, the markets will be more glutted than usual, because the number of popish infants is at least three to one in this kingdom; and therefore it will have one other collateral advantage, by lessening the number of Papists among us.

14   I have already computed the charge of nursing a beggar's child (in which list I reckon all cottagers, laborers, and four fifths of the farmers) to be about two shillings per annum, rags included; and I believe no gentleman would repine to give ten shillings for the carcass of a good fat child, which, as I have said, will make four dishes of excellent nutritive meat, when he hath only some particular friend or his own family to dine with him. Thus the squire will learn to be a good landlord and grow popular among the tenants; the mother will have eight shillings net profit, and be fit for work till she produces another child.

15   Those who are more thrifty (as I must confess the times require) may flay the carcass; the skin of which artificially dressed will make admirable gloves for ladies and summer boots for fine gentlemen.

16   As to our city of Dublin, shambles may be appointed for this purpose in the most convenient parts of it, and butchers we may be assured will not be wanting; although I rather recommend buying the children alive and dressing them hot from the knife as we do roasting pigs.

17   A very worthy person, a true lover of his country, and whose virtues I highly esteem, was lately pleased in discoursing on this matter to offer a refinement upon my scheme. He said that many gentlemen of

this kingdom, having of late destroyed their deer, he conceived that the want of venison might be well supplied by the bodies of young lads and maidens, not exceeding fourteen years of age nor under twelve, so great a number of both sexes in every county being now ready to starve for want of work and service; and these to be disposed of by their parents, if alive, or otherwise by their nearest relations. But with due deference to so excellent a friend and so deserving a patriot, I cannot be altogether in his sentiments; for as to the males, my American acquaintance assured me from frequent experience that their flesh was generally tough and lean, like that of our schoolboys, by continual exercise, and their taste disagreeable; and to fatten them would not answer the charge. Then as to the females, it would, I think with humble submission, be a loss to the public, because they soon would become breeders themselves: and besides, it is not improbable that some scrupulous people might be apt to censure such a practice (although indeed very unjustly) as a little bordering upon cruelty; which, I confess, hath always been with me the strongest objection against any project, how well soever intended.

But in order to justify my friend, he confessed that this expedient 18 was put into his head by the famous Psalmanazar,[5] a native of the island Formosa, who came from thence to London above twenty years ago, and in conversation told my friend that in his country when any young person happened to be put to death, the executioner sold the carcass to persons of quality as a prime dainty; and that in his time the body of a plump girl of fifteen, who was crucified for an attempt to poison the emperor, was sold to his Imperial Majesty's prime minister of state, and other great mandarins of the court, in joints from the gibbet, at four hundred crowns. Neither indeed can I deny that if the same use were made of several plump young girls in this town, who without one single groat to their fortunes cannot stir abroad without a chair, and appear at the playhouse and assemblies in foreign fineries which they never will pay for, the kingdom would not be the worse.

Some persons of a desponding spirit are in great concern about that 19 vast number of poor people who are aged, diseased, or maimed, and I have been desired to employ my thoughts what course may be taken to ease the nation of so grievous an encumbrance. But I am not in the least pain upon that matter, because it is very well known that they are every day dying and rotting by cold and famine, and filth and vermin, as fast as can be reasonably expected. And as to the younger laborers, they are now in almost as hopeful a condition. They cannot get work, and consequently pine away for want of nourishment to a degree that if at any time they are accidentally hired to common labor, they have not

[5][a French impostor claiming to be from Formosa, now Taiwan]

strength to perform it; and thus the country and themselves are happily delivered from the evils to come.

20   I have too long digressed, and therefore shall return to my subject. I think the advantages by the proposal which I have made are obvious and many, as well as of the highest importance.

21   For first, as I have already observed, it would greatly lessen the number of Papists, with whom we are yearly overrun, being the principal breeders of the nation as well as our most dangerous enemies; and who stay at home on purpose to deliver the kingdom to the Pretender, hoping to take their advantage by the absence of so many good Protestants, who have chosen rather to leave their country than stay at home and pay tithes against their conscience to an Episcopal curate.

22   Secondly, the poorer tenants will have something valuable of their own, which by law may be made liable to distress,[6] and help to pay their landlord's rent, their corn and cattle being already seized and money a thing unknown.

23   Thirdly, whereas the maintenance of an hundred thousand children, from two years old and upwards, cannot be computed at less than ten shillings a piece per annum, the nation's stock will be thereby increased fifty thousand pounds per annum, besides the profit of a new dish introduced to the tables of all gentlemen of fortune in the kingdom who have any refinement in taste. And the money will circulate among ourselves, the goods being entirely of our own growth and manufacture.

24   Fourthly, the constant breeders, besides the gain of eight shillings sterling per annum by the sale of their children, will be rid of the charge of maintaining them after the first year.

25   Fifthly, this food would likewise bring great custom to taverns, where the vintners will certainly be so prudent as to procure the best receipts for dressing it to perfection, and consequently have their houses frequented by all the fine gentlemen, who justly value themselves upon their knowledge in good eating; and a skillful cook, who understands how to oblige his guests, will contrive to make it as expensive as they please.

26   Sixthly, this would be a great inducement to marriage, which all wise nations have either encouraged by rewards or enforced by laws and penalties. It would increase the care and tenderness of mothers toward their children, when they were sure of a settlement for life to the poor babes, provided in some sort by the public, to their annual profit instead of expense. We should see an honest emulation among the married women, which of them could bring the fattest child to the market. Men would become as fond of their wives during the time of

[6][seizure of property to pay off debts]

their pregnancy as they are now of their mares in foal, their cows in calf, or sows when they are ready to farrow; nor offer to beat or kick them (as is too frequent a practice) for fear of a miscarriage.

Many other advantages might be enumerated. For instance, the addition of some thousand carcasses in our exportation of barreled beef, the propagation of swine's flesh, and improvement in the art of making good bacon, so much wanted among us by the great destruction of pigs, too frequent at our tables, which are no way comparable in taste or magnificence to a well-grown, fat yearling child, which roasted whole will make a considerable figure at a lord mayor's feast or any other public entertainment. But this and many others I omit, being studious of brevity. ₂₇

Supposing that one thousand families in this city would be constant customers for infants' flesh, besides others who might have it at merry meetings, particularly weddings and christenings, I compute that Dublin would take off annually about twenty thousand carcasses, and the rest of the kingdom (where probably they will be sold somewhat cheaper) the remaining eighty thousand. ₂₈

I can think of no one objection that will possibly be raised against this proposal, unless it should be urged that the number of people will be thereby much lessened in the kingdom. This I freely own, and it was indeed one principal design in offering it to the world. I desire the reader will observe, that I calculate my remedy for this one individual kingdom of Ireland and for no other that ever was, is, or I think ever can be upon earth. Therefore let no man talk to me of other expedients: of taxing our absentees at five shillings a pound; of using neither clothes nor household furniture except what is of our own growth and manufacture; of utterly rejecting the materials and instruments that promote foreign luxury; of curing the expensiveness of pride, vanity, idleness, and gaming in our women; of introducing a vein of parsimony, prudence, and temperance; of learning to love our country, in the want of which we differ even from Laplanders and the inhabitants of Topinamboo;[7] of quitting our animosities and factions, nor acting any longer like the Jews, who were murdering one another at the very moment their city was taken;[8] of being a little cautious not to sell our country and conscience for nothing; of teaching landlords to have at least one degree of mercy toward their tenants; lastly, of putting a spirit of honesty, industry, and skill into our shopkeepers, who, if a resolution could now be taken to buy only our native goods, would immediately unite to cheat and exact upon us in the price, the measure, and the goodness, ₂₉

---

[7][a place in the Brazilian jungle]

[8][When the Romans captured and destroyed Jerusalem in A.D. 70, the Jews were fighting among themselves.]

nor could ever yet be brought to make one fair proposal of just dealing, though often and earnestly invited to it.

30   Therefore I repeat, let no man talk to me of these and the like expedients, till he hath at least some glimpse of hope that there will ever be some hearty and sincere attempt to put them in practice.

31   But as to myself, having been wearied out for many years with offering vain, idle, visionary thoughts, and at length utterly despairing of success, I fortunately fell upon this proposal, which, as it is wholly new, so it hath something solid and real, of no expense and little trouble, full in our own power, and whereby we can incur no danger in disobliging England. For this kind of commodity will not bear exportation, the flesh being of too tender a consistence to admit a long continuance in salt, although perhaps I could name a country which would be glad to eat up our whole nation without it.

32   After all, I am not so violently bent upon my own opinion as to reject any offer proposed by wise men, which shall be found equally innocent, cheap, easy, and effectual. But before something of that kind shall be advanced in contradiction to my scheme, and offering a better, I desire the author or authors will be pleased maturely to consider two points: First, as things now stand, how they will be able to find food and raiment for an hundred thousand useless mouths and backs. And secondly, there being a round million of creatures in human figure throughout this kingdom, whose sole subsistence put into a common stock would leave them in debt two millions of pounds sterling, adding those who are beggars by profession to the bulk of farmers, cottagers, and laborers, with their wives and children who are beggars in effect; I desire those politicians who dislike my overture, and may perhaps be so bold to attempt an answer, that they will first ask the parents of these mortals whether they would not at this day think it a great happiness to have been sold for food at a year old in the manner I prescribe, and thereby have avoided such a perpetual scene of misfortunes as they have since gone through by the oppression of landlords, the impossibility of paying rent without money or trade, the want of common sustenance, with neither house nor clothes to cover them from the inclemencies of the weather, and the most inevitable prospect of entailing the like or greater miseries upon their breed forever.

33   I profess, in the sincerity of my heart, that I have not the least personal interest in endeavoring to promote this necessary work, having no other motive than the public good of my country, by advancing our trade, providing for infants, relieving the poor, and giving some pleasure to the rich. I have no children by which I can propose to get a single penny; the youngest being nine years old, and my wife past childbearing.

USING THE DICTIONARY: Modern readers of Jonathan Swift's eighteenth-century essay encounter words and meanings that are no longer in frequent or common use. Check in your dictionary each of the words italicized in the following phrases. Find the meaning that fits the context. 1. *professed* beggars (3) 2. schemes of other *projectors* (4) 3. *wanting* food (4) 4. food and *raiment* (4) 5. I *apprehend* there cannot be many (6) 6. *protested* he knew too few examples (6) 7. a *prolific* diet (13) 8. *popish* infants (13) 9. *repine* to give ten shillings (14) 10. skin *artificially* dressed (15) 11. *shambles* for butchers (16) 12. a prime *dainty* (18) 13. *mandarins* of the court (18) 14. a single *groat* (18) 15. stirring abroad without a *chair* (18) 16. an Episcopal *curate* (21) 17. talk of *expedients* (29) 18. animosities and *factions* (29) 19. will not *bear* exportation (31) 20. pounds *sterling* (32)

THE WRITER'S AGENDA:

Satire employs exaggeration and ridicule to hold things that are objectionable up to scorn. But a satirist like Swift does not merely make us laugh at what is contemptible. His aim is to make his audience see clearly what is wrong and to point the way toward change for the better. Answer the following questions about his analysis of what is wrong and his proposals for a solution.

1. Swift sets out to shock, by an outrageous imaginary scheme, those who are too callous to be shocked by *horrible realities*. In the opening paragraphs, he makes us see what these horrible realities are. What do we learn in the first six or seven paragraphs about conditions in Ireland?

2. Much satire owes its comic effect to its *extreme exaggeration* of a basic truth. According to Swift, who is really "devouring" Ireland? Where does he say? By earnestly presenting his gruesome proposal, what attitudes does he attribute by implication to those responsible for Ireland's plight?

3. Satirists are sometimes accused of criticizing shortcomings but offering little positive advice. Explain and discuss the *positive proposals* that Swift pretends to reject toward the end of his essay.

4. Throughout his mock-serious discussion of his "proposal," Swift never lets his audience lose sight of the *basic theme* of poverty and neglect. What are some striking details that he adds as he continues

beyond the picture that he has painted at the beginning? How does he summarize his indictment at the end?

5. In a famous essay, the English philosopher Bertrand Russell discussed our tendency to *glorify* the oppressed—to see in them virtues that are lacking in their exploiters. Does Swift glorify the Irish? Or does he criticize them? If so, where and how?

FOR DISCUSSION OR WRITING:

1. Who do you think is the major audience for whom Swift intended his satire—the oppressed Irish? their English exploiters? a combination of both? Defend your answer.

2. In his satirical writings, Swift often uses a coarse outspokenness and a slashing, cruel humor that are not for the squeamish. Do you think many readers would be offended by the gruesome or grotesque details of this essay? Do you think their reaction would lessen the persuasiveness or effectiveness of Swift's satire?

3. Can you think of a clear and present evil about which the audience of the modern mass media has become too complacent or fatalistic? What would it take to break through the crust of complacency or apathy? (Your instructor may ask you to write a paper in which you try.)

4. Write your own modest proposal on a topic like the following:

♦ how to reduce juvenile delinquency

♦ how to end prostitution

♦ how to combat anti-American feeling abroad

♦ how to combat crime in the cities

♦ how to end the arms race

♦ how to combat unemployment

5. Eighteenth-century writers were fond of the pointed saying that would be remembered and quoted by others. Study the following examples. Use several of them as *model sentences.* For each, write a very similar sentence on a topic of your own choice. Follow the structure of the original as closely as you can.

a. All looks yellow to the jaundiced eye. (Alexander Pope)

SAMPLE   All tastes sour to people with vinegar in their dispo-
IMITATION: sition.

b. To err is human; to forgive, divine. (Alexander Pope)

c. An honest man's the noblest work of God. (Alexander Pope)

d. We have just religion enough to make us hate, but not enough to make us love one another. (Jonathan Swift)

e. When a true genius appears in the world, you may know him by this sign, that the dunces are all in confederacy against him. (Jonathan Swift)

f. The stoical scheme of supplying our wants by lopping off our desires is like cutting off our feet when we want shoes. (Jonathan Swift)

g. No one ever yet became great by imitation.(Samuel Johnson)

h. Fame cannot spread wide or endure long that is not rooted in nature, and manured by art. (Samuel Johnson)

BACKGROUND: One of the great books in American literature is *Walden* by Henry David Thoreau (1817–62). In describing how he wrote the book, the author said, "I lived alone in the woods, a mile from any neighbor, in a house which I had built myself, on the shore of Walden Pond, in Concord, Massachusetts, and earned a living by the labor of my hands only." *Walden* records Thoreau's search for a simpler, more self-sufficient life that would provide an alternative to the hectic pace and petty worries of commercialized and industrialized modern society. Thoreau was a leading representative of the New England tradition of individualism. He lived in Concord, a few miles from where the first shots of the American War of Independence were fired. He studied at Harvard College and was a friend of Emerson and other leading New England scholars and writers of his time. He wrote his first books about boat trips and hikes he took to explore the New England countryside. Thoreau spoke and wrote in opposition to slavery and the war against Mexico and was briefly jailed for refusing to pay taxes in support of an unjust government. His essay "On the Duty of Civil Disobedience" (1849) is a classic in the literature of dissent. It championed the right of the individual to resist the tyranny of the majority and to disobey unjust laws. The essay reprinted here is one of the early chapters of *Walden*. It is written in a very personal style, frequently using the personal pronouns *I* or *me*. As Thoreau said, "It is, after all, always the first person who is speaking." But the essay frequently shifts from the personal *I* to the more inclusive *we* or *us,* talking about "our" lives and how to improve them. Thoreau thus assumes that he and his audience share common interests and much common experience. He expects that his readers will all take to heart such portions of his account "as apply to them."

Henry David Thoreau

Where I Lived, and What I Lived For

GUIDE TO READING: Thoreau asks his readers to take a fresh look at their lives and at the world around them. He looks at many subjects from an unconventional personal **point of view.** As he moves from one subject to another— farming, the arts, newspapers, the railroads—pay special attention to how his remarks reflect his personal attitude toward life.

AT A CERTAIN season of our life we are accustomed to consider 1
every spot as the possible site of a house. I have thus surveyed the
country on every side within a dozen miles of where I live. In imagination I have bought all the farms in succession, for all were to be
bought, and I knew their price. I walked over each farmer's premises,
tasted his wild apples, discoursed on husbandry with him, took his
farm at his price, at any price, mortgaging it to him in my mind; even
put a higher price on it, took everything but a deed of it—took his word
for his deed, for I dearly love to talk—cultivated it, and him too to
some extent, I trust, and withdrew when I had enjoyed it long enough,
leaving him to carry it on. This experience entitled me to be regarded
as a sort of real-estate broker by my friends. Wherever I sat, there I
might live, and the landscape radiated from me accordingly. What is a
house but a *sedes,* a seat?—better if a country seat. I discovered many a
site for a house not likely to be soon improved, which some might have
thought too far from the village, but to my eyes the village was too far
from it. Well, there I might live, I said; and there I did live, for an hour,
a summer and a winter life; saw how I could let the years run off, buffet
the winter through, and see the spring come in. The future inhabitants
of this region, wherever they may place their houses, may be sure that
they have been anticipated. An afternoon sufficed to lay out the land
into orchard, woodlot, and pasture, and to decide what fine oaks or
pines should be left to stand before the door, and whence each blasted
tree could be seen to the best advantage; and then I let it lie, fallow
perchance, for a man is rich in proportion to the number of things
which he can afford to let alone.

My imagination carried me so far that I even had the refusal of 2
several farms—the refusal was all I wanted—but I never got my fingers
burned by actual possession. The nearest that I came to actual possession was when I bought the Hollowell place, and had begun to sort my
seeds, and collected materials with which to make a wheelbarrow to
carry it on or off with; but before the owner gave me a deed of it, his
wife—every man has such a wife—changed her mind and wished to
keep it, and he offered me ten dollars to release him. Now, to speak the
truth, I had but ten cents in the world, and it surpassed my arithmetic
to tell, if I was that man who had ten cents, or who had a farm, or ten
dollars, or all together. However, I let him keep the ten dollars and the
farm too, for I had carried it far enough; or rather, to be generous, I
sold him the farm for just what I gave for it, and, as he was not a rich
man, made him a present of ten dollars, and still had my ten cents, and
seeds, and materials for a wheelbarrow left. I found thus that I had
been a rich man without any damage to my poverty. But I retained the
landscape, and I have since annually carried off what it yielded without
a wheelbarrow. With respect to landscales,

> I am monarch of all I *survey,*
> My right there is none to dispute.

3   I have frequently seen a poet withdraw, having enjoyed the most valuable part of a farm, while the crusty farmer supposed that he had got a few wild apples only. Why, the owner does not know it for many years when a poet has put his farm in rhyme, the most admirable kind of invisible fence, has fairly impounded it, milked it, skimmed it, and got all the cream, and left the farmer only the skimmed milk.

4   The real attractions of the Hollowell farm, to me, were its complete retirement, being about two miles from the village, half a mile from the nearest neighbor, and separated from the highway by a broad field; its bounding on the river, which the owner said protected it by its fogs from frosts in the spring, though that was nothing to me; the gray color and ruinous state of the house and barn, and the dilapidated fences, which put such an interval between me and the last occupant; the hollow and lichen-covered apple trees, gnawed by rabbits, showing what kind of neighbors I should have; but above all, the recollection I had of it from my earliest voyages up the river, when the house was concealed behind a dense grove of red maples, through which I heard the house dog bark. I was in haste to buy it, before the proprietor finished getting out some rocks, cutting down the hollow apple trees, and grubbing up some young birches which had sprung up in the pasture, or in short, had made any more of his improvements. To enjoy these advantages I was ready to carry it on; like Atlas, to take the world on my shoulders— I never heard what compensation he received for that—and do all those things which had no other motive or excuse but that I might pay for it and be unmolested in my possession of it; for I knew all the while that it would yield the most abundant crop of the kind I wanted if I could only afford to let it alone. But it turned out as I have said.

5   All that I could say, then, with respect to farming on a large scale (I have always cultivated a garden) was that I had had my seeds ready. Many think that seeds improve with age. I have no doubt that time discriminates between the good and the bad; and when at last I shall plant, I shall be less likely to be disappointed. But I would say to my fellows, once for all, "As long as possible live free and uncommitted." It makes but little difference whether you are committed to a farm or the county jail.

6   Old Cato, whose "De Re Rustica" is my "Cultivator,"[1] says, and the only translation I have seen makes sheer nonsense of the passage, "When you think of getting a farm turn it thus in your mind, not to buy

---

[1][Cato the Elder (234–149 B.C.) was a Roman statesman who wrote the book mentioned here as a guide to farmers, or "cultivators."]

greedily; nor spare your pains to look at it, and do not think it enough to go round it once. The oftener you go there the more it will please you, if it is good." I think I shall not buy greedily, but go round and round it as long as I live, and be buried in it first, that it may please me the more at last.

The present was my next experiment of this kind, which I purpose   7
to describe more at length, for convenience, putting the experience of two years into one. As I have said, I do not propose to write an ode to dejection, but to brag as lustily as Chanticleer in the morning, standing on his roost, if only to wake my neighbors up.

When first I took up my abode in the woods, that is, began to spend   8
my nights as well as days there, which, by accident, was on Independence day, or the Fourth of July, 1845, my house was not finished for winter, but was merely a defense against the rain, without plastering or chimney, the walls being of rough weather-stained boards, with wide chinks, which made it cool at night. The upright white hewn studs and freshly planed door and window casings gave it a clean and airy look, especially in the morning, when its timbers were saturated with dew, so that I fancied that by noon some sweet gum would exude from them. To my imagination it retained throughout the day more or less of this auroral character, reminding me of a certain house on a mountain which I had visited a year before. This was an airy and unplastered cabin, fit to entertain a travelling god, and where a goddess might trail her garments. The winds which passed over my dwelling were such as sweep over the ridges of mountains, bearing the broken strains, or celestial parts only, of terrestrial music. The morning wind forever blows, the poem of creation is uninterrupted; but few are the ears that hear it. Olympus is but the outside of the earth everywhere.

The only house I had been the owner of before, if I except a boat,   9
was a tent, which I used occasionally when making excursions in the summer, and this is still rolled up in my garret; but the boat, after passing from hand to hand, has gone down the stream of time. With this more substantial shelter about me, I had made some progress toward settling in the world. This frame, so slightly clad, was a sort of crystallization around me, and reacted on the builder. It was suggestive somewhat as a picture in outlines. I did not need to go out doors to take the air, for the atmosphere within had lost none of its freshness. It was not so much within doors as behind a door where I sat, even in the rainiest weather. The Harivansa[2] says, "An abode without birds is like a meat

---

[2][Thoreau makes several references to the sacred writings of ancient India, such as the Vedas. The Hindu epic called the *Harivansa* tells the story of how the god Hari or Vishnu appeared in human form as Krishna, called later in the essay Damodara.]

without seasoning." Such was not my abode, for I found myself suddenly neighbor to the birds; not by having imprisoned one, but having
caged myself near them. I was not only nearer to some of those which
commonly frequent the garden and the orchard, but to those wilder
and more thrilling songsters of the forest which never, or rarely, sere-
nade a villager—the wood-thrush, the veery, the scarlet tanager, the
field-sparrow, the whippoorwill, and many others.

10   I was seated by the shore of a small pond, about a mile and a half
south of the village of Concord and somewhat higher than it, in the
midst of an extensive wood between that town and Lincoln, and about
two miles south of that our only field known to fame, Concord Battle
Ground; but I was so low in the woods that the opposite shore, half a
mile off, like the rest, covered with wood, was my most distant horizon.
For the first week, whenever I looked out on the pond it impressed me
like a tarn high up on the side of a mountain, its bottom far above the
surface of other lakes, and, as the sun arose, I saw it throwing off its
nightly clothing of mist, and here and there, by degrees, its soft ripples
or its smooth reflecting surface was revealed, while the mists, like
ghosts, were stealthily withdrawing in every direction into the woods,
as at the breaking up of some nocturnal conventicle. The very dew
seemed to hang upon the trees later into the day than usual, as on the
sides of mountains.

11   This small lake was of most value as a neighbor in the intervals of a
gentle rain storm in August, when both air and water being perfectly
still, but the sky overcast, mid-afternoon had all the serenity of evening,
and the wood-thrush sang around, and was heard from shore to shore. A
lake like this is never smoother than at such a time; and the clear
portion of the air above it being shallow and darkened by clouds, the
water, full of light and reflections, becomes a lower heaven itself so
much the more important. From a hill top near by, where the wood had
been recently cut off, there was a pleasing vista southward across the
pond, through a wide indentation in the hills which form the shore
there, where their opposite sides sloping toward each other suggested
a stream flowing out in that direction through a wooded valley, but
stream there was none. That way I looked between and over the near
green hills to some distant and higher ones in the horizon, tinged with
blue. Indeed, by standing on tiptoe I could catch a glimpse of some of
the peaks of the still bluer and more distant mountain ranges in the
north-west, those true-blue coins from heaven's own mint, and also of
some portion of the village. But in other directions, even from this
point, I could not see over or beyond the woods which surrounded me.
It is well to have some water in your neighborhood, to give buoyancy to
and float the earth. One value even of the smallest well is, that when
you look into it you see that earth is not continent but insular. This is as

important as that it keeps butter cool. When I looked across the pond from this peak toward the Sudbury meadows, which in time of flood I distinguished elevated perhaps by a mirage in their seething valley, like a coin in a basin, all the earth beyond the pond appeared like a thin crust insulated and floated even by this small sheet of intervening water, and I was reminded that this on which I dwelt was but *dry land.*

Though the view from my door was still more contracted, I did not 12 feel crowded or confined in the least. There was pasture enough for my imagination. The low shrub-oak plateau to which the opposite shore arose, stretched away toward the prairies of the West and the steppes of Tartary, affording ample room for all the roving families of men. "There are none happy in the world but beings who enjoy freely a vast horizon,"—said Damodara, when his herds required new and larger pastures.

Both place and time were changed, and I dwelt nearer to those 13 parts of the universe and to those eras in history which had most attracted me. Where I lived was as far off as many a region viewed nightly by astronomers. We are wont to imagine rare and delectable places in some remote and more celestial corner of the system, behind the constellation of Cassiopeia's Chair, far from noise and disturbance. I discovered that my house actually had its site in such a withdrawn, but forever new and unprofaned, part of the universe. If it were worth the while to settle in those parts near to the Pleiades or the Hyades, to Aldebaran or Altair, then I was really there, or at an equal remoteness from the life I had left behind, dwindled and twinkling with as fine a ray to my nearest neighbor, and to be seen only in moonless nights by him. Such was that part of creation where I had squatted—

> There was a shepherd that did live,
> And held his thoughts as high
> As were the mounts whereon his flocks
> Did hourly feed him by.

What should we think of the shepherd's life if his flocks always wandered to higher pastures than his thoughts?

Every morning was a cheerful invitation to make my life of equal 14 simplicity, and I may say innocence, with Nature herself. I have been as sincere a worshipper of Aurora as the Greeks. I got up early and bathed in the pond; that was a religious exercise, and one of the best things which I did. They say that characters were engraven on the bathing tub of King Tching-thang to this effect: "Renew thyself completely each day; do it again, and again, and forever again." I can understand that. Morning brings back the heroic ages. I was as much affected by the faint hum of a mosquito making its invisible and unimaginable tour through my apartment at earliest dawn, when I was sitting with door and windows open, as I could be by any trumpet that ever sang of fame. It was Homer's requiem; itself an Iliad and Odyssey in the air, singing its own wrath and wanderings. There was something cosmical about it; a standing advertisement, till forbidden, of the everlasting vigor and fertility of the world. The morning, which is the most memorable season of the day, is the awakening hour. Then there is least somnolence in us; and for an hour, at least, some part of us awakes which slumbers all the rest of the day and night. Little is to be expected of that day, if it can be called a day, to which we are not awakened by our Genius, but by the mechanical nudgings of some servitor, are not awakened by our newly-acquired force and aspirations from within, accompanied by the undulations of celestial music, instead of factory bells, and a fragrance filling the air—to a higher life than we fell asleep from; and thus the darkness bear its fruit, and prove itself to be good, no less than the light. That man who does not believe that each day contains an earlier, more sacred, and auroral hour than he has yet profaned, has despaired of life, and is pursuing a descending and darkening way. After a partial cessation of his sensuous life, the soul of man, or its organs rather, are reinvigorated each day, and his Genius tries again what noble life it can make. All memorable events, I should say, transpire in morning time and in a morning atmosphere. The Vedas say, "All intelligences awake with the morning." Poetry and art, and the fairest and most memorable of the actions of men, date from such an hour. All poets and heroes, like Memnon, are the children of Aurora, and emit their music at sunrise. To him whose elastic and vigorous thought keeps pace with the sun, the day is a perpetual morning. It matters not what the clocks say or the attitudes and labors of men. Morning is when I am awake and there is a dawn in me. Moral reform is the effort to throw off sleep. Why is it that men give so poor an account of their day if they have not been slumbering? They are not such poor calculators. If they had not been overcome with drowsiness they would have performed something. The millions are awake enough for physical labor; but only one in a million is awake enough for effective intellectual exertion, only one in a hundred millions to a poetic or divine life. To be awake is to be alive. I have never yet met a man who was quite awake. How could I have looked him in the face?

15   We must learn to reawaken and keep ourselves awake, not by mechanical aids, but by an infinite expectation of the dawn, which does not forsake us in our soundest sleep. I know of no more encouraging fact than the unquestionable ability of man to elevate his life by a conscious endeavor. It is something to be able to paint a particular picture, or to carve a statue, and so to make a few objects beautiful; but it is far more glorious to carve and paint the very atmosphere and medium through which we look, which morally we can do. To affect the

quality of the day, that is the highest of arts. Every man is tasked to make his life, even in its details, worthy of the contemplation of his most elevated and critical hour. If we refused, or rather used up, such paltry information as we get, the oracles would distinctly inform us how this might be done.

I went to the woods because I wished to live deliberately, to front 16 only the essential facts of life, and see if I could not learn what it had to teach, and not, when I came to die, discover that I had not lived. I did not wish to live what was not life, living is so dear; nor did I wish to practice resignation, unless it was quite necessary. I wanted to live deep and suck out all the marrow of life, to live so sturdily and Spartan-like as to put to rout all that was not life, to cut a broad swath and shave close, to drive life into a corner, and reduce it to its lowest terms, and, if it proved to be mean, why then to get the whole and genuine meanness of it, and publish its meanness to the world; or if it were sublime, to know it by experience, and be able to give a true account of it in my next excursion. For most men, it appears to me, are in a strange uncertainty about it, whether it is of the devil or of God, and have *somewhat hastily* concluded that it is the chief end of man here to "glorify God and enjoy him forever."

Still we live meanly, like ants; though the fable tells us that we 17 were long ago changed into men; like pygmies we fight with cranes; it is error upon error, and clout upon clout, and our best virtue has for its occasion a superfluous and inevitable wretchedness. Our life is frittered away by detail. An honest man has hardly need to count more than his ten fingers, or in extreme cases he may add his ten toes, and lump the rest. Simplicity, simplicity, simplicity! I say, let your affairs be as two or three, and not a hundred or a thousand; instead of a million count half a dozen, and keep your accounts on your thumb nail. In the midst of this chopping sea of civilized life, such are the clouds and storms and quicksands and thousand-and-one items to be allowed for, that a man has to live, if he would not founder and go to the bottom and not make his port at all, by dead reckoning, and he must be a great calculator indeed who succeeds. Simplify, simplify. Instead of three meals a day, if it be necessary eat but one; instead of a hundred dishes, five; and reduce other things in proportion. Our life is like a German Confederacy,[3] made up of petty states, with its boundary forever fluctuating, so that even a German cannot tell you how it is bounded at any moment. The nation itself, with all its so-called internal improvements, which, by the way, are all external and superficial, is just such an un-

---

[3][Unlike such unified nation-states as France or England, Germany remained until later in the nineteenth century a loose confederation of smaller kingdoms and petty principalities.]

wieldy and overgrown establishment, cluttered with furniture and tripped up by its own traps, ruined by luxury and heedless expense, by want of calculation and a worthy aim, as the million households in the land; and the only cure for it as for them is in a rigid economy, a stern and more than Spartan simplicity of life and elevation of purpose. It lives too fast. Men think that it is essential that the *Nation* have commerce, and export ice, and talk through a telegraph, and ride thirty miles an hour, without a doubt, whether *they* do or not; but whether we should live like baboons or like men is a little uncertain. If we do not get our sleepers, and forge rails, and devote days and nights to the work, but go to tinkering upon our *lives* to improve *them,* who will build railroads? And if railroads are not built, how shall we get to heaven in season? But if we stay at home and mind our business, who will want railroads? We do not ride on the railroad; it rides upon us. Did you ever think what those sleepers are that underlie that railroad? Each one is a man, an Irishman, or a Yankee man. The rails are laid on them, and they are covered with sand, and the cars run smoothly over them. They are sound sleepers, I assure you. And every few years a new lot is laid down and run over; so that, if some have the pleasure of riding on a rail, others have the misfortune to be ridden upon. And when they run over a man that is walking in his sleep, a supernumerary sleeper in the wrong position, and wake him up, they suddenly stop the cars, and make a hue and cry about it, as if this were an exception. I am glad to know that it takes a gang of men for every five miles to keep the sleepers down and level in their beds as it is, for this is a sign that they may sometime get up again.

18   Why should we live with such hurry and waste of life? We are determined to be starved before we are hungry. Men say that a stitch in time saves nine, and so they take a thousand stitches today to save nine tomorrow. As for *work*, we haven't any of consequence. We have the Saint Vitus' dance, and cannot possibly keep our heads still. If I should only give a few pulls at the parish bell-rope, as for a fire, that is, without setting the bell, there is hardly a man on his farm in the outskirts of Concord, notwithstanding that press of engagements which was his excuse so many times this morning, nor a boy, nor a woman, I might almost say, but would forsake all and follow that sound, not mainly to save property from the flames, but, if we will confess the truth, much more to see it burn, since burn it must, and we, be it known, did not set it on fire—or to see it put out, and have a hand in it, if that is done as handsomely; yes, even if it were the parish church itself. Hardly a man takes a half hour's nap after dinner, but when he wakes he holds up his head and asks, "What's the news?" as if the rest of mankind had stood his sentinels. Some give directions to be waked every half hour, doubtless for no other purpose; and then, to pay for it, they tell what they

have dreamed. After a night's sleep the news is as indispensable as the breakfast. "Pray tell me anything new that has happened to a man anywhere on this globe"—and he reads it over his coffee and rolls that a man has had his eyes gouged out this morning on the Wachito River; never dreaming the while that he lives in the dark unfathomed mammoth cave of this world, and has but the rudiment of an eye himself.

For my part, I could easily do without the post office. I think that there are very few important communications made through it. To speak critically, I never received more than one or two letters in my life—I wrote this some years ago—that were worth the postage. The penny-post is, commonly, an institution through which you seriously offer a man that penny for his thoughts which is so often safely offered in jest. And I am sure that I never read any memorable news in a newspaper. If we read of one man robbed, or murdered, or killed by accident, or one house burned, or one vessel wrecked, or one steamboat blown up, or one cow run over on the Western Railroad, or one mad dog killed, or one lot of grasshoppers in the winter, we never need read of another. One is enough. If you are acquainted with the principle, what do you care for a myriad instances and applications? To a philosopher all *news,* as it is called, is gossip, and they who edit and read it are old women over their tea. Yet not a few are greedy after this gossip. There was such a rush, as I hear, the other day at one of the offices to learn the foreign news by the last arrival, that several large squares of plate glass belonging to the establishment were broken by the pressure—news which I seriously think a ready wit might write a twelvemonth or twelve years beforehand with sufficient accuracy. As for Spain, for instance, if you know how to throw in Don Carlos and the Infanta, and Don Pedro[4] and Seville and Granada, from time to time in the right proportions—they may have changed the names a little since I saw the papers—and serve up a bull-fight when other entertainments fail, it will be true to the letter, and give us as good an idea of the exact state of ruin of things in Spain as the most succinct and lucid reports under this head in the newspapers: and as for England, almost the last significant scrap of news from that quarter was the revolution of 1649; and if you have learned the history of her crops for an average year, you never need attend to that thing again, unless your speculations are of a merely pecuniary character. If one may judge who rarely looks into the newspapers, nothing new does ever happen in foreign parts, a French revolution not excepted.

What news! how much more important to know what that is which was never old! "Kieou-he-yu (great dignitary of the state of Wei) sent a

19

20

---

[4][Don Carlos and Don Pedro, as well as the Infanta (or daughter of the king), were for a time possible choices for the next monarch of Spain.]

man to Khoung-tseu to know his news. Khoung-tseu caused the messenger to be seated near him, and questioned him in these terms: What is your master doing? The messenger answered with respect: My master desires to diminish the number of his faults, but he cannot come to the end of them. The messenger being gone, the philosopher remarked: What a worthy messenger; What a worthy messenger!" The preacher, instead of vexing the ears of drowsy farmers on their day of rest at the end of the week—for Sunday is the fit conclusion of an ill-spent week, and not the fresh and brave beginning of a new one—with this one other draggle-tail of a sermon, should shout with thundering voice,— "Pause! Avast! Why so seeming fast, but deadly slow?"

21   Shams and delusions are esteemed for soundest truths, while reality is fabulous. If men would steadily observe realities only, and not allow themselves to be deluded, life, to compare it with such things as we know, would be like a fairy tale and the Arabian Nights' Entertainments. If we respected only what is inevitable and has a right to be, music and poetry would resound along the streets. When we are unhurried and wise, we perceive that only great and worthy things have any permanent and absolute existence,—that petty fears and petty pleasures are but the shadow of the reality. This is always exhilarating and sublime. By closing the eyes and slumbering, and consenting to be deceived by shows, men establish and confirm their daily life of routine and habit everywhere, which still is built on purely illusory foundations. Children, who play life, discern its true law and relations more clearly than men, who fail to live it worthily, but who think that they are wiser by experience, that is, by failure. I have read in a Hindu book, that "there was a king's son, who, being expelled in infancy from his native city, was brought up by a forester, and, growing up to maturity in that state, imagined himself to belong to the barbarous race with which he lived. One of his father's ministers having discovered him, revealed to him what he was, and the misconception of his character was removed, and he knew himself to be a prince. So soul," continues the Hindu philosopher, "from the circumstances in which it is placed, mistakes its own character, until the truth is revealed to it by some holy teacher, and then it knows itself to be *Brahme*." I perceive that we inhabitants of New England live this mean life that we do because our vision does not penetrate the surface of things. We think that that *is* which *appears* to be. If a man should walk through this town and see only the reality, where, think you, would the "Mill-dam" go to? If he should give us an account of the realities he beheld there, we should not recognize the place in his description. Look at a meeting house, or a courthouse, or a jail, or a shop, or a dwelling house, and say what that thing really is before a true gaze, and they would all go to pieces in your account of them. Men esteem truth remote, in the outskirts of the

system, behind the farthest star, before Adam and after the last man. In eternity there is indeed something true and sublime. But all these times and places and occasions are now and here. God himself culminates in the present moment, and will never be more divine in the lapse of all the ages. And we are enabled to apprehend at all what is sublime and noble only by the perpetual instilling and drenching of the reality that surrounds us. The universe constantly and obediently answers to our conceptions; whether we travel fast or slow, the track is laid for us. Let us spend our lives in conceiving then. The poet or the artist never yet had so fair and noble a design but some of his posterity at least could accomplish it.

Let us spend one day as deliberately as Nature, and not be thrown off the track by every nutshell and mosquito's wing that falls on the rails. Let us rise early and fast, or break fast, gently and without perturbation; let company come and let company go, let the bells ring and the children cry—determined to make a day of it. Why should we knock under and go with the stream? Let us not be upset and overwhelmed in that terrible rapid and whirlpool called a dinner, situated in the meridian shallows. Weather this danger and you are safe, for the rest of the way is down hill. With unrelaxed nerves, with morning vigor, sail by it, looking another way, tied to the mast like Ulysses. If the engine whistles, let it whistle till it is hoarse for its pains. If the bell rings, why should we run? We will consider what kind of music they are like. Let us settle ourselves, and work and wedge our feet downward through the mud and slush of opinion, and prejudice, and tradition, and delusion, and appearance, that alluvion which covers the globe, through Paris and London, through New York and Boston and Concord, through church and state, through poetry and philosophy and religion, till we come to a hard bottom and rocks in place, which we can call *reality,* and say, This is, and no mistake; and then begin, having a *point d'appui,*[5] below freshet and frost and fire, a place where you might found a wall or a state, or set a lamp-post safely, or perhaps a gauge, not a Nilometer,[6] but a Realometer, that future ages might know how deep a freshet of shams and appearances had gathered from time to time. If you stand right fronting and face to face to a fact, you will see the sun glimmer on both its surfaces, as if it were a cimeter, and feel its sweet edge dividing you through the heart and marrow, and so you will happily conclude your mortal career. Be it life or death, we crave only reality. If we are really dying, let us hear the rattle in our throats and feel cold in the extremities; if we are alive, let us go about our business.

[5][a firm support]

[6][A "Nilometer" would measure the level of the River Nile, whose annual flooding kept the adjoining agricultural lands fertile in Egypt.]

23   Time is but the stream I go a-fishing in. I drink at it; but while I
drink I see the sandy bottom and detect how shallow it is. Its thin
current slides away, but eternity remains. I would drink deeper; fish in
the sky, whose bottom is pebbly with stars. I cannot count one. I know
not the first letter of the alphabet. I have always been regretting that I
was not as wise as the day I was born. The intellect is a cleaver; it
discerns and rifts its way into the secret of things. I do not wish to be
any more busy with my hands than is necessary. My head is hands and
feet. I feel all my best faculties concentrated in it. My instinct tells me
that my head is an organ for burrowing, as some creatures use their
snout and forepaws, and with it I would mine and burrow my way
through these hills. I think that the richest vein is somewhere here-
abouts; so by the divining rod and thin rising vapors I judge; and here I
will begin to mine.

 USING THE DICTIONARY: A. Check expressions that are less
common now than in Henry David Thoreau's time: 1. *husbandry* (1) 2. have the *refusal* of (2) 3. *conventicle* (10)
4. be *wont* to (13) 5. *paltry* (15) 6. *sleeper* (17) 7. *supernumerary* (17) 8. *avast* (20) 9. *freshet* (22) 10. *cimeter* (22)

B. Thoreau makes frequent use of **allusions**—he mentions a
name or incident that brings to mind a familiar story. For
instance, mention of Ulysses chained to the mast brings to
mind Homer's story of how Ulysses succeeded in resisting
the fatal attraction of the sirens' song. How much help does
your dictionary provide with allusions like the following?
11. ready like *Atlas* to take the world on my shoulders (5)
12. brag as lustily as *Chanticleer* (7) 13. *Olympus* is but the
outside of the earth everywhere (8) 14. All poets and heroes,
like *Memnon,* are the children of *Aurora* (14) 15. an *Iliad*
and *Odyssey,* singing its own wrath and wanderings (14)

THE WRITER'S AGENDA:

   In reading Thoreau's essay, we hear the voice of a strongly individual writer who yet seems confident that what he says will strike a responsive chord with many of his readers. Answer the following questions about what makes Thoreau's writing fresh and provocative.

   1. Thoreau's central thesis was "Simplicity! Simplicity! Simplicity!"
Look at his introductory discussion of farms and farming, of his "abode
in the woods," and of places to live. How does it prepare us for his
central thesis?

2. Many of Thoreau's most memorable sentences make us look at things from a new and different **point of view**. What makes the perspective the author adopts in each of the following sentences unusual? Explain the full meaning of each as it is developed or supported by the author in its context in the essay.

a. "A man is rich in proportion to the number of things he can afford to let alone."

b. "As long as possible live free and uncommitted."

c. "The morning wind forever blows, the poem of creation is uninterrupted, but few are the ears that hear it."

d. "To affect the quality of the day, that is the highest of arts."

e. "We do not ride on the railroad; it rides on us."

f. "Men say that a stitch in time saves nine, and so they take a thousand stitches today to save nine tomorrow."

g. "To a philosopher all news, as it is called, is gossip."

h. "God himself culminates in the present moment, and will never be more divine in the lapse of all the ages."

3. Thoreau often looks beyond the practical meaning of things to their symbolic significance. They become **symbols** of how we live or should live. What to him is the symbolic significance of morning? What is his objection to Sundays? What to him makes the railroads a symbol of a new industrial civilization?

4. Thoreau often uses **figurative language** that is rich in visual and emotional associations. Many of his figurative expressions are sustained or extended metaphors that trace the same imaginative comparison through several related details. Explain as fully as you can the images and feelings that examples like the following bring to mind.

a. "Let us settle ourselves, and work and wedge our feet downward through the mud and slush of opinion, and prejudice, and tradition, and delusion, and appearance . . . till we come to a hard bottom and rocks in place, which we can call reality."

b. "The intellect is a cleaver; it discerns and rifts its way into the secret of things."

c. "Time is but the stream I go afishing in. I drink at it; but while I drink I see the sandy bottom and detect how shallow it is. Its thin current slides away, but eternity remains."

FOR DISCUSSION OR WRITING:

1. Thoreau was an outstanding representative of the New England tradition of individualism and nonconformity. Prepare a personal portrait of Thoreau based on your reading of this essay. What traits or personal qualities are you going to emphasize? What evidence from the essay are you going to use?

2. In recent years, there has been a strong revival of one of Thoreau's basic themes: the theme of *self-sufficiency*—of doing without nonessentials, of doing as much as we can for ourselves. Where have you had a chance to observe or to test this ideal? Argue for or against self-sufficiency as an ideal for our times.

3. Like Thoreau, many young people today are searching for a personal philosophy that would provide an alternative to our modern materialistic civilization. Discuss one such spiritual or religious orientation that you know well.

4. Both Swift and Thoreau were moralists appealing to their readers' better moral or spiritual selves. Compare and contrast the way these two authors view, and appeal to, their audiences.

5. Thoreau often develops his ideas in balanced sentences packed with examples or details that are arranged in grammatically parallel fashion. Use three of the following examples as *model sentences*. For each, write a sentence on a subject of your own choice, following the structure of the original sentence as closely as you can.

   a. Men think that it is essential that the nation have commerce,
           and export ice,
           and talk through a telegraph
           and ride thirty miles an hour . . .
    but whether we should live like baboons
                    or like men
      is a little uncertain.

   b. If we read of one man robbed,
           or murdered,
           or killed by accident,
                or one house burned,
                or one vessel wrecked,
                or one steamboat blown up,
                or one cow run over on the Western Railroad . . .
    we never need read of another.

   c. Shams and delusions are esteemed for soundest truths,
       while reality is fabulous.

d. When we are unhurried and wise,
   we perceive
that only great and worthy things have any
   permanent and absolute existence—
that petty fears
and petty pleasures
are but the shadow of the reality.

BACKGROUND: George Orwell (1903–50) was a British socialist who had observed British imperialism at first hand in India and Burma and who had fought against fascism in Spain. (See the introduction to "Shooting an Elephant" in unit 2 for biographical details.) In *Homage to Catalonia* (1938), he documented what he saw as the betrayal of the Spanish working classes by both the Western democracies and Stalinist Russia. He became one of the great critics of the rival totalitarian movements that in the thirties and forties were stringing barbed wire across most of Europe. In his novel *1984* (published in 1949), he predicted a totalitarian society of the future where Big Brother told everyone what to think and what to say; where records of undesirable people disappeared down the memory hole; and where history was constantly being rewritten to follow the zig-zags of the party line. Telescreen and print were dominated by doublespeak, with the headquarters of the secret police called the Ministry of Love and with the war department called the Ministry of Peace. Orwell's heroes were the lone individuals who were struggling to reserve a corner of their lives for their own honest needs, who still found a way to express their own honest feelings. Although banned by school boards playing Big Brother, *1984* is still one of the most widely read books of our time. In 1948, Orwell had published "Politics and the English Language," an essay that developed a theme central to his nightmare vision of the future: the manipulation and debasement of language in contemporary politics. Orwell addressed his essay to an audience tired of propaganda and doublespeak. Many of his readers were ready to share his belief that if we get rid of bad verbal habits we "can think more clearly," and that "to think clearly is a necessary first step towards political regeneration."

George Orwell

Politics and the English Language

GUIDE TO READING: Orwell's central assumption in this essay is that style is more than just "a matter of style." How we talk affects how we think, and how we think affects how we act. Study carefully the abuses of language that Orwell analyzes in this essay and the examples he provides for each.

MOST PEOPLE who bother with the matter at all would admit   1
that the English language is in a bad way, but it is generally assumed
that we cannot by conscious action do anything about it. Our civilization is decadent and our language—so the argument runs—must inevitably share in the general collapse. It follows that any struggle against
the abuse of language is a sentimental archaism, like preferring candles
to electric light or hansom cabs to aeroplanes. Underneath this lies the
half-conscious belief that language is a natural growth and not an instrument which we shape for our own purposes.

Now, it is clear that the decline of a language must ultimately have   2
political and economic causes: it is not due simply to the bad influence
of this or that individual writer. But an effect can become a cause,
reinforcing the original cause and producing the same effect in an intensified form, and so on indefinitely. A man may take to drink because
he feels himself to be a failure, and then fail all the more completely
because he drinks. It is rather the same thing that is happening to the
English language. It becomes ugly and inaccurate because our thoughts
are foolish, but the slovenliness of our language makes it easier for us to
have foolish thoughts. The point is that the process is reversible. Modern English, especially written English, is full of bad habits which
spread by imitation and which can be avoided if one is willing to take
the necessary trouble. If one gets rid of these habits one can think more
clearly, and to think clearly is a necessary first step towards political
regeneration: so that the fight against bad English is not frivolous and is
not the exclusive concern of professional writers. I will come back to
this presently, and I hope that by that time the meaning of what I have
said here will have become clearer. Meanwhile, here are five specimens
of the English language as it is now habitually written.

These five passages have not been picked out because they are   3
especially bad—I could have quoted far worse if I had chosen—but
because they illustrate various of the mental vices from which we now
suffer. They are a little below the average, but are fairly representative
samples. I number them so that I can refer back to them when necessary:

(1) I am not, indeed, sure whether it is not true to say that the Milton
who once seemed not unlike a seventeenth-century Shelley had not
become, out of an experience ever more bitter in each year, more alien
[*sic*] to the founder of that Jesuit sect which nothing could induce him
to tolerate.

Professor Harold Laski*
(Essay in *Freedom of Expression*).

* [Harold Laski (1893–1950) was a leading British socialist. John Milton was a mili-
tant English Protestant likened in this passage to the founder of the Jesuit society
and archenemy of the Protestant Reformation.]

(2) Above all, we cannot play ducks and drakes with a native battery of idioms which prescribes such egregious collocations of vocables as the Basic *put up with* for *tolerate* or *put at a loss* for *bewilder.*

Professor Lancelot Hogben (Interglossa).

(3) On the one side we have the free personality: by definition it is not neurotic, for it has neither conflict nor dream. Its desires, such as they are, are transparent, for they are just what institutional approval keeps in the forefront of consciousness; another institutional pattern would alter their number and intensity; there is little in them that is natural, irreducible, or culturally dangerous. But *on the other side,* the social bond itself is nothing but the mutual reflection of these self-secure integrities. Recall the definition of love. Is not this the very picture of a small academic? Where is there a place in this hall of mirrors for either personality or fraternity?

Essay on psychology in Politics (New York).

(4) All the "best people" from the gentlemen's clubs, and all the frantic fascist captains, united in common hatred of Socialism and bestial horror of the rising tide of the mass revolutionary movement, have turned to acts of provocation, to foul incendiarism, to medieval legends of poisoned wells, to legalize their own destruction of proletarian organizations, and rouse the agitated petty-bourgeoisie to chauvinistic fervor on behalf of the fight against the revolutionary way out of the crisis.

Communist pamphlet.

(5) If a new spirit is to be infused into this old country, there is one thorny and contentious reform which must be tackled, and that is the humanization and galvanization of the B.B.C. Timidity here will bespeak canker and atrophy of the soul. The heart of Britain may be sound and of strong beat, for instance, but the British lion's roar at present is like that of Bottom in Shakespeare's *Midsummer Night's Dream*—as gentle as any sucking dove. A virile new Britain cannot continue indefinitely to be traduced in the eyes, or rather ears, of the world by the effete languors of Langham Place, brazenly masquerading as "standard English." When the Voice of Britain is heard at nine o'clock, better far and infinitely less ludicrous to hear aitches honestly dropped than the present priggish, inflated, inhibited, schoolma'amish arch braying of blameless bashful mewing maidens!

Letter in Tribune.

4   Each of these passages has faults of its own, but, quite apart from avoidable ugliness, two qualities are common to all of them. The first is staleness of imagery; the other is lack of precision. The writer either has a meaning and cannot express it, or he inadvertently says some-

be a lack of precision

thing else, or he is almost indifferent as to whether his words mean anything or not. This mixture of vagueness and sheer incompetence is the most marked characteristic of modern English prose, and especially of any kind of political writing. As soon as certain topics are raised, the concrete melts into the abstract and no one seems able to think of turns of speech that are not hackneyed: prose consists less and less of *words* chosen for the sake of their meaning, and more and more of *phrases* tacked together like the sections of a prefabricated hen-house. I list below, with notes and examples, various of the tricks by means of which the work of prose-construction is habitually dodged:

DYING METAPHORS. A newly invented metaphor assists thought   5 by evoking a visual image, while on the other hand a metaphor which is technically "dead" (e.g. *iron resolution*) has in effect reverted to being an ordinary word and can generally be used without loss of vividness. But in between these two classes there is a huge dump of worn-out metaphors which have lost all evocative power and are merely used because they save people the trouble of inventing phrases for themselves. Examples are: *Ring the changes on, take up the cudgels for, toe the line, ride roughshod over, stand shoulder to shoulder with, play into the hands of, no axe to grind, grist to the mill, fishing in troubled waters, on the order of the day, Achilles' heel, swan song, hotbed.* Many of these are used without knowledge of their meaning (what is a "rift," for instance?), and incompatible metaphors are frequently mixed, a sure sign that the writer is not interested in what he is saying. Some metaphors now current have been twisted out of their original meaning without those who use them even being aware of the fact. For example, *toe the line* is sometimes written *tow the line.* Another example is *the hammer and the anvil,* now always used with the implication that the anvil gets the worst of it. In real life it is always the anvil that breaks the hammer, never the other way about: a writer who stopped to think what he was saying would be aware of this, and would avoid perverting the original phrase.

meaningless

OPERATORS OR VERBAL FALSE LIMBS. These save the trouble of   6 picking out appropriate verbs and nouns, and at the same time pad each sentence with extra syllables which give it an appearance of symmetry. Characteristic phrases are *render inoperative, militate against, make contact with, be subjected to, give rise to, give grounds for, have the effect of, play a leading part (role) in, make itself felt, take effect, exhibit a tendency to, serve the purpose of,* etc., etc. The keynote is the elimination of simple verbs. Instead of being a single word, such as *break, stop, spoil, mend, kill,* a verb becomes a *phrase,* made up of a noun or adjective tacked on to some general-purpose verb such as *prove, serve, form, play, render.* In addition, the passive voice is wherever possible used in preference to the active, and noun constructions are used instead of gerunds (*by examination of* instead of *by examining*). The range of verbs is further cut down by means of the *-ize* and *de-* formations, and the banal statements are given an appearance of profundity by means of the *not un-* formation Simple conjunctions and prepositions are replaced by such phrases as *with respect to, having regard to, the fact that, by dint of, in view of, in the interests of, on the hypothesis that;* and the ends of sentences are saved by anticlimax by such resounding common-places as *greatly to be desired, cannot be left out of account, a development to be expected in the near future, deserving of serious consideration, brought to a satisfactory conclusion* and so on and so forth.

7   PRETENTIOUS DICTION. Words like *phenomenon, element, individual* (as noun), *objective, categorical, effective, virtual, basic, primary, promote, constitute, exhibit, exploit, utilize, eliminate, liquidate,* are used to dress up simple statement and give an air of scientific impartiality to biased judgments. Adjectives like *epoch-making, epic, historic, unforgettable, triumphant, age-old, inevitable, inexorable, veritable,* are used to dignify the sordid processes of international politics, while writing that aims at glorifying war usually takes on an archaic color, its characteristic words being: *realm, throne, chariot, mailed fist, trident, sword, shield, buckler, banner, jackboot, clarion.* Foreign words and expressions such as *cul de sac, ancien régime, deus ex machina, mutatis mutandis, status quo, gleichschaltung, weltanschauung,* are used to give an air of culture and elegance. Except for the useful abbreviations *i.e., e.g.,* and *etc.,* there is no real need for any of the hundreds of foreign phrases now current in English. Bad writers, and especially scientific, political and sociological writers, are nearly always haunted by the notion that Latin or Greek words are grander than Saxon ones, and unnecessary words like *expedite, ameliorate, predict, extraneous, deracinated, clandestine, subaqueous* and hundreds of others constantly gain ground from their Anglo-Saxon opposite numbers.[1] The jargon peculiar to Marxist writing (*hyena, hangman, cannibal, petty bourgeois, these gentry, lackey, flunkey, mad dog, White Guard,* etc.) consists largely of words and phrases translated from Russian, German or French; but the normal way of coining a new word is to use a Latin or Greek root with the appropriate affix and, where necessary, the *-ize* formation. It is often easier to make up words of this kind

---

[1] An interesting illustration of this is the way in which the English flower names which were in use till very recently are being ousted by Greek ones, *snapdragon* becoming *antirrhinum, forget-me-not* becoming *myosotis,* etc. It is hard to see any practical reason for this change of fashion: it is probably due to an instinctive turning-away from the more homely word and a vague feeling that the Greek is scientific. [author's note]

(*deregionalize, impermissible, extramarital, non-fragmentary* and so forth) than to think up the English words that will cover one's meaning. The result, in general, is an increase in slovenliness and vagueness.

MEANINGLESS WORDS. In certain kinds of writing, particularly in art criticism and literary criticism, it is normal to come across long passages which are almost completely lacking in meaning.[2] Words like *romantic, plastic, values, human, dead, sentimental, natural, vitality,* as used in art criticism, are strictly meaningless, in the sense that they not only do not point to any discoverable object, but are hardly ever expected to do so by the reader. When one critic writes, "The outstanding feature of Mr. X's work is its living quality," while another writes, "The immediately striking thing about Mr. X's work is its peculiar deadness," the reader accepts this as a simple difference of opinion. If words like *black* and *white* were involved, instead of the jargon words *dead* and *living,* he would see at once that language was being used in an improper way. Many political words are similarly abused. The word *Fascism* has now no meaning except in so far as it signifies "something not desirable." The words *democracy, socialism, freedom, patriotic, realistic, justice,* have each of them several different meanings which cannot be reconciled with one another. In the case of a word like democracy, not only is there no agreed definition, but the attempt to make one is resisted from all sides. It is almost universally felt that when we call a country democratic we are praising it: consequently the defenders of every kind of régime claim that it is a democracy, and fear that they might have to stop using the word if it were tied down to any one meaning. Words of this kind are often used in a consciously dishonest way. That is, the person who uses them has his own private definition, but allows his hearer to think he means something quite different. Statements like *Marshal Pétain was a true patriot, The Soviet Press is the freest in the world, The Catholic Church is opposed to persecution,* are almost always made with intent to deceive. Other words used in variable meanings, in most cases more or less dishonestly, are: *class, totalitarian, science, progressive, reactionary, bourgeois, equality.*

Now that I have made this catalogue of swindles and perversions, let me give another example of the kind of writing that they lead to. This time it must of its nature be an imaginary one. I am going to translate a passage of good English into modern English of the worst sort. Here is a well-known verse from *Ecclesiastes:*

[2] Example: "Comfort's catholicity of perception and image, strangely Whitmanesque in range, almost the exact opposite in aesthetic compulsion, continues to evoke that trembling atmospheric accumulative hinting at a cruel, an inexorably serene timelessness. . . . Wrey Gardiner scores by aiming at simple bull's-eyes with precision. Only they are not so simple, and through this contented sadness runs more than the surface bittersweet of resignation." (*Poetry Quarterly.*) [author's note]

I returned and saw under the sun, that the race is not to the swift, nor the battle to the strong, neither yet bread to the wise, nor yet riches to men of understanding, nor yet favour to men of skill; but time and chance happeneth to them all.

10   Here it is in modern English:

Objective consideration of contemporary phenomena compels the conclusion that success or failure in competitive activities exhibits no tendency to be commensurate with innate capacity, but that a considerable element of the unpredictable must invariably be taken into account.

11   This is a parody, but not a very gross one. Exhibit (3), above, for instance, contains several patches of the same kind of English. It will be seen that I have not made a full translation. The beginning and ending of the sentence follow the original meaning fairly closely, but in the middle the concrete illustrations—race, battle, bread—dissolve into the vague phrase "success or failure in competitive activities." This had to be so, because no modern writer of the kind I am discussing—no one capable of using phrases like "objective consideration of contemporary phenomena"—would ever tabulate his thoughts in that precise and detailed way. The whole tendency of modern prose is away from concreteness. Now analyse these two sentences a little more closely. The first contains forty-nine words but only sixty syllables, and all its words are those of everyday life. The second contains thirty-eight words of ninety syllables: eighteen of its words are from Latin roots, and one from Greek. The first sentence contains six vivid images, and only one phrase ("time and chance") that could be called vague. The second contains not a single fresh, arresting phrase, and in spite of its ninety syllables it gives only a shortened version of the meaning contained in the first. Yet without a doubt it is the second kind of sentence that is gaining ground in modern English. I do not want to exaggerate. This kind of writing is not yet universal, and outcrops of simplicity will occur here and there in the worst-written page. Still, if you or I were told to write a few lines on the uncertainty of human fortunes, we should probably come much nearer to my imaginary sentence than to the one from *Ecclesiastes*.

12   As I have tried to show, modern writing at its worst does not consist in picking out words for the sake of their meaning and inventing images in order to make the meaning clearer. It consists in gumming together long strips of words which have already been set in order by someone else, and making the results presentable by sheer humbug. The attraction of this way of writing is that it is easy. It is easier—even quicker, once you have the habit—to say *In my opinion it is not an*

unjustifiable assumption that than to say *I think.* If you use ready-made phrases, you not only don't have to hunt about for words; you also don't have to bother with the rhythms of your sentences, since these phrases are generally so arranged as to be more or less euphonious. When you are composing in a hurry—when you are dictating to a stenographer, for instance, or making a public speech—it is natural to fall into a pretentious, Latinized style. Tags like *a consideration which we should do well to bear in mind* or *a conclusion to which all of us would readily assent* will save many a sentence from coming down with a bump. By using stale metaphors, similes and idioms, you save much mental effort, at the cost of leaving your meaning vague, not only for your reader but for yourself. This is the significance of mixed metaphors. The sole aim of a metaphor is to call up a visual image. When these images clash—as in *The Fascist octopus has sung its swan song, the jackboot is thrown into the melting pot*—it can be taken as certain that the writer is not seeing a mental image of the objects he is naming; in other words he is not really thinking. Look again at the examples I gave at the beginning of this essay. Professor Laski (1) uses five negatives in fifty-three words. One of these is superfluous, making nonsense of the whole passage, and in addition there is the slip *alien* for *akin,* making further nonsense, and several avoidable pieces of clumsiness which increase the general vagueness. Professor Hogben (2) plays ducks and drakes with a battery which is able to write prescriptions, and, while disapproving of the everyday phrase *put up with,* is unwilling to look *egregious* up in the dictionary and see what it means; (3), if one takes an uncharitable attitude towards it, is simply meaningless: probably one could work out its intended meaning by reading the whole of the article in which it occurs. In (4), the writer knows more or less what he wants to say, but an accumulation of stale phrases chokes him, like tea leaves blocking a sink. In (5), words and meaning have almost parted company. People who write in this manner usually have a general emotional meaning—they dislike one thing and want to express solidarity with another—but they are not interested in the detail of what they are saying. A scrupulous writer, in every sentence that he writes, will ask himself at least four questions, thus: What am I trying to say? What words will express it? What image or idiom will make it clearer? Is this image fresh enough to have an effect? And he will probably ask himself two more: Could I put it more shortly? Have I said anything that is avoidably ugly? But you are not obliged to go to all this trouble. You can shirk it by simply throwing your mind open and letting the ready-made phrases come crowding in. They will construct your sentences for you—even think your thoughts for you, to a certain extent—and at need they will perform the important service of partially concealing your meaning even from yourself. It is at this point that the special connection between politics and the debasement of language becomes clear.

13   In our time it is broadly true that political writing is bad writing. Where it is not true, it will generally be found that the writer is some kind of rebel, expressing his private opinions and not a "party line." Orthodoxy, of whatever color, seems to demand a lifeless, imitative style. The political dialects to be found in pamphlets, leading articles, manifestos, White Papers and the speeches of undersecretaries do, of course, vary from party to party, but they are all alike in that one almost never finds in them a fresh, vivid, home-made turn of speech. When one watches some tired hack on the platform mechanically repeating the familiar phrases—*bestial atrocities, iron heel, bloodstained tyranny, free peoples of the world, stand shoulder to shoulder*—one often has a curious feeling that one is not watching a live human being but some kind of dummy: a feeling which suddenly becomes stronger at moments when the light catches the speaker's spectacles and turns them into blank discs which seem to have no eyes behind them. And this is not altogether fanciful. A speaker who uses that kind of phraseology has gone some distance towards turning himself into a machine. The appropriate noises are coming out of his larynx, but his brain is not involved as it would be if he were choosing his words for himself. If the speech he is making is one that he is accustomed to make over and over again, he may be almost unconscious of what he is saying, as one is when one utters the responses in church. And this reduced state of consciousness, if not indispensable, is at any rate favorable to political conformity.

14   In our time, political speech and writing are largely the defense of the indefensible. Things like the continuance of British rule in India, the Russian purges and deportations, the dropping of the atom bombs on Japan, can indeed be defended, but only by arguments which are too brutal for most people to face, and which do not square with the professed aims of political parties. Thus political language has to consist largely of euphemism, question-begging and sheer cloudy vagueness. Defenseless villages are bombarded from the air, the inhabitants driven out into the countryside, the cattle machine-gunned, the huts set on fire with incendiary bullets: this is called *pacification*. Millions of peasants are robbed of their farms and sent trudging along the roads with no more than they can carry: this is called *transfer of population* or *rectification of frontiers*. People are imprisoned for years without trial, or shot in the back of the neck or sent to die of scurvy in Arctic lumber camps; this is called *elimination of unreliable elements*. Such phraseology is needed if one wants to name things without calling up mental pictures of them. Consider for instance some comfortable English professor defending Russian totalitarianism. He cannot say outright, "I be-

lieve in killing off your opponents when you can get good results by doing so." Probably, therefore, he will say something like this:

"While freely conceding that the Soviet régime exhibits certain fea- 15 tures which the humanitarian may be inclined to deplore, we must, I think, agree that a certain curtailment of the right to political opposition is an unavoidable concomitant of transitional periods, and that the rigors which the Russian people have been called upon to undergo have been amply justified in the sphere of concrete achievement."

The inflated style is itself a kind of euphemism. A mass of Latin 16 words falls upon the facts like soft snow, blurring the outlines and covering up all the details. The great enemy of clear language is insincerity. When there is a gap between one's real and one's declared aims, one turns as it were instinctively to long words and exhausted idioms, like a cuttlefish squirting out ink. In our age there is no such thing as "keeping out of politics." All issues are political issues, and politics itself is a mass of lies, evasions, folly, hatred and schizophrenia. When the general atmosphere is bad, language must suffer. I should expect to find—this is a guess which I have not sufficient knowledge to verify— that the German, Russian and Italian languages have all deteriorated in the last ten or fifteen years, as a result of dictatorship.

But if thought corrupts language, language can also corrupt 17 thought. A bad usage can spread by tradition and imitation, even among people who should and do know better.The debased language that I have been discussing is in some ways very convenient. Phrases like *a not unjustifiable assumption, leaves much to be desired, would serve no good purpose, a consideration which we should do well to bear in mind,* are a continuous temptation, a packet of aspirins always at one's elbow. Look back through this essay, and for certain you will find that I have again and again committed the very faults I am protesting against. By this morning's post I have received a pamphlet dealing with conditions in Germany. The author tells me that he "felt impelled" to write it. I open it at random, and here is almost the first sentence that I see: "[The Allies] have an opportunity not only of achieving a radical transformation of Germany's social and political structure in such a way as to avoid a nationalistic reaction in Germany itself, but at the same time of laying the foundations of a co-operative and unified Europe." You see, he "feels impelled" to write—feels, presumably, that he has something new to say—and yet his words, like cavalry horses answering the bugle, group themselves automatically into the familiar dreary pattern. This invasion of one's mind by ready-made phrases (*lay the foundations, achieve a radical transformation*) can only be prevented if one is constantly on guard against them, and every such phrase anaesthetizes a portion of one's brain.

I said earlier that the decadence of our language is probably cur- 18 able. Those who deny this would argue, if they produced an argument at all, that language merely reflects existing social conditions, and that we cannot influence its development by any direct tinkering with words and constructions. So far as the general tone or spirit of a language goes, this may be true, but it is not true in detail. Silly words and expressions have often disappeared, not through any evolutionary process but owing to the conscious action of a minority. Two recent examples were *explore every avenue* and *leave no stone unturned,* which were killed by the jeers of a few journalists. There is a long list of flyblown metaphors which could similarly be got rid of if enough people would interest themselves in the job; and it should also be possible to laugh the *not un-* formation out of existence,[3] to reduce the amount of Latin and Greek in the average sentence, to drive out foreign phrases and strayed scientific words, and, in general, to make pretentiousness unfashionable. But all these are minor points. The defense of the English language implies more than this, and perhaps it is best to start by saying what it does *not* imply.

19   To begin with it has nothing to do with archaism, with the salvaging of obsolete words and turns of speech, or with the setting up of a "standard English" which must never be departed from. On the contrary, it is especially concerned with the scrapping of every word or idiom which has outworn its usefulness. It has nothing to do with correct grammar and syntax, which are of no importance so long as one makes one's meaning clear, or with the avoidance of Americanisms, or with having what is called a "good prose style." On the other hand it is not concerned with fake simplicity and the attempt to make written English colloquial. Nor does it even imply in every case preferring the Saxon word to the Latin one, though it does imply using the fewest and shortest words that will cover one's meaning. What is above all needed is to let the meaning choose the word, and not the other way about. In prose, the worst thing one can do with words is to surrender to them. When you think of a concrete object, you think wordlessly, and then, if you want to describe the thing you have been visualizing you probably hunt about till you find the exact words that seem to fit it. When you think of something abstract you are more inclined to use words from the start, and unless you make a conscious effort to prevent it, the existing dialect will come rushing in and do the job for you, at the expense of blurring or even changing your meaning. Probably it is better to put off using words as long as possible and get one's meaning as clear as one can through pictures or sensations. Afterwards one can

---

[3] One can cure oneself of the *not un-*formation by memorizing this sentence: *A not unblack dog was chasing a not unsmall rabbit across a not ungreen field.* [author's note]

choose—not simply *accept*—the phrases that will best cover the mean-ing, and then switch round and decide what impression one's words are likely to make on another person. This last effort of the mind cuts out all stale or mixed images, all prefabricated phrases, needless repeti-tions, and humbug and vagueness generally. But one can often be in doubt about the effect of a word or a phrase, and one needs rules that one can rely on when instinct fails. I think the following rules will cover most cases:

(i)   Never use a metaphor, simile or other figure of speech which you are used to seeing in print.

(ii) Never use a long word where a short one will do.

(iii) If it is possible to cut a word out, always cut it out.

(iv) Never use the passive where you can use the active.

(v)   Never use a foreign phrase, a scientific word or a jargon word if you can think of any everyday English equivalent.

(vi) Break any of these rules sooner than say anything outright barba-rous.

These rules sound elementary, and so they are, but they demand a deep change of attitude in anyone who has grown used to writing in the style now fashionable. One could keep all of them and still write bad En-glish, but one could not write the kind of stuff that I quoted in those five specimens at the beginning of this article.

I have not here been considering the literary use of language, but merely language as an instrument for expressing and not for concealing or preventing thought. Stuart Chase* and others have come near to claiming that all abstract words are meaningless, and have used this as a pretext for advocating a kind of political quietism. Since you don't know what Fascism is, how can you struggle against Fascism? One need not swallow such absurdities as this, but one ought to recognize that the present political chaos is connected with the decay of language, and that one can probably bring about some improvement by starting at the verbal end. If you simplify your English, you are freed from the worst follies of orthodoxy. You cannot speak any of the necessary dia-lects, and when you make a stupid remark its stupidity will be obvious, even to yourself. Political language—and with variations this is true of all political parties, from Conservatives to Anarchists—is designed to make lies sound truthful and murder respectable, and to give an ap-

*[Stuart Chase, author of the *Tyranny of Words* (1938), was a leading popularizer of the semantics movement, which fought propaganda, gobbledygook, and premature abstraction.]

pearance of solidity to pure wind. One cannot change this all in a moment, but one can at least change one's own habits, and from time to time one can even, if one jeers loudly enough, send some worn-out and useless phrase—some *jackboot, Achilles' heel, hotbed, melting pot, acid test, veritable inferno* or other lump of verbal refuse—into the dustbin where it belongs.

 Using the dictionary: George Orwell says that bad writers often use pretentious words taken over from Latin and Greek or borrowed from other languages. For each of the following examples, find a simpler word derived from Old English or Anglo-Saxon: 1. *egregious* (3) 2. *collocation* (3) 3. *vocable* (3) 4. *expedite* (7) 5. *ameliorate* (7) 6. *predict* (7) 7. *extraneous* (7) 8. *deracinated* (7) 9. *clandestine* (7) 10. *subaqueous* (7). What is the meaning of the following foreign expressions? 11. *ancien régime* (7) 12. *deus ex machina* (7) 13. *mutatis mutandis* (7) 14. *gleichschaltung* (7) 15. *weltanschauung* (7)

THE WRITER'S AGENDA:

Orwell's commitment to honesty in speech and writing often causes him to write **inductively**. He often presents the facts or the evidence first and then goes on to generalize. Answer the following questions about the conclusions he draws from the evidence he presents in this essay.

1. Orwell sets his essay in motion by taking on a familiar or widely shared *assumption.* What is it? How does he deal with it?
we can conciously change lang use

2. One of the two major faults of prose style that Orwell attacks is "staleness of imagery." (What is the other?) Find the different discussions of *figurative language* in this essay, paying special attention to the examples he provides. How does Orwell define the basic function of metaphor? How does he distinguish among fresh, dead, and worn-out metaphors? What are his objections to mixed metaphors? Find and discuss outstanding examples of Orwell's own use of fresh, vivid figurative language. *lack of percision*

3. Describe and illustrate the different kinds of verbal padding and *inflated diction* attacked in this essay. What, according to the author, is their purpose? What is their result?
adds stylib. but lessens meaning exp!

4. What abuses of language does Orwell analyze under the heading of *"meaningless words"*? real, natural, romantic etc.

5. Orwell's analysis of common defects of prose style leads up to his indictment of political speech and writing as "largely the *defense of the indefensible.*" What examples does he use to back up this charge? According to the author, what is the role of euphemisms in the language of politics?   hide truth

6. What *misunderstanding* does Orwell try to prevent at the beginning of his concluding paragraph? (What are some possible misunderstandings that he tried to clear up earlier?) How does his conclusion restate and summarize the key ideas of his essay?

FOR DISCUSSION OR WRITING:

1. Orwell attacked the trite, cliché-ridden quality of the political language of his time. Examine an example of current political language for ready-made phrases or prefabricated expressions. For example, choose an editorial, campaign speech, inaugural speech, or transcript of a press conference.

2. Study the use of euphemisms in current political discussions of subjects that make for bad news, such as unemployment, defense spending, or political oppression in countries allied with the United States.

3. Orwell attacks "meaningless terms" that have come to serve for hypocritical self-congratulation or ignorant abuse. Choose one of the following examples: *fascism, democracy, freedom, justice, equality, Americanism.* Prepare an extended definition designed to give the term an honest meaning.

4. An updated list of words frequently abused in political discussion might include *subversive, progressive, reactionary, bourgeois, terrorist, militaristic, exploitation.* Choose one or more of these and discuss uses and abuses.

5. Where do you think Orwell's ideal reader would stand politically? Support your answer.

Barbara Tuchman

Humanity's Better Moments

GUIDE TO READING: In this essay, the author tries to go against the tide. She tries to counteract our prevailing modern pessimism about human nature and about the future of humanity. How does she proceed? What examples of human achievement or what evidence of positive qualities does she present, and in what order?

1   FOR A CHANGE from prevailing pessimism, I should like to recall some of the positive and even admirable capacities of the human race. We hear very little of them lately. Ours is not a time of self-esteem or self-confidence—as was, for instance, the nineteenth century, when

self-esteem may be seen oozing from its portraits. Victorians, especially the men, pictured themselves as erect, noble, and splendidly hand- some. Our self-image looks more like Woody Allen or a character from Samuel Beckett.[1] Amid a mass of worldwide troubles and a poor record for the twentieth century, we see our species—with cause—as func- tioning very badly, as blunderers when not knaves, as violent, ignoble, corrupt, inept, incapable of mastering the forces that threaten us, weak- ly subject to our worst instincts; in short, decadent.

The catalogue is familiar and valid, but it is growing tiresome. A study of history reminds one that humanity has its ups and downs and during the ups has accomplished many brave and beautiful things, ex- erted stupendous endeavors, explored and conquered oceans and wil- derness, achieved marvels of beauty in the creative arts and marvels of science and social progress; has loved liberty with a passion that throughout history has led men to fight and die for it over and over again; has pursued knowledge, exercised reason, enjoyed laughter and pleasures, played games with zest, shown courage, heroism, altruism, honor, and decency; experienced love; known comfort, contentment, and occasionally happiness. All these qualities have been part of hu- man experience, and if they have not had as important notice as the negatives nor exerted as wide and persistent an influence as the evils we do, they nevertheless deserve attention, for they are currently all but forgotten. 2

Among the great endeavors, we have in our own time carried men to the moon and brought them back safely—surely one of the most remarkable achievements in history. Some may disapprove of the effort as unproductive, too costly, and a wrong choice of priorities in relation to greater needs, all of which may be true but does not, as I see it, diminish the achievement. If you look carefully, all positives have a negative underside—sometimes more, sometimes less—and not all ad- mirable endeavors have admirable motives. Some have sad conse- quences. Although most signs presently point from bad to worse, hu- man capacities are probably what they have always been. If primitive man could discover how to transform grain into bread, and reeds grow- ing by the riverbank into baskets; if his successors could invent the wheel, harness the insubstantial air to turn a millstone, transform sheep's wool, flax, and worms' cocoons into fabric—we, I imagine, will find a way to manage the energy problem. 3

Consider how the Dutch accomplished the miracle of making land out of sea. By progressive enclosure of the Zuider Zee over the last sixty 4

---

[1] [Samuel Beckett's best-known play is *Waiting for Godot* (1954), in which two tramps spend much of their time in aimless conversation, vacillating between self- pity and self-disgust.]

years, they have added half a million acres to their country, enlarging its area by eight percent and providing homes, farms, and towns for close to a quarter of a million people. The will to do the impossible, the spirit of can-do that overtakes our species now and then, was never more manifest than in this earth-altering act by the smallest of the major European nations. Today the *Afsluitdijk,* or Zuider Zee road, is a normal thoroughfare. To drive across it between the sullen ocean on one side and new land on the other is for that moment to feel optimism for the human race.

5   Even when the historical tide is low, a particular group of doers may emerge in exploits that inspire awe. Shrouded in the mists of the eighth century, long before the cathedrals, Viking seamanship was a wonder of daring, stamina, and skill. Pushing relentlessly outward in open boats, the Vikings sailed south, around Spain to North Africa and Arabia, north to the top of the world, west across uncharted seas to American coasts. They hauled their boats overland from the Baltic to make their way down Russian rivers to the Black Sea. Why? We do not know what engine drove them, only that it was part of the human endowment.

6   What of the founding of our own country, America? We take the *Mayflower* for granted—yet think of the boldness, the enterprise, the determined independence, the sheer grit it took to leave the known and set out across the sea for the unknown where no houses or food, no stores, no cleared land, no crops or livestock, none of the equipment or settlement of organized living awaited.

7   Equally bold was the enterprise of the French in the northern forests of the American continent, who throughout the seventeenth century explored and opened the land from the St. Lawrence to the Mississippi, from the Great Lakes to the Gulf of Mexico. They came not for liberty like the Pilgrims, but for gain and dominion, whether in spiritual empire for the Jesuits or in land, glory, and riches for the agents of the King; and rarely in history have people willingly embraced such hardship, such daunting adventure, and persisted with such tenacity and endurance. They met hunger, exhaustion, frostbite, capture and torture by Indians, wounds and disease, dangerous rapids, swarms of insects, long portages, bitter weather, and hardly ever did those who suffered the experience fail to return, re-enter the menacing but bountiful forest, and pit themselves once more against danger, pain, and death.

8   Above all others, the perseverance of La Salle in his search for the mouth of the Mississippi was unsurpassed. While preparing in Quebec, he mastered eight Indian languages. From then on he suffered accidents, betrayals, desertions, losses of men and provisions, fever and

snow blindness, the hostility and intrigues of rivals who incited the Indians against him and plotted to ambush or poison him. He was truly pursued, as Francis Parkman wrote, by "a demon of havoc."[2] Paddling through heavy waves in a storm over Lake Ontario, he waded through freezing surf to beach the canoes each night, and lost guns and baggage when a canoe was swamped and sank. To lay the foundations of a fort above Niagara, frozen ground had to be thawed by boiling water. When the fort was at last built, La Salle christened it Crèvecoeur—that is, Heartbreak. It earned the name when in his absence it was plundered and deserted by its half-starved mutinous garrison. Farther on, a friendly Indian village, intended as a destination, was found laid waste by the Iroquois with only charred stakes stuck with skulls standing among the ashes, while wolves and buzzards prowled through the remains.

When at last, after four months' hazardous journey down the Great River, La Salle reached the sea, he formally took possession in the name of Louis XIV of all the country from the river's mouth to its source and of its tributaries—that is, of the vast basin of the Mississippi from the Rockies to the Appalachians—and named it Louisiana. The validity of the claim, which seems so hollow to us (though successful in its own time), is not the point. What counts is the conquest of fearful adversity by one man's extraordinary exertions and inflexible will. 9

Our greatest recourse and most enduring achievement is art. At its best, it reveals the nobility that coexists in human nature along with flaws and evils, and the beauty and truth it can perceive. Whether in music or architecture, literature, painting or sculpture, art opens our eyes, ears, and feelings to something beyond ourselves, something we cannot experience without the artist's vision and the genius of his craft. The placing of Greek temples, like the Temple of Poseidon on the promontory at Sunion, outlined against the piercing blue of the Aegean Sea, Poseidon's home; the majesty of Michelangelo's sculptured figures in stone; Shakespeare's command of language and knowledge of the human soul; the intricate order of Bach, the enchantment of Mozart; the purity of Chinese monochrome pottery with its lovely names—celadon, oxblood, peach blossom, clair de lune; the exuberance of Tiepolo's ceilings where, without picture frames to limit movement, a whole world in exquisitely beautiful colors lives and moves in the sky; the prose and poetry of all the writers from Homer to Cervantes to Jane 10

[2] [Francis Parkman (1823–93), author of *The Oregon Trail* and of *Pioneers of France in the New World*, was the leading nineteenth-century historian of the American frontier.]

Austen and John Keats to Dostoevski and Chekhov—who made all these things? We—our species—did.[3]

11   If we have (as I think) lost beauty and elegance in the modern world, we have gained much, through science and technology and democratic pressures, in the material well-being of the masses. The change in the lives of, and society's attitude toward, the working class marks the great divide between the modern world and the old regime. From the French Revolution through the brutal labor wars of the nineteenth and twentieth centuries, the change was earned mainly by force against fierce and often vicious opposition. While this was a harsh process, it developed and activated a social conscience hardly operative before. Slavery, beggary, unaided misery, and want have, on the whole, been eliminated in the developed nations of the West. That much is a credit in the human record, even if the world is uglier as a result of adapting to mass values. History generally arranges these things so that gain is balanced by loss, perhaps in order not to make the gods jealous.

12   The material miracles wrought by science and technology—from the harnessing of steam and electricity to anesthesia, antisepsis, antibiotics, and woman's liberator, the washing machine, and all the labor-savers that go with it—are too well recognized in our culture to need my emphasis. Pasteur is as great a figure in the human record as Michelangelo or Mozart—probably, as far as the general welfare is concerned, greater.[4] We are more aware of his kind of accomplishment than of those less tangible. Ask anyone to suggest the credits of mankind and the answer is likely to start with physical things. Yet the underside of scientific progress is prominent and dark. The weaponry of war in its ever-widening capacity to kill is the deadly example, and who is prepared to state with confidence that the over-all effect of the automobile, airplane, telephone, television, and computer has been, on balance, beneficent?

13   Pursuit of knowledge for its own sake has been a more certain good. There was a springtime in the eighteenth century when, through knowledge and reason, everything seemed possible; when reason was expected to break through religious dogma like the sun breaking through fog, and man, armed with knowledge and reason, would be able at last to control his own fate and construct a good society.

---

[3][In her list of great artists, the author includes, along with those who are universally known, the Italian painter Tiepolo (1696–1770); the Spanish novelist Cervantes (1547–1616), author of the mock-heroic *Don Quixote;* the British novelist Jane Austen (1775–1817), author of *Pride and Prejudice;* and the Russian short-story writer and dramatist Anton Chekhov (1860–1904), author of *The Cherry Orchard.*]

[4][Louis Pasteur (1822–95) was the French chemist who pioneered the prevention of disease through inoculation and after whom the process of pasteurization is named.]

Although the Enlightenment may have overestimated the power of   14
reason to guide human conduct, it nevertheless opened to men and
women a more humane view of their fellow passengers. Slowly the
harshest habits gave way to reform—in treatment of the insane, reduction of death penalties, mitigation of the fierce laws against debtors and
poachers, and in the passionately fought cause for abolition of the slave
trade.

The humanitarian movement was not charity, which always carries   15
an overtone of being done in the donor's interest, but a more disinterested benevolence or altruism, motivated by conscience. It was person-
ified in William Wilberforce, who in the later eighteenth century
stirred the great rebellion of the English conscience against the trade
in human beings. In America the immorality of slavery had long troubled the colonies. By 1789 slavery had been legally abolished by the
New England states followed by New York, New Jersey, and Pennsylvania, but the southern states, as their price for joining the Union, insisted that the subject be excluded from the Constitution.

In England, where the home economy did not depend on slave   16
labor, Wilberforce had more scope. His influence could have carried
him to the Prime Minister's seat if personal power had been his goal,
but he channeled his life instead toward a goal for humanity. He insti-
gated, energized, inspired a movement whose members held meetings,
organized petitions, collected information on the horrors of the middle
passage, showered pamphlets on the public, gathered Nonconformist
middle-class sentiment into a swelling tide that, in Trevelyan's phrase,
"melted the hard prudence of statesmen."[5] Abolition of the slave trade
under the British flag was won in 1807. The British Navy was used to
enforce the ban by searches on the high seas and regular patrols of the
African coast. When Portugal and Spain were persuaded to join in the
prohibition, they were paid a compensation of £300,000 and £400,000
respectively by the British taxpayer. Violations and smuggling continued, convincing the abolitionists that, in order to stop the trade, slavery
itself had to be abolished. Agitation resumed. By degrees over the next
quarter-century, compensation reduced the opposition of the West Indian slave-owners and their allies in England until emancipation of all
slaves in the British Empire was enacted in 1833. The total cost to the
British taxpayer was reckoned at £20 million.

Through recent unpleasant experiences we have learned to expect   17
ambition, greed, or corruption to reveal itself behind every public act,

[5] [The Nonconformists were English Protestants who refused to conform to the official Anglican state church and who commanded a strong following among the middle class. G. M. Trevelyan, long a professor of history at Cambridge University, first
published his widely read *History of England* in 1926.]

but, as we have just seen, it is not invariably so. Human beings do possess better impulses, and occasionally act upon them, even in the twentieth century. Occupied Denmark, during World War II, outraged by Nazi orders for deportation of its Jewish fellow citizens, summoned the courage of defiance and transformed itself into a united underground railway to smuggle virtually all eight thousand Danish Jews out to Sweden, and Sweden gave them shelter. Far away and unconnected, a village in southern France, Le Chambon-sur-Lignon, devoted itself to rescuing Jews and other victims of the Nazis at the risk of the inhabitants' own lives and freedom. "Saving lives became a hobby of the people of Le Chambon," said one of them. The larger record of the time was admittedly collaboration, passive or active. We cannot reckon on the better impulses predominating in the world, only that they will always appear.

18   The strongest of these in history, summoner of the best in us, has been zeal for liberty. Time after time, in some spot somewhere on the globe, people have risen in what Swinburne called the "divine right of insurrection"—to overthrow despots, repel alien conquerors, achieve independence—and so it will be until the day power ceases to corrupt, which, I think, is not a near expectation.

19   The ancient Jews rose three times against alien rulers, beginning with the revolt of the Maccabees against the effort of Antiochus to outlaw observance of the Jewish faith.[6] Mattathias the priest and his five sons, assembling loyal believers in the mountains, opened a guerrilla war which, after the father's death, was to find a leader of military genius in his son Judah, called Maccabee or the Hammer. Later honored in the Middle Ages as one of the Nine Worthies of the world, he defeated his enemies, rededicated the temple, and re-established the independence of Judea. In the next century the uprising of the Zealots against Roman rule was fanatically and hopelessly pursued through famines, sieges, the fall of Jerusalem and destruction of the temple until a last stand of fewer than a thousand on the rock of Masada ended in group suicide in preference to surrender. After sixty years as an occupied province, Judea rose yet again under Simon Bar Kochba, who regained Jerusalem for a brief moment of Jewish control but could not withstand the arms of Hadrian. The rebellion was crushed, but the zeal for selfhood, smoldering in exile through eighteen centuries, was to revive and regain its home in our time.

20   The phenomenon continues in our own day, in Algeria, in Vietnam, although, seen at close quarters and more often than not manipulated

---

[6] [The revolt of the Maccabees against the Syrians under King Antiochus took place in the second century B.C. Hadrian was the Roman emperor at the time of the final Jewish rebellion against Roman rule in the second century A.D.]

by outsiders, contemporary movements seem less pure and heroic than those polished by history's gloss—as, for instance, the Scots under William Wallace, the Swiss against the Hapsburgs, the American colonies against the mother country.[7]

I have always cherished the spirited rejoinder of one of the great colonial landowners of New York who, on being advised not to risk his property by signing the Declaration of Independence, replied, "Damn the property; give me the pen!" On seeking confirmation for purposes of this essay, I am deeply chagrined to report that the saying appears to be apocryphal. Yet not its spirit, for the signers well knew they were risking their property, not to mention their heads, by putting their names to the Declaration. 21

Is anything to be learned from my survey? I raise the question only because most people want history to teach them lessons, which I believe it can do, although I am less sure we can use them when needed. I gathered these examples not to teach but merely to remind people in a despondent era that the good in humanity operates even if the bad secures more attention. I am aware that selecting out the better moments does not result in a realistic picture. Turn them over and there is likely to be a darker side, as when Project Apollo, our journey to the moon, was authorized because its glamour could obtain subsidies for rocket and missile development that otherwise might not have been forthcoming. That is the way things are. 22

Whole philosophies have evolved over the question whether the human species is predominantly good or evil. I only know that it is mixed, that you cannot separate good from bad, that wisdom, courage, and benevolence exist alongside knavery, greed, and stupidity; heroism and fortitude alongside vainglory, cruelty, and corruption. 23

It is a paradox of our time in the West that never have so many people been so relatively well off and never has society been more troubled. Yet I suspect that humanity's virtues have not vanished, although the experiences of our century seem to suggest that they are in abeyance. A century that took shape in the disillusion which followed the enormous effort and hopes of World War I, that saw revolution in Russia congeal into the same tyranny it overthrew, saw a supposedly civilized nation revert under the Nazis into organized and unparalleled savagery, saw the craven appeasement by the democracies, is understandably marked by suspicion of human nature. A literary historian, Van Wyck Brooks, discussing the 1920s and '30s, wrote that whereas 24

---

[7][William Wallace (1272–1305) led the Scots in their fight for independence from English rule. Switzerland has through the centuries been the symbol of a small country that successfully defended its independence against powerful neighbors, such as the Austrian-Hungarian empire ruled by the House of Hapsburg.]

Whitman and Emerson "had been impressed by the worth and good sense of the people, writers of the new time" were struck by their lusts, cupidity, and violence, and had come to dislike their fellow men. The same theme reappeared in a recent play in which a mother struggled against her two "pitilessly contemptuous" children. Her problem was that she wanted them to be happy and they did not want to be. They preferred to watch horrors on television. In essence this is our epoch. It insists upon the flaws and corruptions, without belief in valor or virtue or the possibility of happiness. It keeps turning to look back on Sodom and Gomorrah; it has no view of the Delectable Mountains.[8]

25   We must keep a balance, and I know of no better prescription than a phrase from Condorcet's eulogy on the death of Benjamin Franklin: "He pardoned the present for the sake of the future."

 USING THE DICTIONARY: In each of the pairs, a word from this essay appears with a similar or related word. How are the words in each pair related? How are they different or alike? 1. *decadent—decay* (1) 2. *altruism—charity* (2) 3. *manifest—manifesto* (4) 4. *dominion—domain* (7) 5. *adversity—adversary* (9) 6. *promontory—peninsula* (10) 7. *regime—government* (11) 8. *dogma—doctrine* (13) 9. *humane—human* (14) 10. *mitigation—leniency* (14) 11. *disinterested—uninterested* (15) 12. *collaboration—cooperation* (17) 13. *chagrined—annoyed* (21) 14. *apocryphal—apocalyptic* (21) 15. *era—epoch* (22)

THE WRITER'S AGENDA:

In this essay, the author sets out to overcome the modern reader's pessimism about human history and human nature. To overcome the skepticism of her audience, her general strategy is to go from the relatively safe and undisputed to the debatable or questionable. She starts with the accomplishments of builders and explorers, proceeds through human achievements in science and art, and finally looks at the political sphere, where motives and accomplishments are likely to be most suspect to the skeptical modern reader.

1. Look at the way the first three paragraphs set the essay in motion. What is the modern "self-image" that she sets out to counteract? What are major areas or major points in her *preview* of the kinds of human accomplishment that she will discuss?

[8][A symbol for salvation or the promise of eternal life.]

2. Describe the author's *early examples* of the "spirit of can-do," from the Zuider Zee to La Salle's journey. What in this section is familiar or predictable? What is striking or unexpected? What do these achievements have in common?

3. The author labels *art* humanity's "greatest recourse" and "most enduring achievement." How does she define its functions or its purpose?

4. For the author, a profound change in the lives of, and in the attitude toward, the *working class* marks the "great divide" between the modern world and earlier periods. What forces, according to her, brought this change about, and how?

5. Barbara Tuchman pays tribute to *humanitarian reform* as the major legacy of the eighteenth century—the Age of Reason, or the Enlightenment. What data and details does she use to make sure that this judgment will not seem a superficial impression?

6. In the remaining portion of her essay, Tuchman tackles head on our pervading modern pessimism about *politics*—our tendency to "expect ambition, greed, or corruption to reveal itself behind every public act." What are the key examples that she uses in this crucial section? What are striking facts or details that she uses to convince her readers? What are the lessons that she wants them to learn from these examples?

7. Throughout her essay, the author reassures her readers that she is aiming at a *balanced* point of view. She wants them to feel that she is fully aware of the "darker side" of human history, that she is not painting a foolishly optimistic picture. Point out and discuss several of her references to the "darker side."

For discussion or writing:

1. In this essay, Tuchman provides a sweeping survey of the history and accomplishments of humanity. Which of the accomplishments she describes seem most familiar or most convincing? Which to you seem most questionable or subject to interpretation, and why?

2. Tuchman attributes to modern readers a pervading pessimism about history or disillusionment with human nature. Is this pessimistic outlook shared by members of your own generation? In their view of history or human nature, do you feel most people your age tend to be pessimists, fatalists, realists, optimists, cynics? What explains the prevailing view?

3. People in the author's generation often looked to art, architecture, or music for inspiration. They expected art to reveal "the nobility

that coexists in human nature along with flaws and evil." Has art lost this power to inspire or to ennoble for young people today?

4. Much modern history is written by "revisionist" historians—people who reexamine and revise cherished illusions or traditional views. Have you had occasion to revise your own views of American history or world history? How and why?

5. Write an essay in defense of skepticism, pessimism, optimism, or a similar term of your choice.

Alternative Rhetorical
Grouping of Essays

Index of Authors, Essays, and Rhetorical Terms

Note: Definitions of terms appear on pages indicated by bold face. Major essays of authors appear on pages indicated by italics.

Acknowledgments

Maya Angelou, "Step Forward in the Car, Please," is from Maya Angelou, *I Know Why the Caged Bird Sings.* Copyright © 1969 by Maya Angelou. Reprinted with permission of Random House, Inc.

Arthur Ashe, "A Black Athlete Looks at Education," is from *The New York Times.* © 1977 by The New York Times Company. Reprinted with permission of The New York Times Company.

Isaac Asimov, "Nuclear Fusion," is from *Parade,* February 18, 1979. Reprinted with permission of Parade Publications, Inc. and Isaac Asimov.

Sir Roger Bannister, "The Pursuit of Excellence," is from Roger Bannister, *The Four-Minute Mile.* Copyright © 1955, 1981 by Roger Bannister. Reprinted with permission of Dodd, Mead & Company, Inc. This material appeared originally in *Sports Illustrated,* in different form.

Ben Bova, "In Defense of Technology," is from Ben Bova, "Where Do We Go From?" *Analog Science Fiction/Science Fact,* September 1974. Copyright © 1974 by The Condé Nast Publications Inc. Reprinted with permission of Davis Publications, Inc. and Ben Bova.

Lee Burress and Edward B. Jenkinson, "Censorship Attacks Good Books," is from Lee Burress and Edward B. Jenkinson, *The Students' Right to Know,* NCTE, 1982. Reprinted with permission of the National Council of Teachers of English.

Rachel Carson, "Our War Against Nature," is from Rachel Carson, *Silent Spring.* Copyright © 1962 by Rachael Carson. Reprinted with permission of Houghton Mifflin Company.

Stephen Darst, "A Violent Majority," is from *Harper's,* April 1976. Copyright © 1976 by Harper's Magazine. All rights reserved. Reprinted with permission of Harper's Magazine.

Joan Didion, "Bureaucrats," is from Joan Didion, *The White Album.* Copyright © 1979 by Joan Didion. Reprinted with permission of Simon & Schuster, a Division of Gulf & Western Corporation.

Ed Edelson, "Smart Computers—Now They Speak Our Language," is from *Popular Science,* May 1982. © 1982 Times Mirror Magazines, Inc. Reprinted with permission of *Popular Science.*

Gretel Ehrlich, "Wide Open Spaces," is abridged from Gretel Ehrlich, "Wyoming: The Solace of Open Spaces." Copyright © 1981 by The Atlantic Monthly Company, Boston, Massachusetts. Reprinted with permission of Gretel Ehrlich.

Loren Eiseley, "The Bird and the Machine," copyright © 1955 by Loren Eiseley, is from Loren Eiseley, *The Immense Journey,* 1957. Reprinted with permission of Random House, Inc.

Marian Evans (George Eliot), "The Beauty of the Commonplace," *Adam Bede,* 1859.

Otto Friedrich, "Going Crazy," short excerpts from *Harper's,* June 1975. The magazine article is an excerpt from the book *Going Crazy* (New York: Simon & Schuster, 1976). These excerpts are reprinted here with permission of Otto Friedrich.

Paul Fussell, "Speedway," is from *Harper's,* August 1982. Copyright © 1982 by Paul Fussell. Reprinted with permission of International Creative Management, Inc.

Ellen Goodman, "The Company Man" and "Superworkingmom," are from Ellen Goodman, *Close to Home.* Copyright © 1979 by the Washington Post Company. Reprinted with permission of Simon & Schuster, a Division of Gulf & Western Corporation.

Amy Gross, "The Appeal of the Androgynous Man," is from *Mademoiselle,* May 1976. Copyright © 1976 by The Condé Nast Publications Inc. Reprinted with permission of Amy Gross.

Garrett Hardin, "Lifeboat Ethics," is from Garrett Hardin, "Lifeboat Ethics: The Case Against Helping the Poor," *Psychology Today,* September 1974. Copyright © 1974 Ziff-Davis Publishing Company. Reprinted with permission of Ziff-Davis Publishing Company.

Lillian Hellman, "An Only Child," is from Lillian Hellman, *An Unfinished Woman.* Copyright © 1969 by Lillian Hellman. Reprinted with permission of Little, Brown and Company.

Jane Howard, "In Search of the Good Family," is from Jane Howard, "All Happy Clans are Alike," *Atlantic,* May 1978. Copyright © 1978 by Jane Howard. Reprinted with permission of The Sterling Lord Agency.

Pauline Kael, "The Mass Audience and *Citizen Kane,*" is from Pauline Kael, Herman J. Mankiewicz and Orson Welles, *The Citizen Kane Book.* Copyright © 1971 by Bantam Books. This introduction by Pauline Kael, "Raising Kane," appeared originally in *The New Yorker;* copyright © 1971 by Pauline Kael. All rights reserved. Reprinted with permission of Bantam Books.

Sam Keen, "A New Breed," is from Sam Keen, "Lovers vs. Workers," *Quest,* September 15, 1981. Reprinted with permission of Sam Keen.

Martin Luther King, Jr., "I Have a Dream," copyright © 1963 by Martin Luther King, Jr. Reprinted with permission of Joan Daves.

Mark Kramer, "The Ruination of the Tomato," is from Mark Kramer, *Three Farms: Making Milk, Meat and Money from the American Soil.* Copyright © 1980 by Mark Kramer. The essay in this volume is an abridged version of an article that first appeared in the *Atlantic,* January 1980.

Reprinted with permission of Little, Brown and Company in association with the Atlantic Monthly Press.

Fern Kupfer, "Institution Is Not a Dirty Word," is condensed from *Newsweek,* December 13, 1982. Copyright © 1982 by Newsweek, Inc. All rights reserved. Reprinted with permission of Newsweek, Inc.

Robin Lakoff, "Talking Like a Lady," is from Robin Lakoff, "Language and Woman's Place," *Language in Society.* Reprinted with permission of Cambridge University Press, New York.

Susannah Lessard, "The Real Conservatism," is from Susannah Lessard, "Civility, Community, Humor: The Conservatism We Need," *The Washington Monthly,* July/August 1973. Copyright 1973 by The Washington Monthly Company, 2712 Ontario Road, N.W., Washington, D.C. 20009. Reprinted with permission of The Washington Monthly Company.

Carolyn Lewis, "A Different Drummer," is condensed from Carolyn Lewis, "My Unprodigal Sons," *Newsweek,* May 10, 1982. Copyright 1982 by Newsweek, Inc. All rights reserved. Reprinted with permission of Newsweek, Inc.

Charles McCabe, "Muggers and Morals," is from the *San Francisco Chronicle,* September 1981. © 1981 San Francisco Chronicle. Reprinted with permission of the San Francisco Chronicle.

Marya Mannes, "Television: The Splitting Image," is from the *Saturday Review,* November 14, 1970. Copyright © 1971 by Marya Mannes. Reprinted with permission of the author's agent, David J. Blow.

Margaret Mead, "We Need Taboos on Sex at Work," is from *Redbook,* April 1978. Reprinted with permission of Rhoda Metraux and Mary Catherine Bateson.

Peter Meyer, "Land Rush," is from *Harper's* January 1979. Copyright © 1978 by Harper's Magazine. All rights reserved. Reprinted with permission of Harper's Magazine.

Leonard Michaels, "New York, New York," is from Leonard Michaels, "The Visit," *The New York Times,* October 26, 1975. © 1975 by The New York Times Company. Reprinted with permission of The New York Times Company.

N. Scott Momaday, "The Way to Rainy Mountain," is from N. Scott Momaday, *The Way to Rainy Mountain.* © 1969 by the University of New Mexico Press. First published in *The Reporter,* January 26, 1967. Reprinted with permission of the University of New Mexico Press.

Donald M. Murray, "Culture Trading on the Old Silk Road," is from *Today's Education,* November–December, 1981. Reprinted with permission of *Today's Education* and Donald M. Murray.

A. S. Neill, "Punishment Never Cures Anything," is from *Cosmopolitan.* Copyright © 1971 by Hart Publishing Company, Inc. Reprinted with permission of Ena Neill.

Michael Novak, "The Family Out of Favor," is from *Harper's,* April 1976. Copyright © 1976 by Harper's Magazine. Reprinted with permission of Harper's Magazine.

George Orwell, "Shooting an Elephant" and "Politics and the English Language," is from George Orwell, *Shooting an Elephant and Other Essays.* "Shooting an Elephant," copyright

1950 by Sonia Brownell Orwell, renewed 1978 by Sonia Pitt-Rivers. "Politics and the English Language," copyright 1946 by Sonia Brownell Orwell, renewed 1974 by Sonia Orwell. Reprinted with permission of Harcourt Brace Jovanovich, Inc. and the estate of the late Sonia Brownell Orwell and Martin Secker & Warburg Ltd.

S. J. Perelman, "Choc-Nugs Are Loaded with Energy," is from S. J. Perelman, "Tomorrow— Fairly Cloudy," *The Most of S. J. Perelman.* Copyright © 1930, 1945 by S. J. Perelman. Reprinted with permission of Simon & Schuster, a Division of Gulf & Western Corporation.

Richard Rodriguez, "Children of Ceremony," is from Richard Rodriguez, *Hunger of Memory.* Copyright © 1981 by Richard Rodriguez. Reprinted with permission of David R. Godine, Publisher, Boston.

Jonathan Schell, "What Happened at Hiroshima," is from Jonathan Schell, *The Fate of the Earth.* Copyright © 1982 by Jonathan Schell. Originally appeared in *The New Yorker.* Reprinted with permission of Alfred A. Knopf, Inc.

William Strickland, "The Road Since *Brown,*" is from William Strickland, "The Road Since *Brown:* The Americanization of the Race," *The Black Scholar,* September–October, 1979. Reprinted with permission of *The Black Scholar.*

Jonathan Swift, "A Modest Proposal," 1729.

Judy Syfers, "I Want a Wife," is from Judy Syfers, "Why I Want a Wife," *Ms* Magazine, December 1971. Reprinted with permission of Judy Syfers.

Lewis Thomas, "Ant City and Human Society," is from Lewis Thomas, "Social Talk," *The New England Journal of Medicine,* November 9, 1972. Reprinted with permission of *The New England Journal of Medicine.*

Lewis Thomas, "Language and Evolution," is from Lewis Thomas, "Debating the Unknowable," *Late Night Thoughts on Listening to Mahler's Ninth Symphony.* Copyright © 1981, 1983 by Lewis Thomas. The essay in this volume is an abridged version of an article that first appeared in the *Atlantic,* July 1981. Reprinted with permission of Viking Penguin Inc.

Henry David Thoreau, "Where I Lived, and What I Lived For," *Walden,* 1854.

James Thurber, "The Secret Life of Walter Mitty," is from James Thurber, *My World—and Welcome to It,* published by Harcourt Brace Jovanovich, Inc. Copyright © 1942 James Thurber. Copyright © 1970 Helen W. Thurber and Rosemary T. Sauers. Reprinted with permission of Helen Thurber.

Barbara W. Tuchman, "Humanity's Better Moments," is abridged from the *American Scholar,* Autumn 1980. Copyright © 1980 by Barbara W. Tuchman. Originally delivered as a Jefferson Lecture, Washington, D.C., April 1980. Reprinted with permission of Russell & Volkening as agents for the author.

Sabine R. Ulibarri, "The Education of José Pérez," is from a lecture by Sabine R. Ulibarri, "Cultural Heritage of the Southwest," in Philip D. Ortego, ed., *We Are Chicanos: An Anthology of Chicano Literature* (New York: Washington Square Press, 1973). Reprinted with permission of Sabine R. Ulibarri.

E. B. White, "Once More to the Lake," is from *Essays of E. B. White.* Copyright 1941 by E. B.

White. Reprinted with permission of Harper & Row, Publishers, Inc.

George Will, "The Barbarity of Boxing," is from *The Washington Post,* November 21, 1982. Copyright © 1982 by The Washington Post Company. Reprinted with permission of The Washington Post Company.

Tom Wolfe, "The Right Stuff," is from Tom Wolfe, *The Right Stuff.* Copyright © 1979 by Tom Wolfe. Reprinted with permission of Farrar, Straus & Giroux, Inc.

Mary Wollstonecraft, "The Rights of Woman," *Vindication of the Rights of Woman,* 1792.

Jade Snow Wong, "Fifth Chinese Daughter," is from Jade Snow Wong, "Puritans of the Orient," in Thomas C. Wheeler, ed., *The Immigrant Experience.* Copyright © 1971 by The Dial Press, Inc. Reprinted with permission of Doubleday & Company, Inc.